Film Unframed
A History of Austrian Avant-Garde Cinema

Edited by Peter Tscherkassky

Peter Tscherkassky

"There must be something in the water…"

"There must be something in the water…" commented an American festival director a few years ago, with a mixture of puzzlement and wonder. His observation was dropped during a conversation about one of the most vital and multifaceted avant-garde film scenes in the world – that of Austria. This tiny country in the middle of Europe has seen the growth of an art film tradition over the course of the past six decades that can boast a degree of continuity and ongoing productivity seldom realized elsewhere. In the meantime, it is practically commonplace that Austria's most important contribution to film history was and is largely created in the field of avant-garde production. I fear I will not be able to provide a watertight argument as to why it has come to this. But a few – hopefully plausible – explanations can be attempted.

Austria counts eight million residents, of whom roughly a quarter live in Vienna. This disproportionately giant-headed capital is the heirloom of a splendorous time when Austria was an empire covering a surface area outstripped only by Russia. After the First World War, this empire crumbled into numerous nation states – today, twelve occupy the territory of its former dominion. Austria itself became a truncated state – a dwarf, with a sizable estate alongside its oversized metropolis, consisting of a truly remarkable cultural abundance. And we are talking about a cultural legacy that had largely been incubated in Vienna. The modern portion of this heritage – to avoid reaching as far back as maestro Mozart – arose in the last decades before the fall of the monarchy, approximately during the years from 1880 till the outbreak of war in 1914 – in other words, the historical

phase for which the term "fin de siècle" has been coined. Among the main actors of this period, a handful of representative figures may be named: the painters Gustav Klimt, Egon Schiele, Oskar Kokoschka and the internationally still underacknowledged Richard Gerstl; the authors Arthur Schnitzler, Hugo von Hofmannsthal, Karl Kraus, Rainer Maria Rilke, Georg Trakl and Franz Kafka; the composers Gustav Mahler, Arnold Schoenberg, Anton Webern, Alban Berg, Josef Matthias Hauer (who prior to and independently of Schoenberg developed a 12-tone technique); the architects and designers Otto Wagner, Adolf Loos, Josef Hoffmann and Koloman Moser; philosophers such as Ernst Mach and Ludwig Wittgenstein; and of course the founder of psychoanalysis, Sigmund Freud. They all led their lives and created their work fully aware that one era was coming to a close while a new, yet intangible age was on the rise. They searched for ways to express the advent of this epoch, for new forms capable of articulating fundamentally new content. For this reason, it will come as no surprise that the aforementioned artists and philosophically scientific innovators of the fin de siècle were united by an intensively analytical relationship to the world and to their own material of expression. This development naturally continued after the war – the work of Robert Musil and Stefan Zweig comes to mind, as well as the logical positivism of the Wiener Kreis (Vienna Circle) including such philosophers as Moritz Schlick, Rudolf Carnap and Kurt Goedel. But it met with an abrupt end in 1934, when class struggle culminated in bloody conflict, the Right shut parliament down and the young Republic was transformed into an authoritarian, clerical-fascist corporate state. During the subsequent era of Austro-fascism and the relapse into barbarism under the dictatorship of National Socialism from 1938 till 1945, modern vision was packed away into a box labeled "degenerate."

After liberation by the Allies, it became the task of cultural workers to salvage this heritage from the rubble of war. Artists traumatized by the recent past opposed the pathos and emotional drivel of Nazi-sanctified effusions of art with a renewed will to self-interrogation and an analytic approach to forms of language and expression. It had just been made terribly clear how easily "content" could be used to manipulate and control emotions, the consequences experienced in catastrophic terms. Artistic ambition driven by "content" was princi- pally met with distrust. As during the fin de siècle, the call for *new* possibilities of form and *new* designs gained dominance over emotionalism and pathos. All of the historically relevant art produced in post-war Austria – serial music, the abstract painting of the Informel, concrete poetry, etc. – can be traced back to this fundamental attitude of a critical intelligence.

We have not yet reached the field of cinema, but we are looking at the immediate environment in which its roots are to be found. All the pioneers of Austrian avant-garde film cultivated a deep connection to the established arts: to music, the visual arts and literature. And they all shared a social environment of provincialism and meanness that could hardly have been more claustrophobic. Military defeat and the destruction of the Nazi regime had not dispelled the reactionary fog in many minds, despite "denazification." In the bog of this post-war mentality, art thrived that had to rebel. Under these conditions, the radicalism of concrete poetry and the literary performances produced by the Wiener Gruppe (Vienna Group) was not only possible, it was necessary. The emergence of Viennese Actionism was also at its core an expression of resistance. And whoever works his way through the *Heimat* movies and historical romances of the day can see they were conceived to help forget complicity in the horrors of Nazi dictatorship, constructing an Austrian identity with pillars of singing forests, eternal Habsburg glory and diverse references to the ideology of the corporate state. This cinematic environment further contributes to an understanding of what was soon to follow in the field of cinema.

However, a stale atmosphere alone does not give rise to oppositional art. It also required personali- ties such as those of Peter Kubelka, Kurt Kren and Valie Export, with their longing for radically new and innovative forms of moving images. A film industry had not developed in this small country comparable to the potent production systems found in France, Italy, Germany and Great Britain. The European auteur cinema that began to emerge in these countries as of 1945 and absorb creative minds required money and an infrastructure that simply did not exist in Austria. Here, the one path that remained open led into the field of art and territories of the cultural underground. But what ensued was a kind of reinvention of cinema and a preparation of the ground for all subsequent generations – each in its turn inventing its own paths. Which brings us back to what this book is about… So, to put it in a nutshell: it took the cultural heritage of a world empire, intensively analytical and self-reflexive art forms and intellectual disciplines, a reactionary social environment conducive to rebellion, the absence of a film industry and a handful of geniuses disposed to create autonomous art forms. And perhaps there is something in the water.

This book is the first of its kind to present a condensed history of Austrian avant-garde cinema in English. Introductory essays illuminate the prehistory of this tradition, as well as various direc- tions in different phases of development, within which entirely individualistic aesthetic forms unfolded. The main portion of the book consists of 18 chapters presenting the oeuvre of individual artists. Separate chapters are dedicated to cinematic forerunners of the avant-garde and to Austria's autarchic manifestations of expanded cinema developed by a number of filmmakers in the turbulent years of the 1960s. But artists today also live in exciting times: contemporary motion picture makers are able to lead parallel lives engaged in analog film art and new digitally generated worlds. Meanwhile, by replacing analog projection equipment with digital systems, the movie industry is producing a fait accompli without any form of public debate, forcing the art of analog film into a niche existence after more than a century of prominence. The only remaining question is how large and comfortably furnished this niche will be. Within the context of such changes in overall conditions, a longer essay illuminates the multi-faceted manifestations of motion-picture art in Austria today. A concluding essay oriented to more fundamental questions describes the relationship between radical film art and modern art in general. While covering such a broad spectrum, one of our main objectives is also to inspire further research. This purpose is addressed by a comprehensive appendix. It contains biographies, filmographies and biblio-graphical information on all the filmmakers and artists found in this book, whether in chapters dedicated to individual artists or in one of the essays providing an overview.

Naturally, in addition to our esteemed authors many people have contributed to the making of *Film Unframed*. Of these the first to be thanked is Brigitta Burger-Utzer of sixpackfilm for almost singlehandedly executing the herculean task of creating the aforementioned appendix. As a kind of "advisory board" of book-publishing experts, I would like to thank Alexander Horwath, director of the Austrian Film Museum; Brigitte Mayr, managing director of Synema – Gesellschaft für Film und Medien; Michael Omasta, head film critic at Vienna's city newspaper *Falter*; and again Brigitta Burger-Utzer – all well-proven publishers who helped with their advice. We have Charles Ulbl to thank for the – in our humble opinion – beautiful layout of the book, a seasoned and exceptionally engaged graphic designer. I have had the pleasure of working with Charles for over twenty years, during which time he has not only become an expert of Austrian avant-garde cinema, but a real friend as well. Our thanks also to the translators: Fabrice Leroy and Adrian Martin provided wonder-ful translations from the French, while Eve Heller and Steve Wilder did excellent and nuanced translations of writings by stylistically diverse German authors. Our additional thanks to Steve

Wilder for initiating us into the mysteries of English punctuation rules as well as lending our text consistency as copy editor, the great and thorough unifier of a host of innumerable details. Then there is Kellie Rife who joined us on proofreading in the eleventh hour, and to whom we are indebted for her sharp eye in the final scrutinizing of our galleys. And my endless thanks again go to Eve Heller for her editorial labors. As a native German-language author, I would never have been able to do without her writerly skill and meticulous care honing our English text, including her patience and willingness to spend hours brooding over individual German translation riddles and possible improvements.

Last but not least, I would like to thank the filmmakers of this country. It is a pleasure to be an active part of the multifaceted landscape of the motion-picture art they create, ever challenged anew to give my best as a filmmaker.

I Dream of Austria.

Adrian Martin

Austria is a dream to me. Not because of any of the silly, touristic clichés or cheesy national stereotypes. Nothing to do with *The Sound of Music* or beer or folk music or Alps or anything like that. Austria happens to be a haven and a utopia for one simple, remarkable and quite unique reason: it is a country that, culturally speaking, respects its avant-garde filmmakers, present, past and future.

Perhaps some natives of Austria do not, themselves, realize just how extraordinary this situation is. In most countries (mine included), the avant-garde cinema – if it is ever acknowledged at all – receives only token courtesies, issued through the clenched, hissing teeth of mainstream-minded bureaucrats. Perhaps a little "seed funding" here and there – just a safety-valve measure to keep the crazy artists happy in their little ghetto, where they cannot bother anyone. But when it comes to the litmus test of cultural export – a program of films touring various countries of the world, say, or a special film festival retrospective selection – the experimentalists are quickly, quietly shuffled out the back door. It is as if they never existed. And in the eyes of mainstream culture at large, they indeed do not exist. No one hears about them. They struggle to be screened, discussed, promoted, represented. They await, sadly, their footnote in a history book that may never be written with them in mind.

Whoever enters and maintains the cultural infrastructure of Austria seems to have seen things the right way up. It is like a magnificent reversal of the usual, decrepit, established values, at least as they play out in most other places of the world. What is the evident truth is indeed taken to be evidently true – which is some kind of historic miracle. And the truth, even to a distant outsider like myself, is this: although Austria has a handful of notable auteur figures (like Michael Haneke or Michael Glawogger), and probably some more secret popular cinema traditions worth investigating, the one area in which film has incontestably asserted itself, flourished and excelled is that of the avant-garde. From (at least) Peter Kubelka and Kurt Kren, along the far-out feminism of Valie Export and Mara Mattuschka, through to the brave young stylists of today, it seems like an unbroken line of achievement in avant-garde cinema. And, what's more, this cinema is globally accessible – it travels (and often with its makers). In the often wordless wonders of the latest round of Austrian delights unspooling at whatever film festival or art event I attend on the globe, I feel, for a delirious moment or three, that cinema has at last fulfilled its fondest Esperanto dream: it has indeed cracked the code of a universal language. And so I dream of Austria….

Doubtless, the truth will be more complex, the true history of it less smooth. That is why you

← Austria Filmmakers Cooperative, 1968 (left to right):
Gottfried Schlemmer, Valie Export, Hans Scheugl, Ernst Schmidt Jr.,
Peter Weibel (anonymized by unknown hand) and Kurt Kren.

are reading this book, to get a sense of the context out of which this cultural miracle first emerged, and how it actually managed to stay afloat all this time. There must be divisions, sectarian battles, factional armies, ageing parent-figures and rebellious child-figures, subcultures, breakdowns and breakthroughs, renewals and impasses… But, even on this plane, I sense more of a general accord, not such a tense détente, among the practitioners, over the course of generations, in the Austrian dream-scene. When I heard the news, in 2002, that my friend Alexander Horwath – whom I knew through the film-critical adventure of the *Movie Mutations* writing and book project masterminded by Jonathan Rosenbaum – had been gracefully handed the reins of the Austrian Film Museum by Peter Kubelka, I instantly thought to myself: how could this possibly happen anywhere else in the world? How could someone I identified as a certain purist of an old-style, materialist avant-garde (however jolly he might be in person) make such a pact of perfect trust with a relative youngster who militantly mixed up his tastes for narrative, abstraction, Hollywood, radical politics, rock music, spectacular entertainment and severe cinema of all kinds? Only in Austria…

For each of us, our experience of cinema is indelibly linked to sites, places. Not just where and when we saw something as an index to our usual, sentimental life experiences, like growing up or falling in love – but the actual material conditions of viewing, what our bodies did and what our minds processed to finally convert a movie into what Raymond Bellour has recently called a "special memory," a living memory that preserves and transmits the thousand and one pleasurable shocks of cinema.

Between me and the Austrian avant-garde, it has always been an affair of extremes. Firstly, a kind of bunker experience, like being secreted away in a cellar of a Resistance network: in the 1980s, in Melbourne, watching in this way a series of Kurt Kren films being projected, in pristine 16 mm prints, just for me (it was part of a huge, globally touring exhibition of experimental cinema); and then in the early 1990s, in the offices of

sixpackfilm, being exposed to the new works of a new generation I knew scarcely anything about. Bunker viewing, in the life of any serious cinephile, is linked to filmmakers' co-operatives, to ephemeral, no-budget events, to the spluttering energy of an underground – sometimes literally underground. Linked, also, to critical work (pens writing notes in the dark, interviews with the artists, curating or advising for programs back home), to dissemination of knowledge, to the peculiar liberation offered, once upon a time, by hard theory.

But then, secondly, a huge leap into the spaces of cinema spectacle. Siegfried Fruhauf, in widescreen and at top volume, sprayed across the expanse of a vast wall at the Rotterdam Film Festival in the early 2000s. Peter Tscherkassky, in my hometown for the Melbourne Film Festival just weeks ago (as I write this) in 2011 – offering a no less hypnotic sensation of pure cinema. And a story I will probably still be telling on my deathbed: how, in the early 1990s, a rather genteel bourgeois art house cinema in Melbourne projected, unwittingly, some Cannes-derived package of features with shorts attached – and so up came, for an audience utterly unready for it, Martin Arnold's *passage à l'acte* (1993), which caused a near-riot worthy of the fabled premiere of Buñuel/Dalí's *L'Age d'or*, with angry, well-dressed, middle-aged customers shaking the wall of the projection booth and shouting: "This is not a film!"

Oh, but it was a film – a real film, alright. Like so many of the Austrian avant-garde treats I have seen and been in awe of down the years, it worked on intensities, pulses, waves, sensations – and ultimately, emotions, even when it was hard to put an exact or conventional label to the kind of feelings that stirred inside your entire human frame as you watched such monumental objects of form. When I first experienced the Austrian work, I could not quite locate what I was seeing and hearing. It was not drily conceptual (like some British styles I knew well); nor was it chasing the lure of deconstructed, camp narrative (as so many underground Americans were back then). It had what I once described as the *call of fiction*: moments of tension, drama, shock, exhilaration – but in the abstract, or in miniature, just for a fleeting frame or two. And, constantly, a back-and-forth movement between figuration and abstraction, at a velocity and with a particular type of energy I had never witnessed or felt before. The found footage film is a rich tradition in many countries, but the genre was definitely reinvented and enlivened in Austria.

It took me a long time – until I fully grappled with the writings of thinkers like Gilles Deleuze, Jean-Luc Nancy and Giorgio Agamben that touched upon film – to really formulate the specialness of the Austrian avant-garde cinema. Quite simply and literally, these were *films that thought*, they were concepts in action, in motion. Energetic, dynamic thoughts; a material, burning brain. No separation between an idea and its execution; no gap between intention and structure. Maybe not all these filmmakers went in as master theorists (some did), but their films came out as grand theoretical gestures – gestures we are far from exhausting today.

Once, seven years ago now, there was an excellent film from my country called *The Ister* (2004). Made by two young guys with very little money and a digital video camera, traveling along the Danube. An essay-film, a montage-film, a river-film in every sense, featuring brazen interviews with philosophers and artists. Lots of different languages, plenty of subtitles in it. Like nothing else that had ever been made, or has been made since, in Australia. When this film was premiered in Rotterdam, naturally I was there, a proud citizen of my nation. Some guy – a European film critic – stumbled out at the end, dazed. He looked straight at me and said, with no humor intended: "That's a good Austrian film." He had read the credits wrong, skipping a few letters. But I could not bear to correct his misapprehension. Because – in the stateless realm of everything that is bold and new and experimental – wouldn't it be the highest compliment to say of any movie that deserved it: "That's a good Austrian film"?

Ground Survey.
An Initial Mapping of an Expanding Territory.

Peter Tscherkassky

In the Beginning…

You can't draw a line through flowing water – but we'll give it a try all the same. Let the story begin in the early summer of 1955, during an encounter at a café in Linz. Peter Kubelka, a 21-year-old student of film directing, thrilled by Italian Neorealism and enrolled at Rome's Centro Sperimentale di Cinematografia, has just come home for summer vacation in Upper Austria. He is conferring with his friend Rudolf Malik, a liberal-minded priest enthusiastic about art and explicitly interested in film, who has been cultivating their friendship since Kubelka's high school years in Linz. At the age of 17 Kubelka had announced that he wanted to become a filmmaker, and Malik spontaneously offered to play the role of his future producer. Now, four years later, the moment has come. Kubelka tells him about the first film he's planning to make and wants to complete over the summer. It's about unrequited love, poverty and also trust. As promised, Malik agrees to produce the film. He gets thirty of his brethren to reach into their saving accounts and withdraw 1,000 Austrian schillings each. This sum of 30,000 schillings plus a 15,000 schilling subsidy from the educational ministry constitutes the budget of *Mosaik im Vertrauen*. Shooting takes place in a railroad yard in Linz. Operating the 35 mm camera is the young photographer, jazz pianist and aspiring filmmaker Ferry Radax, Kubelka's former fellow student at Vienna's Film Academy.

The 16 minutes of *Mosaik im Vertrauen* premiere on December 9, 1955, at Filmhaus Schöner in Vienna. And here we have it after all, our line in the water, if you will: the birth of Austrian avant-garde cinema, including date and time. Today, *Mosaik im Vertrauen* (*Mosaic in Confidence*, 1955) is considered Austria's first bona fide, domestically produced avant-garde film work.[1] Two years later, in 1957, Peter Kubelka's first metrical film, *Adebar*, followed – the first serial film in cinematic history, its first "structural" film as it later will be termed. What transpired in Austria during the intervening decades is universally acknowledged as constituting one of the most vibrant and productive art film scenes worldwide. The present volume reports on this small world within the world at large.

Naturally, this tradition has a prehistory too, even if it does not reach far back in time. Austria missed out entirely on an interwar avant-garde film movement, such as that which evolved in Italy, Germany and France. In these European countries, a generation of artists passed through the schools of Expressionism, Cubism, Futurism and Dadaism.

---

1 See Stefan Grissemann, "Countdown to Zero. Before the Avant-Garde: Austro-Film Visions 1951–1955," in this book, p. 44 ff: "*Mosaik im Vertrauen* finally liberated Vienna's outsider cinema from the dead weight of mythos and morbidity – and proved to be the onset of Austria's actual avant-garde film history." For a discussion of Peter Kubelka's film work see Peter Tscherkassky, "The World According to Kubelka," in this book, p. 56 ff.

← Peter Kubelka (above), Peter Weibel and Valie Export (below), in **Birth of a Nation** (1997) by Jonas Mekas

Painting had taken a geometric and serial turn in Germany when Walter Ruttmann, Oskar Fischinger, Hans Richter and Viking Eggeling set their scroll drawings in motion by means of the still young technology of cinema. Ruttmann chose *Opus I* as the brittle and simultaneously programmatic title for his first abstract film. The manic pursuit of a pure and universal language of forms inspired Eggeling's *Symphonie Diagonale*, created between 1920 and 1924 by the emigrant Swede during his Berlin exile. At the same time in France during the first half of the 1920s – coinciding with the flowering of Impressionist film whose main exponents included Germaine Dulac, Marcel L'Herbier, Abel Gance, Louis Delluc and Jean Epstein – Man Ray and Marcel Duchamp began to experiment with nitrate film strips. For his *Le Retour à la raison* (*Return to Reason*, 1923), Man Ray sprinkled spices, needles and thumbtacks on negative film stock, exposed it to light, and after processing, ran these "rayographs" through the projector. In 1924 René Clair produced *Entr'acte*, while Fernand Léger and Dudley Murphy created *Ballet mécanique*. These Dadaist films are considered incunabula of the avant-garde and were followed in 1925 by Henri Chomette's Cinemá pur studies, *Jeux des reflets et de la vitesse* [Games on Reflection and Speed] and *Cinq minutes de cinéma pur* [Five Minutes of Pure Cinema], as well as Duchamp's text film, *Anémic Cinéma*, in 1926. In 1927 Germaine Dulac created the surrealist film *La Coquille et le clergyman* (*The Seashell and the Clergyman*) based on a screenplay by Antonin Artaud. Luis Buñuel in turn masterfully

tricked film audiences by exploiting expectations, utilizing the syntax of the feature film and already well-established rules of narrative cinema: he applied these syntactical rules "incorrectly." Buñuel's poetic surrealist films made in collaboration with Salvador Dalí, *Un Chien andalou* (1928) and *L'Age d'or* (1930), caused a huge stir and became world-renowned.

Nothing comparable was happening in Austria. Although *Ballet mécanique* experienced its world premiere in the Vienna of 1924, apparently the event had no significant impact. It would be 1951 before a film was finally produced outside the commercial mainstream then flourishing in Austria: *Der Rabe* [The Raven], a 13-minute visualization of Edgar Allan Poe's eponymous poem. At the time, such a film was termed an "outsider production," and in fact this work by Kurt Steinwendner (alias Curt Stenvert) and Wolfgang Kudrnofsky proved one crucial thing to its contemporary local art scene: film outside the commercial studio system could be creatively used in its own right as a highly personal and expressive medium. *Der Rabe* also demonstrates the pre-avant-garde tendency to make use of literature as a socially accepted art form to legitimate its own endeavors.

Twenty-year-old Herbert Vesely also chose a literary detour in 1951, basing his debut film, *Und die Kinder spielen so gerne Soldaten* [And the Children Love to Play Soldier], on a very free adaptation of Franz Kafka's novella, *In the Penal Colony*. Georg Trakl's poem "The Young Maid" served as the basis for his second short film completed one year

Peter Kubelka
Mosaik im Vertrauen
1955

Ferry Radax
Das Floß
1954

Herbert Vesely
nicht mehr fliehen
1955

later, _An diesen Abenden_ [On These Evenings].
It is Vesely's 70-minute film _nicht mehr fliehen_
[Flee No More] from 1955 that is regarded as his
most important work prior to the dawn of avant-
garde cinema. Funded with German money but executed by Austrian artists Vesely, Hubert Aratym
and Gerhard Rühm, it exhibits a highly independent
film aesthetic in its attempt to visualize existentialism under the sway of Albert Camus. Contemporary
reviews reacted favorably, especially acknowledging
the economic risk of such an enterprise in the context of a filmic wasteland comprised almost entirely
of the most tawdry and miserable entertainment
vehicles – it would take another seven long years
before the Oberhausen Manifesto declared "Papas
Kino ist tot" [Papa's cinema is dead].[2]

Vesely's _An diesen Abenden_ gave Ferry Radax
his first opportunity to work as a camera assistant.
Two years later, in 1954, Radax proceeded with his

own independent foray into filmmaking, _Das Floß_
[The Raft]. The film remained a fragment, but it
gave the avid photographer further opportunity
to master the film camera. In 1955, he proved what
he had learned when Peter Kubelka engaged him
as director of cinematography for his own debut:
Mosaik im Vertrauen is a beautifully shot film.
In 1955, as an avant-garde film, it remained one of
a kind.

Next, Please!
In 1956, the next person who would later come to
stand alongside Peter Kubelka – as the second
acknowledged pioneer of Austrian avant-garde film
– grabbed a camera: Kurt Kren. Unlike Kubelka,
who had cut to the chase and started shooting on
35 mm, Kren initially experimented with 8 mm film
before getting himself a 16 mm Bolex in 1957 and
creating the first official work in his filmography:
1/57 Versuch mit synthetischem Ton (Test) (1/57 Test
with Synthetic Sound). Fifty further films followed,
until his untimely death in 1998. Like Kubelka,
Kren circulated within the modest dimensions
of Vienna's art scene and its equally navigable

2   See "In der Zone Null," _Der Spiegel_, no. 29, July 13, 1955,
pp. 37–38. In regard to the Oberhausen Manifesto see
http://en.wikipedia.org/wiki/Oberhausen_Manifesto. On the films
of Kurt Steinwendner and Herbert Vesely, see Stefan Grissemann,
"Countdown to Zero," especially p. 44 ff.

infrastructure.[3] Everyone knew everybody. This situation fostered artistic exchange and crossover productions of all kinds. Kren shot one of his early 8 mm films, entitled *Klavier Salon 1. Stock* [Piano Salon, 1st Floor] (1956) with Konrad Bayer, poet and member of the legendary Wiener Gruppe (Vienna Group), and he created two other works with the sculptor and Op-artist Marc Adrian: *Das Walk* [The Walk] (1956) and *Mobiles* (1957), both on 16 mm film.[4] The collaboration with Bayer did not expand

beyond its experimental 8 mm dimensions. On the other hand, from the very beginning Kren was directly involved with Marc Adrian's career as a filmmaker: Adrian's first three films, *Black Movie* (1957), *1. Mai 1958* [May 1, 1958] and *Wo-da-vor-bei* [Where-there-in front-next to] (both 1958) were created in collaboration with Kren. *Black Movie* is particularly noteworthy. The film consisted of variously colored strips of leader. Originally dated 1957–1963,[5] a "first version" of *Black Movie* was later dated 1957.[6] It was only shown privately because it existed solely as an original, and the edit points of the film had the unfortunate tendency of coming undone during projection. So Adrian and Kren simply set up a laundry basket behind the projector into which the hand-numbered strips of film would drop.[7] In Adrian's early films we again encounter a concern with literature, as several works hinge on concrete poetry including *Text 1*

3   In addition to Kubelka's producer, Rudolf Malik, the liberal wing of the Catholic Church in the person of Monsignor Otto Mauer can be attributed with playing no small part in supporting post-war art in Austria: In 1953, Otto Mauer, Dean of St. Stephen's Cathedral, founded a neighborhood gallery called Galerie nächst St. Stephan as a forum for modern art, focusing on the abstract paintings of the so-called Informel art movement and creating one of the most important forums for art in Vienna at the time. It not only presented one of Arnulf Rainer's first exhibit but also hosted Vienna's first public Kurt Kren screening (organized by Peter Kubelka) in March of 1961. To this day, currently under the direction of Rosemarie Schwarzwälder, Galerie nächst St. Stephan is considered one of the most important galleries in the city. Additionally, Vienna's Cathedral and Diocesan Museum has Otto Mauer to thank for a comprehensive collection of 3,000 works spanning classical and modern art.
4   On the work of Kurt Kren, see Stefan Grissemann, "Fundamental Punk. On Kurt Kren's Universal Cinema," in this book, p. 92 ff. On Kren's earliest films see Thomas Korschil, "Die ersten, die letzten, soweit," in *Ex Underground. Kurt Kren, seine Filme*, ed. Hans Scheugl (Vienna: PVS Verleger, 1996), pp. 24–50. The Vienna Group (1954–1964) "can be considered one of the most radical modernist moments in Europe during the second half of the 20th century, alongside the Situationist International and the [British] 'Independent Group.' " See http://de.wikipedia.org/wiki/Oswald_Wiener. An image of the exceptional radicalism of the Vienna Group is conveyed in *the vienna group – a moment of modernity, 1954–1960*, ed. Peter Weibel (Vienna and New York: Springer, 1997).

5   See *Neuer Österreichischer Film*, ed. Kuratorium Neuer Österreichischer Film (Vienna: Kuratorium Neuer Österreichischer Film, 1970), p. 48; see also *Subgeschichte des Films. Lexikon des Avantgarde-, Experimental- und Undergroundfilms*, ed. Hans Scheugl and Ernst Schmidt Jr. (Frankfurt am Main: Suhrkamp, 1974), p. 32.
6   Starting with Ernst Schmidt Jr., *Österreichischer Avantgarde- und Undergroundfilm 1950–1980*, Vienna: Österreichisches Filmarchiv, 1980, p. 10.
7   See Wolfgang Lehner and Bernhard Praschl, "Stellen Sie sich einen österreichischen Film vor! Zur Entwicklung des Avantgarde-, Experimental- und Undergroundfilms in der Zweiten Republik," in *Medienkultur in Österreich*, ed. Hans Fabris and Kurt Luger (Vienna, Cologne and Graz: Böhlau Verlag, 1988), pp. 199–250. The accusation raised by Peter Kubelka in this essay regarding the predating of certain films (p. 214) is possibly based on the eventuality that these films might have only been presented in private, which could explain why he failed to register such an event.

Marc Adrian
Das Walk
1958

Marc Adrian
1. Mai 1958
1958

(1963). But these films engage the written word in specifically filmic entanglements. _Random_ (1963), on the other hand, takes abstract painting as its touchstone. _Random_ also happens to be the first European film created by means of a computer, used to facilitate its random generation.[8]

A First Generation

For many years now, three generations have been distinguished within the historiography of Austrian avant-garde film. The leading figures of the first generation have already been acknowledged with the naming of Peter Kubelka, Kurt Kren, Marc Adrian and Ferry Radax. The only one who eventually wandered off into commercial realms was Ferry Radax, but not before completing _Sonne halt!_ [Sun, Stop!] (1959/1962), a central work of the first generation.[9] However, apart from this late surrealist flowering, the most significant aesthetic paradigm introduced in the early work of the first generation is clearly the metricalization and serialization of film. Above all, it was Peter Kubelka's metric films, followed by the mathematically structured films of Kurt Kren organized according to strict serial scores, that were the first of their kind in the world and created a radically new film aesthetic – namely Kubelka's _Adebar_ (1957), _Schwechater_ (1958) and _Arnulf Rainer_ (1960), and Kren's _2/60 48 Köpfe aus_

dem Szondi-Test (2/60 48 Heads From the Szondi Test), _3/60 Bäume im Herbst_ (3/60 Trees in Autumn, both 1960), _4/61 Mauer pos.-neg. und Weg_ (4/61 Wall pos.-neg. and Path, 1961), and _5/62 Fenstergucker, Abfall, etc._ (5/62 People Looking out of the Window, Trash, etc., 1962).[10] In these works the relationship of the medium to all pro- and extra-filmic content is entirely redefined: it emancipates itself from these "realities." One could say that the medium of film finds its own identity _as an art form_ in these works – its own entirely specific and particular language, its own utterly unique voice that cannot be heard in any other art form. The German philosopher and cultural theorist Theodor W. Adorno developed an unprecedented and radical theory of autonomous art, through which he interpreted modern art as implicitly expressing _in its very form_ a fundamental critique of our alienated social order. Although Adorno had a lifelong interest in film, he regarded it as incapable of reaching the level of an autonomous modern art form – due to what he considered its "restrictive dependency on reality": "The photographic technology of film, primarily representational, places a higher intrinsic significance on the [represented] object, as foreign to subjectivity, than on aesthetically autonomous types of processes [i.e., music, literature, painting]; this is the retrogressive aspect of film in the historical development of art. Even where film

---

8   In regard to Marc Adrian's work, see Norbert Pfaffenbichler, "Shadow Burns," in this book, p. 114 ff.

9   In regard to _Sonne halt!_ by Ferry Radax see Peter Tscherkassky, "The Halted Sun of Ferry Radax," in this book, p. 82 ff.

10   These early works by Kurt Kren (as well as numerous later films) have been released on DVD under the title _Kurt Kren, Structural Films_, Index DVD Edition 002.

Ferry Radax
Sonne halt!
1959/1962

Peter Kubelka
Schwechater
1958

dissolves and modifies its objects as much as it can, the disintegration is never complete. Consequently, [the photographic technology] does not permit absolute construction: The elements, into which it disassembles, always retain something reified; they are never pure values." [11] Metric and serial films grant precisely this capacity to film: the ability to constellate its elements as "pure values." With metric film, cinema meets Adorno's expectations of an "aesthetically autonomous process."

Be this as it may, Peter Kubelka, Kurt Kren and Marc Adrian went their filmically artistic ways without being diverted by the "generationalizing" of film history. It should be kept in mind, when the topic of Austria's three generations of avant-garde filmmakers arises, that this organizing principle is not based on personal biography or individual filmography. Instead, it refers to the three fundamental aesthetic paradigm shifts that transpired, roughly speaking, in the mid-1950s, mid-1960s and the second half of the 1970s. And this explains how Kurt Kren also came to play a central role in the subsequent generation.

A Second Generation

Kurt Kren had mainly worked with 16 mm from the start. This might not seem very important at first glance, but given the prevalent use of 35 mm by the first generation throughout the 1950s, Kren was a logical bridge to the second generation for whom 16 mm became the format of choice. This switch

strikingly demonstrates how seemingly incidental modifications of the material of expression (in this case a change of format) strongly influences artistic expression within the medium (in our case the cinematic medium). During the formation of the third generation in the second half of the 1970s it would be Super 8 that served as a catalyst. And the most recent generation – even if no one has yet named it the "fourth" – cannot be imagined without electronic imaging and computer processing. The discourse regarding "analog versus digital" must be considered from this perspective (a discourse which basically started with the introduction of the electronic medium of video for home use, long before the rise of digital computer systems). Each generation, despite all differences of individual voice and style, exhibits a specific and identifiable aesthetic that is profoundly linked to an associated format and its specific possibilities.

Viewed in terms of production dates, the first renowned representative of the second generation is Ernst Schmidt Jr., who picked up a 16 mm camera and started shooting in 1963. He was soon followed by Hans Scheugl, joined shortly thereafter by Peter Weibel, Valie Export and Gottfried Schlemmer; and finally Kurt Kren stepped into the picture. He had gotten a little lost sitting around in Vienna in the mid-1960s and was taken on the next leg of the journey by the upcoming young filmmakers. [12]

By this time, subsequent to his early serial films, Kren had already completed a second and very spectacular group of works, his so-called "Action films," which he undertook with Otto Muehl and Günter Brus. This engagement with Viennese Actionism would prove to have a formative impact upon the development of a new filmic aesthetic – especially the Actionism of Otto Muehl and Günter

11 T. W. Adorno, "Filmtransparente," in *Ohne Leitbild. Parva Aesthetica* (Frankfurt am Main: Suhrkamp, 1967), p. 83: "Die photographische Technik des Films, primär abbildend, verschafft dem zur Subjektivität fremden Objekt mehr an Eigengeltung als die ästhetisch autonomen Verfahrensarten; das ist im geschichtlichen Zug der Kunst das retardierende Moment des Films. Selbst wo er die Objekte, wie es ihm möglich ist, auflöst und modifiziert, ist die Auflösung nicht vollständig. Sie erlaubt daher auch keine absolute Konstruktion; die Elemente, in die zerlegt wird, behalten etwas Dinghaftes, sind keine reinen Valeurs." A somewhat problematic English translation of this passage can be found in T. W. Adorno, "Transparencies on Film," *New German Critique*, no. 24/25, special double issue on New German Cinema, (Autumn, 1981–Winter, 1982), p. 202. Published by Duke University Press Stable, http://www.jstor.org/stable/488050. For a closer examination of the relationship between film, modernity and modern art, see Peter Tscherkassky, "The Framework of Modernity. Some concluding remarks on cinema and modernism," in this book, p. 310ff.

12 On the work of Ernst Schmidt Jr. see Peter Tscherkassky, "The Generalist: Ernst Schmidt Jr." in this book, p. 140ff. On the work of Hans Scheugl see Stefan Grissemann, "Time Slice, Space Block. The Synthetic Realities of Viennese Filmmaker Hans Scheugl," also in this book, p. 154ff, as well as Index DVD Edition 029, *Hans Scheugl, The Seconds Strike Reality*. On the work of Valie Export see Maureen Turim, "VALIE EXPORT: The Female Body in Myriad Frames," in this book, p. 164ff. Three of her short films were released on *VALIE EXPORT, 3 Experimental Short Films*, Index DVD Edition 004.

Brus.[13] It was undoubtedly Kurt Kren who forged the most profound bond with Actionism. His Action films, almost all realized in the years 1964 and 1965, can be seen as a catalyst for those artists of the second generation who would soon go on to create a radical form of what was to be called "expanded cinema." Originally, Kren had been invited by Muehl and Brus to record their Actions on film.[14] Decades later Kren narrated with a grin how Muehl turned pale at the premiere of *6/64 Mama und Papa* (1964): Kren had applied his serial editing technique to the footage he shot of Muehl's Actions. In an outrageously time-consuming and complex editing marathon, Kren interlaced a host of continuous takes; he continually returned to significant shots as leitmotifs, and throughout the film interlinked chronologically disparate images and movements that formally mirrored one another. Kren wove the frenzy of the Action that had unfolded before his lens into geometric figures of compression and condensation, requiring painstaking meticulousness. Alternating shot/countershot sequences that jump between single frames edited

by hand (!), the Actionist tumult was ornamentalized into geometric patterns. In other words, with his cut-up techniques Kren took on a kind of artistic rivalry with the Actions – that is to say, the film vehemently manifests its artistic independence in regard to the object of its depiction, the Actions.

What Muehl presumably expected was a documentation of the spectacular event that had transpired in front of the camera. Instead, Kren destroyed the spatial and temporal continuity of the Happening. While the Actionists carried out a sensually relished and thorough decimation of the concept of traditional fine art, Kren paralleled this breakdown on the level of its filmic "documentation." In so doing, Kren defined a radically new approach to the cinematographic act in relation to the object of its representation. Kren does *not* document – instead he *competes*. The Actionist's annihilation of the concept of fine art as the production of pretty pictures for the living room is transferred to the level of its reproduction and places the notion of filmic "reproduction" in general in question. And this, in turn, anticipates the breakdown of classical film found in expanded cinema, in material film and in conceptual film.[15]

---

13 Hermann Nitsch and Rudolf Schwarzkogler did not play a significant role in the avant-garde film scene. However Nitsch found an early supporter in Peter Kubelka, and a lifelong friend. To this day Kubelka uses a wing in Nitsch's castle in Prinzendorf, Lower Austria, to house a portion of his voluminous collection of early and late Neolithic artifacts.
14 On the first encounter between Muehl and Kren see Otto Muehl's vivid description in a letter he wrote from prison in 1995, "Begegnung mit Kurti im Café Merkur" [Encounter with Kurti in Café Merkur] in *Ex Underground. Kurt Kren, seine Filme*, ed. Scheugl, p. 95ff. (Muehl was serving a seven-year sentence for sexual abuse of minors during the time of his Friedrichshof Commune. See http://en.wikipedia.org/wiki/Otto_Muehl)

---

15 Muehl and Brus themselves soon began to document their Actions on film. What had been accomplished on the level of their Actions – the release of the materials of fine art from traditional and restrictive confines, the transgression of representation and its means in space, etc. – was relinquished on the level of their own films, ultimately resulting in relatively conventional representational realism. These documentations could never have afforded the aesthetic conditions that became crucial for expanded cinema. Their considerable relevance as documents of Viennese Actionism however remains unquestionable. Kren's Action films were released on DVD: *Kurt Kren, Action Films*, Index DVD Edition 001.

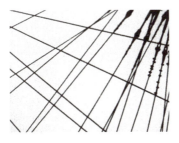

Ernst Schmidt Jr.
P.R.A.T.E.R.
1963–1966

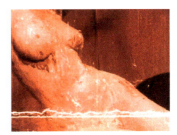

Kurt Kren
6/64 Mama und Papa
1964

Expanded Cinema

The aesthetic leitmotif of the second generation was transgression. The first generation had been concerned with establishing film as an autonomous art form equal to the other modern arts. But now, in the midst of the sociocultural revolution of the 1960s, it was again time (as in the days of Dadaism and Surrealism) to try to destroy the separation between life and art, to integrate art into life, and bring day-to-day life into art. The notion of an autonomous and refined high art was perceived as an anachronistic relic from a bourgeois era. Transgression: the Actionists had demonstrated how it was to be done in the field of fine art. The corresponding gesture in film art was called "expanded cinema."[16]

A historical evaluation of expanded cinema that does not take the social environment of the time into consideration would be doomed to fall short. A fundamentally revolutionary transformation of social conditions was the order of the day. This battle was taken on by resorting to the well-established Viennese tradition of linguistic criticism.[17] Every form of language was understood as an instrument of domination, and as such was to be artistically identified and interpreted. The illusion apparatus of film and cinema were obvious and equally worthwhile targets. Expanded cinema as well as what later became known as material film[18] attempted to disassemble this apparatus into its component parts in order to reveal its every aspect, and that means its fundamental basis. This not only included material aspects of the film-

strip, but also elements such as the conditions of reception in the movie house or preconceived expectations of the audience. It could take place peacefully as in *Ein Familienfilm von Waltraud Lehner* [A Family Film by Waltraud Lehner] (1968, by Weibel and Export): two actors sit in the movie theater and treat the public like guests in their private home (Waltraud Lehner is the civil name of Valie Export). But it could also definitely get violent as in *Exit* (1968, Weibel and Export). Aluminum foil was tautly spanned in place of the movie screen. After the public was seated and, in place of a film, observed themselves reflected in the foil, fireworks shot out at them from behind the "screen": In a panic, they rushed for the "exit."

In retrospect, the Austrian avant-garde film scene of the 1960s gives the impression of a "movement" because of the group formation that began to take shape at the time. Here again, we can attempt to diagnose a dawning and to name a date: this time it is January 26, 1967. On this very day at Vienna's Palais Pálffy the first joint appearance of the most important representatives of the second generation took place. The program that had been scheduled consisted of a mix of 16 mm films by Kren, Scheugl, Schmidt Jr., as well as the first expanded cinema actions by Peter Weibel – *Action Lecture No. 1* and *Nivea*, a "direct commercial": "For *Nivea* he held up a Nivea beach ball while standing in front of the screen, in the flickering white light of the projector accompanied by the sound of a camera motor played by a tape recorder." Weibel hereby released the "constituent elements of film – director, light, sound, camera, projector – from their illusionistic unity."[19]

The group experience of this evening, and its repeat performance the next day, had a formative impact. The self-awareness of a new generation was strengthened, henceforth to be theoretically nourished by the eloquent chief ideologist of the group, Peter Weibel, whose pointedly radical manifestos and essays still make for lively reading. The artists got on board and set sail.

16 On the history and aesthetic of Austrian expanded cinema, see Hans Scheugl, "Expanded Cinemas Exploding," in this book, p. 154 ff, as well as Scheugl's *Erweitertes Kino. Die Wiener Filme der 60er Jahre* (Vienna: Triton Verlag, 2002). A comprehensive presentation of the international expanded cinema movement in English can be found in the catalogue *X-Screen. Film Installations and Actions in the 1960s and 1970s* for an exhibition of the same name that took place at mumok in Vienna, 2003/2004, edited by Museum Moderner Kunst Stiftung Ludwig Wien and Matthias Michalka (Cologne: Verlag der Buchhandlung Walther König, 2004).
17 At this time the art scene was avidly engaged with the language philosophy of Viennese philosopher Ludwig Wittgenstein, whose *Philosophical Investigations* had been published posthumously in 1953.
18 Hans Scheugl, "Expanded Cinemas Exploding," in this book, p. 154 ff, as well as Hans Scheugl and Ernst Schmidt Jr., *Subgeschichte des Films*, p. 584.

19 Hans Scheugl, "Expanded Cinemas Exploding," in this book, p. 154 ff.

A Boat Called "Underground"

Nine months later, in October 1967, P. Adams Sitney introduced a comprehensive selection of the New American Cinema in Vienna. The series screened at the Austrian Film Museum, which Peter Kubelka had co-founded with Peter Konlechner in 1964. Contemporary witness Hans Scheugl says in retrospect: "For us filmmakers in Austria, the delayed encounter with the American films was of little relevance, insofar as the development of a new film language in Austria had already advanced very far and the films we got to see did not deliver any new insight for our own work. The situation was different in Germany, Italy and Great Britain where, until the mid-1960s, there was absolutely no avant-garde film. The influence of the Americans accordingly had a strong effect on the films of Werner Nekes, Wilhelm and Birgit Hein; Alfredo Leonardi, Massimo Bacigalupo and Antonio De Bernardi; Malcolm Le Grice, Peter Gidal and Stephen Dwoskin. But the US filmmakers were undoubtedly important to us, too, because of how they saw themselves as a part of the social upheaval occurring in America and because of how adrenalized their art movement was; this stimulated and strengthened our own filmic radicalism."[20] Such a somewhat blanket statement

could perhaps permit selective fine-tuning on closer analysis. Scheugl's evaluation might have been colored by a conflict brewing at the time between the Austrian Film Museum and the new generation of filmmakers: Kubelka and co-director Konlechner refused to show the work of the second generation at the Film Museum, instead giving preferential treatment to their American colleagues.[21] On the other hand, the evaluation can be accepted *cum grano salis*: In Vienna back then a highly autarchic film aesthetic had evolved – an independence that had even been registered and appreciated by contemporary criticism, however sparse.

In this age of the Internet and an historically unprecedented abundance of festivals worldwide, the significance of individual international meetings back in the day can only be grasped with a concentrated effort of the imagination. The flow of oral and written information was also very meager, as Hans Scheugl succinctly describes,[22] let alone the chance of seeing the actual films of colleagues from abroad. This makes it all the easier to retro-

---

20 Hans Scheugl, *Erweitertes Kino*, p. 77.

21 This conflict culminated in the occupation of the Film Museum on January 14, 1969. But works by yesterday's antagonists are now an integral part of Peter Kubelka's recurring cycle of 63 programs, What Is Film?, shown at the Austrian Film Museum every Tuesday night.

22 See Hans Scheugl, "Expanded Cinemas Exploding," p. 154 ff.

Ferry Radax, Hans Scheugl, Peter Weibel, Kurt Kren,
Peter Kubelka, Ernst Schmidt Jr. (from left to right)
At Studio Praml, December 25, 1966

spectively put one's finger on the few salient events of the time. This includes the five editions of the EXPRMNTL festival organized by Jacques Ledoux in Belgium (twice in Brussels, three times at the beach resort of Knokke-Le-Zout). The first edition took place in 1949 under the name Festival international du cinéma expérimental et poétique and was primarily dedicated to the historical avant-garde movements, though it also included contemporary works by the Canadian Norman McLaren, as well the early US avant-garde: Maya Deren, Sydney Peterson, James Broughton, Gregory Markopoulos, James Whitney, John Whitney and Kenneth Anger. The next EXPRMNTL festival took place nine years later, in 1958, and together with the first edition in Knokke at the turn of the year 1963/1964, provided several American films with European premieres – whereby 1963/1964 showed "almost the entire New American Cinema (...) Stan VanDerBeek, Gregory Markopoulos and Ed Emshwiller received prizes, only Brakhage wasn't given an award, despite the many films he had running."[23] At these

two editions of the festival Austria was represented solely by Peter Kubelka, but this was to change.

In September of 1966, the Destruction in Art symposium took place in London, intervening between Knokke 1963/1964 and 1967/1968. Judging by its publicity, it had no less of an impact. It brought lasting international renown to the films of Kurt Kren (as well as to the Vienna Actionists), but on the whole was not attended by enough filmmakers to have a structural impact on the community. This role was left to Knokke-Le-Zout in 1967/1968, which was dominated for the first time by European filmmakers. The Austria Filmmakers Cooperative was founded only a few days after the festival, modeled on co-ops already established in New York, London, Hamburg and Amsterdam. "The effect Knokke had was astounding. The energies suddenly released on the European film scene led to a veritable explosion of organization in terms of screenings, the production of films and finally, also publicity. In no year before or since were as many films produced as in 1968."[24]

What came next is now history, presented in the individual essays to be found in this book. In conclusion, let us summarize: The emergence of the second generation had the quality of a sudden

23 Scheugl, *Erweitertes Kino*, p. 87. In his *Movie Journal* Jonas Mekas describes the tumult surrounding the prohibited presentation of Jack Smith's *Flaming Creatures* (1963) at Knokke, which instead took place in the underground of the underground, namely a hotel room. See *Movie Journal. The Rise of a New American Cinema, 1959–1971* (New York: Collier Books, 1972), p. 111ff.

24 Scheugl, *Erweitertes Kino*, p. 95.

Peter Weibel
Action Lecture No. 2
1968

Occupation of the Austrian Film Museum.
Above: Oswald Wiener (with hat);
to his left, Otto Muehl.
Below: Ernst Schmidt Jr., Peter Weibel
(both standing),
Valie Export (right of Weibel).
January 14, 1969

Quiet Days in Vienna

From today's vantage point the early 1970s seem like a quiet period in the wake of the preceding radicalism of the 1960s, and in comparison it undoubtedly was. Nevertheless, new filmmakers entered the scene, circumspectly presented by the chronicler of the Austrian avant-garde, Ernst Schmidt Jr., in a film series entitled Austrian Avant-Garde and Underground Film 1950–1980 at Vienna's Z-Club.[26] Naturally, the catalogue accompanying this retrospective also includes artists whose work remained of a modest scope, or who subsequently turned to other artforms or more conventional types of filmmaking. But others came to stay. Maria Lassnig, Linda Christanell and Christiane Adrian-Engländer, alias Moucle Blackout, joined Valie Export in opposing the traditional male dominance within the field. In faraway New York Maria Lassnig, although completely unacknowledged in Austria, created a body of animation films throughout the 1970s – practically a new film each year.[27] Moucle Blackout meanwhile had made a debut in 1969 with her serial study *Walk In*, showing a single shot of Marc Adrian walking into a room that was repeated in a serially predetermined variety of lengths over the course of 12 minutes. Blackout's *Die Geburt der Venus* (*Birth of Venus*, 1970–1972) was a pioneering act, a wild dance of naked bodies constructed out of a montage of photographs: "Moucle Blackout's experimental animation film *Die Geburt der Venus* captures the spirit of the 1960s. A psychedelic aesthetic, Pop-art and pop music, free love and feminist probing present a portrait of the era. On the other hand, the impressive filmic language Moucle created through the use of fantastic stop-motion and mirroring effects makes the film a genuine classic of the Austrian avant-garde. *Die Geburt der Venus*, along with the early anima-tion films of Maria Lassnig, count as the first solo efforts by women artists in Austria. Like Lassnig, Moucle Blackout dares to venture into a highly

eruption, and its passing seemed even more abrupt. This was in part due to the context of a failed social revolution, but it also had to do with the nature of the works. Many had assumed a demonstrative character, and at some point, everything had already been demonstrated. A continuation of the act of unmasking would have been doomed to freeze into a pose. And with the failure of the efforts made by the "generation of 1968" to revolu-tionize society, the dream of a fundamental "transformation of film culture also seemed over. After almost 20 expanded cinema Actions in the year of 1968 alone, Hans Scheugl lists only a single Action for 1969 (Schmidt Jr.'s *Hell's Angels*), and for 1970 none.[25]

---

25 Scheugl, *Erweitertes Kino*, p. 200

---

26 See also Peter Tscherkassky, "The Generalist: Ernst Schmidt Jr.,"
p. 140 ff.
27 In regard to the films of Maria Lassnig see Maya McKechneay,
"Two Telephone Books, a Lightbulb, a Glass Plate," in this book,
p. 176 ff.

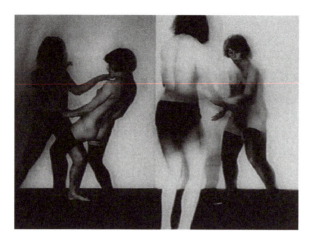

Valie Export
Die Praxis der Liebe
1984

Moucle Blackout
Die Geburt der Venus
1970–1972

personal terrain of imagistic language when she radically addresses sexual fantasies," writes animation filmmaker Sabine Groschup.[28]

A feminist-inspired cinema is also to be found in the numerous works of Linda Christanell. Christanell has dedicated herself to the art of the filmic tableau: arrangements of erotically and sensually loaded as well as ambivalently charged objects, all potentially serviceable as fetishes, are lit with subtlety and subject to minimal movement. "Lately I often use pieces of jewelry and make fetishes of them, trying to bring these things into a new context in which they radiate energy and endeavoring to reveal their sexual meaning."[29] With close to 30 titles dating from 1975 to 2012, Christanell is one of the most productive filmmakers in Austria. Her films have been honored and presented in numerous retrospectives, and a

comprehensive monograph dedicated to her work was published in 2011.[30]

Coming from a diametrically opposed cinematic angle, the experimental writer Hermann J. Hendrich created structural film studies, including *49 Steine* (*49 stones*, 1971), *14 long shots* (1974), and *gray day* (1973), a film based on an Action by Valie Export. Hendrich most successfully implemented his ideas in 1986 with the realization of *mnemosyne* – dedicated to Valie Export, for whom Hendrich worked as business manager on her dramatic features *Unsichtbare Gegner* (*Invisible Adversaries*, 1977), *Menschenfrauen* (*Human Females*, 1979) and *Die Praxis der Liebe* (*The Practice of Love*, 1984).

In 1971 Kurt Kren moved to West Germany and resolutely continued with his work. Fundamentally changing his style, he followed up his restless, fast-edited early work with quiet, concentrated studies of time. The masterpieces he created during this period include *31/75 Asyl* (*31/75 Asylum*, 1975), *32/76 An W+B* (*32/76 To W+B*, 1976) as well as the

28 "ASIFAKEIL präsentiert die Avantegardefilmerin Moucle Blackout im quartier21/MuseumsQuartier," http://www.ots.at/presseaussendung/OTS_20101111_OTS0077/asifakeil-praesentiert-die-avantegardefilmerin-moucle-blackout-im-quartier21 museumsquartier.
29 Linda Christanell, quoted by Claudia Gehrke in *Rote Küsse. Frauen-film-Schaubuch*, ed. Sabine Perthold (Tübingen, Germany: konkursbuch, 1990), p. 200.

30 *Linda Christanell – Wenn ich die Kamera öffne, ist sie rot*, ed. Synema (Vienna: Synema, 2011). Nine of Christanell's films have been released on *Linda Christanell, The Nature of Expression*, Index DVD Edition 025.

first film he made after emigrating to the US in 1978, *37/78 Tree again*.

Moving in very different directions, Valie Export and Ernst Schmidt Jr. undertook early crossovers to other genres. They created two seminal works of the 1970s, both premiering in 1977: Export's afore-mentioned *Invisible Adversaries* and Schmidt Jr.'s cunning two-hour city portrait *Wienfilm 1896–1976* (*Vienna Movie 1896–1976*).[31] Like Kurt Kren, both had remained active after 1970. Export in particular was able to interweave hard won liberties of filmic expression and the use of her own body to refine her feminist perspective. *Mann & Frau & Animal* (*Man & Woman & Animal*, 1970–1973) and *....Remote....Remote....* (1973) constitute the mate-rial evidence of this work period. The experience Export gleaned from her pioneering video art was applied to her narrative feature *Invisible Adversar-ies*. This brings us to our own domestic *chronique scandaleuse*, which of course the Austrian avant-garde film scene must and most naturally does have. Schmidt Jr. had already made his contribution back in 1968, with his film *Kunst und Revolution* (*Art and Revolution*). *Kunst und Revolution* was Schmidt's filmic treatment of an eponymous Action by Messrs. Muehl, Brus, Weibel, Oswald Wiener and an individual in disguise which took place on June 7, 1968 at Vienna's university, during which "several taboos [were violated] at once: nudity, defecation, masturbation, whipping, self-mutilation, the smear-ing of one's own excrement on one's own naked body, and vomiting (...) – all the while singing the Austrian national anthem on an outspread national flag."[32] Valie Export effected a scandal of no less consequence with her dramatic feature *Invisible Adversaries*. Export had already come into conflict with the law in 1971 (on the side of Peter Weibel),

as co-editor of the book *Wien – Bildkompendium Wiener Aktionismus und Film*, leading to their con-viction and suspended prison sentence – all of this happened at a time when Oswald Wiener and Günter Brus had long since fled to Germany to avoid sentencing for their participation in the *Kunst und Revolution* Action – after having been held in prison for two months pending trial.[33] Actionism constantly stirred up a rabid tabloid press, accompanied by police deployment or legal epilogues. Reactions of this kind were undoubtedly taken into account, and provocation was part of the game. But all this was outdone by the scandal caused by *Invisible Adver-saries*. Although this time around the lawsuits immediately pending resulted in acquittal, Austria's biggest tabloid had already begun to whip up an ongoing frenzy on the basis of certain provocative scenes in *Invisible Adversaries*, resulting in an unin-terrupted 27-week run in a Vienna movie theater,[34] an unprecedented success that no avant-garde film

---

33   Today, Austria has a museum dedicated exclusively to the work of Günter Brus, as well as one devoted to Hermann Nitsch. And Brus has been honored with the Grand Austrian State Prize, the highest distinction for artistic achievement the Republic can bestow – as well as Nitsch, as well as Oswald Wiener. In a sense this is a perfectly Austrian fate – although the demise of the individual in question is usually awaited before they are hon-ored with their own museum – to which the actor and cabaret artist Helmut Qualtinger (1928–1986) once said: "In Vienna you've got to die before they celebrate you and let you live it up – but then you live long!"

34   The campaign started on October 20, 1977, with the headline "Where Shit Is Subsidized." (Richard Nimmerrichter aka "Staberl," *Neue Kronenzeitung*).

---

31   Both films are available on DVD: *Wienfilm 1896–1976*, dir. by Ernst Schmidt Jr., was released on *Der österreichische Film*, # 41, 2006 (Vienna: Der Standard/Hoanzl, DVD Edition); Export's film was released on *Valie Export, Invisible Adversaries*, Index DVD Edition 021.

32   "Kunst und Revolution," http://de.wikipedia.org/wiki/Kunst_und_ Revolution. Based on a mix-up, the tabloid press wrongly accused Kurt Kren with authorship of the film ("University obscenity now in cinemas also!" was the headline of the smear sheet *Blauer Montag*) and led to Kren's being fired by the National Bank.

Linda Christanell
Aline Carola
1990

has since attained in this form. The film was exhaustively honored with numerous debates in Parliament and the recommendation by an independent commission of experts to award Valie Export the annual Award of Honor for *Invisible Adversaries* was not accepted by the Social Democrat minister for cultural affairs.

While all this excitement was going on, a new avant-garde movement was subcutaneously picking up speed – much later it would become known as the "third generation."

Subjective Cameras
When the third generation emerged, it was armed with Super 8 cameras. At the time Super 8 was experiencing a worldwide boom, and Austria was no exception: In October 1982, when Vienna's Stadtkino dedicated a weekend to Super 8 film, the 16-hour program exclusively presented domestic films produced in 1981 and 1982.

Regular 8 had already made inroads within the ranks of the avant-garde long before Super 8 was introduced to the market in 1965. In the US, Gregory Markopoulos, Kenneth Anger and Curtis Harrington had produced their first 8 mm films in the 1940s. With a small-gauge body of work that evolved over the course of a decade, the brothers George and Mike Kuchar staged 8 mm productions starring mom and all the neighbors they could lay their hands on in a kind of topsy-turvy Hollywood in the Bronx – in perfect anonymity until 1963, when Ken Jacobs and Jonas Mekas discovered their wonderfully grotesque mini-melodramas to the delight of New York's underground. In 1964, Jacobs and Stan Brakhage temporarily switched formats from 16 mm to Regular 8. Brakhage's 8 mm cycle of *Songs* produced between 1964 and 1969, including his *23rd Psalm Branch* (1966–1967), belong to the canon of the New American Cinema.

Over the course of the 1970s, Super 8 equipment matured into high-tech products thanks to the gigantic amateur market that made it viable. Over the years close to one thousand different camera models were developed and produced for this market. And the bright, crystal-clear light of a Xenon Super 8 projection had little in common

with the rather intimate living-room experience of a Regular 8 film screening. It was this projection technology that motivated festivals to include Super 8 productions at the time.[35] In the 1970s, the technically matured medium of Super 8 also provided an upcoming generation of artists in the US, including Saul Levine, Vito Acconci, Marjorie Keller, Joe Gibbons, Lenny Lipton, Vivienne Dick and many more, affordable equipment to produce their own work. "The most innovative post-structural (or anti-structural) films of the Seventies were produced in super-8."[36] The really big boom that presented a serious flipside to daddy's home movies was delivered by the punk-inspired youth movement of the late 1970s and early 1980s, its continental European center located in Berlin. The rebellion took place under the motto "No future!" and when it came to the form thousands of these films assumed, the motto was simultaneously "No history": How they looked had more to do with the simple handiness of the equipment and low production costs than with the Absolute films of the 1920s, Robert Wiene's *Cabinet of Dr. Caligari* (1920) or the work of important German avant-garde filmmakers of the 1960s and 1970s such as Werner Nekes, Wilhelm & Birgit Hein, Klaus Wyborny, or Heinz Emigholz. For the most part, extremely rapid sequences of images were used to celebrate an attitude towards life which in Berlin had an adrenalized high-speed quality connected with an ongoing struggle for housing (at times more than 200 buildings were occupied by mostly punk squatters, wresting them from real estate speculators and creating an atmosphere of collective upheaval). Seen by an historically trained eye these works evinced a good deal of déjà vu, but they could lay claim to representing the authenticity of a large-scale celebration of the moment.

---

35 When Lisl Ponger showed one of her films at the Oberhausen Short Film Festival, the projectionist calculated that the screen reflected an enlargement two million times the size of her Super 8 film frames.

36 J. Hoberman, "The Super-80s," in *Film Comment*, May/June 1981, reprinted in J. Hoberman, *Vulgar Modernism: Writing on Movies and Other Media* (Philadelphia: Temple University Press, 1991), pp. 129–136.

Ernst Schmidt Jr.
Kunst und Revolution
1968

In Austria, things were really different. Here a very recent and most radical past had to be acknowledged and "the scene" was simply not big enough to allow itself a rehash. The terrain of structural film as well as the expansive forms of the 1960s had been thoroughly elaborated, executed on a highly advanced aesthetic level. To follow in these footsteps would have come across as a naive regression. But there is a "but" to the story: Although the collective effort of the second generation to destroy traditional cinema had not led to what one might consider a "unified aesthetic," it did forge an identifiable bond in the form of a basic artistic attitude toward the medium and its emancipated use. This double-sided situation had two results: First, potentials specific to the medium could again be freely explored and utilized detached from ambitions in regard to sociocultural struggles. And secondly, weighed down by its heritage in terms of film history and the exhaustion of a collective aesthetic attitude, our heavily-laden protagonists developed a multiplicity of personal styles and individual aesthetics of unprecedented abundance here in Austria. You looked over your colleague's shoulder and developed your own form of expression. While it is problematic to use a single term to categorize the films of the 1950s and 1960s (an expression

such as "structural film" falls hopelessly short; the characterization "expansive forms" used for expanded cinema is also insufficient), it is utterly impossible to find a common conceptual denominator for the work produced by the third generation.[37] Of its many filmmakers (the vast majority of whom started with Super 8), a few are herewith named, including the production year of their filmic debuts: Dietmar Brehm (1974), Karl Kowanz (1975), Robert Quitta (1977), Herwig Kempinger (1979), Lisl Ponger (1979), Angela Hans Scheirl (1979), Peter Tscherkassky (1979/1980), Gustav Deutsch (1982), Mara Mattuschka (1983, 16 mm), Ursula Pürrer (1984) and Martin Arnold (1985, 16 mm).[38]

[37] Who exactly came up with the designation "third generation" (and invented the "generation principle" to begin with) is not known. From the standpoint of current research, first written mention was made by Peter Weibel in 1984: "In the early 1980s a third generation continued the tradition of avant-garde filmmaking on Super 8," in "Der Traum von der Freiheit," in *Der Kunst ihre Freiheit. Wege der österreichischen Moderne von 1880 bis zur Gegenwart*, ed. Kristian Sotriffer (Vienna: Edition Tusch, 1984), p. 223.
[38] Available on Index DVD Edition: *Mara Mattuschka, Iris Scan*, 006; *Peter Tscherkassky, Films From a Dark Room*, 008; *Lisl Ponger, Travelling Light*, 010; *Gustav Deutsch, Film ist. (1–12)*, 012; *Dietmar Brehm, Black Garden*, 016; *Martin Arnold, The Cineseizure*, 018; *Pürrer/Scheirl, Super-8-Girl Games*, 026; *Ursula Pürrer, A. Hans Scheirl, Dietmar Schipek, Flaming Ears*, 031; and *Mara Mattuschka, Chris Haring, Burning Down the Palace*, 038.

Found Footage

From today's perspective, if you nonetheless take a step back and try to recognize *a single* common bond within this new and multifaceted landscape of the third generation, one phenomenon in particular catches the eye – the widespread use of found footage. Working with found footage played a pivotal role in emancipating the younger generation from the legacy of the first and second, and it still does so to this day.

An anecdote comes to mind: In 1960, when Peter Kubelka's mother attended her first screening of his film *Arnulf Rainer* – consisting entirely of black-and-white film frames, silence and white noise – she is reported to have exclaimed, "Such a thing only happens to my boy: Now the projector is broken!" The avant-garde has repeatedly been attributed an iconoclastic tendency. And if this reasoning were sound, its iconoclasm could hardly be better encapsulated than by this little story. An untrained eye must necessarily perceive *Arnulf Rainer* as the breakdown of the entire cinematographic apparatus: The images seem to have been erased and even the machine for their transportation appears to have abandoned its function. But in fact the rebellion of the avant-garde is not directed against the image in itself, but rather the overall perception of the image as a stand-in for reality. The concept of "film as a window onto the world," famously formulated by André Bazin precisely demarcates the standpoint the avant-garde opposes. This "transparent" window robs the image of its "self," and it is precisely this integrity of the image in itself which concerns the avant-garde. Upon closer examination, the supposed iconoclasm of the avant-garde reveals itself as the exact opposite, namely as a turning *toward* the image, to restore its reality *as image*. In contrast to the seeming naturalness of the relationship between the film image and that which it represents – the basis of cinematic illusionism – it stresses the character of the *contrivance*, of the *created* nature of the image. This implies a position radically opposed to that of industrial cinema. While the latter tinkers on a "window to the world" in an effort to make us forget the window, the structural film allows for the recognition of how this supposed window invents the sense and meaning of the world it shows; it reveals the mechanisms that are used to construct sense and shows the creation of meaning *in statu nascendi*: the moment of its unfolding. In terms of "iconoclasm" one could at most claim that structural film is able to display a relative indifference to what is portrayed. By definition, its main concern is with its own structure, and in order to demonstrate this structure, the specific content of imagery might occasionally appear interchangeable.

With the self-referential exposition of filmic sign structures, the troops of the 1960s had established an elementary aesthetic knowledge that is historically irreversible. But whoever subsequently persists in a pure exploration of sign systems inevitably lands in a territory of formalism – a fate met by more than just a few works across the globe in the 1970s ... In contrast, for the third generation the filmic medium and its specific sign systems continued to be resonant issues, but no artist felt these concerns alone were enough to adequately substantiate a film. And it is precisely at this historical point in time that found footage came into the picture. It enabled a new generation to return to the *content* of images, without appearing naive. To stay with the metaphor: The prior generation had been concerned with the window and its construction; now the gaze *through* the window was thematized. This implies perceptual processes as well as what is perceived. Instead of the window, what the window renders visible now served as artistic material, including all of its codes.

What this means shall be illustrated by a description of a short film created by Dietmar Brehm. Brehm is one of the most distinguished and simultaneously productive representatives of the third generation – the length of his oeuvre currently clocks in at around 40 hours.[39] His work always

---

39 Thanks to Dietmar Brehm the city of Linz is registered as another hotspot of innovative film production on the map of Austria, and currently joined by the outstanding filmmaker Siegfried A. Fruhauf (see Nicole Brenez, "Is This the Precise Way That Worlds are Reborn?", in this book, p. 276 ff). Among many other Linz compatriots are Sabine Hiebler & Gerhard Ertl, who collaboratively created found footage films in the 1990s, including *Schönberg* (1990), *General Motors* (1992) and *komakino* (1996), which received acclaim touring international festivals.

Dietmar Brehm
Pool
1989

includes a central interest in processes of perception. Initially, this comes down to the original "perceiver" – the camera as a "recording organ." Brehm never makes unmediated use of found footage. Instead, his images are usually the result of an elaborate process of rephotography. During refilming, the asynchronous shifting of phases between the rotating shutters of projector and camera result in pulsating exposure values. In all Super 8 cameras this pulsating remains invisible during shooting – with one exception, and that is the Beaulieu camera. Thanks to an oscillating mirror shutter unique to its construction, this pulsation becomes visible in the viewfinder during shooting and is adjustable given the Beaulieu's stepless speed control. Brehm can thereby inscribe rhythms of tempo and flickering into images during the process of refilming. He calls the resulting visual effect "pumping screen": pulsing, fragmented images of movement often stretched to extremes of slow motion. By means of this pumping screen, Brehm never simply shows images, but also the seeing of these images – his gaze, our gaze, the gaze of the camera.

Pool was created in 1989 and is three minutes long. *Pool* contains very few image elements: people in bathing suits hang around a swimming pool, a roofed terrace structure with peculiarly triangular windows is seen, as well as several tropical plants. The people are sitting on stools, swimming or standing in small groups; a few are seen diving into the water. The movements are slowed down. This slow motion stands in contrast to the restless camera work of the scanned material. Pans to the left are dominant; the lens zooms in on imagery several times, only to rapidly zoom back out. The process of refilming causes the edges of the images to get frayed: While their center remains bright, the periphery sinks into darkness. We get the impression of peering through a telescope at grounds in the distance. On the whole, the film conveys a highly "unreal" atmosphere. The use of slow motion, the fragmented closeups of movement (a man seems to be flailing at something with his towel), bodies seen in repeated phases of diving – all this contributes to a mood that makes events inexplicable, as if the people and their actions are lacking any kind of motivation. On the other hand, the zooms and pans suggest a searching movement, as if the camera were trying to discover something that might evade the fleeting gaze. Vegetation including palm trees with long, sharply pointed leaves, seems to especially magnetize the gaze of the camera's scan. The overall sense of a latent threat arises, heightened by an acoustic background reminiscent of jungle sounds. Yet the people do not react to the situation we observe them to be in, and their apparent indifference stands in sharp contrast to the atmosphere of looming danger.

What is Brehm doing here? He is reacting to the content of his material as if scrutinizing a text in a language entirely foreign to him. Instead of reading this text "properly," he stares at the individual, isolated "words" that thereby lose the meaning of their original context and begin to refer back to themselves. The gestures and small events of the characters lose all recognizable, or even vaguely comprehensible meaning. *Pool* starts effecting the sense of watching a camp of lost souls from a safe distance: people who have been banished to a state of pointless existence and endless waiting, as if arisen from a work by Samuel Beckett and trapped in Dante's purgatory.

To recognize Brehm as the quintessential existentialist of the third generation might require more than these three minutes of *Pool*.[40] Yet this short work exhibits the subtle re-semantization of film art typical of the third generation. While Ernst Schmidt Jr. of the second generation programmatically proclaimed, "The medium itself is first and foremost the subject matter of the filmmaker,"[41] in *Pool* one encounters a reflexive use of the medium, but the film is not entirely consumed by this reflexivity.

sixpackfilm

The year *Pool* was created, 1989, was also the year of the completion of Martin Arnold's *pièce touchée* – and *pièce touchée* was to herald major changes.

At this point in time the third generation was sitting pretty, if you will, in the saddle. Thanks to tireless efforts that went into organizing both domestic and international group shows (spearheaded first and foremost by Lisl Ponger), as well as the help of the Austria Filmmakers Cooperative

(which had been reanimated in 1982), the work of the third generation had achieved extensive exposure and its artistic identity – gained through a fundamental shift of aesthetic paradigms – was firmly established. In these years a new generation also arose within the ranks of film criticism, and the attention of this new guard of critics accompanied the young avant-garde filmmakers from the very beginning. For the first time, filmmakers and film critics were on the same wavelength – and this has remained unchanged to this day. Innovative filmmaking receives in-depth coverage by serious media in Austria. Period.

Also, the festival Österreichische Filmtage, which was dedicated to domestic film production and took place annually since 1984 in Upper Austria's Wels, presented avant-garde films on an equal footing with other genres. And the same can be said without reservation of its successor festival since 1993, the Diagonale.[42] In 1987, Lisl Ponger got the third generation's first big retrospective on its legs with a presentation at Vienna's Museum of the 20th Century called Die Schatten im Silber (Shadows in Silver, including catalogue), and one year later we presented ourselves at the same location in a self-conscious dialogue with the second generation. This screening series was entitled Das Licht der Peripherie (The Light of Periphery, my first meaningful job as curator and catalogue editor), and it was so popular that we had to repeat each of the "peripheral light" shows ad hoc because the cinema was continually overrun and sold-out.

Another year later, in 1989, the third generation landed its first international mega-hit with Martin Arnold's *pièce touchée*. This occasion led to the founding of sixpackfilm, and it signaled the beginning of a new era. But first things first.

The battle waged by filmmakers for adequate financial support had begun in the 1960s, as strikingly evidenced by furious pamphlets penned by Ernst Schmidt Jr. and Peter Weibel. It was in 1970 that a first law was passed establishing funding for film production in Austria. A distinction was

---

40 For an analysis of Brehm's masterly seven-part cycle, *Schwarzer Garten* (1987–1999), see Bert Rebhandl, "The Garden of Delights," in this book, p. 186 ff, as well as Peter Tscherkassky, "Sucking Camera. Found Footage in der Filmkunst Dietmar Brehms," in *Dietmar Brehm: Perfekt*, ed. Gottfried Schlemmer (Vienna: Sonderzahl, 2000), pp. 159–176. The entire cycle can be found on the aforementioned Index DVD 016, *Dietmar Brehm, Black Garden*.
41 Scheugl and Schmidt Jr., *Eine Subgeschichte des Films*, p. 820

42 A fact that continues to baffle international guests who come to visit the Diagonale in Graz for the first time.

established at the outset between support for feature-length movies produced by the commercial film industry on the one hand, and the funding for non-commercial, low-budget films on the other.[43] In 1981 the Austrian Film Institute (ÖFI) was founded, which distributes funding for the production of commercial, feature length films. ÖFI accordingly funds films based on guidelines of the *Film* Funding Act; on the other hand, the Cultural Section of the Ministry for Education, Art and Culture distributes film subsidies according to guidelines of the *Art* Funding Act. The so-called "small" film fund is administered by this ministry, and as stipulated by law, requires "projects that are of an innovative character." Each of these two domains – the "big" as well as the "small" funds – is overseen by its own independent commission of experts. The small fund jury for innovative projects processes approximately 300 applications annually; roughly 25 percent of these are recommended for funding. Their costs range from a few hundred to one hundred thousand euros. This sums up the situation of film subsidy in Austria, which, while appearing chronically underfinanced here at home, seems luxurious to visitors from abroad. This it is not, but when it comes to artistic filmmaking, the situation here is still better than in most other European countries, not to mention the US. However, at the end of the 1980s what was still missing was a professional distribution and rental organization. And this brings us back to *pièce touchée* ...

sixpackfilm was originally founded for the sole purpose of mounting a large-scale found footage film festival. This was supposed to be organized by the young cultural manager Brigitta Burger-Utzer and me. For legal reasons, we needed a non-profit association as subsidy recipient. In the fall of 1991 the festival took place in Vienna's Stadtkino and met with great success. At this time Arnold's *pièce touchée* was touring festivals around the globe with the help of an American promoter, and was garnering one prize after another. It was all too clear to Arnold that this tour of success would have been logistically impossible without the professional support of his promoter. So after the found footage festival was over and sixpackfilm was about to be dissolved as initially planned, Arnold suggested that it be restructured into an organization that would submit a selection of the best new non-commercial films of all genres to international festivals, as had been done with *pièce touchée*. Naturally this selection of films would also correspond to many of the works funded by the Ministry of Art and Culture. And this is precisely what happened. At that time Herbert Timmermann was the ministry official responsible for such matters – a man who accomplished great things across the board for independent filmmaking in Austria thanks to his commitment and unbureaucratic engagement. Timmermann immediately recognized the win-win nature of the proposition and secured the necessary financial support for founding of the festival distribution company.

---

43 That the production of a so-called "commercial" film requires public funding at all is due to the fact that the German-language market is too small for box-office income to cover production costs. If film production were not subsidized, there would be no European auteur cinema – there would simply be no European film industry *at all*. This is exactly why the US vehemently attempted to forbid the funding of film production during GATT negotiations in recent years, concerning further so-called liberalization of world trade. In the end European film was saved only after laboriously achieved exemption clauses in the GATT treaty.

Martin Arnold
pièce touchée
1989

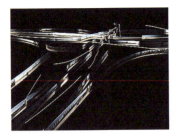

Dietmar Offenhuber
Besenbahn
2001

Dietmar Offenhuber
kapitel 3 aus Berlin 10439
2005

Stadtmusik (S. Auinger, D. Offenhuber, H. Strobl)
m18 felsen
2005

Over the years, the one-woman enterprise of sixpackfilm has evolved into a mid-size organization with eight employees dividing five full-time jobs, plus a sixpackfilm representative in the US. Together they create a level of public exposure that one could not have dared dream of in the past. An alternating jury of independent experts selects what they perceive to be the most convincing current productions chosen from all genres – short narrative, documentary, animation, video and digital art, avant-garde. The selected works are subsequently submitted to festivals all around the world. At this time, well over 100 festivals regularly receive submissions from sixpackfilm, and each year hundreds of films and videos are invited to participate. So sixpackfilm takes on labor in the non-commercial domain assumed by the global distribution companies of commercial films, to an extent that the individual filmmaker could never come close to managing (or financing, if you consider the shipping costs involved). In addition to its non-commercial festival distribution activities, in 1996, sixpackfilm also became a rental organization. All films in festival distribution, on an average of two years, are subsequently assimilated into its rental catalogue. Furthermore, many domestic avant-garde classics are available for rental.

In addition to festival work, sixpackfilm has organized cinematic events from its outset. The aforementioned found footage festival was soon followed by the three-week series Unknown Territories, presenting new and independent American avant-garde films in Vienna. This was followed by the counter-move of a program of Austrian films curated by Steve Anker[44] that toured some of the most prominent venues in Europe and the US. Thanks to catalogues that accompany such occasions, sixpackfilm has also earned a name for itself as a publisher.

sixpackfilm continues to organize screenings. Of its regularly programmed events, the In Person series is especially noteworthy and illuminating. International artists are invited to personally present their work in Vienna. This means includes filmmakers such as Pat O'Neill, Kenneth Anger, Phil Solomon, Matthias Müller, Ivan Ladislav Galeta, Mike Hoolboom, Su Friedrich, Leslie Thornton, Craig Baldwin, Sadie Benning, James Benning, Bruce McClure, Tony Conrad, Nathaniel Dorsky, Lis Rhodes, Irit Batsry and Ernie Gehr, just to name a few.

---

44 At the time Anker was a professor at the San Francisco Art Institute and director of the San Francisco Cinematheque.

Astrid Ofner
Sag es mir Dienstag
2007

Thomas Baumann, Josef Dabernig, Martin Kaltner
Gehfilmen 6
1994

And finally in 2004, in cooperation with the Medienwerkstatt Wien, sixpackfilm established the DVD label Index. The Index catalogue has 38 currently available titles, including a selection of international artists along with Austrian productions.[45]

Today
Naturally, an efficient distribution infrastructure providing public exposure contributes to the development of the wide variety of work being produced, as well as ensuring its continuity in the long run. But let us rather pose a question as to whether the variety out there represents something like a fourth generation. At least so far, no one has named it as such. This might be attributable to the unprecedented diversity of the contemporary scene. As Barbara Pichler points out in her heroic attempt to master and do justice to this abundance, there is a lack of homogeneous subcultures according to

which the work could more easily be classified.[46] Equally relevant is her observation that "various types of interaction between film, art and pop-culture phenomena have increased in intensity," and previously distinct domains overlap with accelerating frequency. Meanwhile, as a consequence of the growing commitment of art academies, electronic motion pictures are also extending ever further into the realm of the white cube. Today, Dietmar Offenhuber's magnificent and yet latently apocalyptic visions of current urban development (*Besenbahn*, 2001; *kapitel 3 aus Berlin 10439*, 2005; *m18 felsen*, 2005) meet with Astrid Ofner's poetic, luminously grainy Super 8 Kafka essay blown up to glorious 35 mm, *Sag es mir Dienstag* (*Tell Me On Tuesday*, 2007); famous film settings generated on computer by Constanze Ruhm and artificially emptied of all action (*Evidence*, 2000) parade alongside the super-eccentric and intentionally funky, low-contrast *Gehfilmen* series by Thomas Baumann and Martin Kaltner (such as *Gehfilmen 6* [*Walking Film 6*, 1994], in which two gentlemen can be observed in

---

45 http://www.index-dvd.at. The Medienwerkstatt is a foundation established in the early days of video to "provide access to electronic media and promote their artistic application," as indicated on its website, handles rental distribution for art and documentary videos produced in German-speaking regions, and programs related events (http://www.medienwerkstatt-wien.at/).

46 See Barbara Pichler, "Avant-Garde Now: Notes on Contemporary Film Art," in this book, p. 294 ff.

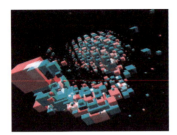

Didi Bruckmayr
trendfollower
2008

Johannes Hammel
Die Badenden
2003

an Eastern Bloc satellite town walking with utmost earnestness, though without apparent goal or motivation, on artificial "green islands" of grass along paths of comparable pointlessness between hideous prefabricated cement block buildings[47]; highly artificial computer-animated sculptural images like those generated by Didi Bruckmayr (*My Personality Hates Me!*, 2007; *Flexible Cities*, 2008; *trendfollower*, 2008) stand side by side with found footage films by our domestic expert of chemical film treatment, Johannes Hammel, like *Die Badenden* (*The Bathers*, 2003); *Die Liebenden* (*The Lovers*, 2004); *Abendmahl* (*Last Supper*, 2005); and *Jour sombre*, 2011.

Amidst such new masters there are four that have essays dedicated to their work in this book, and who have engaged for many years in hybrid realms. Michaela Grill generates live video to live performances of music. In the case of Josef Dabernig, there seems hardly a creative activity he wants to leave out. Alongside film, Dabernig has received wide acclaim in the arts of photography, literature, object art and architecture. The filmmaker Norbert

Pfaffenbichler is equally creative as a visual artist and curator. And Siegfried Fruhauf, whose work most convincingly synthesizes classical analog film and computer-based image processing, also publishes poetry and regularly does white cube exhibitions of his art. The other thing these four have in common: their work has nothing in common.

If, despite all odds, one tries to discover the semblance of factions within the pluralistically fragmented scene of motion picture art in Austria, it is relatively easy to hone in on the animation artists. Thanks to Maria Lassnig and Hubert Sielecki, a strong tradition has unfolded over the years with fringes that lap into avant-garde territory.[48] This might be explained by the influence of animators such as Thomas Renoldner in the Austrian section of the Association Internationale du Film d'Animation (ASIFA Austria). Renoldner's filmic roots reach back to the Super 8 movement of the early 1980s, when he staged late manifestations of expanded cinema utilizing the small-gauge format. Alongside artists such as Mattuschka, whose animation films have been unconditionally appreciated

47 Works by Ruhm are available on Index DVD Edition 009: *Constanze Ruhm, Video Works 1999–2005*. The *Gehfilmen* series by Baumann/Kaltner was released as *Gehfilmen* on DVD Edition Der Standard/Hoanzl, Der österreichische Film, #123.

48 See Maya McKechneay, "Two Telephone Books, a Lightbulb, a Glass Plate. How Maria Lassnig's Lo-Fi Animated Film Art Influenced an Entire Generation of Animation Filmmakers," p. 176 ff.

as avant-garde work, innovators such as Martin Reinhart and Virgil Widrich must be mentioned. Reinhart, a veritable technical genius, even invented his own patented motion-picture processing technology, whereby time and space axes are transposed: "Normally, each individual frame of film depicts the entire space, but only a moment in time (1/24 second). With tx-transformed films, it is just the opposite: Each frame shows the entire time, but only a tiny portion of space – if one cuts alongside the horizontal space axis, the left portion of the picture turns into the 'the before,' the right one into 'the after'." [49] What this means – in other words, what it looks like – can be marveled at in the 35 mm film *tx-transform* (1998) by Reinhart and Widrich.

Widrich's vivacious animation film *Copy Shop* (2001) even earned an Oscar nomination. His subsequent *Fast Film* (2003) went one step further. A wild chase sequence is seen, pieced together out of 300 scenes from different classics of motion-picture history. *Fast Film* is based on no less than 65,000 (!) different photocopies of individual frames from Hollywood movies. However, these stills were splintered into fragments, and resolved into cohesive images only when folded into objects – like a car or an airplane: In other words, thousands upon thousands of paper objects had been folded together and imprinted with still frames that only

became recognizable upon reassembly. These image-objects were shot frame-by-frame using a digital camera and animated using a computer. Every individual frame of *Fast Film* shows at least three such paper objects: a background image, a foreground image and a border area in between. In select sequences this density of layers escalates, with up to 30 different image components. And the story of *Fast Film* (about a happy couple, the she of which is kidnapped, the ensuing chase sequence and concluding rescue) plays out on the surfaces of paper objects … The resulting extravaganza was too much even for the Academy to handle.

The Austrian film-funding system enables – in moderation, but nonetheless – a cinema freed from the pressures of commercial viability. This not only creates conditions for the further development of film production anchored in the classical avant-garde tradition, it also supports the cultivation of borderline territories, such as the threshold between experimental and essayistic cinema. In this context Michael Pilz comes to mind, with his poetically woven observational marathons, or Manfred Neuwirth, whose 90-minute *[ma]Trilogy* counts among the most moving works in the production landscape. The first part, entitled *Tibetische Erinnerungen* (*Tibetan Recollections*, 1988–1995), is a kind of Tibetan road movie in slow motion, showing the strange and outlandish beauty of an ethnically threatened culture in occupied territory; *manga train* (1998) proceeds

---

49   http://www.tx-transform.com/Eng/index.html and http://www.tx-transform.com/.

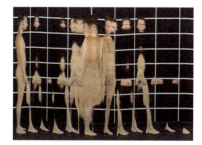

Martin Reinhart, Virgil Widrich
tx-transform
1998

Virgil Widrich
Fast Film
2003

Manfred Neuwirth
Tibetische Erinnerungen
1988–1995

Manfred Neuwirth
manga train
1998

to Japan; and *magic hour* (1999) returns to his homeland of Lower Austria – Neuwirth's path unfolds in a way that allows the most obscure detail to assume a central role: a real eye-opener.[50]

Michael Palm has also developed a completely unique style of filmmaking. The visual and aural levels of his work often seem to lead perfectly autonomous, parallel lives. In his 30-minute narrative film *Sea Concrete Human* (2001), a post-apocalyptic investigation of our Earth is narrated from the perspective of a vaguely defined entity, audible as a text-to-speech computer voice reporting on a search for the cause and effects of the global disaster. The starting point of this search is provided by diary-like audio and image recordings of a female explorer of Antarctica, the only one who had briefly managed to survive the mysterious catastrophe. In fact the visuals, usually grainy Super 8 images blown up to 35 mm as well as innumerable photographs, seem like incidental recordings of an extended hike across a vacant landscape of coastal dunes and abandoned concrete beach buildings whose functions have long been forgotten. Palm uses these artfully artless images to convey his apocalyptic and suspensefully told story, including numerous references to the destructive effects of global warming.

In Palm's most recent work, *Low Definition Control* (2011), he presents a 90-minute, 35 mm CinemaScope essay on the topic of an increasingly overregulated and intrusively monitored society. Again one sees images – often assuming an aesthetic resembling that of surveillance cameras – distinct from their aural accompaniment, consisting of off-screen commentary voiced by critical minds. These respond to questions about immigration, foreignness, the relationship between the State and the individual, the expansion of police authority, unforeseen consequences of medical diagnostics in regard to pre-natal as well as prospective medical conditions (such as the discovery of the inevitable future onset of Alzheimer's in a seemingly healthy patient), further coupled with questions regarding how such knowledge should be managed, on the part of the attending physician as well as the individual in question. And all this culminates in the question of a "world film" as a new version of Big Brother, in which all this accumulated knowledge is stored – transformed into digital codes. Running parallel to the voice articulating this idea, we see grainy black-and-white images, as if gazing into a no longer valid reality: upon unsuspecting passersby, children at play, participants in an urban marathon, children sledding. And it is only logical that the last images of the film quote post-apocalyptic beach images from *Sea Concrete Human* ...

Alongside advanced hybrid forms of documentary-essayistic-narrative, animation and digital

50 Films by Neuwirth and Pilz are available on DVD: *Manfred Neuwirth, [ma]Trilogy*, Index DVD Edition 011; and *Michael Pilz, Facts For Fiction. Parco Delle Rimembranze*, Index DVD Edition 027.

Thomas Draschan
Encounter in Space
2003

image magic, there of course can be found a bio-tope cultivated by the friends and defenders of analog film, who despite a digitally dominated age refuse to relinquish its inimitable and irreplaceable qualities. It will not be surprising that the rules of the analog purity law[51] find special respect in prox-imity to Master Kubelka. Of the Austrians who made pilgrimages to Germany in order to participate in Kubelka's master class, Film and Cooking as Art-form, at the Frankfurt Academy of Fine Art, the Städelschule, Thomas Draschan is counted among

the most prolific. In many of his works Draschan attempts a kind of eclectic "Kurt Kren meets Bruce Conner" mix for post-modernists. The pool of images from which Draschan draws seems inex-haustible. An obsessed found footage collector is obviously at work here, one who comprehends and manages the content of his huge holdings by means of an elaborate system of categorization. Otherwise, his tour de force cascades of pictures gleaned from the most diverse film sources would hardly be pos-sible, as the montage usually is oriented upon imag-istic analogies, whether based on form or content. Meanwhile Draschan does not shy away from funky jokes (i.e., "porno-penis meets crocodile throat") – always entertainingly catchy. Like Kren, Draschan practices single-frame editing and explicitly works in the tradition of Bruce Conner when he, too, helps himself to Brian Eno and David Byrne's album "My Life in the Bush of Ghosts," but instead of Conner's use of "America Is Waiting" visualizes the track "Mea Culpa" in his film _Encounter in Space_ (2003).

On the other hand, Albert Sackl, also a Kubelka graduate, has committed himself wholeheartedly to single-frame animation and associated possibilities of condensing time. Like the stop-motion artist Mara Mattuschka, Sackl usually acts in front of and

---

51   http://en.wikipedia.org/wiki/Reinheitsgebot.

Michael Palm
Low Definition Control
2011

for the camera. *Vom Innen; von aussen* (*About the Inside; from the Outside*, 2006) exhibits the naked Sackl, and with him the borderline masochism of his willingness to submit to incredibly time-consuming production processes, often under physically grueling conditions. At first Sackl appears in front of a neutral black background, standing in upright position, like a Muybridge figure, but ordered not to move. By means of stop-frame animation, Sackl begins to rotate on his body's vertical axis as he moves through the pictorial space, soon transitioning to the outdoors through the sleight of hand rendered by a camera pan into refreshing green landscapes, the heat of summer, through fall and snowy winter. And always right in the middle of it all, the naked Sackl, stiffly upright and rotating, barreling through time and space. The camera pans back indoors and the jerkiness typical of stop-motion photography continues: through living rooms and studio, Sackl always as the driving force in the midst of the wandering scene, his body spinning, time and again split into three figures, cohabiting distinct spatial positions between individual frames, and then again merging into one figure, like a failed hologram unable to expand into 3D. The leaps in time become ever more extreme looking out the studio window at the racing traffic on the street or at the fog-covered meadow. If ever the statement of Richard Wagner's Gurnemanz character, "Time here becomes space," materialized into a film, this would be it.

It comes as no surprise that Sackl quotes Étienne-Jules Marey in *Vom Innen; von aussen* with a demonstratively outspread book of Marey's

groundbreaking photographic studies. In all of his works Sackl aspires to a high level of artificiality, and kindred to Marey, what interests him about the artificiality of film is the ability to make realms visible that are normally hidden from natural perception (or to create them in the first place). In radical contrast stands the self-observational style that Günter Zehetner forged in Kubelka's smithy. Zehetner is a master of artlessness, executed with such nerve that some viewers are left clueless – especially in response to his most recent videos. *Fernsehen, Christine und ich* (*TV, Christine and I*, 1993, silent): Titled as if to give itself away, Zehetner and his girlfriend are seen on a couch watching an off-screen TV, but not with great concentration. She files her fingernails, he pages through a newspaper and occasionally leaves the scene only to return and stare off at the tube. The End. *Schlafen II* (*Sleeping II*, 1993, Super 8, silent): Our couple is seen sleeping via time-lapse photography, captured by camera mounted on a tripod shooting over the course of one night. But the documented sleep of changing bodily positions radiates a character of infighting more than restorative tranquility. And as a kind of one-hour magnum opus from Zehetner's Super 8 period, *Die Zeit heilt alle Wunder* (*Time Heals All Wonders*, 1997): This time the film was shot with synchronous sound and a camera either set down in front of Zehetner or held with outstretched arm – almost always aimed at his own face unabashedly gazing back into the lens: capturing him boozing it up with friends, loudly singing to Beatles music; hung over the next day; the visit of a female acquaintance; in bed in front

Albert Sackl
Vom Innen; von aussen
2006

Günter Zehetner
Schlafen II
1993

Günter Zehetner
Die Zeit heilt alle Wunder
1997

Eve Heller
Ruby Skin
2005

of the TV (which we now get to watch at length: Peter Falk, Robert Redford, et al.); Zehetner pissing into the toilet; home alone, expressively dancing for the camera to radio hits that evidently move him deeply, and once again steadfastly gazing into the camera. Zehetner presents himself as a creature of everyday life, aiming the camera at himself with such candor that we cannot help being put into the position of voyeurs (even without the half-erect penis of *Schlafen II*). However, unlike images from the vacation films of home moviemakers, these views of an everyday protagonist convey a feeling of abandonment and depressive melancholy with an intensity that could only be equaled by maestro Antonioni. But in Zehetner's work, he steps into the place assumed by "art," and with an authenticity quotient of 100 percent.

Also "new acquisition" Eve Heller, a US film-maker with dual citizenship based in Austria since 2005 – who can boast teachers including Paul Sharits, Tony Conrad, Keith Sanborn, Peter Hutton, Peggy Ahwesh and Abigail Child – has remained true to analog (and occasionally hand-processed) film. In many of her works Heller proves herself to be a master of the optical printer – incidentally, a device that has played a surprisingly rare role in the history of Austrian avant-garde filmmaking. Using a JK optical printer she imported to Austria,

Heller penetrates found footage frame by frame, enlarging the details of images – at times to extremes bordering on abstraction. Through her painstaking editing of slowed-down imagery and layers of multiple images, Heller re-contextualizes the visual vocabulary of her source material, rendering dreamlike atmospheres that distill entirely new poetic and narrative implications while making palpable the materiality of her 16 mm medium. However, for *Ruby Skin* (2005) – the first film she completed here in Austria – Heller worked without the aid of a printer, hacking directly into a 1970s educational film about creative writing to exploit the 26-frame discrepancy between image and sound characteristic of 16 mm analog film. Editing the material into brief fragments, Heller divorced the intended marriage of sound and picture, revealing its illusion by breaking down and reshuffling the elements. In a manner reminiscent of William Burroughs' cut-up technique, she thereby materially generated a rhythmical poetry teetering on the borderline between sense and nonsense. It makes yet a deeper and different kind of sense that the daughter of a refugee from Nazi Austria, upon moving back to her father's native Vienna, presented her very first and previously unreleased films to the public on the occasion of her retrospective at the Austrian Film Museum: *One* (1978/2010),

Juice (1982/2010) and *Self-Examination Remote Control* (1981/2010), all of them Super 8 originals carefully reprocessed to 35 mm; as if the historical gap between flight and a kind of representative homecoming found a bridge in Heller's own history, previously hidden and herewith revealed. *Self-Examination Remote Control* in particular is a delicate self-portrait of the young filmmaker at 18 that engages in a dialectic of self-revelation and hiding. Heller's current project is a 35 mm, black-and-white CinemaScope film generated from footage she shot in an abandoned Jewish cemetery in Vienna: a film about negative space as the presence of absence, and a document about the double death of the forgotten.

Also "new" on the scene, and then again not, is the appearance of filmmaker Friedl vom Gröller: Behind this artist's name stands the photographer Friedl Kubelka, who first became well-known for a number of photographic series she undertook in the early 1970s, at that time as Friedl Bondy. Over the course of a year she shot a photographic self-portrait every day, and this process has been repeated once every five years. She undertook similar portrait studies, though with different temporal intervals, involving her then husband Peter Kubelka, their daughter Louise and in 1980 a one thousand-part portrait featuring her own mother.[52]

Friedl vom Gröller's films arise within a strictly simple setting. All are 16 mm, silent, black-and-white, shot with a camera mounted on a tripod, each has a running time equivalent to one 30-meter daylight spool of film, which is two and a half minutes of screen time. As a filmmaker, the artist vom Gröller remains true to her general subject of the "portrait," setting strangers or close associates in front of the camera, whom she joins (especially in her recent works) once the camera is running – significantly distinguishing her one-reelers from Andy Warhol's *Screen Tests* (1963–1966). It is evident that this shifting of positions on the fly is very

Eve Heller
Self-Examination Remote Control
1981/2010

important to vom Gröller. Just as her photographic self-portrait series demonstrate an unrestrained willingness to reveal herself, she also favors the documentation of intimate moments in her films. In *Passage Briare* (2009) vom Gröller sits with a middle-aged man on the street – up to that time clearly a stranger – whose mouth contains one last tooth, and while the camera is running, removes her dentures, very shyly and evidently herself painfully embarrassed. One is witness to a self-revelation that momentarily engenders a claustrophobic sense similar to being with a stranger in an all too narrow elevator. But then the tables turn and we are enabled to accept the proximity of our relatedness, conjoined in the inevitability of aging (effects already seen at work in her early film *Peter Kubelka und Jonas Mekas* from 1994, in Mekas' fight against nodding off to sleep while the camera is running [as the filmmaker dashes into the scene to plant a kiss on Peter Kubelka's lips]).

We encounter the filmmaker's new spouse, Georg Gröller, in *Der Phototermin* [The Photo Shoot] (2010). The two are seen in their living room during a photo session. The camera is rolling, a female photographer shoots photographs and the Gröllers act in an appealingly unprofessional manner for both of the recording devices, oscillating between high spirits and self-consciousness. Friedl G. is entirely without embarrassment and continually provokes Georg G. to react: first a kiss, and then in a second shot outside on the balcony, a modest slap

---

52 Some of her striking photographic portrait work can be found in Friedl Kubelka, *Portraits of American independent filmmakers, 1971–1981*, ed. Pip Chodorov (Paris: Re:Voir Video & The Film Gallery, 2006).

in the face that comes as a complete surprise and provokes absurdly awkward counter-reactions from GG. Two people love each other, they tease each other ... and we get to watch. In the end, we see a few of the still images from the photo shoot, which are considerably different in mood from what we just experienced in motion.

This all might sound somewhat old-fashioned, and it undoubtedly is, which is precisely what constitutes its charm. It is a game with naivety (but entirely conscious: both Gröllers are trained psychoanalysts), with a specific quality rooted in unconditional self-exposure. This defenselessness is what releases emotional reflexes in the viewer. And it is precisely these feelings that are treated in the cinema of Friedl vom Gröller – as if one were no longer in the seat of a movie theater, but lying on her couch instead. One only has to give way to it.

Friedl Kubelka can also be credited with the founding of Vienna's School for Independent Film in 2006, which she operates out of her small studio (alongside her School for Creative Photography founded in 1990). Here a whole new generation is flourishing underground, unrelentingly practicing filmmaking and holding on to Super 8, 16 mm and hand-processed film, firmly believing in its irreplaceability. In the meantime, former students have merged into the filmkoop wien, which has its own production studio housing editing tables, a Crass animation stand, darkroom, screening space, etc. This also seems to be a necessity of each genera-

tion – the creation of its own infrastructure to meet its specific needs. And groups like this allow us to see into the future of the Austrian avant-garde: It will not only be digital, it will not only be analog – it will have many faces.

The attempt to write a history about independent film in Austria without being guilty of omissions is doomed to fail. There are simply too many actors, works and facets. Please forgive the unavoidable gaps. If one looks back far enough into the past, it is as if one sees a coherent film running. But that film is born and shaped by the erosive powers of history, grinding down myriad details, players on the scene, films, events and struggles back in the day – particulars worn away and left behind. The closer we get to the present and the more nuances we see, the more this film starts to stutter and quake in an abundance of high-resolution still frames that begin to take its place. Many years from now these individual images of today will have merged into the next sequel of history's film, and some of the images still visible now will also have been swallowed up by time and disappear. Till then, let us enjoy the pleasures of a multi-faceted shimmering present and the vibrant and profound film offered by history: Indeed, the whole spectacle is far more than the sum of its parts.

Translated by Eve Heller

Friedl vom Gröller
Passage Briare
2009

Friedl vom Gröller
Der Phototermin
2010

Countdown to Zero. Before the Avant-Garde:
Austrian Visionary Film 1951–1955.

Stefan Grissemann

Reeds are a surprising yet central motif to the post-war art scene in Austria, a signal of breaking away, albeit carrying ominous metaphorical weight: Who-ever heads for the reeds first has to wade in the water, and whoever takes this step might well suffer from heavy existential fatigue.[1] In Vienna after 1945, not only the decision to make art but also to live off it implied a real leap of faith, it meant embarking on virgin territory, possibly to await dire consequences. The few formally advanced films made in the early 1950s pay tribute to this atmosphere. They are sinister and elusive productions that tend toward mythic-historical or futuristic-apocalyptic scenarios, and they are entirely out of the ordinary. Their pessimism appears to constitute their modus operandi and serves as their point of departure.

Reeds are everywhere: Herbert Vesely's film fable entitled *An diesen Abenden* [On These Evenings] made in 1951/1952 begins and ends with scenes in a landscape of reeds; painter and object artist Kurt Steinwendner directed a village crime thriller in 1953 that unfolds in the vicinity of Neusiedler Lake, explicitly naming his second feature film *Flucht ins Schilf* [Escape into the Reeds]. This title served as an apt motto outside the film world as well. Vienna's young artists

showed up every night at a club with makeshift walls plastered with reeds from the Burgenland. Thanks to this site, the exact beginning of the story of avant-garde film in Austria can be dated: In the middle of December in the year 1951, a locale opened in the heart of Vienna called the Strohkoffer [Straw Suitcase], taking its name from the reeds that lined its walls. It was situated in the cellar of the Kärntner Bar (today named after its interior designer, the groundbreaking Austrian pioneer of modern architecture, Adolf Loos, the Loos Bar), and functioned both as a night gallery and club room. As of 1952/1953 it became the regular meeting place for the Art Club founded in 1947 by a circle of artists including Arik Brauer, Ernst Fuchs, Albert Paris Gütersloh and his son Wolfgang Hutter, Rudolf Hausner, Friedensreich Hundertwasser and Maria Lassnig. With a capacity for 60 people, 6 by 8 meters in size and outfitted with three tables, one piano and a few stools, the Strohkoffer became *the* meeting place for Vienna's bohemians, and soon reached beyond fine artists to be infiltrated by writers, musicians, photographers and filmmakers. The language artist and dandy H. C. Artmann, the young poser and poet Konrad Bayer, the composer and lyricist Gerhard Rühm – each soon to make their mark as representatives of the Wiener Gruppe (Vienna Group) – enlivened the place with literary Actions, often accompanied by the ubiquitous author Jeannie Ebner. The multifaceted relation-

---

[1] *Ins Wasser gehen*, "to go into the water," is a German euphemism for committing suicide by drowning.

ships between artists at the Strohkoffer branched out of cliques woven into "a net by threads of sperm,"[2] as avant-garde artist Marc Adrian once observed, and laid the groundwork for collaborations that bridged schisms and long outlasted the two years the den was open. In the second half of the 1950s, Marc Adrian together with Kurt Kren would begin to redefine cinema; and Ferry Radax met Konrad Bayer at that basement locale, both of them going on to shoot the famous film *Sonne halt!* (*Sun Stop!*) in 1959. As the author Gerhard Fritsch put it, the Strohkoffer provided quarters for "downright un-Austrian hopes and expectations."[3]

Progressive art played down in the basement, in this nocturnal asylum of the Viennese art world where Joe Zawinul and Friedrich Gulda made music, and people like Jean Cocteau and Orson Welles stopped by. In 1947, Kurt Kren had returned from forced exile to Vienna where his father was bestowed the "reparation" of being allowed to acquire his son a position at the National Bank. According to Kren he had already taken up filmmaking by 1950,[4] but these first 8 mm films are unaccounted for. Kren got to know the artists Padhi Frieberger, Arnulf Rainer and Peter Kubelka at the Strohkoffer, and also Marc Adrian who started to acquaint himself with the substance of film around 1953, although initially without producing concrete results. By 1953, the Strohkoffer hype was already over. Certain artists had already distanced themselves from the Art Club, including photographer and eventual author Wolfgang Kudrnofsky, who was part of the surrealist Hundsgruppe [Dogs Group] together with Arnulf Rainer and Ernst Fuchs. Others now wandered over to the stylized Dom-Café. The Straw Suitcase was history.

After two decades of time that had been lost to Austro-Fascism, National Socialism and their aftermath, the breakthrough of modern cinema took place in Vienna with astonishing informality. The European avant-garde that had transpired between the two World Wars had never seen the light of day in Austria. In the first decade after World War II, "the present was missing," as Hans Scheugl writes.[5] Austria was an artistic wasteland. In painting, Surrealism arrived belatedly as "Fantastic Realism," and blossomed into a lyrical inwardness. People interested in cinema could only read about the works of Sergei Eisenstein or Dziga Vertov – the films were nowhere to be seen.

Nonetheless, avant-garde film pioneer Peter Kubelka does not recall the 1950s in Vienna without pleasure: It was "the most meaningful decade for the development of the post-war avant-garde in Austria," he says. "That's when a foothold was gained." In the 1950s, "important things happened that were consolidated and became established in the 1960s. It was a veritable heyday." While theoretician P. Adams Sitney writes that, in reaction to Austrian conservativism "a climate of pessimism and negativity"[6] prevailed in Vienna's avant-garde circuit, Kubelka adds, "it was also an inspiring and ecstatic time because we really got something going with our work."[7] The class taught by sculptor Fritz Wotruba was a locus of inspiration for Kubelka. "For me, the people who were important aside from Fritz Wotruba himself, were Joannis Avramidis, Andreas Urteil – who died young – and Alfred Hrdlicka, who represented a style very different from Wotruba. Of the poets it was Albert Paris Gütersloh, Heimito von Doderer and the young Vienna Group, consisting of among others H.C. Artmann, Gerhard Rühm, Friedrich Achleitner – who had shifted from architecture to literature – and later Oswald Wiener." Kubelka was also friends with Vienna's painters, "especially the group around the Galerie nächst St. Stephan: Arnulf Rainer, Josef Mikl, Wolfgang Hollegha and Markus Prachensky." As he ascertains, "We understood one another; after all, we were in the same boat – floating in the

2   Maria Fialik, *"Strohkoffer" – Gespräche* (Wien: Zsolnay, 1998), p. 195.
3   Fialik, p. 225.
4   Hans Scheugl, *Keine Donau. Kurt Kren und seine Filme* (1988; on Index DVD Edition 020, *Kurt Kren, Which Way to CA?*).

5   Hans Scheugl, *Erweitertes Kino. Die Wiener Filme der 60er Jahre* (Vienna: Triton, 2002), p. 10.
6   P. Adams Sitney, "Eine dreißigjährige Freundschaft," in *Peter Kubelka*, eds. Gabriele Jutz and Peter Tscherkassky (Vienna: PVS Verleger, 1995), p. 13.
7   This Kubelka quote and the following are taken from an interview by Stefan Grissemann with Peter Kubelka on February 3, 2010, in Vienna.

remote waters of post-war Austria. I viewed Wotruba as my teacher, although I didn't study with him. But I developed a philosophy under his influence, and a relationship to art." On the other hand, Kubelka describes his social position as dismal. He was so poor he could not even afford to rent a room. "The material situation was devastating. There were practically no jobs. You could not simply take up work somewhere as a waiter. Waiters at that time began their trade at the age of 11. These were regulated professions. For fourteen years, from 1952 to 1966, I usually did not know how I was going to pay for my glass of wine or where I was going to sleep."

After WW II the Austrian film industry had gotten off to a sluggish start. Escapism ruled the day with near complete sovereignty. Kitsch melodramas played in the movie houses alongside sentimental "Heimat" productions, films with regional backdrops made by former Nazi entertainers such as Géza von Cziffra, E. W. Emo, Gustav Ucicky, Karl Hartl, Luis Trenker and Wolfgang Liebeneiner. At the same time, the post-war debutant Franz Antel concentrated on alpine slapstick films with erotic innuendos starring Hans Moser, Paul Hörbiger and Maria Andergast. The 1950s witnessed a switch to teen films and popular song vehicles, as well as the "Sissi" fairytales. The notion of "film as art" was fundamentally misunderstood in conformist films that trivialized high culture, such as those by Walter Kolm-Veltée (*Eroica*, *Franz Schubert*, *Don Giovanni*). Georg Wilhelm Pabst proved to be the one exception, making a serious effort to deal with Austria's dark contemporary history in such films as *Der Prozess / Im Namen der Menschlichkeit* (*The Trial*, 1948) and *Der letzte Akt* (*The Last Act*, 1955). Furthermore, between 1952 and 1955 the Rosenhügel film studios under soviet aegis not only produced standard musicals, revue and opera films, but also made more topically current movies, for instance Aldo Vergano's neorealistic working class drama *Schicksal am Lenkrad* [Fate at the Steering Wheel] (1954), and Alberto Cavalcanti's eccentric Brecht adaptation, *Herr Puntila und sein Knecht Matti* (*Herr Puntila and His Servant Matti*, 1955/1960).

Aldo Vergano
Schicksal am Lenkrad
1954

Kubelka reports about a formative experience at the studios in 1952: "I was first allowed to visit the Rosenhügel Studios as a film student, while a production was in progress. As soon as I crossed the threshold I knew, this was not for me. This is not where I wanted to be. This is not how I wanted to make films. Naturally a large number of former Nazis were employed by the film industry, since one could not get rid of them all as of 1945. They now directed films under Russian patronage, but continued in the taste of 1938. When liberation came in 1945, it in no way implied that everything would instantly become normal, democratic and enlightened. In fact it took ten years for the knowledge of what had taken place in the interim to reach Austria. For example, I had been informed about James Joyce by my German teacher in 1947. But naturally I could not get a copy of *Ulysses* anywhere: it was nowhere to be bought. It was a famous work, but it had not found any reception in German speaking countries. With cinema it was exactly the same, take for instance Dziga Vertov: One knew *Man With A Movie Camera* existed, but it was nowhere to be seen."

For a decade after the Nazi terror, Austria remained a desolate place for cinema – ignorance and hostility toward art maintained rule. Reconstruction needed no culture, just dissipation and lots of harmony. However, a clandestine counter-movement was already taking shape. Not even 20 years old, art history student Herbert Vesely (1931–2002) founded the avant-garde Studio Peripherie 50, together with painter and architect Leo Tichat, in order to produce their own short film, *Und die Kinder spielen so gern Soldaten* [And the children love to play soldiers] in 1951. This 10-minute anti-war film lost to posterity was a very loose adaptation of Franz Kafka's short story *In the Penal Colony*. Vesely presents the execution of a prisoner of war as a serial event that happens over and over again, ad nauseum. As of this project, Tichat worked as set designer and occasional co-author for Vesely, here also appearing in front of the camera as an actor together with H.C. Artmann. Gerhard Rühm contributed his Musique concrète to the soundtrack.

In the same year, the late-Cubist Kurt Steinwendner (1920–1992) together with Wolfgang Kudrnofsky (1927–2010) dared to undertake his first project, a morbidly expressive short film entitled *Der Rabe*, based on Edgar Allan Poe's narrative poem "The Raven" from 1844.[8] Kudrnofsky was cinematographer, Steinwendner directed. Their budget: 28,000 schillings. The film premiered in May of 1951 at the Forum-Kino in Vienna where it not only inflamed Ferry Radax's passion for cinema – the film was and remains effective to this day, despite a certain excess of pathos. The poetic narrative that circles around the tantalizing remembrance of a deceased woman is made alien and sinister through the electronic music of Paul Kont as played on a heliophone. Shadowy photography renders distorted images and unreal atmospheres that abruptly transition into an abstract play of light. *Der Rabe* has an abundance of death motifs. At the very outset a rat is seen feeding on the corpse of a rotting cat. The wooden voice of the off-screen narrator signals a sense of antiquated cinema, but the restlessness of the trembling camera and the irritation arising from obscured images, close-ups and intermittent negative

photography speak a different, modernist language. In the end, the pictures in motion are reduced to a torn photograph walked on by the occasional rat. *Der Rabe* is about shattered and disturbed perception. The famous dictum "Nevermore" cawed by the winged messenger of death in Poe is written here in chalk on a wooden floor. Already in 1951, Austria's conservative film establishment was being given the official word in writing: We do not want to go back to grandpa's cinema – nevermore!

The Austrian film avant-garde that took up duty in these days became conspicuous as a mini-movement bent on anti-realism, in part under the influence of writings by the Hungarian film theoretician Béla Balázs. They took abstraction, mythomania and Surrealism as their call to arms. Literature was used as an anchor, as a means to legitimize the fundamental pessimism of the filmmakers. Echoes of the war are clearly evident in these early endeavors, poetically transformed and stylized in the form of allegories, distanced from actual conditions. An expressly subjective poetic is at work in the films of Vesely, Steinwendner and Kudrnofsky, exhibiting a freely associative, contrapuntal relationship between image and sound, and representing a new form of psychodrama. Painting, sculpture and music inform these works: Steinwendner was a fine artist who called himself Curt Stenvert as of 1969, and like Marc Adrian studied with Fritz Wotruba; the filmmaker and jazz pianist Ferry Radax, like Peter Kubelka, found his initiation in the Vienna Boys Choir.

Unlike Steinwendner who was soon to utilize a more naturalistic film style, Vesely, from an upper middle class family, initially stayed with associative literary psychodramas. *An diesen Abenden* is based on Georg Trakl's poem "Die junge Magd" ("The Young Maid"). The production was subsidized by the foreign office of the Federal Chancellery, the Austrian UNESCO Commission, as well as industrialist and patron of the arts, "Dr. h.c. Ing. Manfred Mauthner Markhof," as the opening credits painstakingly note. It is added: "This is a play of the grim reaper and the maid." One hears Gerhard Rühm's lonely xylophone tinkling, an avant-garde ringing – Arte Povera. Vesely adapts Trakl without

8   *Wienerinnen* and *Der Rabe*, dir. by Kurt Steinwendner; Vienna: Der Standard/Hoanzl, DVD Edition *Der österreichische Film*, # 44.

Kurt Steinwendner
Der Rabe
1951

Harald Röbbeling
Asphalt
1951

quoting the original text. In keeping with silent film tradition, the director utilizes faces and landscapes to tell the story of a maid's fall from grace. He employs powerful choreography and dramatic visual compositions as if having studied the work of Sergei Eisenstein and Carl Theodor Dreyer, as well as closely examining the films of Maya Deren. The film opens with the figure of a young woman turned away from the camera. A cloudy sky and gently swaying reeds are seen. She slowly turns her head to the side. The camera follows the direction of her gaze, panning quietly to the right – and then back again. An edit now reveals the unhappy face of the maiden (played by Mara Ghosta) in the foreground and two reapers in the distance – farm laborers at work in the field, one of whom is played by Ferry Radax. The maid shoulders a heavy sack of straw as village bells toll. *An diesen Abenden* is not a contemporary narrative: The archaic setting of the village is more reminiscent of Renaissance painting.

The abject maid is under observation in her sparse home. A lascivious farm hand spies through the window, watching as she washes herself. Rühm deploys the monotone, saw-like bowing of a viola

to accompany their erotic encounter. She finds his desire alluring, and in a dancing pantomimical gesture appears ready to give herself to him – before she is distracted from the outside world by a man in prayer – lured away by religion and the realm of piety and faith. *An diesen Abenden* negotiates the atavistic conflict between God and drive. The film at times appears almost like a dance piece constituted by artificial movements, measured and ghostly, unfolding as if in a trance: a play of seductive gazes, a melodrama of desire. While Vesely constructs his work with narrative conservativism, it is at the same time formally challenging. Similar to Steinwendner's *Der Rabe*, Vesely sketches a mystical world, creates a work of ominous images and sounds in which symbolism and modernism hold each other in check. In some instances the French avant-garde of the 1920s becomes resonant. The movement of a young farm laborer with a sickle is repeated three times and hearkens back to Fernand Léger's *Ballet mécanique* (1924). The skewed shots and slowed dramaturgy render a film that is visually multifaceted and atmospherically wrought. It communicates almost without a word,

Herbert Vesely
An diesen Abenden (pictured: Ferry Radax)
1951/1952

which especially accentuates its universality and the weight of its imagery.

Mara Ghosta's strictly ritualized presentation of the heroine's tragic case resembles that of a performance artist. She begins to sing, kneeling and praying, while light-hearted girls play seductively and the sand of time slips through the hourglass. Finally, physical contact is made when the maid and the farmhand express their longing by dancing back to back, delivering substitute images for the hardly representable act of sexual intercourse. Vesely shifts between positive and negative stock, thoroughly illuminating the figures and transforming their bodies into x-rays. After having sex, the disillusioned woman returns to work but threatens to be on the verge of madness, cradling an imaginary baby in her arms, screaming and rolling in the dirt. Weeping, she retreats into the reeds in existential anguish. In her windblown linen dress she stomps through the fields to meet her doom, accompanied by the monotone singsong of a medieval ballad reworked by Gerhard Rühm. A bell tolls and the reapers withdraw under the cover of dark clouds floating over the scorched

earth... The Vienna Film Academy rejected Vesely on the basis of his stylistic forwardness, while *An diesen Abenden* was awarded the main prize at a New York film festival in 1954.

Already in 1951, formal deviations were taking new positions. A decisive countermovement announced itself in the form of an unexpected naturalism, the very antithesis to Vesely and Steinwendner's metaphor-laden avant-garde work. In Harald Röbbeling's genre picture of youth entitled *Asphalt*, a Viennese post-war neorealism begins to take form. Röbbeling (1905–1989), son of Vienna's Burgtheater director Hermann Röbbeling, is an Austrian figure that has almost been lost to German-language film history. He debuted as an actor at Hamburg's Thalia Theater and worked as an editor, author and assistant director during the 1930s. As of 1947, he directed films himself. *Asphalt*, made in 1951, was his fourth feature film before he realized 17 shorts at the East German DEFA studios for the satirical series *Das Stacheltier* [The Porcupine]. Röbbeling endeavored to direct his films according to a neorealist model, with a low budget and incorporating non-actors, always shooting outdoors on the street and under the open sky. *Asphalt* reports on the "Endangerment and Protection of Metropolitan Youth" in five episodes. The film takes the form of a reportage based on police records, integrating expressionist methods of the 1920s with the newsreel style of the early 1950s. Röbbeling presented the work as "a socially engaged avant-garde experiment,"[9] shot with lay actors and without a conventional script. The result is a risky, also speculative endeavor. At the same time it is a visually powerful cross between a city symphony, educational and "rubble film," in equal parts a semi-documentary and moralistic under-taking. The film, not without bigotry itself, fell victim to its times. It was altered and censored by the State, and banned to young people. Heavily changed, *Asphalt* was distributed to movie houses in 1959 under the title *Minderjährige klagen an* [Minors File Complaint]. A certain Rudolf Lubowski was named as director and author, the name of Röbbeling was consistently suppressed. The original version was considered lost until 2001 when a print was discovered in France.

Kurt Steinwendner turned to neorealism in 1952. *Wienerinnen – Schrei nach Liebe* [Viennese Women – Scream for Love] turned out to be a small masterpiece of anti-sentimental realism.[10] Like Röbbeling, Steinwendner employs an episodic form to depict the "other Vienna" – a city of barracks and of the proletariat, vehemently renouncing the saccharine quality of "official" Vienna films. One central location of *Wienerinnen* is a brickmaking factory: a site of rising towers signifying a stark, inhuman city. The association cannot be mistaken. The exterminating industry of the Nazis was in the air to such a degree that Steinwendner needed only to contrast his documentary factory images against touristic views of Vienna to generate immense aggression. Austria's capital is here seen as inhospitable, feral, depressive, criminal and unspeakably ugly. The cumulative and by no means

unrealistic desolation in this film even distorts the Prater amusement park into a zone of trauma. In *Wienerinnen* a radical modernism is positioned against the delusions of the Heimat films. The vinous Viennese waltz of the credit sequence is soon underhandedly replaced by atonal electronic music, again composed by Paul Kont. In 1953 Steinwendner further developed the thriller and noir elements of his *Wienerinnen* film with *Flucht ins Schilf* [Escape into the Reeds], and for the first time reached a wider audience. As in the case of *Asphalt*, the young Viennese Walter Partsch was the cinematographer. *Flucht ins Schilf* is about a murder case at Neusiedler Lake, the landscape lending the crime thriller local color. The Pannonian village is modeled on a typical Western town. In less than three years Steinwendner had passed through every station leading from art to the mainstream, shifting from the avant-garde (*Der Rabe*) to experimental social psychodrama (*Wienerinnen*) to the genre film – in 1953 he even directed a low-grade comedy with Paul Löwinger (*Die fünf Karnickel/ Im Krug zum grünen Kranze*). After that he only sporadically engaged in filmmaking.

Ferry Radax (born in 1932) learned his craft working with Vesely as well as from his experience as a press photographer and creator of various union and community sponsored documentaries. He debuted in the summer of 1954 working in Italy as a feature filmmaker. In Radax's first film four young people flee from an atomic war to the open sea, but are as unsuccessful in their endeavor as the film project itself proved to be: *Das Floß* [The Raft] was planned as a 60-minute experimental narrative film, but was never completed.

Meanwhile Herbert Vesely further pursued his examination of fragmented avant-garde storytelling in Germany. The existential science fiction film *nicht mehr fliehen* [Flee no more] is a borderline case of Austrian cinema: a German production completed by a crew that primarily consisted of Austrian artists, shot in Spain during the Summer of 1954, with a budget of roughly 90,000 German Marks – an unheard of sum for an underground art film – thanks to its German producers. Vesely made no compromises. He described his film as a "psycho-

---

9   Christian Dewald, *Der Wirklichkeit auf der Spur. Essays zum österreichischen Nachkriegsfilm "Asphalt,"* ed. Christian Dewald (Vienna: Filmarchiv Austria, 2004), p. 7. See also http://www.filmarchiv.at/rte/upload/filmhimmel_pdf/fh_061.pdf.
10   See footnote 8.

Kurt Steinwendner
Wienerinnen – Schrei nach Liebe
1952

physical final situation,"[11] and composed it in a quasi-musical fashion along the lines of a fugue (from the word *fuga*, also meaning "flight"), working with repetition and variation, precisely emulating the style of the "nouveau roman." The somewhat sedate dramaturgy Vesely used to stretch his riddled story to the near feature film length of 67 minutes is integral to its nihilistic game plan. The painter Hubert Aratym drafted the screenplay together with Vesely; Gerhard Rühm contributed a twelve-tone composition to the soundtrack. Textual commentary was provided by quotations from texts by Albert Camus as well as US journalist and atomic bomb historian William L. Laurence.

nicht mehr fliehen begins with overlapping radio transmissions accompanied by images of an empty, silver glistening landscape. A truck drives through a wasteland of rock. A warning sign augurs "Danger," but also could read as "Dancer," as in Man Ray's *Le Retour à la raison* (1923), since the choreography of Vesely's figures creates a highly stylized impression. The truck breaks down, a classy lady named Sapphire (Xenia Hagman) heads off into the no man's land, the proletarian driver (as Gerard: Héctor Mayro) reluctantly in tow carrying her heavy luggage. Are they trying to escape? Presumably, but this is never clarified. *nicht mehr fliehen* mainly offers atmospheric images of being lost in the torrid heat, with evocative and sometimes searing, often percussive music. The stranded duo reaches a ghost town on the railroad tracks. A lonely child plays in the wide open emptiness of the landscape. Echoes of Italo-Western films are unmistakable – 16 years later Roland Klick's hippie outlaw drama *Deadlock* fishes in the same visual pool. Vesely's allegorical staging complies with cinematic modernism of the day. The director references Cocteau's *Orphée* from 1949 while anticipating stylistic devices of films like Alain Resnais' *Last Year in Marienbad* from 1961. *nicht mehr fliehen* "is not free of fashionable philosophy and stylistic puerilisms," a German critic

wrote in 1957, but "the strength of the composition that directly addresses the unconscious easily outweighs these small faults."[12] Vesely explicitly quotes the paintings of Giorgio de Chirico in the architectural geometry of the film, and he posits abruptly dramatized montage, staging brief emotional outbursts: a corpse, a weapon, excitement. Only the lady keeps a cool watch on the events that unfold. In an attempt to interpret the action that is transpiring, an off-screen voice repeats, "The place does not exist," several times. *nicht mehr fliehen* paints a picture of a post-nuclear apocalypse. The world is deserted, zero, meaningless, a "scenery of the absurd." The dialogue is multi-lingual, taking place in French, German and Spanish. A bar with a motel appears in the middle of nowhere like a fata morgana. A room is rented in this outpost of civilization where the patron haggles over money. The actions are symbolic, the fragments of communication laden with meaning and rich with philosophical ambition. A second woman by the name of Ines (Dittah Folda) appears. Being all too curious, he drags her off to the train tracks where he has sex with her on the hard rocks between the rails. Subsequently she is pelted with stones like a stray dog, aimed at preventing her from returning to the bar. Later the man lays under the truck doing repair work, oil dripping on his face, while the voice of the off-screen narrator recites Albert Camus' *The Myth of Sisyphus*, telling the tragic tale of his eponymous hero. Vesely suspends the image of Gerard's oil-smeared face as a freeze frame, penetrating its photographic texture. The woman polishes her nails, the man loads his gun, the child plays with shells. In a double exposure Sapphire dances with herself in front of a mirror, attired in the haute couture fashion she brought along. The child lies in the sun as if dead, the woman wanders back to the car in a floor length gown, posing like a photo model. The world goes blurry before her and our eyes. The man shoots several times at the young woman who is still in pursuit of him. The model looks unperturbed and slowly strides into the

11 Hans Scheugl, *"Der Film der frühen Jahre. Herbert Vesely und der neue deutsche Film,"* in *Viennale International Film Festival*, catalogue (Vienna: Viennale International Film Festival, 2006), p. 255.

12 Anonymous, "Veselys *Nicht mehr fliehen*," Filmkritik 1/57, January 1957, pp. 14–15.

Herbert Vesely
nicht mehr fliehen
1955

emptiness. The camera rocks back and forth as if on the open sea, observing the dead girl. Four policemen approach but do not concern themselves with the murderer, as if they already know what game is being played out here. Only Sapphire is missing, she has vanished. The police assert with annoyance that she should have signed out. Gerard merely gives a tired shrug of his shoulders. Numbers are counted down for the remaining 60 seconds of the film to the irritating back and forth movement of the camera, approaching the "zero second." "Warning, world: This is Zero," declares a voice accompanied by electronic peep tones. Insert: End. *nicht mehr fliehen*, positioned between Surrealism, existentialism and the Theater of the Absurd, records the pointlessness of flight and discusses a very concrete fear of nuclear annihilation at the time – from one war to the next.

Austrian avant-garde film does not represent a break with narrative cinema, if one considers the early works of Vesely and Steinwendner as constituting its first forays. It rather derived from and within this tradition by boldly expanding its possibilities. Vesely's individual path led to the television entertainment industry. His countdown-to-zero study *nicht mehr fliehen* was completed at the beginning of 1955 and reached movie houses by the end of June. A few weeks later, in August of 1955, 21-year old Peter Kubelka shot his first film at a freight train yard in Linz, with the energetic support of Ferry Radax. That film is a 16-minute obstacle course of associations, a structural work, a story in ruins without the slightest shred of sentimentality. It accomplished an artistic quantum leap in film: *Mosaik im Vertrauen* (*Mosaic in Confidence*) finally liberated Vienna's outsider cinema from the dead weight of myth and morbidity – and proved to be the onset of Austria's actual avant-garde film history.

Translated by Eve Heller

Peter Kubelka at
Centre Pompidou in 1975,
standing in front of his film
Arnulf Rainer (1960).

The World According to Kubelka.

Peter Tscherkassky

For over 20 years I have had the honor and above all the pleasure of being able to count Peter Kubelka among my friends. It is a distinct pleasure because Kubelka is an individual who unites an exceptional depth and array of personal qualities: On the one hand, he is extraordinarily charming, hospitable, generous, profoundly humorous, a grandiose storyteller and entertainer; on the other hand Kubelka is the most critical oppositional spirit imaginable. There seems to be virtually *nothing* accessible to our senses that escapes his wide-awake, considered and contemplative judgment. Without exception, Kubelka approaches things from a critical distance, forming his own opinion according to a highly developed system of values. The praise of others regarding any topic whatsoever seems to make him wary. Kubelka wants to discover things (and their sum: the world) for himself, with unbiased judgment. And since he is not willing to make any concessions whatsoever to the so-called Zeitgeist, many of Kubelka's opinions and evalua-tions turn out to be deviant: some astonishingly conservative (in the original sense of the word), others radically progressive. In Kubelka, this basic attitude combines with a truly comprehensive (and not surprisingly autodidactically acquired) wealth of knowledge, as well as an impressive ability to consider the most various things and aspects and place them in entirely unexpected constellations. Let us take an arbitrary example from a host of

possibilities: A tavern, for instance, is not a tavern, but a "machine modeled upon the nursing mother – the waiter is her hand that puts her breast to your lips. We are in paradise, spared all worldly toil at a well spread table. It is like an island of the blessed, where everything is edible and the dishes come to us (...) You do not have to do anything to procure nourishment – even the nomad who unerringly found a tree rife with fruit had to make an effort. Being fed in this way returns us to the stage of being at mother's breast, which is in fact the first and only time you receive something without having to do anything. And this earliest paradisal condition is induced in the tavern – food appears as at mother's breast – not only milk but the entire edible universe, all the worlds mankind has created, such as roast pork with dumplings and sauerkraut, mashed potatoes and meatloaf."[1] But also a person's *own* cooking contains a deeper, fundamen-tal meaning through which he comprehends the cosmos available to him. See for instance the example of the Scottish coastal farmer and his oyster stew, enthroned as the ruler of his kingdom, cooking his "oysters robbed from the ocean" in the mother's milk of the cow he "forces to live with him": "He could just as well eat his oysters on the open sea, and drink his milk when he is back home.

[1] Peter Kubelka, "Interview V: Das Wirtshaus, die Küche," in *Peter Kubelka*, eds. Gabriele Jutz and Peter Tscherkassky (Vienna: PVS Verleger, 1995), p. 187.

But cooking presents options extending beyond mere sustenance," and so he unites the oyster with milk, and "sprinkles it with exotic pepper. And now comes the big moment: He takes a spoonful of oyster and milk and puts it in his mouth – at the very same moment in time he tastes, synchronously, his universe – he tastes who he is: He is the master of the ocean, and the master of the meadow. And additionally he is master of the ships that travel to the Orient to bring him, a farmer in Scotland, pepper. With this single bite and swallow the farmer enjoys and exalts his existence on earth, he puts it down in writing. He creates his own coat of arms: 'This is I.'" [2]

This abridgement might sound like metaphorical banter, but in Kubelka's exposition there is always a logical conclusion to his far-reaching, well-founded, inductive unfolding of thought, proceeding from the smallest matter (i.e., the oyster) and concluding with the greatest (not infrequently the cosmos). Kubelka zooms in and pulls back again. Herein the genius of the artist (as opposed to the scientist) can be recognized: in his highly creative capacity to shift measures and perspectives bridging entire eras, cultures and academic disciplines.

In short, an evening listening to Kubelka – and Kubelka likes to talk, despite his skepticism in regard to spoken language – is an evening as if spent in an alternate, parallel world. You take part in (or are imparted) a fundamentally *other* point of view, and this is always in the spirit of a worldview in search of the original, the authentic, the fundamental, in short, the *root* of the matter.

I preface with this thumbnail sketch in an attempt to create an image of the *person* Peter Kubelka, because it is precisely these qualities of character that at the end of the 1950s enable the 23-year-old to reinvent and redefine the already well over 60-year-old Lady "Cinema" from the ground up… But first things first.

Born in 1934, Peter Kubelka spent his childhood and youth in the province of Upper Austria, in Taufkirchen. His mother was a housewife, his father a musician – a recognized violin virtuoso. Kubelka attaches great significance to his ancestral bloodline of farmers, gunsmiths, glass blowers, bakers, millers, doctors, female teachers, etc. For example, he ascribes his "Indian serenity," as he calls it, to his great-great-grandmother, an Indian-Portuguese mestizo.[3] In the world of the kitchen, the women of the family socialized Kubelka: mother, grandmother and great aunt, each an excellent cook. Art came to him via music, namely under the guidance of his father, Ferdinand, a perfectionist intolerant of mistakes. From 1944 to 1947 his son Peter sang in the world-renowned Vienna Boys' Choir, and at this time aspired to become a musician – until he turned 17 and returned to his first love, "film," whose acquaintance Kubelka had made as a child, through the visit to his hometown of a traveling cinema. By then he had already realized that in the realm of music, "a person could only be 1/100th as good as Schubert." The medium of film, however, still seemed to be waiting for its Schubert. With characteristic perseverance and consistency, from that moment on Kubelka pursued his goal of wresting an autonomous art form from this relatively young medium, something corresponding to what he had learned to expect through his musical schooling. After graduating from Wels high school, in 1952 Kubelka moved from Upper Austria to Vienna to study at the Film Academy, which at the time was organized and run as a humble night school. In 1954, he relocated to Rome where he studied directing at Centro Sperimentale di Cinematografia. During summer vacation in 1955, the 21-year-old realized his debut film: *Mosaik im Vertrauen*. He engaged his colleague Ferry Radax as cameraman, whose acquaintance he had made at the Film Academy and who later had followed Kubelka to the Centro Sperimentale. Radax, 23 at the time, had already collaborated on

---

2   Peter Kubelka, "Was bedeutet Essen und Kochen für die Menschen," transcript of a 1978 lecture, reprinted in Jutz and Tscherkassky, pp. 170–185; quote p. 177.

3   As a soldier Kubelka's great-great-grandfather wound up in the south of Brazil, where he married and founded a zwieback bakery. His son returned to his father's homeland, became an innkeeper – and thereby also contributed in a significant way to the genetic makeup valued by Kubelka.

several documentaries as a camera assistant, and had also acted in one of the few pre-avant-garde films produced in Austria, Herbert Vesely's *An diesen Abenden* [On These Evenings] (1952). Radax's first independent effort, *Das Floß* [The Raft] (1954), remained a 60-minute fragment.[4] One year later, Kubelka and Radax went to a remote railroad yard in Linz to realize Kubelka's screenplay in 35 mm. Today, *Mosaik im Vertrauen* (*Mosaic in Confidence*, 1955) is deemed the first Austrian avant-garde film – the very beginning of what this book is about.

Mosaik im Vertrauen has six characters: the railroad stationmaster, Johann Bayer; his young daughter; an Italian vagabond called Putnik (played by a fellow student from Rome); a Teddy Boy type named "Leo" in the end credits; the elegant lady Michaela; and her chauffeur, played by the poet Konrad Bayer.

The plot is simple: Putnik spends his days in a railroad yard. From an appropriate distance he pines after the stationmaster's daughter. The stationmaster wants to drive the irksome hobo away. Additionally Putnik is faced with the competition of Leo, who is also courting the stationmaster's

daughter. Eventually, Michaela arrives on the scene, together with her chauffeur in a luxurious car. The latter remain silent observers as events unfold. They never interfere, though their arrival seems to have a negative influence on the course of things.

One night around the campfire, Putnik and the stationmaster grow friendly. They get to talking and railroad man Bayer begins to tell a bit about his life. The men stay together till the light of dawn. The film ends with the departure of the Lady: The disc of the rising sun cuts to Michaela's broad-brimmed hat as she presses it to her head in the wake of the convertible's wind stream. As the end credits roll, the car disappears into the distance.

If only told the plot of the film, no one would likely suspect the seed of an extraordinary avant-garde tradition lying at its core. Yet in the *construction* of this mosaic there already stirs an absolute determination to realize a fundamentally new form – the desire of a young film student fascinated by Italian Neorealism to recreate and redefine the medium of cinema from scratch, which resulted two years later in metrical film, a completely unprecedented cinematic form.

But one step at a time: The mosaic as a picture composed of many parts can serve as an analogy for any "normal" or conventional film. However, in this case it applies specifically to the unique way in

---

4   See Stefan Grissemann's text "Countdown to Zero. Before the Avant-Garde: Austrian Visionary Film 1951–1955" in this book, p. 44 ff.

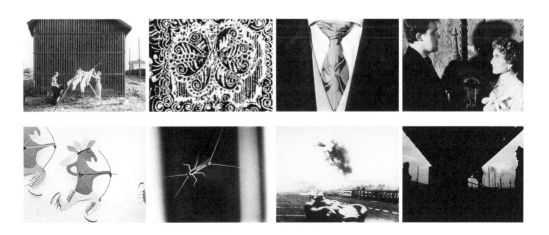

Peter Kubelka
Mosaik im Vertrauen
1955

which the parts of this film are presented, stressing their existence as *individual* elements: The montage does not adhere to conventional editing patterns, it largely refuses established narrative film codes that commonly determine how individual shots are composed to render the appearance of a homogenous narrative flow. Instead, shots appear strangely singular, like isolated statements. The *suture*, as it will later be called in film theory, does not really function here. Simply said, after seeing the film only once without advance information one will hardly be able to comprehend its narrative. Only upon repeated viewings do individual parts fuse into a recognizable whole, into a story. The formal construction of the film, its emphatic stress upon individual components and their meaning in regard to a complexly woven whole, is designed to redefine the relationship of the part to the whole. The entirety of the film no longer consists of a sequence of individual parts, but rather, the film attempts to realize a kind of simultaneity of its components – much like a musical work composed of individual elements that likewise stand in a well-defined, anticipatory and retrospective relation to all the other elements of the composition.

Within the first minute of the film the main elements of the story are introduced. The opening shot presents Putnik's hand drawing an ornament in chalk on the side of a boxcar. Instantaneously, his conflict with the stationmaster becomes audible: "Get up and walk!" yells the voice of the railroad man (an echo of Christ's words to Lazarus that seems to speak to the beginning of the film itself.) The next shot shows Putnik in flight, running between parked boxcars, leaving stationmaster Bayer behind threateningly shaking his fist. The chauffeur of the elegant automobile later to arrive is glimpsed standing on a railway bridge high above the scene, cupping his hands to his eyes like a pair of binoculars, as if watching the two men in the distance. But instead of his view of the men, a "countershot" follows, showing newsreel footage with a superimposed title announcing "La Catastrophe des 24 Heures du Mans – Gaumont Actualités," a report on the 24-hour Le Mans race of 1955 during which 84 spectators were killed in a

catastrophic automobile accident. This found footage is a material witness to the very process introduced by *Mosaik im Vertrauen*, heralding a central characteristic of avant-garde narrative technique: the condensation of content through the metaphorization and metonymization of events. The collision of the race car with the grandstand full of spectators, which is seen later, can be read as a metaphor for the mosaic of the film itself: It intrudes upon the public in a manner that in no way meets with the expectations of its audience…

The start of the car race is edited to coincide with the beginning of the film's story: Several race cars speed into the picture from the right, crosscut with a locomotive barreling in from the left. "Brake, BRAKE!" yells a voice off-screen: Wham! We see a race car collide with the perimeter of the racetrack, accompanied by a pained "Ow!" spoken off-screen: Le Mans and the tiny world of the railroad yard become parallel realities.[5]

Next the object of desire and conflict is revealed: the beautiful daughter of the railroad stationmaster. Putnik helps her gather freshly washed laundry from the clothesline. "Sie sind *sehr* gut" ("You are *very* good"), he says; "Meinen Sie?" ("You think so?"), she coyly asks in return. In the background the boards of a barn loom like the bars of a cage; the clothesline hung with white shirts threads through the middle and foreground of the image – a threshold Putnik will fail to cross.

In stark contrast to the pitiable world of the hobo, the story continues with glamour boy Leo's first appearance. A long shot of his nighttime tête-à-tête, with the daughter standing in front of a massive house door, is preceded by a blast of thunder introducing a series of phallic symbols seen in close-up: a man's flashy patterned tie, an enormous cigar and a transistor radio – the latter was quite a rarity at the time and a status symbol. A close-up of Leo's impressive shoes cuts to the dainty high heels of the stationmaster's daughter, then to her face. A skewed shot lends him the superiority of looking down upon her: "You are a

---

5   Kubelka will later use a nearly identical montage of sound and image in *Unsere Afrikareise*: At the instant a zebra is shot, a woman reacts with an "Ow!", seemingly to a mosquito bite.

Peter Kubelka
Mosaik im Vertrauen
1955

devilishly dangerous girl." A brief found footage shot intercuts of men examining a motorcycle after an accident. "You think so?" she asks coquettishly (the formal "Sie" used with Putnik here gives way to the familiar "du," in speech exchanged with the dashing gentleman). A stranger hastily pushes himself between the man and woman, disappearing through the doorway – its ornamentation can be interpreted as genital symbols. The opening of the house door seamlessly rhymes with the subsequent shot of a limousine door opening as the elegant leg of a lady emerges: "Madame Michaela," announces a nasal voice. The scene jumps back to Teddy Boy at the doorway, proclaiming, "You will fall prey to me"; the young woman has meanwhile slipped down to the lower half of the screen, her eyes barely able to peer above its bottom edge.

Such a "fall" might imply what is shown in the next sequence, which takes place in the station-master's house: Papa Bayer screws a light bulb into a lampshade in the kitchen and speaks to his (neither visible nor audible) wife. "There. Now it burns again." The lampshade is seen from below; the light bulb shines like an artificial sun illuminat-ing the kitchen table and the following monologue in dialect: "Wås redst denn nix? Waas eh wåst wüst: an Persianermuff und an Ami-Wågen mit an blau'n Auspuff! Fia wås bin i denn vaheirat? Damit i an Kaffee trink? Koid is ma aa." ("Why don't ya say nothin'? I git exactly what ya want: a Persian muff an' American wheels with a blue muffler! Why the hell am I hitched? To get a cup of java? Freezing my ass off, too.") The filament of the bulb glows icily in an extreme close-up.

Cut back to the front door where the admirer demonstrates the functions of the radio to his Dulcinea. Extremely short cuts follow: the face of the woman, the face of the man, the close-up of a strange insect, behind it the swinging pendulum of a clock, cartoonish drawings of several Indians with oversized noses,[6] as well as Putnik bent forward and peering out between his legs. Each of these

elements is cut so tightly that they seem to melt into one another. This rapid montage sequence was edited according to the clock's swinging pendulum, the tempo of which invisibly continues to keep time and not miss a beat "behind" the inserted image components: The concept of the metricalization of filmic sequencing can here be discovered in a nutshell, especially as found three years later in the basic structure of *Schwechater*. The sequence ends with a completely blurry close-up of the woman's face that can read as the resolution phase of this metaphorically implied sexual encounter.

This shot becomes superimposed with a traveling shot en route to the railyard, ultimately arriving upon the sad gaze of Putnik. His ornament appears again, only now a stylized butterfly can be discerned in its center as if caught in a net, superimposed on the merciless bars of Putnik's caged reality: the railroad tracks on which Putnik, like a prisoner, is obliquely seen to stagger and sway. The object of his desire is further beyond his reach than ever. For a moment the story seems to come to a standstill.

Then the vigorous honking of a horn announces the limousine that is to deliver "Madame Michaela." Shot from the hood of the car as it approaches a cordoned barrier to the rail yard, the backlit railroad turnout briefly flashes as it is switched – which seems to trigger the catastrophe of Le Mans: The notorious accident is seen during which an explo-ding car sped into the spectators and killed over 80 people. With gruesome precision the camera swings in tandem with the engine block as it mows down the masses and the car bursts into flames. Motionless and indifferent "Madame" and her chauffeur peer through their windshield. As a corpse is carried away in Le Mans, the chauffeur gets the hiccups – "Pardon!" – and opens the car door. The shot of Michaela's elegantly heeled leg swinging out of the limousine is repeated; in the instant of her contact with the street a high rain of sparks flares up in Le Mans; a coquettish swinging of the lady's hips is accompanied by the words "...fallen prey..., ...fallen prey...," again as spoken by Leo. Briefly our couple is seen standing before the house door. But the race continues, as if nothing has happened.

---

6   The size of a man's nose is commonly equated with penis size; arrows unambiguously indicate those of Cupid. Additionally, in Italian slang the word "frecce," arrow, is used for "sperm" (as told by Ferry Radax in an interview with the author).

The subsequent scene leads to the most conciliatory sequence of the film, Putnik's encounter with the stationmaster at the nightly campfire. "Should I chase you away once again?" asks Johann Bayer. But now the men grow more friendly. In a handful of words Bayer seems to convey advice to the lovesick Putnik, alluding to his own unhappy marriage. He speaks about putting a good word in for Putnik with railroad management about a job. Solitary men in race cars round their seemingly senseless laps in the morning twilight dawning at Le Mans, and the sun rises above the horizon at the railyard. Life is a race: you win, or you lose. Michaela looks back across the hood of her convertible; as the car starts up with a jerk she falls back into her seat. The hat she holds on her head against the driving wind assumes the position of the rising sun that had just occupied the screen, disappearing as a progressively diminishing disc into the distance. As these silent spectators depart the scene, 16 minutes after its commencement, we, too, are left behind with the rolling of the end credits.

Narrative films are called "hermetic" if their story is not accessible upon first viewing. In this sense *Mosaik im Vertrauen* is indeed a hermetic

Peter Kubelka
Mosaik im Vertrauen
1955

film, and the above rough reconstruction of its story is intended to serve as a kind of navigational aid. But the most exciting aspect of the film lies in the way Kubelka tells his small drama of poverty, wealth and unrequited love – the *construction* of this mosaic that was so fundamentally other to the familiar movie fare of the early 1950s. How can this "otherness" be described?

I would like to distinguish the following aspects of the film: a) the temporal structure, b) the character of the story, c) the narrative strategies, d) the sound, e) the tendency toward abstraction.

a) Temporal structure

A chronologically linear sequence of events is dispelled at the very outset of *Mosaik im Vertrauen*. The foreshadowing and later repetition of individual plot motifs does not compare to flashbacks in dramatic feature films in which such images are almost always legitimated as the memories of a character. The method of *Mosaik* can best be compared to musical techniques of announcing or repeating compositional themes. If on initial viewing the impression arises of an unsolved jigsaw puzzle, disordered pieces lying all over the place, the placement of each element has actually been precisely determined and melds into an overall structure. At the expense of a story with a linear narrative, this method of montage stresses the meaning of the overall construction, a meaning that

does not in effect disappear seamlessly and without a clue behind the story. There is a story, but one has to work at it, by thinking through the relationship of the individual part to the whole. What we see here is an elementary anticipation of Kubelka's first metrical film, *Adebar* (1957). But more on that, later.

b) The character of the story

The film is extremely anti-psychological. All the actors appear as toy figures.[7] Within this free space won at the expense of psychology, the film points to itself and its own formal construction. (It is reported of the Austrian emigrant Josef von Sternberg that he deliberately searched for "dumb" plots that, as he put it, would not distract too much from the abstract play of light and shadow.) Herewith a direction is taken in Peter Kubelka's filmography that will be perfected in 1958 with *Schwechater*: Form and its beauty triumph over subject.

c) The strategies of storytelling

The most conspicuous is the tendency toward condensation of the narrative through the use of metaphor and metonymy. To cite an example, Leo is solely characterized by the use of such devices: the "powerful" tie, the cigar and his impressive footwear; and the transistor radio connotes the cliché of the male as master of technology. Putnik and his ornament present the antipode: a captured butterfly, poorly scribbled on the wall of a boxcar. Then again the boxcar and train condense the entire hobo motif (except that neither Putnik nor his train ever make any headway).

Metaphors and metonymies can be accounted for in every feature film. Their unique application in *Mosaik im Vertrauen* derives from their tendency to assume the primary narrative voice of the story. This correlates to language usage in poetry: Poetry also neglects rules of grammar and conventional syntax, instead concentrating on the basic element of linguistic expression – the individual word – and inventing its own, new rules for the combination of words. "The poetic (…) is characterized by

a multifaceted weaving of relationships of equivalence (repetitions, parallelisms, etc.) between the elements of syntagmas [i.e., single words], lending it a quality of density that incidentally is also responsible for its ambiguity."[8] This description reads like an abbreviated characterization of *Mosaik im Vertrauen*. Here, too, metaphors and metonymies, displacement and condensation, suppress a "realistic" narrative style and unfold a filmically poetic discourse.

d) Sound

The composition of the soundtrack also contributes to this condensation of narrative form. Like Kubelka's later films, *Mosaik* already demonstrates the possibilities of sound not merely synchronized to image as "supporting material." The dialogue is reduced to a few sentences that sketchily condense essentials for understanding the story. "Not one word too many!" seems to be the modus operandi. On the whole, *Mosaik* unfolds an aural landscape that is never subservient to representational realism, but rather exists as an equal partner to the image in the construction of meaning.

e) The tendency toward abstraction

"Abstraction" here refers to that which foregrounds form at the expense of content. Figurative representation rests on a network of codes and expectations linked to them as developed by a culture. Whether something is accepted as a realistic reproduction depends on how many of these expectations are met. These codes not only include codes associated with the image itself, but also encompass codes beyond the image, such as narrative codes, which in turn are recognized and understood as filmically narrative through filmic codes. There are few established narrative codes to which *Mosaik* still adheres. The narrative strategies of condensation and displacement conveyed by the use of metaphor and metonymy additionally host a seed of abstraction since they only function if understood as "devices" that include double meanings: The image they employ (whether linguistic or visual) points beyond itself

---

7   A fast-motion sequence of energetic arms playing a relished game of table soccer is shown twice – maybe a metaphor for the director and his cameraman manipulating the figures of the story.

8   Gabriele Jutz, "Eine Poetik der Zeit. Kurt Kren und der strukturelle Film," in *Ex Underground. Kurt Kren, seine Filme*, ed. Hans Scheugl (Vienna: PVS Verleger, 1996), p. 106.

to a deeper meaning. One has to abstract from the content of the image's surface to penetrate its intended meaning.

In summary: *Mosaik im Vertrauen* is composed in a way that emphasizes the importance of its basic parts, the individual shots. The method of their combination does not obey any standardized, conventional pattern, but instead follows its own rules as conceived by the artist, referring reflexively to the construction of the film as a whole. It seemingly aspires to redefine the relationship of its component parts to the whole. The leitmotif: condensation. To put it in a nutshell, *Mosaik im Vertrauen* leads us directly to the portal of *Adebar*, the first, as Kubelka calls it, "metric" film, and the first truly structural film.

With *Adebar*, Kubelka remains faithful to the theme of his debut film – the encounter of the sexes and their parting: "The need to touch one another and the difficulties of this. There is this one silhouette where the couple stands motionless, the man above, and with him the head and shoulders of the woman, very simple, and then comes this dance movement, the woman glides out of the picture and the man remains standing alone, that is the end phase. This is a completely clear theme that has to do with life."[9]

At the same time, Kubelka now presses on to what he calls the "essence of film." Behind this ontological formulation lies Kubelka's basic hypothesis: Over the course of its history, mankind developed various languages in order to communicate (including spoken language as merely one of many). Naturally art also communicates, namely in the most various media. Every artistic medium has its *own language* with an *irreducible* core: this core is something *solely* featured by this language. And this core *cannot be translated into any other language*.

With *Adebar*, Kubelka wants to reveal the core of film, in other words, the characteristics fundamentally and *solely* specific to film, and therefore *not translatable* into other languages.

9   Peter Kubelka, "Interview III: Prosa und Poesie," in Jutz and Tscherkassky, p. 70.

How is *Adebar* structured?

Eight different shots serve as the basic material of *Adebar*. These show silhouettes of people dancing. The sound derives from a 26-frame phrase of pygmy music that is continually repeated as a loop and also provides the basis for the length of each shot: The duration of a shot either totals 26 frames, or is halved to 13 frames or doubled to 52. All eight shots are utilized both in positive and negative. Six of these shots show movement. Of the seventh shot only the first and last frame exists;[10] the eighth shot displays only a single freeze frame. Kubelka additionally fabricated freeze frames from the first frames of two shots depicting motion, as well as from the very last frames of five of the moving shots. These additional freeze frames also have lengths of 13, 26 and 52 frames.

Adebar consists of 16 sequences; each sequence is composed of four different shots.

10   Because of the similarity of these two frames it is clear they originate from one continuous shot.

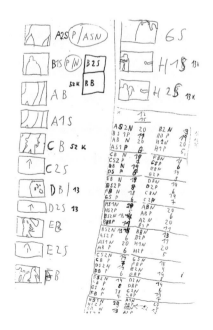

Peter Kubelka
Adebar sketch

The Structure of *Adebar*

Legend

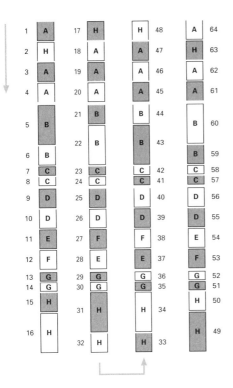

□ Negative   □ Positive

| A | Shot of dancers in motion

| A | Freeze frame from the first frame of a shot

| A | Freeze frame from the last frame of a shot

Description of shot content

A Legs of dancers **B, D** and **E** Medium shot of dancers shot from slightly low angle **C** Close shot of young woman dancing to rock and roll and turns under her own arm **F** (Freeze frame) Two dancers in close proximity on the right, shot from waist up (barely recognizable) **G** (Freeze frame) On the left two dancers, on the right an arm reaching into the image **H** A dancing couple shot from the waist up; in the end the woman dances to the left and out of the picture

The length of each sequence always amounts to a total of 104 frames. To be precise, the combination of 26/26/26/26 frames appears eight times, and the combinations 52/26/13/13, 13/13/26/52, 26/52/13/13 and 13/13/52/26 are each seen twice. As easily calculated, the film has a length of 16 x 104 frames, equaling 1,664 frames in total. This equals a running time of 69.3 seconds. The succession of the 16 sequences is based on their inner structure – i.e., the length of individual shots, positive or negative and image content – and corresponds to the musical composition forms of theme, retrograde, inversion and retrograde inversion.

The second eight sequences mirror the first eight sequences. The axis of this mirroring runs through the exact middle of the film, between the eighth and ninth sequence: Here the film turns in on itself, or, to put it more precisely, the structure of the film turns back on itself, unfolding in mirror image back to the beginning. Thus the first shot of the ninth sequence repeats the last shot of the eighth sequence, and the last shot of the entire film repeats the very first. Shot duration, image content and form (that is, moving or still) are each faithfully mirrored; only positive becomes negative and negative becomes positive.

Without more closely considering the complex architecture of the film,[11] I will proceed with a discussion of *Adebar* in terms of a) film as organization of time, b) film as movement and stasis, and c) film as sculpted light.

a) Film as organization of time

In the history of narrative film the content of a shot normally determines its duration (you see a talking head, and when it is done speaking: cut!). *Adebar* became the first film in history based purely on a mathematically rhythmic montage strategy from beginning to end: As in the case of a musical

11 For a precise analysis of Kubelka's metrical films see Stefano Masi, "Peter Kubelka, scultore del tempo" [Italian], in *B&N. Rivista del Centro Sperimentale di Cinematografia*, 1/1984, Rome, pp. 27–80; French version: "Peter Kubelka, sculpteur du temps," in *Peter Kubelka*, ed. Christian Lebrat (Paris: Paris Expérimental Editions, 1990), pp. 97–155; German version, translated and revised in Jutz and Tscherkassky, pp. 73–122. The latter also contains an analysis by Dominique Noguez, "Der Welt-Mensch" [German], pp. 129–149.

Peter Kubelka
Adebar
1957

composition, a precise and predetermined rhythm provides the basis for the temporal progression and unfolding of the *entire* work. The possibility of employing a temporally rhythmicalized editing strategy, a "metricalization" of montage, as the basis for the construction of an entire film was unknown before *Adebar*. It is a groundbreaking film in terms of its unprecedented artistic reflection upon the intrinsic characteristic of the cinematographic apparatus to divide time with utmost precision.

b) Film as movement and stasis

The base units of this rhythmic metrical structuring are the static individual "photographs" of the filmstrip. In the temporal unfolding of *Adebar*, the (illusion of) movement and its basic unit, the individual static photograph of the film frame – represented as freeze frames – are given equal artistic weight.

c) Film as sculpted light

Kubelka had the shots of the dancers printed on a high contrast film stock so that all details were effaced and only silhouettes remain visible. The proportions of the figures in relation to one another remain the sole trace of a perspectival illusion of space. The film itself is reduced to light and shadow. As mentioned, over the course of the film each shot is seen in both positive and negative form, and, thanks to the mirroring at its central axis, both forms are seen in equal length. This establishes an exact equivalence of light and dark values, not only in terms of total time, but also in terms of space/surface: At the conclusion of the film, every inch of the screen has received the exact same quantity of light and the exact same quantity of darkness. Considered in these terms, *Adebar* in its totality can be imagined as a perfect balance that comes down to one white and one black frame. Once again the tension between motion and stasis becomes discernable, between the space of time and the point in time. With this imagined compression of the inner structure of the film down to the point in time of two individual imaginary frames (black and white), *Adebar*'s structure flares up and vanishes into pure light and darkness (and anticipates *Arnulf Rainer*).

In summary: With *Adebar*, Kubelka first achieved what he had learned in the field of music and what to his mind meets the standard of an autonomous art form. *Adebar* is the first film constituted by a totality resulting from a precisely defined relationship between its component parts in relation to one another and to the whole: The overall construction of *Adebar* is such that each shot and every individual frame correspond and stand in an indissoluble relationship to one another. This overall construction is based on and deduced from fundamental characteristics and specific possibilities unique to the medium of film and the cinematographic apparatus. In other words, the core of the newest language possessed by mankind at the time – namely film – articulated itself in *Adebar*, a core that cannot be translated into *any* other language already in existence.

One year later, Kubelka demonstrated how this core is *not* generated out of movement as claimed in the platitude "film is movement." With *Schwechater* (1958) he turned to the questions of a) stasis, b) the equivalence of image and non-image and c) filmic dynamism. Just four shots form the basic material of *Schwechater*. In accordance with the material's original purpose as an advertisement for a beer of the same name, we see an abstract looking close-up of foaming beer [shot A], a hand in the foreground lifting a glass [B], a group of youthful people at a restaurant table [C], and a couple sitting at a table [D]. These four shots have different lengths. The foaming beer of [A] is a one-minute continuous take, [B] consists of 30 frames, [C] 16 frames, [D] 90 frames. All four shots are used both in negative and positive. Again, high-contrast printing abstracted the images, though not as extremely as *Adebar*.

The entire film displays a continuous shifting between image and non-image: Each image sequence is always followed by the equivalent length of non-images (either black or red film). These sequences have lengths of 1, 2, 4, 8, 16 and 32 frames. This order is precisely maintained throughout the film, alternatingly increasing and diminishing in length: 1/1/2/2/4/4/8/8/16/16/32/32/ 16/16/8/8/4/4/2/2/1/1/2/2 and so on, nine times in

total. In fact, *Schwechater* begins and ends with
a segment of 16 frames. The total running length
of the film consists of 1,440 frames, which equals
exactly one minute of projection time (the length of
a standard commercial at the time).

Kubelka made as many positive and negative
copies of the three short shots [B], [C] and [D], so
that each shot totaled the entire running time of
the film when strung together. In other words, he
had 48 copies printed of the 30-frame long shot [B],
(30 x 48 = 1,440); 16 copies of the 90-frame shot [C],
(16 x 90 = 1,440); and 90 copies of the 16-frame
shot [D], (90 x 16 = 1,440), each printed both as
positive and negative. These six one-minute long
filmstrips, plus the positive and negative version of
the continuous one-minute shot [A], constitute the
basis, the bedrock of the film *Schwechater*. Running
quasi "underneath" *Schwechater*, the images of
six virtual film sequences (plus the positive and
negative beer foam from [A]) rise up into the film
as if from beneath the surface. A score generated
by a highly complex system determines from which
of the eight shots the next frame or sequence of
frames will be derived: This is then the exact frame
that would be found on the filmstrip virtually
running in tandem to the film. For instance: If the
system of the score determines that frame #31
from the 30-frame long shot [B] is required, then
the first frame from shot [B] is used.

Each sequence of images is a combination of
film frames from one or several shots. In fact, the
longest, continuous frame sequence derived from
one single shot is nine frames long.[12]

Independent of the nine-image sequences
continuously expanding and contracting in duration,
there are 14 phases with a length of 30 frames
tinted red – regardless of whether this red phase
coincides with an image segment or a non-image
segment. These red phases appear ever more
frequently over the course of the film: The first red

---

12 To complicate the matter further, these four threads do not
begin at their respective first frames; [B] begins with frame #19.
The second image in *Schwechater* is derived from [B] and is accordingly frame #20 from [B], incidentally in positive. See Jutz and
Tscherkassky for a precise description and reproduction of the first
216 frames of *Schwechater*, pp. 88–97.

Peter Kubelka
Schwechater
1958

The black wave

	4	image frame
	4	non-image frame
	2	image frame
	2	non-image frame
	1	image frame
	1	non-image frame
	2	image frame
	2	non-image frame
	4	image frame
	4	non-image frame
	8	image frame
	8	non-image frame
	16	image frame
	16	non-image frame
	32	image frame
	32	non-image frame
	16	image frame
	16	non-image frame
	8	image frame
	8	non-image frame
	4	image frame
	4	non-image frame
	2	image frame
	2	non-image frame
	1	image frame
	1	non-image frame
	2	image frame
	2	non-image frame
	4	image frame
	4	non-image frame
		and so on

The red permeation

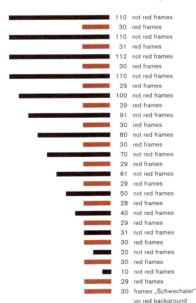

	110	not red frames
	30	red frames
	110	not red frames
	31	red frames
	112	not red frames
	30	red frames
	110	not red frames
	29	red frames
	100	not red frames
	29	red frames
	91	not red frames
	30	red frames
	80	not red frames
	30	red frames
	70	not red frames
	29	red frames
	61	not red frames
	29	red frames
	50	not red frames
	28	red frames
	40	not red frames
	29	red frames
	31	not red frames
	30	red frames
	20	not red frames
	30	red frames
	10	not red frames
	29	red frames
	30	frames „Schwechater" on red background

Diagram of the two waves
of **Schwechater**

phase occurs 110 frames into the film, while between the last and second to last red phase there are only 10 frames that are not tinted red. This means that the film becomes increasingly red. At the end of the film, after the last segment of red frames, there are 30 frames of the Schwechater logo (with red background) to be seen.

Running parallel to every red sequence, a low hum is heard, accompanied by one, two or three high-pitched, signal-like sine tones, or none. A high-pitched sine tone is continuously sustained during the Schwechater logo at the end of the film.

Two waves thus permeate the entire film: a pulsing wave of image/non-image, and an intermittent wave of red that rises up and grows ever more prevalent, acoustically accentuated by the accompaniment of sine waves. The rising crest of this red wave ultimately breaks and flows into the Schwechater logo.

The score that determines which image from which shot is seen, and whether in negative or positive form, adheres to an extremely complex set of rules that, so far, has been examined in literature written about *Schwechater* only in regard to shot [B]. According to this analysis for example, whether a frame from shot [B] is seen in positive or negative follows the rhythmical pattern of a sestina. The sestina is a 12th century Provençal song that adheres to the scheme A-A-B-B-C-D (E-E-F-F-G-H, et cetera.).[13] There are a great number of such rules that determine the appearance of *Schwechater*, though these are subject to a hierarchy. That is, there are stronger rules that overrule weaker ones. Thus within the two waves described, the red-tinted rule is stronger than the "non-image" rule: If the system of the score determines "red," the "non-image" sequence that would be black changes to red.

Kubelka has often pointed out that he wants to make films that have the power and beauty of natural occurrences. For *Schwechater* he cites the example of the glittering of the sun in a flowing

---

13 Compare also Masi; Kubelka himself destroyed all the notes and scores of his metric films in 1962. Insofar the exact structural plan of *Schwechater* will probably remain unknown. On the poetic form of the sestina see http://en.wikipedia.org/wiki/Sestina.

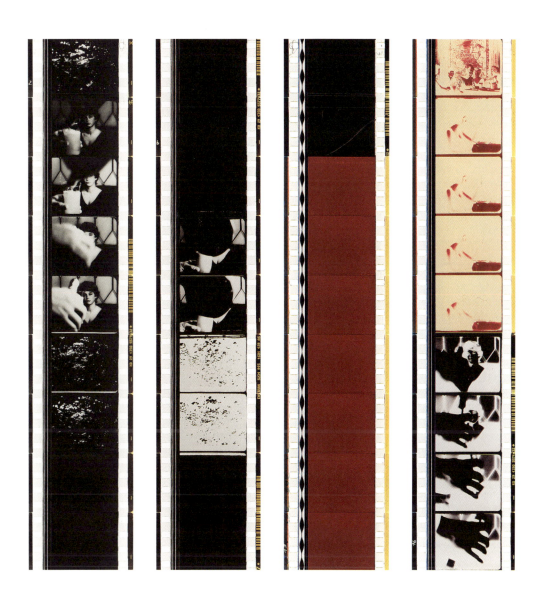

Peter Kubelka
Schwechater
1958

brook under a canopy of leaves stirred by the wind. The shimmering appearance of this stream is predetermined by a host of overlaid and mutually interpenetrating laws of nature, and it is this mutual interlacing of nature's laws that serves as the model for the appearance of *Schwechater*.[14]

Now to the abovementioned central themes:

a) Stasis: "Cinema is not movement. This is the first thing. Cinema is not movement. Cinema is a projection of stills."[15] This aesthetic credo serves as the key to the entire formal construction of *Schwechater*. This film leaves a most profound visual impression of the ephemeral character of the individual frame. The objectively evident passage of time appears to be overruled by the looping repetition of all movements: *Schwechater* visualizes the speeding of time in the instant.

b) Filmic dynamic: Despite this concentration upon the static individual frame, Kubelka helps himself abundantly to the possibilities offered by montage to render filmic dynamism. In addition to the durational contraction and expansion of individual film sequences, it is particularly the mounting crescendo of the red wave, heightened by accompanying signal tones, that builds up suspense over the course of the film, ultimately culminating in the red of the logo as a kind of climax. *Schwechater* can be seen as a continually repeating cross consisting of a diachronic horizontal movement of increasing density permanently intersected by the verticality of instantaneously flashing images.

c) Equivalence of image and "non-image": The capacity of the cinematographic apparatus to photographically record reality in motion and produce the illusion of movement is *one* aspect of its construction. In place of this illusion, *Schwechater* integrates red or black non-image

segments as equivalent to the image. *Schwechater* does not constitute a logical, compositional or aesthetic step between *Adebar* and *Arnulf Rainer* (in terms of aesthetics, the films might rather be viewed as the three points of an equilateral triangle). However, the equivalence of pure light or darkness to image – that is, this aspect of the film to impart equal gravity to the non-image – points directly to Kubelka's next film, *Arnulf Rainer*.

Arnulf Rainer (1960) is the logical result of an aesthetic development based on an increasing disinterest in profilmic reality. This ultimately provoked the relinquishment of the camera in order to reach the purest possible essence of the cinematic apparatus.

Arnulf Rainer consists of black-and-white film frames, silence and white noise (the entire audible sound spectrum). Kubelka mathematically generated all possible combinations of these elements based on 2, 4, 6, 8 and 12 film frames, as well as several combinations of 24. For example, with two basic image options of either black or white, this comes down to a choice of two-frame sequences consisting of black-black, black-white, white-black, white-white. The same applies to sound options: silent-silent, silent-sound, sound-silent, sound-sound. The shortest possible combination of sound and image consisting of one single frame offers the options white/silent, white/sound, black/silent, black/sound. From the total of possible combinations, Kubelka created a pool of visual and acoustic "themes" based on lengths of 2, 4, 6, 8, 9, 12, 16, 18, 24, 36, 48, 72, 96, 144, 192 and 288 frames. For the shorter frame sequences he used every possible combination. When it came to the longer frame sequences he limited his options (12 frames would have generated 4,096 possible frame combinations, alone resulting in a film 34 minutes in length). *Arnulf Rainer* consists of 16 sections, each with a length of 576 frames. This equals the length of a filmic second squared (24 x 24) and constitutes a framing device for the "themes" based on their length: 288 x 2 = 576, 192 x 3 = 576, 144 x 4 = 576, 96 x 6 = 576 and so on. Within each individual section Kubelka utilized various themes from his pool of combinations. Within each of the

---

14 See Peter Kubelka, "The Theory of Metrical Film," in *The Avant-Garde Film: A Reader of Theory and Criticism*, ed. P. Adams Sitney (New York: Anthology Film Archives, 1978), p. 154; German version in Jutz and Tscherkassky, pp. 46–67.
15 In Jonas Mekas, "Interview with Peter Kubelka," in *Film Culture*, no. 44, Spring 1967; reprinted in *Film Culture. An Anthology*, ed. P. Adams Sitney (London: Secker & Warburg, 1971), pp. 285–299; and in *Structural Film Anthology*, ed. Peter Gidal (London: BFI Publishing, 1976), pp. 98–108; quote from p. 103.

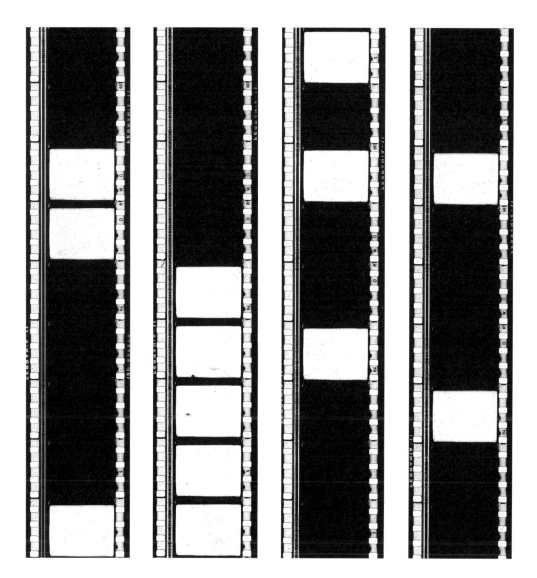

Peter Kubelka
Arnulf Rainer
1960

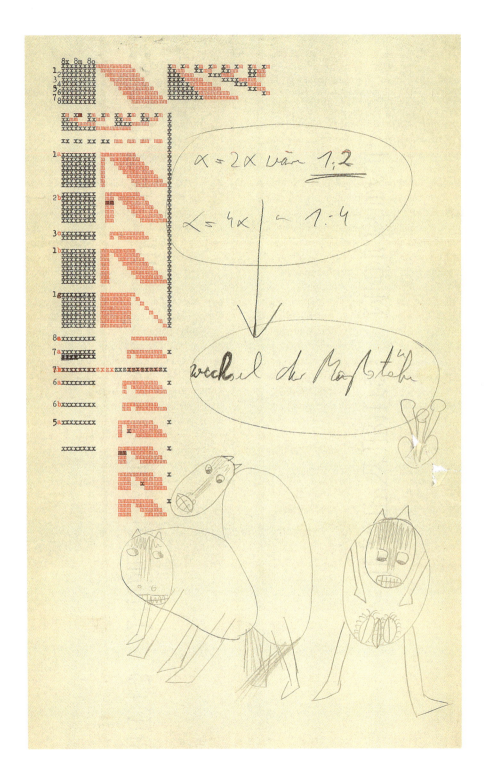

Peter Kubelka
Arnulf Rainer sketch

16 sections, the longest theme is always at the beginning and then steadily proceeds to a shorter theme.

With *Arnulf Rainer*, his third metrical film, Kubelka arrived at the most elemental components of cinematography – namely light, absence of light, sound, silence. These are the four poles from which all of cinema, all of film is suspended. Stretched to their utmost limits, all illusionism is driven out. The last trace of a spatial reproduction is extinguished. And the illusion of movement based on visual similarities of sequential frames (whose minor differences disappear upon projection and thanks to the sluggishness of perception are transformed into an illusion of continuity) is also obliterated. Instead of employing similar frames, this film seeks out the greatest possible *difference*, between silence and blasting sound, white light and pitch darkness. Representation is replaced by presence and absence, by the most sudden change possible between individual instants of the filmstrip, tugged frame by frame through the time machine called the "projector." Kubelka: "Here in the structure of the film was pictured what I wanted to say, and not in image content."[16] And: "'Content' is not content."[17] With *Arnulf Rainer*, form and content converged.

During a lecture at New York University in 1974 Kubelka explained, "I wanted to put cinema where it could stand with every musician and every painter. I wanted to be able to count cinema as a

force which could compete with these arts. Also, I wanted to get to the absolute basis of my medium, and to handle it as purely as possible."[18] Kubelka accomplished exactly this with his metrical films.

All three metric films originated as commissioned work: *Adebar* promised to be a commercial for a dance bar of the same name; *Schwechater* was supposed to advertise a beer; and in the case of *Arnulf Rainer*, a documentation of Rainer's painting work was requested. The impetus for the next film, *Unsere Afrikareise* (*Our Trip to Africa*, 1966), also resulted from a commission. In 1961, Kubelka accompanied a handful of nouveau riche Austrians on a safari to Sudan. The group wanted documentation of their bloodbath in the bush. Naturally they never suspected they would thereby go down in film history. For the first time in his filmmaking career Kubelka used a portable 16 mm camera, for obvious reasons. He came home from his journey with 1,300 shots and several hours of sound recordings. Considering the energetic force of his metrical films, *Unsere Afrikareise* might appear regressive at first glance, a step backward. But in fact these 12.5 minutes of film have a formal density easily equal to his metric works. *Unsere Afrikareise* is without a doubt one of the most complex and poetically resonant films of sound/ image montage in the history of cinema.

The groundwork for *Afrikareise* was prepared over the course of five years (!) dedicated to analyzing and memorizing the source material. In addition to working with rushes, Kubelka glued

---

16 Peter Kubelka in his lecture "Filmbau" [Film Construction] at the Audi Max of the Vienna University of Technology, delivered December 5, 2001.
17 Peter Kubelka in a lecture at Toronto's Cinematheque, Ontario Canada, March 22, 2002.

---

18 Peter Kubelka, "Theory of Metrical Film," in *The Avant-Garde Film: A Reader of Theory and Criticism*, ed. P. Adams Sitney (New York: New York University Press, 1978), p. 156.

Peter Kubelka
Unsere Afrikareise index card

Metaphors from
Unsere Afrikareise
elucidated by
Peter Kubelka.

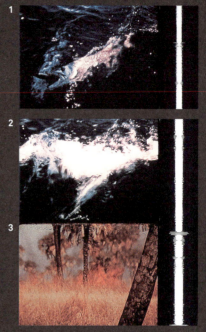

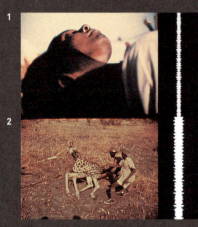

1   Dancing Arabian woman. Original Arabian music replaced by US American music. When the music reaches a long, sustained leading note, the dancer lays her head back in a gesture of surrender.

2   The ensnared giraffe is BRUTALLY yanked to the ground by the hunters. BRUTALLY triumphant laughing begins at the same pitch that ends the romantic surrender of the music, synchronously accompanying the falling of the giraffe.

Montage Metaphors:

Image 1 / Sound 1: The American pop song synchronized to the movement of the dancer heightens the SURRENDER conveyed by the leaning back of her head.

Image 2 / Sound 2: The giraffe is YANKED to the ground, in sync with the cadence of the laughter.

Image 1 / Image 2: The downward flow of movement from above is initiated by the SLOW LEANING BACK of the head and continues with the VIOLENT YANKING TO THE GROUND of the giraffe.

Sound 1 / Sound 2: The continuous aural event is initiated with the long sustained leading tone of the MUSIC that is continued at the same pitch with the LAUGHTER of the expedition member.

1   Text (with Arabian accent): "I put it inside." The word "inside" coincides with the appearance of the stretched out body of the silvery fish, risen to the surface of the deep blue ocean.

2   A GUNSHOT rings out.

Coinciding with the sounding of the gunshot, the fish is yanked out of the water, generating a white watery SPRAYING UP of foam.

3   Flames BLAZE UP in the dried out, yellow elephant grass. The bush fire crackles under palm trees.

Montage Metaphors:

The aural event of the "shot" ringing out yanks the fish out of the water and sparks the bush fire.

Image 1 / Image 2: An explosively released image event of upward movement starting from down below begins with the foaming up of the spray and is continued with the flaming up of the fire.

Sound 1 / Sound 2: The silence of the sea turns into the crackling flames of the bush fire. The cool blue of the sea becomes the yellow of the dried grass, white spray turns to burning, fire red.

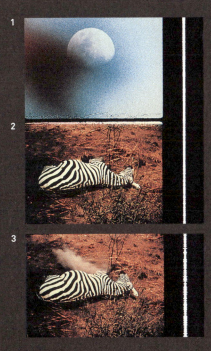
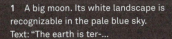
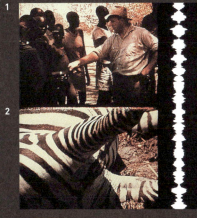

1   A big moon. Its white landscape is recognizable in the pale blue sky.
Text: "The earth is ter-…

2   Text: …-ra."
The dying zebra, motionless in the landscape of its striped hide, lies in the burned red dust of the earth.

3   The impact of the gunshot that puts the animal out of misery releases a fountain of dust. At the same time, the exclamation of a female hunter is heard: "Ow!" as triggered by a mosquito bite.

Montage metaphors:

The educated hunters identify the cool, high moon as "terra" (earth). This error yanks our gaze back down to earth with the dying of the zebra. Equally erroneous is the accompaniment of the sounding gunshot, killing the zebra, with an annoyed "Ow." The irreversible tragedy of death is contrasted to this exclamation that applies to the passing of a minor hurt.

1   The white hunter shakes hands with the indigenous people. Thunder sounds in sync with the movement of the hands.

2   In place of the NATIVE'S HAND, the HOOF OF A ZEBRA is shaken. We do not see by whom.

3   A zebra's leg is skinned by white hands using a knife. The shaking movement continues.
All shaking gestures continue to be accompanied by the synchronous sound of thunder. The knife's cutting movement release calls of "Hurrah" by the indigenous people.

Montage metaphors:

Image 1 / Sound 1: The exact analogy of the shaking movement and the thunder demonstrates that the shaking of hands causes the thunder sound. The Great Hunter thunders with the "Moors."

Image 1 / Image 2 / Image 3: The handshaking event, consisting of the up and down movement of hands, begins on an upswing with the hunter and the indigenous people and is replaced on the downswing with the zebra leg. In other words, he thunders with man and animal.

[Cut to image 3]: We see the zebra leg at another point, continuing the shaking movement.
The cause of the movement is the hand of the hunter with the knife who is skinning the zebra.

the first and last three frames of every single shot – nice and neat – onto index cards: six shots to a card. Each index card related to one of the various themes of the film. This collection of cards constituted his dictionary and became the basis of his filmic vocabulary in abbreviated form. His sound recordings were also protocolled in extensive detail, including the notation of discussions, music and sounds – again providing the basis for memorization. This elaborate process allowed for a comprehensive penetration of the source material and a thorough evaluation of all available content in regard to a number of issues: image content, image composition, color, vectors of movement, atmospheric mood and so on. This in turn enabled a metaphorical weaving of the material, achieving a density that has repeatedly been compared to the writings of James Joyce.

Every aspect of each shot, every snippet of conversation, each fragment of sound, was closely considered in Kubelka's construction of meaning through montage. He employs the idea of "articulation" in considering this kind of montage: "The poet writes a sequence of words: Cow night running rain. As you can see, with each word we add to the series, what we envision changes. Now let us assume that the poet wrote (...): Cow cutlet night. Our imagination is bowled over: There is no longer a cow, all that remains is a little thing, a small piece of meat. The image of the cow has disappeared. How is this possible? (...) It is because the content of the poetic image is determined by articulation: It is not found *in* the words, but rather *between* the words. The words are the same for everybody. But it is our synthesis of the words which makes all the difference in what is said."[19] This statement perfectly elucidates how Kubelka achieves articulation in his films: He connects his images and sounds in unexpected ways, like a poet might construct his sentences – and also images with images, sounds with sounds, through the entire course of the film. He interrupts single shots only to resume them at another point, repeat them and

successively, through articulation, imbues the images with metaphorical meaning.[20]

Taking all aspects in sum, the 186 shots of *Afrikareise* constitute a lyrical poem about the inhumanity of profoundly arrogant people who, out of the sheer pleasure of slaughter, go marauding through a landscape colonialized by them and their kind. It is a film in which colors, forms, movements, gestures and facial expressions coalesce in transformative poetic implications. Even death itself comes to rhyme with tango through Kubelka's deployment of contrapuntal montage: *Unsere Afrikareise* is a singular masterpiece.

In 1967, the year after completing *Afrikareise*, Kubelka began what he calls his "despecialization." We are indebted to this despecialization – after 15 years of unconditional commitment to film – for Peter Kubelka the music maker, cook, assiduous Neolithic artifact collector, teacher and lecturer.[21] Already in 1958, at Jacques Ledoux's EXPRMNTL festival in Brussels, Kubelka had met his American colleagues Stan Brakhage, Kenneth Anger, Gregory Markopoulos and Robert Breer. Five years later, in 1963, he got to know P. Adams Sitney and Jonas Mekas at EXPRMNTL's next edition, which by then had moved on to the resort town of Knokke.

In 1966, shortly before finishing *Unsere Afrikareise*, Kubelka took a first and fateful visit to America. This trip initiated his lifelong and profound connection to the US. Jonas Mekas had organized a show at the Film-Maker's Cinematheque in New York, which turned out to be a resounding success, attended by the likes of Robert Rauschen-

---

19 Peter Kubelka in a conversation with Stefano Masi, November 1979, quoted in Jutz and Tscherkassky, p. 111.

20 Compare with Dominique Noguez's analysis of shots 56–75, which imply an erotic encounter between a member of the safari group and a local resident (including the realization of the cuckolded partner), in Jutz and Tscherkassky, pp. 141–144. See also Dominique Noguez, *Une renaissance du cinéma. Le cinéma underground americain. Histoire, économie, esthétique* (Paris: Klincksieck, 2000).
21 Over the years Kubelka has collected thousands of early and late Neolithic tools and idols as well as artifacts from recent, so-called primitive cultures, with which he intends to make the specifically human ways of accessing the world palpable: how the human animal changed the world to prepare it for his own purposes. A tour guided by Kubelka through a selection of his artifacts is a truly revelatory experience. Taking a Neolithic hand axe into one's own hand while he explains its painstaking production thousands of years ago makes the specifically human and wondrous achievement of its invention tangible in the literal sense of the word.

berg, Claes Oldenburg and Andy Warhol. It was at this time that Kubelka made the acquaintance of artist colleagues such as Ken Jacobs, Ernie Gehr, Jack Smith, Harry Smith, Ken Kelman, George Landow and Paul Sharits, some of whom became instant friends, and it was during this stay that he put the finishing touches on *Unsere Afrikareise* as Stan Brakhage's guest in Boulder, Colorado. On October 14, 1966, the film had its world premiere at the Film-Maker's Cinematheque – and met with tremendous success. A few years later, in 1970, he co-founded Anthology Film Archives with Mekas, Sitney, Brakhage and Jerome Hill, and established the first of three "Invisible Cinemas." The United States became a second home to Kubelka, and, as he never tires of pointing out, the country came to his rescue. The possibility of establishing a relatively secure existence as a film artist in Austria seemed hopeless, and after all, by 1966 Kubelka had already fathered five of his six children. It was in the US that he began lecturing on his "non-verbal worldview." To this day, beginning with his first public lecture in 1967 at Harvard University, Kubelka has given lectures at over 50 American universities. In addition, he has appeared at innumerable other venues. Kubelka was the first avant-garde film theoretician ever invited to speak at the Museum of Modern Art in New York, giving a seven-part lecture series in 1977 entitled "The Essence of Cinema." We can only imagine the impact such appearances had then and still have to this day.[22] In 1977, Kubelka also premiered *Pause!* at the Museum of Modern Art. Shot on 16 mm color film outdoors with a handheld camera and sync sound, *Pause!* shows Arnulf Rainer in numerous takes, shot from shifting proximities standing in front of old walls, expressively grimacing – worthy of Franz Xaver Messerschmidt[23] –articulating a physical body language that Rainer also used as the basis for his own photographic *Face Farces*. Ultimately

Peter Kubelka
Pause!
1977

Rainer found that his photos did not adequately depict his emotional states and therefore painted over them, while with *Pause!*, Kubelka succeeded in rendering an emotional kaleidoscope that is simultaneously disturbing and cathartic.

Kubelka's lectures provided the basis for an intensive concern with the other arts within the context of his "despecialization": "In the wake of demand for lectures in America I started to concern myself with other art forms because I wanted to defend film as an autonomous art and therefore needed the criteria of other arts that are established as autonomous arts. During the course of this activity I became conscious of the tremendous restriction one accepts as a mortal individual being if one lives as a specialist. I believe in the uniqueness of the life of the individual, and value this unique individual life as a tremendous treasure – and only a fragment of it is used if one lives as a specialist."[24] So Kubelka began anew to make music (leading to the founding of his own ensemble, Spatium Musicum, in 1980), concerned himself

---

22 The number of lecture invitations has by no means diminished since Kubelka's retirement from teaching; on the contrary, in recent years it has steadily increased.
23 Franz Xaver Messerschmidt (1736–1783) was a German-Austrian sculptor famous for his "character heads," a collection of busts with extremely contorted facial expressions,
http://en.wikipedia.org/wiki/Franz_Xaver_Messerschmidt.

---

24 Peter Kubelka in a conversation with the author, April 2004.

Peter Kubelka
Dichtung und Wahrheit
1996/2003

intensively with art history, literature and with – cooking. Kubelka had been interested in the preparation of food and its consumption since his childhood. Now he began to interpret the meaning of how foods are prepared and consumed as a fundamental expression of mankind's relationship to the world and reality in his lectures. This led to unadulterated food lectures, attaining an early highpoint in 1972 with a 90-minute live broadcast on public television in New York entitled "Eating the Universe." And finally, it resulted in the renaming of his master class at Frankfurt's art academy Städelschule, where Kubelka had been appointed professor in 1978, to "Class for Film and Cooking as Artform." To this day Kubelka is proud that cooking was thereby acknowledged to be an equally valid artform by an art academy.

Kubelka's later film work, the aforementioned *Pause!* (1977) and *Dichtung und Wahrheit* (*Poetry and Truth*, 1996/2003), does not exhibit the formal density of his early films. In the case of *Dichtung und Wahrheit*, Kubelka himself said that it required courage to release this found footage film (he himself says it is "not found, but gathered film" [25]). *Dichtung und Wahrheit* is based on rushes from a total of three different advertisements that Kubelka presents largely unaltered, albeit meticulously assembled, as a film without sound. The title refers to the difference in facial expression and gesture of the actors before and during the shooting of the performance, those seconds during which the camera is already rolling but the actors are not yet behaving "as if," and those seconds when they start poeticizing ("dichten"), after the director calls "Action!" and they slip into their roles. Kubelka is

---

25 Peter Kubelka in a conversation with the author, September 2003.

hereby not interested in a cheap critique of the aesthetic of advertisements. He instead assumes the distanced position of an archeologist, knowing how to pursue the specific capabilities of film. In the continual repetition of the passage from truth to poetry, Kubelka recognizes that everything in life arises from repetitive patterns that are compressed into rhythms, cycles and myths. These "building blocks of paradise" as Kubelka calls them, tell of the shining hero who checks his outward appearance before freeing the damsel; of mother-hood and of the child who is already practicing the role of mother; of the immaculate conception as a motif of numerous mythologies of mankind, in the form of an unconditional giving of the mouth of the woman, in which a chocolate is placed.

At the origin of all art stands the ready-made, says Kubelka. As an example he cites the typical Inuit sculptor. On finding an interestingly shaped stone, he carries it with him until he discovers a form in it and through a few spare interventions makes this form visible for others. Kubelka wanted to shape a ready-made in this manner with *Dichtung and Wahrheit* – and at the same time leave enough room for future archaeological and anthropological questions that we cannot yet formulate.

Whether we will have questions in the future regarding his unfinished film, *Denkmal für die Alte Welt* [Memorial for the Old World], remains to be seen. In the early 1970s, Kubelka had started working on this 16 mm film, and its premiere had been announced for January 30, 1977, at MoMA. Yet his "standards were not satisfied by the form it was in," [26] and so Kubelka withdrew the film on short notice, premiering *Pause!* instead. *Denkmal für die Alte Welt* has been repeatedly revised since its cancelled premiere. Whether it will ever find a form that meets with Kubelka's artistic demands can only be hoped.

In 2012 Kubelka completed a new film, as what he calls a "counterpart" to *Arnulf Rainer*. *Antiphon* is an inversion of his third metrical film, both on a visual as well as an auditory level:

Light becomes darkness, darkness becomes light, sound becomes silence and silence becomes sound. But according to Kubelka, *Antiphon* is intended to come across even more aggressively than *Arnulf Rainer*. It is to be presented as part of a work entitled *Monument Film*, which will encom-pass a multiple projection experience consisting of both films. Initially, they will be projected individually – *Arnulf Rainer* to be followed by *Antiphon*. They will then be projected side by side, their individual soundtracks alternating between two separate speakers. Finally, both films will be projected at once, so as to entirely overlap, using only one speaker. Theoretically the resulting effect will be a continuous projection of white light and continuous sound. But there will be a slight time delay between the two projections due to the idiosynchratic nature of analog technology, and this will further enable a heightened physical experience of the medium. With this work, Kubelka intends to enable an experience of the essence of film, thus ensuring its survival: Film as *film* and not involving the doomed attempt to convert film to any other motion-picture medium – whether digital or whatever else might arise. These fleeting media are solely the interim result of an economic war, not waged in search of the best technological solution, but purely out of financial interest. In August 2011, Kubelka vehemently expressed to me that he does not want to throw his work into this maelstrom: "None of my films can be transferred to another medium because none of them would make any sense. No other media can convey the message of the works and the thoughts that they trigger. It has to be film or not at all. This is why I will not permit my films to be transferred to video or digital media. If film goes under, then I want to go under with my work, too." Concluding words, indeed.

Translated by Eve Heller

---

26 Peter Kubelka, "Interview IV: Die Räume der Musik," in Jutz and Tscherkassky, p. 161.

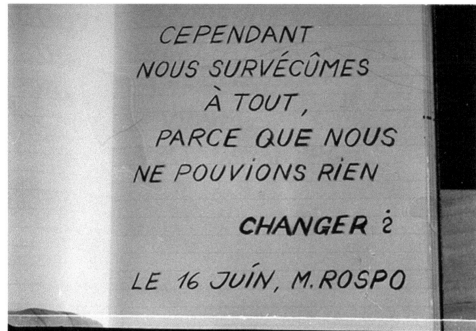

CEPENDANT
NOUS SURVÉCÛMES
À TOUT,
PARCE QUE NOUS
NE POUVIONS RIEN

CHANGER ¿

LE 16 JUIN, M. ROSPO

The Halted Sun of Ferry Radax.

Peter Tscherkassky

"We spent three days at the editing table earnestly trying to explain the plot of the film. But the more we tried to explain the story, the more inexplicable everything became – so we gave up."[1]

It's not quite as bad as Ferry Radax, author and director of _Sonne halt!_ (_Sun Stop!_, 1959/1962), here makes it out to be. After all, a few years ago he took the time to sit down with me and more or less unravel the narrative of _Sonne halt!_ The film counts as an Austrian avant-garde classic, even if its quasi-surrealist narrative technique did not inspire a formal school or style. Ultimately Radax himself turned to more conventional forms of filmic expression after completing a number of semi-experimental documentaries and dramatic films, namely _Am Rand_ (_On the Edge_, 1961–1963), _Große Liebe_ (_Great Love_, 1966) and _Testament_ (1967/1968).

Sonne halt! was shot at the turn of the year 1959/1960 in beautiful 35 mm black-and-white. The third and final 26-minute version from 1962 is available on DVD with English subtitles.[2] The film is more entertaining and better appreciated when its convoluted story can be followed and its characters identified as intended by their creator. Hence my attempt herewith to provide a map through the winding maze of its narrative…

The "we" in the Radax quote above refers to the poet and author Konrad Bayer, member of the legendary Wiener Gruppe (Vienna Group) until his suicide in 1964, who collaborated on films by Peter Kubelka, Kurt Kren and Ferry Radax, thereby accompanying as well as influencing the awakening of the Austrian avant-garde. Radax himself – along with Kubelka, Kren and Marc Adrian – is one of the central representatives of a first generation of avant-garde filmmakers in Austria. Born in 1932, he had already taken an interest in Vienna's art scene as a teenager experimenting with photography. His biography exhibits qualities that seem characteristic of the artistic intelligentsia of post-war Vienna. There were a few local hangouts where the scene met – the Strohkoffer [Straw Suitcase] was the most well known, alongside Adebar and Café Hawelka, and including daytime pubs such as the Stambul. Artists of all stripes met there, together in pursuit of what they had missed during the Nazi regime and what was new, searching for a second dawn of modernism. They assumed an elitist self-awareness for protective purposes, given that their social environment was perceived, quite rightly so, as dismissive or even antagonistically disposed. As a jazz pianist, Radax gained access to the entertainment clubs of US forces and thereby to US culture, especially Hollywood.

1 Ferry Radax quotation from Michael Omasta, "Stichwortlexikon zu Bayer, Radax, _Sonne halt!_", in _Avantgardefilm Österreich. 1950 bis heute_, eds. Alexander Horwath, Lisl Ponger and Gottfried Schlemmer (Vienna: Wespennest, 1995), p. 153.
2 _Ferry Radax, Sonne halt!_ DVD Edition Der Standard/Hoanzl, _Der österreichische Film_, #91, Vienna.

At the Kolosseum, a 1,200-seat movie palace run by the Americans, Radax got to know the original English language versions of hundreds of Westerns and similar entertainment vehicles in glorious Technicolor. Radax's study of film began at this time. He took his 9.5 mm film camera into the cinema and filmed at a rate of two frames per second. At home, using a viewing box he had especially constructed, he projected the film and fastidiously traced a distinctive still frame from the original movie, shot for shot. He sat in the "moonlight of the movie screen" (Jean Cocteau) for hours on end, transcribing the complete dialogue and adding it to the notebook of his film frame reproductions. The effectiveness of such a study is easy to imagine. It subsequently enabled Radax to work as a camera assistant on various documentary films and to create dynamic opening credit sequences with a certain degree of artistic freedom.

Two European film productions helped Radax to finally recognize the realistic possibility of his own creative filmmaking: *Orphée* (1949) by Jean Cocteau, shown in Vienna as of 1950, followed one year later by the local Austrian production *Der Rabe* [The Raven] by Kurt Steinwendner. Soon thereafter, Radax was working as a camera assistant on a then so called "outsider production," namely Herbert Vesely's short film *An diesen Abenden* [On These Evenings] (1951/1952).[3]

In 1954, the wait was over – his first endeavor was *Das Floß* [The Raft]. From the start, Radax took up the existential subject of diffuse fear over world catastrophe that would become a thread in all of his subsequent films, till the end of the 1960s. In the film, a group of young people attempt to take flight on a boat after a third World War. It capsizes. The shipwrecked make a renewed attempt to set sail on a raft, but upon landing they recognize that they have been traveling in a circle and are right back where they started from. The flight was a failure, the film remained a fragment, but it led to a collaboration with Peter Kubelka.

Radax and Kubelka met in 1953 at the Vienna Film Academy, which was at that time still operating as a night school. Kubelka had recently moved from Upper Austria to Vienna to study filmmaking. He and Radax were among the first dozen students that attended the academy three times a week. In 1955, Radax followed Kubelka to Rome and the Centro Sperimentale di Cinematografia to continue his studies. After showing Kubelka the footage of *Das Floß* on an editing table, Kubelka decided to engage his colleague as a cameraman for his own debut film, *Mosaik im Vertrauen* (Mosaic in Confidence, 1955).

In 1959, after a few years in Switzerland during which Radax made several formally advanced commercials, he made a second attempt to create his own independently produced film. Given a small grant from the Ministry of Education, he set off on November 20, 1959, together with three actors, headed to Monterosso al mare in the Italian Cinque Terre, a location with which he was already familiar from the shooting of *Das Floß*. It was here that the footage for *Sonne halt!* was shot over the course of seven weeks.

The differences between Kubelka's *Mosaik im Vertrauen* and Radax's film are striking. While *Mosaik* is concerned with a precise construction and extreme distillation of the story, *Sonne halt!* is the opulent, baroque product of a voluptuous imagination whose navigating impulses are almost lost entirely as the film seemingly develops a life of its own. *Sonne halt!* has the charm of being nearly incomprehensible and will never entirely submit to an exhaustive hermeneutic interpretation. A plot like that found in *Mosaik* is barely recognizable. Literature on the film offers the following brief synopsis: A dandy who is also a sailor endeavors to court two women; both differ markedly in appearance and style – the one elegant, the other in tune with nature. To impress both, the dandy first shoots the sun and subsequently the moon out of the sky. When he nonetheless fails to succeed in conquering either woman, he leaves town to set sail.

Accordingly, we are faced with the following characters: the double-role of dandy/sailor played by the poet Konrad Bayer; the elegant lady

---

3   See Stefan Grissemann, "Countdown to Zero. Before the Avant-Garde: Austrian Visionary Film, 1951–1955," in this book, p. 44 ff.

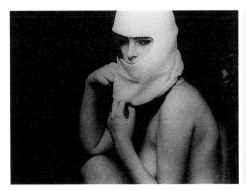

Ferry Radax
Sonne halt!
1959/1962

(Suzanne Hockenjos); a kind of "Eve" as embodiment of the earthy female (Ingrid Schuppan); and a bit part taken on by an Italian friend, the real life sailor Alberto "Jolly" Giogli who acts as a guard at the gates of Paradise. The soundtrack – a mix of language, music and noise – is dominated by Konrad Bayer reciting fragments off-screen from his novel *the sixth sense* with great verve and know-how, as if on-stage.[4] We encounter the names of several characters from the novel ("Oppenheimer," "Braunschweiger," et al.), but who have no apparent connection to the film. In his recital, Bayer often switches between Austrian dialect and a consciously over-the-top inflection of high German – the contrast between "naturalness" (Eve and sailor) and exaggerated artificiality (lady and dandy) thereby made audible. Bayer's collage-like style of storytelling is reminiscent of language cut-up techniques, and effects a radicalization of those literary stylistic devices that, beginning with William Faulkner, assimilated montage strategies characteristic of film. On the other hand, the montage in *Sonne halt!* is oriented to Bayer's spoken text. In the third version of the film, this is

joined by numerous French sentences seen as writing in a notebook (appropriately dated June 16, the Joycean "Bloomsday"), leafed through by a hand and inserted as intertitles.

The following is an attempt to descriptively contain the plot of the film.

"Plot" is perhaps saying too much. There is not a lot of interaction between the different characters. The respective identities of the main actor, sometimes shifting within a single shot, are determined by language off-screen: Dialect marks the sailor as opposed to high German indicating the dandy. Bayer also uses high German to assume the third person voice of an omniscient narrator. *Sonne halt!* accompanies Konrad Bayer as his double character of dandy/sailor embarks on a foray into a small Italian village and surrounding countryside. Here is an attempt to follow hot on his heels.[5]

---

4   Konrad Bayer, *der sechste Sinn*, in Konrad Bayer, *Sämtliche Werke*, ed. Gerhard Rühm (Vienna: Klett-Cotta, 1985); English: Konrad Bayer, *the sixth sense* (London: Atlas Press, 2008).

5   Radax produced a total of three very distinct versions of *Sonne halt!*. The following describes the third and final, authorized version which is 26 minutes long, assembled in 1962. The first version had a running time of 60 minutes. The second version was 35 minutes long; some connoisseurs such as Kubelka prefer this somewhat more abundant version in comparison to the final one. There are indeed strong differences. The film was not only shortened, but image and sound montages were markedly altered. A negative only exists of the third version. The rest of the negative was destroyed by Radax. The Austrian Film Museum retains the only intact print of the second version.

"Franz Goldenberg went to the cinema. Suddenly he recalls his six senses and the events appear in a different light." This is the first sentence to be heard in the film. It accompanies a pan across a harbor; the film concludes with an image of the same harbor. "The dandy," Franz Goldenberg, arrives at a solitary villa on the coast high above the sea. Meanwhile, a parallel sequence of shots shows the dark-haired woman who will later appear in Paradise as the embodiment of the archetypical female. The narrator tells of how Franz Goldenberg hopes to arrive before dusk. While Bayer rambles through the city and peers into a gallery window, he suddenly starts speaking in a heavy dialect about the relationship of art to individuality, not necessarily making much sense. The use of dialect signals Goldenberg's identity switch to sailor. In a parallel montage we see the dark-haired woman. Eve's appearance here establishes a kindredness between the sailor and the archetypical woman. In the morning light of the next day, the dandy leaves his house. The sailor excitedly begins to talk about individual being: "It's a load of twaddle. The masses don't understand, but it's individual being... what brings the circle closer... and – whereby, you get... art! Of course. Through art being created, you get man, and – because man exists, I mean, – and because he's very close to the divine sphere, I mean human beings, *real* human beings, a philistine – I dunno exactly, but who cares. (...) So maybe I can't spell, so what? I don't need to – I introduce individuality into the school..." "Individuality" is one of the sailor's favorite topics, always recited as impetuously as possible. In contrast, the dandy exercises noble restraint as he passes through the city: "I observed everything silently." Emotion on the part of the dandy is first perceived when he eats pizza in a restaurant. There he encounters the surreal collage of a hand on a plate from which the eyes of a woman gaze out at him. A congenial passage from *the sixth sense* is heard, the reciting of a detailed account about eating intended to provoke disgust: "I take the plate with the apfelstrudel and sit down a little to one side. I introduce the fork into the apfelstrudel I bend my head and slowly, very slowly... lick the sugar off

the crust. It is true! Absolutely fresh, soft, sweet apple-flesh. My saliva and the apple-flesh are a soft sweet mush. Suddenly I swallow apple-flesh. More and more saliva collects in my mouth. The prongs sink quickly into the apple-flesh. My head jerks forward, and with a flick of my tongue, I tear the shreds of apple-flesh from the prongs of the fork. Hastily, I swallow strudel. I stab into the strudel, swallow, stab into the strudel. My tongue digs into the dough." [6]

After the meal, Goldenberg plays golf on the shore. Here the motif of the sun in the form of a little controllable ball is introduced. Goldenberg sets a golf ball on a tee. In a series of jump cuts it repeatedly disappears, and reappears just as unexpectedly, as does Goldenberg who continually swings at the ball (countless jump cuts thread throughout the entire film). "Now!" cries a voice at the exact moment the ball first disappears. It is the same "Now!" that later accompanies the shooting down of the sun.

The first encounter between the dandy and the lady takes place at night. She is lying on her hotel bed, he is playing a banjo in the courtyard and singing a kind of Minnelied: "And when they then are dead and gone, I'll never mend them again! Sleep little dolly, Lise go to sleep, I am so tall! And you are so petite! You're such an awfully nervous child, you smash up all the dolls! And when they then are dead and gone, you never mend them again!" After a cut to the lady courted by song and visibly unimpressed, we encounter Goldenberg in a cemetery. A shaky pan across rows of tombstones is followed by a shot of the dandy gazing into the entry hatch of an underground charnel house where candles are alit on skulls. "This is Franz's panoramic world-view!" says Goldenberg. Meanwhile, back at the hotel, the lady has arisen and dances a few steps to the music. Suddenly Goldenberg stretches his upper body through the open window; he is armed with a rifle. He takes aim and shoots at the woman. The flash of gun fire is scratched by hand into the emulsion of the film – as will later be the case when the sun is targeted – lending the

6   Bayer, *der sechste Sinn*, p. 221.

Ferry Radax
Sonne halt!
1959/1962

Ferry Radax
Sonne halt!
1959/1962

imagery a cartoonish quality that detracts from its cruelty.

Over the course of various flashbacks to the villa, pizza oven and other motifs, we continually move in on Alberto Jolly dressed as a sailor, keeping watch at an almost entirely overgrown gate under a bridge. He appears to be observing the dandy through a pair of binoculars. The latter finds himself on a wooden footbridge that is supported by an oversized figure – the "giant" [7] – stretching toward the sea. In the context of the film it resembles a launching platform. The soundtrack recalls the first American space program: "Cape Canaveral! Ten years ago this name was known only by a few people! Now it is known …," a recorded voice proclaims in English, steadily slowing down and getting deeper. Conrad, as named in the screenplay at this juncture, is again armed with a weapon – but this time it is aimed at the sun. [8]

Hit on target, the disc of the sun drops at high speed via time-lapse photography behind a hill. (This shot was filmed in the spring of 1959, when Radax visited Monterosso on his own to make a five minute film about the sun – without actors and using stop motion photography; back home the footage was mistakenly destroyed by a film lab; the only surviving shot shows the descent of the sun.) The resulting global darkness is represented by the superimposition of negative and positive versions of identical images, creating a solarization effect. Ocean waves lap the shore of Monterosso: "At first, single raindrops fell. The rain grew heavier and heavier. Then the water fell in one great mass onto the street. Dobihal asks a question: Were we

living under a river? Suddenly everything was awash and the fish ate the tomato salad off our table." While Billie Holiday intones, "I would gladly give the sun to you," the dandy appears to emerge from a magically unreal, solarized grove, encountering Eve directly for the first time, as she bounces a ball (Radax: "the sun") against the wall of a villa. As the ball falls to the ground the dandy also grabs for it – unmoving, he and Eve stand facing each other, their outstretched hands wrapped around the ball. Thereupon night falls across the globe. Time-lapse sequences of the full moon are seen, street traffic, passersby hastily rushing around as if in panic; again Goldenberg aims his weapon; bullet shots sound: the assassinated moon now also falls from the sky. A rapid series of photographs flares up, fragmented, negative in part, some footage poorly exposed or entirely abstract; these images are supposed to evoke an atmosphere of collective, post-catastrophic chaos.

Yet, the disaster does not last. The sun reappears. In the abundant garden of an Italian villa, Goldenberg encounters Eve once again. With a foreign accent he boldly announces: "The red Indian grabs the lady in red by the chin." Apparently this is not agreeable to Eve – she strikes him with a forceful blow, that knocks him to the ground. Undiscouraged, Goldenberg rushes after the fleeing woman. The chase leads over the bridge under which the guard Jolly sits with his binoculars, where he observed the assassination of the sun. Jolly shoots a harpoon at the people running overhead, missing both thanks to jump cuts that catapult them out of the picture, in the nick of time. During his ongoing search for Eve, Goldenberg stumbles upon the gate. Jolly has disappeared and Goldenberg can freely step through the entryway. Beyond the gate, a densely overgrown valley is revealed. Dressed in a fur coat and cap, he begins to traverse the countryside, accompanied by the exotic sounds of Gamelan music. To Radax, this valley symbolizes the Garden of Eden. The ball of the sun is now in Goldenberg's possession. He approaches an old, weathered stone house. Nobody responds to his knocking at the door. He throws the sun into a small brook where it sweeps away a tiny "bridge" constituted by a flute.

---

7   Today that footbridge is made of stone.
See http://static.panoramio.com/photos/original/10451001.jpg.
8   A so called "script excerpt" of this sequence ending with the assassination of the sun is printed in *Neuer österreichischer Film*, special catalogue of the Viennale 1970, edited and published by Kuratorium Neuer Österreichischer Film (Vienna, 1970), p. 78 ff.; reprinted in "Über Ruinen zu neuem Leben," in *Filmhimmel Österreich*, eds. Christian Dewald/Filmarchiv Austria, no. 68, June 2007, pp. 8–10. In fact this "script excerpt" is a transcript of the finished film; in Monterosso the crew worked without a screenplay. Radax and Bayer decided the night before what they were going to shoot the next day. The differences between version 2 and 3 of the film make it especially clear that the story of *Sonne halt!* is a pure product of the editing table.

Suddenly, Goldenberg is holding the flute in his hands, and tries to play it. As he fails, he looks into the flute and discovers Eve and himself, leaning their heads over a weathered stone wall. A small window at waist level exists between their invisible lower bodies, presenting an opening that becomes a frame for a kiss. This unambiguous metaphor has the effect of a promise: continuing his journey through Paradise, Goldenberg comes upon Eve naked at a well, and takes her by surprise. As soon as she realizes she has been discovered, Eve pulls a magic hood over her head and disappears for good.

Wearing the horned mask of a devil, Goldenberg returns to reality on the elevated terrace of a dilapidated restaurant overlooking a beach. As the mask falls off, he discovers an elegantly dressed lady wading in the sea down below. She comes up from the beach to keep him company. His fear of being touched appears to be stronger than the allure of the erotic silhouette of her reclining body. Goldenberg dances drunkenly across the terrace ("After they had drunk hundreds of beers… they danced with very simple steps"), drops into a chair ("My legs are pumped full of sodawater"), grabs a Chianti bottle and dashes it furiously to the floor: "He – Bang! – Stands up – Explodes!" He thereby triggers a further catastrophe, visualized by a montage of extremely brief components: unclear, shaky, underexposed, negative photos ("A dull roar. Vibrating walls. The mobile scenery turns on its axis… and his children tore out the grass with plyers.") It is especially with these abstract visualizations of catastrophe that Radax finds his greatest creative freedom and *Sonne halt!* formally achieves its most advanced expression.

This time too, the catastrophe quickly subsides. Yet dazed by fear, dandy and lady begin to laugh heartily. All-clear sirens collide with a love song sung in Yiddish. The laughing of our protagonists becomes extremely artificial… Is there really a good reason for the all-clear signal? [9]

---

9   The film here refers to the Nazi regime for a second time. Early on and without apparent narrative motivation, a photograph shows an attack of German Wehrmacht soldiers accompanied by a threat in the soundtrack: "'We are *more* than just a back-drop,' roared the captain."

The film's last sequence involves a futile attempt to become more intimate, followed by separation. It is the woman who now takes the initiative to win Goldberg for herself. He evades her. While she tries to follow him into a bar, he makes a phone call to sign up on a ship. They encounter one another a final time, on a stairway that steeply descends to the sea. We see her make the strenuous climb while he walks down to the harbor. "Why don't you come with me?" a voice asks off-screen as they encounter one another on the stairway. No answer. The ending of the film commences with a view of the harbor. Three boys are seen in an empty open-air cinema playing soccer. A hand leafs through the notebook to the last French intertitle as Bayer narrates, "Everyone shook each others' hands amidst general handshaking. The three of us stand in the middle of the cinema. The events show themselves in a new… LIGHT!" Precisely cut to the word "light," a hand turns the page and the screen turns a brilliant white. The film is over.

Ferry Radax was not only a photographer, musician and filmmaker, he was also a painter. Members of the art world in Vienna were among his friends and acquaintances. His numerous filmic portraits of colleagues in later years substantiate his interest in all forms of art. In this light, one might view *Sonne halt!* as the labyrinthine result of a wide variety of influences. The attempt to tread on new filmic territory by connecting with radical experimental literature lead *Sonne halt!* to become an extremely open work; a wildly proliferating, surreal game of confusion. If one takes the interplay between visual content and free associative off-screen text in *Sonne halt!* versus the precise construction of Peter Kubelka's *Mosaik im Vertrauen* as two prongs of a forking road, there is no doubt that the direction toward condensation and formalism realized in *Mosaik* determined the path the avant-garde would take in Austria for many years to come. The surreal sun of Ferry Radax came to an early halt.

Translated by Eve Heller

Fundamental Punk.
On Kurt Kren's Universal Cinema.

Stefan Grissemann

1 Space/Man

"Sometimes I think of me as a tourist in the universe making snapshots with my films... (laughs)."[1] It was in 1993 that Kurt Kren made this statement, five years before his death. Understatement was Kren's second nature. His films were meant to have the lightness, casual beauty and candidness of snapshots, but as a rule they were meticulously planned, calculated and executed with great perseverance – often over a period of many weeks and without the slightest degree of certainty. *50/96 Snapspots (for Bruce)*[2] is the name of Kren's last film, the final snapshot of a cosmic traveller. A tourist views other tourists. Kren films visitors to Vienna standing in front of the golden kitsch monument to Johann Strauss shining in Vienna's sunstruck Stadtpark as they posture individually or in groups, assuming conventional or self-consciously original poses. But it is not the flaunting of individuals that Kren is getting at – he condenses each of these appearances into two or three single frames that speed by – it is the carefree simplicity of the touristic gaze. Photographic amateurs only see what they are supposed to see: themselves smiling on their journey through the music capital of Vienna, evidence of their own presence in a standardized image designed for that very purpose.

As in his prior film, *49/95 Tausendjahrekino* (*49/95 thousandyearsofcinema*), Kren illustrates a situation being illustrated. He photographs the photographed. But while *Snapspots* concentrates on models in *front* of the camera, *Tausendjahrekino* is about the touristic gaze *through* the camera: Kren films people shooting photographs. The soundtrack comes from Peter Lorre's sole directorial endeavor, *Der Verlorene* (*The Lost One*, 1951). Lorre's voice is heard sarcastically speaking. Poisoned by guilt for having committed a murder, he drunkenly exposes a Nazi war criminal: "I know you. I don't know where I know you from, but I know you... I've seen those eyes somewhere before... Mistake? Impossible. I know those eyes." Because his behavior is not socially acceptable, he is dismissed: "What a vulgar person." Kren's accompanying images consist of shaky, split-second views that speak to the imagemakers themselves: They show Vienna tourists in staccato, their cameras aimed at a tourist attraction. In the end, an air raid warning sounds, "All men to the hero's cellar," Lorre jeers, and Kren places the object of photographic desire into the trembling picture: St. Stephen's Cathedral itself. History lives, murder does not fall under a statute of limitations – a film about seeing, recognition and the politics of sight.

[1] Kurt Kren in an interview with Andre Stitt, *Kinokaze* (London), no. 1, 1993, quoted in Hans Scheugl, "A tourist in the universe. Biographie," in *Ex Underground. Kurt Kren: Seine Filme*, ed. Hans Scheugl (Vienna: PVS Verleger, 1996), p. 150.
[2] Kren numbers his films as of *1/57 Versuch mit synthetischem Ton (Test)*: The first number indicates the chronological work number, the second indicates the year of its production.

"Et cetera…" flickers on the screen at the end of *Snapspots (for Bruce)*, the film that brings Kren's career to a close. At the exact instant the work of the filmmaker is to break off, it extends into infinity with all the ambivalence of an unlimited gift to the world. "Et cetera," must here mean it could have gone on. But also: It goes on.

2   Start

Already as a child Kren liked to play with film, getting into it physically by drawing on the medium after steaming the emulsion off 8 mm film material he found in his childhood home. In 1939, the Nazi terror abruptly intervened in his existence. Born in Vienna in 1929 to a German mother and an Austrian father of Jewish descent employed at a bank, Kurt Kren was brought to Rotterdam via Kindertransport. In a village not far from the city, he experienced the bombing of his second home "from a distance." He first returned to Vienna in 1947, when his father was allowed to secure him a position at the National Bank as a form of "restitution." Already in 1950, he began filming with Normal 8, as he himself maintained. In the mid-1950s, he got himself a 16 mm camera, because it was too difficult to do fast cuts with the smaller gauge film. In 1956, Kren shot his first 8 mm "efforts" as he called them, obsessed with the radicalism of the contemporary art scene – including a project with the poet Konrad Bayer. As a member of the legendary Vienna Art Club, Kren got to know artists Marc Adrian, Padhi Frieberger, Arnulf Rainer and Peter Kubelka. In March of 1961, he showed his films in Vienna for the first time, at a screening organized by Peter Kubelka at the Galerie nächst St. Stephan. Kren chose the concept of "filmmaker" as his occupational title, like Kubelka: a hand-craftsman of disembodied images.

Kurt Kren
50/96 Snapspots (for Bruce)
1996

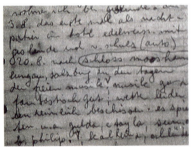

Kurt Kren
34/77 Tschibo
1977

Kurt Kren
29/73 Ready-Made
1973

Kurt Kren
36/78 Rischart
1978

3 Self Portraits

The degree to which Kurt Kren took his formally and mathematically predetermined cinema personally became clear by the 1970s at the latest, with a series of works organized as self-portraits. *29/73 Ready-Made* was the first to place the diminutive figure of the director at the center of attention in a Kren film. Outtakes from a documentary staged by Hans-Christoph Blumenberg (*Die lange Nacht von Casablanca*, 1973) show a bearded Kren in a jean jacket at a television studio, as an awkward reader of three sardonic letters that Groucho Marx wrote to the Warner Brothers Studios in Hollywood. Kren treats the scenes as an *objet trouvé* consisting of puzzling documents from an aborted mission. He shows each interminable repetition and linguistic variation of the deficient television performance without the slightest attempt to explain the situation. Self-portrait as TV marionette: Vanity is not a category in Kren's body of work. The offensively unprocessed form of the film stands in marked contrast to the rest of Kren's work. With a running time of 13 minutes, *Ready-Made* is also the longest production in his filmography.

36/78 Rischart reads like an antithesis to *Ready-Made*: Kren turned the camera on himself, superimposing handheld self-portraits – a bald and bearded man with circular, wireframe glasses standing in the sunlight of a winter day on the open street, looking into the camera and smoking. In *Rischart*, rapid fades as well as multiple exposures render a fragile, hurriedly dissolving image world: the portrait of an intangible person, an artist who moves as quickly as the cinema machine allows.

Four years later Kren staged a completely different way of appraising life in *34/77 Tschibo*. *Tschibo* leafs through each page of Kren's scribbled calendar notes from 1968 through 1977, one frame at a time.[3] Towards the end of *Tschibo*, calendar entries are joined by characteristic Kren frame diagrams as well as a very brief street scene at night deriving from the first failed attempt of the film *33/77 Keine Donau*. Kren noted film experiences ("*Chelseagirls* by Andy Warhol – very good"), his own presentations, and everyday occurrences ("Lent Weibel 10 German Marks"). He meticulously listed nightly visits to Viennese locales like the Griechenbeisl, the Savoy, the Alt Wien and Voom Voom. *Tschibo* is a record of the humble life of an artist – and a growing frustration: "Shit Vienna!"

3　A very similar albeit more elaborate endeavor is premiered by the German filmmaker Heinz Emigholz under the title *The Basis of Make-Up* in 1983: an exhaustive image by image exposure of each page of his journals as of 1973.

Kurt Kren
33/77 Keine Donau
1977

reads one of the first calendar entries at the beginning of 1968. With information that rushes by at light speed upon projection, the film was naturally not conceived for single frame examination, but by now every DVD player makes this possible.[4] Yet the insight Kren affords into his private life is fragmented, his notes hardly legible, even upon an "unauthorized" freeze-frame viewing of the film. *Tschibo* is a paradoxical act of self-exposure and -concealment.

Thomas Korschil already interpreted Kren's earlier *1/57 Versuch mit synthetischem Ton (Test)* (*1/57 Test with Synthetic Sound*) as a hidden self-portrait[5] – as an abstract first person narrative that flirts with the panic of isolation, self-erasure and "newfound vitality." It is a bit difficult to follow this analysis. The film does not show much more than a brick wall and a cactus, shot at various distances to the camera, accompanied by thin, white noise and a scraping sound. The notion of a "test" is not coincidentally noted in the title: The official number one project in Kren's filmography is a classic test film, a sounding puzzle of images.

Three American films Kren ironically titled *bad home movies* are also autobiographical, shot

---

4   Three DVDs with films by Kurt Kren were released on the DVD-label Index: Index DVD Edition 001: *Kurt Kren, Action Films*; Index DVD Edition 002: *Kurt Kren, Structural Films*; Index DVD Edition 020: *Kurt Kren, Which Way to CA?*
5   Thomas Korschil, "Die ersten, die letzten, soweit," in Scheugl, *Ex Underground*, p. 36.

from 1981 through 1982. *40/81 Breakfast im Grauen* can be understood in particular as a very direct working out of an alternative way of life. Kren himself again steps into the picture, as a bare chested worker in a cap – a working class filmmaker chatting with a friend under an open sky during a lunch break in New Hampshire, standing in the ruins of a demolished house. These three, three-minute long "Krenish" home movies take a completely unpretentious look at America, people and machines, work and leisure time, art and nature. These are nomadic films, Americana studies. *39/81 Which Way to CA?* is an amateur film of the highest caliber, profound clarity and simplicity – a work about unsentimental, prototypical places – diners and highways on the road from Vermont to California. *41/82 Getting warm* offers a renewed, light cinema, this time in color, showing workers in the sun, the parking lot in front of a supermarket, impressions of Kren's trip from New England to Texas. These productions are in no sense formless and without structure as Kren aficionados once disappointedly described them. On the contrary, with effortless virtuosity they celebrate coincidental and ephemeral instants with a love of detail and an eminent sense for filmic condensation – the likes of which in US avant-garde film history had perhaps best been captured by Joseph Cornell. This little trilogy holds time and place in suspense, it transmits no sense of succession or comprehensible geography. It does not point to a there and

Kurt Kren
1/57 Versuch mit synthetischem Ton (Test)
1957

Kurt Kren
40/81 Breakfast im Grauen
1981

Kurt Kren
39/81 Which Way to CA?
1981

Kurt Kren
41/82 Getting warm
1982

Kurt Kren
41/82 Getting warm
1982

then, to vary Michael Palm's phrase,[6] but rather to a here and now. Kren's *bad home movies* are really *good road movies* – or simply the *home movies* of a homeless person, a universal tourist.

4   Face/Man

His own face was not the only one Kren took as a point of departure for his filmic research. In *2/60 48 Köpfe aus dem Szondi-Test* (*2/60 48 Heads From the Szondi Test*), 48 grainy photographs of anonymous faces are set in motion, shot single-frame at varying ratios and in differing sequences. Kren rephotographs these pictures from a scientific publication about the diagnosis of psychological drives, according to a precisely determined schematic diagram, single-framing each photo between one to eight times. In this way no shot is held longer than one third of a second. At the same time, Kren zooms in on the photos, stressing their graphic nature and flatness, as well as the halting rhythm of the cinematographic machine. Kren begins with extreme close-ups of the printed mouths and noses, gropes his way to the eyes, back and forth to mouth areas, foreheads, hair parts and ears: skull measurements. Nothing comes of the head study, just a rhythm of images, a visual pulse. Kren perverts the methods of racial science experts who attribute human characteristics to particular skull forms, by reinterpreting their cult of superfici-

---

6   Michael Palm, "Which Way?", in Scheugl, *Ex Underground*, p. 127.

ality according to an inner logic of filmic montage. He speeds up and slows down, remaining rhythmically erratic as the grey images of faces threaten to melt into one another – a film from the prehistory of morphing technology. Kren's *48 Köpfe* ends with the dissolution of facial fragments into the pixels of their graphic presentation.

5   Single Frame

The individual film frame is the time capsule of cinema. Avant-garde film has always considered its medium in terms of the single frame. One works on 24 images to produce one second of film, and each frame is to be considered in its own right. Kurt Kren knew this. In *3/60 Bäume im Herbst* (*3/60 Trees in Autumn*) he studies the textures of bare tree tops for five full minutes, using the single frame capacity of his camera to shoot a maximum of eight frames at a time, as in *Szondi-Test*. He films up close and from a great distance, shooting focused and blurred takes and uses variable in-camera editing techniques, all of which results in a remarkable effect of abstraction and a pure play of form, while the subject of the images at the same time remains recognizable and intact. The branches and leaves appear like lightning against the pale sky, like strange signs, yet they are merely lines and spots on the light gray Eastman-Kodak film, at times filigree, then again thick. In contrast to *Szondi-Test*, *Bäume im Herbst* is a sound film, with a soundtrack that does not come across as synthetic but almost

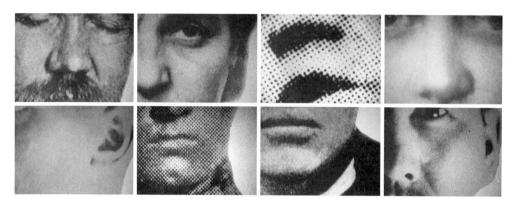

Kurt Kren
2/60 48 Köpfe aus dem Szondi-Test
1960

Kurt Kren
3/60 Bäume im Herbst
1960

sounds organic – as if the wind was knocking an unshielded microphone. Yet it is in fact highly artificial: Kren painted the soundtrack onto the film using India ink, as he had with *Versuch mit synthetischem Ton*. Abstraction and two dimensionality get deeper in *4/61 Mauer pos.-neg. und Weg* (*4/61 Wall pos.-neg. and Path*) with its close-ups of patina covered wall structures in negative and positive exchange, and the lively crossroads of a hiking path seen from great distance, all shot according to a strict film frame score rendering a painterly effect. Kren's cinematic Tachism paints

atavistic signs on the wall as if during a lightning storm of flashbulbs, indecipherable like cave paintings or prehistoric maps.

Eighteen years later Kren returned to the central motif of *Bäume im Herbst* with his first American film. This time the self-ironically titled *37/78 Tree Again* keeps a distance, not showing the details of trees but rather presenting a long shot of Vermont countryside – a slice of nature in full bloom filmed single-frame using time-lapse photography, and recording wild leaps in time and atmosphere. Clouds in the sky fly by, tree tops

Kurt Kren
20/68 Schatzi
1968

tremble, a pair of horses fitfully move across the meadow and the sunshine pours glitteringly into the flashing, flickering images. To create three and a half minutes of cinema Kren shot for 50 days, repeatedly rewinding the film according to a precise score that allowed him to shoot on portions of previously unexposed frames of film, seamlessly inserting "delayed" images – all the while reckoning that in the end he might wind up empty-handed since he was shooting very old, expired infrared film stock somebody had given him.

The exploration and rhythmicalization of still frames that began with *Szondi-Test* stays with Kren. In *11/65 Bild Helga Philipp* he processed the work of the Viennese Op-Artist by expanding the bold lines and geometric forms of her paintings into nervous picture puzzles, creating a filmic abstraction of abstraction. In contrast, *20/68 Schatzi* and *24/70 Western* are adaptations of photographs.

In the first film one sees an unsightly picture fog: milky textures, nervous flickering. Slowly a uniformed figure emerges from the gray – a Nazi officer looking across a field of corpses. The image trembles and tips repeatedly to black as the gaze of the camera approaches the man. The shot cannot be held still because, as an image, it is literally indefensible, unbearable. Kren transforms the static image into a moving image, one even seems to perceive motion in the original photo. In contrast, *Western* shows an unfocused and trembling scan of a photographic poster detailing a snapshot of the massacre in My Lai. The presence of dead bodies is only gradually recognizable, but the big picture remains incomprehensible. After three minutes scanning the poster, Kren inserts a completely different image for a split second: a long shot out a window capturing the serene image of a Viennese housing development in the green.

6   Mathematic

Kurt Kren entertained a close relationship to numbers – his comprehensively numbered filmography is just one proof. He meticulously transcribed his film frame scores on millimeter-ruled paper, and he composed metric films that stand in diametric opposition to Peter Kubelka's emphatically pure cinema with its tendency toward abstraction. An obscure mathematic began to take effect in the pulse of Kren's work: For *5/62 Fenstergucker, Abfall etc.* (*5/62 People Looking out of the Window, Trash, etc.*) he invented a kind of "golden ratio of editing rhythm," first extending the duration of the shot from one frame to two, and then adding the number of the prior two shots to determine the duration of

Kurt Kren
11/65 Bild Helga Philipp
1965

Kurt Kren
24/70 Western
1970

Kurt Kren
37/78 Tree Again
1978

the next shot – after the three frames resulting from this addition of one and two, there follow shots consisting of 5, 8, 13, 21 and 34 single frames. *15/67 TV* presents four minutes of soundless image music, created from a few seconds of film: Unquestionably one of Kren's major works, it is perhaps his masterpiece.[7] Five short scenes are continually being rearranged in relation to one another, shot from the same perspective. The view stems from inside a café in Venice, gazing out at three girls dallying on a pier. In the foreground of the cafe we see the silhouettes of two customers. In one shot a customer moves in such a way as to block the outside view. Keeping these human shadows and the window frame in mind, Kren stages six different spatial depths of field at once: In the water behind the girls a ship is gliding by, and in front of the

window people with children pass through the image. *TV* consists of 21 montage sequences based on these five original shots. Each montage sequence consists of five shots with different arrangements and repetitions of one or more of the original shots, based on a hermetic system. There are only two montage sequences that show all five original shots (the first and last sequences). All shots are separated from each other with a few frames of black leader and a slightly longer black spell between each "fiver" montage sequence. The interplay of movement, from the rapt turning of one of the girls, the passage of the ship and the abrupt darkening of the image effected by the bending down of a man at the edge in the foreground – as well as the brief black pauses – results in a kind of rondo, a subtle, coincidental dance of things and bodies.

7   No Future

The idea of pure virtuosity never appealed to Kurt Kren. The measures he took against filmic purity,

---

7   This is also what P. Adams Sitney thinks: "His best film, *15/67 TV*, successfully explores the new formal territory that had been entered upon by *Adebar*." P. Adams Sitney, "The Standing Ovation," in Gabriele Jutz and Peter Tscherkassky, eds., *Peter Kubelka* (Wien: PVS-Verleger, 1995), p. 204.

Kurt Kren
5/62 Fenstergucker, Abfall etc.
1962

Kurt Kren
18/68 Venecia kaputt
1968

Kurt Kren
15/67 TV
1967

against the big idea, are often first discovered after taking a second look. He knew to appreciate residual images, the "unsuitable" suited him best. Kren was already making underground films in 1962, long before the notion had seeped into trendy newspapers. With _5/62 Fenstergucker, Abfall etc._ he created an aggressive hymn to garbage, the city and death, Vienna's everyday voyeurs constituting its leitmotif. Disgruntled community residents lean out of their windows to catch a look at what's going on down below, but Kren's camera looks back at them without pity. _Fenstergucker_ is a short, tightly edited and thereby pointed _city symphony_, a delayed reflex and swan song of works by Walter Ruttmann, Dziga Vertov and Alexander Hackenschmied (aka Alexander Hammid). His title does his film justice: He shows retirees looking out of windows, broken

glass, paper, aluminum and plastic, empty bottles, a dead bird and other garbage lying in the grass. Kren's aggression is the driving force. No future, nowhere: Kren was a punk before his time. _18/68 Venecia kaputt_ can also be seen as a troublemaker. Kren painted onto film footage showing the view of a Venetian alleyway with a US warship in the distance: The city of Venice sinks symbolically in a film only lasting a few seconds.

8   Action Films (I): Kicking like a Muehl

After two film-less years Kurt Kren returned to cinema in 1964, making a dramatic change to his earlier thematic register with work on two of Otto Muehl's Material Actions. In 1995, the artist recalls how, after having proposed the idea of a Material Action film to Kren in a coffee house, the frustrated

Kren derisively explained that he'd officially given up his film career, and that he did not earn enough pay as a humble bank employee to afford film-making anymore. His schizophrenic existence split between job and art had come to an end since he had pawned his camera: "Damn filming!" So Muehl decided to redeem Kren's camera and returned him to filmmaking. "You're a crazy dog," "Kurti" declared to Muehl, and he turned his attention to making his first Action film. Kren's biography is rife with people who claim to have rescued or freed him.

At first he "wasn't that thrilled" by Muehl's assignment, Kren admits in 1988,[8] but he agreed anyway, under the condition that he could film the Actions however he liked. *6/64 Mama und Papa* was Kren's first Action movie, and was the first time he experienced a Material Action. He found it "very liberating." The film lovingly approaches its subject by way of semi-melodic repetitions: a sacrificial table with a big mess freshly arranged especially for the camera. Muehl empties blood red paint by the bucketful, mud and all kinds of semi-fluid liquids on the body of a naked blond model. Flower and earth are added, eggs are cracked over the body of the woman, flowers pinched between her buttocks, fluids pissed onto

8   Kren in *Keine Donau. Kurt Kren und seine Filme* (1988), dir. Hans Scheugl (Index DVD Edition 020: *Kurt Kren, Which Way to CA?*)

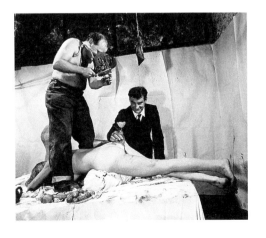

her body and mud licked off her nipples. Muehl concentrates on the primary and secondary sex characteristics of his subject, to which he adds materials reminiscent of bodily secretions. He stages a golden shower ritual, brings synthetic menstrual blood and creamy trickles to wend their way through thickly applied ersatz excrement on the skin of the woman. The artist ironically casts himself as an overgrown infant and libertine with happily smeared face who takes turns sucking at Mama's breasts and specially prepared milk bottles. An isolated pair of red lips on a pure white screen speaks inaudible words on and off. Kren's extremely fast cutting thwarts the voyeurism of the viewer. Whatever is perceived as lurid imagery – in the moment it is registered by the brain of the viewer it is already two or three cuts back in the film. Kren does not linger or provide an overview. He documents less the individual steps of the Muehlish material choreography, and more the hysteria, the transgression itself of the Action.

The few photos remaining of the *Mama and Papa* film shoot show Kren with a bare chest standing behind his camera, visibly ready to physically give himself fully to Muehl's Action. But Kren does not so much celebrate actionistic libertinism as cinema itself, a new way of seeing that flies in the face of the spattered, painted and aestheticized physicality: Kren's Action films are "not only about the liberation of the body, but also a liberation from the body," as Peter Weibel writes.[9] The work process of the Action films was new to Kren. He learned to improvise, to shoot quickly and without establishing a frame score in advance.

In *7/64 Leda mit dem Schwan* Muehl varies only the principles of the prior Action as he works on the heaving body of his model (prepared with a living swan), albeit with fewer organic props. He sprinkles nails on the belly of the woman and covers select body parts with plastic planes. Because the protagonist prematurely breaks the Action off, Kren subsequently sprinkles a few inserts from *Mama und Papa* into the film as filler. The Greek mythology

9   Peter Weibel, "Kurt Krens Kunst: Opseo- statt Kinematographie," in Scheugl, *Ex Underground*, pp. 84–85.

Kurt Kren
filming Otto Muehl Action
Mama und Papa (1964).

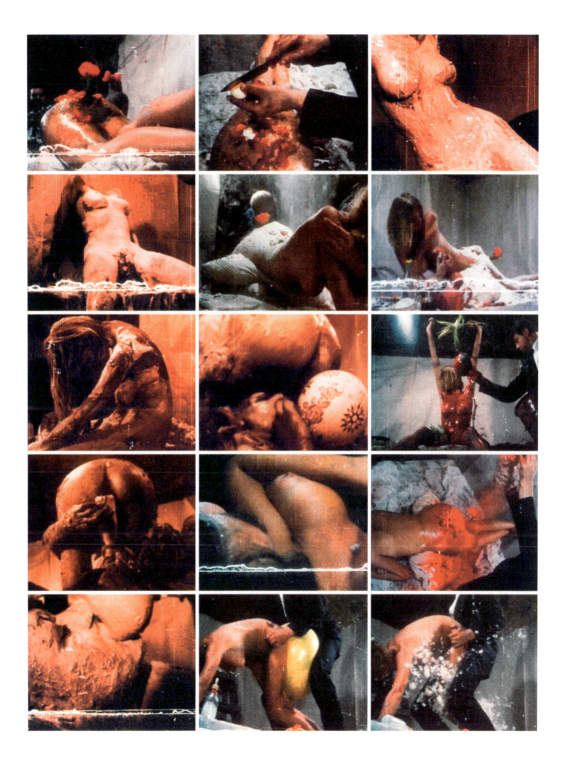

Kurt Kren
6/64 Mama und Papa
1964

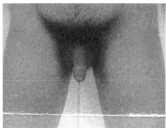

Kurt Kren
8/64 Ana – Aktion Brus
1964

Kurt Kren
16/67 20. September
1967

Kurt Kren
10c/65 Brus wünscht euch seine Weihnachten
1965

that provides *Leda mit dem Schwan* with its title
and central motif remains superficial. Here the swan
is not the animal incarnation of Zeus, and he does
not even impregnate the heroine symbolically. As
a living prop who has stumbled into an inexplicable
ceremony, the swan merely stretches its dirtied
neck in perplexity. Kren casually reveals the driving
force of chauvinism behind the Action: As master
of ceremonies in a dark suit, Muehl enjoys helping
himself to the nameless naked women who place
themselves fully at his disposal in the name of the
avant-garde, who in the case of the Leda Action he
literally tars and feathers. Kren's Action films are
elementally dirty movies and in more ways than one.

9   Action films (II): At the Brus-stop

In the mid-1960s, Günter Brus and Kurt Kren liked
to frequent the Café Sport to hatch joint projects.
Brus wrote in 1995: "Café Hawelka was the manor
house of the artistic estate. Café Sport was the pig
pen." "Back then in Vienna, everyone was wounded,"
further noting, "even Kurt Kren's camera was covered with bandaids."[10] Together with Günter Brus,
Kren realized five films between 1964 and 1967,
interestingly all in black-and-white – as if he
understood Brus as an opposite pole to Muehl,
with whom he exclusively shot in color. *8/64 Ana*
is the title of the first collaboration between Brus
and Kren: a painting Action that is transformed

into a moving, semi-abstract painting. The title
refers to Anni Brus, the wife of the artist. She
initially appears in *Ana* sitting on top of a ladder,
allowing her naked body to be painted black before
Brus, in white make-up like a Butoh dancer with
black rings under his eyes; his frenetic painting
extends to the walls of the studio and his own
body. Because Kren only had one roll of light sensi-
tive reversal film ready, he shot in single frames,
intuitively and without a frame score. The film
begins with very bright pictures, out of focus and
up close, showing the artist at work and in action,
but soon Kren shifts his interest to black paint
spots, surfaces, streaks and splatters on the walls
and skin. The bars of a bicycle are brought into
the Action, mixing with the smeared people into a
surreal sculpture, before the film gets completely
lost in Brusian informal painting.

Along with *Ana*, *10/65 Selbstverstümmelung*
(*10/65 Self-mutilation*) is the main work of the
Brus/Kren collaboration: Clearly more elegiacally
framed than the Muehl films (and thereby more
documentary than its highly impressionistic filmic
predecessors), *Selbstverstümmelung* circles around
a solo by the artist. With a shaking camera Kren
observes the suffering figure of Brus who, with
contorted expression, attacks his own body with
razors and crowbars – not yet spilling blood – and
in the throes of death, rolling around in art mud:
a work of auto-destructive pathos, almost a horror
film. As the whitely-chalked art mutant Brus pulls
a viscous mass off over his head like a second skin,

10   Günter Brus, "Filmzerstückler und Selbstverstümmler,"
in Scheugl, *Ex Underground*, p. 91.

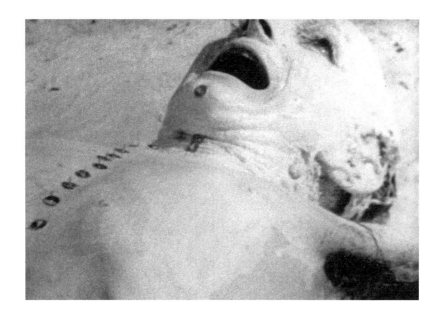

he goes at himself with a host of "surgical" instruments, clamps, scissors, thumbtacks and razors. A sense of bitter humor does not fail him: a smoking cigarette intermittently dangling out of his eye, ear *and* mouth.

16/67 20. September is Kren and Brus' metabolism film. A man urinates in parallel montage with pictures of a meadow where people in the distance answer to the call of nature. After a good minute, third and fourth visual elements appear in rapid cuts: Feces push out of an anus in close-up, a glass of beer pours into the mouth of a man. The last visual element soon hooks in: Food dripping with fat is forked into a mouth. The actor is Brus himself. The stretching of time becomes an ordeal. Assimilation and excretion take close to seven minutes total in Kren's working of the material.

16/67 20. September shows "an alarmingly leaking body,"[11] but is a film "that had to be done," as

11 Michael Palm, "Which Way?", in Scheugl, *Ex Underground*, p. 118.

Kurt Kren
10/65 Selbstverstümmelung
1965

Kurt Kren
32/76 An W+B
1976

Kren laconically determined in 1967,[12] "even if many of my friends will hate me for it." The punk gesture cannot be overlooked: Günter Brus is misspelled in the opening credits (as "Günther"), and afterwards it says "copiright Kren."

What Otto Muehl, Günter Brus and Kurt Kren shared was a joy in the cynical disassembling of middle class togetherness (most clearly in the sarcastic title *Mama and Papa*) and familial ritual (in *9/64 O Tannenbaum* a slack penis is messed with and served up in Material Action fashion, providing for an anti-Christmas atmosphere, a genital panic grotesque). In Actionism everything without exception took place bodily: In the casually improvised time-lapse dance/wrestle film *10c/65 Brus wünscht euch seine Weihnachten* (*10c/65 Brus Wishes You His Christmas*), Brus allows "Nur der traute hochheilige Bauch" ("Only the trusted, highly holy belly") to be written on his upper body.[13]

12 Stephen Dwoskin, *Film Is: The International Free Cinema* (New York: Overlook Press, 1975), p. 200.
13 A bastardisation of a line from the originally Austrian Christmas carol "Silent Night, Holy Night" (composed by Franz Xaver Gruber in 1816 in Oberndorf, Salzburg): "Nur das traute, hochheilige Paar", the holy pair of Mary and Jesus replaced by the holy belly.

10   Filming places

Kren edited his first Material Action films using rewinds and a magnifying glass during his work hours at the National Bank, where he also composed his first "scores," the complex graphs of his film frame schemata. In the spring of 1968, he ended the "schizophrenia of his civil service career" by resigning. However, he was relieved of his job ahead of time thanks to unfounded accusations in the newspapers defaming him as one of the gang leaders of the notorious Action "Art and Revolution" (vulgo "Uni-Piggishness") in Lecture Hall 1 of Vienna University's new building on June 7. Now he had no choice: He had to live with and off his art. For a few years Kren's career experienced an upward trend. The underground flourished, the pop and film revolution grew to become a worldwide movement. In 1968, Kren traveled for the first time to North America and attended screenings of his films in New York and St. Louis. In 1971, he showed his work at the Cannes Film Festival. Soon after he moved to Germany, "more as a matter of coincidence than anything else." Hans Peter Kochenrath brought him to Cologne in 1971. He lived in Germany for seven years, pressing ahead with his filmmaking and watching up to five films a day. He moved further into Saarland before heading for Munich in 1976.

During these years Kren turned to a new genre: a bold filmic reprocessing and transformation of local scenes where he lived. Michael Palm writes that Kren thereby developed methods "to conquer time," in reference to the films *31/75 Asyl* and *33/77 Keine Donau* – works that "create an alienated, diffused physics of time."[14] In his masterpiece *Asyl*, Kren documents his life in Saarland, a sanctuary for the city person. His sense of peace is vague, "possibly I wasn't that happy with life in the country," and, "maybe I got a little crazy out there."[15] In *Asyl* Kren presents a static shot of a landscape filmed over the course of 21 days, under varying weather conditions, in sun, rain and snow, using five variable masks that render a moving picture puzzle: He exposed a single 400 foot magazine that

14 See Michael Palm, "Which Way?" in Scheugl, *Ex Underground*, pp. 120–122.
15 In Scheugl, *Ex Underground*, p. 180.

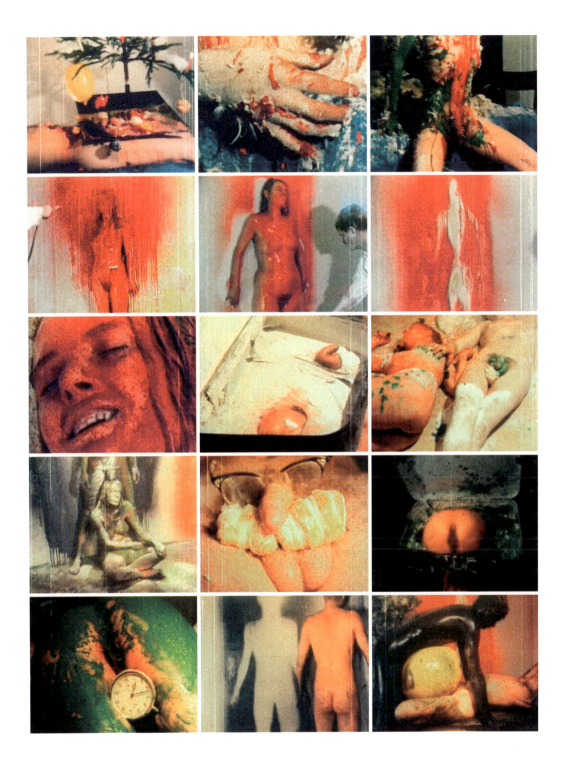

Kurt Kren
9/64 O Tannenbaum
1964

he rewound each day to begin anew. The (nature) space reproduced through the holes of the mask in front of the camera is only seen in excerpts, in rips or tears – and it is also temporally deconstructed. A world of synthetic synchronicity results – snow, no snow, rainfall, no rain, more *and* less light permeating the scenery of a Brueghel-like landscape with bare trees, a path and fenced in tract of land – occasional people appear and disappear, walking along the path like phantoms, slightly transparent. Details tremblingly pop up in various sections of the image, giving view to fragments of the landscape. Only for a few seconds toward the end of the film is the natural, unprocessed space of the scene presented to view. The concept of the leap in time is condensed to one image and instantly comprehensible on sight – the artificial coexistence of different time frames in cinema is put in a nutshell.

When Kren made films, he bent nothing less than the laws of nature. He boldly dissolved times into one another and created artificial spaces, an upside down world. For *32/76 An W+B* he shot out a window in a Munich gallery through a large photographic negative of the same view mounted on the front of his camera, thereby confusing our sense of what is really happening on the street with the negative image. The gaze falls upon an alley along the Isar river, rendering a "trip between the outer world of the real and the inner world of the camera." [16] The film is built up out of various depths of field, as was *15/67 TV*. Parked cars, flowing traffic and people walking in front of the alley of trees, beyond which the park lies where passersby are to be seen. Kren gently zooms back and forth on this shot, shifting focus between the negative "backdrop" attached to the camera, and the lively scene beyond. The film is dedicated to his colleagues Wilhelm and Birgit Hein.

Silent film makes sense for Kren. "I'm less audio, more visual," [17] he observed in 1988. Only eight sound films are to be found among the 50 extant works Kren realized between 1956 and 1996. The first three of his films are not numbered

(*Das Walk*, 1956; *Klavier Salon 1. Stock*, circa 1956; *Mobiles*, 1957). Five works are either expanded cinema or immaterial, conceptual cinema, or are considered lost. Filmmaking was an adventure to Kurt Kren. He never exactly knew what would emerge in view of the formal risks he loved to take on. He was "not like other artists," who "keep repeating the one angle schtick they discovered." [18]

11 No Film

In April of 1978, Kren traveled to North America and met Marnie Rogers who he married. They separated after being together for close to a year. He then set his sights on the life of a vagabond and transient worker. Kren called his American car his "rolling home": He was often homeless and slept in his car although he was invited to do film screenings and guest lectures at colleges and film schools, and his works from the 1970s were given full retrospectives at prestigious places like New York's Museum of Modern Art. He could not live off film. In the Spring of 1981, Kren worked as a nail remover in New England, "a super time," as he later recalled. He tore down wooden houses to sell as building material with a few friends. At the end of the year, with the onset of a tough East coast winter, he moved to Texas. Kren lived "like a migratory bird," always in search of warmer climates, his trip first leading him from New England to California, and on to Austin where he settled down at the end of 1981.

In 1982, Kren skidded into a major economic crisis that perfectly paralleled the US American recession of the Reagan era. Existential fear had been his companion since his early years. But he found a new social context and solidarity in the vital art scene in Houston where he lived as of 1983, moving into his first American apartment. He acted in independent films, took part in performances and worked with Texan rock bands who deployed projections of his films in combination with their music. The museum job that film activist Ralph McKay got him in March of 1983 saved his life – and over the years made him miserable, as Hans Scheugl's *Keine Donau* shows, a documentary shot

---

16 Gabriele Jutz, "Eine Poetik der Zeit," in Scheugl, *Ex Underground*, p. 108.
17 Scheugl, *Keine Donau*.

---

18 Scheugl, *Keine Donau*.

Kurt Kren
31/75 Asyl
1975

in Houston in 1988: The filmmaker Kurt Kren as a security guard in a museum punches his time card and informs his colleagues that he's "fucking tired." He contemplates the breadwinning day ahead of him without illusion: "Same shit, only worse." *42/83 No Film* is correspondingly a product of depression and inertia. Three seconds long, only the title, no movement, just three writing tablets (dark letters on a light background, white writing on a black background, and once again, a question mark), in the end: a film after all.

For close to six years Kren wandered through the Museum of Fine Arts in Houston as a uniformed security guard. He threatened to despair in the monotonous work of the exhibition rooms, in counting the minutes that did not slip by, and that in fact were "the seconds of my life." "My brain is going more and more sour," he wrote Wilhelm and Birgit Hein in 1985. In 1984, halfway cleaned up financially, he invested $190 in an Atari video recorder and a computer at which he likes to sit in the cell of his Houston living space. The aesthetic of the monitor consequently informed the next two films realized in 1984 and 1985, before withdrawing from filmmaking for five long years. After his short Reagan TV treaty *43/84 1984*, he only loaded one roll of film for his *44/85 Foot'-Age Shoot'-Out*, commissioned by the San Francisco Cinematheque. It shows street traffic by day and by night, texts wander over his monitor. He films himself naked in the mirror, and in his security guard uniform. Trashing is the basic attitude of the film. He signals rage at the pressure the filmmaker Kren is feeling. He shoots shaking images of the skyline, a street sign and turns the camera's lens to the floor.

12   Finale

The last shot in Scheugl's film shows Kurt Kren at the harbor of the city, pacing back and forth in the golden light of dusk in front of a giant freighter, as if ready for departure. And the time comes: In 1988, Kren was rediscovered in Vienna through a big showcase of his work at the Stadtkino. One year later, after living in America for over a decade, he returned from Houston to his hometown. Old friendships were still in place. In January of 1989, Valie Export and Hans Scheugl organized Kren's retrieval to Vienna where he got an apartment in a subsidized housing development, and in March of the same year, was honored with an award in recognition of his film art. He began to teach at Vienna's Academy of Applied Arts, as instigated by Peter Weibel. In the early 1990s, he answered all questions about future film plans dismissively: He said he's filmed empty and burned out, in his typically factual tone. He couldn't imagine reaching for a camera again. Yet in the few years left he let himself be talked into making a few last films, almost all were commissioned works. *46/90 Falter 2* was created in 1990 in a Vienna subway station,

Kurt Kren
42/83 No Film
1983

Kurt Kren
44/85 Foot'-Age Shoot'-Out
1985

Kurt Kren
43/84 1984
1984

Kurt Kren
46/90 Falter 2
1990

a commercial conveying the fleeting hustle and bustle of subway passengers, a mercurial, single-frame urban study of characteristically gentle nervousness. In 1995/1996, Kren shot his last two works in peace and quiet, snug in Vienna's art scene, embraced by a circle of friends and artists, his lifework secure and well looked after.

In 1997, Kren took a little trip together with his colleague Gustav Deutsch, the latter later distilling their time into a video essay entitled *K & K & K* (1999). Kren and Deutsch go in search of Robert Klemmer's grave, a painter who had died in 1971 at the age of 33. Kren talks of Klemmer as his "drinking buddy" and how he had filmed his funeral but fell into technical difficulties: The film jammed in the camera. Kren removed the defective roll of film and threw it into the open grave of his friend, burying his *Klemmer* (a German word for something stuck) together with the other Klemmer – and called his film *25/71 Klemmer und Klemmer verlassen die Welt* (*25/71 Klemmer and Klemmer Leave the World*). Only after a longer search do

Deutsch and Kren find the site: Dornbacher Cemetery, Group 42, Row 5, Grave 3. During the search Kren muses over his own death. It isn't that much fun to tramp around in cemeteries anymore, he says laughing, since one is already "so close to the end oneself." In the early Summer of 1998, it was indeed his turn. Kurt Kren died in his apartment, and despite everything it is surprising. He was only 68 years old. Hundreds of friends and acquaintances attended his burial at Vienna's Central Cemetery. No film was thrown into his grave.

13   Wild Gift

In the end everything was very simple. Kren didn't need detours, his humility did not block his basic trust in his own work. In an interview/performance back in 1967, Hans Scheugl and Peter Weibel asked their older colleague, "What are you giving to the world." Kren's dry answer: "Me."

Translated by Eve Heller

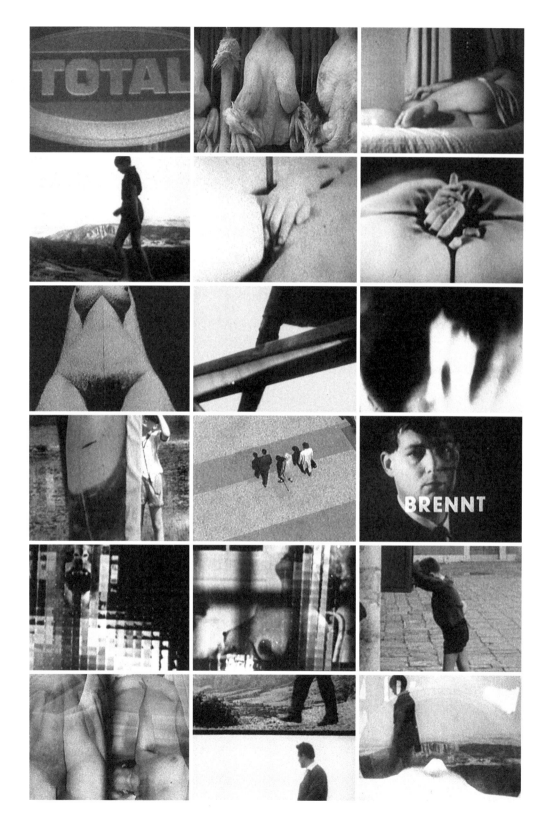

Shadow Burns.
Notes on the Film Works of Marc Adrian.

Norbert Pfaffenbichler

There are artists who do more or less the same thing all their lives – they develop a single technique and/or style and never manage to leave this path. And there are other artists who attempt to reinvent themselves with each new work, employing a wide variety of media and materials, consciously trying to avoid repeating themselves, taking on completely new challenges after completing an experiment, and pursuing their own interests and obsessions without compromise. In terms of market strategy the first category is probably more efficient and "profitable," as the resulting work can be evaluated and categorized more easily by the public, critics and dealers. Marc Adrian undoubtedly belongs to the second category. He was the kind of artist who never worried about the market or prevailing fashions and instead unconditionally worked in conformity with his own artistic ethos. An extremely versatile artist, Adrian demonstrated comparable levels of virtuosity in a number of different areas. Having studied under the renowned sculptor

Fritz Wotruba in Vienna, he created sculptures (mostly kinetic works), produced abstract visual compositions (Op Art), did photo collages, and wrote literary, dramatic and theoretical texts. His theory of "methodical inventionism" deserves special mention.[1] His film work in itself is extremely heterogeneous, marked by an unmitigated desire to experiment and a radical approach in terms of form and content. Particularly conspicuous is the difference between his early works (film blocks 0–2)[2] and the later films. Over the course of time they increased in length significantly, and became much more personal and obsessive. His late works are also characterized by extensive use of found footage, much of it pornographic, and the application of a wide variety of visual strategies to alter images. Adrian manipulated his source material using an optical printer and developed most of the films himself. While his early film work fits in the canon of post-war avant-garde film, the categorization of his later efforts is much more difficult since it is hard to find anything comparable either in Austria or in the rest of the world. Perhaps precisely this variety is one reason Adrian has yet to receive the

---

[1] "As in most of my works, my operational modus was methodical inventionism, i.e., the works are placed on a pre-drawn blueprint. In this way, all personal and aesthetic touches are rendered impossible in the final product, and total loss of control is assured." Marc Adrian in a radio interview, San Francisco, 1970, speaking about his early films, quoted in Peter Weibel, "Expanded Cinema: Material Films, Film Actions (without Film), Project and Concept Films," in *Beyond Art: A Third Culture. A Comparative Study in Cultures, Art and Science in 20th Century Austria and Hungary*, ed. Peter Weibel (Vienna and New York: Springer Verlag, 2005), p. 148.

[2] Film block 0: *Black Movie I* (1957), *1. Mai 1958* (1958), *Wo-Da-Vor-Bei* (1958), *Schriftfilm* (1959/1960), *Black Movie II* (1959). Film block 1: *Random* (1963), *Orange* (1962–1964), *Go* (1964), *Text I* (1963), *Text II* (1964). Film block 2: *Text III* (1966), *Total* (1964). Film blocks 0–2 and other films by Marc Adrian are available on DVD: *Marc Adrian, Das filmische Werk 1 + 2* (Zurich: Art Adventures, 2004 and 2005).

international renown he deserves, despite his pioneering accomplishments.[3]

Black Movie I (1957), **Black Movie II** (1959), **Black Movie III** (1969) // Adrian dated the start of his film work at 1957. In collaboration with Kurt Kren he produced a silent short film with the polemic title *Black Movie*. This first work already reveals the radical views held by the two friends and artists. The film consists of different monochrome color fields rendered by 16 mm film leader – easily available and inexpensive – which Adrian and Kren projected according to a precise rhythm that had been graphically mapped out beforehand.

Adrian produced two more versions of this color film experiment, *Black Movie II* (1959) and *Black Movie III* (1969). The third version, made at the invitation of the Museum of Modern Art in New York, was given a soundtrack. The colors that appear in the film were read aloud and edited to the images according to chance. There is no correspondence between the color seen and the name of the color synchronously heard.

1. Mai 1958 [May 1, 1958] (1958) // His second film, *1. Mai 1958* was also a joint effort with Kren, and its title indicates the day of shooting. The two friends, "armed" with a camera, rode bicycles in Vienna's Prater and filmed traditional May Day festivities, in the style of newsreels popular at the time. The film was shot without sound, which Adrian later regretted. All available effects to alter the imagery were used, including freeze frames, time lapse photography, superimpositions, etc. Their great desire to experiment is quite obvious in this "documentary," as is the enthusiasm with which the two young artists worked.

Wo-Da-Vor-Bei [Where-there-in front-next to] (1958) // Production of *Wo-Da-Vor-Bei* marked the beginning of many years during which Adrian used writing, that is to say, text, as filmic material.

At the time the artist was in close contact with the Wiener Gruppe (Vienna Group), consisting of the writers H. C. Artmann, Gerhard Rühm, Konrad Bayer, Friedrich Achleitner and Oswald Wiener. Despite mutual inspiration, Adrian's text films have little in common with the Vienna Group's literary output – they are entirely independent and unique works. Interestingly enough, at approximately the same time France's Lettrists also began using text as raw material for films.[4] There was however no exchange between these contemporaneous avant-garde groups in Paris and Vienna. For Adrian's experiments the genuinely filmic phenomena of movement and montage were central. His love of mathematical systems is clearly apparent in the text films as well. Letters, words and word fragments are not arranged according to conventional grammatical or syntactic rules, but instead ordered on the basis of mathematical permutations.

In *Wo-Da-Vor-Bei* the eponymous sequence of letters are set into a continuous stream of motion. The letters become larger and then smaller (zoom effect), are variously combined, reflected horizontally and shown in positive and negative. This "silent sound poem" confronts the spectator with seemingly unsolvable riddles, and the absence of any punctuation makes interpretation even more difficult. Methods of animation and montage are applied to the syllables of filmic time and space so that the title can be understood in different ways: Wo? Da! Vorbei. (Where? There! Gone.) and Wo? Da? Vor? Bei? (Where? There? In front? Next to it?) are equally possible. The mirroring of this sequence of letters adds to the confusion, as back and front are interchangeable.

Schriftfilm [Script Film] (1959/1960) // In his next work Adrian showed a series of two-word combinations, one above the other, in capitals and of identical size: The upper half of the picture contains a noun, the lower half an adjective or verb. The arrangements of the words undergo permutations, resulting in all possible combinations. In contrast

---

3   This essay will concentrate on a selection of the artist's films. The most comprehensive presentation of Adrian's artwork is to be found in the 400-page catalogue *marc adrian* [German/English], eds. Anna Artaker and Peter Weibel (Graz: Ritter Verlag, 2007).

4   The first Lettrist films were *Traité de bave et d'éternite* by Isidore Isou and *Le Film est déjà commencé?* by Maurice Lemaître, both made in 1951.

Marc Adrian, **Black Movie I**, 1957

Marc Adrian, **1. Mai 1958**, 1958

Marc Adrian, **Wo-Da-Vor-Bei**, 1958

Marc Adrian, **Schriftfilm**, 1959/1960

to the rigid system of word permutation, the length of time that the words appear on screen was determined randomly. Due to the inflexibility of combinatorial possibilities, some meaningful phrases are produced, such as "Frau geht," "Mann fällt" and "Stein bricht" [woman goes, man falls, stone breaks], while others are wholly absurd, such as "Stein schreit," "Wasser geht" [stone shouts, water goes] and "Schatten brennt" [shadow burns]. Adrian employs the means afforded by mathematics and also film to attack the "medium of language." In doing so he packs his criticism into a highly lyrical filmic work.

Text I (1963), **Text II** (1964), **Text III** (1966) // In *Text I* the terms "hammer," "wind" and "butter" are written in lowercase and scattered across the screen in an aleatoric manner. The letters' size remains constant, while the arrangement of the words and the amount of time they appear is random.

In *Text II* Adrian's systematic destruction of text goes even further. Two adjacent letters fill the screen at a time, and the pairs change constantly. While finding meaning in these random combinations is normally impossible, every time the sequence j-a ("yes" in German) appears, Adrian interrupts the flow of images briefly. *Text I* and *II* are accompanied by purely synthetic sounds.

In *Text III* Adrian deals with the themes of war and death in his own characteristic manner. The film suggests a despairing and simultaneously martial requiem. He dedicated the work to a female wireless radio operator who lived with the Adrians during the Second World War and was killed during an air raid on Vienna. Adrian combined text fragments he had photographed, newspaper articles from the *Kleine Wiener Kriegszeitung* [Little Viennese War Newspaper] in Old German script, and manipulated stills from Sergei Eisenstein's epic propaganda film, *Battleship Potemkin* (1925). The inverted texts were blown up and accelerated by means of montage to such an extent that they are barely legible, solely isolated words such as "Volk" [the people] and "Schlacht" [battle] occasionally catch the spectator's eye. The stills from *Battleship Potemkin* continually interrupt the flow

of text. They are always mirrored vertically, and the two halves of the image curve together or apart in various formations. The soundtrack comprises recordings of the Tibetan *Book of the Dead* recited in the original language.

Random (1963) // *Random* is a groundbreaking work which anticipated innovations that were further developed many years later. The film is considered one of the world's first entirely digitally generated computer animations. Completely abstract, it was created with the aid of an IBM computer normally used for medical research. A cathode ray was used to animate dot grids of varying sizes, that were subsequently transferred both as positive and negative images to 35 mm black-and-white film. The title is indicative of the intention: All parameters of the work, such as the visual motifs, their duration and the synthesized soundtrack, were pre-determined by a random number generator.

Orange (1962–1964) // *Orange* is an associative collage of sounds and images that Adrian once again edited according to chance operations. The work's central visual motif is a still life with an orange, cut in half and placed on a tray in the picture's upper left. A knife is seen jutting into the lower right portion of the frame, wobbling menacingly on the tray's edge. The light that illuminates the scene is in constant motion, giving the shot a dynamic quality. The sexual connotations of this ensemble are unequivocal and are further emphasized by the addition of freeze frames showing a couple copulating and a detail shot of a vagina. On the soundtrack a voice can be heard reciting a dictionary entry for the term "orange."

Go (1964) // His next film, the motion study *Go*, is also based on a principle of random montage. We see nothing other than a woman's and a man's pair of legs. The actors move within the tight frame in a linear direction, toward and away from each other in all possible combinations. This minimalistic choreography provided Adrian with sufficient raw material for his mathematically based, aleatoric montage. The action is shown in both positive and

 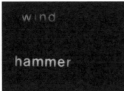 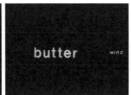 

Marc Adrian, **Text I**, 1963

Marc Adrian, **Text II**, 1964

Marc Adrian, **Text III**, 1966

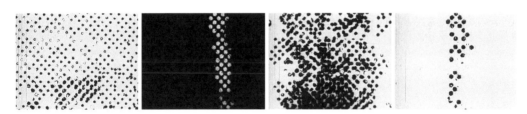

Marc Adrian, **Random**, 1963

   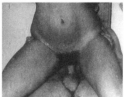

Marc Adrian, **Orange**, 1962–1964

negative images, which increases the number of possible combinations.

Total (1964–1968) // *Total*, a thoroughly complex and personal film, is divided into three chapters, "Childhood and Youth" I & II and "Coda." In a wild collage of sound and image Adrian combines private material and found footage, inserts photographic collages and adds text. The film possesses a wealth of formal ideas: multiple exposures, reflections, solarization, repetitions, shifting frame lines, changes in film speed; individual scenes are run backward and forward, a glass screen with grid-like divisions serves as a filter, etc. Thus Adrian anticipates stylistic devices that later generations of film artists will come to perfect. The combination of pornographic film with original material is a method that will provide the basis for many of Dietmar Brehm's films. Repeatedly rephotographing a sequence in forward and reverse motion without omitting a single frame will later be a method masterfully realized by Martin Arnold. Furthermore, Adrian added animated text to the work. On the one hand he quotes himself by employing fragments from *Schriftfilm*, on the other hand he adds speech balloons to the picture, a reference to that other great sequential art form, the comic strip. These speech balloons contain the following text: "My momma cares for me. My dad cares for me. Just everyone cares for me. What the hell is wrong?" and "My boy cares for me. Just everyone cares for me. What the hell is wrong?" This is Adrian's expression of his deep mistrust of social conventions, such as the Western concept of the nuclear family. Adrian's son appears frequently, and the artist himself can be seen at different ages.

The strategies employed in *Total* include shock and provocation. For example, the fact that a large amount of pornographic material appears next to footage taken on family vacations is particularly disturbing. Also memorable are the frequent close-ups of a bleeding penis with a nail sticking through it. The shock effect these images must have produced can only be imagined nowadays, given our thoroughly "sexualized" society in which all types of pornography are easily obtainable at any time.

Blue Movie (1969) // *Blue Movie* returned Adrian to abstraction. He proceeded with color experiments he and Kurt Kren had initiated with the *Black Movie* series. *Black Movie III* and *Blue Movie* were completed the same year. In contrast to the earlier works, *Blue Movie* does not consist of monochrome sequences. With this film Adrian was primarily interested in the phenomenon of how colors mix. He animated rectangles of different sizes in the primary colors, red, blue and yellow, on a black background. These figures' sides all have the same ratio, equal to a film frame, and overlap frequently – thereby producing compound colors. As a guiding principle of construction and composition Adrian employed the "golden section." Like the films that preceded it, *Blue Movie* was created according to a predetermined and strictly calculated score. The purely synthetic soundtrack was conceived to run in sync with the images.

Mund [Mouth] (1965) // The film begins with a closeup of a man's head, his lips have been taped shut with an adhesive bandage. This image is accompanied by credits read off-screen in English, rather than rolling in text form as is normally the case. As a result, an immediate reference is made to one of the important functions of the mouth, as an organ of speech. This is followed by an insert reading "ein lehrfilm" [an educational film]. Adrian collaged documentary, medical and pornographic imagery with his own footage to deliver a wild parody of scientific and sex education films. The uses to which the human mouth can be put is demonstrated in detail. The film's provocative potential is enormous, particularly in light of the time it was made. For example, we see a shaved vagina with vampire teeth, homosexual fellatio, a man standing on his head while urinating into his own mouth through a plastic tube, and a closeup of an anus defecating, with the excrement smeared across it by a second person as it leaves the body. Adrian crosscut these scenes with a shot of him eating a dollar bill. The theme of gender is broached, in a scene during which a bearded man applies red lipstick. The stream of images is repeatedly interrupted by inserted text such as "Darf ich ihnen in den Mund

Marc Adrian, **Go**, 1964

Marc Adrian, **Total**, 1964–1968

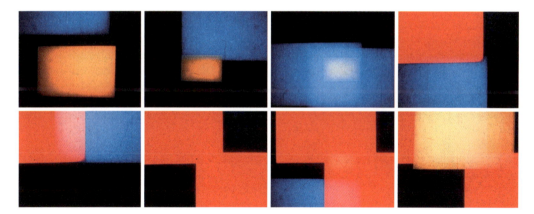

Marc Adrian, **Blue Movie**, 1969

Marc Adrian, **Mund**, 1965

scheissen mein Fräulein?" [Miss, may I shit into your mouth?] and "excurs über die vergeblichkeit" [excursus on futility]. The soundtrack is also collaged, though consists mainly of sounds made by an organ and accompanied by a man singing a song by Adrian, in an English that is difficult to understand. _Mund_ is a furious parody and frontal attack on the bourgeois morals and values of its time.

Theoria (1971) // This color film begins with a text insert reading "ein Ritus" [a rite], which is followed by the dedication, "für Ede Wolf" [for Zeke Wolf, aka the Big Bad Wolf], a villain from Walt Disney's cartoon empire. Subsequently the figure's face appears, accompanied by resounding laughter. The first sequence follows, during which Adrian is seen sitting at a table and smoking a pipe as he calmly cooks a spoonful of heroin over a candle and then injects it into his thigh. This unambiguous introduction is followed by a rush of sounds, images and collaged text. The filmmaker combines ethnographic and pornographic material with scenes of wild animals such as vultures and hyenas and battleground footage from the Second World War. Again and again he appears in the heterogeneous stream of images, dressed in turban and caftan while sitting in his room, writing. The numerous sequences showing naked bodies in action are highly altered in that they are shown in negative, solarized or tinted with shades of intense red or blue.

uarei (1977) // _uarei_ is another experiment with color footage, and Adrian's last abstract film. It begins with a quote from Flann O'Brien's novel _The Third Policeman_, as spoken by the fictional character of DeSelby: "Human existance [sic] being an hallucination containing in itself the secondary hallucination of day and night (…) it ill becomes any man of sense to be concerned at the illusory approach of the supreme hallucination known as death." This text emerges from complete blurriness, then disappears back into it. The visual vocabulary Adrian chose for the film is solely comprised by basic geometric shapes, circle, square and line. Only one is shown at a time and, strictly centered, they slowly increase or decrease in size. Pastel shades are employed so that the visual compositions are tone on tone; in other words, figure and background contrast solely in terms of their color's intensity. The delirious effect of this work is underlined by the psychedelic soundtrack and the film's considerable length.

der regen [the rain] (1983) // Back in 1957, Adrian and Kurt Kren had started working on a surrealistic film based on the former's play, _der regen. ein stück in rhythmischen proportionen_ [the rain. a play in rhythmic proportions]. Kren eventually lost interest in the project, but in 1983 Adrian completed _der regen_ by himself. While the text was originally intended for the stage, it was considered "unperformable." Adrian, an avant-gardist through and through, in response: "The impossibility of executing something has never held me back from conceiving a project."[5] Material shot with Kren was supplemented with found footage and scenes Adrian created himself. Adrian appears as the protagonist at various ages. The theme is no less than the human condition, life from cradle to grave. Adrian takes up the classic motif of the "three ages and death," which has frequently been used in the visual arts, to create an extremely personal film version of this visual typology. Documentary footage of a birth is juxtaposed with shots of dying animals, human mummies and funeral scenes. These are punctuated by "Adrians" of various ages who walk around, stagger and fall, lost in the blazing color of a flood of images. The entirety of the film material is heavily altered, having been superimposed several times and immersed in garish color. The visually opulent action is acoustically accompanied by Adrian's experimental, metric text, expressionlessly recited by a male and a female voice in unison, plus a wide variety of sound fragments (shots, explosions, pop music, etc.). He succeeds in presenting an equally hermetic and hypnotic work in which methods taken from a broad spectrum of genres such as surreal, structural, essayistic and psychedelic film are successfully united in a single work.

5 Otto Mörth, ed., _Marc Adrian. Das filmische Werk_ (Vienna: Sonderzahl, 1999), p. 95.

Marc Adrian, **Theoria**, 1971

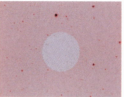

Marc Adrian, **uarei**, 1977

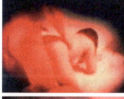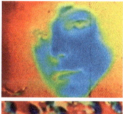

Marc Adrian, **der regen**, 1983

Pueblo (1979/1989) // Marc Adrian: "Pueblo, that's the village, the people, that's what everybody has in common." In his longest film work the filmmaker thematizes the phenomenon of "belonging to a group of outsiders,"[6] as Adrian put it. His status as an artist is compared and contrasted with the lives of North America's native residents: Both lead an existence on the edge of society, beyond standardized, conventional ways of life. The film is a mixture of all kinds of material, both found footage and film Adrian shot himself. Particularly memorable are the innumerable scenes showing ritual dances performed by members of different Native American tribes. As he had received a government subsidy to make this work, Adrian felt an obligation to make it as accessible as possible to a wide audience, in contrast to his previous films. For this purpose he integrated a few figures who provide commentary on what happens on-screen. For example, a conservative, "average" couple is shown sitting on a living-room couch, apparently watching the film on television at the same time as the film audience. They enjoy the "nice Indians, they're just like children," and gripe about corrupt politics. Another figure, sitting on a raised chair and never clearly visible, symbolizes the hegemony of the state. Interviews with native North Americans and the artist's own statements complete the associatively structured and extremely subjective film essay.

Bilderbruch 1, Kiln [Image Quarry 1, Kiln] (1990) // *Kiln* attempts to capture the mood of the 1980s and 1990s. The motifs in its mystic stream of images are dominated by the elements of fire and water. Images of a kiln and blazing flames are frequently combined with others of water surfaces, sailboats and gondolas. The motifs and image editing match: Adrian "fuses" and "liquefies" his film material by means of multiple superimpositions, manipulation of time, reflections and intensive tinting. Red, green and blue dominate. Despite the fact that his raw material came from a variety of sources, the film seems to have been "poured from the same mold," especially in comparison with earlier works.

6   Mörth, p. 102.

In addition to the nudity typical of his later films, including a woman's laced-up breasts, detail shots of vaginas and the frequently employed closeup of a baby being nursed, one scene especially recurs, in which a man's feet can be seen. The actor, who is spinning on his own axis most of the time, is wearing a hiking boot on one foot, and on the other an old black shoe with a long extension that resembles a penis. Haunting music composed by Markus Brandt accompanies the film and is in itself as multifarious and yet harmonious as the suggestive flood of images.

Stadt-Werk-Statt (1990) // This rhythmic montage experiment is based on the principles of dialectic and repetition. Two entirely distinct but equally claustrophobic spatial settings serve as the raw material for this fast-paced black-and-white montage film. In one scene we see footage of the aftermath of a violent performance from 1989, by artists Markus Binder, Thomas Lehner, Georg Ritter and Gotthard Wagner at Vienna's culture center WUK. These four artists from Linz, and associated with its alternative culture center, Stadtwerkstatt, used a plow to tear a longitudinal furrow in a gallery's concrete floor. The actual performance is not shown in the film, only the brutally torn-up floor and the foreboding plow appear. The second setting shows two women, one blonde and the other brunette (filmmakers Linda Christanell and Moucle Blackout, respectively), standing next to each other in a huge hospital room. A storm is created by means of impressive wind and fog machines. The camera, alternately positioned behind and in front of the women, incessantly zooms in on their heads.

Again and again the words "FRUCHTBAR" [fertile] and "UNFRUCHTBAR" [infertile] appear briefly to punctuate the rapidly edited scenes. These adjectives evoke associations with the almost surreal visual motifs and disturbing interior situations (a plow: infertile concrete rather than fertile soil; a hospital: delivery room, deathbed, etc.). A plow and a storm being transferred from the "natural" and "fertile" outdoors to sterile, architecturally designed interiors torpedo conventional experiences of enclosed rooms. In addition, the

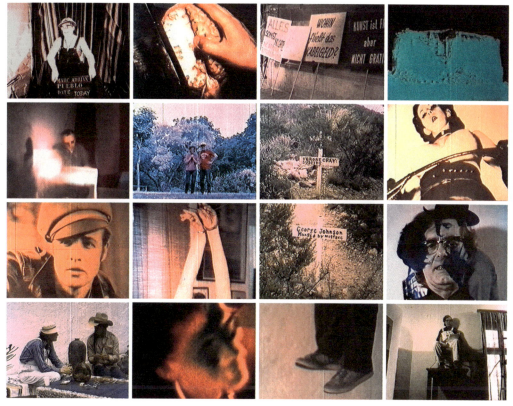

Marc Adrian, **Pueblo**, 1979/1989

Marc Adrian, **Bilderbruch 1, Kiln**, 1990

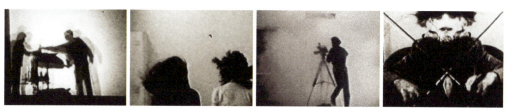

Marc Adrian, **Stadt-Werk-Statt**, 1990

"filmic space" is broken up and "liquefied" by means of the camera techniques employed (zooms, tracking shots and pans), the frequent image inversion, the reversal of movement and the dynamically repetitive montage. The soundtrack is also an assembly of disparate elements: Miscellaneous noise is juxtaposed with music by Peter Ruzicka, and a brief passage from a text, fragments of which are repeated incessantly: "Each work of art is a message about an experience. The art must be controlled during the whole process. I have to begin again."

Nachfilm [Follow-up Film] (1995) // *Nachfilm* is an oppressive study on the theme of coming to terms with Austria's past. On a visit to the Mauthausen concentration camp, now a memorial, the artist ran into two individuals who apparently lived nearby during the Second World War, when the camp was in operation. Their statements played down and even went so far as to deny what happened, which shocked Adrian. He immediately wrote down the dialogue of the two elderly women and later had a professional actress recite the transcript for the film. This accompanies scenes showing the camp, both in the past and present, interrupted by extended sequences of black.

Istigkeit [Isness] (1996) // *Istigkeit*, named after a term coined by Meister Ekkehard about 1220, represents an attempt to "couple film and poetry." Writer Petra Ganglbauer reads one of her texts, to which Adrian filmically responds. A variety of images are superimposed several times over a closeup of Ganglbauer reading, with the intention of expanding the extent of lyrical associations. Text and film create strong mutual references. Certain sentences and terms such as "Wie kam die Figur zu ihrer Gestalt?" [How did the figure get its form?], "Manifestation und Sprache des Lichts" [Manifestation and language of light], "Wir treten in die Nacktheit ein, wie man eine Bühne betritt" [We enter nakedness the way one takes a stage], "Die Leinwand als Narbe" [The screen as scar] and "Ich Kino" [I cinema] are direct references to the medium of film. Adrian visualizes certain portions of the text in an illustrative manner, and others

associatively. When, for example, the word "fish" is heard, a fish-shaped keychain fob is shown. The flow of images subsequently veers away from the text, taking its own path. Frequently images appear of living and dead crows, under water shots, and a spinning top. Text and images conform to the same lyric principle, paralleling the writer who intentionally disregards grammatical rules. Adrian treats his film material using means of associative montage while also altering the image through dissolves, tinting and manipulating film speed.

Four Short Pieces (1997), **Conundrum** (1998), **Taos** (2000) // Adrian's last films were inspired by Sergei Eisenstein's essay "The Dynamic Square," which deals with the question of the aspect ratio in cinema.[7] Rather than the "American" widescreen format, Eisenstein argues in favor of the "dynamic square screen." While in terms of content all three of these works primarily focus on the culture of native North Americans, the trilogy also contains found footage, derived for example from medical educational films. Sound and picture are associative and mounted in a collage-like manner. Though the visual content remains the same, the framing changes constantly during individual shots, abruptly switching from widescreen to square and then circular framing. On the one hand this represents a criticism of preset industrial standards, which includes the aspect ratio, on the other it demonstrates the potential for manipulation and interpretation of images by means of the part shown.

In 2008 Marc Adrian died in Vienna at the age of 77 without having received the international recognition he undoubtedly deserves for his pioneering films.

Translated by Steve Wilder

The author wishes to thank Anna Artaker, Christian Dewald, Olaf Möller, Otto Mörth, the Austrian Film Museum and the Filmarchiv Austria.

7   Sergei Eisenstein, "The Dynamic Square," in Sergei Eisenstein, *Film Essays and a Lecture*, ed. and trans. Jay Leyda (Princeton: Princeton University Press, 1982), pp. 48–65.

Marc Adrian, **Nachfilm**, 1995

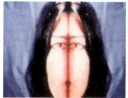   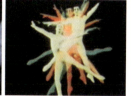

Marc Adrian, **Istigkeit**, 1996

 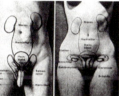 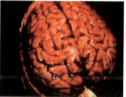 

Marc Adrian, **Four Short Pieces**, 1997

Marc Adrian, **Conundrum**, 1998

Marc Adrian, **Taos**, 2000

Expanded Cinemas Exploding.

Hans Scheugl

A new realism characteristic of art in the 1960s superceded the abstraction of post-war years with its multi-layered metaphysical depths, rising to the surface of social and political reality by means of new technologies and materials. Novel associations were sought, especially between different art forms. Film became an important element as a technical medium in Pop Art and Happenings, especially in the US – this also included experimental film, which had characteristically been an isolated player in the art world. Since the early 1960s, the Happenings staged in New York by Robert Whitman, Carolee Schneemann and Aldo Tambellini (Electromedia Theatre) consisted of an interaction between performance and film projection. They were conceived as visual, non-verbal theater pieces. As of 1966, E.A.T. (Experiments in Art and Technology), founded by Billy Klüver and Robert Rauschenberg to nurture the collaborative work of artists and technicians, assumed an influential role. It led to a large number of technical, electronic and other diverse media projects.

In 1965, Stan VanDerBeek offered a related form of film presentation in which the spatial integration of the audience was a central issue, utilizing a dome-shaped projection space for his Movie-Drome. And the following year, the multi-media event of *Andy Warhol's Exploding Plastic Inevitable* integrated music, dance, live performance and the light effects of diverse projections to create a psychedelic "Gesamtkunstwerk"; realizing the liberating goal of art to break the boundaries of accustomed forms. The opposite of these sensuous, experiential spaces and their thirst for acceleration was presented by the Fluxus Movement. The Fluxus films were characteristically short and produced with simple means. They offered an intellectual, formally conceptual, minimalist and contemplative approach which often manifested an ironic examination of the film medium itself.

In the Summer of 1966, a special edition of the journal *Film Culture* appeared under the title *Expanded Arts*. All forms of filmic alternatives, in Europe later termed "film happenings," were subsumed under the category of "expanded cinema," including popular multi-media events and light shows, and the neo-Dadaist manifestations of Fluxus.

In preceding years, not only actual knowledge but mere reports of the New American Cinema had led to an artistic restlessness in Europe. Warhol's marathon films roused as much interest as the sexual freedom of the underground. Already as of 1958, early New American Cinema films (e.g., by Stan Brakhage, Kenneth Anger, Robert Breer) were shown at the 2nd EXPRMNTL Film Festival organized by the Belgian Cinémathèque in Brussels. In 1964, a selection of around 30 films toured European capitals. A second, expanded program was presented in Vienna in 1967. In 1963/1964, at

Above: Austria Filmmakers Cooperative, 1968. (from left:) Peter Weibel,
Ernst Schmidt Jr., VALIE EXPORT, Gottfried Schlemmer, Hans Scheugl, Kurt Kren.
Below: Peter Weibel, **Nivea**, 1967

Ernst Schmidt Jr.
Tonfilm
1968

Ernst Schmidt Jr.
Filmreste
1966/1967

the 3rd EXPRMNTL Festival, relocated to Knokke-le-Zout, the large number of films generated by the New American Cinema movement still overpowered a more humble European output. But by the following festival of 1967/1968, a stronger showing of the European film avant-garde diminished the ratio of Americans to one third of the event. At the same time, expanded cinema was not a topic of discussion during the few days the festival lasted. Multi-media Happenings by Americans could not travel to Europe for technical as well as financial reasons and consequently remained largely unknown. The Dutch staged occasional filmic events and presented rudimentary conceptual forms, but no one could afford anything equivalent to the complexity of the American projects. But what *was*

a critical topic at Knokke was the political significance of art. Leftist students not only attacked feature films, but also denounced experimental films as escapist and conformist. Meanwhile, European filmmakers had their first opportunity to get acquainted with one another and consider new cooperative alternatives in an active effort to dismantle established structures of commercial art. In fact, Knokke got a few things started. While the London Film-Makers' Co-operative had already been founded in 1966, based on the New York Film-Makers' Co-operative, similar operations were now established in Amsterdam, Hamburg and Vienna.

Immediately after Knokke in January of 1968, the Austria Filmmakers Cooperative was founded by Ernst Schmidt Jr., Hans Scheugl, Kurt Kren,

Peter Weibel, Valie Export and Gottfried Schlemmer. In succeeding months they were joined by Marc Adrian, Otto Muehl and Otmar Bauer. Over the course of 1968, several filmmaker meetings served to present and view new films made by European filmmakers. The two largest gatherings took place in February in Hamburg, and November in Munich. In March, filmmakers Wilhelm and Birgit Hein together with others founded X-Screen, a cinema for independent film in Cologne. X-Screen opened with a program of works by Viennese filmmakers. "As the smallest group," wrote Birgit Hein, "the Austrian cooperative had the most coherent character and could stage the most effective show."[1] She indicated that from their inception as a group within a highly conservative environment, the Austrians could pursue goals of cultural politics with greater vehemence and were able to collaborate artistically on a number of fronts.

This collaboration had already begun the year before, in January of 1967, when a film club in Vienna invited Kren, Schmidt Jr. and Scheugl to show their films. Peter Weibel opened the program with an *Action Lecture* and presented *Nivea* as a "direct commercial film." For *Action Lecture No. 1*, Weibel stood in front of the screen reading a theoretical text aloud while 8 mm films were projected on him. For *Nivea* he held up a Nivea beach ball while standing in front of the screen, in the flickering white light of the projector accompanied by the sound of a camera motor played by a tape recorder. The intention behind both Actions was to release constituent elements of film – director, light, sound, camera, projector – from their illusionistic unity and reconstellate them. It was on this occasion that Weibel first formulated the basic principles of his artistic concept of reality. He and Valie Export, with whom he lived and worked, went on to demonstrate this concept in a rapid succession of various Actions and projects in 1968: "The notion of reality does not exist for the filmmaker. What is given to the filmmaker is not nature but the film material. The decisions the filmmaker makes within the

realm of celluloid possibility result in the film."[2]

Weibel's position early on lent a different slant to, what P. Adams Sitney two years later would term, "structural film."[3] For Sitney, and generally in America and Europe, structural film essentially implied films that were not determined by narrative guidelines but rather by formal issues of their own construction. The form these films take is shaped by their predetermined structure. First generation avant-garde filmmakers in Vienna had already composed film scores according to this principle in the 1950s, namely Peter Kubelka, Kurt Kren and Marc Adrian. For the next generation of filmmakers in the 1960s – and including Kren – other parameters became important. In their avant-garde film encyclopedia, *Eine Subgeschichte des Films* [A Sub-history of Film],[4] Schmidt and Scheugl therefore introduced the concept of "material film." This term implies a different direction, departing from a structural strategy and approaching the open forms of Happenings, which in Vienna were shaped by Actionist Otto Muehl's idea of Material Action. Just as Muehl transformed the human body into the material of his Actions, the return of film to its material components led to new signifying strategies within an altered context. This was not only the aim of expanded cinema but also determined the anarchistic methods used by Ernst Schmidt Jr. Like Kren, Schmidt Jr. filmed some of Muehl's Actions. He messed with the material by painting on it, scratching and punching holes in the very celluloid of films such as *Einszweidrei* (*Onetwothree*, 1965–1968), *Filmreste* (*Film Scraps*, 1966/1967), *Weiß* (*White*, 1968) and *Tonfilm* (*Sound Film*, 1968).

These artists did not want to surrender to the challenge raised by the camp of leftist students in Knokke for art to take a political stance – they wanted to face it head on. They were unanimous: Art as an ethical or moral calling had long since been exhausted as an idea and was ineffective.

---

1   Birgit Hein, *Film im Underground* (Frankfurt am Main, Berlin and Vienna: Ullstein, 1971), p. 141.

2   Peter Weibel's program notes in Hans Scheugl, *Erweitertes Kino: Die Wiener Filme der 60er Jahre* (Vienna: Triton, 2002), p. 85.
3   P. Adams Sitney, "Structural Film," *Film Culture*, no. 47, 1969.
4   Hans Scheugl and Ernst Schmidt Jr., *Subgeschichte des Films. Lexikon des Avantgarde-, Experimental- und Undergroundfilms*, 2 volumes (Frankfurt am Main: Suhrkamp, 1974).

Far greater potential rested in gaining a distance to every kind of language that held or sought power.

The investigation of language use has a long tradition in Vienna. It penetrated the art world with the work of Ludwig Wittgenstein and found further ground in the late 1950s with the poets of the Vienna Group, including Oswald Wiener who participated with Otto Muehl, Peter Weibel and others in various Actions. Like Wittgenstein, Wiener and company saw the examination of language as an elemental investigation of the human being, and they sought new forms of expression to modify language and thereby, change the individual's world view.

Weibel perceived reality as the ruler of language – and language administered by society as the ruler of reality. Once this kind of control is recognized, the repressive authority of language must be rebelled against. Karl Marx had pointed out that language is the expression of consciousness and therefore a product of social conditions which are to be changed. The rebellion of art was not directed against the economic foundation and its political superstructure but rather against its instruments and therefore remained an act of subjective consciousness raising. Language here stands for all forms of expression, including the imagistic language of film. "Language is determined through the character of its sign, the construction of sentences and through the conditions of their transformation. All of this depends upon agreement and agreements are freely made. The secret of film syntax is nothing other than just such a freely chosen resolution as to the elements that constellate 'film.' I can take any number of accessible elements from that constellation and redefine their usage." [5]

In the latter days of the hippie movement in America, theoreticians like Gene Youngblood identified expanded cinema with a "New Age" – a new culture of community, facilitated by a breaking of media boundaries, where "art, science and metaphysics are reconverging." [6] The Austrian filmmakers were far removed from this addiction to harmony. They were not interested in a "synthaesthetic synthesis" of technical concepts leading to a universal language, or what is more, an "oceanic consciousness"; nor were they in search of the "pansexual universe" that Youngblood believed he discovered with Andy Warhol's scene. [7] In films, expanded cinema Actions and theoretical essays they instead sought an analytic approach that would not accept the idea of "reality" as "an invisible environment of messages." [8] Expanded cinema offered a broad bandwidth of possible investigations into the vocabulary and accordingly, syntactical connections available to film. This included works and projects that playfully and with apparent didactic rigor made film production or its presentation their topic, and sought to confront the audience. In this respect, their work resembled Fluxus films and Actions, which additionally had the great advantage of being inexpensive to produce. Their highly theoretical underpinnings required strategic costuming, while on the other hand, some Actions demanded a theoretical lining in order to avoid being seen as banal.

One Action by Valie Export entitled *Abstract Film No. 1* (1968) was reminiscent of pre-cinematic light art. The image on screen arose from reflections created by a flashlight aimed at water running over a mirror. The meaning of the material displayed by the "film" was more relevant than what appeared on screen. The idea of the editing process was taken up by Export in *Cutting* (1968), demonstrating the convergence of mediation and reality in the sense of slicing and opening: A scissor cuts the window of a projected house facade "open," making the reality behind the window visible, but also Weibel's body is laid bare by a cutting open of his clothing and a cutting off of his body hair. The technical possibility of slow motion was realized in reality and conveyed to the audience with *Der Kuss* (The Kiss, 1968) and *Schütten* (Pouring, 1968). In *Splitscreen-Solipsismus* (1968) by Valie Export, a mirror effected a boxer fighting with himself.

---

5   Peter Weibel, "Nimm eine Handvoll Zelluloid (Teil 3),"
Film, November 1969, abridged.
6   Gene Youngblood, *Expanded Cinema* (New York: Dutton, 1970),
p. 45.

7   Youngblood, pp. 77, 81, 92 and 117.
8   Youngblood, p. 45.

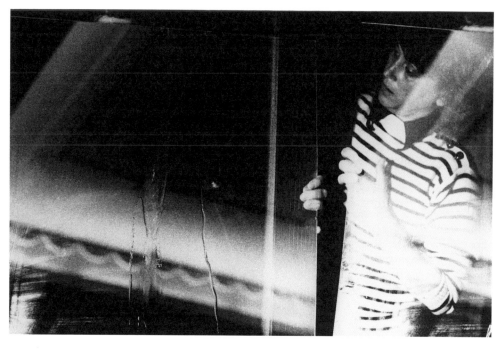

above: VALIE EXPORT, **Cutting**, 1968
below: VALIE EXPORT, **Abstract Film No. 1**, 1968

For Ernst Schmidt Jr. and myself, film also meant film history itself. In *Hell's Angels* (1969), Schmidt Jr. folded film programs into a flock of paper airplanes that he let sail into the "movie heaven" of the theater, throwing their shadows across the screen, bright with the projector's light. He dedicated the film to Howard Hughes who had produced a movie by the same title, directed by Howard Hawks. Another one of cinema's greats was referenced in *hommage à alfred hitchcock* (1968), a project I undertook in the form of a "movie environment." The individual viewer is led to the end of a passageway where a steel plate is charged with a high voltage current, as he or she is expressly warned. As with Hitchcock's heroes, their life experience has not prepared them to decide how far they should engage in the adventure. The case is solved upon stepping onto the plate.

The importance of confronting the audience is made clear by considering that not only Weibel and Export, but all the Co-op's founding members sought to directly engage and challenge the public. The inclusion of the viewer in the event had its deceptive side, since the participation offered did not assure the kind of consumer satisfaction that comes with cooperation. Instead, it was far more likely to manifest a breakdown of such expectations. If anything, the aggression that surfaced during some of the Actions was supposed to make people insecure about their position as faithful participants within the emerging art event, if not drive them away entirely. The refusal to include public participation in a symbolic order of art was supposed to move it beyond its passive irresponsibility, leaving it to the insecurity of an open-ended concept of art, without the guidance of the artist.

The breakdown of audience participation and the deceptive security of its promise was thematized by Weibel in his *Action Lecture No. 2*. It was performed in Cologne in March of 1968 and served to introduce his and Valie Export's first appearance in Germany. *Action Lecture No. 2* was a technically expanded variation of his *Action Lecture No. 1* that had taken place in Vienna the year before. As in the first performance, several 8 mm films were projected onto his body and onto the projected image

of him on-screen. This time the audience could "control" the light of the projector as well as the sound, which he carried on his person in the form of a portable tape recorder, by shouting. The yelling had to get loud enough to be registered by a light dependent resistor which in turn signaled the light and sound machines. But under these conditions of noise and bright light, Weibel's speech was barely audible and the images projected onto him were hardly visible. The participation promised absurdly led to a communication breakdown: "…in the automated closed circuit of volume, the patient or state cripple experiences the nausea of his communication, the gear shift of our democracy: tautology or antinomie, affirmation or annulment, sink or swim."[9]

For *Instant Film* (1968), Weibel and Export distributed pieces of transparent PVC foil to members of the audience who were supposed to make their own art by looking through it and framing a picture of their choosing. However, this self-determined "film image" only confirmed the world view they had always had. The freedom of choice was worthless.

The illusory nature of this freedom was also clearly revealed by Export's *Ping Pong* (1968). An 8 mm film casts shifting spots on the wall, which the player is supposed to hit using a racket and a ball. What is introduced invitingly as a "play film (feature film)"[10] is in fact "a provocation of motor reflexes and reactions, and these are not intelligible or emotional. The authoritarian character of the screen as a manipulative medium could not be exposed more clearly than this: No matter how much the viewer tries to be part of the game, his status as a consumer is hardly changed."[11]

The title of Weibel's *Glanz und Schicht des Zelluloids* [Splendor and Emulsion of Celluloid] (1968) includes a pun: The German word *Glanz* speaks to the shiny base side of the film strip and would literally translate as "shine," but here

---

9   Weibel quote in Peter Weibel and Valie Export, *Wien. Bildkompendium Wiener Aktionismus und Film* (Frankfurt am Main: Kohlkunst, 1970), p. 258.
10   The German word for feature film is *Spielfilm*, which literally translates as "play film."
11   Weibel and Export, p. 262.

above: VALIE EXPORT, **Ping Pong**, 1968
below: VALIE EXPORT, Peter Weibel, **Instant Film**, 1968

is translated as "splendor," to play upon the title of Honoré de Balzac's *The Splendor and Misery of Courtesans* as in Weibel's title. The filmstrip's emulsion and shiny base were alternatingly edited together, and accordingly the perforation side of the film was intermittently on the wrong side. The film thereby kept losing its loop in the projector and getting torn, each time losing footage until it was entirely consumed in the end.

Ja/Nein (*Yes/No*, 1968) by Ernst Schmidt Jr. also expresses in its title the contradiction between the fulfillment and denial of an expectation. The film shows the curtain of a movie screen opening and closing, while the actual curtain opens and closes at the same time, in sync with the projected film. The film that we would see once the projected curtain is open will never start. On another occasion, Schmidt Jr. promised nothing short of a *Schöpfung* (*Creation,* 1968), but without being able nor desiring to live up to the sophistication of an artistic act. First he showed a blank screen by running clear leader through the projector while he drew upon the film with a felt pen as it wound onto the take-up reel. Subsequently, the result was presented to the audience. Schmidt's ironic commentary: "It was not difficult to get into a discussion after this very minimal film work, although it was not that instructive for everyone."[12]

Stephen Dwoskin viewed the contribution Gottfried Schlemmer made to the Munich gathering of filmmakers with humor: "Gottfried Schlemmer showed a film where the audience of filmmakers knew exactly how long to stay out of the cinema, yet while doing so experienced the film. This was *8h01–8h11* (1968), a 10-minute film of a clock running continuously for ten minutes. Everyone waited outside looking at their watches for ten minutes and then went back in."[13]

Kurt Kren presented the expanded cinema Action *19/68 White – black* at New York's Judson

Gallery in May of 1968. A film projector cast white light onto a screen while a tape recording was heard endlessly repeating a Mao quote. At the same time Kren was busy spanning strips of film across the entire space of the room where they were ultimately wound around the projector to be burnt and destroyed.

I conceived *zzz: hamburg special* for the 1968 Hamburg Film Show. I gave Ernst Schmidt Jr. a spool of thread to take with him to Hamburg. He was supposed to let it run through the projector instead of a film so that the moving shadow of the thread was seen on screen in CinemaScope. This resulted in the first readymade film and at the same time, "the last film in film history," as I announced: *zzz* was then and ever since guaranteed its place at the very end of every alphabetical listing of film titles. The duration of the show depended upon the patience of the audience, while the movement of the thread and consequently its shadow on screen was left to the projectionist. *zzz: hamburg special* was selected by the German journal *Film* as one of the ten most important films of the year 1968; the collaboration of the projectionist was expressly acknowledged.

We not only strived for viewers, our target was also the media. Films and Actions only became existent through their recognition. Artistic provocation thereby won the significance of a political demonstration. In 1968, the German press was glad to get in on the scene. The most aggressive Action to which the public was subject happened at the Munich Filmmaker Meeting in November 1968 at a cinema. Weibel gave it the fitting title of *Exit*. Export, Kren, Schmidt Jr., Scheugl and Schlemmer set fire to missiles and firecrackers attached to a screen consisting of aluminum foil. The smoking and spark-spraying projectiles flew into the audience while Weibel shouted out texts about the aggression exercised by the State and society against the freedom of the individual. As was to be expected, the public fled for the exit. Besides ending as planned, the real success of the Action was achieved when the press gave it extensive coverage ("Go Ahead and Shoot at the Audience!").

---

12 *Ernst Schmidt Jr. Drehen Sie Filme, aber keine Filme! Filme und Filmtheorie 1964–1987/Ernst Schmidt Jr. Shoot Films, But No Films! Films and Filmtheory 1964–1987* [German/English], eds.Linda Bilda/Secession (Vienna: Triton, 2001), p. 127.
13 Stephen Dwoskin, *Film Is: The International Free Cinema* (New York: Overlook Press, 1975), p. 89.

above: Hans Scheugl, **zzz: hamburg special**, 1968
below: VALIE EXPORT, **Tapp- und Tastkino**, 1968

However, the reverberation of this Action in the media was far exceeded by the staging of *Tapp- und Tastkino* (*Tap and Touch Cinema*, 1968), by Valie Export and Weibel the day before at a public square in Munich. A miniature cinema with stage curtains was strapped to Export's bare chest, with an opening only for two hands. Instead of being in the darkened cinema, the visitors had to enjoy their film experience in broad daylight and in front of everybody. The direct, haptic experience held the promise of unalienated sexuality, yet was interrupted after 12 seconds by Weibel with a megaphone, in order to guard against a relapse into the passive consumerism characteristic of conventional cinema.

I myself staged two Actions with the intention of raising sexuality into the public domain, aiming at the same time to motivate the public to take an active role in the process. One of these Actions took place in Munich as well. *Sugar Daddies* (1968), was a film of writings and drawings I shot off a toilet wall in the University of Vienna. This film was subsequently screened on the wall of a toilet in the Munich Künstlerhaus. On another occasion I filmed the public screening and edited the new material into the existing film. Theoretically, *Sugar Daddies* thus could have gone on perpetually. In *Der Voyeur* (1968), I stood in front of a full size movie screen with an 8 mm projector and screened a pornographic film. The image was so small on the giant screen that it could not be recognized from the audience as more than a small square of light. Whoever wanted to see the film had to acknowledge their role as a Peeping Tom by joining me on stage.

We were unable to realize many projects for technical reasons. Such was the case with *Testfilm* as planned by Export, Kren, Scheugl, Schmidt Jr., Schlemmer and Weibel in 1968, to test the attention span of the audience. The participants were to film each other according to a sign system agreed upon in advance, albeit with built-in mistakes that were supposed to be discovered by viewers who would thereby win prizes. The project failed because it was impossible to locate six cameras that were available at the same time.

The discrepancy between artistic and political demands and what was actually possible to realize led Weibel and Export to formulate a series of utopian projects. These were aimed at enhancing the senses and subjugating the technically pre-pared individual to the terror of surgical interven-tions. Such was the case with two projects among several: Weibel's *Lasermesser* [Laser Knife] (1969) and Export's retinal radiation in *Proselyt* (1969), both realized yet a further escalation of the potential aggression of *Exit*. Not without reason. The filmmaker's situation was precarious. Public agencies not only withheld support, they paid negative attention in the form of bans and legal trials accusing the artists of "creating a public nuisance," among other, similar charges.

A multi-media expansion that had long since succeeded in the US was first implemented in Austria as of 1969: Weibel and Export turned to video and television. In 1970, they were represented by video works and tele-actions at the Underground Film Festival in London. Their tele-actions trans-formed expanded cinema with video etc., from a projection system to a general picture processing and generating machine, as Weibel wrote in his "Videology" program on the occasion of the fifth and last Knokke festival of 1974/1975.[14] In 1969, the production of films, public appearances and Actions by the Vienna filmmakers rapidly declined and by the following year, the brief but explosive period of expanded cinema was over.

Translated by Eve Heller

---

14 *peter weibel. das offene werk 1964–1979,* eds. Nadja Rottner and Peter Weibel (Ostfildern: Hatje Cantz Verlag, 2006), p. 689.

above: Hans Scheugl, **Sugar Daddies**, 1968
below: Hans Scheugl, **Der Voyeur**, 1968

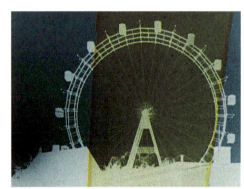

The Generalist: Ernst Schmidt Jr.

Peter Tscherkassky

If I had to name a single Austrian filmmaker who to this day has not received the international recognition he deserves for the artistic level his work attained, I would unhesitatingly name Ernst Schmidt Jr. When he died in 1988, at the early age of 50, Ernst Schmidt Jr. left behind a body of work that could hardly be more multifaceted. Close to 100 work titles were to be found in the catalog of his posthumous exhibit at the Vienna Secession in 2001, and are subsequently listed at a home-page dedicated to the artist, designed and maintained by his half brother Helmut Benedikt.[1] Schmidt Jr. has proven to be one of Austria's most productive film artists of his time. Additionally, Schmidt Jr. belonged to that irreplaceable species that looks beyond the nose of its own film work, actively championing an infrastructure to provide support for non-commercial film – in the US, Jonas Mekas is a perfect example of this type. Schmidt Jr. was just such a rare specimen, a passionate and splen-did jack-of-all trades. The universal film encyclope-dia to which he dedicated almost thirty years of his life remained unfinished at the time of his death, but Schmidt Jr. produced influential publications throughout his career. In 1964, he initiated the film

journal *Caligari* – which resulted in only two edi-tions. But as of 1965 he wrote for the Viennese film magazine *action*, and as of 1966, he regularly contributed to the influential German periodical *Film*, in which he published the first German lan-guage compendium of underground film entitled *Das andere Kino – Ein Lexikon des neuen europä-ischen Films* [The Other Cinema: A Dictionary of the New European Film].[2] Two years later, Schmidt Jr. contributed a comprehensive film chronology to *Neuer Österreichischer Film* [New Austrian Film],[3] a catalog accompanying a Viennale retrospective in 1970 by the same name. It presented a timeline of Austrian film production that reached well beyond the avant-garde. Schmidt Jr. commences his history with the year 1800 and the Phantaskop projections of Belgian inventor Etienne Gaspard Robertson. Robertson included Vienna as a site to present his improved version of the Magic Lantern to the world, much like the Lumières who would come to grace Austria with its first film screening on March 27, 1896 – exactly three months after the brothers had staged the world's very first film projection in Paris.

As of the 20th century Schmidt Jr.'s chronology records filmically relevant events of each individual year, especially noting the titles of significant pro-

1   Ernst Schmidt Jr. Drehen Sie Filme, aber keine Filme! Filme und Filmtheorie 1964–1987/Ernst Schmidt Jr. Shoot Films, But No Films! Films and Filmtheory 1964–1987, eds. Linda Bilda and Secession (Vienna: Triton, 2001).
The website: http://www.ernst-schmidt-Jr.net/home.html.

2   In the yearbook for the journal Film (Velber/Hannover: 1968).
3   Neuer Österreichischer Film, ed. Kuratorium Neuer Österreich-ischer Film (Vienna: Kuratorium Neuer Österreichischer Film, 1970), pp. 5–35.

ductions, including those of Austria's numerous emigrants (the most prominent in early years including Fritz Lang, Michael Curtiz [Kertész], Erich von Stroheim, Max Fleischer, G. W. Pabst, Josef von Sternberg, Fred Zinnemann, Otto Preminger, and Billy Wilder). Naturally he notes the world premiere of Fernand Léger's *Ballet mécanique* on September 24, 1924, at Vienna's International Theater and Musical Festival, even though it bore no influence on local film production: A classical avant-garde tradition as that which took place between the two world wars in such countries as Germany and France (with *Ballet mécanique* as a central work), was entirely missing in Austria.

The most productive and artistically expressive phase of the second generation of avant-garde filmmakers to which Schmidt Jr. belonged undoubtedly took place between 1967 and 1969. In this sense, the 1970 catalog *Neuer Österreichischer Film*, which intended to accompany as well as signal the beginning of a new film culture, unintentionally drew a premature conclusion. The revolution that had been hoped for was not forthcoming – neither on a social nor on a filmmaking level. Capitalism and commercial film only flagged momentarily.

But not Ernst Schmidt Jr.! Barely four years later he had accomplished a mammoth publishing feat in the form of an encyclopedia of avant-garde film co-written with Hans Scheugl.[4] This 1,300 page encyclopedia was published in 1974 by Suhrkamp, one of the biggest German publishing houses. The two volumes include almost everything and everyone who in some way was associated with film as an artform. Long since out of print, Schmidt Jr. and Scheugl's *Sub-history* remains an irreplaceable reference work for those lucky enough to possess a copy. By the time Schmidt Jr. had another comprehensive retrospective going in 1980 at the Z-Club (one of the few cultural hotspots in an otherwise sleepy Vienna of its day), the dream of a fundamentally altered film culture was truly over.

What remained was an ongoing battle waged by the avant-garde for recognition and respect. This retrospective spectacle was accompanied by another catalog penned by Schmidt Jr.: *Österreichischer Avantgarde- und Undergroundfilm 1950–1980*.[5] Schmidt Jr. had the foresight to include some of the earliest works by several representatives of an upcoming third generation of filmmakers, such as Karl Kowanz, Herwig Kempinger, Robert Quitta, and Lisl Ponger. They all utilized Super 8, a technology fully developed by the second half of the 1970s. The historical accomplishment of this one-week event and accompanying exhibit at the Austrian Film Archive consisted in the introduction of Austria's film art achivements of the past three decades to a younger audience and new generation of filmmakers: from Kurt Steinwendner's surreal film poem *Der Rabe* [The Raven] (1951) to Peter Weibel's first expanded cinema Action *Nivea* (1967), restaged at the Z-Club by Weibel himself. A film historical consciousness was raised and the search for a formally new and independent expression provoked, underlining the imperative to avoid falling back on a level of articulation in film art that had already been attained. Herein lay Schmidt Jr.'s greatest contribution next to his accomplishments as a film artist: He played a central role in establishing the basis for the continuity of film art production in Austria.

He also secured his own filmmaking continuity, unlike any other of his colleagues. Schmidt Jr. dated 1963 as his beginning. In the subsequent quarter century up until his death in 1988, his oeuvre grew to include close to 100 titles as mentioned above. A good two thirds of these works are films presentable along traditional lines, varying from a few meters in length to a two-hour documentary film and a regular feature. The rest are expanded cinema Actions, conceptual films, projects and unfinished or lost films. In 1970, Schmidt Jr. tried to get a taxonomic handle on his overflowing abundance. He assigned every film title a consecutive opus number (as did Kurt Kren). This number was conjoined with a letter that designated a specific style or work group:

---

4   Hans Scheugl and Ernst Schmidt Jr., *Eine Subgeschichte des Films. Lexikon des Avantgarde-, Experimental- und Undergroundfilms* [A Sub-history of film. Lexicon of Avant-Garde, Experimental and Underground Film] (Frankfurt am Main: Suhrkamp, 1974).

5   Ernst Schmidt Jr., "Österreichischer Avantgarde- und Undergroundfilm 1950–1980," *Schriftenreihe des Österreichischen Filmarchivs*, no. 6, Vienna, 1980.

a) Documentary films that primarily achieve their rhythmic structure through editing.

b) Also documentary films, albeit more extensively processed and alienated via the insertion of alien material (*Einszweidrei*) or white frames (*Bodybuilding*).

c) Films that reflect their materiality (*Filmreste* actually lies somewhere between b and c).

d) Films that reflect cinema.

e) Films that expand film formally.

f) Collective films

g) Text films

h) Abstract films

i) Films that are in the process of creation or are continually changing.

j) Documentary films (like a), yet produced in collaboration with all involved (usually do not succeed).

k) Political films

l) Series *The Long March*

m) –

n) TV

o) Expanded movies

p) Feature films

q) Photos/drawings

r) Slides[6]

One might be reminded of Jorge Luis Borges' famous citation of a taxonomy of the animal kingdom in the fictional Chinese encyclopedia entitled the *Heavenly Emporium of Benevolent Knowledge*. Here, too, the attempt is made to submit something to a system of order that, in its abundance and heterogeneity, essentially resists the regulating power of categorization.

But actually it had all started in a more or less straightforward way. Schmidt Jr.'s first completed film, the half-hour long *Steine* (*Stones*, 1964), presents itself as an ordinary documentary film about a sculpture symposium in the St. Margarethen rock quarry, not far from Vienna. In the middle of a rubble landscape of sandstone, modern sculptors create work which is made accessible to the public in the framework of a symposium.

Steine shows the arrival by car, the quarry, the outlying countryside, artists at work, an observing public and primarily, the abstract or strongly abstracted sculptures themselves. Jazz music is heard, a dynamic piano/bass combination (Dieter Glawischnig, Ewald Oberleitner), some "concrete" and highly programmatic poems by Gunter Falk and Harald Sauter about the art of sculpture, the sync sound of stones being chiseled, the cry of rook crows in the surrounding Pannonian Basin, as well as some off-screen comments by the visiting public.

The acoustic spine of the film consists of jazz music and its driving cadence. The opening arrival to the site is edited to the rhythm of the music. It is filmed from a car, capturing the landscape, village houses along the way, traffic signs and the boundary line of the open road. Schmidt Jr. often shoots at a sharp angle so that the car appears to be racing behind a steep vanishing point. Hardly a single shot is held for longer than two seconds. Often three shots are compressed into a single second. He zooms in on objects to the point of blurring recognition, and turns the camera on its optical axis. The arrival at a dusty parking lot is accompanied by the first of several poetic texts recited in an insistent tone: "One can take a stone and strike it. One can take a stone and strike it to give it form. Every stone has a form. Every stone has a coincidental form. Every thing has a form. Every thing has its coincidental form. One can take a stone and strike it to give it a different, not coincidental form." Meanwhile, a lot of cars have arrived. Now the music mixes with commentary from the visitors according to a motto of puzzlement along the lines, "I often can't imagine what this is supposed to represent."

Contact with the stone artwork is rendered by a tour of the sculpture garden. Faces are recurringly seen – questioning, critical, skeptical gazes. Meagerly well-intentioned comments in dialect are followed by rejection: "It's over the top, crazy." "That's something no normal person could understand." "I can't think of what to make of it, intellectually."

6 Ernst Schmidt Jr., "Ernst Schmidt Jr.," in *Neuer Österreichischer Film*, p. 92.

Ernst Schmidt Jr.
Steine
1964

"The person who thought this up has a different way of looking at things." "Whoever can make something out of this isn't normal." "Either we are crazy or the sculptors are crazy." "Crazy, yeah," etc. In a rapid montage of comments, Schmidt Jr. gives voice to their disappointed expectations. The one continually recurring criticism regards the failure of mimetic function. A sculpture that does not represent something through and beyond itself, is dismissed as nonsense, as lunacy.

This collage of public commentary provides Schmidt Jr. with a point of departure for his own encounter with the sculptures. First he immerses himself again in the landscape, lays flat down in the meadow with the camera, shooting foliage and the sky above, which is intermittently edited with the randomly chiseled walls of the rock quarry: we see "nature" and its "coincidental form." A fade-out/fade-in marks the transition to culture and its "non-coincidental forms": the sculptures. They are presented in montage sequences of varying lengths, tackled from the most diverse angles and axes. Schmidt Jr. exclusively employs a hand-held camera and exercises every imaginable form of movement. He fundamentally exhausts the "coincidence" of the filmic shot by shooting at a wide range of proximities, from the long shot to the macro, creating cascades of quick cuts that get down to two frames at a time. In effect, the filmmaker himself is transformed into a kind of sculptor. The repetitive gesture of shooting many shots from similar positions or using similar camera movements renders a visual impression far less chaotic than this description perhaps suggests. Schmidt Jr. dedicates hundreds of brief shots to single sculptures, thereby conveying a far greater plasticity than a static shot would afford. He creates multiple exposures using images shot from the same vantage point but with one of the layers rapidly zooming in on its subject. Schmidt Jr. increasingly concentrates on the role light plays in his perspective of the stones. Some of the works have schisms that leak sunlight. He shoots these bright spots single-frame, exposing the film up to four times in order to show the sculpture upon a fifth pass in its entirety, as a dark monument standing in contrast to the backlight of the sky. The sculpture's leaked points of light thus begin to dance insanely, lending the static block of stone the filigree charm of a rollicking congress of photons.

Steine concludes in an evening ambience, quite romantically. Once again the aforementioned poem about stone and its form is heard, and then image and sound cut out. Schmidt Jr. commenced his life-long reflection on the art of film with a consideration of another art form – sculpture, the plastic art. *Steine* involves a conventional macro structure: travel, arrival, the official tour, the nature/culture theme, artists at work, a filmic exchange with particular sculptures and finally the dialogue of film and stone through Schmidt's use of techniques specific to his cinematic medium. In addition to its documentary ambition, the film explicitly broaches a question concerning the mimetic function of art. Schmidt Jr. establishes his position on the matter and provides an answer beyond the clueless public in his endeavor to film-ically render the primary process of the psyche as articulated in the stone sculptures. He leaves the renunciation of mimesis to his colleagues in the sculptor guild. His film does not question whether to represent reality but *how* to do so. The film is assigned the task of representation – it has not yet become its own material. This is reflected in the title: The stones are the material of the sculptors.

This is not the case with his next film, about Vienna's Prater. The written form of the title *P.R.A.T.E.R.* (1963–1966) itself announces that only a fractured representational realism is intended. Schmidt Jr. shifted his attention from the site of high culture in *Steine* to the place where the

medium of film entered the world – the amusement park. Schmidt Jr. wanted to help usher the delayed second birth of film into the modern age. Originally planned as a project for the film academy, the administration could not begin to comprehend how Schmidt Jr. wanted to implement "different techniques of montage and 16 mm camera strate-gies, in part utilizing tachist dissolution," and "a soundtrack consisting of fragmented field recordings of the world, scraps of noise, fragments of interviews and inserts of sound poems by Ernst Jandl."[7] Funding was refused; Schmidt Jr. dropped out of school in protest.

Like *Steine*, *P.R.A.T.E.R.* is marked by a strongly repetitive cadence. Schmidt Jr.'s main interest did not lie in the attractions of the amusement park, but in its visitors, their facial expressions and gazes. The half-hour film consists of two parts. While the first effects an expose of central themes, the second intensifies their processing and dissolu-tion: Shots get increasingly fragmented and ran-dom; for the first time Schmidt Jr. inserts negative footage. While the soundtrack in *Steine* was pains-takingly composed according to customary stand-ards, the sound in *P.R.A.T.E.R.* is constantly fading in and out, even the collages of speech are heard as fragmented snatches randomly thrown together.

---

7   From Ernst Schmidt Jr.'s synopsis for *P.R.A.T.E.R.*

Ernst Schmidt Jr.
P.R.A.T.E.R.
1963–1966

Schmidt Jr. radicalized this direction appreciably in subsequent works. The nine minutes of *Bodybuilding* (1965/1966), based on footage from two Material Actions by Otto Muehl, highlight what will follow in the wake of Kurt Kren's elaborately structured, serial Action films. Schmidt Jr. subjects the footage to an anarchic work process. A chaotic ordering of the material stands in the stead of Kren's precisely calculated editing strategies. Paralleling the extreme deployment of the human body in Muehl's Actions, Schmidt Jr. submits the filmic body of the footage to attack. Blank film is repeatedly inserted, positive and negative material equally valued and deployed, poorly exposed material is retained. And while Kren focused on the visual with noble acoustic restraint, Schmidt Jr.'s soundtrack is a wild collage of the most various, randomly chosen aural sources. The magnetic sound stripe itself is further subject to intermittent erasure through the use of a magnet. *Bodybuilding* reads like an early formulation of an aesthetic program aimed at leading toward the dissolution of traditional cinema.

Schmidt Jr.'s *15. Mai 1966* (1966) could also be interpreted as a documentary film in the broadest sense. But the subject – a drive from Vienna's Schwechat airport at the edge of town into the inner city on May 15, 1966 – is pretty minimal. There is no point other than the occasion to make a film. It opens with negative shots of people at the edge of a field who appear to be preparing for a film shoot. Commands like "Cut sound!", "Camera rolling!" and "Attention!" are repeated throughout the entire film as if an attempt is continually being made to finally get the film going. What is seen is what was there to be seen, without the slightest attempt on Schmidt Jr.'s part to capture anything uniquely characteristic of the stretch between Schwechat airport and Vienna. Instead, he was far more interested in the details offered by faded advertising billboards that could have been found *anywhere*. And after night falls all that remains are the trails of colorful neon lights captured by Schmidt Jr.'s wild camera pans. One might describe *15. Mai 1966* as a documentary film that lost its subject along the way and makes a spectacle of itself as a practical demonstration on techniques

of expression, guaranteed to be inappropriate for a documentary film.

Schmidt Jr.'s next film, *Einszweidrei* (*Onetwothree*, 1965–1968), is comprised of three parts as the title suggests. Again shots of diverse Muehl Actions dominate, combined with found footage: A film about brass music with a whole lot of young men attired in traditional Austrian folk costume who seem to appreciate Muehl's spectacle with the critical and highly observant gaze of experts; Valie Export takes Peter Weibel out for a walk on all fours, leading him on a leash down Vienna's most elegant shopping boulevard, the Kärntnerstraße (the Export/Weibel scandal Action *Aus der Mappe der Hundigkeit* [From the Portfolio of Doggieness]); naturally followed by found footage about a dog breeding kennel; shots of Vienna's streets, passersby, traffic signals, cars. A formally new gesture in Schmidt Jr.'s oeuvre was introduced – the destruction of the film material itself. For the first time he painted and drew directly onto the filmstrip – and not delicately, but in thick smears of felt marker down the length of the film, posing a serious challenge to the images. He punched holes into the footage, and in some places, vertically sliced the filmstrip, taping it back together so that it was slightly misaligned. Pieces of film never intended for projection were included in the mix, such as handwritten marks made by the film lab, academy leader, white and black leader. The use of multiple exposure precisely calculated to represent objects in *Steine* is deployed here to increasing excess, until Muehl seems to disintegrate: His elaborate Material Actions can barely be recognized in the resulting, fiercely dynamic, white haze of complete over-exposure.

Filmreste (*Film Scraps*, 1967) generated the highpoint in the direction Schmidt Jr.'s work was taking, and delivers on the title's promise. Here the unformed, unfinished, already rejected and broken triumphs. The images consist of actual film remnants stemming "primarily from *P.R.A.T.E.R.* and *Einszweidrei* according to Schmidt Jr., and some border on the edge of recognizability, partly rendered indecipherable by the application of paint and other physical methods of filmic intervention.

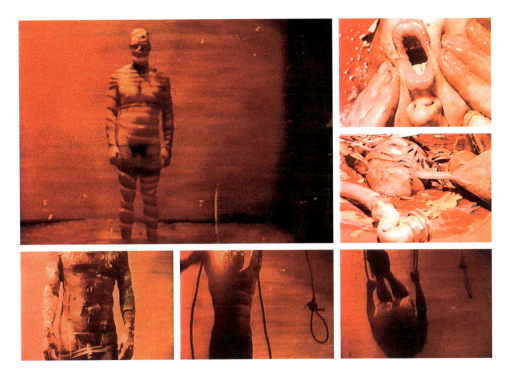

Ernst Schmidt Jr.
Bodybuilding
1965/1966

Ernst Schmidt Jr.
15. Mai 1966
1966

The soundtrack is comprised of a Gospel phrase ("…and a thing called love. Ooouh…!"), a few sentences from a radio news program ("…columns of Israeli troops on the move … south of the desert airstrip…"), a single, continuously repeated piano chord, diverse humming and static noises, as well as Schmidt Jr. himself announcing double-digit numbers. With *Filmreste*, Schmidt Jr. reduced the base and emulsion of film to their material status, stripping the sign carrying medium "film" of its signs. Suddenly the medium behind its destroyed message was rendered visible – becoming the message itself. One last requirement remained: The film had to be able to make it through the printing machine.

Einszweidrei and *Filmreste* are the culmination of what had started with the Action films of Kurt Kren. Kren went far beyond a purely documentary ethos with his Action films, creating autonomous artworks parallel to the Actions themselves. It was precisely the extraordinary, in-depth structuring of his films (some involving hundreds of single-frame edits which Kren cement-spliced by hand, and which were readily apparent upon projection) that lent them an aura that could not but compete with what was depicted. And especially because one might very well have expected these films to be documentations, they reclaimed the independence of film as an autonomous art form. Nevertheless, a balance is maintained in these films, a relationship

in the form of a dialogue with the Material Actions. Ernst Schmidt Jr. went one step further in shedding the imperative to depict the external world: With his work, even Otto Muehl's spectacular Actionism was tossed overboard.

It is finally Schmidt Jr.'s seventh film, *Tonfilm* (*Sound Film*, 1968),[8] that is abstract – and then again it isn't. One sees colored surfaces or blurry and unrecognizable monochrome objects. Schmidt Jr. names colors off-screen: "Red. Yellow. Orange. White…" but that do not correspond with the colors on screen – except in the case of "Black," a blurry, dark grayish cat that could perhaps pass for "black" stares into the camera. While the colors were originally intended to correspond with the colors announced on the soundtrack, diverse mistakes during the developing and processing of the print led to color distortions. Schmidt's synopsis: "A film to be improved."[9]

In summary, with these seven works a trajectory can be detected that leads to an increasing "materialization" of the films, as well as a playful (and definitely humorous) stepping out from the narrow confines of traditional cinematic regulations.

---

8   Discrepancies regarding the chronology of Schmidt Jr.'s films are to be found in secondary literature regarding his work. The above is in accordance with Schmidt Jr.'s own specifications in *Neuer Österreichischer Film*, p. 92 ff; in *Subgeschichte des Films*, p. 813, as well as in *Österreichischer Avantgarde- und Undergroundfilm 1950–1980*, p. 43 ff.
9   Schmidt Jr., *Neuer Österreichischer Film*, p. 93.

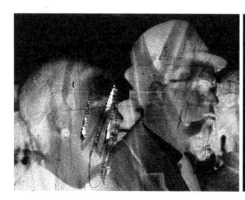

Ernst Schmidt Jr.
Filmreste
1967

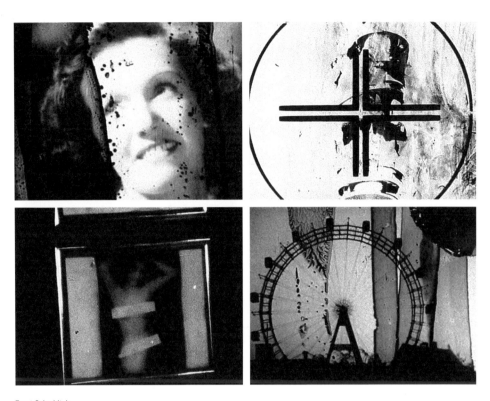

Ernst Schmidt Jr.
Filmreste
1967

After probing specific film effects in *Steine*, with *P.R.A.T.E.R.* Schmidt Jr. begins to violate rules, destructively interfering with the customary coherence of the marriage of picture and sound in film. *Bodybuilding*, *Einszweidrei* and *Filmreste* signaled his debate with Viennese Actionism. The great influence Viennese Actionism had on the second generation also made itself evident in films which had nothing to do directly with Actionism. A driving force behind the emergence of Actionism was the need of its protagonists to break away from the cultivated "artificiality and elitism of abstract painting in the 1950s"[10] – the so called "Informal" art movement in Vienna. In the same way, repre-

sentatives of the second generation were concerned with breaking out of the corset of metric film, serialism and similar systems of regulation established by the first generation.[11]

The paradoxical significance of the use of various materials in Actionism – the human body, food, paint, excrement, blood, objects – consisted in the fact that they no longer served a sign system: These materials did not indicate a signified beyond

10 Robert Fleck, "Der Wiener Aktionismus," in *Kunst in Österreich*, eds. Noemi Smolik and Robert Fleck, (Cologne: Kiepenheuer and Witsch, 1995), p. 54.

11 This fundamental shift of aesthetic paradigms found expression in rather intense arguments, partly carried out in public. It also led to personal quarrels. From today's vantage point, *post festum*, these conflicts present themselves as the logical and coherent manifestation of the traversal and conquest of an aesthetic battlefield, namely film art. However, its protagonists were naturally denied such an historical perspective, and experienced these conflicts as quite painful. To this day, some wounds inflicted upon certain parties seem to have only healed superficially.

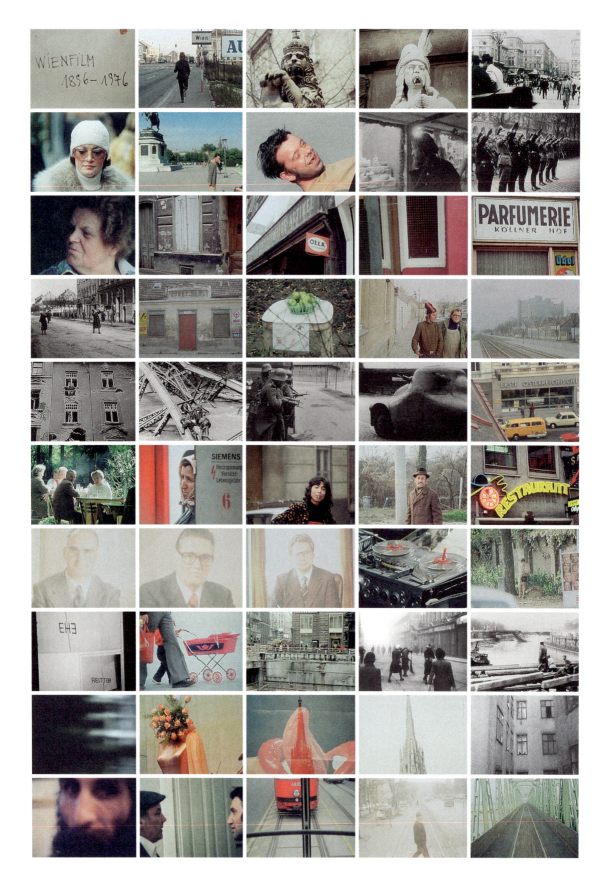

themselves. Instead, they were simply used for what they were: An egg is an egg, and the color red is red, not blood. On the other hand, the medium of film based on photographic technology is deeply inscribed with a semiotic character, practically inherited at birth, and it is precisely this semiotic character that Schmidt Jr. began to undermine. He placed it in question by wreaking havoc, both in sound (as in the crude erasure of portions of the magnetic soundtrack in *P.R.A.T.E.R.*), as well as in image. The latter is treated far more explicitly and clearly: He painted over footage, scratched and fragmented the flow of images via montage.[12]

Within the brief period between 1963 and 1967, Schmidt Jr. attained an unprecedented level of artistic freedom in relation to his material, that is, to every single constituent part of a whole we call "cinema." And he never looked back. The year 1968 was to be his most productive, with 21 titles listed in his catalog of works, including expanded cinema Actions, film projects, conceptual films, experimental documentary films and material films.[13] With each of these works, Schmidt Jr. wanted his chosen medium of film to lead back to its materiality, to its fabricated nature (and always with a great deal of humor and irony). His main message: Film, especially "normal" film, is manipulative – but it also can be radically manipulated, shaped and formed.

This included the presentation of film. *Demonstration* (1968) demonstrated the movie auditorium. This expanded movie consisted of instructions according to which the auditorium lights were to be turned on and off, the masking of the screen adjusted to accommodate different formats, the stage curtains opened and closed while the house lights were on. The curtains were also to be opened and closed in the dark, illuminated only by the light of the projector, while the auditorium exits were briefly opened and closed, intermittently letting the daylight in. In short, the functions and variables of

the movie auditorium were presented and declared to be the actual film. *Demonstration* concluded with the audience being called upon to rise from their seats, thereby making the body itself and its position in the movie house setting part of the movie.

In *Ja/Nein* (*Yes/No*, 1968) Schmidt Jr. assigned the curtain the starring role. A film was projected showing a curtain that opens and closes. The task of the projectionist was to open and close the actual curtain of the movie house in conjunction with the opening and closing of the projected curtain.

Schmidt Jr. also practiced appropriation art of an extreme kind. For his concept film *Lumière Films* (1968) he wrote: "My oldest films may be obtained as follows: borrow the following films by the Lumière brothers from a good cinémathèque: *La Sortie des Usines Lumière, La Voltige, La Pêche aux poissons rouges, Le Débarquement au Congrès de photographie à Lyon, Les Forgerons, L'Arroseur arrosé, Le Repas de bébé, Le Saut à la couverture, La Place des Cordeliers à Lyon, La Mer.* Cut out the subsequently inserted, superfluous captions and present the program."[14]

Schmidt Jr.'s *Fernsehen* (*Television*, 1968) was "every television program": "My project happens when one turns on the television set at home. Every television program is *29/n Fernsehen*."[15] Such conceptual overabundance was contrasted with nothing in *Nothing* (1968), which, as the title promises, was nothing. Two years later, when Schmidt Jr. wanted to produce a film version of *Nothing* consisting of a whiteness that was gradually and imperceptibly to shift to black, the film lab thought the negative was faulty and stayed with the original, that is: it copied – nothing.

In addition to these and similar conceptual films, Schmidt Jr. produced material films such as *Weiß* (*White*) in 1968: pure, raw stock perforated with holes by way of an office hole punch. It is always the original with holes that is projected. The vertical scratches resulting from the wear and tear of projection are also seen *within* the holes thanks to the slowness of the human eye, thereby proving

---

12 Here Schmidt Jr.'s work can be seen as deeply relating to the significance of the fragment in modern art. To return to the topic of Schmidt Jr.'s debut film, *Steine: An early example in the field* of sculpture would be Auguste Rodin's *The Walking Man* (1878), a fusion of parts no longer invested in creating the illusion of a coherent whole.

13 Bilda, p. 273 ff.

14 Schmidt Jr. in Bilda, p. 121.

15 Schmidt Jr. in Bilda, p. 72.

persistence of vision and making the physiological basis of our perception of motion in film apparent.

Up until the early 1970s, Schmidt Jr. realized expanded cinema Actions, created conceptual films, shot several lettrist text films, and began work on his wonderful *Wienfilm 1896–1976*, a two-hour documentary Schmidt Jr. called "a kind of anthology about Vienna, from the discovery of film up until the present time."[16] The list of participants reads like a who's who of the avant-garde and underground scene in the Austria of its day.

Four years later in 1981, Schmidt Jr. produced his only feature film, *Die totale Familie,* based on Heimito von Doderer's novel *The Merovingians or the Total Family*. It did not attain the artistic niveau of Schmidt Jr.'s avant-garde work. Doderer's magnificent and very Viennese black humor does not really come across, and the staging has a strangely wooden quality. But in 1987, one year before his death, Schmidt Jr. succeeded where before he had failed, when he attempted a collective film project (based on the story of Dracula) in 1968. This time his group effort was to succeed. As in the case of the Doderer project, Schmidt Jr. dared to approach a literary artwork of formidable dimensions: the 600-page work, *Memoirs of My Nervous Illness* by Daniel Paul Schreber. These memoirs are nothing other than the very detailed description of a deeply paranoid and simultaneously ingeniously surreal, entirely self-enclosed, logically consistent world view according to which Schreber influences the entire world order through his direct contact with God. The paranoid schizophrenic Schreber wrote the book to prove his sanity and be released from a mental institution.[17]

In the 1980s, a lively animation scene had established itself around Vienna's Academy of Applied Arts thanks to Maria Lassnig and Hubert Sielecki. Schmidt Jr. invited the movers and shakers on the scene as well as younger avant-garde film-makers such as Dietmar Brehm, Lisl Ponger and myself to take part in filming the Schreber material, later to assemble our contributions and his own material into a feature length film. Schmidt Jr. pragmatically divided the screenplay into three parts. Each participant was assigned a segment to visualize. Schmidt Jr. subsequently compiled these contributions into part 1 of *Denkwürdigkeiten eines Nervenkranken (The Memoirs of My Nervous Illness)*.

During the final edit of the second part of the film, Schmidt Jr. died of organ failure due to diabetes resulting from alcohol abuse. His editing assistant Susi Praglowski proceeded to complete part 2.

In 1993, Schmidt Jr.'s half brother and legal heir Helmut Benedikt granted me permission to produce part 3 posthumously, given that Schmidt Jr. had not only left behind the complete screenplay, but also the pre-recorded music and the Schreber monologue for all three parts.

Film artists who had been involved in part 1 and/or part 2 were invited to participate, as well as two artists Schmidt Jr. had originally asked to collaborate, but who had declined for insignificant reasons at the time – namely Kurt Kren and the painter Christian Ludwig Attersee (the latter had taken over Lassnig's class at the time). Our efforts succeeded. Part 3 of *The Memoirs of My Nervous Illness* was finished in late autumn of 1993 and premiered at Austria's national film festival, the Diagonale, with great success. Whether Schmidt Jr. would have been pleased with the result I will never know…

What remains of Ernst Schmidt Jr.? His extensive writings have been properly archived in their entirety. Some of it has been published, and some has yet to see the light of day. However, his film work is readily available and waits to be discovered on an international level.

Translated by Eve Heller

---

16   Schmidt Jr. in Bilda, p. 168. The film is available on DVD on *Der österreichische Film*, DVD Edition Hoanzl/Der Standard #41 (2006).
17   An undertaking that incidentally succeeded. His book also later became quite renowned thanks to Sigmund Freud's essay *Psychoanalytic Notes Upon an Autobiographical Account of a Case of Paranoia*, as well as an in-depth analysis in *Crowds and Power* by Elias Canetti and Walter Benjamin's *Bücher von Geisteskranken*.

Time Slice, Space Block.
The Synthetic Realities of Viennese Filmmaker
Hans Scheugl.

Stefan Grissemann

Back when Divine Wrath was still of use, art was momentarily forced to renounce the humor to which it actually is entitled. In September 1969, a scolding of the public took place on television: A young film-maker created an anti-bourgeois spectacle via Austria's public broadcasting service (ORF).[1]
It is an impressive image. Literally speaking from the underground of a construction pit in front of Vienna's town hall, he directs his diatribe at the TV audience, and begins to throw stones and rubble at the distant camera which continually zooms in on him. Fury drives him forward, vexed by provincial, art-loathing Austria and its "fascist, reactionary cultural functionaries." The man's name is Hans Scheugl and he is one of the main proponents of Vienna's expanded cinema impulse, an art move-ment that assumes cinema has dimensions that can be expanded into public space, into performance, into a live situation.

Today people don't talk about "degenerate art" anymore, the angry young man yells at the camera, but instead they say "art is degenerating." "To us this is praise," he continues, because in Austria, anyone who is "abnormal is on the right path." "*You* are the normal ones, you slobbering television zombies" and "all you up there in the morgues that you call theaters and universities." Not to be normal, he rages, "is the only choice."

---

1   Televised in an episode of the weekly series *Apropos Film*.

Austrian conditions are felt to be horrible and murderous. Scheugl announces he is going to lay out memorial stones for two suicide victims, but he continues to hurl rocks toward the camera: stones for the poet Konrad Bayer and the Actionist Rudolf Schwarzkogler (who Scheugl here mistakenly calls Helmut), but also for Günter Brus, Hermann Nitsch, for H.C. Artmann and Gerhard Rühm "who emigrated to foreign countries," and for Otto Muehl, Oswald Wiener, Kurt Kren and Ernst Schmidt Jr., "who carry on and resist." But the real scandal of the broadcast took place subsequent to Scheugl's appearance. Back in the studio, anchor Dietmar Schönherr is laughing sarcastically and comments "Yep, something like this actually exists." Stone throwing for "these kind of people is apparently a routine part of their job." Hans Scheugl is 29, he rants on, and – "would you believe it ?!" – archivist at the Austrian Film Archive. In Austria during the late 1960s, artists were not only thus ridiculed and denigrated for entertainment purposes, but simultaneously, more or less covertly mobbed out of their humble living conditions. Scheugl has been awarded a "sizable prize from the Austrian Art Fund" and, Schönherr continues, is part "of a new social order calling itself 'Underground.'" The representatives of this movement love all kinds of drugs but hate "war and order." And even though nobody can explain what it is, "the Underground has already installed itself on all fronts: there is an

Underground press and naturally the Underground has its own art," it even has its "own hospitals and universities." Which drugs Schönherr imbibed prior to broadcast is not divulged.

In any case, the art scene and the (petite) bourgeoisie had become increasingly entrenched. The resulting furor benefited the avant-garde. In the 1960s, the "new social order" that had quietly evolved over the course of the prior decade began to grow out of control, into a nightmare for the middle class. Artists increasingly put themselves on the line, declaring the act of making art to be the work of art itself. They dissolved sculpture and painting into material slaughters and Actionism, and they transformed traditional film into expanded cinema. Hans Scheugl experienced this development up close and first hand. He was socialized in the Vienna of the late 1950s, a veritable no man's land in terms of art. Against all odds he acquired a cultural education, through books, movies and the limited avant-garde to be found in niche galleries and cafés in the city. He came in contact with Kurt Kren and Ernst Schmidt Jr., Valie Export and Peter Weibel – and after completing his studies at the Vienna Film Academy, in the mid-1960s he began his own creative work. In 1967, after carrying out a few camera jobs for Schmidt Jr. and completing a short experimental narrative, *Miliz in der Früh* [Militia in the Morning] (1966), he created two important structural works: *Wien 17, Schumanngasse* and *Hernals* were both shot in the 17th district of his hometown, and one is the exact antithesis of the other. The trembling gaze of the camera in *Wien 17, Schumanngasse* is conveyed by a car steadily

driving straight down a street heading out of town. The path is the goal: Scheugl's film shows nothing but the street, its entire length covered in just over two and a half minutes. *Wien 17, Schumanngasse* presents a simple documentary form, but also shows things rarely seen at the movies: the continuity of movement conveyed by a not so attractive street on a grey winter day in the middle of January; mounds of dirty snow piled up on the side; stores, taverns and middle class cars of the 1960s; a tram intersecting the street; a church, a shoe factory, passersby with and without baby carriages – coincidental movie extras. At the end of the two and a half minutes it takes to shoot a 100 foot roll of 16 mm film, the ride reaches the end of Schumanngasse at the edge of town, in those days still looking pretty rural. For a split–second a street sign reading "Schumanngasse" flashes up, barely legible, in the last, flickering white flare of the film.[2]

In 1993, Scheugl did a formal flashback on his *Schumanngasse* film with the late work *(Calcutta) GO*, albeit taking a ride that is a good three times as long and incomparably more intense, through the streets of the Indian metropolis. *(Calcutta) GO*: that means full speed ahead through a whirl of people and vehicles, bikes and mopeds. It is a film run riot: wild, chaotic, colorful and loud – not empty, colorless and slow like *Wien 17*. Cinema is seen as a chain of movements, a calculated sensory overload. The eye of the camera in the car, like the willing ear of the microphone, registers

2   *Wien 17, Schumanngasse* as well as most of the other films here discussed are available on Index DVD Edition 029: *Hans Scheugl, The Seconds Strike Reality*.

Hans Scheugl
Calcutta (Go)
1993

Hans Scheugl
Wien 17, Schumanngasse
1967

the city passing by: people and machines, scraps of music and voices, motors and horns – acoustic fragments of everyday life mixed in the fleeting motion of the motorized passenger. _Calcutta (GO)_ consists of a nine-minute tracking shot: It is a documentary city portrait, a discourse also about the possibility of overtaking at high risk of collision, about tactical driving under time pressure.

The investigation of complex relations between real time and film time and between real space and depicted space are motifs central to Scheugl's work (e.g., the equation between the length of an actual street and the length of a 100 foot roll of film). While the director of _Wien 17, Schumanngasse_ and _Calcutta (GO)_ appears to artlessly record unedited

forward movement, his highly musical montage film _Hernals_ presents cinema as synthetic, a kind of cubist artform that can double, stretch and fragment time and space – and where fact intermingles with unsolicited fiction. Scheugl presents serial and occasionally polemical slices of everyday life in Vienna, in a manner perhaps informed by Kubelka's _Unsere Afrikareise_ (_Our Trip to Africa_, 1966). Scheugl runs two cameras to capture Valie Export and Peter Weibel acting in brief, dramatic scenes that take place on the street and in a supermarket, as well as several unstaged scenes in public spaces. By continually jumping between two different perspectives that repeat the same scene and utilizing short interludes of black, the documentary form of the film is made rhythmic and thereby rendered synthetically contrived, as "filmed." One sees construction workers, observes old ladies looking out windows, women with children, and hears fragments of Viennese dialect. A house is torn down, the city covered with rubble as if it were year zero. Vienna appears to be lying in ruins. In *Hernals*, also shot in the 17th and partly in the 18th district of Vienna, another tram intersects the street – this time filmed in color, from two angles and with sound, it becomes a main attraction at the outset of the film. *Hernals* is a film of perspectival leaps and dislocations. Valie Export is targeted, pursued and monitored by Scheugl's camera upon exiting an apartment. Images of Austria in 1967 are seen on a sunny day: Scheugl films passersby, cigarette machines and storefronts, children at play and old fashioned merchants – ethnographic documents of Vienna. But *Hernals* is also a public piece of Actionism, a run-through of short choreographies (including minor slips like the soundman edging into a scene): Weibel waits for Export on a street corner and slaps her in the face. Later she strides through a small supermarket, he punches a Nivea balloon hanging from the ceiling and throws a can of food to her in passing. In Scheugl's topography of Vienna the settings are in close proximity to one another. A small grocery on the corner of Beheimgasse and Hörmayrgasse is portrayed, out-side a streetcar rattles by in staccato montage. Schumanngasse is only three blocks away.

Structuralism alone does not satisfy Scheugl. He also intended to investigate the dominant narrative cinema. "In Austria things progressed radically to formal, material filmmaking,"[3] he remarked in 2008: "Storytelling features fell entirely by the wayside." In 1968, Scheugl's pressing interest in commercial cinema led to a work with a title indicating its base material while doing anything but playing it safe: *Safety Film* consists of a Hollywood Western shot directly off a movie screen and restored to its raw form – an act that strips the film of its narrative, reduces its size and drains all color from the CinemaScope and DeLuxe Color Western *The Way West* (1967) starring Kirk Douglas, Robert Mitchum and Richard Widmark. Scheugl's method is penetration: He focuses on details, filling the screen with faces and facial features, textures of rock, the flanks of horses – with mouths, eyes and congregations of people way too close and out of focus (plus silent) to "narrate" anything. The flickering, grainy, black-and-white material of the film is intercut with extremely short positive and negative shots of a Viennese movie house facade, conveying the impression of a document: The interior (the Western) is set against the exterior (the movie house) – the inner and the outer logic of the machine of cinema.

After *Safety Film* Scheugl turned his attention to expanded cinema, which he construed with an accent on minimalism. *zzz: hamburg special* (1968) presents nothing but the live dance of a simple piece of twine, which the projectionist is given to thread through his projector and its white light.

---

3 Dietmar Schwärzler, "Das amerikanische Kino als Metaerzählung. Interview with Hans Scheugl," *Kolikfilm*, special edition no. 9, 2008, p. 67.

Hans Scheugl
Safety Film
1968

Hans Scheugl
Eroticon sublim
1968

Hans Scheugl, **Hernals**, 1967 →

Hans Scheugl
Sugar Daddies
1968

Scheugl calls this "the last film in film history,"[4] and also, ironically, his "Faden-Film." The Austrian word conveys a double-entendre as "faden Film" means "boring film," while "Faden" is the word for thread. *Eroticon sublim* is a silent monochrome work Scheugl made in 1968 out of red leader, celebrating the pure sensuousness of color film. He challenges his viewers more directly with *Der Voyeur* (1968): Shouldering an 8 mm projector, Scheugl throws a porno film from close range onto a giant movie screen, thereby rendering a tiny image. The voyeur, already addicted to the easily accessed violation of taboo provided by the Underground, has to emerge from the audience and come close to get their money's worth.

Also shot in 1968, *Sugar Daddies* is Scheugl's third "erotic" reflection. It is the document of an Action (he himself calls the work a "psychological Action film"), and renews the expansion of the filmic to a filmic beyond. The director shoots toilet graffiti and personal contact information off the wall of a men's lavatory at the University of Vienna. He subsequently projects this film onto the wall of a urinal in a train station which he then shoots again, thereby disturbing urinating men whose reactions are captured by his cameraman. This staging of a public nuisance is just as much a form of art cruising. According to artist and theoretician

Stephen Dwoskin, *Sugar Daddies* presents a prime example of expanded cinema. A film showing toilet graffiti is presented in a particular public environment and on that occasion reconverted into film, and the wall onto which the original film was projected is suddenly a wall inscribed with writing. "Everything was moved and shifted, only to return to itself. The wall per se was unimportant, the graffiti was unimportant, even the film itself was insignificant, but the space thereby created by Scheugl, that threw the movable projected image into the world – that was important."[5] With the homoerotic overtones of his work, Scheugl also agitates against the conspicuous chauvinistic attitude of Viennese Actionism and the Austrian avant-garde. The film is dedicated to those great makers of mayhem, Laurel & Hardy, taking its title from an early work by the genius slapstick duo. A certain humor is already evidenced in the opening title sequence: The insert "Hans Scheugl presents" is projected onto the water tank of a toilet.

Practically everything Scheugl and his comrades worked on at this time seems like a manifesto. Every text is programmatic, every film is a declaration of principles. Creating art is by no means made more easy, though. The artists' demands are so high that even the best intentions and utmost talent can hardly hope to meet

---

4   Hans Scheugl, *Erweitertes Kino. Die Wiener Filme der 60er Jahre* (Vienna: Triton, 2002), p. 102.

5   Stephen Dwoskin, *Film Is: The International Free Cinema* (New York: Overlook Press, 1975), pp. 242–243.

Hans Scheugl
Prince of Peace
1993

Hans Scheugl
Black/White
1990

expectations. "We, the Austrian Filmmakers'
Cooperative, as heir to film history and its revolutionary subject, direct the following address to the
German public," as Weibel scribbles the collective
voice of a meeting on a slip of paper: "Through our
existence + Action we are securing the destruction
of the film industry, its lackeys, film critics, film
distributors and movie house owners, and we are
activating the consciousness of the public."[6]

As co-founder of the Austria Filmmakers'
Cooperative in 1968 (together with Ernst Schmidt,
Peter Weibel, Valie Export, Kurt Kren and Gottfried
Schlemmer), publicist and film theoretician,
Hans Scheugl engages in various spheres of activity
in addition to his filmic practice. He finds the
cultural climate for film at the end of the 1960s
to be hopeless, given that "formal film had reached
its end point and there was no access to feature
filmmaking."[7] In 1969, after a mere three years of
cinematic activity, he withdrew into theory and
shifted his focus to writing books. Two major
works appeared in 1974: the avant-garde film
encyclopedia he composed with Ernst Schmidt Jr.,
entitled *Eine Subgeschichte des Films* [A Sub-
history of Film], as well as his study on the myths
of US cinema, *Sexualität und Neurose im Film*
[Sexuality and Neurosis in Film].[8]

Sixteen years later Hans Scheugl returned
anew to film practice: *Der Ort der Zeit* (*The Place
of Time*, 1985) is a narrative documentary fiction
film that honorably commences the second phase
of his filmmaking career with an intelligently
formalized analysis of filmic space and its effect
upon time within the space of film. A path is traced
in brief, spatially overlapping jump-cuts to the
right, a course that seems entirely unrelated to the
cryptic plot. *Der Ort der Zeit* is a film about the
illusion of space/time continuity. The machine of
the film moves unswervingly forward, shifting
steadily to the right (and evermore surprisingly),
from inside to outside, from day to night, "on a
labyrinthine path," as Alexander Horwath writes,[9]
entirely without regard for what is happening in
front of the camera. Time strides forward, as is its
wont. Scheugl allows his story fragments to be
enacted by amateurs, the narrative remains as
incomprehensible as its location, which itself is
reduced to innumerable shots of details, while the
plot of an entire day is condensed into 40 minutes
of running time. *Der Ort der Zeit* displays how a
sequence of very simple images in cinema can
become very difficult to read – even more to the
point: If we take cinema seriously, this must remain
its elemental state. Scheugl's narrative drama is
open-ended on all possible formal (and intellectual)
fronts, activating the viewer's pleasure to freely
associate.

6   Scheugl, *Erweitertes Kino*, p. 97.
7   Schwärzler, "Das amerikanische Kino als Metaerzählung," pp.67–68
8   Hans Scheugl and Ernst Schmidt Jr., *Eine Subgeschichte
des Films. Lexikon des Avantgarde-, Experimental- und Undergroundfilms*, 2 volumes, (Frankfurt am Main: Suhrkamp, 1974).
Hans Scheugl, *Sexualität und Neurose im Film. Die Kinomythen von
Griffith bis Warhol* (Munich: Hanser, 1974).

9   Alexander Horwath, in *Falter* 23/85, Vienna, 1985, cited from
info sheet no. 10, 16th Internationales Forum des Jungen Films, Film
Festival Berlin, 1986.

Hans Scheugl
Keine Donau – Kurt Kren und seine Filme
1988

Hans Scheugl
Der Ort der Zeit
1985

The methodical deconstruction of traditional cinematic fictions remains Hans Scheugl's domain. After completing four subsequent medium and full length feature film productions including *Was die Nacht spricht – Eine Erzählung* (*What the Night speaks – a Story*, 1986) and *Rutt Deen* (1993), plus a television work about avant-garde pioneer Kurt Kren (*Keine Donau – Kurt Kren und seine Filme*, 1988), and the double film *Black/White* (1990), Scheugl refers back to *Sugar Daddies* in 1993 with his eight-minute *Prince of Peace*. He shows men stepping into a public lavatory in Vienna. As the camera zooms in on them church bells sound. In a parallel montage, Scheugl fades in a sequence of partially concealed gay porn photos. One of the protagonists of these images has a tattoo of Jesus on his upper arm. This sexually charged image transforms the lavatory into a Catholic place of worship. In the end, the faceless men behind the glass door get ready to leave the lavatory, very slowly, almost with mythical implications.

Scheugl has since been writing up every biotope from which either he himself originated or which he has steadily reinterpreted in his own film work. *Erweitertes Kino. Die Wiener Filme der 60er Jahre* [Expanded Cinema. Viennese Films of the 60s] from 2002 recapitulates the history of Vienna's underground film movement in the 1960s and the productive Actionism of the youthful Vienna film art scene. *Das Absolute. Eine Ideengeschichte der Moderne*[10] [The Absolute. A History of Ideas of Modernity] attempts nothing less than an intellectual history of modern art, while his 2007 *Sex und Macht*[11] [Sex and Power] undertakes a "meta-narrative on 20th century US American film" – a remix and update of his book *Sexualität und Neurose im Film*. Aside from a video work that has yet to be released, since 1993 Scheugl seems to be solely engaged in writing theory. A third phase in the film career of time/space explorer Hans Scheugl remains to be seen.

Translated by Eve Heller

---

10 Hans Scheugl, *Das Absolute. Eine Ideengeschichte der Moderne* (Vienna and New York: Springer-Verlag, 1999).
11 Hans Scheugl, *Sex und Macht: eine Metaerzählung des amerikanischen Films des 20. Jahrhunderts* (Stuttgart: Schmetterling Verlag, 2007).

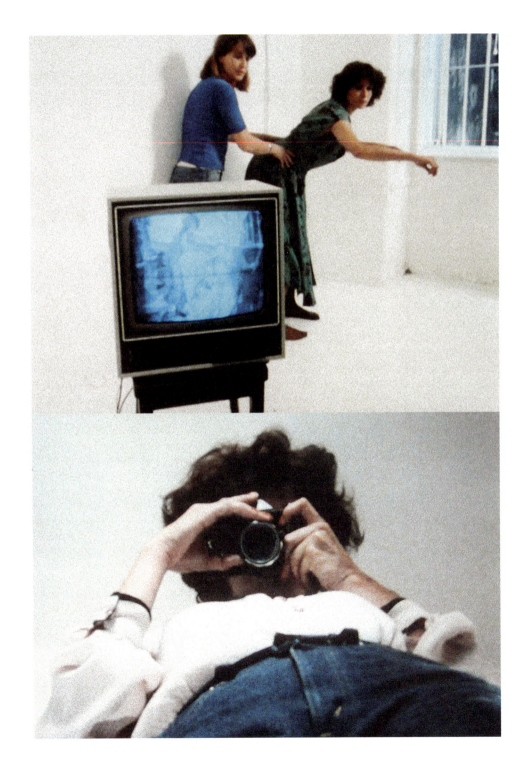

VALIE EXPORT:
The Female Body in Myriad Frames.

Maureen Turim

VALIE EXPORT has gained international recognition as a major performance, film and media artist who emerged as a female counterpoint to Vienna's largely male Actionist art movement. In fact her own essay, "Aspects of Feminist Actionism," clearly lays out the historical and theoretical parameters for her art.[1] She was one of several women performance and media artists to emerge in the 1960s from within male-dominated avant-gardes; a striking parallel may be drawn in her early career to that of Carolee Schneemann, and to the emergence of other female performance artists in the context of New York Fluxus. This female artistic flowering coincided with second-wave feminist movements in the US and Europe, but also with what was called the "sexual revolution" in the US. This context of cultural and sexual liberation led innovative artists like EXPORT to make framing her body and its pleasures into a pioneering emblem of this moment: Dada Material Action films active in the assault on taboos.

So let us start with the body and pleasure, yet note that in EXPORT's work pain will also become an issue. _Orgasm_ (1966-1967), one of VALIE EXPORT's first films, sets out, perhaps, to subjectively record a sexual intercourse of the artist and her lover. I say perhaps, because the fragmentary montage of images leaves much ambiguity about the events

in this sexual encounter. First, we concentrate on close-ups of breasts, then a close-up of a vulva, open and displayed for the camera. A female hand appears, massaging the open flesh of the vagina with an outstretched finger, offering an image of boldly asserted masturbation. When we cut to a close-up of a man's face, shot from below, we find him apparently in the throws of sexual arousal. Does this series of shots constitute an alternation between two partners, the shots of one presumably shot by the other? The orgasm of the title may well be the woman's. The shot that ends the film is of her vulva, fluids oozing from her vagina. We have then a sex procedural, imaged through fragmentation; sex here plays less for romance, or for the arousal of the spectator. Instead, the film remains a curious statement of visual erotica, with the emphasis on my term "statement," for here sexuality offers itself through conceptual rendering. Contrast this to Schneemann's _Fuses_ (1965), that seeks to express in the author's own description of the film, "the intimacy of the lovemaking" through the "materiality of film" that corresponds to "the energies of the body."[2] EXPORT refuses such expressive correlation.

---

1   VALIE EXPORT, "Aspects of Feminist Actionism,"
New German Critique, no. 47, Spring–Summer, 1989, pp. 69–92.

2   From the description of the film on Schneemann's website: http://www.caroleeschneemann.com/fuses.html. These ideas are further articulated in Kristine Stiles, Dan Cameron and David Levi Strauss, _Carolee Schneemann: Up to and Including Her Limits_ (New York: New Museum of Contemporary Art, 1997), and Carolee Schneemann, _Carolee Schneemann, Imaging Her Erotics: Essays, Interviews, Projects_ (Cambridge: MIT Press, 2002).

For her, form serves as enigma, emphatically stating the body and its gestures; energies are stopped, posed. They do not express intimacy, nor palpable energies, but rather the visual evidence of sex and they reclaim the anatomy of the female. On this last point a comparison could be made to Anne Severson's _Near the Big Chakra_ (1971), which features extreme close-ups of thirty-eight vulvas of various aged women. Clearly, the visual reclamation of female sex organs was among the concerns of women filmmakers in the early phases of second-wave feminism, before such images were incorporated into mainstream pornography.

EXPORT's still photography work in relation to _Orgasm_ is palpable. Although these images move, they are held in their frames in a manner similar to her photos, as is evident when one compares the shot of the vulva and vaginal opening in the film to EXPORT's still photos of female genitalia.

To understand this emphatic framing and its assertion of body parts depicted as statements, it is perhaps useful to jump ahead in EXPORT's career to _Mann & Frau & Animal_ (Man & Woman & Animal, 1970–1973). The film begins with close-ups of gleaming chrome plumbing, as a female hand turns on the faucet. Given the context of EXPORT's work, this shot may already be seen as a visual joke, and even more so in the context of the developing sequence, as a later close-up of water flowing over her clitoris and vulva has the extended faucet serve as a tool of orgasm. The film emphasizes the rather tranquil flow of water as well as the sensitivity of female genitalia to such flow. However, images of fluidity and cleanliness will be supplanted by shots of the vagina excreting fluids. First the vaginal area is adorned in ejaculate. This gives way to an image that makes it clear that EXPORT is having fun with the clean/dirty paradigm, as menstrual blood then permeates the vaginal image. With the linking of this close-up through montage to a photo of the vagina in a developing bath into which blood drips, EXPORT highlights her punning connections of filmmaking and photography, the bath event sequence and the development bath, the blood flowing outward to be visible in the image, and the blood dripped onto the photo in the bath, which becomes the filmed image of an inverted rhyming.

In between _Orgasm_ and _Mann & Frau & Animal_ comes _Aktionshose : Genitalpanik (Action Pants : Genital Panic_, 1969). It was first presented as a performance at the Stadtkino in Munich. The costume worn, a leather jacket and tight pants associated with males, had an area cut away exposing nude female genitalia. Striding up and down the rows of spectators, she brandished a machine gun and challenged the male audience to engage with a "real woman" instead of with an image on a screen. VALIE EXPORT confronted voyeurs with a body that returned the gaze.

From the performance she produced the poster "Actionshose : Genitalpanik" and a photo series. The poster, especially, recalls a famous 1968 poster

VALIE EXPORT
Tapp- und Tastkino
1968

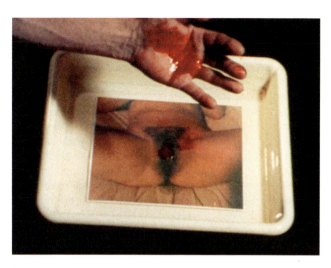

VALIE EXPORT
Mann & Frau & Animal
1973

of Huey Newton, co-founder and leader of the Black Panther Party for Self Defense, posed with a gun and a ceremonial spear sitting in an African-style chair. EXPORT's *Genital Panic,* with its sly reference to Freud's castration theory, which it then inverts into a celebration of female genital power, was notably reanimated by artist Marina Abramovic in 2005, but as a wordless performance in a museum setting, in which she sits before her spectators as they stare at her. For Abramovic this was a way of acknowledging how much her performance art has in common with the precedents set by EXPORT, while transforming the piece by placing it in the suspended temporality of long-duration posing of her own performance pieces.

Prior to *Aktionshose : Genitalpanik*, EXPORT staged another piece that took the pornographic theater's use of the voyeuristic touch room into the streets, performing *Tapp- und Tastkino* (*Tap and Touch Cinema*) in ten European cities from 1968 to 1971. EXPORT wore a boxed-shape "movie theater" around her naked upper body, so that her body could not be seen, but could be touched by a participant reaching through the curtained front

of the "theater." Gertrud Koch, in her essay on VALIE EXPORT entitled "A Pain in the Body, a Pleasure in the Eye,"[3] extensively explores theoretical implications of this performance action, which substitutes unseen, but framed touching for the cinema's voyeuristic sightlines. Limiting the groping through the curtain to only 12 seconds was yet another aspect of the performance. Duplicating the clock of prostitution and the peep show even while freeing the female body from its visual pornographic display, the performance is a complex intervention, and one specific to a moment in history. Later, similar motifs find their way into popular culture as Madonna's *Open Your Heart* music video of 1984 plays with granting a performative power to the exotic dancer in a circular room/peepshow club; she seems to enjoy her Thierry Mugler-bedecked dance performance in front of a wide variety of spectatorial windows, then befriends a little boy

3   Gertrud Koch, "'A Pain in the Body, a Pleasure in the Eye.' Somatische Performativität und filmisches Dispositiv in VALIE EXPORTs 'Spielfilmen,' " in *VALIE EXPORT: Mediale Anagramme*, ed. Neue Gesellschaft für Bildende Kunst (Berlin: Akademie der Künste, 2003), pp. 123–126.

with whom she escapes, suggesting that what is at stake is women's control and choice concerning the display of the body. Given this intertextuality with pornographic parlors and their inscription in film and video, I have questions about simply assuming that VALIE EXPORT's timed touching is the opposite of cinematic visual voyeurism. If fondling, or in the colloquial, "copping a feel," is a common public harassment of women, if the Tokyo subway finally instituted women-only cars meant to forestall unwelcome hands, if Merzak Allouache's 1996 _Salut, Cousin_ comically satirizes a Pigalle peepshow with a touch component whose timing device locks on the arms of Algerian immigrant, Allio (played to comic perfection by Gad Elmaleh), as an image of entrapment in Western culture, then we can see more clearly how EXPORT's performance gains its feminist audaciousness primarily by her willingness to take the scene to the street with all the self-consciousness entailed by her act of reframing. In retrospect, particularly taking into account how commercial pornography has expanded its representation since the late 1960s, our perspective now highlights how the strategies of freeing the female body from constraints by pioneering artists such as EXPORT were contingent demonstrations; valid for their good-humored, yet serious intervention in what sometimes still seems an impossible task of freeing the expression of sexuality from oppressive gender, class and race relations.

In _Asemie – die Unfähigkeit, sich durch Mienenspiel ausdrücken zu können_ (1973), mimesis itself is

the problem EXPORT addresses, which translates as "Asemia: The inability to express oneself through mimicry." _Asemie_ is a record of a performance. First, EXPORT, clothed, writes out her opening credits on a chalkboard, in the introductory style that characterized most of her early work. Then she returns, nude, and mounts the small platform that is draped in a white sheet. She takes a parakeet out of a small box, then ties it with a string to a support string that has been secured to the sheeted platform. She pours a pot of hot wax over the bird, which struggles to fly. Visual abstract expressionist aesthetics mix with an abject dread, as we hear the parakeet squawking and see it struggling, until silence and lack of motion signals that the bird has been executed. The camera lingers on the pattern formed by the wax and the corpse of the bird. The artist then pours the rest of the wax over her feet. With a new pot of wax, she pours wax over her left hand, then uses her mouth to manipulate the pot to pour wax over her right hand. The two wax hands are positioned on either side of the bird, as she waits for the wax to dry, first remaining crouching, then on all fours. Finally she picks up a spackle knife with her mouth, with which she breaks the wax off her hands. Then she departs, while a high angle lingers on the top of the platform.

Roswitha Mueller suggests in _VALIE EXPORT: Fragments of the Imagination_ that the bird was already dead before the performance.[4] She illustrates her brief discussion of the performance and its film with stills that appear to be from another performance, as EXPORT in these stills is clothed. The visual evidence from the tape suggests that the parakeet was very much alive when the hot wax was poured over the bird. Further, the performance is referenced and defended in EXPORT's later feature, and perhaps her most famous work, _Unsichtbare Gegner_ (_Invisible Adversaries_, 1977), a film I will later discuss at length. For now, let me point out the sequence in which she includes an insert of the newspaper coverage of the original performance of _Asemie_: An image of the pot of wax

---

4   Roswitha Mueller, _VALIE EXPORT: Fragments of the Imagination_ (Bloomington: Indiana University Press, 1994), p. 44.

VALIE EXPORT
Asemie
1973

looming over the live parakeet and another of a dead parakeet in a small open box appears in news photos accompanied by the headline "Die Kunst, Vögel zu martern" [The Art of Torturing Birds], recalling the photo layout of amassed coffins accompanied by the headline "Unsichtbare Gegner" used for the opening credits. Over this insert of the newspaper story covering *Asemie*, EXPORT's voiceover says, "If you are creative in Vienna, the police suspect you." That line is preceded by the citation "The Viennese Golden Heart beating faster for a dog than an artist." By reiterating this incident in *Invisible Adversaries*, where it is linked to scathing critiques of the Austrian post-war government, EXPORT insists on its political significance.

The performance of pain and abjection was an Actionist preoccupation, and in *Asemie*, EXPORT displays her roots in that movement. She seemingly refuses female masochism with a foray into sadism, under the title that suggests the absence of definitive meanings for the series of actions entailed. Asemia is also the term for the medical condition of being unable to understand or express any signs or symbols. Aphasia, the less severe, but related condition, the inability to understand linguistic signs, has been the object of much theoretical attention, most notably by Alexander Luria in the Soviet Union, who studied trauma post WWII.[5] Later, it was introduced into semiotic studies by Roman Jakobson.[6] Roland Barthes evoked asemia in his analysis of the "contre-écritures" of Henri Michaux, while the artwork of Cy Twombly stands as the most famous example of many artists who work in this area of undecipherable traces of textuality.[7] From Abraham and Torok's

psychoanalytical writings, Derrida derived his discussion of the related term anasemia.[8]

So, in entitling her work *Asemie*, which can mean "having no specific semantic content," EXPORT is calling on this intellectual and artistic tradition, just as she evokes semiotics with her title *Syntagma* (1983) and rhetoric with *Hyperbolie* (1973). Asemic writing creates a void that the reader may interpret. All of this is similar to the way one would deduce meaning from any abstract work of art. Multiple meanings for any given symbolism are another possibility for an asemic work, and this might be EXPORT's aim.

Yet I want to challenge that the acts depicted achieve their role as traces beyond meaning as the title seems to imply. The violence may be senseless, but it is hardly outside referential cultural meaning. It mimics a most primitive and foundational ritual for the creation of meaning, animal sacrifice. The act of casting her hands in wax may be understood as doing to herself what she did to the bird, except the wax would never kill her as it does the bird. Is this the displacement of the violence of self-mutilation? Certainly, the bird's torturous death creates an intensity, in the sense of the term *Libidinal Economy* introduced by Jean-Francois Lyotard.[9]

Today, the work might be received in a new context, that of crush films that present women killing small animals and birds as an erotic fetish, sometimes with their high heels, supplying a niche market on the Internet. Currently such films are frequently in the news, as the US Supreme Court overturned a 1999 law outlawing the display of crush films for profit, despite the cruelty to animals, on the grounds that the law was too broadly construed, and violated freedom of speech.[10] New

---

5   A. R. Luria, *Traumatic Aphasia: Its Syndromes, Psychology, and Treatment* (The Hague: Mouton, 1970).
6   Roman Jakobson, "Child language. Aphasia and phonological universals" (1968), in *Selected Writings* (Berlin, New York and Amsterdam: Mouton, 1987).
7   Roland Barthes, *L'obvie et l'obtus* (Paris: Seuil and Schama, 1982); Cy Twombly, Simon Schama and Roland Barthes, *Cy Twombly: Fifty Years of Works on Paper* (New York: Whitney Museum of Art, 2005). See also David H. T. Scott, *Semiologies of Travel: from Gautier to Baudrillard* (Cambridge: Cambridge University Press, 2004.); Raymond Bellour, *Henri Michaux* (Paris: Gallimard, 1986); and Nina Parish, *Henri Michaux: Experimentation with Signs* (Amsterdam: Rodopi, 2007), p. 134.

8   Nicolas Abraham and Maria Torok, *The Wolf Man's Magic Word: A Cryptonymy* (Minneapolis: University of Minnesota Press, 1986), with foreword by Jacques Derrida.
9   Jean-Francois Lyotard, *Libidinal Economy* (London: Continuum, 2004).
10   Adam Liptak, "Justices Reject Ban on Videos of Animal Cruelty," *The New York Times*, April 20, 2010, p. A1. See also Andrew A. Beerworth, "United States v. Stevens: A Proposal For Criminalizing Crush Videos under Current Free Speech Doctrine," *Vermont Law Review* 35:901, Summer, 2011. Also "Crush videos outlawed, again," *Journal of the American Veterinary Medical Association*, 238, no. 3, February 1, 2011, pp. 262–263.

VALIE EXPORT, **Syntagma**, 1983   →
VALIE EXPORT, **Unsichtbare Gegner**, 1977   → →

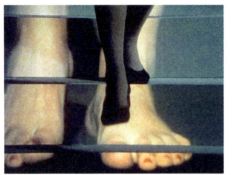

legislation that would redefine the commerciali-
zation of images of animal cruelty is pending in
the US, while the Hollywood film industry has
adopted self-regulation regarding the abuse of
animals (though originally birds and rodents were
specifically not included, as the main thrust of
protection was horses).[11] So the very issues that
EXPORT evokes of animal sacrifice and sadism
towards defenseless creatures are loaded with
cultural meanings.

It is fascinating to compare *Asemie* to
....Remote....Remote.... (1973), a film which
juxtaposes a performance of self-mutilation with
an enlarged photo of two young siblings clasping
each other's hands. The photo was first published
in the Vienna papers to illustrate children being
rescued from abusive parents. In this staged
setting, EXPORT's unrelenting slicing at her cuticles
with an exacto knife seems to evoke self-mutilation's relationship to child abuse; female cutters,
according to psychologists, are often trying to
release an interior pain, then become addicted
to the endorphins released when the body is
wounded.[12] Of course, from a psychoanalytical point
of view, which we know interests EXPORT from
her other works and writings, we can analyze her
play with Freud's essay, "A Child is Being Beaten."[13]
A split self re-enacts parental or other abuse
towards another part of the self, a punishment
which one might imagine they deserve. Agencies
enmesh in warfare within a split subjectivity.

What to make of the bowl of milk sitting on
the artist's lap, into which she inserts a bleeding
middle finger? Given that the close-up of the bowl
also frames her crotch, doesn't it echo the finger
inserted into the close-up of the vagina in *Orgasm*?
Clearly, EXPORT works with such visual echoes. The

wax hands from *Asemie* become the plaster hands
of Paris in *Delta. Ein Stück* [Delta. A Play] (1976),
for example, and circulate in many of the photos.
Also, we might note intertextual traces, from this
bowl of milk to the one in Georges Bataille's *Histoire
de l'oeil (The Story of the Eye)*, the passage that
chronicles Simone's squatting naked to dip her
vagina into a bowl of milk.[14] So if we admit this
intertextually, the finger is doubly associated
with the vagina in EXPORT's film. Self-mutilation
is placed in relation to the memory of child abuse,
but also to female sexuality; this display conjoins
disgust with visual fascination. In "Violence of
Desire in the Female Avant-garde," I wrote about
the expressive relationship between innovative film
cutting and female cutters, women who engage in
self-mutilation.[15] Creative innovation that has a
violent force, may, like self-mutilation, release pain.

As we have noted, EXPORT's work repeatedly
addresses the psyche through its representations
of the body. When she takes on a shift in strategies
by making a feature-length narrative film for theatrical release, it is to female paranoic hysteria that
she turns, having her artist protagonist, Anna,
imagine that alien beings, "Hyksos," have taken
over the psyches of the people around her. Hyksos,
EXPORT has told us, is a term she borrowed from
the memory of an Art History class she took in the
early 1960s: "The Hyksos were an Asiatic tribe that
moved into the Egyptian empire and usurped the
southern part of Egypt. (...) The only thing lasting
about their presence was the 'petrified' memory."[16]
What EXPORT is referencing here is the famous
statue of a female Hyksos, originally made of wood,
but now petrified, and therefore preserved as one
of the few extant artifacts of this foreign rule in the
south of Egypt.

This flirtation with art history recalls EXPORT's
early film *Selbstportrait mit Kopf* [Self-Portrait with

11 Susan Orlean, "Animal Action," *The New Yorker*,
November 17, 2003, pp. 92–93
12 Mary E. Williams, *Self-mutilation* (Detroit: Greenhaven Press
and Favazza, 2008); and Armando R. Favazza, *Bodies Under Siege:
Self-Mutilation And Body Modification in Culture and Psychiatry*,
(Baltimore: Johns Hopkins University Press, 1996).
13 Sigmund Freud (1919), "'A Child is Being Beaten': A Contribution
to the Study of the Origin of Sexual Perversions," in *The Standard
Edition of the Complete Psychological Works of Sigmund Freud*,
vol. XVII, (London: Vintage, 1975) pp. 175–204.

14 Georges Bataille, *The Story of the Eye* (London: Penguin, 2001).
15 Maureen Turim, "Violence of Desire in the Female Avant-garde,"
in *Women And Experimental Filmmaking*, eds. Jean Petrolle and
Virginia Wright Wexman (Urbana and Chicago: University Of Illinois
Press, 2005), pp. 71–90.
16 Scott MacDonald, "VALIE EXPORT on *Invisible Adversaries*,"
in *A Critical Cinema 3. Interviews with Independent Filmmakers*
(Berkeley: University of California Press, 1998), p. 257.

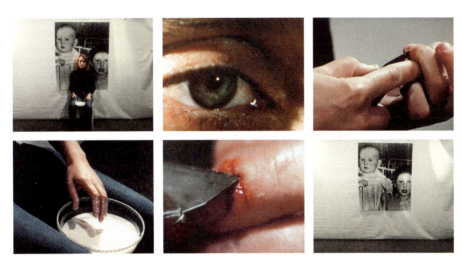

VALIE EXPORT
....Remote....Remote....
1973

Head] (1966/1967), in which EXPORT's head on the right shares a close-up with a sculptural portrait on the left to which she bears a striking resemblance. As the artist slowly moves, the comparison of physiognomy is abetted with violets and a Victorian lamp also visible in the frame. For me, the props evoke the Gibson Girl, a turn of the century ideal of female beauty made famous by US illustrator Charles Gibson. Many films have used this association of female with statuary: For example in "Greta Garbo and Silent Cinema: The Actress As Art Deco Icon," Lucy Fischer notes, "in this scene, the Art Deco statue is Leonora – and Leonora is Garbo."[17] Similarly, Jean Renoir in *Rules of the Game* (1939) associates Geneviève de Marras (Mila Parély) with a statue of Buddha. The association of the female with statuary from the past, rendered by framing them together, becomes EXPORT's whole film, her self-portrait.

So in *Invisible Adversaries*, EXPORT has her artist heroine revive many of EXPORT's own artistic ventures, seeking a relationship to art history through images of the body on the one hand, and the psyche on the other. This includes a scene in her lit darkroom in which Anna has tacked the images she will collage of contemporary objects, women and men within famous paintings, through layering of images. Eventually, by dissolve, she will link an image fragment of a Piera della Francesca fresco to Anna and her companion Peter in the same pose talking about the Hyksos. Later, the film returns to the combining of art images and contemporary models posing, this time in a video studio setting, layering, then demonstrating, the process by fading between the images taken by two different cameras. By making Anna obsessed with Hyksos and with the reduplication of art images, EXPORT is reworking much of her earlier artistic production in fictional form. This narrative trope is a means, as EXPORT expresses it, "to create an experimental avant-garde sense of content and form into a feature film." It also serves to document EXPORT's intermedia approach to image making, alternating between and blending performance, still photography, film and video.

The bath scene in *Invisible Adversaries* compares to *Mann & Frau & Animal*. The scene begins

17 Lucy Fischer, "Greta Garbo and Silent Cinema: The Actress As Art Deco Icon," *Camera Obscura 48*, vol. 16, no. 3, 2001, p. 106.

with a brief close-up of Anna's hair being pissed on, followed by a shot of the sink faucet running water over her head. What follows is some sexual play in which Peter rubs first her pubic area, then her buttocks and finally, her armpit with his head, saying he is drying it. Anna's dialogue quotes Claude Lévi-Strauss on a Sioux myth in which two triadic units are opposed homomorphically, one consisting of scalp, braid ornaments and pubic hair, with the other triad being sun, moon and stone. The visual joke is that in the sexual play that accompanies Anna's exposition, she touches Peter's pubic area at the moment she quotes Lévi-Strauss's mention of pubic hair. When asked about this sequence in the interview, she connects this to another passage in Lévi-Strauss in which he tells of certain native societies where urine is used to wash someone's hair or in ritual cleaning of the body. This is another example of how EXPORT incorporates theory into her film, linking the scatological aspects of Actionism with anthropological observations theorized structurally. Let me add that both versions of Lévi-Strauss, in the film and in the interview, seem somewhat fanciful. Lévi-Strauss discusses Hidatsa and Mandan myths (tribes of Sioux-speaking Native Americans) comparatively in the chapter on "Myths and Rituals of Neighboring Peoples," but not as represented in the film. Another chapter, "The Sex of the Sun and the Moon," compares mythic treatments of these astronomical bodies across North and South Native American peoples, but again, there seems to be considerable poetic license in the configurations with which EXPORT plays.

When asked about her film as a reworking of Don Siegel's 1956 sci-fi thriller, EXPORT maintains, "I had not seen *Invasion of the Body Snatchers*, and had not heard about it." Still, Christine Holmlund writes convincingly of the intertextuality, seeing *Invisible Adversaries* as an avant-garde feminist film reworking of the last third of Siegel's film, "rewriting it from Becky's point of view at the very moment when she is about to mutate."[18] She notes,

also, "A strong fear of totalitarianism thus subtends both narratives, though what constitutes totalitarianism differs."[19]

Anna's reflection in the mirror takes on a life of its own, applying lipstick, while she merely watches. Holmlund contends that following this visual observation of her double, "Anna sets out to observe and document her own, her lover Peter's (Peter Weibel), and others' transformations into aliens,"[20] but my sense is that the film pursues this with far more ambiguity: as to whether this apparition is itself a psychoanalytic symptom, and at what stages Anna's struggle to make art while experiencing hysteric symptoms isn't another way of looking at the film. EXPORT reminds us that throughout her career, "I, as the centerpoint for the performance, position the human body as a sign, as a code for social and artistic expression."[21] Here she uses narrative, the sci-fi story, as a bearer of signs and symbols, in addition to the way in which the surrogate female artist's body navigates within this narrative.

Speaking of that navigation, she revitalizes the body in the urban-environment framings, reinscribing elements of *Körperkonfigurationen in der Architektur* (*Body Configurations in Architecture*, 1972–1976) and *Syntagma* in *Invisible Adversaries*. EXPORT ingeniously frames the body in urban space, interior and exterior, adding here a series of shots of various couples arguing in cars. For those who have traced the car in films, these series of pointless mobile arguments are a particularly amusing variation on this setting.

The vestiges of the cutting/violence paradigm I mentioned earlier is treated in this film as a visual joke on the woman's relationship to the kitchen: Anna's slicing of vegetables is intercut with images of small animals about to be cut with knives. Ice skates worn in Anna's dream that is projected above her bed finally slice down her thigh, leaving a thin trail of blood, montaged with abstract drawings first with red, then white lines. So individual

18 Christine Holmlund, "Feminist Makeovers: The Celluloid Surgery of VALIE EXPORT and Su Friedrich," in *Play it again, Sam: Retakes on Remakes*, eds. Andrew Horton and Stuart Y. McDougal (Berkeley: University of California Press, 1998), pp. 217–237.

19 Holmlund, p. 220.
20 Holmlund, p. 220.
21 VALIE EXPORT, "Expanded Cinema as Expanded Reality," *Senses of Cinema*, www.sensesofcinema.com/2003/28/expanded_cinema/

sub-segments of the film each supply their variations on longstanding EXPORT images and concerns.

EXPORT's interview with Helke Sander for Sander's video *Wann ist der Mensch eine Frau?* (*When Is a Human Being a Woman?*, 1976) becomes incorporated into *Invisible Adversaries*, as a way of underlining the common political threads of their films.

Finally, EXPORT's film ends with a mobile crane shot, just as it began, moving out from the window of Anna's apartment to pan across Vienna, only this time the pan takes place in the darkness of night. In fact, much of the film folds in half, with rhymes in the second half repeating and varying the sequences in the first half. Despite the narrative premise, this mirror structure simply repeats the alienation from the city's inhabitants, and the geopolitics that cradle this city in an ominous series of news reports from the world beyond. In the last of these, meant to verbally illustrate the power of cruise missiles if they were aimed at St. Stephen's Cathedral, the film image dissolves into a photo, which a woman's hand tears to close the film. EXPORT tears at the city, to warn the city, to urge the city to protest.[22]

The recent foregrounding of EXPORT's work in the Musee de l'art Moderne Centre Pompidou's "elles" exhibit and catalogue emphatically reminds us of her importance to women's artmaking and to feminist art making. EXPORT's work may be compared to that of other, often beautiful women who performed, often naked, to arouse the art world to women's potential as artists. They explored their own sexuality, sometimes their masochism, often their violence, but always their aim at expression from a woman's point of view.

VALIE EXPORT is still making art today, most notably her installation at the Arsenale of the Venice Biennale 2007. The performance piece she did for the opening has become the basis of her

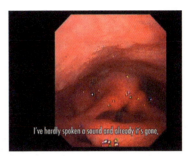

VALIE EXPORT
I turn over the pictures of my voice in my head
2008

video, *I turn over the pictures of my voice in my head* (2008). In the performance the artist read a text while her vocal cords were being filmed through a medical scope. Similar images were part of an installation at the Biennale called *Glottis*, in which circularly framed images of vocal chords were on suspended monitors. From its very beginning the text spoken takes on many of the verbal images familiar from EXPORT's work, aligning them now with her focus on the voice: "The voice is suture, the voice is seam, the voice is cut, the voice is tear, the voice is my identity, it is not body or spirit, it is not language or image, it is sign, it is a sign of the images, it is a sign of sensuality. It is a sign of symbols, it is boundary. It speaks the 'split body,' it is hidden in the clothing of the body, it is always somewhere else." The images accompanying these words, indeed the images, which are of the body parts in real time, producing the words, take us back to *Orgasm*, as they recall that film's focus on the labia and the vaginal opening in the final images, and the several times EXPORT has returned to female genitalia over her career of image exploration. That the vocal organs visually rhyme with female genitalia, that when they are in use, they create a fascinating flow of movement and change, makes this work a compelling new iteration by an artist who has given voice to her female body through a myriad of frames.

---

22 VALIE EXPORT's short films *Mann & Frau & Animal*, *....Remote.... Remote....* and *Syntagma* are available on Index DVD Edition 004: *VALIE EXPORT, 3 Experimental Short Films*; her feature film *Unsichtbare Gegner* is available on Index DVD Edition 021: *VALIE EXPORT, Invisible Adversaries*.

Two Telephone Books, a Lightbulb and a Glass Plate.
How Maria Lassnig's Low-Fi Animated Films Influenced
an Entire Generation of Animation Filmmakers.

Maya McKechneay

"The lady minister was so smart and nice,
She brought me back home.
Women should have important jobs,
that's how it should be,
Professors can make their students famous."
(From *The Ballad of Maria Lassnig*)

Maria Lassnig had worked as an artist for decades. And she waited. Fame caught up with the painter late in her career. Lassnig did not become well known until 1980, when she was invited to represent Austria at Venice's Biennale at the age of 60, together with Valie Export, who was 20 years younger. In the meantime, Lassnig's works have been included in some of the most significant collections of contemporary art. At auction they represent the crème de la crème of living Austrian artists.[1] On her 90th birthday, in 2010, Austria's media honored Lassnig with numerous tributes. In the same year, Munich's Lenbachhaus gave her a major one-woman show, focusing on current self-portraits. Lassnig still paints to this very day.

Lassnig is not as well known for her filmmaking as she is for her painting. She herself often plays down the importance of her films in interviews: "The king of film in New York, the one with the film archive – Jonas Mekas – once said to me, 'Stick with painting!' In his opinion I'm a better painter than filmmaker,"[2] as she recalls. At another point: "I exhibited my work for the first time in conjunction with my animation films at the Biennale in Venice, in a small room. I noticed that in my exhibition space people stopped and stood still. (...) But they sat down to watch the animation films, and they stayed for hours on end. I became jealous of my own animation films."[3] Despite her ambivalence toward filmmaking, Lassnig has influenced an entire generation of Austrian animation filmmakers, as a professor heading the master class on Experimental Design at Vienna's Academy of Applied Arts from 1980 to 1989. But first things first.

Born in Krappfeld, Carinthia, in 1919 Lassnig attended a convent school according to her autobiographical street-ballad film, *Maria Lassnig Kantate* (*The Ballad of Maria Lassnig*, 1992). As of

---

1 In 2007 her oil painting entitled *Mit einem Tiger schlafen* was sold at a Palais Kinsky auction for 230,000 euros. That same year, the highest bid for the mythological panel painting *Samson* (1983) came in at 200,000 euros.

2 Taken from an interview Mara Mattuschka and Sabine Groschup conducted with Lassnig in 2009. An abridged version was published in Christian Dewald, Sabine Groschup, Mara Mattuschka and Thomas Renoldner, eds., *Die Kunst des Einzelbilds, Animation in Österreich – 1832 bis heute* (Vienna: Verlag Filmarchiv Austria, 2010).

3 Maria Lassnig, video interview with Ully Aris and Wilfried Reichel for Vienna's Museum of Modern Art mumok exhibition *Maria Lassnig – Das neunte Jahrzehnt*, February 13 – May 5, 2009, http://www.youtube.com/watch?v=ucgovs7VPmk

1941, she studied painting at Vienna's Academy of Fine Arts (under Wilhelm Dachauer, Ferdinand Andri and Herbert Boeckl), until Dachauer expelled her in 1943. The reason he gave was that she corrupted her fellow students with her "degenerate" colors. In the early 1950s she joined Vienna's progressive artist group known as the Art Club and associated with Monsignor Otto Mauer and the artists he exhibited at his newly founded Galerie nächst St. Stephan, including Arnulf Rainer. In 1961, she moved to Paris, and from there proceeded to New York in 1968 where she took a class in animation at the School of Visual Arts (SVA) in the early 1970s.[4]

"We learned the most basic kind of animation there, animation for beggars, so to speak," as Lassnig describes her educational situation in retrospect. "They taught us how to do it at home, using two telephone books supporting a glass plate with a lightbulb underneath, one animation cel after another. It's really easy, just move it a little at a time. (…) At home I had a big cable spool like the ones used for telephone cables, they were just lying around on the street, so I dragged one home (…) and then for ten dollars you could get an animation stand, a kind of column you attach a camera to, and of course I bought a Single 8 camera right away, a simple 8 mm camera. After that I got a Super 8 camera and finally a 16 mm Bolex."[5] Lassnig, who suffered from chronic poverty at the time, claimed that she hoped to earn some money with animation film: "I painted in the mornings, and in the evenings I drew and shot animation," is how she described her daily routine. She spent a great deal of time at the Millennium Film Workshop, a film art center founded in 1966 that offers visitors workshops and access to technical equipment in addition to holding regular screenings. There Maria Lassnig first encountered, among others, the works of Stan Brakhage.

Between 1970 and 1976 Lassnig attended meetings of a feminist women's film group[6] and completed nine of the ten short films that constitute her entire body of film work. According to Lassnig, her films were well received by New York City's film scene, as evidenced by frequent invitations from the Film Forum, run by Karen Griffin and her husband, animation filmmaker George Griffin.[7] Especially her *Selfportrait* (1971) toured widely and was distinguished with an award from the New York State Council on the Arts.

Perhaps because cartoons were perceived as a "minor form" (especially in the US of the 1970s) and primarily as a product of popular culture (despite the efforts of New York cartoon and Pop artists such as Robert Crumb and Roy Lichtenstein to blur these boundaries), Lassnig was able to allow herself a great deal of directness and humor in her work. Lassnig's *Selfportrait*, said to be the first self-portrait in cartoon form ever, owes its effectiveness to a clash of picture and sound. Lassnig's face is at the center of the film, drawn in cartoon style. From off-screen we hear the artist's drowsy, elegiac voice, half singing and half speaking in English with a heartbreaking Austrian accent. Her timbre is somewhat reminiscent of the singer Nico: "It's already over and doesn't matter, but…" Whereas classic cartoons on television present emotions through exaggerated facial expressions, and extreme emotions in an overall physical excess including smoking skulls and bulging eyeballs, Lassnig depicts her own face as expressionless. Rather than a mirror of affect motivated from within, we see an experimental field exposed to various influences: Lassnig's drawn head is wrapped in cellophane, stuck in a

---

4   Other former students of this institution, founded in 1947 as the Cartoonists and Illustrators School, include Keith Haring and Joseph Kosuth. Lassnig left the school before graduating: "I dropped out after realizing that I couldn't learn anything more from them, and it also didn't look like they were going to teach me how to shoot film." Maria Lassnig, interview with Mara Mattuschka and Sabine Groschup, 2009.

5   Maria Lassnig, interview with Mattuschka and Groschup, 2009.

6   At the invitation of feminist performer and experimental filmmaker Carolee Schneemann and Olga Spreitzer, a pupil of Ernst Fuchs (renowned painter and co-founder of the Vienna School of Fantastic Realism), and with whom she later would share an apartment.

7   Maria Lassnig, interview with Mattuschka and Groschup, 2009: "And then there was also a movie theater on the right side of New York, I can't remember what it was called. There was a couple that ran it, and she managed the theater and he was an animation filmmaker. And they invited me there, I showed my films there often." Thanks to Azazel and Ken Jacobs, as well as Jonas Mekas, who kindly clarified to which theater Lassnig refers.

cage, blown off-screen line by line and cracked in two, hatching the face of her, in contrast, broadly smiling mother: "When my mother died, I became she. She was so strong." Precisely by not expressing emotion through facial expression here, but rather through sound and the mechanical manipulation of face and body, Lassnig denies the viewer the "feast of recognition" so typical of comics and cartoons. The minimal facial surface here does not become an easily legible display of basic emotions. Instead, as part of "the 'body vessel' that I inhabit" (in Lassnig's terms from an interview in 1970), it remains rigid and object-like. Nonetheless, it does resist external forces and their symbolic attacks through constant self-regeneration – and in this way the illustrated Lassnig does resemble a classic cartoon hero.

In *Shapes* (1972), created one year later, Lassnig used a stencil spray technique to pose human torsos – bodies without heads – in front of the camera. Jubilant Baroque music in the background demands "high culture," and at first the figures obediently assume the fixed posture of ancient heroes: discus throwers, spear throwers, the ideal of the naked Olympian. However, among the male outlines are also females, and they will not be denied the same poses. After a short interlude of animated sculptures, the male and female bodies – the one recognizable by its extended member, and the other by the apple she presents – merge in an ironic happy end, in a (still) headless fusion.

Lassnig's nine-minute film, *Couples* (1972), again demonstrates an interplay of various animation techniques, and in terms of content is

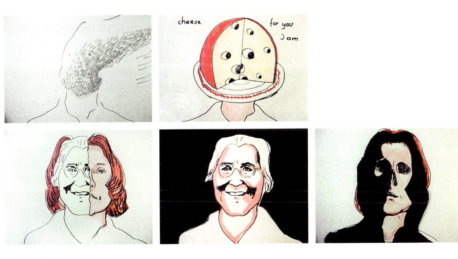

Maria Lassnig
Selfportrait
1971

Maria Lassnig
Shapes
1972

perhaps Lassnig's clearest (and also funniest) confrontation with male-female communication (and copulation) breakdowns. Pink, promiscuous, sketched genital protuberances crawl toward one another, but do not come together, like misfit puzzle pieces, and alternate with an animated collage of illustrated images. Although the end of the film again attests to the triviality of the entire topic with its flaming, pierced and blood-dripping scrawled hearts, there is nonetheless a tragic core in the middle part: In verse-like repetition, a little pen drawn man gropes toward the telephone booth to snarl in the receiver, "Mary, I have to see you. We're involved." Whereby Lassnig's voice interjects, "But you don't LOVE me": which does not at all disturb the seemingly automatic responses of the male, until – in the same pseudo-rationalist phrasing – it comes to a break-up in the final verse ("I can't be involved with you anymore. There are other people in my life."). The dialogue that Lassnig puts in the mouth of her "couples" (who are reduced to fleshy organ creatures), also settles the score with efficiency-driven phrases of the "Free Love" generation: Her: "Why can't you be more tender?" Him: "Sex is not servitude." Her: "Oh, you have no heart." Him: "I have my needs and desires. But you are not my universe."

In 1980, Lassnig was still living in New York and making animation films when Austria's culture minister, Hertha Firnberg,[8] invited her to become the first female professor at Vienna's Academy of Applied Arts with her own master class.[9] The Master Class of Experimental Design offered Lassnig was originally intended for the performance artist Joseph Beuys, but he chose to stay in Düsseldorf. Mara Mattuschka, who joined Lassnig's class in 1983, believes that the name of the master class itself played no minor role in Lassnig's decision to offer something other than painting. Lassnig herself has explained how the

decision to offer instruction in animation film was somewhat accidental.[10] In 1982, an animation studio was set up and run by Hubert Sielecki, given Lassnig's "innate fear of machines," as she put it.[11] Viennese animation artist, painter and writer of crime novels Sabine Groschup, who became a Lassnig pupil in 1981, remembers that, "In our class Hubert was in charge of technical know-how. All we had was one tiny room, 12 square meters in size, that at the same time served as the assistant's space. It was extremely tight, but that was where we worked." Mara Mattuschka, filmmaker, performance artist and painter, emphasizes how primitive the original animation studio was in the beginning: "But that was actually a good thing, because that way we practically experienced the birth of cinema. With Hubert came a little equipment: a Bolex, and an electronic sequencer that he mounted onto a tripod. You had to constantly hold onto certain little wires so that the contact would not break. We did a lot of experimentation back then. A lot of stop-motion animation using the human body, including a film in which Lassnig, holding a brush in her mouth, crawls through the picture like a dog with a bone."[12] By May of 1987 a total of 78 films, more than five hours of footage, plus some three hours of practice films, were made in this tight space. That same year 16 students, including Mattuschka, collaborated on the 45-minute animation film *1x1 des Glücklichen Lebens* (*ABC of Happyness*), which was commissioned by the ORF and broadcast on the art magazine *Kunst-Stücke*,

---

8   Firnberg, a Social Democrat, was a minister in the cabinet of Bruno Kreisky from 1970 to 1983.
9   In Austrian art academies, a professor heads, as a "master," a so-called "master class," made up of a small number of students at different phases in their studies. Graduates are replaced by seven to ten new students each year. Also, all additional teachers within such a "master class" are chosen by the master professor.

10   "A young English woman who wanted nothing more than to study film came to the class. I thought, why not, I can do that. A class in animation film was approved, and so was an assistant who gradually got all the equipment from the Academy, while I was so backwards and made animation like in the Stone Age, with two telephone books supporting a glass plate with a light underneath, even in Vienna. I advised the students artistically while they did their animation, and encouraged them – that worked." Maria Lassnig, in an interview with Dieter Ronte, in *Mit eigenen Augen. KünstlerInnen aus der ehemaligen Meisterklasse Maria Lassnig / With their own eyes. Former Students of Maria Lassnig*, ed. Gerald Bast [German/English] (Vienna: Springer/Edition Angewandte, 2008), p. 15.
11   Maria Lassnig, interview with Mattuschka and Groschup, 2009.
12   Mara Mattuschka in an interview with the author, Graz, March 2010.

and also screened at international film festivals such as the Berlinale.[13]

While Lassnig showed her own films once in a while in class, technique was taught primarily by Hubert Sielecki: "Sielecki was in touch with the scene in Łódź and invited some of its members to Vienna, like Zbigniew Rybczyński,[14] who visited our class several times. That was really interesting. So

many possibilities: He used a different mask for every scene. No outlines. That was a multiple exposure consisting of 80 passes, incredibly complex. And *that* was what he tried to teach *us* how to do."[15]

Lassnig required her students to exclusively draw the first year and exclusively paint the next – primarily human models, but also still lifes – in order to learn technique from scratch. Animation seems to have primarily represented an extension of the study of painting to her, an additional tool to be used in studying movement. Mattuschka

13 See Hubert Sielecki, "Der Animationsfilm," in *Katalog zur Ausstellung der Meisterklasse für Gestaltungslehre – experimentelles Gestalten, o. Prof. akad. Maler Maria Lassnig* (Vienna: Hochschule für Angewandte Kunst, 1989).
14 Polish animation artist whose short film *Tango* (1983) received an Oscar.

15 Sabine Groschup in an interview with the author, Vienna, May 2010.

Maria Lassnig
Couples
1972

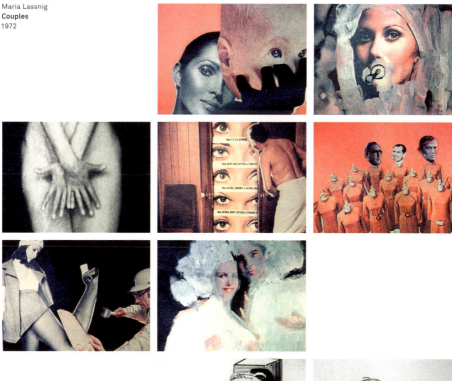

explains that she never thought about anything like an independent film scene: "It was only by chance that I submitted several works to the Oberhausen film festival. And right away three of them were accepted and screened. I just had different priorities…"[16] Compared to the media-oriented master class taught by Peter Weibel,[17] in which theory came before practice, Lassnig's class was said to be more down to earth: "The people who took Weibel's class were all dressed stylishly and carried briefcases to the Academy, and they used lots of electronics. Lassnig, on the other hand, liked to admit students from the countryside. There was a completely different atmosphere: Just one floor below Weibel, and you thought you were in a different century… In our class it smelled of sheep's wool."[18] Nevertheless, both Groschup and Mattuschka stress that it was precisely this classical training and the personality of Lassnig with her clearly defined approach that influenced their work most. It was also important as a source of friction. The more traditional the classroom atmosphere, the more eccentric and off-beat the class' performances and parties.[19]

From 1980 to 1989 Lassnig accepted over 70 regular students to her class. These were joined by a number of others who audited her class, several of whom she had approached after observing them copying famous masterpieces in museums. The students who attended Lassnig's classes include a number of individuals who later significantly influenced animation film in Austria, or still do: Martin Anibas (1987), James Clay (1984), Johanna Freise (1987), Sabine Groschup (1981), Paul Horn (1987),

Renate Kordon (1983), Mara Mattuschka (1982), Bady Minck (1982), Thomas Renoldner (1988), Roland Schütz (1980), Ulf Staeger (1987), Thomas Steiner (1986), Stefan Stratil (1982) and Nana Swiczinsky (1989). No generalizations can be made about the film works produced by the "Lassnig School," though one could say that variety is the one characteristic they share, a result of the opportunity to experiment freely and find one's own personal style, without expectations of technical perfection. Even today, the film works of Sabine Groschup, for example, stand out as hand-crafted products. Her film *Gugug* (*Peekaboo*, 2006) was drawn by hand, frame-by-frame, with a felt-tip pen directly onto film. The images are accompanied by the warm voice of Groschup's grandmother who talks about how, as a young girl, she believed that babies were washed up on the bank of a stream. In one scene, which Groschup drew line-by-line and dot-by-dot to fit her grandmother's childlike perception, she used an "unprofessional" felt-tip pen like that used by children, to apply the ink irregularly. When projected onto the movie screen, it is precisely this irregularity that causes the animated colored field to take on an abstract quality, becoming a riot of color. *Gugug* employs a selection of motifs that are both naïve and clever.

One of Lassnig's students who has enjoyed the most international success is Luxembourg native Bady Minck. In 1988, while still attending the academy, she and Stefan Stratil made the eight-minute *Der Mensch mit den modernen Nerven* (*Man with Modern Nerves*). Shot on black-and-white 16 mm film, Minck and Stratil created an animated model of a city hall in Mexico City, designed by Adolf Loos, that was never built. Rotation, shifts, high-contrast lighting and reflection create the illusion of a metropolis of infinite size. In 1986, Minck, Stratil and Groschup, working as a team, were the first of their class to attempt commercial work, making an ad for Tichy-Eis, a company that makes ice cream: "We even won a few awards with that, and we thought, OK, let's ride this success," remembers Groschup. "But none of us, and nobody in the class, was really able to make a living with animation film, that never worked. Many of us are currently

---

16 Mattuschka interview, Graz, March 2010.
17 Artist and theoretician Peter Weibel heads the Department for Media Art at Vienna's Academy of Applied Arts since 1984.
18 Mattuschka interview, Graz, March 2010.
19 "Our regular performances were a kind of outlet. I appeared at the discotheque U4 with an armband worn by blind people… I wanted something to counteract this constant pressure from Maria Lassnig. At every party we had performances, operas in banana costumes we made ourselves. In addition to classic painting we put on lots of art Actions. Lassnig found it all amusing, she had a generous way of looking at things, even if they weren't part of what she had planned. Sometimes there were pretty direct provocations from her students. For the theme 'animal,' Christian Macketanz drew himself fucking a goat." Mattuschka interview, Graz, March 2010.

Martin Anibas
am land
1991

Sabine Groschup
Liebe
1988

Renate Kordon
Malerinnen
1984/2008

Bady Minck
Attwengerfilm
1995

Stefan Stratil
I'm a Star
2002

Thomas Renoldner
Lonely Cowboy
1992

Nana Swiczinsky
WIEDER HOLUNG
1997

Nana Swiczinsky
Lezzieflick
2008

Bady Minck,
Stefan Stratil
Der Mensch mit den modernen Nerven
1988

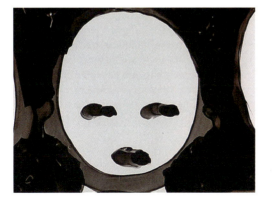

Sabine Groschup
Gugug
2006

teaching."[20] Among other things Stratil later made music videos for the German pop band Der Plan. Minck's trailer for the Austrian distributor Polyfilm, produced in 1994, is still shown before all screenings of the company's films, probably making it the most frequently seen Austrian animation film of all time. "Actually, everybody who began by doing animation film still is,"[21] said Groschup when talking about her former fellow students. For example, the board of the Austrian chapter the international animation society ASIFA (Association internationale du film d'animation), consists exclusively of Lassnig pupils.[22]

The works of Thomas Steiner, a native of Linz, such as *Camping Cézanne* (2010) and *TAU II* (2006) continue the tradition of Lassnig's *Art Education* (1976) when he sets classical paintings in motion. In 2005, Harald Hund was invited to show *All People is Plastic*, a pessimistic vision of the future consisting of complex animation (produced by Paul Horn), at the most important short-film festivals in the world. Mara Mattuschka, who combines performance, live action film and various animation techniques, created a new sub-genre with her surrealistic works, now 45 in number, which have impudent titles such as *Unternehmen Arschmaschine* (*Project Arse Machine*, 1997). Her sub-genre has always been elastic, in tune with the motto of her teacher, Maria Lassnig: " Forget your style. Use a different one each week!"[23] Mattuschka's latest works, created in collaboration with Viennese choreographer Chris Haring, occupy the boundary between performance and dance. Members of Haring's Liquid Loft theater group bow to the camera as it assumes unusual angles. And Mattuschka frequently intervenes at the digital editing bench by speeding up or slowing down action. Even more than in her earlier films, she

successfully synthesizes painterly and filmic approaches in her work, *Burning Palace* (2009). Shot inside an old hotel, Mattuschka plays with odd angles and depths of field, the temperature of the rooms' colors and surreal poses of the dancers, who move with seemingly superhuman elasticity. Surrounded by dark-red velvet wallpaper and soft shades of gold, they resemble something by Vermeer, the only painter from whom, as Lassnig once told her class, they could learn anything.

"Professors can make their students famous," sings Lassnig in the 1992 self-ironic look back at her life, *The Ballad of Maria Lassnig*, the last animation film she has made to date. In fact, some of her pupils have far surpassed their former professor in terms of fame in the film sector. But this was not especially difficult to accomplish since it has only been in the past few years that Lassnig was rediscovered as a filmmaker. Her 10 short films have now been transferred and copied onto more stable media, and new 16 mm prints have been struck for use at festivals and museums, plus a DVD of all her works was released in 2009.[24] When seen together, Lassnig's works seem strangely inhomogeneous, as if she were constantly experimenting with new techniques, making sketches, examining how her experiments worked, as with masking and multiple exposures or stencils, and once she got it, moved on. But if one takes a closer look at the pumping bodies of various types of seats in *Chairs* (1971) one will immediately recognize them to be ancestors of the dancing objects in Bady Minck's Polyfilm trailer. And on closer examination of Mara Mattuschka's (film) bodies, distorted through the use of extreme lenses and video filters, they reveal themselves to be descendants of the strangely shaped emotion creatures in Lassnig's *Couples*. While one could say that the works of Lassnig the filmmaker represent nothing more than the sketchbooks of Lassnig the painter, these sketches contain the seed from which an entire crop of Austrian animation filmmakers has grown.

Translated by Steve Wilder

20 Groschup interview, Vienna, May 2010.
21 Groschup interview.
22 Stefan Stratil: chairman; Renate Kordon: deputy chairman; Sabine Groschup: treasurer; Thomas Renoldner: secretary; Daniel Suljic: deputy secretary; Nana Swiczinsky, Thomas Renoldner: studio/technology, as of 2011.
23 Quote from *Maria Lassnig, Gemalte Gefühle*, TV-portrait for the art magazine *Kunst-Stücke*, produced by Andrea Schurian, 1994.

24 All of Maria Lassnig's films were released on Index DVD Edition 033, *Maria Lassnig, Animation Films*.

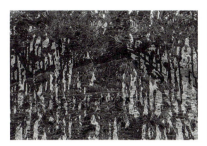

Thomas Steiner
Camping Cézanne
2010

Thomas Steiner
TAU II
2006

Harald Hund
All People is Plastic
2005

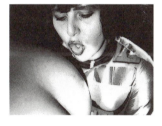

Mara Mattuschka,
Gabriele Szekatsch
Unternehmen Arschmaschine
1997

Mara Mattuschka,
Chris Haring
Burning Palace
2009

Maria Lassnig
Chairs
1971

Maria Lassnig
Art Education
1976

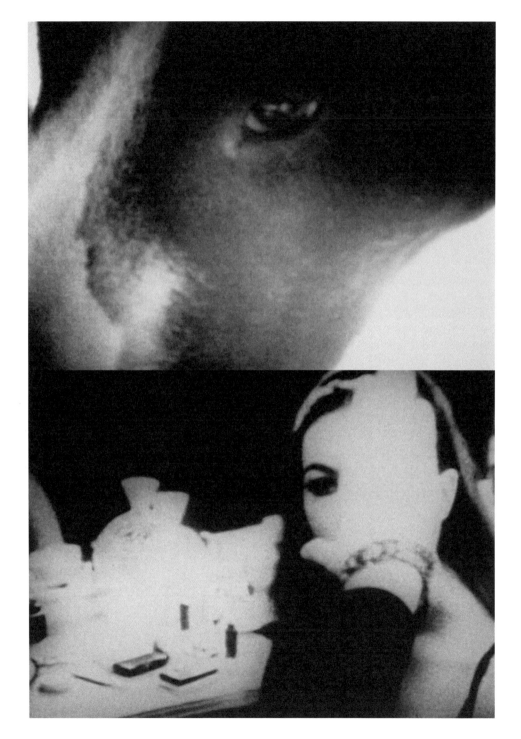

The Garden of Earthly Delights.
On the Films of Dietmar Brehm.

Bert Rebhandl

Dietmar Brehm's extremely prolific body of films reaches back to the year 1974. Repeatedly, Brehm returns to previous concerns whereby new versions of older films are generated and through refilming and reprocessing, entire series of films are placed into a larger context. I will not attempt to do justice to the historical evolution of this work, but instead limit myself to describing a few films of central importance, and, essentially, use them as examples in a discussion of three questions.

1) How do Dietmar Brehm's avant-garde films compare to narrative cinema, or in simpler terms: How narrative are they?

2) To what extent do these films represent medial analogies to psychological or organic processes and forms of logic?

3) Is there a place in the history of cinema for Brehm's project, assuming it can be described as such in light of the first two questions?

Brehm himself defined the *Schwarzer Garten* cycle (*Black Garden*)[1] as a type of central inventory of his work, in which crucial notions appear (mystery, Blicklust [a term Brehm coined, similar to scopophilia], and organics), and in which he condenses corresponding elements from various

phases of his work. As these six films are readily available, I will use them as primary subject matter for observation. They should also be regarded as embodying Brehm's aesthetic program, as they contain the greatest possible density of his most important methods. They also develop, in a quite ambivalently attractive way, a figurative inventory of his films. The quintessential Brehm film could be imagined as a constellation of elements derived from far-flung parts of *Schwarzer Garten*: raw material consisting of images from old films, many of them pornographic, frequently chopped up and assembled into sequences in which the narrative context is lost and everything complements the intensity of the scene being shown (coitus, a woman in sexual bondage, a close-up of genitals, an erotic pose). Through processes of rephotography Brehm further heightens this intensity, filmically penetrating the footage and thereby distancing and objectifying the material. These images are often joined by others showing everyday, banal scenes and activities that connect in a variety of ways with the highly charged scenes, though none that could be put into simple words. In almost all instances the soundtrack leads a life of its own – it is what truly makes Brehm's films a complete auratic experience, in which the sound of a storm or even flowing water can take on an "erotic" quality similar to that of the image of a vulva emerging from the film material's grain.

---

1   The cycle *Black Garden* consists of six films: *The Murder Mystery* (1987/1992), *Blicklust* (1992), *Party* (1995), *Macumba* (1995), *Korridor* (1997) and *Organics* (1998/1999). Available on Index DVD Edition 016: *Dietmar Brehm, Black Garden.*

1   Narrativity

The question of the narrative character of Brehm's films has specific significance in two different respects. It is relevant in light of a general tendency of avant-garde film to turn away from commercial cinematic forms, not least in its unwillingness to stick to basic narrative patterns. In addition, there is also Brehm's trademark, his frequent use of pornographic material. He hereby relates to a special case of cinematic narration, namely to a rigidly codified sequence of sexual acts with a minimum of narrative context, that instead follows a principle of repetition and leads to a physical and mimetic resolution (ejaculation, "cum shot") – but not in a dramatic sense that would be tied to the conventions of narrative cinema. Pornography is based on a protocol, while classic narrative film is derived from the creation of a subject and his or her experiences and crises.

The first film in *Schwarzer Garten* is entitled *The Murder Mystery* (1987/1992). The fact that this title was chosen is a significant indicator, in light of the viewing method that would be developed for it. While this title is a genre label, it is employed in this instance for a specific 16-minute film subsumed, on the one hand, under the genre as a result. On the other hand it serves as a kind of virulent question concerning content throughout viewing. While a murder must always be solved, it must be committed first. *The Murder Mystery* indeed contains a scene in which divers remove a corpse from a body of water, but this moment is relatively inconspicuous compared to the visual motifs comprising the lion's share of the film: close-ups of women's genitals from pornographic movies, other images from this genre and intermittently repeating countershots of the filmmaker (blurry but easily identifiable due to his trademark sunglasses).

The most perplexing image is the recurring shot of an Asian man with no apparent connection to the other images. A pulsating mass of red structures *The Murder Mystery*, and it seems to explode at the film's conclusion. The soundtrack fails to provide an answer to the visual riddles presented. As in other films by Brehm, the mood before a storm dominates a world outside events that seem to be taking place in a separate, secret area. In *Blicklust* [Lust of Looking] (1992) an image of a naked woman appears; her hands and feet are tied, her back is to the camera. She stands there, erotically bound to a scaffolding with arms and legs spread, as if waiting for something to happen. She is the closest we get to the resemblance of a narrative subject. Conventional expectations established by commercial film would have us wondering what will happen to her – who will approach her, help her, untie her? Brehm repeatedly contrasts these images with scenes of an operation showing a lower arm being cut open, followed by numerous splayed bodily orifices with medical devices and other objects inserted into them. The visual analogy of the surgical wound to the female vulva is obvious, and at the same time the relationship between the images of the woman's tied-up body and the gaping flesh is such that the one cannot "replace" the other. Brehm holds his film's narrative tendency in check by consciously creating a numb area of association.

It would be natural to attribute a narrative strategy to Brehm's work resembling that of dreams, whereby elements are selected from material provided by consciousness and – according to principles described by Sigmund Freud – structured into open-ended texts. But the syntax of Brehm's films falls considerably behind the logic of both waking and dream narrative. It is determined by acts of display whereby individual elements are isolated from the flow of action, and, in a sense, endowed with meaning – such as the tree in *Korridor* (*Corridor*, 1997), the snake in *Macumba* (1995), and the Zorro mask in *Organics* (1998/1999). The image gains the character of a fetish in a game in which the filmmaker privileges emphasis over connections. While Brehm occasionally allows himself to be led by narrative subtexts (most obvious in *Macumba*), his films' logic is one of repetition, produced through the obsessive allocation of meaning to details. The narrative is potentially there, but it never gets underway, as its constitutive elements are all too strong to be linked. For this reason they coexist and, with the sovereignty of fetishes, reject all attempts at integration.

Dietmar Brehm
The Murder Mystery
1987/1992

2   Mediality

Brehm works on and with films, found footage and his own, old and new. His works interweave the materiality and content of films. He himself coined the term "pumping screen" to describe the throbbing effect rendered by his labor intensive process of refilming footage, thereby bringing images to light that then instantly disappear. The analogy to the basic cinematographic principle of *fort/da* involving the exposed frame and intervening frameworth of darkness is obvious and reveals a countermovement to the exhibitory effect of Brehm's shots. Pumping renders a continual withdrawal of the object, which is in fact the subject of the image. Conceiving an alternative formulation, Christa Blümlinger writes, "In the blinking of the 'flickering,' the unity of filmic withdrawal is so to speak condensed: Rather than after a shot or a scene, the bodies briefly disappear repeatedly within a single scene."[2] In addition, Brehm employs other means of effecting disappearance, for example masks that cover parts of the image. Such is the case with the

African-American couple in *Macumba*, who represent a kind of narrative core in *Schwarzer Garten*. But nothing can emerge from this core because the dispositif withdrawal inscribed in the filmic material repeats on the level of framing and syntax.

One could maintain that Brehm, like few other avant-garde filmmakers, most elementally couples two potentialities unique to cinema in a non-abstract manner (as did Peter Kubelka in 1960 with *Arnulf Rainer*): the highlighting of brightness and the disappearance into the void of darkness. Blümlinger considers this process melancholic and allegorical, that it leads to an "ambivalent pandemonium of filmically 'shape-shifting mummies' comprised of 'found' material." At the same time, however, she takes into account the fact that pumping always represents a "mortifying process of assimilation."[3] I would continue by saying that it represents a kind of displacement compared to recognition of the image as a medium of profilmic reality. Brehm repudiates this mediality by intensifying it. He works on the image as if it were an organism, though instead of advancing to a substance, he repeatedly discovers new layers of the reference's withdrawal – what the image

---

2   Christa Blümlinger, *Kino aus zweiter Hand. Zur Ästhetik materieller Aneignung im Film und in der Medienkunst* (Berlin: Vorwerk 8, 2009), p. 125. For a brief technical description of Brehm's "pumping screen" see Peter Tscherkassky's text "Ground Survey" in this book, p. 31.

---

3   Blümlinger, p. 132.

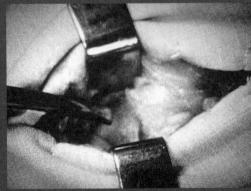

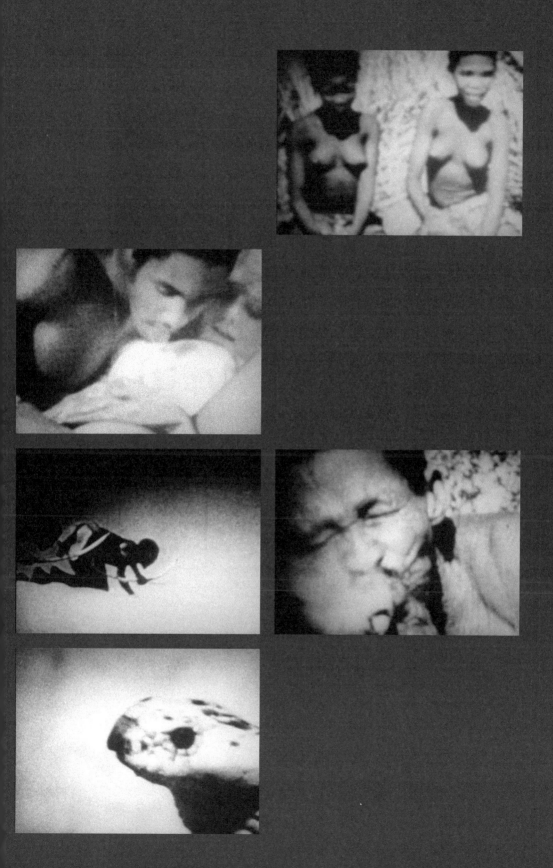

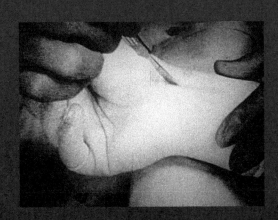

related to at one time disappears in the process of penetration. An analogy can be found in the many images of surgical procedures during which skin is opened, flesh is sliced apart and openings are created, though nothing is found inside other than more tissue, more fissures, more material.

On an organic level this corresponds to the futile attempt to find something resembling a solid position or an Archimedean point in the unconscious. The processes of consciousness involving desire, cathexis and rejection play out on a basic level where the affect and the somatic unite, and become unattainable. The mediality of Brehm's films can be recognized as a material analogy to substance ontologies of Western tradition – which when conveyed by means of the invention of cinematography disintegrate in a wholly concrete way. At the same time, these substance ontologies are returned to their rightful place, not as totalizing concepts, but as detail shots, as fetish particles of their essential nature. An equally ironic and contingent instance of this can be seen in Brehm's "pumping" of Linz's cathedral, a neo-Gothic stone monument created by a religion based on physical and spiritual resurrection. This was undertaken not for the purpose of criticizing religion, but because the building is just around the corner from his apartment – thereby belonging to the external world that occasionally intrudes into his laboratory, and which he assimilated into the material of his experiments, as if he himself were the medium of this material.

3   Historicity

Writing a history of avant-garde or experimental film is a difficult task. Many projects are too distinctive for easy inclusion in a linear or systematic narration of development and regression, expansion or innovation. Moreover, as avant-garde film has repeatedly regarded itself as a critical inscription in the systems of commercial cinema, its timelines and evolutions must also be considered. Thus, the history of avant-gardes often becomes a story of absolute beginnings and end points at which certain gestures culminate in a "last" or final treatment of a certain body of material. It is clear from the above descriptions of Dietmar Brehm's project that he has no interest in such forms of logic.

His work contains neither consistently abstracting gestures nor more explicit moments of a conceptual recapitulation of work already performed on cinema's corpus (even his references to Andy Warhol's pre-narrative exhibitionistic films remain preconceptual). When seeking to locate his project in (film) history, one has to consider a number of factors that are not easily unified. On the technical level of filmmaking, Brehm certainly belongs to an era characterized by small-gauge formats currently becoming extinct, such as Super 8 and 16 mm; refilming footage from a screen and filmically altering material are important methods belonging to the pre-digital era, which Brehm has in no way abandoned, instead integrating them into his work

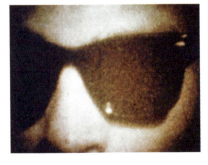 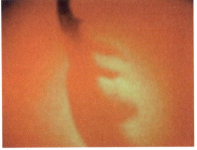

Dietmar Brehm
The Murder Mystery
1987/1992

 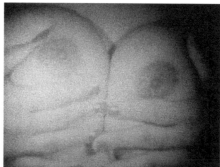

Dietmar Brehm
Party
1995

processes. On the level of characteristic motifs, rather than focusing on commercial cinema for his system of references he expressly chose a number of cinematographic subsystems that are closely associated with the primary representational character of chemically based, analog motion pictures: scientific film in the broadest sense (medical, anthropological, nature, etc.); pornography; and in terms of narrative cinema, a preference for the 1960s and 1970s can be seen, though this could just as well reflect the fact that a wealth of material from this period is still available.

A film like *Macumba* provides a prime example of the combination of all these elements and is at the same time one of Brehm's few works that contain fairly specific historical indices. An African-American couple appears several times in a context that would seem to indicate integration into Western life. The boarding of a bus is an extremely charged act in light of the civil rights movement in the US. But Brehm counteracts this scene by intercutting an offensive image showing a sexual act that involves a white woman. In *Macumba* the relatively clear reference to 20th century history conceals, an even bigger story that intimates relevance to natural history, though not in terms of

a quasi-Darwinist perspective on the filmmaker's part. Instead, it must be seen as resulting from the simultaneous presence of a variety of material: The film images eliminate the historical distance between the bushman smoking his pipe (linked via associative montage to a snake and a man's genitals) and the African-American couple in a living room. These figures are thus made contemporaries on another level, which in fact marks the historicity of Brehm's films: They belong to an era of cinematographic post-history in which what was an imprint of time becomes material.

In Brehm's case the reference is irretrievably lost, its traces merely confirm its complete withdrawal. The *Schwarzer Garten* cycle allows for the concretization of Blümlinger's suspicion concerning the principally allegorical and melancholic character of this work. It is an allegory that presents the end of historicity, instigated by cinema as a pumping medium of universal synchronicity (and its constant withdrawal). *Schwarzer Garten* is a garden of earthly delights, a timeless paradise, a purgatory without a destination.

Translated by Steve Wilder

Lisl Ponger's Cinema.
The Lessons of Ignorance.

Jonathan Rosenbaum

The lessons that can be learned from Lisl Ponger's cinema take many forms, but perhaps one could claim that most of them are separate versions of the same lesson about becoming conscious of our own ignorance. This is already apparent in the most elementary way in the earliest Ponger film I've seen: _Film – An Exercise in Illusion 1_ (1980) is a travelogue in which any precise sense of what is traveling or moving becomes ambiguous: Is it the camera? the camera's aperture? the scenery? More specifically, if the essence of film in general and film illusion in particular is motion, these three silent minutes of Super 8 film shot from a moving boat in Venice – or maybe it's one shot and/or filmed from several moving boats – feature movement within the apparatus of the camera as well as outside it, registering extreme changes in light. Which is another way of saying that we don't really know what we're watching even if it's the nature of film illusion to persuade us that we think we know, conning us into superimposing some touristic narrative upon whatever it is that we're seeing.

This lesson becomes more intricate and is made far more explicit three years later, in Ponger's _Film – An Exercise in Illusion 2_ (1983). This time the camera seems to be located at the front of a moving train. Our sense of the passing scenery is complicated by a rainbow arcing in the upper left portion of the frame. But then a hand very quickly enters at the upper right – so quickly it shatters the illusion of a continuous take – and removes a transparent sheet in front of the camera that had superimposed the rainbow. Changes in light then cause the picture to bleach out, followed by a shift to a blurry image that now appears to be moving in reverse. Is it the film that's running backward, or the train? Is any part of the footage being repeated? Then a clear "window" appears successively in various portions of the blurred image, further confusing our overall sense of the frame as a window in its own right. And at the end, a left pan across a scenic vista arrives at what appears to be a "real" rainbow. But what do we mean at this point by "real"? This is the question most of Ponger's films ask – in one way or another, and at one point or another – even though any resemblance to an academic exercise as demonstrated in _Film – An Exercise in Illusion 1_ and _2_ is largely left behind. The answer to the question typically turns out to be that we don't know. One could argue, of course that it's the business of most artists to expose our ignorance – at least indirectly – by exposing us to things that we don't already know. Getting us acquainted with the fact of our own ignorance is often the first, necessary step in this process.

By the time we arrive at _Passages_ (1996), a decade later, Ponger's methods for structuring the delayed recognition of our ignorance have become far more elaborate and taken on a good deal more

Lisl Ponger
Film – An Exercise in Illusion 1
1980

ideological weight. From the outset of the film we hear the voices of people recounting details of their travels while we see various touristic images that momentarily seem to match these accounts, but much more often contradict or collide with them. Very gradually, we come to realize that amateur travel films have in fact been combined with the oral history of refugees and displaced persons to create a disquieting unity that spooks the supposed innocence of leisurely travel while indicating troubled personal histories as well as perturbing the cosy pleasure of home movies. This evokes a lesson imparted by William S. Burroughs in the final section of *The Ticket That Exploded* (1968), in a chapter entitled "the invisible generation":

"what we see is determined to a large extent by what we hear you can verify this proposition by a simple experiment turn off the sound track on your television set and substitute an arbitrary sound track prerecorded on your tape recorder street sounds music conversation recordings of other television programs you will find that the arbitrary sound track seems to be appropriate and is in fact determining your interpretation of the film track on screen people running for a bus in Piccadilly with a sound track of machine-gun fire looks like 1917 petrograde you can extend the experiment by using recorded material more or less appropriate to the film track for example take a political speech on television shut off sound track and substitute another speech you have prerecorded hardly tell the difference isn't much record sound track of one danger man from uncle spy program run it in place of another and see if your friends can't tell the difference it's all done with tape recorders consider this machine and what it can do..."[1]

When I first started teaching film thirty-three years ago, I terminally alienated some of my students during a lecture course on film aesthetics with the following lesson in materialism. I showed them Luis Buñuel and Salvador Dalí's silent film *Un Chien andalou* (1929) several times, each time with a radically different musical accompaniment. Then I asked them on a quiz whether the statement, "The use of different kinds of music to accompany a silent film changes the film profoundly," was true or false. Afterwards I explained that such a statement could only be false because the film remained the same regardless of whatever music accompanied it: The music changed only the way we looked at and "read" the film, not the film itself. I'm not recommending this as a teaching method, especially if you want your contract renewed (mine

---

1   William S. Burroughs, *The Ticket That Exploded* (London: Corgi Books, 1968) p. 181.

Lisl Ponger
Passagen
1996

wasn't), but I'm bringing it up to illustrate the degree to which a certain amount of mystification about the relationship between image and sound is firmly entrenched in the way we routinely think about and experience film.

As a way of demonstrating how the ear leads the eye and vice versa, Michel Chion usefully begins his book *Audio-Vision*[2] with two modest proposals: Analyze the opening non-narrative sequence of Ingmar Bergman's *Persona* (1966) with and without the sound, and analyze a characteristically naturalistic beach sequence from Jacques Tati's *Les Vacances de Monsieur Hulot* (1953), with and without the image. Chion observes that in the soundless first case, not only does the opening sequence of *Persona* lose its rhythm, its unity and its meaning – it also looks different: A "shot" of a nail driven into a hand becomes three separate shots, and a narrative exposition of bodies in a morgue, minus the sound of dripping water, becomes a disconnected series of stills without reference to either space or time. In the second case, the apparent boredom, discomfort and inertia of vacationers witnessed on a beach are transformed into the sound of lively children enjoying themselves without the image to "mislead" us.

What Burroughs and Chion are both getting at in different ways is our mental reflex to normalize and smooth over discontinuities between sound and image, yielding what Ponger indicates as film

"illusion," even before she incorporated sound into her films. Each of these exercises demonstrates that what we see or don't see is largely determined by what we hear or don't hear, and sometimes vice versa. We might even call it our propensity for converting films into "movies," seamless blocks of narrative continuity, regardless of whether or not the separate materials actually belong together in a mutually reinforcing relationship. This is only the first step Ponger sets up in *Passages*, of an overall process of displacement and dislocation that our brain typically seeks to "correct" by forging a more homogeneous block of time, space and experience – an expedient illusion that serves our ideological assumptions about both the luxury of tourism and the horrors of involuntary exile, by keeping them comfortably separate – at least until Ponger obliges us to recognize that we're conning ourselves into believing we're seeing and hearing the accounts of tourists instead of people forced to flee their homes and countries. And this recognition is brought about in such a way that it creeps up on us very slowly, in fits and starts of which we cannot be sure. Ponger exercises an intricate care in editing images and sound to build a cohesive and relatively peaceful atmosphere while creating pressure points of deeply troubling and poignant subtexts. In a certain sense we ourselves become dislocated and our cognitive insecurity speaks to the uprooted predicament intimated by voices in the film.

The seductiveness of such filmic sound/image strategies shouldn't lead us to divorce Ponger's films either from her still photography or from some

2   Michel Chion, *Audio-Vision: Sound on Screen*, trans. and ed. Claudia Gorbman (New York: Columbia University Press, 1994), pp. 3–4.

Lisl Ponger
Imago Mundi – Das Gültige, Sagbare und Machbare verändern
2007

of her other relevant activities, such as selling second-hand clothes at Vienna's flea market (a market she reportedly helped establish in the 1970s). For instance, the ironic, self-implicating incorporation of herself in some of her so-called "travel" photographs (e.g., *Gone Native*, *Out of Austria*, *The Big Game*, and *Lucky Us*, all from 2000, and *From the Wonderhouse*, two years later). These should be seen in contrast to her less exhibitionistic and more incidental appearance as part of a study group in her 2007 film *Imago Mundi – Das Gültige, Sagbare und Machbare verändern* (*Imago Mundi – Challenging what is accepted*). Arguably one might also trace aspects of a flea-market orientation in her use of *bricolage*, her penchant for recycling certain objects and materials in different works, e.g., the way in which the photographic display in her book *Fremdes Wien*[3] in 1993 becomes reconfigured in her 2004 film *Phantom Fremdes Wien* (*Phantom Foreign Vienna*), or the way in which her 2005 photograph *Destroy Capitalism* appears to be an offshoot of her subsequent 2007 film *Imago Mundi*.

Insofar as it's also the business of criticism to teach us things we don't already know – or else to teach us things that we *do* already know, even if we don't realize that we do – it could be argued that art and criticism are fundamentally concerned with the same agenda. But unfortunately it's the usual pretense of critics, whether they're journalists or academics, to impart knowledge of some kind and

not to expose their own ignorance. And it's at this point that criticism and art, far from offering two separate versions of the same exploration, often wind up diverging, because the standard etiquette of criticism is to disavow positions of ignorance, not own up to them.

Furthermore, distinctions should be made between the kind of ignorance revealed to me by Ponger and the kind revealed to me by critics writing about her films. In *Souvenirs* (1982), when she cuts to create a kind of rhyme effect between the color shot of a Nazi officer briefly hopping and a black-and-white shot of a touristic photographer stooping down in a park to take a photo, she is playing with various kinds of absent knowledge – including (especially) the fact that the apparent Nazi officers are, as later revealed, only extras in a film shoot, and the fact that we don't know exactly what the photographer in the park is photographing. On the other hand, if I point out that *Souvenirs* begins with the camera moving around the exterior of a pre-Columbian temple, I can only make this claim because a catalogue description I read explained to me that this is a pre-Columbian temple – otherwise I wouldn't have known (assuming that this identification is correct). The first kind of ignorance is far more pertinent to Ponger's project than the second.

Also, it would be a serious mistake to assume that all of Ponger's films can be identified by their utilization of the viewer's ignorance – even though this overall strategy reaches a certain apotheosis in her 23-minute *déjà-vu* (1999), and the issue of

3   Lisl Ponger, *Fremdes Wien* (Klagenfurt: Wieser Verlag, 1993).

ideological innocence remains pivotal in the works that follow. But another climax is reached three years later in her 37-minute *Imago Mundi – challenging what is accepted* (2007), her longest film to date. Here the strategies she uses more closely approach the challenging ways Jean-Luc Godard confronted his viewers in the 1960s with various forms of cultural history and ways of articulating that history in political and spatial terms. This is above all true in *La Chinoise* (1967) and *La Gai Savoir* (1969), which also employed young performers at work and at leisure in claustrophobic surroundings (including a mutable studio space in the latter film), but also in *Week End* (1967) and *1+1* (1968) – better known under the title of its unauthorized version, *Sympathy for the Devil*. The rougher "underground" techniques and methodologies of Ponger's earlier work are supplanted by the conditions of industrial filmmaking, including such screen credits as "makeup," "costume," "production manager" and even "catering" – not to mention the employment of cinematographer Caroline Champetier, whose other credits include several Godard films, and other works by such filmmakers as Jean Eustache, Philippe Garrel, Jacques Rivette and the team of Jean-Marie Straub and Danièle Huillet, all of whom straddle the usual divisions of industrial and experimental filmmaking. And, as with all these French-language filmmakers, extensive use of citation or allusion are prominent:

In this case including Spanish Baroque painter Antonio de Pereda's canvas *The Knight's Dream* (from the mid-17th century – a still-life imitated and "updated" in the film); a scene from Georg Büchner's unfinished play *Woyzeck* (1836–1837), performed twice in succession; a passage read aloud from Dimitré Dinev's contemporary novel *Engelszungen*; and a closing printed quotation from a contemporary collection by bell hooks. Superficially, one might say that *Imago Mundi* collapses time and history in much the same way that the earlier *Phantom Foreign Vienna* collapses space and geography, although in fact space-time and geography-history are creatively collapsed as well as expanded in both films. And in both cases, our ignorance as well as the means by which our limited knowledge is constructed becomes an integral part of Ponger's subject.

But an actual manipulation of the viewer's ignorance and innocence in *déjà-vu* is central to what this film is about and how it functions. To clarify precisely what the viewer is ignorant and innocent about, it would be helpful to quote a knowledgeable critic, Tim Sharp: "There are eleven native languages in *déjà-vu*, each reflecting a distinctive way of thinking and the cultural assumptions of those who speak them. Viewed historically, some of those languages (English, French, German, Portuguese) represent major export items – spreading the word with missionary

Lisl Ponger
Phantom Fremdes Wien
2004

zeal in the interest of the politics of power, economic efficiency and cultural presumption. In this post-colonial era we are still only half aware of the hierarchies which language creates. It is also worth considering the physical environment in which one watches the film. We are (willing) prisoners captured by flickering images. The soundtrack, however, turns us temporarily into colonial subjects. Fixed firmly in your seat you can escape neither the desire to understand, nor the improbability of having mastered eleven languages. This linguistic helplessness, coupled with possible annoyance or frustration, creates an emotional counterpoint to the seductive nature of the images and reproduces on a small scale the feelings of puzzlement and powerlessness which is the daily fare of the colonized."[4]

One of the most impressive achievements of *Phantom Foreign Vienna* – for me, Ponger's masterpiece – is the way it combines the formal concerns of her earliest works with the postcolonial interrogations of such works as *Souvenirs* and *déjà-vu*. To indicate the material being worked with, we should turn again to the discourse of a knowledgeable critic – in this case a Brigitte Huck essay: "On a world journey through Vienna [Ponger] filmed over seventy different cultures and nations. She was present at a Philippine church service in the second district, at a New Year's festival in a Sikh temple. She discovers Sudan and Ghana in the fourth district, and the Togolese living in the sixth. Vietnamese weddings; Taiwanese dance events; the Succoth festival at Beth Chabat, the Jewish school; the Swedish festival of light; Polish scouts; Croatian singers; Armenian clerics who commemorate the forty days of the Musa Dagh at Franz Werfel's grave."[5]

This is an abbreviated summary of a compilation that can be described as genuinely global, even if the film paradoxically never extends beyond the boundaries of Vienna. And the key issue of how these separate documentations are combined – an

issue that is simultaneously formal and ideological, an issue of *mapping* – is at the heart of the film's activity. Narrating the footage in the separate German and English versions of the film, Ponger foregrounds this question by drawing information and anecdotes from her diary and her memories, recalling the methodology of Chris Marker (while retaining a first-person narration, unlike Marker). At first her ordering is chronological and set by her diary entries, then it becomes geographical (in relation to districts of Vienna rather than the globe – Vienna in this case effectively, that is to say ideologically, *becoming* the globe), afterwards it returns to chronology. Then she signals formally determined transitions, such as cutting from "orange to orange," and, later, "the criteria of light, reflection, shadow," then "the category of music." This process becomes more labyrinthine when the succession of one nationality after another becomes complicated by nationalities within nationalities (e.g., the "Swedish Saint Lucia celebration"). Subsequently, a series of different New Year celebrations (taking place at different times of the year) is followed by a strategy of cutting between separate Turkish weddings held a year apart in which the sound of one wedding is used to accompany the images of another. Finally, and climactically, Ponger announces, "When the background sound, the synchronized sound, and the image match up, the result is a filmic unity, a constructed reality" – in short, an ideology. And immediately afterwards, we're offered images shot at the Peace Pagoda, background sounds taken from a BBC archive and drum beats that were added later.

In fact, what Ponger is both explaining and demonstrating here is that maps of all kinds – meaning all systems of arrangement, including catalogues, exhibitions and compilations – are ideological constructions. Some are voluntary and conscious and others are involuntary and unconscious, but all are profoundly political. And the exploration proposed by Ponger's cinema is ultimately spurred by how little we know about them.

4   Tim Sharp, "Travelling Shots: Notes on the Films of Lisl Ponger," *Austria Kultur*, vol. 11, 1/2001, p. 17.
5   Brigitte Huck, "Lisl Ponger," essay in accompanying booklet to *Lisl Ponger, Travelling Light*, Index DVD Edition 010, p. 10.

Lisl Ponger
déjà-vu
1999

Lisl Ponger
Souvenirs
1982

Lisl Ponger
Phantom Fremdes Wien
2004

Works of Dreams and Shadows.
The Films of Peter Tscherkassky.

Maureen Turim

Dream Work might be an apt title for any and all of Peter Tscherkassky's densely evocative films, but happily he has chosen intriguing individual titles for each, with multilingual puns that open up a host of implications for the viewer. That said, let me begin my examination of Tscherkassky's films with *Dream Work* (2001), the third film in his *CinemaScope Trilogy*. I will then work backwards across the trilogy, before proceeding to newer films as well as mixing in others that preceded them, an achronology that serves my analytical and theoretical desires. It is telling that Tscherkassky named his film *Dream Work* instead of "Traumarbeit." Though from Vienna like Sigmund Freud, he cites his compatriot across a foreign language. "Traumarbeit" is one term recognized by intellectuals the world over, so the question is why? English breaks the compound into two words and estranges "Traumarbeit" for a German speaking audience. "Dream Work" also connects with the productions of US studios or "dream factories." Also "work" can be translated both as "Werk" and "Arbeit," allowing for a pun on the "work of art," which finds its German equivalent in "Kunstwerk."

"A woman goes to bed, falls asleep and begins to dream. This dream takes her to a landscape of light and shadow, evoked in a form only possible through classic cinematography," [1] Tscherkassky

tells us, explaining he intends an analogy to Freud's concepts of displacement (*Verschiebung*) and condensation (*Verdichtung*), the two main mechanisms of dreamwork introduced in *The Interpretation of Dreams*. In this sense Sidney J. Furie's *The Entity* (1982), from which *Dream Work* is derived, might be seen as a parallel to Freud's waking reality from which material is selected and "displaced" in the "dream," or in this case, Tscherkassky's film. Condensation is rendered through contact printing up to seven layers of film from the original movie, precisely isolating and recombining elements from individual frames using a laser pointer, so that every single frame of the new film is an entirely unique coalescence.

Tscherkassky utilizes contact printing as a creative tool for many films, while specifically dedicating *Dream Work* to Man Ray, "who, in 1923 with his famous rayographs in *Le Retour à la raison* was the first artist to use this technique for filmmaking, creating the image by shining light on physical objects placed on the film stock." [2] In this context, consider a passage by art historian Barbara Zabel: "To create *Clock Wheels* (...) Man Ray dismantled a clock, a procedure that may have been inspired by Picabia's anarchistic act of dipping a clock's mechanisms into black ink and imprinting them on paper in *Reveil Matin* (1919).

[1] See notes by Peter Tscherkassky on "Dream Work," available at http://www.tscherkassky.at/content/films/theFilms/DreamWorkEN.html

[2] Ibid.

Man Ray's rayograph presents not only a figure-ground reversal but also a positive-negative reversal in technique. By applying ink to paper via metal objects, Picabia implied their materialization. Man Ray, on the other hand, reversed the process: images of objects appeared because they prevented light rays from hitting the paper. After exposure to light, he removed the objects, and shadowy, white images appeared during the developing. In effect, he dematerialized the mechanical, suggesting only the objects' ghostly absence."[3]

The opposition Zabel finds between Picabia's printing with objects and Man Ray's use of objects as light-shielding shadow capture is perhaps not as strong or as absolute as she suggests. In Tscherkassky's work, by contact printing positive and negative images off the same strip of found footage, he specifically undercuts any neat oppositions between the material and dematerial, achieving a transformation of this opposition into a continuum. He creates shadows of film layers. His images are haunted as other to themselves, as traces that are not dematerialized entirely (they

remain the same in substance, film images), even while they are clearly altered. They display the traces of their transformation. The negative/positive basis of photography central to Tscherkassky's contact printing underlies his alternation of these two versions of the film image, inversions of the values of each other. In juxtaposing, recomposing, layering and alternating positives with negatives, Tscherkassky plays with the space of development and the time of fixing an image; if the negative is the ghost of the positive in our perception, the positive is just as much the ghost of the negative when we produce film images. Tscherkassky seems to love these paradoxes, ghosts that fly by as he creates cinema image by image. This substance of filmic matter stands in sharp contrast to video or digital production in which negative images are rendered in post-production, not involving a direct trace of their creation. Tscherkassky insists on the materiality of the filmic image, its negative and positive double existence. He revels in the materiality of image production unique to his process of filmmaking and fully exploits its elemental qualities.

Dream Work opens with a shade pull swinging in a window, a familiar *film noir* icon and a little like a miniature noose. A gauzy curtain blows in the breeze. Window pull and curtains dance as in other avant-garde works, such as the insistent framings of interior spaces in the films of Barry Gerson. In fact, the curtains here echo those that waft in the second story bedroom window of Maya Deren's bungalow in *Meshes of the Afternoon* (1943). *Dream Work* does not look like found footage, gleaned from a color Hollywood horror movie. Even as *The Entity* originally framed the window, it did not give this window pull the reiterative swagger it gains on re-inscription. Repetition and variation establish new rhythms as the window frames the image flows to follow. As a woman walks across the carpet and slips out of her high heels, we perhaps begin to recognize the footage as found, but we also come upon another Tscherkassky strategy. He taps into dated commercial images of women to unfreeze the moment their sexuality was sold, to reanimate it, to let it reiterate itself, ironically. His film lingers on this low angle shot and the next, as our protagonist

3   Barbara Zabel, *Assembling Art: The Machine and the American Avant-Garde* (Jackson: University Press of Mississippi, 2004), pp. 74–75.

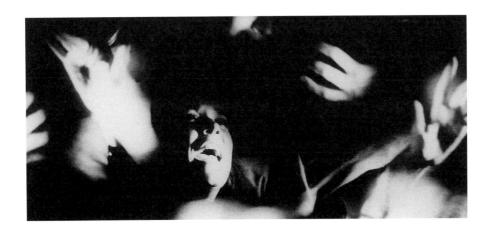

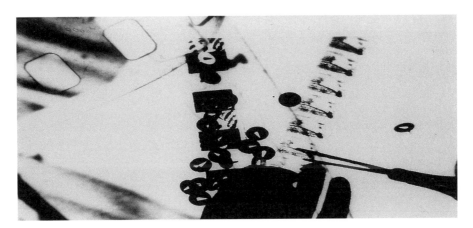

Peter Tscherkassky
Dream Work
2001

line of intelligible dialogue, spoken by *The Entity*'s psychiatrist as he accompanies our protagonist into her home, having shifted from doctor to private investigator. Reframed within the ominous context of her unfolding dream, an unconscious mixture of psychiatrist, investigator and filmmaker iterates this question to the image of a woman whose dream he will invent. Add Alfred Hitchcock and Salvador Dalí to the Deren mix, as Tscherkassky self-consciously combines camp with historical avant-garde, emphasizing by implication the historicity of this interpenetration of filmmaking modes, a cross-fertilization evidenced not only in such pure found footage films as Joseph Cornell's *Rose Hobart* (1936), but also in Jack Smith's *Flaming Creatures* (1963), and Su Friedrich's *Damned if you Don't* (1987), among many others.

The bra being stripped calls forth a rain of tacks – the first direct reference to rayographs – super-imposed over another image we recognize as an allusion to Man Ray, to the nude torso of Kiki as it appears in *Le Retour à la raison*. Pained moans, explosive sounds, a vague noise that recalls muffled meshing gears and yelps further summon a rain of nails and abstracted expressions of light. Sprocket holes twist across the image. Superimpositions, doubling, shadowing, echoing: images occur as reiterations. The movements of our protagonist in space are blurred and overlap, traces of each visual signifier reverberating as a multiplicity, as if the page of Freud's Magic Writing Pad were being lifted to expose wax impressions as the page hovers above and off to the side.

A series of beautiful images of the artist in his "dark room" follows: A light table glows underneath the filmstrips we just saw and still see via super-imposition, as these strips are manipulated by the hands of the filmmaker. Dziga Vertov seems to have been invited to Man Ray's celebration when a scissor cuts the filmstrip, simultaneously setting off the ringing of an alarm clock. Instantly our protagonist awakes, seeming, as she looks up and smiles, to be addressing the filmmaker off-screen. She opens the window shade in staggered slow motion. A coda of multiple exposures ensues, as if the film were still inside the dream after all.

removes her pantyhose to toss them into a hamper. This striptease, incidental and naturalized in *The Entity*, was of course always strategically placed. In Sidney J. Furie's film, vulnerable female sexuality serves as a prelude to alien attacks: horror erotica. Tscherkassky's appropriation emphasizes this sexual come-on as it turns into a prelude to a dream. Later it will echo within the dream, in negative and positive flicker, becoming a poem of high-heel abandonment and our protagonist slipping out of her bra. The striptease will be repeated as dream fragments. A poetics of appropriation raises the question of who the dreamer may be: the dreamer we're watching or the one whose dream was to re-create her.

Soon our protagonist drifts to sleep, shadows flickering across her face accompanied by ticking noises and chiming clocks intercut with abstracted images. Image and sound[4] mesh into what appears to be a kind of sculptural machine, but in fact may be re-worked images of shadows on Venetian blinds. "Would you like to show me where those attacks took place?" is heard as *Dream Work*'s first

4   The soundtrack was created by Iranian composer Kiawasch Saheb-Nassagh, in part using segments of the original optical soundtrack that were contact printed by the filmmaker in the darkroom.

Peter Tscherkassky
Outer Space
1999

Peter Tscherkassky
Outer Space
1999

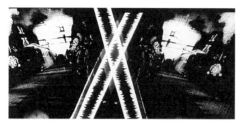

Finally, crystalline grains of salt gradually cover the image, a return to Man Ray as well as an allusion to the sleep the sandman delivers, increasingly obscuring the window that opened *Dream Work* and rendering a handmade fade to black. Condensation and displacement, then of not only the filmstrip, but in a historical sense, of previous gestures of the avant-garde: appreciation fosters the renewal of desire to forge inventive images from old. Of course, the visual/verbal play of the strip (tease) is another poetic pun on the filmstrip.

Stills from *Dream Work* as well as Peter Tscherkassky's other darkroom films are exhibited in galleries as art works in their own right. Two consecutive frames are displayed to highlight the contrast and dynamic exchange between frames, the tensions between representation and abstraction, and the conceptual aesthetics of compositions. Tscherkassky also exhibits filmstrips mounted on lightboxes to illuminate graphic patterns and variations. One is invited to see beyond the frameline and to understand the creative process Tscherkassky employs as accompanying DVD monitors display lightbox excerpts in motion. Ultimately these works are elegant and original pieces of serial photography and creative graphic design, installation art objects that materialize

what passes ephemerally before one's eyes during the films' temporal unfolding. Tscherkassky's DVD *Films From A Dark Room* makes it tempting to stop his rapid image flow in the privacy of one's own home and focus on particular frames to see what is happening "underneath" the projected images, frames that can never be fully absorbed during the film's projection.[5] This possibility transforms the films entirely, for as films they have an aesthetic of the fleeting and the partial, the hidden underneath-and-between-the-frames only passes ephemerally before one's eyes, even if it is crucial to the films' function.

Dream Work's strategies of reshaping provide a link to *Outer Space* (1999), its predecessor in the CinemaScope Trilogy that is also derived from *The Entity*. The film opens outside a house and follows our protagonist as she enters her "private space," where the interiority of subjectivity gives way to a cubist fragmentation of her body under attack and in duress, rendered again via Tscherkassky's contact printing. A storm rips through the interior, shattering windows. The "inner space" of a story traditionally "contained" by the parameters of the film frame is deranged by the "outer space" of Tscherkassky's filmic interventions. The individual frame is made to contain a fugue of story elements while the filmstrip twists and turns, trembles and shakes, sprocket holes and jagged fragments of the optical soundtrack tearing into our protagonist's space that is under attack by the medium of film itself. In addition to the title, aspects of Tscherkassky's image-layering echo Andy Warhol's *Outer and Inner Space* (1965), in which Edie Sedgwick is filmed overlapping with images of herself on video, blending moments and aspects of her self. At the end of the film, Tscherkassky's sense of outer space seems to coincide with all of space beyond the eyes, as spotlighted faces and then eyes alone indicate a bodily entity that defines the outside. In writing on Maya Deren,[6] I have looked at how

5   Index DVD Edition 008: *Peter Tscherkassky, Films From A Dark Room*.
6   Maureen Turim, "The Interiority of Space: Desire and Maya Deren," in *Avant-Garde Film*, eds. Alexander Graf and Dietrich Scheunemann (Amsterdam and New York: Editions Rodopi, 2007).

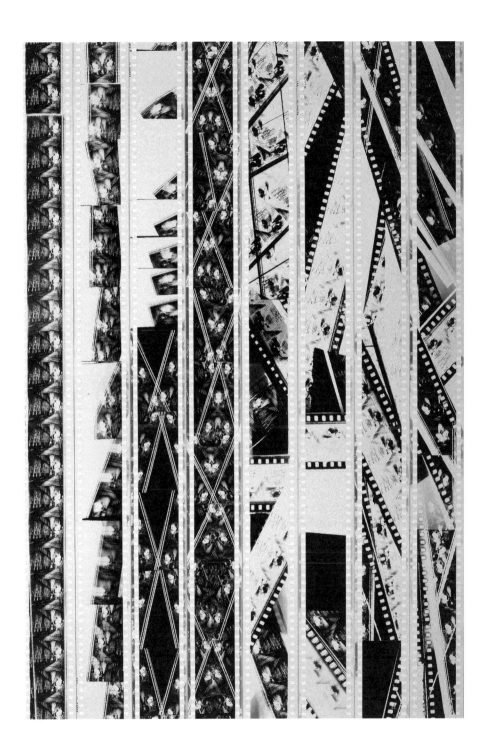

Peter Tscherkassky
L'Arrivée
1997/1998

Peter Tscherkassky
tabula rasa
1987/1989

Peter Tscherkassky
Erotique
1982

space itself is rendered as interiority in her films. *Outer Space* evokes Deren in this sense, just as *Dream Work* did.

As to the opening film of the trilogy, *L'Arrivée* (1997/1998) announces the arrival of film itself: Images of a train arriving at a station echo the Lumière brothers' *L'Arrivée d'un Train à La Ciotat* (1895), shot and shown at the dawn of the medium when it drove audiences to dive under their chairs to avoid full impact, according to legend. Tscherkassky's contact prints the filmstrip of a train's arrival so that it slowly glides across the screen from out of nowhere, visually and aurally conveying a physicality of the medium with a different impact, albeit reminiscent of its forefather. As the image of film within the image of *L'Arrivée* meets and retreats, as the train approaches and the station becomes discernable, we first see the hint of a woman looking out a compartment window. Stepping off the train, she is caught between the

sprocket holes of the film; in my inverted reading of the trilogy I see her as announcing the woman of both *Outer Space* and *Dream Work*. Only by working back across the trilogy do we recognize her first appearance, before she enters the house, before she enters the dream.

The *CinemaScope Trilogy* is a formal invocation of cinema, exploring its history, materiality and relation to dream. These films also center on women as beheld from a self-conscious male perspective, recalling earlier Tscherkassky films such as *Erotique* (1982), *Liebesfilm* (*Film of Love*, 1982) and *tabula rasa* (1987/1989). Tscherkassky sustains the male artist's preoccupation with the female form and suffuses it with a self-consciousness informed by film theory and feminist theory. Already in his early Super 8 films, Tscherkassky explored what happens to a voyeuristic aesthetic when formal elements of film restructure one's relationship as viewer to the image of woman offered to view.[7]

Parallel Space: Inter-View (1992) opens with the reading of a note the filmmaker seems to have left for a friend, and introduces just this sort of self-awareness: "Originally I was going to make a purely structural film, but it turned out to be the most personal I have made." This self-consciousness continues with various forms of writing and inscription, as "Physics of Seeing," and "Physics of Memory" are penned before our eyes, reshot and edited in abstracted multiplicity, superimposed with a photo of a room containing a classical psychoanalytic set-up of furniture, curiously draped. A computer screen scrolls text word by word: "All I remember is: I was looking for you." Granular images of furniture follow, joined by a small frame floating within the big picture. As this frame within the frame enlarges to encompass the frame that once enclosed it, we see that the filmmaker, framed nude in a medium shot, appears to be adjusting his camera as if shooting out at us.

7   See Alexander Horwath, "Singing in the Rain. Supercinematography by Peter Tscherkassky," in *Peter Tscherkassky*, eds. Alexander Horwath and Michael Loebenstein (Vienna: FilmmuseumSynema-Publikationen, 2005), pp. 32–34. Also available at http://www.sensesofcinema.com/2003/28/tscherkassky/

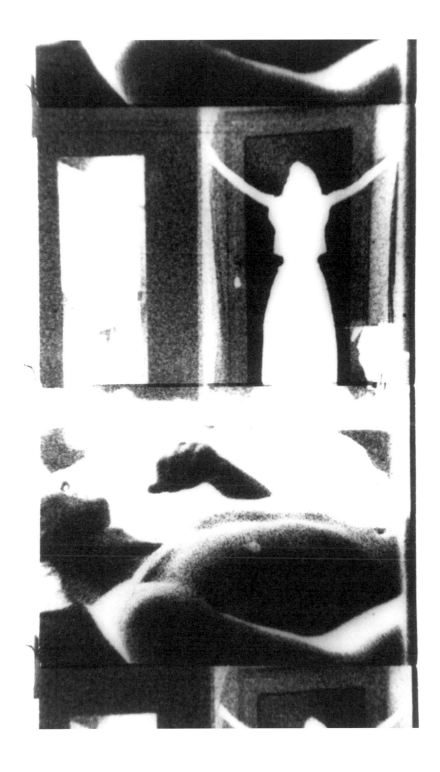

Peter Tscherkassky
Parallel Space: Inter-View
1992

In fact he is moving in on a mirror's reflection until the lens touches its surface.

In title and substance, *Parallel Space: Inter-View* invites the sort of perspective Anne Friedberg entertains in her consideration of windows, frames and screens as devices and metaphors.[8] Her ongoing argument favors multiplicity, pointing to cubism and montage within the shot as welcome alternatives to representational realism. She takes to task the ideological critique of the imaginary entrance provided by perspective, because she sees its premise as an exaggeration of the ability of the apparatus to uniformly contain the viewer. Whether single point or multiple, perspective ceases to be seen as having the power to position the perceiver – it only offers a vantage point that one visits and then leaves, for the next shot, painting or photo, which operates differently. The theoretical connection between Friedberg's writing and *Parallel Space* lies in the film's play with frame and perspective. The film was entirely shot with an analog photo camera. The size of a 35 mm movie image is exactly half the size of a 35 mm photographic image. When a 35 mm photographic filmstrip is projected as film, its images are split in two. The projection resembles a flickering superimposition of parallel spaces that seem to merge, yet remain distinct. In Peter Tscherkassky's film, a photographic instant capturing a coherent space is divided into two dimensions, paralleling the condition of being part of the world, while also being separate from it. Images are further abstracted by the black-and-white

pointillism of the photographic grain. A montage of hands reach out to flesh and faces kiss in the wake of family photos, while philodendron leaves recall Henri Matisse paintings and cut-outs. Abstract fragments and still frames grabbed from the sequence, showing the frightened face of a baby, are stacked one on top of the other. Joined by the image of an older boy, these read as self-portraits. As stills of the computer monitor lyrically return to the scrolling text fragments, "I was" and "for you," a hand writes "looking" on a card before pushing it up and out of the frame and itself disappearing.

This handmade lyrical poem of the self, recollected as trajectory towards the other, finds a parallel in a formal restructuring of found footage at the center of *Parallel Space: Inter-View*. In Elia Kazan's *Wild River* (1960), an emotionally charged scene takes place between a government agent who has come to wrest a house for the Tennessee River Dam project, and his love interest, the granddaughter of a woman who is defending her home. A television provides the interface for the Kazan movie, and the film we have been watching is now interspersed with this "televised" footage that echoes its troubled yearning. The flickering of images is so rapid we sense a complete interpenetration of alternating fragments revealing images hinting at sexuality and desire. At the same time we are preoccupied with the dramatic and somewhat desperate embrace of the fictional couple. Tscherkassky's film traces the relationship of the boy to the man, and the man to the other, as a desire for pairing, for the couple, refracted through media and writing. This is a story of desire: "I was looking for you."[9]

Tscherkassky's reframing targets a purely male world in *Instructions for a Light and Sound Machine* (2005), while further expanding on the nature of the film medium central to each of his films. The reworking of a beat up print of Sergio Leone's CinemaScope classic *The Good, the Bad, and the*

---

8   See Anne Friedberg, *The Virtual Window: From Alberti to Microsoft* (Cambridge: MIT Press, 2006).

9   See also Gabriele Jutz, "The Physics of Seeing. On Peter Tscherkassky's film *Parallel Space: Inter-View*" and Amy Taubin, "Flash Floods. On Peter Tscherkassky's film *Parallel Space: Inter-View*," both available at
http://www.tscherkassky.at/content/txt_ue/ue_text.html

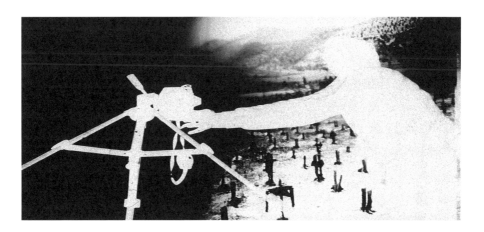

Peter Tscherkassky
Instructions for a Light and Sound Machine
2005

Ugly (1966) juxtaposes concrete signifiers from the Western with an aesthetic of conceptual abstraction until concrete representations are released as a cinematic poem, lyrical on an entirely different register. A standard focus grid lies behind the film's title shot, as the name of the film appears in shaking, hand-etched letters. The grid contains circles at each corner that mark the distinct challenges of getting the edges of the CinemaScope image in focus. The film commences with a reflection on a window that opens to reveal a man wielding a spyglass seen in negative, followed by an iris emulating what the man sees: a rider in the distance. The filmmaker used a circular hole punch to perforate black leader for a matte that renders the telescope's "sight." Its elliptical shape as opposed to the traditional circle expected from a telescope is a witty manifestation of CinemaScopic decompression. Another joke on film syntax follows: Each time a shot alternates with the peering spyglass, the countershot gains an oval until there are several irises at once, each revealing disparate views of horseback riders in the distance. The increasing swarm of iris cut-outs gathering the posse gradually eats up the entire screen, revealing a CinemaScopic desert landscape.

A shot/countershot exchange between the protagonist and his enemies glaring at one another in the barren landscape and sweltering environment of locust sounds heightens the suspense of an imminent showdown. Tscherkassky's film responds by bursting out of its frame, slicing the horizontal and splicing frames into staccato duplications. Gun barrel dynamics in opposing diagonals form a highly original negative/positive weave that serves as homage to both Sergei Eisenstein's *Battleship Potemkin* (1925) and Peter Kubelka's *Adebar* (1957). Machine gun and helicopter sounds perhaps recall the Vietnam War occurring during the making of Sergio Leone's film, and an extreme escalation of US bombing in response to a NLF attack on a US helicopter base. War is evoked by the soundtrack (created by German composer Dirk Schaefer), while Tscherkassky emphasizes the surrealist heritage of the action images as he emphatically reframes the gouging of eyes.

Horizontally constellated gunplay culminates in a deathly ode to rope. Our protagonist hangs in his noose as the strip of film swings back and forth across the screen, till the vertical axis of the film appears to snap in the gate. We live through the death of film as white and silent absence, a suspenseful void before film and image gradually sputter back. Our hero reappears, resurrected in a hovering graveyard that is a haunting image of death looming behind every action. Tscherkassky overlays right and left pans of our protagonist on the run in an inspired play on how camera movement is perceived in relation to the movement of figures, a concern which links Sergio Leone to Akira Kurosawa. Musique concrète-like train sounds, bells and industrial rhythms accompany his desperate flight, opening a paradigm of man versus machine, of the wild versus the industrial landscape. We witness the poetic folding of the outside of the film into its gut as head and tail leader, countdown clocks and random filmstrip calligraphy intercede in the flow of narrative images, including a pair of scissors again openly hungry to accentuate the montage. A bulls-eye focus targeting seconds in a countdown is cleverly alternated with guns taking aim. Ultimately, our protagonist is consumed by the spiraling teeth of the tombstone vortex he cannot escape. The iconography of Leone's already densely poetic and self-conscious film serves in Tscherkassky's cinematic reanimation as a black-and-white reconfiguration offering a new displacement: No longer a story about men in the post-Civil War era, or a Western, it becomes an elegy to male cinematic figuration.

Coming Attractions (2010) takes its name both from the movie industry's advertising mechanism of the trailer and Tom Gunning and André Gaudrault's "Cinema of Attractions," which conceptualizes the emphatic "showing" of itself by early film, its direct connection to the audience, its frontal address of the camera, and bald use of cinematic "tricks." Tscherkassky explains, "At some point it occurred to me that another residue of the 'cinema of attractions' lies within the genre of advertising. Here we also often encounter a uniquely direct relation between actor, camera and audience. The impetus

Peter Tscherkassky
Coming Attractions
2010

for *Coming Attractions* was to bring the three together: commercials, early cinema and avant-garde film."[10]

Instead of being spun from a narrative feature, *Coming Attractions* was made out of rushes from commercials shot in the 1970s and 1980s. This footage represents a cinema of trial and error consisting of long, continuous takes, models repeating gestures and expressions for a few choice seconds in a commercial. The performers' inability to act lends a deeply amateurish atmosphere to the material, perfectly collaborating with the directors' apparent lack of artistic ambition. Tscherkassky reworks the rushes using various contact printing techniques and takes full advantage of long, uninterrupted takes. The result is something between amusing and hilarious, and it is as demonstrative and exhibitionist as early cinema aimed to be. Here, too, cinema displays the fact of itself. But, like all of Tscherkassky's films, this is a meta-filmic endeavor revealing basic cinematic mechanisms.

Coming Attractions opens with a rear-view mirror reflecting the image of a man looking at us, followed by a female model seen in countershot, looking back at him (and us). She indicates the other half of the film frame where segments of what we are about to see are "previewed." The film that follows is divided into eleven individually titled chapters that playfully "look back" at early cinema. Some pay quirky tribute to the magic enabled by motion picture technology through allusions to

films by Georges Méliès: "La Femme à la tête de caoutchouc" tips its hat to *L'Homme à la tête de caoutchouc* (*The Man with the Rubber Head*, 1901) which utilized a zoom and superimpositions to render an expanding head that ultimately explodes. Here instead we see a woman wearing a plastic hair dryer, demonstrating its inflation and deflation mechanism, until it stops working to her dismay. "La Femme orchestre" refers to Méliès *L'Homme orchestre* (*The One Man Band*, 1900) in which the maestro used seven superimpositions to conjure the illusion that he alone is playing all the instruments in an orchestra. Tscherkassky shows the model wearing her inflatable hair dryer bonnet, repeating the senseless gesture of raising and lowering a saxophone, *ad absurdum*, while music intermittently plays.[11] Tscherkassky makes his own material magic in segments that allude to Standish D. Lawder's *Cubist Cinema* that conjoins classical avant-garde film with modernist painting.[12] "Cubbhist Cinema #3: The Path is the Goal (Natura morta with Guitar, Tulips, Pork Roast & My Wife in the Bush of Hosts)" collages motifs common to cubist painting as a woman repeatedly runs across a meadow, seemingly without any goal she can attain. "Cubist Cinema #2: Rough Sea at Nowhere" is a kinetic contact-printed collage of rushes showing a carbonated water maker at work. Multiple layers of wave-shaped cut-outs reveal water spraying in many directions, resulting in a cubist miniature that stands in charming contrast to the

---

10 Peter Tscherkassky, "*Coming Attractions* – Notes by the director," available at http://www.tscherkassky.at/content/films/theFilms/ComingAttractionsEN.html

11 Soundtrack again composed by Dirk Schaefer.
12 Standish D. Lawder, *Cubist Cinema* (New York: New York University Press, 1975).

Peter Tscherkassky
Coming Attractions
2010

Peter Tscherkassky
Coming Attractions
2010

ocean of its documentary antecedent, _Rough Sea at Dover_ (1895, by Birt Acres and Robert W. Paul).

Coming Attractions also pays tribute to famous films of the historical avant-garde. "Ballet monotonique" plays on Fernand Léger's _Ballet mécanique_ (1924). The original avant-garde classic includes the shot of a laundress carrying laundry up a stairway from the Seine, repeated 27 times. Tscherkassky superimposes horizontal lines of a high contrast stairway on rushes of women hanging laundry from a soap detergent commercial, directly addressing the camera and exclaiming, "Yes!" Stroboscopic images render a hallucinatory claustrophobia. Tscherkassky explains that the figures are "caught in a cage built up of stairs, subject to the tedium of their daily routine (and as actresses caught in a prison of repeated takes)."[13] Jean Cocteau's _Le Sang d'un poète_ (1930) resonates in "Le Sang d'un poème," which takes place entirely in negative. A creamy substance is poured into a row of small cups seen in a series of superimpositions that convey a sense of ritual and transfigured time, further charged with erotic tension as a few drops spill, and a woman's hand strokes her long stockinged leg. The medium shot of a man watching is framed by inexplicable diagonals; this may be read as a mirror's reflection, until he walks out of the frame, or perhaps into the mirror, reminiscent also of Jean Cocteau's _Orphée_ (1950). "Deux minutes de cinéma pur" pays homage to a milestone of the

early avant-garde cinema, _Cinq minutes de cinéma pur_ (1926) by Henri Chomette. Tscherkassky montages outcast scraps from rushes without apparent rhyme or reason, but with perfect rhythm. The abandoned remains of what we might call "unintentional cinema" include actors waiting for cameras to roll, set lights being turned off and end slates; cinematically speaking, these shots are pure in the truest sense of the word – they were never meant to be seen – and here they constellate into a perfectly wordless poem.

What does it mean to make _Films From a Dark Room_, as Tscherkassky entitled his DVD anthology? His use of two words for "darkroom" clearly signals he is not simply indicating where he makes his films. It might be useful to recall that the French phrase "chambre noire" means darkroom as well as what we call a "camera obscura" (from Latin), to indicate the photographic apparatus itself. He may, however, also want to connote films made subsequent to photography, through contact printing. However, returning to my opening assertion, even in their highly thought out structural ploys and art-historical inter-textuality, these films are themselves a kind of Traumarbeit, emanating from that dark room we call the unconscious, and they are all the more powerful for that provenance.

---

13 Tscherkassky, "_Coming Attractions_ – Notes by the director."

The Filmic Convulsions of Mara Mattuschka.

Christa Blümlinger

Since the early 1980s, Mara Mattuschka has produced a multimedia art of grotesque poses, satire and reappropriation. This Bulgarian native has transformed the legacy of body art and performance in an entirely original way through the use of animation film techniques. With brilliant humor and combining a variety of acting and staging methods, Mattuschka starred in almost all the films she made in the 1980s and 1990s. She invented a neo-Dada form of referencing for avant-garde film at a time when such strategies were being discussed in the field of photography as a form of feminist reappropriation. The visual intensity of her filmic miniatures is derived from an "exhibitionism transformed into art"[1] and a precise eye for composition in time and space. Mattuschka never dwells excessively on a movement or a pose, and she always maintains a distance to self-promotion through the use of montage, visual contrasts, the artificial nature of animated movement and makeup. Mattuschka's short films in particular evidence a strong sense of rhythm. Birgit Hein fittingly attributes them with a self-contained plasticity through which tension is maintained from beginning to end.[2]

Over the course of three decades Mattuschka has made some 45 films, mostly shorts. A film, performance and visual artist, she studied Painting under Maria Lassnig,[3] the doyenne of Austrian animation film, after studies in Mathematics, Linguistics and Ethnology. In her early work, Mattuschka primarily employed stop-motion to shoot movement broken down into component parts, resulting in a restructured form in time and space upon reanimation. This method not only brings the ironic aspect of her performances to a head, it also gives them an autonomous, profoundly filmic form. The masquerades and poses seem compulsive and convulsive, the movements of her body and the motion of the images resemble the aesthetic of a mechanical doll. Mattuschka's jerky performances as Mimi Minus or Madame Ping Pong are in line with a concept of film seemingly inspired by chronophotographic studies of movement (Étienne-Jules Marey) and the use of close-ups to create pathos (Sergei Eisenstein). In a 1929 homage to Marey which was inspired by Eisenstein, dance journalist André Levinson wrote that cinema is unable to reproduce the natural rhythms of the human body, and for this reason dance's dizzying spins and ecstatic stomping should be portrayed by means uniquely inherent to film. According to

1   Peter Tscherkassky, "Filmavantgarde in Österreich," in *Austria (In)Felix* [German/Italian], ed. Francesco Bono (Graz: Edition blimp/aiace, 1992), p. 50.
2   Birgit Hein, "Mara Mattuschka," in *Die Schatten im Silber. Österreichische Avantgarde-Filme 1976-1987*, ed. Wolfgang Drechsler and Lisl Ponger (Vienna: Museum of the 20th Century, 1987), pp. 16–17.

3   At Vienna's Academy of Applied Arts (now called University of Applied Arts).

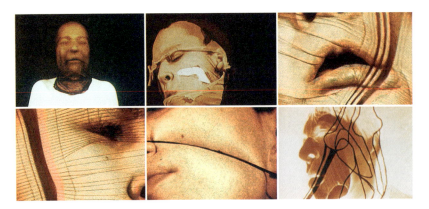

Mara Mattuschka
NabelFabel
1984

Levinson, this entails frequent changes in angle and "eloquent enlargement of details."[4] This idea happens to encompass two significant formal elements central to Mattuschka's work: Single-frame animation and enlargement of details create a kind of intensified montage that, in accordance with Levinson, contravenes the portrayal of natural movement. An excellent example can be seen in *NabelFabel* (*NavelFable*, 1984), in which layers of paper and stocking are peeled off Mimi Minus' veiled movements, as hideous details of her deformed mouth and nose intermittently fill the picture.

Mattuschka's short films are fragmentary and heterogeneous in two senses. Firstly because of the animated images' halting movement, and secondly due to their mixture of various artistic techniques. In *Der Untergang der Titania* (*The Sinking of Titania*, 1985), in which a live-action stop-motion sequence of Titania (Mattuschka) taking a bath is combined with hand-drawn animation, the collage aesthetic is particularly striking. Peculiar little men and devils frolic on the tiles and in the tub, apparently products of the woman's imagination. These fantasies revolve around the drain, which provides

a link to excretions from other bodies.[5] The caricaturization, of bodily motifs in particular, articulates the idea of a liberated body and a carnivalesque culture, described by Mikhail Bakhtin as a countercultural strategy.[6]

Since 2005, Mattuschka has repeatedly collaborated with choreographer Chris Haring and his performance group, Liquid Loft. Haring, too, works with combinations of various art genres. The rhythm and expression of his theatrical body performances evidence a certain affinity to Mattuschka's staging of her self. The choreographer uses collaged sounds and ironically appropriated gestures to develop an aesthetic of the cry, to stress the ugly, the painful and also the lustful. In *Part Time Heroes* (2007), for example, the perform-ers resemble puppets in constantly varying poses and outfits. Would-be stars are holed up in thin-walled hotel rooms, connected by telephones,

---

4   André Levinson, "A la mémoire de Jules Marey – Le Film et la danse," *Pour vous*, no. 8 (10 January 1929), p. 11, quoted in Laurent Guido, "Entre corps rythmé et modèle chorégraphique: danse et cinéma dans les années 1920," *Vertigo*, "Danses" (October 2005), p. 26.

5   In reference to the metaphor of the drain, Mattuschka explains that it links Titania "with all asses," as if in a telephone network; see Peter Tscherkassky, "Mimi Minus oder die angewandte Chaosforschung. Mara Mattuschka und ihre Filme," in *Gegenschuß. 16 Regisseure aus Österreich*, ed. Peter Illetschko (Vienna: Verlag Wespennest, 1995), p. 105.
6   Andrea B. Braidt and Barbara Liebhart point out the parallel with Bakhtin's studies on laughter during the Renaissance. See Andrea B. Braidt and Barbara Liebhart, "Logik der bewussten Unschuld. Die Filmemacherin Mara Mattuschka," in *Diagonale 2009*, catalogue (Vienna, 2009), p. 180. See Mikhail Bakhtin, *Rabelais und seine Welt* (*Rabelais and His World*) (Frankfurt am Main: Suhrkamp, 1990), p. 76 ff.

radios and an elevator, which is supervised by a central mechanic. The use of mirrors and glass surfaces makes it clear that their seductive poses are a matter of projection. Duplication of actions and gestures frozen in time reveal the clichéd nature of their postures. Rather than employing live-action animation, the film adaptation of the performance depicts the dancers' twists and turns and convulsions as functions of time and space, which then determines the montage. Jerkiness and suddenness is a product of the relationship between camera and body performance. Insistent framing on the one hand and expressive appeals gaped into the camera on the other reveal the situative dynamic of the shots. Frontality, extreme close-ups, distortions of perspective and emphatically static shots serve in this case to illustrate the variability of the poses, both as dance performance and visual configuration.

Mattuschka skillfully reveals how film works. For example, at the beginning of _Burning Palace_ (2009) the dancers' physical performance engages in a complex interplay with the power of cinema as a technology of animation and projection. Silhouettes of tableaux vivants herald the scenes that follow, in which the fantasies of waking hotel guests are staged as grotesque poses and physical

transgressions. The dark outlines of dancers warming up backstage appear on the closed stage curtain, as an illusion of unleashed erotic postures. When the shadow projections dovetail with the slow movements of real bodies, the imaginative power of filmic shots is revealed: What lies off-screen is always part of the spectator's imagination. Mattuschka's theatrical prelude is reminiscent of scenes from Arthur Robison's _Schatten_ (_Warning Shadows_, 1923), in which silhouettes serve as allegories for manifestations of hypnotic projections or personal obsessions.

By stepping behind the curtain – and by implication, the screen – _Burning Palace_ exposes the interrelationship between the performer and the apparatus filming the performer, to which the performer reacts with subtle gestures and glances. The camera's position and thereby that of the filmmaker is staked out through obsessive compositions and angles, as well as perspective – by means of light and optics. Neither the sound – obviously altered in post-production – nor the image is intended to visualize the performance in a documentary manner. Rather than realistically, sound is used as if pre-recorded, mixed and dubbed. Media and technology have played a supporting role in Mattuschka's films from the very start.

Mara Mattuschka
Der Untergang der Titania
1985

Metamorphoses and Masquerade

Along with painting and other visual media, Mattuschka employs film as a reservoir of multifaceted appropriation and metamorphosis. For example, at the beginning of *S.O.S. Extraterrestria* (1993) she gives her stockinged face the attributes of zombies and monsters. As a huge elephant woman, Mimi Minus bursts into the world right before the apocalypse, just to enjoy watching the little people in the big city. As a giant she covers the Eiffel Tower with a condom and triumphantly mounts it, while the soldiers' world of war is wiped out at her feet. From her vantage point as an alien astride this pleasure-giving phallus, the desperate doings and downfall of the tiny humans below are of little importance. Terrific bolts of lighting heighten the monster's organic pleasure. With Mimi as a female Gargantua, or King Kong in this case, a visual perspective is outlined, one which was not intended in the original film footage gleaned from all kinds of American disaster, war and pirate movies.

Mara Mattuschka is especially fond of close-ups. The variety of her visages dispenses with traditional forms of representation and facial communication, by continually disappearing, changing or becoming veiled. In a number of her films and variations Mimi Minus demonstrates the act of masking and the application of makeup, and the transformations her face undergoes designate diverse matters. For example, the liquefying paint

in *Es hat mich sehr gefreut* (*It Was a Pleasure*, 1987) is a reference to sexual satisfaction. The black that covers everything literally blots out the female body as a "brain detergent" in *Cerolax II* (1985). Repeatedly the grimace is pushed into the foreground as a moment of frozen ugliness. In *Loading Ludwig* (1989), Mattuschka employs mirrors, lenses and glass to dramatize the disfigurement of her face. This is employed again in *Burning Palace* when a protagonist glides along a glass plate and then plunges his face into an indeterminate zone between human and animal. In this case the head seems to be deformed or eaten away from within, similar to Francis Bacon's figures or Ana Mendieta's photographic self-portraits. The body's insides leave a trail on the glass, thereby materializing the invisible wall separating figure and spectator.

Mattuschka appears in almost all her films from the 1980s, though in a variety of changing identities and pseudonyms, some of them male – she never seems to be the same individual. Even though we are aware we are watching Mara Mattuschka, what we witness is only (most importantly) this figure's ability to transform itself, which is related to the photographic self-staging of Martha Wilson or Cindy Sherman. In her short films, Mattuschka's face provides a venue for an encounter with the *Other*, though not as a conventional reflection of a reaction to plot or dialogue; rather it takes on the form of an unending metamorphosis. Mattuschka's acting exaggerates and multiplies conventional and still dominant gender attributes, also found in contemporary advertising. The emphatic play of masquerade acknowledges the mask as the decorative cover of a non-identity, as Mary Ann Doane writes about Claire Johnston.[7] Existing figurations are questioned.

7   In a similar way, the figure of the femme fatale in film noir must be regarded as illustrating men's desire to force women into a certain stereotypical identity. See Claire Johnston, "Femininity and the Masquerade: *Anne of the Indies*," in *Psychoanalysis and Cinema*, ed. E. Ann Kaplan (New York and London: Routledge, 1989 [1975]), p. 70 (Johnston refers to the films of Jacques Tourneur; the text was written long before the so-called performative turn and the appearance of queer theory in the humanities); and Mary Ann Doane, "Film and the Masquerade: Theorizing the Female Spectator," in Mary Ann Doane, *Femmes Fatales: Feminism, Film Theory, Psychoanalysis* (New York: Routledge, 1991 [1982]), pp. 17–32.

Mara Mattuschka, Chris Haring
Part Time Heroes
2007

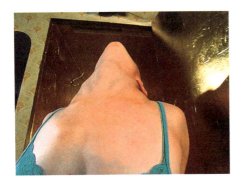

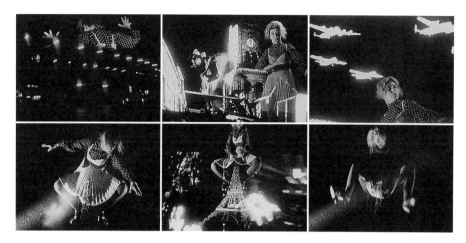

Mara Mattuschka, **S.O.S. Extraterrestria**, 1993

Mara Mattuschka, **Cerolax II**, 1985

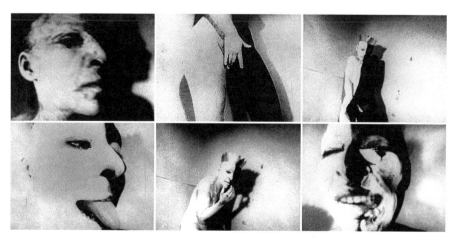

Mara Mattuschka, **Parasympathica**, 1985

In a few of Mattuschka's films the fragmentary nature of these identities is revealed as a schism, by means of light and movement and figurative opposites such as light/dark and black/white. In *Parasympathica* (1985) the artist divides her body into two halves, one black and the other white, with everything held together by a crown she wears. This "split" figure rotates jerkily by means of single frame animation. As Mattuschka spins on her own axis in a movement resembling a butterfly, the contrasts between the two divisions of the autonomic nervous system, the sympathetic and the parasympathetic, are blurred. The poses, ironically termed "Provocativa," "Riservata," "Triste," and so on, refer to traditional ideas concerning the character of women.[8] Mattuschka's portrayal of moodiness in the immobilized instants of single-frame animation reference the iconographic tradition of female insanity as staged for the theater, in particular the affective expressions of hysterical women in the late 19th century. The halting and mechanical motion reveals such figurations of frozen or cramped female bodies as a manipulation and a kind of a game, in the same way that they were presented by Jean-Martin Charcot at the Salpêtrière. Mattuschka's visual stuttering subjects formulas of pathos from cultural history to merry criticism, referring at the same time to the technique of serial photography, which Albert Londe employed to dissect the movements of his female patients. Moreover, the irony applies to certain gestures in male Action art, which in the wake of Surrealism celebrated images from the Salpêtrière as a poetic sublimation of automatism.

The Body of the Images

Mattuschka's humor does not evoke loud laughter. Instead it creates, as Birgit Hein writes, "a distance to a person's own problems." According to Peter Tscherkassky, this brand of humor arises from "the extraordinary nature of the images."[9] These films'

straightforward but effective means are what make the spectator laugh. Frequently, the joke can be found not so much in the comedy of the situation or the body's pose, as in the specific filmic means employed: the decoupling of sound and image, the exaggerated camera angles, the conscious violation of visual continuity or the effect produced by collage.

At times the performances of Mimi Minus are also self-ironic. By means of precisely timed visual or acoustic interventions Mattuschka creates a filmic distance to her performance. This is done in a particularly impressive manner in the two-minute miniature *Es hat mich sehr gefreut*. A nude Mimi Minus engages in autoerotic activity while the camera distances itself, in leaps and bounds, to the point that Mimi's white figure is tiny and eventually disappears in a glaring, high-contrast mountain landscape. Her echoing laughter transitions to a sensuous moan. But at the conclusion, after the climax suggested on the soundtrack, she reappears, clearly visible and close to the camera. She removes her sunglasses and directs her tear-stained, smeared face at the spectator. The farewell comes from off-camera, in the loaded Viennese phrase, "Thank you, it was a pleasure."[10] Mattuschka appropriates this imperial quote in the same nonchalant fashion that she reappropriates gestures or written symbols, ideograms or film images from a variety of eras and cultures.

For Mattuschka writing always also implies image, in other words drawing or a typographic process and therefore the trace of a physical gesture. In the short film the artist describes as an "ode to IBM," *Kugelkopf* (*Ball-Head*, 1985), the body itself is turned into a machine, the head a matrix. A spectacular event takes place early on: In a jerky live-action animation sequence in high-contrast black-and-white, Mattuschka shaves her head with a razor blade, which cuts the skin, producing bloody colored matter. The razor scene is, as Tscherkassky

---

8   Mattuschka claims that this alludes to an evaluation of character traits published in Spain by the Catholic Church. See Tscherkassky, "Mimi Minus oder die angewandte Chaosforschung," p. 100.
9   Hein, p. 17; and Tscherkassky, "Filmavantgarde in Österreich," p. 51.

10   "It was very beautiful, it was a pleasure": This was a statement consistently used by the Austrian Emperor Franz Joseph I on cultural occasions after the suicide of Eduard van der Nüll. The architect took his own life after the ruler expressed his disapproval of Nüll's design of the Vienna State Opera House.

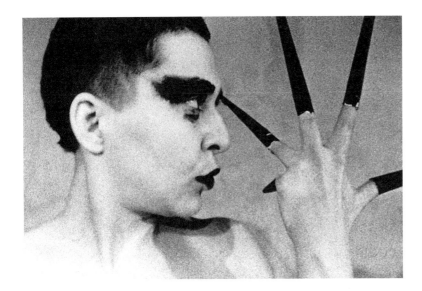

Mara Mattuschka,
Michael Petrov
Loading Ludwig
1989

notes, a brilliant quote of Carl Theodor Dreyer's _La Passion de Jeanne d'Arc_ (_The Passion of Joan of Arc_, 1928),[11] though it can also be read as a feminist appropriation of Günter Brus' Actions of the 1960s, for example, in which scissors and razors were employed and there was a transition from painted line to cut flesh. The metrical condensation of Mattuschka's single frame animation is rhythmically organized by images of actual machine parts. Completely wrapped in bandages, the artist's head becomes a typewriter's golf ball. It jerks forward, printing letters on an invisible glass wall and then deleting them. The concept of the typewriter is taken in an historically literal sense, both as machine and the woman who types, artistically transcending the context of media archeology.[12] The illegible typography of Mimi Minus does not serve as a transcription of some man's speech, but rather results from a female's performance. Thinking and writing coincide in this example of Action Painting. The writing, impossible for the spectator to decipher, becomes material in a filmic sense, if nothing else due of the demonstrative use of the glass plate as a basis of animation film technique.

On the whole, the visual form assumed by Mattuschka's films emphasize the physical body, both human and filmic: Her animation films are smeared and choppy, they are the product of a rough manual working method that leaves visible traces.[13] And precisely because these works are hybrids, moving between photography and film, straddling theater, dance and painting, they are able to develop an independent form, like the "dizzying spins" of bodies envisioned by André Levinson in the 1920s. When Mattuschka subsequently began to collaborate with Chris Haring, abandoning her handmade approach and the animation studio, she developed a new aesthetic of the cry and the pose, convulsion and metamor-

---

11 Tscherkassky, "Filmavantgarde in Österreich," p. 51.
12 Cf. Friedrich Kittler, _Grammophon Film Typewriter_ (Berlin: Brinkmann & Bose, 1986), p. 314.

13 Cf. Gabriele Jutz, _Cinéma Brut, Eine alternative Genealogie der Filmavantgarde_ (Vienna and New York: Springer Verlag, 2010).

phosis. Mattuschka's most recent works involve a change in visual strategies because she has switched to a new motion picture technology and withdrawn behind the camera. Now that her films are no longer created in the studio and developing lab, they conform to digital principles of directly controllable photography and the multi-faceted possibilities of post-production processing. The reflexive moments of interruption and pause, repetition and reflection are introduced within the pro-filmic performance, and become accentuated by means of mise en scène (spatial arrangement, perspective, framing, light), as well as montage and digital postproduction processes. The vibration of the image is no longer owing to the individual frame. Through the transition to digital technology it has instead shifted to loops and virtually any section of the image. This change finds its aural equivalence in digital sound editing, which relies on sampling and sequencing to create effects such as direction reversal, minimalistic loops and deceleration. Sound and image remain entirely autonomous, just as in Mattuschka's early works. This is illustrated in a sequence of central importance to *Burning Palace*, in which three Sphinx-like beings pervade the hotel's mirrored staircase with a cascade of grotesque cries and outbursts, demonstrating the extent to which Mattuschka's disjunctive approach to montage and mixing is indebted to her distinctive sense of rhythm.

Mara Mattuschka is a pioneering artist who not only unites the distinct cinematic worlds of live action and animation film aesthetically, but also knows how to translate such artistry into new digital forms that exploit capabilities unique to the medium. In this sense her most recent works break new ground in the field of animation.[14]

Translated by Steve Wilder

---

14 Mattuschka's early films are available on Index DVD Edition 006: *Mara Mattuschka, Iris Scan*. Her film *Legal Errorist* (2004), made with Chris Haring, is available on Index DVD Edition 023: *As She Likes It. Female Performance Art From Austria*. *Part Time Heroes* and *Burning Palace* are available on Index DVD Edition 038: *Mara Mattuschka/Chris Haring, Burning Down the Palace*.

Mara Mattuschka
Kugelkopf
1985

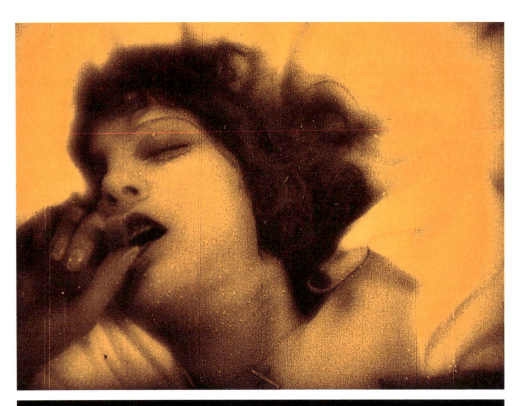
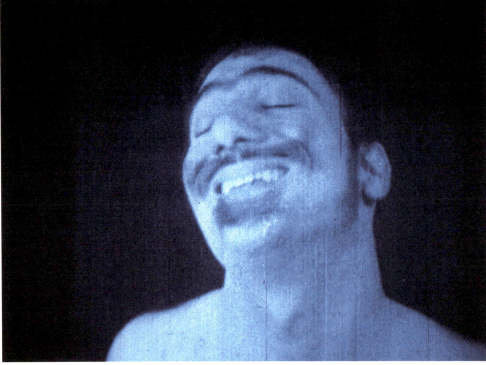

Gustav Deutsch, Visual Thinker.

Livio Belloï

In 1995, on the heels of the centennial celebrations of the Lumière cinematograph, Gustav Deutsch threw himself headlong into the elaboration of *Film ist.*, a project which, under its deceptively minimalistic title, was to become one of the most vibrant visual adventures of our time. In truth, the filmmaker's work underwent a profound shift at the start of the 1990s. From *Adria* (1989) onward, and after various video and (mainly Super 8) film productions, Deutsch indeed began to take a close interest in the practice of found footage film, in keeping with the critical legacy of filmmakers such as Bruce Conner and Ken Jacobs.

From the outset, Deutsch conceived *Film ist.* as an attempt to define cinema through its own material, with and in the very flesh of images. The filmmaker's purpose is to discuss film using film,[1] to rely on the expressive possibilities of the medium itself in order to illuminate its mechanisms from within. In this respect, *Film ist.* can be considered as a methodical and multifaceted cinematic answer to the famous ontological question that French critic André Bazin[2] placed

at the center of theoretical discussion in the 1950s. To define cinema by means of its own material is without a doubt a virtually endless enterprise, which has immersed its creator in the web of an ongoing *work in progress* of considerable magnitude.

Fifteen years after the initial formulation of this project, *Film ist.* presents itself today in the shape of a trilogy, the respective sections of which are each articulated around an overarching theme. Elaborated between 1996 and 1998 as the result of extensive research through mostly Austrian and German archives, *Film ist. [1–6]* principally consists of fragments borrowed from scientific, educational and industrial films, and focuses primarily on cinema as a *laboratory invention*. Composed between 1999 and 2002, *Film ist. [7–12]* approaches cinema rather as a *popular spectacle* and ponders two other birthplaces of the cinematograph: the fairground and the music hall. This provides Deutsch with the opportunity for a prolonged immersion in the world of silent film, with a marked predilection for the infancy of cinematographic art (i.e., for the most part, cinema before 1920). In terms of structural organization, each of these first two sections is divided into six chapters individually numbered (respectively from 1 to 6 and from 7 to 12), and bearing two titles (one in German and one in English), a configuration which imparts to the whole the characteristics of a genuine

---

1   Gustav Deutsch, interview with Scott MacDonald: "I try to speak with film about film," in *Gustav Deutsch*, eds. Wilbirg Brainin-Donnenberg and Michael Loebenstein, German/English (Vienna: FilmmuseumSynemaPublikationen, 2009), p. 82.
2   Cf. *Qu'est-ce que le cinéma?*, T. I: *Ontologie et langage*, T. II: *Le cinéma et les autres arts* (Paris: Éditions du Cerf, 1958 and 1959). In English see André Bazin, *What is cinema? Vol. 1 & 2*, trans. and ed. Hugh Gray (Berkeley: University of California Press, 1967–1971).

Gustav Deutsch
Film ist. a girl & a gun
2009

nomenclature.[3] Divided yet again into numbered segments (7.1, 7.2, 7.3, etc.), each chapter aims to complete the open title of the project and presents itself as an attempt to formalize – always in a partial yet illuminating manner – the very notion of cinema. More recently, the project was yet again augmented by a thirteenth chapter entitled – according to an expression generally attributed to David W. Griffith – *Film ist. a girl & a gun* (2009), itself divided into five acts and compounding all kinds of images from the first forty-five years of cinematographic production (including films preserved by the Kinsey Institute for Research in Sex, Gender and Reproduction), and punctuated by citations from Hesiod, Plato and Sappho.

Reduced to its essence, Deutsch's work pertains equally to an art of finding and to a science of editing. His art of selecting found footage is the fruit of a tireless labor of patience and the product of long viewing hours (often working together with his partner and artistic collaborator Hanna

Schimek), in search of the images, either forgotten or better known, which could potentially be integrated into the project. Deutsch's work, at the same time, relies on a unique science of editing, which is evident in the carefulness with which the film-maker recombines the source material on the basis of extremely varied relationships (analogy, contrast, metaphor, visual shock, etc.). With *Film ist.*, Deutsch has undeniably rethought in depth the analytical potentialities of montage. His subtle visual equations adhere to several recurrent principles, which I will discuss – albeit not exhaustively – in the typology below, primarily based upon the central panel of the triptych.

Series

As the first and most elementary form of assemblage, serial montage has the distinguishing property of aggregating in clusters various images, which, despite their heterogeneous origins (fiction films, local views, newsreels, ethnographic footage, etc.), share at least one given element. Alternatively, this common denominator appertains to objects, actions or formal properties. For instance, segment 7.1 assembles images from various sources, but which nonetheless fit together rather naturally due to their thematic analogy: the opening sequence featuring doors is followed respectively by the series "ladder," "bicycle" and "water hose," each with their share of collisions and falls. In this particular instance, the image fragments link up on an equal basis, without any hierarchy; they form virtually unlimited associative bouquets, to

Gustav Deutsch
Film ist. a girl & a gun
2009

---

3   As a reminder, in chronological order: [1] "Bewegung und Zeit/ Movement and Time"; [2] "Licht und Dunkelheit/Light and Darkness"; [3] "Ein Instrument/An Instrument"; [4] "Material/ Material"; [5] "Ein Augenblick/A Blink of an Eye"; [6] "Ein Spiegel/A Mirror"; [7] "Komisch/Comic"; [8] "Magie/Magic"; [9] "Eroberung/ Conquest"; [10] "Schrift und Sprache/Writing and Language"; [11] "Gefühl und Leidenschaft/Emotions and Passion"; and, finally, [12] "Erinnerung und Dokument/Memory and Document." Available on Index DVD Edition 012: *Gustav Deutsch, Film ist. [1–12].*

which other fragments of a similar nature could agglomerate themselves.

However, this type of assemblage – whose basic principle is reminiscent, albeit in another context, of various experiments conducted by Matthias Müller (*Home Stories*, 1990) and Christian Marclay (*Telephones*, 1995) – remains problematic for Deutsch as far as his archival explorations are concerned. As the filmmaker once noted: "I cannot use the normal archive system; archives usually work by title, by author, by year. What I'm looking for is special scenes and particular actions: somebody closing a door, somebody climbing up a staircase, somebody reading a letter ..." [4] Between the classification system favored by film archives and the specific fragments sought by Deutsch, lies an obvious methodological gap, which the filmmaker can sometimes narrow by soliciting the enlightened advice of those who, in his words, "have the archive in their heads." [5]

A similar principle of serial assemblage governs the structure of segment 7.5, which however does not deal with recurrent objects, but with actions, all of which are linked to the general theme of oral activities: in chronological order, eating and drinking, smoking and kissing. Elsewhere, the images aggregate themselves on the basis of common formal properties, as in the context of segment 9.1, where fragments of panoramic views (all subsumed, by definition, under the organizing principle of a moving frame) latch onto each other. In such associative bouquets, images interconnect precisely because they resemble each other. This type of montage attests to two simultaneous objectives on the part of the filmmaker: one iconographic and the other taxonomic, two tendencies which run through the entire *Film ist.* project.

Collisions

Although alternation is also present in serial montage, it raises more complex questions in all the sequences where Deutsch creates collisions

between shots or fragments of a highly heterogeneous nature, whether in terms of genre, geographical location, texture, general tonality, etc.

As an example, segment 10.4 opens with a fairly damaged ethnographic view, obviously belonging to the practice of *record footage* as it was formalized by the great anthropologist, filmmaker and theoretician David MacDougall. [6] In a certain sense, this view even presents a double form of *record footage*, in that the image not only records an African man sitting bare-chested, but also shows him in the process of recording his voice in front of a phonograph horn. In the euphoria inspired by the trad*i*tional chant that he is voicing (but which the film does not make available to its viewer, replacing it with a vaguely South American-sounding track [7]), the African man sitting in front of the phonograph cannot refrain from accompanying his words with corresponding gestures, punctuating this recording session with ample arm and hand movements, which give his demeanor the appearance of an imprecation or an invitation to dance.

With this opening ethnographic view, Deutsch juxtaposes a shot taken from a fiction film of an entirely European nature. Sitting on a nondescript table and framed in medium shot, a character with a familiar face appears: this is indeed burlesque actor Ferdinand Guillaume, famous for his recurrent character of Polidor (or Tontolino in Italian productions). [8] In this particular occurrence, the character appears to be in a rather morose mood, as he delivers for the viewer a string of facial expressions and gestures imbued with dejection and incomprehension. By all appearances, the vexation expressed by the character derives from the mail that he is holding in his hands, presumably a break-up letter.

---

4   Interview with Scott MacDonald, p. 86.
5   MacDonald, p. 86. In this particular case, Deutsch refers to Nico de Klerk and Mark-Paul Meyer, who guided his research in the rich collections of the Nederlands Filmmuseum (Amsterdam).

---

6   David MacDougall, *Transcultural Cinema*, (Princeton: Princeton University Press, 1998), pp. 180–181. By *record footage*, MacDougall refers to the visual material that an anthropologist stores for essentially descriptive purposes, as the image equivalent of fieldwork notes.
7   As for the whole of *Film ist. [7–12]*, this music was composed by Christian Fennesz, Werner Dafeldecker, Burkhard Stangl and Martin Siewert.
8   Deutsch already used this character in the context of the same chapter [10], more specifically at the end of segment 10.2, where Polidor appears as a spectator sitting in a movie theater.

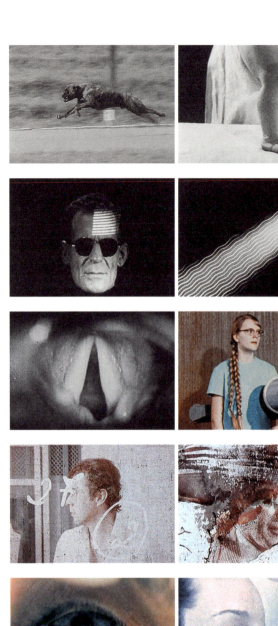

Film ist. 1

Film ist. 2

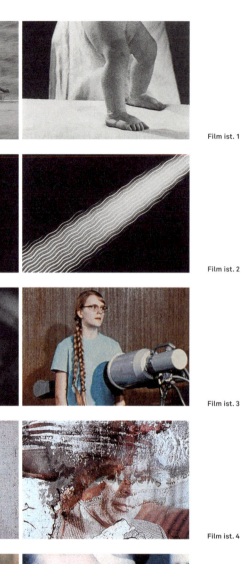

Film ist. 3

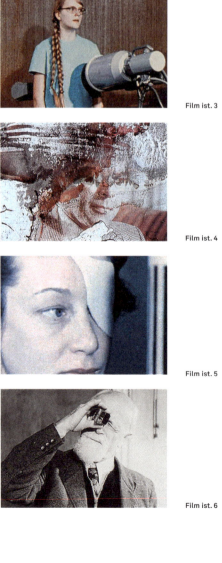

Film ist. 4

Film ist. 5

Film ist. 6

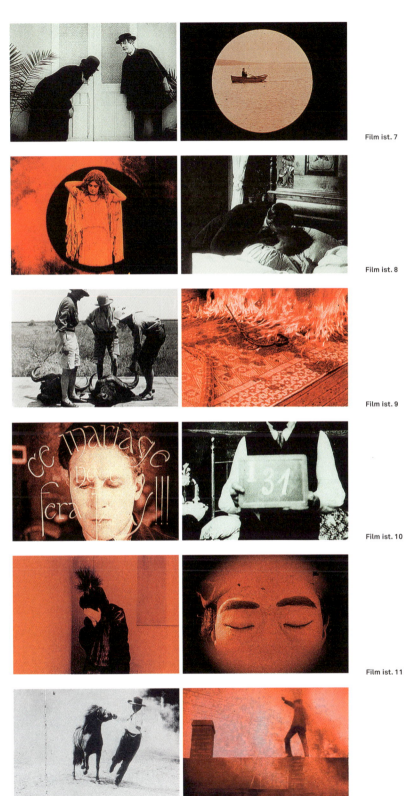

Film ist. 7

Film ist. 8

Film ist. 9

Film ist. 10

Film ist. 11

Film ist. 12

Gustav Deutsch
Film ist. [1–6]
1996–1998

Everything (including geographic location, purpose, texture, overall tonality, etc.) seems to set these two images as polar opposites. Nonetheless, Deutsch submits these two shots to a process of repeated binary alternation. Through this pendulum movement, a correlation is gradually woven between the two heterogeneous fragments that the filmmaker chose to conjoin. By way of the montage, the two shots eventually come to synchronize themselves gradually, with sound functioning as a cement between the images, as the rhythm of the music fictionally emanating from the African man and his phonograph inevitably tends to permeate the interpolated shot. The same musical composition, continuously infusing both images, creates between them a sort of bridge and shapes the terms of a small geographic utopia. Between these two visual units, which are absolutely foreign to each other, the relationship functions according to the mode of musical transportation, of redemption through rhythm. By virtue of his gesturing activity, but also because of the sound machine that he appears to be operating, the man with the phonograph indeed becomes akin, in the course of the montage, to a kind of contemporary disc jockey, above all preoccupied with making his audience dance by preaching by example in a rhythm-induced trance. Only, in this case, the sole audience of the improvised disc jockey is none other than

Polidor, a character given to despair, but whom the African with the phonograph seems to want to comfort, thanks to the music that he appears to be broadcasting, as the montage suggests. It is, therefore, rhythm that ensures the communication between the two correlated fragments. Under its influence, the geographic utopia imagined by Deutsch creates the conditions of a *cross-distance empathy* or fraternity, traversing continents and cultures, as music is conceived to be a language that, by nature, transcends frontiers (which is, in another sense, also true about montage, as the filmmaker consistently demonstrates).

Gravitations

Comfortably lying on a loveseat, a young middle-class woman is absorbed in the reading of what appears to be an illustrated magazine or a *roman-photo* (segment 11.3). While the spectator is spontaneously expecting a reverse shot of the magazine page under her gaze, Deutsch inserts instead a rather enigmatic image at first glance. Within a long shot, at the very back of the image, a wide double-door opens slowly to reveal a female silhouette covered in a white veil, who, with eyes half-shut, begins to walk forward toward the camera. While the opening of the door clearly echoes the start of segment 7.1, the body inhabiting this image immerses us in the universe of the *diva* film, which Deutsch, following Peter Delpeut,[9] has thoroughly explored. In this ghostly character, one will recognize the Italian actress Lyda Borelli, captured here in a key scene from *Rapsodia satanica* (Nino Oxilia, 1915), a cinematographic variation on the Faustian myth.[10]

Between these two introductory shots (the reader, the *diva*), the relation initially appears to be problematic. If we limit ourselves to these two images, the editing maneuver that merges them together seems at first to produce an effect of contiguity, as if the *diva* was opening a door located near the room where the female reader is dwelling. But the following shot immediately contradicts this first hypothesis: It shows, in an image uniformly tinted in blue, a valiant knight hooded with a dark cape, who is none other than Tristano (or, at least, Tristano's ghost), one of the two brothers in love with Alba, the character played by Lyda Borelli in Nino Oxilia's film.

Such a sudden opening toward an outdoor shot compels us to reinterpret the nature of the links woven between the image of the reader and the shots that are agglomerated with it. All things considered, the connection between the two juxtaposed series of images is not of a spatial order, but belongs rather to the realm of imagination or fantasy. In the same fashion as the female dreamer appearing in chapter 8, the reader functions, by means of the montage, as a center of production of images. Herein lies a mode of assemblage relying on a gravitational structure, which Deutsch employs on more than one occasion. Satellite images – here designed to represent the impressions that reading generates in the languid female character – alternately gravitate around a focal image (from the Latin *focalis*, derived from "focus"), which serves as an anchoring point for the sequence. Once this equation is established, Deutsch can conveniently take advantage of the visual lever that the focal image provides, and vary the satellite images in its periphery. After Alba's death, two scenes are thus grafted around the shot of the reader, each featuring crimes of passion (one involving a pistol, the other a knife), and here again expressing the effects of reading on the tortured imagination of the young woman. In contrast to associative bouquets and to montage by collision, gravitational montage therefore supposes a hierarchical relation between the sampled images. Without the fixed point provided by the focal image, it would be impossible for the satellite images to express the daydreams to which this modern Madame Bovary has surrendered. In other words, it is indeed the montage that determines the conditions of her domestic reverie.

Variations, hybrids

Evidently, the assemblage formulas discussed thus far – associative bouquets, collisions, gravitations – rarely exist in monolithic or isolated form. During the course of *Film ist.*, each model can allow for variations and combine freely with other montage configurations within a given segment. Nowhere can the unique science of montage according to Gustav Deutsch be experienced more distinctly than in this double operation of modulation and hybridization.

In this regard, segment 9.4 is particularly revealing. As a reminder, chapter 9 as a whole deals with the connections between cinema and the notion of "conquest" (Eroberung), manifested in four distinct forms: (1) spatial conquest, evoked through the early genre of the panoramic view (in this case filmed from a moving train); (2) air conquest, by means of aerial views,[11] directly inspired by the aerostatic pictures taken by French photographer Nadar from 1855 on; (3) conquest in the ethnographic sense, under the influence of which early cinema replayed the abuses inherent to colonialism and to its corollary ethnocentrism (this is what filmmakers Yervant Gianikian and Angela Ricci Lucchi, whose judgment is similar to Deutsch in this regard, eloquently call "vandal tourism"[12]); (4) conquest in the most expected and

---

9   See his *Diva Dolorosa* (1999).

10 About this film, see Angela Dalle Vacche, *Diva. Defiance and Passion in Early Italian Cinema* (Austin: University of Texas Press, 2008), pp. 240–241 (among others).

11 Among which *Panorama pris d'un ballon captif* (Lumière, circa 1898).

12 Yervant Gianikian and Angela Ricci Lucchi, "Tourisme vandale. Deux projets," *Trafic*, no. 38, summer 2001, pp. 63–65.

warlike meaning of the word, evident in the relationship that cinema has chosen to share with the
military corps and weapons of war.

Within the framework of this last segment,
Deutsch first develops a variation (almost in the
musical sense) around serial montage. From one
image to the next, it is no longer the same object,
action, or formal property that functions as a
transitional object; it is rather a general isotopy.
Such a device can be recognized in segment 7.3,
in which fragments of various kinds of chases (on
foot, on horse, by car or side-car, etc.) are assembled in the form of a *crescendo*, in what amounts to
a frantic ode to movement. The same phenomenon
recurs in segment 12.4, which, by stringing together
images of burning buildings and firemen in action
(obtained from non-fiction and fiction films alike),
pays homage to the early genre of the fire film,
the best-known specimen of which remains *Life of
an American Fireman* (Edwin S. Porter, Edison,
1902/1903). Yet this type of montage – which
one could label as *categorical* [13] – is perhaps best
explored within the framework of segment 9.4.

In this section devoted to military representations, the use of categorical montage allows
Deutsch to literally *inspect the troops*. The segment
first exhibits scenes of cavalry in action showing
soldiers marching either in perfect line or in more
dispersed order. Sometimes, a fairly frontal framing
prevails, which enhances the impression of
presence and mass gathering, as the cavalrymen
are forced to exit the frame by brushing against one
of its sides. At other times, by contrast, the framing
becomes more lateral and captures the charging
cavalry in profile, which serves as an opportunity
for Deutsch to allude to one of the birthplaces of
the classical Western's rich iconography.

In this imaginary army raised from scratch by
the filmmaker, cavalrymen are followed by foot
soldiers who are either moving in line or assembled
in clusters, forming a single and almost indistinct
mass, spiked with raised rifles. From shot to shot,

all soldiers appear to be glancing at each other,
aiming their fire at each other, and preparing to
kill each other (the jubilation caused by this anticipation already shows on some faces).

By virtue of a deliberate progression, Deutsch
continues his troop inventory and sets his sights
next on *heavy artillery*, by lining up shots of cannons
in action, in theatres of operations situated on
both land and sea. In this context, the fundamental
editing pattern of alternation tends to model itself
after the military logic of shooting (cause) and
reaching a target (remote effect). What Deutsch
means to emphasize is the unfortunate intrinsic
cinegeny of the shooting of a weapon, with its deto-
nations and violent metallic convulsions, all elements which fall under an aesthetic of shock. The
same can be argued about the target itself, hit and
blown into pieces by bombs, all of which pertains
to an aesthetic of dislocation and pulverization.
When, after a sub-aquatic explosion, the human
form reappears at the other end, on the side of the
target, it takes on the shape of a group of military
officers, political leaders and weapons salesmen,
all gathered in the same image and all expressing
joy at the sight of the intense spectacle of destruction that the bomb presented to their eyes.

Progressing from the most human and immediate military device (cavalry, infantry) to the most
mechanical and remote one (cannons of various
sizes, on land or aboard warships), this inventory,
made possible by the inherent flexibility of categorical montage, reaches its *climax* – and its *anti-
climax* as well – in the imaging of two weapons
which are more sophisticated and maneuverable
than the previous ones: on one side, a rapid-fire
cannon and on the other, a machine gun resting on
its carriage. By common knowledge, the cannon and
the machine gun are not only saturation weapons,
but also repeating weapons characterized by a high
rate of fire. At the end of this segment, Deutsch
facetiously transfers the technical properties of
these two weapons to the film itself. For the filmmaker, it is time to discard the visual combinations
of categorical montage in order to eventually favor
a new form of assemblage, more apt to express the
potential enclosed in the two sampled fragments.

---

13 This expression is inspired by the notion of "categorical form"
proposed by David Bordwell and Kristin Thompson. On this topic,
see *Film Art: An Introduction,* 7th ed. (New York: McGraw-Hill, 2003),
pp. 133–134.

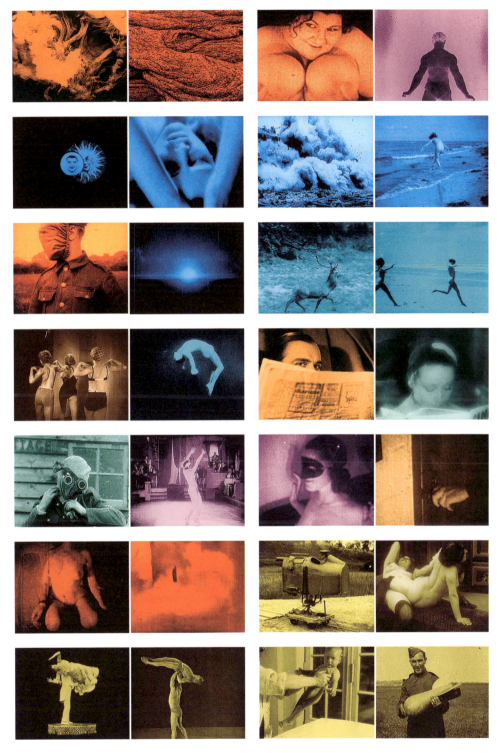

Gustav Deutsch
Film ist. a girl & a gun
2009

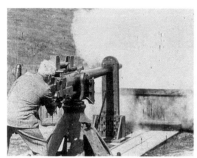

Gustav Deutsch
Film ist. [7–12]
1999–2002

Here, Deutsch puts to use short advertising films, through which arms manufacturers aim to visually demonstrate the supposed efficiency of their respective inventions. If repeating weapons have the capacity to sustain rapid fire, then, according to Deutsch, editing must employ similar techniques. Accordingly, the binary alternation pattern makes its return at the end of the section, but it also undergoes a significant variation: in this case, the editing no longer alternates between two entirely disparate images (as was the case in segment 10.4 above), but, ironically, juxtaposes two images that are paradoxically too *similar* and redundant, which Deutsch moreover integrates into the pattern of a generalized *repetition*.

This repetition first takes place within the images themselves. The same operation is system-atically at play in the two shots correlated by the filmmaker: Framed in a long shot, two men with white hair and white beards respectively work the rapid fire cannon and the machine gun. As a matter of fact, these two fake soldiers strangely resemble each other – it is undoubtedly for this reason that they have eventually been combined together. In truth, both characters form a single individual. On each side of the cut, Deutsch summoned none other than Hiram Maxim (1840–1916), the inventor of the first entirely automatic machine gun, which he named after himself as a pun (Maxim gun).

This fearsome weapon, with its high rate of fire, would later become widely used on the battlefields of the Great War.

Taken separately within their original contexts, these two images did not involve the depiction of any target. Their primary purpose was to show the weapons in action, independently from their potential impact. When fused together by Deutsch, and inscribed within a repeating pattern, as though in dialogue with each other, these very same images take on another, unexpected and altered meaning. First, they tend to construct a short, temporary fiction according to which each of the characters plays in turn the part of the shooter or that of the target. Spurred by the very technical properties of these weapons themselves, the diegetic repetition thus also coincides with an incisive form of enunciative repetition. All evidence considered, the montage beats the two images at their own game and tends to ridicule the sinister warmonger by confining him as a captive of circular time and tautology. Even better yet, by taking advantage of the ballistic power of montage, Deutsch affords himself the luxury, through the calculated play of his cuts, of turning the weapon *against* its own inventor, thus creating a singular case of *backfire*. Such images seem to echo Henri Bergson's famous theory on laughter: "any arrangement of acts and events is comic which gives us, in a single combination, the illusion of life and the distinct impression of a mechanical arrangement."[14] Appropriately, Deutsch therefore concludes his exploration of the notion of conquest on a humorous and particularly biting note.[15]

If this segment 9.4 unquestionably imposes itself as one of the most memorable moments of *Film ist.*, it is because it attests that found footage filmmaking cannot be reduced, in Deutsch's eyes, to a simple mind game or purely formal recreation. By unearthing these images and setting them within an ironic mirror-like alternation, Deutsch, underneath his ferocious humor,[16] formulates a politically conscious and firmly antimilitaristic discourse, which reaffirms the critical and uncompromising spirit of the great pioneer of found footage that was Henri Storck. Notably in his *Histoire du soldat inconnu* (1932), the Belgian filmmaker juxtaposed fragments of newsreel footage from 1928 in order to express his disgust toward war and violence.

All throughout *Film ist.*, the spectator can also encounter fairies and witches, bathing beauties and capuchin monks, Pope Leon XIII and Roscoe "Fatty" Arbuckle, men walking on their heads or on the ceiling, flying women and spider-women, mischievous dogs and menacing snakes, ghosts and hangmen, reversed and slow-motion gestures, metaphors and visual palindromes, etc. Yet there is absolutely nothing in *Film ist.* that falls under the category of a simple and vaguely post-modern patchwork. In its anatomy as well as in its logic, *Film ist.* does rather resemble a Mendeleïev table in motion, in which the periodic elements have been replaced by images or image juxtapositions.

If film can be more than film,[17] then Gustav Deutsch is undoubtedly more than a filmmaker: his work is that of a visual thinker.

Translated from the French by Fabrice Leroy.

The author wishes to thank
Michel Delville and Lara Delage-Toriel

---

17 This phrase is an allusion to *Film ist mehr als Film*, the film trailer that Deutsch produced for the 1996 Viennale; it is also an allusion, more widely, to all the parts of his work that deal with images without falling under the umbrella of film, such as the CD-ROM *Odyssey Today* (2000), the atlas *Licht – Bild – Realität* made in collaboration with Hanna Schimek (and directly inspired by the work of the great art historian Aby Warburg), and architectural projects (such as the fascinating camera obscura built on the Greek island of Aegina).

---

14 Henri Bergson, *Le Rire* [1899] (Paris: Presses Universitaires de France, 1985), p. 53.
15 The same question is treated in a distinct but complementary fashion in the segment "Thanatos" of *Film ist. a girl & a gun*, where Deutsch makes battle scenes collide with pornographic material (military conquest vs. physical conquest).
16 In this case, Deutsch's humor is based on repetition, but also on a verbal pun. By coupling these two images, the filmmaker indeed produces a "shot/countershot" in every sense of the expression, according to a process that, in its play on literal meaning, evokes the film of the same name produced in 1987 by Peter Tscherkassky. On this point, see Alexander Horwath, "Singing in the Rain. Supercinematography by Peter Tscherkassky," in *Peter Tscherkassky*, eds. Alexander Horwath and Michael Loebenstein (Vienna: FilmmuseumSynemaPublikationen, 2005), pp. 32–34. Also available at http://www.sensesofcinema.com/2003/28/tscherkassky/ For Horwath, *Shot – Countershot* "is one of the best jokes in the history of film (as well as film theory)." The end of segment 9.4 of *Film ist.* could easily fall into the same category.

Gustav Deutsch
Film ist. [1–6]
1996–1998

Reanimator, Stutterer, Eraser.
Martin Arnold and the Ghosts of Cinema.

Steve Anker

Martin Arnold's cinema is a world of paradox and contradiction, hidden mysteries and revelations, sensual delights intertwined with provocative psychological and cultural implications. The films and installations Arnold made between 1989 and 2011 constitute a body of work that bridges avant-garde film and popular culture. It spans theory and art while rediscovering a sense of magic that returns us to the wonders of early cinema.

Born in 1959, Arnold grew up during the later years of Austria's modernist avant-garde film movement. By the 1980s, the essentially formal, often abstract, anti-narrative masterworks of Peter Kubelka and Kurt Kren, among others, had become well known within contemporary art circles. Meanwhile, cinema's own history had inspired an approach to avant-garde filmmaking that re-con-textualized narrative "found footage" (i.e., pre-exist-ing material), as exemplified by the work of artists such as Joseph Cornell, Len Lye, Bruce Conner and Ken Jacobs. Both of these artistic directions – formal, medium-specific explorations and found-footage-based reinvented narratives – continue to be practiced both by established as well as younger filmmakers. What began as pure approaches by such pioneers as Kubelka and Conner in the 1950s and 1960s led to a broadening and increasingly frequent combination of these concerns with newer artistic strategies in the experimental cinema of the 1980s and 1990s. Arnold's world of sound and images brings an intricate formalism to material drawn almost exclusively from Hollywood movies – some well-known, others long forgotten. His realization of form, however, is not predetermined by an overarching abstract strategy. Instead, form develops organically from the investigation of each film's content, and like the earlier formalists, he also creates precise scores. "When you look at a strip of film, you will at first see a regular sequence of rectangular frames that represent a three-dimensional space," says Arnold. "Those are the tracks the camera left behind; the apparatus inscribed itself into the material. If you look more closely 'into' the frame, you will see tracks of people and objects which were in front of the camera at the time of the recording." [1] Arnold's approach differs from the Bruce Conner tradition which combined snippets of material from disparate sources into a new linear flow, while highlighting suggestive actions and the authentic flavors of the original films. By contrast, Arnold limits himself to one source, either a specific original film or an inter-related series for each of his works, and explores it microscopically. In this way his work is closer to that of Ken Jacobs, but Arnold's particular sense of humor, formal playfulness, and focus on hidden psychological

---

1 Scott MacDonald, "Sp...Sp...Spaces of Inscription: An Interview with Martin Arnold," *Film Quarterly* 48, no. 1 (Fall 1994), p. 5.

meaning make his approach to using pre-existing material distinctly his own.

For Arnold, discovering dark undertones of meaning that are implicit but unexpressed can be liberating, especially when this process creates a burlesque of disarming hilarity and invites new ways to experience the original material. "The cinema of Hollywood is a cinema of exclusion, reduction and denial, a cinema of repression," Arnold says. "Consequently, we should not only consider what is shown, but also that which is not shown."[2] Arnold's filmmaking becomes a form of critique that transcends didactic analysis and invites repeated viewings allowing multiple interpretations and revelations.

Arnold's first three found footage films, *pièce touchée* (1989), *passage à l'acte* (1993) and *Alone. Life Wastes Andy Hardy* (1998), each had a powerful impact beyond avant-garde film audiences and raised issues rarely encountered in artist-made cinema.[3] Each centers on intimate, ordinary domestic situations, involving complex modes of interpersonal exchange. While limited to minutely detailed minimal action, they offer subversive experiences that are engrossing and viscerally pleasurable. The first two, if not all three, are, as Scott MacDonald notes, "… exhilarating, often laugh-out-loud funny short films that demonstrate that avant-garde work can be as much fun — for a good many viewers at any rate — as any other form of cinema."[4]

pièce touchée is a 16-minute film based on an 18-second shot from a detective melodrama, *The Human Jungle* (1954), directed by Joseph M. Newman. In the scene, a woman is seated in the foreground reading a magazine as a man opens a door behind her, turns out the hall light, enters the room and moves toward her and the camera. He leans over as she looks up and they kiss. She then rises and follows him across the living room.

2   Arnold in MacDonald, p. 7.
3   Before these works Arnold completed two structural film studies based on abstract, geometrical color paintings: _O.T. 1_ [Untitled 1], completed in 1985 but never released, and _O.T. 2_ (1986). _O.T. 3_ remained unfinished. The 16 mm films here discussed are available on the co-released Re:Voir Video/Index DVD Edition 018: *Martin Arnold, The Cineseizure.*
4   MacDonald, p. 2.

The lighting and décor are B-level generic, with the sense of space barely developed. All of the visual elements are further flattened by the thinly detailed black-and-white quality of the images created by the homemade optical printer Arnold used to re-photograph the original footage. Having attended as a young man Peter Kubelka's lectures about the single-frame essence of cinema, and understanding the exciting combustion that can happen when the sequence of frames is unexpectedly altered, Arnold studied and memorized every combination of movement and shape shifting that occurred between the scene's frames.

Over the course of 18 months Arnold photographed 148,000 film frames, and finally composed these into a 200-page score that included incremental movements at different speeds, forward and reverse repetitions and multiple kinds of image reversals. The result is an astonishing realization of cinema as mechanical ballet. Simple gestures become ominous, ironic and visually spectacular. When first seen, the woman is static for more than a minute, as the soundtrack, a rhythmic and aural distortion of a synchronous sound drones on. Her fingers begin to twitch and the viewer's eye becomes riveted to this small detail until the rear door begins to open. Then, through a series of repetitions, the man opens the door and turns out the light while the woman looks up, mouths an inaudible word and flutters her eyelashes. These actions go on for several minutes as their gestures, the light flashing on and off, and the opening and closing of the door become maniacally repeated, often by selecting parts of single gestures and alternating reversals of the same frame. What keeps the viewer entranced is, on one level, Arnold's graphic sensibility — a wealth of surprising and ever changing rhythms (the actor's gestures, a shadow on the wall, the hallway light flickering on and off) that activates the entire composition.

On another level, the interface becomes an increasingly menacing dance of power and domination. Even before the man enters, the woman's increasing finger movements seem mechanical and controlled. As he approaches from behind, his presence becomes dominant and threatening, and her repeated head movements seem connected to him as he reaches over the chair. The simple interplay of two competent actors becomes a cat and mouse play of power: When he bends over for a kiss she blinks in unison, and this is repeated mercilessly for several seconds. Then, 10 minutes into the film, they walk across the room, moving into medium close-up as the man leads (although this becomes ambiguous as reverse movements ironically undermine his forward thrust). One of the film's most brilliant moments erupts as the woman, halted and centrally positioned, begins turning in a circular motion, with her moving arms echoing the spinning of her torso. This creates a moment of direct kinetic delight and the recognition that this human image is the product of

an insensate machine. Psychologically speaking, she could be undergoing a schizophrenic "break."[5] This also turns her even more into a marionette with neither the will nor ability to function on its own. After further interplay as the actors move across the flattened space, the woman returns to her seated position. The man again looms overhead, having positioned himself for a kiss. Interestingly, their lips never meet in Arnold's version.

---

5   Arnold's cinema has been psychologically analyzed in essays by James Leo Cahill, "The Cineseizure," booklet accompanying the DVD *Martin Arnold, The Cineseizure*; Akira Mizuta Lippit, "Cinemnesis: Martin Arnold's Memory Machine," *Afterimage* 24, no.6, May/June, 1997; and Thomas Mießgang, "Beyond the Words," in *Martin Arnold * DEANIMATED* [German/English], catalogue, eds. Gerald Matt and Thomas Mießgang (Vienna and New York: Kunsthalle Wien/Springer Verlag, 2002).

Martin Arnold
pièce touchée
1989

Martin Arnold
passage à l'acte
1993

With *pièce touchée*, Arnold achieves a formal concentration comparable to the great structural works of the past. It also references a range of emotions we associate with the movies: Threatening action, romantic exchanges, sexual tension, absurd parody and amazing transformations are condensed into a nearly abstract construct. The title has multiple meanings: The original footage and characters' actions have been unrelentingly touched; in chess, once a piece is touched it must then be moved, an off-handed gesture that can have devastating consequences; and in fencing, a successful hit is announced by "touché." Arnold has noted: "The structure of space in conventional narrative cinema is as much at a deadlock as the structure of gender and because of that I felt great pleasure in thoroughly shaking up that space."[6]

Although *passage à l'acte* is only 12 minutes long, it is as dense as *pièce touchée* and it expands Arnold's artistic territory. *passage* also centers on a domestic event, and uses material taken from a Hollywood feature film. But there are important differences: Here an entire scene rather than a single shot is dissected. This scene, from one of Hollywood's most lauded depictions of racism, Robert Mulligan's *To Kill A Mockingbird* (1962), is stationary. It involves four characters at a kitchen table, and the original film's sync soundtrack serves as a key organizing device. Once again re-photographed with his homemade optical printer, images move backward and forward, frame by frame, creating minutely considered rhythmic interplays that are reinforced and punctuated by percussive sounds, which are looped at varying lengths. Arnold has acknowledged the influence of sound art, notably hip-hop scratching and cut-up collages by John Zorn and Christian Marclay, and it is remarkable how this succession of image and sound loops reveals unintended meanings within a relatively minor section of the original film.

The title refers to "transition to action," an antiquated psychoanalytical term meaning the impulsive action of a violent character: In *passage* characters are filled with aggressive energy that at times appears repressed but often becomes explosive. Arnold wanted a scene that could represent a typical morning family routine. In the original, a female neighbor visits the protagonist (Gregory Peck) and his children as they eat and prepare to leave for school. The tomboyish girl is uncomfortable in a new dress; the boy demands that she hurry; the neighbor is distressed by the children's behavior; and the father tries to maintain order. Despite evident tensions, this is a happy family whose foundation is maintained by the Peck character's unflappable calm and paternal wisdom. In Arnold's reshaping, the unit becomes a nuclear family with the neighbor as stand-in mother. As in *pièce touchée*, Arnold's great strength is his ability to move between a succession of delightful kinetic actions that simultaneously reveals troubled relationships. Arnold transforms a bland Hollywood scene into a fantasia of magical effects: A screen door facing the camera becomes a repetitive musical instrument each time it opens and slams shut; the father's head swivels sternly with uncanny spatial depth; the children enact a series of duets through slowed and repeated gestures, first as the boy enters to sit at the table, then through alternating close-ups with both mouthing syllables that gradually become discernible ("Well, hurry up" and "I'm trying to"). The four actors are activated in connection with one another and become soloists in a *Symphony Concrète* of visual and aural delights. Here, incidental sound effects that would normally be missed carry equal weight with abstracted vocal sounds, transforming a conventional soundtrack into a radically new musical composition. Arnold maintains the original shot sequence, allowing the original narrative progression to give the picture and sound patterns additional meaning.

The scene also becomes an absurdly funny depiction of a family at war, with kitchen table as battleground. Each gesture seems threatening or belittling, compulsively manic, and the figures turn into grotesque caricatures. After sitting down, the boy jerks his hand as though masturbating; the girl obsessively and repeatedly squawks at the boy while hitting her fork against the table; the boy squints and utters a guttural scream; the father

6   Arnold in MacDonald, p. 5.

points with machine-like emphasis (accompanied by sounds like gunshots) for the boy to sit down; and the "mother" maintains a strained, desperate grin as she helplessly looks on. Arnold has described the repetition and jerkiness of their actions as a form of stuttering or twitching – as if the actual intention behind each movement is in conflict with the one physically manifested. "I inscribed a symptom into [the material], which brings some of the aspects of repression to the surface," says Arnold, "or (…) which gives an idea of how behind the intact world being represented, another not-at-all intact world is lurking." [7] With *passage à l'acte*, Arnold creates an analogue of the unconscious mind by invading the surface of narrative film.

In *Alone. Life Wastes Andy Hardy*, Arnold lifted material from three films in the *Andy Hardy* series produced between the late 1930s and 1940s that starred Mickey Rooney as the All-American teenager. Immensely popular at the time though now virtually forgotten, the series embodied middle-class ideals during the late Depression, and was a precursor to television family dramas soon to saturate early TV. All three films co-starred the young Judy Garland, who, along with Rooney, was an icon of youthful wholesomeness. As in his previous films, Arnold reveals moments pregnant with unintended meaning, but here with a psychological complexity that more deeply reveals troubling emotional entanglements. Again filmmaking becomes an act of liberation and reclamation. Using three separate sources, Arnold creates a unified visual tapestry that blends Garland's singing, generic background music and dramatic dialogue into the new amalgam of a bizarre musical.

The ensemble includes Andy (Rooney), his archetypical mother and father and Andy's girlfriend, Betsy (Garland). In a mere 15 minutes this perfectly normal world becomes overridden with Oedipal lust, implied incest, maternal suffocation, paternal violence and the dangers of romantic love. The first image is a slow motion, medium close-up of Mom facing the camera, with Andy slowly but forcefully embracing her from behind. As he

repeatedly presses her shoulders, she responds in unison with her eroticized lips opening and closing and eyebrows lifting in eager anticipation. Swelling musical phrases reinforce the sexual innuendoes. The entire scene becomes a barely suppressed expression of orgiastic desire, and it is both comical in its absurdity as well as horrific in the suggestion of taboos being broken. A long shot then shows the two of them in a kitchen, again connected through erotic body gestures, and this is percussively intercut with a close-up of Andy, clearly from another scene, in tears. This is soon intercut with a shot of Dad slapping Andy's face, possibly an implied response to his son's actions, and the father's scream of the first audible line, "Shut up!" The slap is mechanically repeated, and Andy's response gradually evolves into "All right… Dad."

The film moves on to Betsy, positioned centrally in the frame, angelically lit and wearing a dress with a heart-like plunging neckline outlined with lace. Her fragmentary and repetitive singing slowly reveals the word "alone," leading to the rest of the line, "on a night that was meant for love," after which "love" breaks up into exaggerated syllables and utterances. Each character is alone and cut off from accepted social bonds, but Betsy is most vulnerable as the submissive object of desire. In another sequence, she sings with outstretched arms, "There must be someone waiting," and this is rapidly intercut with Mom, looking back at Betsy with her hands extended, selfishly grasping. The film concludes with Andy leaning over Betsy as the two prepare for a kiss. But rather than leading to a gratifying romantic climax, their lips and eyes stutter back and forth, and their kiss is a light peck that is mechanically repeated. Finally their lips part, baring fang-like teeth, and sighs become animalistic snarls. Romantic background music is automatically fragmented with each cut, becoming abrasive and ironically antithetical to the original emotional intent.

This trio of films has been richly analyzed from many vantage points: as critiques of Hollywood's puncture-proof sense of perfect order and heightened expectation within ordinary life; as critiques of gender roles and power hierarchies in intimate

---

7   Arnold in MacDonald, p. 11.

situations; and as formal dissections of compelling but hidden narrative film technique. At a glance, these films can be seen as superficial parodies, or simply as technical feats of labor-intensive virtuosity.[8] But Arnold's constructions work on an immediate level as a kind of vaudeville and become more meaningful the more you dig. A great strength of Arnold's cinema is its duality: the original material maintains its fascination and much of its original power as cultural and photographic artifact, even as the smallest details are being critiqued and made transparent.

Early in the new century Arnold took a new approach to working with old black-and-white Hollywood material. In 2002, the filmmaker created three durational installations that employed subtle digital manipulation and moved beyond the traditional theatrical viewing situation. The simplest, *Dissociated*, positions at opposite ends of a room looped close-ups of two Hollywood stars from Joseph L. Mankiewicz's *All About Eve* (1950). Each character expresses a set of shifting facial emotions that range from indifference to brooding consternation. Slight movements are imperceptibly repeated, so that eyebrow raises and slow turns of the head become meaningful in themselves, reminiscent of Joseph Cornell's *Rose Hobart* (1936), but here enacted by the more glamorized and familiar faces of Bette Davis and Anne Baxter. A second installation, *Forsaken*, is taken from one of Hollywood's most successful Westerns, Fred Zinnemann's *High Noon* (1952), and it uses an astonishing technique through which actors within shots are completely erased. In the course of nine minutes echoing between two facing screens, the climactic shoot-out happens with the only visual evidence being gunshots hitting dirt, and with one of the principals suddenly lying upon the ground. Laid bare, however, are quickening camera movements and editing that reveal generic Western locations (store fronts, barn, wooden sidewalks, saloon) and railroad cars of people (including a central character) moving inexorably into the

distance. Seeing carefully executed compositions that include innumerable details but exclude the main action is a disquieting experience, especially since the environment that is left is a strange reminder of what many of us grew up watching and accepted as a kind of reality. *Deanimated (The Invisible Ghost)* (2002) is the most innovative of the three installations because it creates a radical new experience of an entire feature film and its genre, while managing to preserve the distinctive character of the original. Here, Arnold chose a slow-paced, low-budget B horror film directed by Joseph H. Lewis, *Invisible Ghost* (1941), and transformed it by erasing characters and dialogue, and through subtle repetitions. While a cheaply made, clichéd and often ludicrous potboiler, *Invisible Ghost* is also an intricate psychological horror story with strikingly original touches, that belongs to an era fascinated with subliminal (i.e., invisible) forces lurking beneath the conscious mind. It involves an aging widower, Kessler (Bela Lugosi), living with his daughter and servants in an old dark house they are unable to leave due to his attachment to his wife's memory. She is a seeming hallucination with whom he re-engages each wedding anniversary. This memory, however, is false on different levels. His wife supposedly died in a car crash while leaving with another man, but in fact she is living with amnesia while being kept hidden by the well-meaning gardener. Occasionally leaving her hiding place at night in a trance, only Kessler sees her fleetingly through his window. These real "visions" arouse his repressed anger and drive him to momentary madness and the murdering of his servants. Kessler's daughter is engaged to a man wrongfully accused of one of the murders. After he is summarily tried and executed, his exact replica, a twin brother (though more wooden and deathlike) appears and resumes his part in the drama. The film is frequently punctuated by a painting of Kessler's wife as a young woman, a portrait that is in marked opposition to the ragged and aging zombie that drives him to psychotic senselessness. The daughter bears a striking resemblance to the painting of her youthful mother, adding an incestuous note to the father-daughter relationship. One of

---

8   At the conclusion of the Chicago opening of the series Austrian Avant-Garde Cinema, 1955–1993, an annoyed viewer said to me that *passage a l'acte* was no different than MTV.

Martin Arnold
Alone. Life Wastes Andy Hardy
1998

the most interesting figures is the black butler who is on hand to wittily serve and organize the other servants, and discover dead bodies. The backdrop to all of this is a gothic environment of maze-like corridors and rooms, dark nooks and crannies punctuated by multiple candelabras. Redolent with the moodiness of its genre, the film was a natural choice for Arnold to transform through image manipulation and effacement.

Deanimated (The Invisible Ghost) removes or minimizes most of the supporting characters except the butler. All of Kessler's murderous escapades, several sub-plots and most of the dialogue between the main characters disappear. Just enough is included of the actors and their movements to convey the true strangeness of the original. Decidedly low-key, given the lugubrious pacing and largely wooden acting, Deanimated is a somnambulant landscape, a matrix of mysterious glances and pointless gestures amidst a flow of establishing shots, camera pans and close-ups that have no contextual meaning and are returned to without purpose. What remains seems like an insider's partial view of the film or a strange memory of how an old Hollywood movie was supposed to feel. The actors are exposed as real people only capable of barely trained posturing, lost within a patently artificial house and invasively dominating mise-en-scène. We are reminded of Jack Smith extolling the virtues of Maria Montez or the title character in Gore Vidal's Myron. Myron actually finds himself transported onto the set of a Montez movie that he had watched on television a hundred times, seeing the extras' sweat and cheap backdrops for the first time. Arnold was fascinated by the kind of "hanging out" acting Deanimated reveals: "They look as if they are relaxing, dreaming, waiting for the part they can act out, but they're either too early or too late." [9]

The skill with which language and lip movements are removed and the seamlessness with which characters have been erased creates a new sense of the uncanny in Deanimated. In the original,

Virginia enters her father's study, asking "Guess what?" to tell him of her impending engagement. Here, instead a silent series of suggestive and inexplicable facial and head gestures follows, and the father exclaims, "I'm so happy for you my dear." As the film continues, the action and body following each murder is removed, leaving only surrounding elements: shadows moving on windows, doors mysteriously opening, delirious camera movements through walls and up staircases, abrupt shifts to blurred focus and suspenseful music. In the original, Evans serves as Kessler's most faithful companion and the general overseer of unfolding events – the black servant as shadow figure. He also provides comic relief and is the most compassionate character, but even he becomes de-animated as all traces of liveliness vanish and there remain only vague responses to invisible people and events. One of Evans' original purposes is to discover the murder victims, but in this version his shocking "discoveries" consist of thin air. Upon entering the kitchen, Evans is stopped in his tracks, reaches down to touch nothing (originally the strangled gardener), and runs to the study to make a call. Asking for the operator, his dialogue is reduced to "no," "yes," and "alright." Kessler enters with a warm "Good morning," and seeing the butler's dismay, asks, "What's the matter…" Evans sways intently with an expression of horror as the two stare silently for several seconds before exiting the frame. The relationship between the two has been reconfigured and given a new twist by Arnold.

The actors' presences are subsumed by the movie set and camerawork, both having an apparent life of their own, and few shots contain human activity. There is a pan across a table from one set of candles to another; the kitchen is an empty constructivist arrangement of white and black rectangles, across the surface of which the camera aimlessly glides; close-ups of wallpaper coexist with incoherent framed wall paintings; and editing within scenes that would normally intensify moments becomes meaningless, as only peripheral objects remain within the frame.

What serves as the final line, "Now what?" is uttered by the detective as a fuse blows and the

9   Arnold quoted by Akira Mizuta Lippit, "----MA," in Martin Arnold * DEANIMATED, p. 32.

Martin Arnold
Deanimated (The Invisible Ghost)
2002

house goes dark. The film's original climactic section in which Kessler is revealed as the killer, becomes a delirious nine-minute weaving through a maze of spaces and close-ups, all made more eerie through Arnold's decision to darken the frame (further heightening the gothic quality of the candle-lit dark recesses) and to remove characters and dialogue other than a brief moment when the missing wife falls mysteriously to the ground. One is reminded of the miraculous spaces created by Louis Feuillade more than 100 years ago, with an unending maze of impossible spatial connections and invisible doorways. "The End" title is followed by six minutes of complete blackness punctuated only by visual noise and scratchy ambient sounds from the original tail leader of the film.

As with his earlier work, Arnold's _Deanimated_ can be interpreted in cultural, psychological and deconstructive narrative terms. But it is also a chance to have a delirious, post-Warholian

contemplation of "pure" cinema that wouldn't have been possible before the advent of the computer. In an early statement about the installation Arnold said, "What I want is to create the impression that the audience is also lost – not only the actors. So what I'll do is put in tons of rows of chairs, and usually there won't be more than 10 people in the whole theater. It will be like a cheap, outdated, countryside movie space, showing an outdated film where the actors are getting lost."[10]

However, while _Dissociated_ and _Forsaken_ clearly depend on specific installation settings to create a maximum effect, _Deanimated_ can be seen as a film unto itself. It is as full of marvelous nuances and revealing magic tricks as the filmmaker's earlier trilogy, but in this case these are revealed through extended rather than compressed time and embed-

[10] Interview with Martin Arnold by Mika Taanila, Avanto/Helsinki Media Arts Festival 6, http://www.avantofestival.com/avanto2001/2001_screenings/fv_arnold_interview.html; November 11, 2001.

ded within an elongated form that emerges from an older and almost antiquated time and sensibility.

Black ironies underlie all of Arnold's work and in a recent group of short films, he discovers sinister underbellies in that most popular form of family entertainment, animation, and in its most iconic Disney character, Mickey Mouse. *Shadow Cuts* (2010), *Soft Palate* (2011) and *Self Control* (2011) all are limited to a small amount of material but use relentless repetition and abstracted details to create horrific alternates of slapstick cartoons. In *Shadow Cuts*, a continually pulsating flicker and an iris opening and closing reveal Mickey and his dog Pluto on a bed, locked in an embrace that hovers between homoerotic and helpless attachment. Mickey wears an idiotically fixed grin, his red tongue sticking out lasciviously, while Pluto looks at him with an equally unyielding smile. There is a death-like futility to the spasmodic repetitiveness of partial head and arm gestures that are even

more pronounced since black bands replace the eyes. Eyes suddenly appear, but are isolated and within a field of black, and these flicker alternately with the locked-in figures. A rhythmically complex and lewd dance ensues, and the soundtrack of pants, cries and high-pitched tones is bound to every movement. The second two films further abstract the original material and create harrowing descents into animation hell. *Soft Palate* isolates Mickey's white-gloved hand, gaping mouth and shoes moving within frames of utter blackness; his face is a death mask alternating hypnotically with his abstracted torso. *Self Control* takes fragmented elements of violent actions – hands clutching black space where a head would be, a tongue sticking out in agony and a red brick hitting the top of a skull – looping them all into combinations of fevered repetition. As with all of Arnold's work, what could be tiresome exercises in animation deconstruction are riveting, alternately

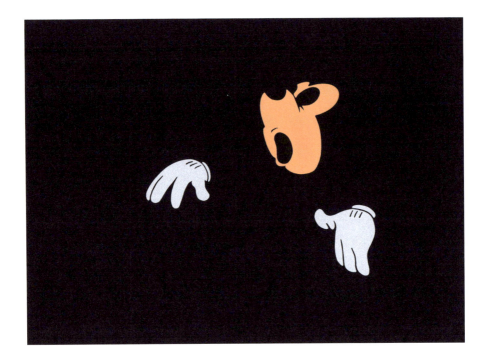

Martin Arnold
Soft Palate
2011

terrifying and hilarious animation experiences
that were wholly unintended in the original.
Easily overlooked details have been surgically
removed and entirely re-imagined.

    Cinema is a world unto itself, one with its own
history, widely varying practices and larger-than-
life personalities. As a mass medium, it is deeply
reflective of the culture that has produced it and
has become a primary source for artistic creation
and social investigation. The films of Martin
Arnold bridge profound analysis with aesthetic
experience, sensory delight with caustic immersion
and raucous humor with disquieting revelation.
Arnold is a quintessential artist of the moment,
one who appropriates and gives new life to what
already exists and is unafraid of confronting dark
subtexts where least expected. In Arnold's world,
a pipe may be a pipe, but its uses and means of
depiction are broken down and reconfigured in
ways that can only be achieved through cinema.

Martin Arnold
Shadow Cuts
2010

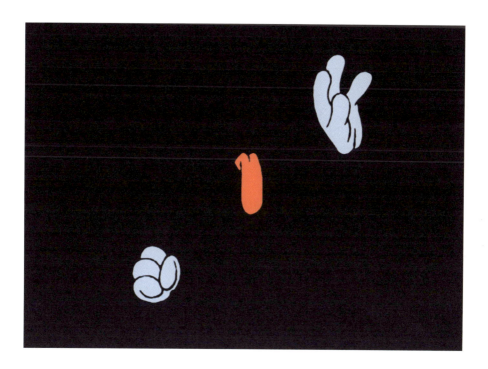

Martin Arnold
Self Control
2011

Viva Voce.
Josef Dabernig's Operatic Avocations.

Andréa Picard

Is Josef Dabernig the Monsieur Hulot of the Austrian avant-garde, or rather Jacques Tati, the scrupulous creator and embodiment of the ubiquitous and gangly, seemingly innocent and slightly unaware character appearing in the French filmmaker's incomparable works? A strange hypothesis, perhaps, but not entirely unfounded (based on the two filmmakers' ultra-precise and ambitious working methods and big dreams, and the themes and concerns of their works – the collision of old and new, the fallibility and absurdity of human communication in a world constantly made strange, the humour in a side-step, etc...), and which allows for a rather matter-of-fact assertion regarding the nature of the avant-garde itself – that it flouts boundaries of all kinds and its impulse can exist nestled within classical structures. That a filmmaker of shorts and artist commonly considered experimental, especially within (or perhaps despite) a national, deeply celebrated and honoured tradition of rigourous formalism, pioneering structuralism and graphic abstraction, can harness the vanguard nature inherent in European modernist cinema from the early 1960s onward and pare it down to a beginning-less and end-less core, and be recognized and admired for his unique, indefinable works is in itself a major achievement.

Since the late 1990s, Josef Dabernig has been granted numerous film retrospectives and festival screenings, solo and group exhibitions, including appearances at the Venice Biennale (2001 and 2003). His art, much like his career, is defined by its amorphous, protean traversals: across fields, disciplines, registers and categories. Dabernig has guest curated both film and art, and is known for his work in installation design, architecture, sculpture, photography and for his cultural theory, which reads as modernist-inflected Gnosticism. Mystery, meticulousness and dry wit define his vocational focus on avocations. This is gusty terrain for an artist for whom interstice allows for freedom of expression, matched by defiance, expressed through an odd comedic charge running through his films – a register of absurdity often aligning him with a certain Eastern European tradition. His work is more camp than kitsch, however, and the self-conscious performances that characterize his films are careful gesticulations of monotony, a physical disenchantment responding to the unfulfilled promise of modernism's proposed but immanently impotent utopia, and the body's attempt to skirt gravity-induced inertia, and maybe even a dose or two of mental fatigue. Human interaction is shown to be fraught by minutia and internalized anxiety, but the solitariness of Dabernig's characters escape their solitude – they venture forth to commune with something, whether it be people, nature, a task or a simple, repetitive gesture.

Josef Dabernig
Rosa coeli
2003

The films have concurrent themes and motifs. An unlikely cross between the aforementioned Tati, Béla Tarr, Samuel Beckett, Aki Kaurismäki and the more distended and elliptical side of Michelangelo Antonioni, these works ranging in length between 6 and 24 minutes, rely on a certain decadent minimalism (an austere, yet sumptuous 35 mm sheen, whether in colour or black-and-white) to fashion portraits of modernist decay and the banal scenarios that occur amidst its strange, introverted structures. As much about architecture and history in place as they are about the tentative absurdity inherent in ritualistic exchange (between people, landscape, technology), Dabernig's films exhort contradictions with every twist of road, eluding the neatness of placement, pronouncement and, joyfully, of watchfulness.

A dry, deadpan treatment of these scenarios further distorts a definitive worldview, which, while puzzling, is alluringly bizarre, often times foreboding and rife with acerbic suspense. The farcical elements, often physical, are laced with a dark, existential confusion – not only one that questions existence, but also social interaction and the pre-scribed decorum attendant in perpetual exchange and societal customs. A Monsieur Hulot-type character, played by Dabernig himself, reappears in the work, embarking on a set task, which seemingly

exists in a fully formed universe where the viewer is welcomed mid-way through. Much remains muddled (chestnuts like story, plot, character relations, mise-en-scène!), but the repetition of imagery – of automobiles, trains, traces of football, atrophying settings, the absence–presence dichotomy and the recurring appearance of Dabernig's family members – suggests an ongoing narrative whose structural expectations are all but abbreviated in any given film. Difficult to situate, Dabernig's films limn the boundaries of both narrative and avant-garde filmmaking, resting unsure of either's hypothetical position in today's art world; instead, they proffer an experience that adheres to an essential notion of cinephila, which swiftly dispenses with genres or categories.

Wisla (1996) begins with a colossal concrete structure jutting into the composition, a ruin standing proud despite its obvious state of neglect. The camera pans insistently to the left, surveying tops of structures barely penetrating the frame whose outline is drawn from an imposing, leaden sky. Shot in ashen black-and-white, the film has an old, burnish feel to it, with textures from a time past. Two men donning suits and ties stride through the concrete catacombs of a dilapidated, brutalist football stadium, to the coach's bench, "Wisla" clearly labeled on the side of the glass shelter where they settle and sit. This is the home of the famous Polish football team; off-screen jeering (Italian!) erupts as the game gets underway. Boisterous cheering and loudspeaker refereeing vividly conjure the visuals of the match as the camera remains focused on the two men who are somewhat clumsily playing out the clichés of a grossly animated soccer coach and his training assistant. Registering nervousness and frustration, their gestures are exaggerated and somewhat dubious. And yet, they are amusing, never preposterous, nor nearly as unbelievable as the real thing. Dabernig's character gets up, calmly walks to the edge of the playing field and signals to his make-believe players, as the camera responds to his order by quickly panning up to reveal row upon row of empty seats. The swimming sea of humanity, alas, does not exist. This game (both the imaginary football match and the film's precise sound-image play) continues a few minutes more until the two men rise, walk up through the bleachers and greet dignitaries watching the game. A series of handshakes takes place, and the two Wisla members walk off-screen, the camera pulling out to expose the barren stadium. *Wisla* ends as the Italian football commentary continues through the credits, which appear at the end of all of Dabernig's films in a typewriter-like, anachronistic font. An introduction into Dabernig's self professed "no-man's land," *Wisla* depicts the un-depicted,

where familiarity is elided in exchange for the geometry of human-made interventions into the natural order, further explored in later films like the sedate, ultra-hermetic *Aquarena* (2007) and *Hotel Roccalba* (2008), a charming, offbeat roaming family portrait that takes place in a hotel where Dabernig's extended family is inexplicably gathered, each engaged in a solitary activity while seemingly on vacation.

Two years after *Wisla*, Dabernig co-directed *Timau* with Austrian artist Markus Scherer, a 20-minute, black-and-white, tripartite vignette, which has been called a "workers' melodrama." The first shot reveals two men driving in a car through a beautiful, but treacherous, mountainous landscape, with lyrical light play being performed upon their car's windshield. The sleepy passenger shifts to reveal a third person in the backseat – the entire film, like all of Dabernig's, relies on a revelation-concealment structure. As they drive, we hear the distinctive but undetermined sounds of the car radio and see wondrous ruins from a distant era. Driving through tunnels, the passengers are alternatively obscured by darkness and obliterated by sunshine, this chiaroscuro peek-a-boo exchange acting as dramatic highpoint to the film's uncertain storyline and suspenseful progression. Finally, they park next to a rock face displaying a mysterious rectangular delineation drawn with chalk – an outline of a football goal net, a remnant from *Wisla*

Josef Dabernig
Wisla
1996

and a personal obsession of the artist repeating throughout his entire filmography as a *clin d'oeil* to the initiated – , and fetch their gear from the trunk. As the tension for narrative builds, the second section of the film draws out the desire for story and simultaneously refuses quick fulfillment. The three men, dressed in some kind of uniform, continue their journey on foot, lugging briefcases. *Timau* adopts a silent film aura as they mount the brush ever upward, their steps unheard, the soft quiet contradicting the arduousness of their hike. This oddly tranquil ascent seems to go on forever until eventually they reach a dark tunnel and the sound is restored. The light from the opening casts their plodding outlines in sharp contrast, and there is very little to see on the screen except for shafts of light alternatively illuminating the top of their heads and feet. Laborious and claustrophobic, their trudging is enhanced through the sounds of belabored breathing. When they at last emerge into daylight, the camera explores the jagged rock face and catches a slithery snake as it cowers beneath a rock, this observational gaze belonging to none of the men.

The third section reveals what the three men have come to do, an uncanny denouement, which is sealed through a formal pact. Deed done, wistful romantic music concludes this odd, elegant tale, the end of which one dares not spoil. But it is a typical Dabernig motif: the paradoxical coming together of old and new worlds, conspiring in a tension befitting contemporaneity. Unsurprisingly,

his oeuvre has occasionally been read as a fabled Western excursion into the East; his camera and Hulot-esque character representing the European sophisticate (though awkward and misplaced) casting a peculiar look upon former Soviet states stuck in a time warp. While the aesthetic collision of rural and urban, and of traditional structures and modernist buildings recurs, the dividing line between old and new is not the dominant theme. Anything askew is, and therein lays the sly, *nervoso* beauty of the work.

Jogging (2000) is wickedly strange. The stereo plays twentieth-century orchestral music composed by Olga Neuwirth as a car travels through a decrepit landscape marked only by unidentified communist architecture; the mood grows steadily eerie. The music, now haunting and pseudo-gothic, grows louder as the skittish camera voyeuristically glances through the side view mirror, glimpsing the reflection of buildings hovering in the background, the driver's hands and peering out the windshield from the backseat. The editing grows quicker as the collage of uncanny imagery (barking wild dogs foaming at the mouth, a herd of goats) increases with the intensity of the music, culminating in an overwhelming state of disquiet. The ultimate destination is Renzo Piano's UFO-inspired Stadio San Nicola, built for the 1990 World Cup. The car suddenly stops, and the Adidas-sporting driver, whose face is never revealed, steps onto the pavement with his puffy black sneakers. The camera goes mad! Swirling out of control, the ethereal music

Josef Dabernig
Wars
2001

Josef Dabernig
Jogging
2000

Josef Dabernig,
Markus Scherer
Timau
1998

still soaring, the camera finally rests upon the big blue sky as the film ends in an extended finale shot reminiscent of Antonioni's *L'Eclisse* where the doom of modernity hangs indeterminately in mid-air.

Three modest works followed: *Wars* (2001), *Parking* (2003), a vehicular, masculine miniature, and the collaborative *automatic* (2002), before Dabernig completed the ambitious *Rosa coeli* from 2003. A man (Dabernig's brother Wolfgang, a recurring figure in several of the works) sits on a train ostensibly reading a newspaper. German voiceover recites his private thoughts; a dense, stylized and poetic text written by Bruno Pellandini (also the author of the arch stage play voiced in 2009's *Herna*), which lasts the duration of the film. En route to a small Moravian town, his birthplace, to bury his recently deceased father, the protagonist conjures his past inside his head as he physically goes through the motions of settling the formalities over his father's death. A rumination on childhood, tinged with regret, sorrow and existential longing, the beauty of the text is rendered elegiac through masterful compositions highlighting the wonders of the land. As the village's past and the ruining of its eponymous monastery, named the Celestial Rose (after which the wine of the region was christened), emerges through this internal monologue, the camera dissects this snowy, sleepy town, its feeble-bodied villagers and the anachronisms of its interior design. Like *Timau*, the signing of a pact is the concluding gesture, but *Rosa coeli* is imbued with the weight of psychological solitude,

Baudelairian recoil for which there can be little sense of accomplishment. A cloaked sense of irony lies hidden amidst this picaresque tale, but as it's so different from Dabernig's other works, it's difficult to detect.

The same cannot be said of his magisterial-farcical *Lancia Thema* (2005). Dabernig plays a tourist driving through a damp, lush and kaleidoscopic landscape – in South-Lazio, Campania and Basilicata where Francesco Rosi shot *Christ Stopped at Eboli* (1979) – listening to arias on his stereo as the viewer is treated to the astonishing splendour of the scenery. Suddenly, he pulls over by a rock face and gets out of his Lancia, fumbles with his analog photo camera and begins photographing his car. The film's gaze strays from the protagonist and contemplates the painterly, awesome surroundings. This gesture is repeated several times between lengthy stretches of driving, which recall so many angst-induced European art films whose tension builds along highways, *autobahns* and *autostradas*. An omnipotent eye oversees the world, is conscious of its geometries (and vestiges, like that of football of course!) of what is present, absent and celestial. The Bel canto emerges from the audiotape, but it is the landscape that really sings, allegorically but also in an otherworldly accord – the enigmatic pull that figures in all of Dabernig's works cannot be contained or explained. *Lancia Thema* is bathed in a *sfumato* sensuousness and hints at a forsaken paradise of purity. But its grandeur is promptly

Josef Dabernig, G.R.A.M.
automatic
2002

Josef Dabernig
Parking
2003

Josef Dabernig
Hotel Roccalba
2008

Josef Dabernig
Lancia Thema
2005

wrested by an unsettling, dry humour, and the meta-cinematic embrace of its own eccentricities.

Aquarena (2007), which Daberning co-directed and wrote with his wife, Isabella Hollauf, demonstrates the tensions between nature and human endeavour via an atypical essay on the Socialist policing of water dissemination, its potential for contamination and waste, and the erosion of public works. An extreme close-up of a typical Alpine illustration, Saint Florian (patron Saint of fire-fighters) bearing a bucket of water to douse a housefire, is peculiarly cropped and headless, painted as a large mural on a concrete façade. A montage of oblique cuts follows the enigmatic pull of water. In a starkly barren, hexagonal pool existing in the middle of a traffic roundabout, a woman (Hollauf) climbs in and begins to swim in the crystalline water as a high-pitched, electronic drone emerges from the soundtrack. A voice-over, rather stern, rather stale, reading codes and sections from a Socialist policy on water management provides the counterpoint, as the camera alternates between static shots of water repositories and the director-swimmer. Despite the instructional text, *Aquarena* rests far from the educational film. Bifurcated into two, it has a peculiar midpoint, as the camera suddenly shoots from inside a high-rise, peering from the window to survey a claustrophobic cluster of concrete blocks. Another abrupt cut leads us back outside where a male swimmer (Dabernig) emerges and climbs into a different pool, in a courtyard surrounded by towering apartment buildings. His swim is less athletic, but the same disquieting music attends his desultory dip into shady waters. *Aquarena* – a portmanteau combining aqua and arena – is one of Dabernig's most beautifully shot films, masterly composed, resolutely elusive and beguiling, its message as subtle as it is obvious.

A darker vision is expressed in *Herna* (2010), which poignantly signals an alarming family breakdown when a young father abandons his wife and child to their vehicle, for an obsessive and interminable round of slot machines in a roadside bar. The bleak premise and suffused miserablism (the kind one encounters in a Béla Tarr film, or a

Elfriede Jelinek novel) are thrown into dialogue with a salon-era radio play written especially for the film by Bruno Pellandini, in which four gossips commiserate about life and death. The seamy outskirts (Czech, perhaps, given that *Herna* is Czech for casino or gambling room) and vacant stare of the disheveled man exist in shocking contrast to the arch, stylized, over-articulations effectively throwing the film out of whack with voice-over contradictory to the film's images. The deep-seeded melancholia is thus prohibited from reaching mature fruition (or an approaching domestic explosion). The blinking lights of the games offer little hope as the gambler clicks and clicks away like an automaton, with no concept of time or emotion. Hence, two parlor games in one – and no two could be so different, so much so, that *Herna* risks foundering from the extremes of its disjunction. Yet similar themes of possession and loss emerge from the parallel stories and conspire to create a complex exploration of existence that delves beneath the surface hovering near the real-life intersections of tragedy, melodrama and silliness.

"If people did not sometimes do silly things, nothing intelligent would ever get done," opined Ludwig Wittgenstein. Like Tati, Dabernig's form of humour has a shade of the theoretical and emerges from a sophisticated aesthetic sense, which drives his complete artistic expression. Despite the recurring image of Dabernig in so many of his films, an unseen presence encapsulated by the camera's point-of-view looms larger, effectively reminding us that there indeed exists something greater than time and matter; a force or energy that has the power to evade causality and logic. However daunting, these we must accept as modernity's grand narratives and structures betray their promises. Creators of comedy ultimately reveal themselves to be the tricksters and taxonomists of melancholia: twin peaks forever, if perilously, scaled.

This essay is a revised and updated version of
"In a Matter of Time: Josef Dabernig"
by Andréa Picard, *Cinema Scope*, no. 28, 2006.

Josef Dabernig,
Isabella Hollauf
Aquarena
2007

Josef Dabernig
Herna
2010

Weapon of Choice. Notes on Notes on Film.
Or, The Man Who Is Squidward Tentacles.
On the Works of Norbert Pfaffenbichler.

Christoph Huber

1 Say Hello to the Ultimate Fun: _Wirehead_

"Please make your choice." The animated woman's face repeats this sentence with gentle persistence. A smooth mask, chin to eyebrows, adorns an interface. Her pokerfaced promise seems as inscrutable as the eyes sunk in dark recesses. Surrounding this face are rudimentary control units and function keys to click on, and a 3D logo with the letters C, E and A, which are revealed elsewhere to be an acronym: Critical Entertainment Agency. Various pictographs are located at the top of the screen, next to the Home button, and one is selected: Entertainment. A series of smaller icons appears, while the initial command is repeated again and again: "Please make your choice." Cartoons is clicked on and the interface dissolves into pixels, then goes black: "Say hello to the ultimate fun." A commercial for the Loonatic Converter is shown.[1] Some examples demonstrate the obvious fun potential of this mysterious before-and-after process: A photograph of Groucho Marx turns into a cartoon drawing of his brother Harpo; Woody Allen's picture mutates into the crazed dodo from Looney Tunes masterpieces such as Bob Clampett's _Porky in Wackyland_ (1938). Who could say no to that? The woman's face returns promptly: "Please make your choice."

A click on Movie takes us to the actual opening credits: _Wirehead_ (1997), the first film Norbert

Pfaffenbichler and Timo Novotny co-directed, was a heterogeneous assembly of material, which resulted from how it was created.[2] It also represents a quasi-narrative shot through with loops and variations. The theme of difference and repetition, which Pfaffenbichler passed off as his work's leitmotif almost as tirelessly as the woman's face, is established within two minutes. The 22-minute early work intimates the conceptual line to be found in Pfaffenbichler's work; the rough, cyberpunk-like appearance somewhere between industrial ruins and remainders of plot, ancient-looking effects and wildly sprawling, channel-surfing aesthetic present stark contrasts to the elegant and for the most part minimalistic thoroughness of his later productions. Not only is the humor appealingly anarchistic, the interludes in _Wirehead_ include (in addition to the recurring "Please make your choice" animation, which was actually the work of Pfaffenbichler) the cartoon featuring a dog, "Unnecessary Surgery," the style of which resembles the work of the brilliant creator of _Ren & Stimpy_, John Kricfalusi; an ego shooter with vector graphics; and promises typically made in

1 Can be ordered at 1-800-555-NEURO.

2 The film is a collection of tests and finger exercises that Pfaffenbichler and various fellow students produced during his early years at the University of Applied Arts, for the master class in Visual Media Design. And so, _Wirehead_ is a metaphor for itself: The title comes from the cyberpunk idea of directly coupling the human brain to a network ("Please make your choice"), and the various contributions are like different inspirations.

Norbert Pfaffenbichler,
Timo Novotny
Wirehead
1997

commercials, such as "multiple joy… multiple partners." All this is cobbled together by the story of an illegal intruder entering an abandoned warehouse where individuals with cyber goggles, cable terminals and barcode stamps and connected to monitors enjoy their own private deliriums. They are all under the supervision of none other than Kurt Kren, humble master of the Austrian avant-garde.[3] With no-budget casualness, the two young directors play with virtually every idea imaginable, from images that seem to have been captured by a surveillance camera to snatches of fragments and movements changing color, which are accompanied by a sizzling sound, including the intruder's Looney Tunes-esque pursuit of himself, and a big finish in which everything once again speeds through an eye in fast motion. In conclusion, a bandaged wirehead stares into the camera in a countershot, behind him and to the right we can see a poster showing a comic character, its brain smoking. _Wirehead_ was made by a university

student: Uneven and full of energy, it astonishes as a source of raw material for later use by its creators, in their matured ideas.[4]

2   Austrian Abstract: Toward _36_

Norbert Pfaffenbichler was born in Steyr, Upper Austria in 1967, trained as a teacher for the handicapped and initially worked in Vienna. In 1992, he began theater studies at the university, then transferred to the Academy for Applied Art. Thanks to Austria's national film festival, the Diagonale, he became a key figure in the filmmaking scene as curator of the new series Austrian Abstracts, which concentrated on the booming production of

---

3   Pfaffenbichler studied under Kurt Kren, among others. As he recalls, the lesson often consisted, in modest mastery, of the wordless presentation of films by Jörg Buttgereit or Shinya Tsukamoto. The body-cinema cascades created by Japanese stylist Tsukamoto, in particular the techno-transformations in his _Tetsuo_ films, clearly left their mark on the visual world of _Wirehead_. These and all other comments by Pfaffenbichler are from a May 2010 interview with the author, conducted in Vienna.

4   The wealth of abstruse ideas is to an extent grounded in the sound provided by the Sofa Surfers, an Austrian electro-rock formation whose tours Novotny and Pfaffenbichler made visuals for. Novotny's amusing black-and-white music video entitled _The Plan_ (1997), which Pfaffenbichler shot, shows the band's bus skidding through curves in slow motion, and in the end the armed musicians storm a shop – only to find empty shelves. Freewheeling tour life became too much of a strain for Pfaffenbichler, and he explored different environments for his abstraction. He remembers that Novotny tended toward a Pop style, while he was more interested in fine art and the avant-garde. In 2006, at the Austrian film festival Diagonale, the duo premiered their first full-length films: Novotny's _Life in Loops (A Megacities RMX)_ (2006) is a poppy remake of Michael Glawogger's documentary _Megacities_ (1998) as a digital city symphony, and Pfaffenbichler's _Notes on Film 02_ represents the provisional culmination of his engagement with Modernity.

Norbert Pfaffenbichler,
Lotte Schreiber
36
2001

 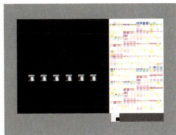

abstract digital videos.[5] His two-minute _36_ (2001), produced with his partner Lotte Schreiber, could be described as the aesthetic essence of the Austrian Abstracts movement. His filmography to that point included two collaborations with Jürgen Moritz in which Pfaffenbichler's basic concern with the interplay of sound and image was refined, and also demonstrated his concern with cinematic history and structural and serial film in particular: In addition to Kren the influence of Peter Kubelka must be mentioned, and Pfaffenbichler was a frequent visitor of the latter's cyclical program of almost exclusively avant-garde classics at the Austrian Film Museum's Invisible Cinema.[6]

The five-minute _Santora_ (1998) combines geometric shapes and a soundtrack by Christian Fennesz. A gray line appears on a white background, above the lower quarter of the picture, followed by a striped block in the middle that then triples in size, extending right and left. Accompanied by a rhythmic electronic staccato, the size and number of these rectangles vary, and the line, disconnected at irregular lengths, stutters. The diagonal movement of a figure is then projected into the block, and its direction is occasionally

mirrored, while its speed changes constantly. The repetitive sequence and the impossibility of making out details are again reminiscent of surveillance images. At the conclusion, unexpected spots of color in the large field surprise the spectator.

The spectrum of variations is increased by _traxdata_ (1998), in which Moritz and Pfaffenbichler, to the accompaniment of Fennesz's spiraling electronic sound, have a split, multi-colored rectangle mutate on a black background. In its left half lines vibrate, making the spectator think of blurry cue cards, bar codes or a score of modern music. On the grayish-blue right half, a pattern evokes abstract geometric forms as well as blurry images (a sunrise, a stylized typewriter's golf ball, even a flood of lava when the picture turns yellow). For a space of four minutes minimalistic mutations parallel the music: reflections, alterations in the color, changes in the pattern. The vibration of sounds, forms and intensity of perception calls to mind avant-garde predecessors, simultaneously expressing a new joy in digital experimentation.

_36_ creates an apotheosis of digital reduction in captivating geometric clarity and conceptual beauty. The picture, framed in gray, is divided into three fields according to form/space, area/color and rhythm/time. Thirty-six horizontal and vertical lines appear inside a large black square to the upper left,[7] change in a variety of binary patterns of movement and then consolidate into six squares

5   The job came relatively unexpectedly, soon after he met with directors Christine Dollhofer and Constantin Wulff bringing along a plastic grocery bag full of VHS tapes.

6   Peter Kubelka's cycle What Is Film is a series of 63 film programs curated by Kubelka that repeats annually, shown at the Austrian Film Museum in Vienna every Tuesday night. See _Was ist Film. Peter Kubelkas Zyklisches Programm im Österreichen Filmmuseum_, eds. Stefan Grissemann, Alexander Horwath and Regina Schlagnitweit (Vienna: FilmmuseumSynemaPublikationen, 2010).

7   All the elements of the mathematical-graphic composition in _36_ are based on the eponymic number.

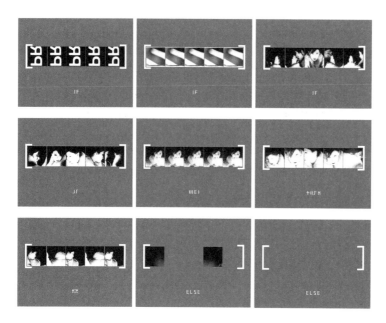

Norbert Pfaffenbichler
notes on film 01 else
2002

on which amorphous patterns appear. In the rectangular section to the right a palette of color fields – reminiscent of Gerhard Richter's *Ten Large Color Panels* (however horizontal rather than vertical) – undergo constant change or pulse and produce flicker effects. In the narrow strip at the picture's bottom, a square containing a smaller square moves from left to right: This is the video's temporal axis. When the upper surfaces' border is crossed, the most radical change of all takes place, also in terms of the sound as Stefan Nemeth's music harmonizes with the picture's structure. As casually as *36* takes up traditions of geometric films, abstract painting and the charmingly blocky aesthetic of early video games, it just as easily overloads the spectator's perception, even after repeated viewings, employing just three precisely marked areas – although the elegance of the processes always ensures a complete overview. *36* is a perfect film. What next?

3 Super Voyeur: *Else* and Beyond.

The six-minute jewel and Pfaffenbichler's main work, *notes on film 01 else* (2002),[8] is the beginning of a cycle:[9] *Notes on Film*, film notes, filmed notes, provides both commentary and supplementary information relating to film, abstractions of live-action images, found footage – which in this case was refilmed with appropriate Pfaffenbichleresque irony. A scene from Paul Czinner's beautiful silent-film adaptation of Arthur Schnitzler's *Fräulein Else* (*Miss Else*, 1929) fascinates him, though it is too short. So Pfaffenbichler shot his own footage with cinematographer Martin Putz, a semi-transparent mirror and actress Eva Jantschitsch.[10] The black-

---

8   This is incidentally Pfaffenbichler's first solo work.
9   Of note when discussing this work is Pfaffenbichler's CD-ROM *notes 01* (2000), an invitation to play with various notation systems that make use of writing, geometry and music.
10   Under the pseudonym Gustav, Jantschitsch experienced her breakthrough a few years later in Austria's electro-pop scene.

Norbert Pfaffenbichler
notes on MAZY
2003

and-white images showing Jantschitsch are arranged according to the principle of a five-part canon. The upper half of the picture, framed by brackets, has a "cubistic" split-screen effect formed by five small fields:[11] They contain five different views of a young woman looking at the audience, which at the same time is observing her. Her poses alternate between enticing and dismissive; her looking at the spectator and then looking away represents the idea of the early cinema of attractions in condensed form. The movements of her face and hands accentuate the game with the spectator, while at the same time notes with increasing numbers and her hand clapping, a simulation of the clapboard, remain purely material elements of the picture, worthy of a Warhol *Screen Test*. The attraction of the moving image is communicated directly and multiplied, though the bracketing is not the only thing that creates intellectual distance: Wolfgang Frisch's synthetic orchestra music alternates between exaggerated emphasis and the fragmented style characteristic of modern music, and in the lower half of the picture runs a series of symbols undergoing hieroglyphic transformations. The word IF in block letters moves, forms strange symbols that look like a system of notation in an unfamiliar language, though familiar numbers

and letters, such as OR, THEN and ELSE, appear at intervals (commands for creating loops in programming languages such as Basic). Repetition as an option: In Pfaffenbichler's *Notes on Film* series it takes on an almost utopian quality that goes beyond the merely analytical – cinema in the subjunctive. What Pfaffenbichler said at the time, that the multiplied gaze in *else* is "super voyeuristic," can also be interpreted in a positive sense. It does justice to the work's ambivalence.

This new perspective was soon employed in a longer work, after completion of two self-confident films that were commissioned: *notes on MAZY* (2003) is part of a trilogy of shorts[12] that interpret a dance piece by Willi Dorner.[13] The quartered screen shows the body of dancer Helga Guszner[14] inside two relatively large rectangles (upper left and lower right), completed by two square fields showing her face. The large block of four squares is framed by the blue of the empty input signal. The dance movements' dynamic produces interference in the picture,[15] at least one of the windows shows the original footage at all times: a pas de deux of the

11 Pfaffenbichler actually employed different kinds of film stock and video, but the differences are barely noticeable due to the images' small size.

12 The two others are by Johannes Hammel and Michaela Schwentner.
13 Pfaffenbichler had already made videos based on Dorner's stage choreographies for years.
14 Guszner's T-shirt is quite amusing: the face of fat Elvis on the front, a number 1 and The King on the back.
15 Such interference is the result of the poor compression caused by the film being imported and exported a number of times.

woman depicted in the fields and her digital image, accompanied by Heinz Ditsch's variation on the choreography's original music. In *Piano Phase* (2004) Steve Reich's music provides the point of departure: Pfaffenbichler and Lotte Schreiber created a series of black-and-white loops in two fields that mutate rhythmically to blocks of a single color, which accompanies a composition for two time-delayed pianos. At certain angles the fragmented Super 8 footage of a swarm of birds takes on confusing dimensions; for example, they resemble animated images of a joint's swinging movement or particles floating in some kind of liquid before they can be identified: The movement of individual elements and mass deformation represent a vision of a world wavering between order and chaos.

4   Talk to Me: *Notes on Film 02*
For his debut feature length film Pfaffenbichler looked to a period in cinematic history during which the world's chaos was met with images of alienation: Michelangelo Antonioni's *Tetralogia dei Sentimenti* [16] was an inspiration, as was Jean-Luc Godard's sci-fi fable *Alphaville* (1965), which Pfaffenbichler wanted to make a variation on at first. After failing to obtain a subsidy, he finally started production with only enough money for a test – and found a suitable beginning point, or "cipher story": Robert Frank's 30-minute reply to Antonioni, *OK End Here* (1963). The core of Pfaffenbichler's 96-minute opus, *Notes on Film 02* (2006), is a seven-minute short film, shown in its entirety (though even then the view is not complete) during the final sequence. A young woman (Ursula Strauss) wakes up in bed and speaks the film's sole line of dialogue: "Talk to me." Her relationship has gone into rigor mortis: Twenty-five subsequent scenes show her engaging, for the most part, in a relatively emotionless exchange with her partner (Lutz Wiskemann). She watches the cartoon *SpongeBob SquarePants*, he reads Horkheimer/Adorno in the bathtub wearing a Belmondo hat. He works, she smokes. A card game with visual motifs

from the worlds of film and art remains a mysterious association, a gentle embrace from behind represents the height of emotion. In the end both of them leave the apartment, and while walking through the city the woman gets lost in a forest of empty high-rises à la Antonioni. But the shots are serial and arranged according to an alphanumeric principle: Every time a scene is added, the film starts over again. *Notes on Film 02* begins with shot A, a close-up of the woman turning over in bed, and her line, "Talk to me." This is followed by the first variation on shot A, then follows shot B: She steps up to him in the kitchen, he leaves. The sequence is A.1 → A.2 → B.1 → A.3 → B.2 → C.1 → A.4 and so on, until in the final sequence all the film's shots, from A.26 to Z.1, add up to result in the whole seven-minute film, a panorama of the urban area in which the protagonist, who is seen at increasing distances, disappears. In its captivating black-and-white images shot by Dariusz Kowalski and accompanied by Bernhard Lang's uncommon soundtrack (including a chanson during the final credits!), this refined experiment is an association-rich game with modernity, while at the same time going beyond mere modernism: Pfaffenbichler's historical references are intended to do more than create a sense of nostalgia. The variations are subtle [17] and deserve intense concentration. Indeed, the video is incomparably more effective on the big screen, and Pfaffenbichler more or less agrees with Andy Warhol's notion that the spectator may leave the theater and return as they please. In any case, the splintered self-confidence of modern narrative cinema is shattered:[18] The obsession with determinism and chance, indulged to such an extent in contemporary cinema (including in Austria), is set up against a radical idea of freedom. Again, subversive potential grows from Antonioni's artfully conservative studies of ennui. Each new shot provides a

---

16 *L'Avventura* (*The Adventure*, 1960), *La Notte* (*The Night*, 1961), *L'Eclisse* (*The Eclipse*, 1962) and *Il Deserto rosso* (*Red Desert*, 1964).

17 Pfaffenbichler told his actors to avoid simple contrasts such as shouting/whispering.
18 Assignments to a particular genre are also deconstructed in an apparently casual manner: Even images that seem "documentary" (the recurring closeup of an old woman on the street; different arrangements of tschotschkes, including a SpongeBob doll, on the head of the bedstead) turn out to be fragments of a fiction that has been cracked open.

different option, a new opportunity. Behind the narrative's melancholy and loss of self, a hope, a possibility becomes tangible: It is all too fitting that the film's loudest scene features a song dedicated to contemporary pop culture's surreal embodiment of innocence, the cartoon figure SpongeBob, with the opening credits of the German version, "SpongeBob Schwammkopf!" (repeated 23 times). According to Pfaffenbichler, this was supposed to have the same effect as Haydn's kettledrum.[19]

5 What He Saw on the Screen: *Mosaik Mécanique*

Notes on Film 02 works better when screened at a theater, and the same can be said of the third film in the *Notes* series, *Mosaik Mécanique* (2007), due to the miniscule size of its parts. Pfaffenbichler, a lover of silent films, chopped Charlie Chaplin's

one-reeler *A Film Johnnie* (1914) up into its 96 individual shots. The final result is 98 visual fields, including head and tail leader, arranged in a 14×7 grid in CinemaScope format, and shown simultaneously. Each shot is looped for the original film's duration of nine minutes, while Bernhard Lang's soundtrack consisting of 98 layers of player-piano phrases create an uncanny tension. The original material has been "spatialized," liberated from the constraint of time, and "put in written form," which makes it "legible" in all directions.[20] Sequences of light and movement, shot-countershots and other filmic building blocks correspond and reveal themselves with a clarity that could only be guessed at up to that point, and elements unquestioned as being essential to the narrative are turned upside down: More happens within the head and tail leader than in the static intertitles – amusingly enough, the first one says, "What He Saw on the Screen."[21] The intertitles are uninteresting black stains on the

---

19 This great feat was followed by another commissioned work, Pfaffenbichler's only film that does not refer to something other than itself: *a1b2c3* (2006) was made with Lotte Schreiber while the two were in the process of ending their relationship and pressed for time. In Pfaffenbichler's view they settled upon the "lowest common denominator." This five-minute video shows a white grid on a blue background that moves along the four main axes at various speeds. The parameters are based on the monitor's digital video format (720×576) – just like the modulations in Bernhard Lang's whistling synthesized sound. A few colored afterimages and variations in the lines' thicknesses that involve the physiology of perception resemble the possibilities beyond the preset grid.

---

20 By comparison, the raw material shrinks to the dictates of a puny standard when projected as originally intended: read line by line, from upper left to lower right.
21 While Pfaffenbichler considered other silent comedies, he finally settled on *A Film Johnnie* for legal reasons involving rights, and also because it involves filmmaking: The theme heightens his film's concept.

Norbert Pfaffenbichler
Notes on Film 02
2006

Norbert Pfaffenbichler
Conference. notes on film 05
2011

vibrant mosaic that lifts the film from its linearity, making it a rag rug for contemplation, an intellectual garden of diverging paths.

While the title is a reference to Kubelka's *Mosaik im Vertrauen* (*Mosaic in Confidence*, 1955) and Fernand Léger's only film, *Ballet mécanique* (1924), more latitude for associations opens up, involving for example the filmstrips that Paul Sharits hung in art galleries. Pfaffenbichler is frequently involved with art shows, both as a curator and artist. His plan for a film adaptation of one of Sophocles' *Oedipus* plays, involving blind actors in static closeups that ensure a total concentration of the drama on the spoken word, never came to fruition due to a lack of funding.[22] But he presented the *Silent Alien Ghost Machine Museum* show in Graz in 2010, in which a number of elements from his film works turn up.[23] Another example is the

installation *o. T.* (*Untitled*), which shows portrayals of Hitler from various feature films: This anticipates his next film project, *Conference*. Fourth in the *Notes* series, it will present the most common figure in cinematic history in dialogue with himself: a looped series of silent shot-countershots of Adolf Hitler played by a variety of actors.[24] A total hyperbole of Hitler's cinematic image, it is potentially spooky and grotesque in equal proportions.

This combination of elements, apparently paradoxical at first, then productive, is typical for Pfaffenbichler: *Mosaik Mécanique* demonstrates, in passing, the mechanical cruelty and surreal power of silent-film comedians by transplanting them into a different force field, which, at initial contact, destroys the conventional comprehension of film. "Is this what it looks like inside the mind of David Bordwell?" asked critic Michael Sicinski, referring to the effortless analytical brilliance of an important US film theorist. Sicinski's conclusion commands no less awe: "As is the case with all great structuralism, *this film was completely inevitable*." But I say, no, it takes a Norbert Pfaffenbichler. *Please make your choice.*

Translated by Steve Wilder

---

[22] Though the 20-minute test for *Ödipus Monument* (*Oedipus monument*, 2008) looks absolutely breathtaking.
[23] The projection of shots from the Chaplin comedy *Dough and Dynamite* (1914) into a grid drawn on a wall closely resembles *Mosaik Mécanique*. The game with postcards in *Notes on Film 02*, among other elements, appears in five different variations as video installations, just as collectible figures and the wall masks from the film apartment are used in different contexts – the latter, for example, in a tribute to Pier Paolo Pasolini and his crowning grotesque short, *La terra vista dalla luna* (1967), with god of the *commedia* Totò. Pfaffenbichler's sense of humor is demonstrated in his magnificent triple self-portrait as Squidward Tentacles, the hapless octopus from *SpongeBob SquarePants*.

---

[24] The original images are filmed off a monitor with black-and-white Super 8 in order to homogenize the material.

Norbert Pfaffenbichler
Mosaik Mécanique
2007

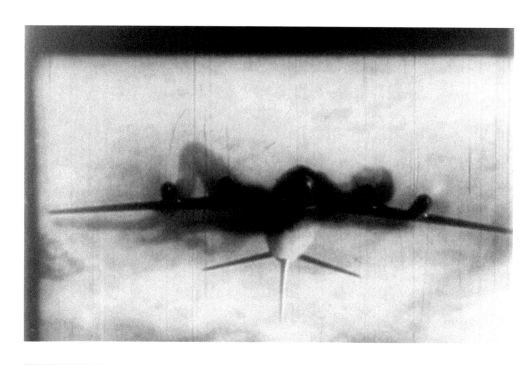
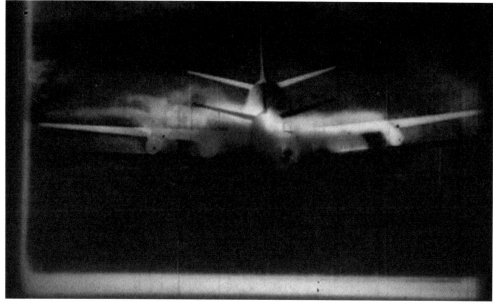

"Is This the Precise Way That Worlds are Reborn?"[1]
The Films of Siegfried A. Fruhauf.

Nicole Brenez

"I defy nature to stop the production of these material and personal, servile tracings. I give it permission to use up the sum of probabilities, without missing a single one. As soon as it's at the end of its roll, I will shut it off from the infinite, and I will summon it to pay up – that is, to endlessly execute duplicates."[2]

As an artist, Siegfried A. Fruhauf has tackled a historical problem that is as fascinating as it is perilous: a brilliant inheritor of structural cinema – this international movement which has explored the specific properties of cinema for four decades – he now finds himself in the position of confronting this legacy at the moment of cinema's transition to digital. *Mutatis mutandis*, we can compare his position to that of the directors and actors of the silent era who had invented and then brought their art to the point of perfection – but suddenly had to rethink it all because of the dissemination of the talkie. How has Fruhauf navigated this passage, which has come from outside of him? On the basis of which postulates has he conceived of it, reflected upon it, worked it through? Between analog cinema and the digital is there a passage, a transference, a rupture, a fall, a mixture, an interweaving, a turning point – or all of the above?

1 Louis-Auguste Blanqui, "Eternity According to the Stars," trans. Matthew H. Anderson, *CR: The New Centennial Review*, vol. 9, no. 3, Winter 2009, p. 25 (translation revised by author and translator).
2 Blanqui, p. 46.

What are we led to grasp of the *argentic* (from the French *argentique* or silver-based emulsion) and the digital in the initiatives taken by the maker of *Exposed* (2001)?

The Argentic Heritage

The heritage of structural cinema is as rich as it is complex. To explore the elements of cinema can mean many different things – starting with the strategic choices made as to what those basic elements actually are. On this level, Fruhauf works within a structuralism inherited simultaneously from Paul Sharits and Peter Tscherkassky, in the sense that their structuralism is not an *objectivism*. In fact, Fruhauf does not restrict himself to the *material* elements of the cinematic dispositif (celluloid, camera, projector, etc.); rather, he integrates, in the footsteps of his elders, three elements that are *immaterial* but wholly defining of the project: the artist's *subjectivity*, the reality of the *regard* that forms the final synthesis of the image created by its circuit of fabrication and the *historical* dimension of images.

La Sortie (1998), *Blow-Up* (2000), *Exposed* and *Mirror Mechanics* (2005): These four films represent as many superb extensions and renewals of structural propositions. Each in a different way, these four films also offer classical stylistic traits: mathematical rigor, seriality, progressive argumentation, sensual materialism.

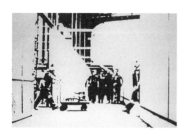

Siegfried A. Fruhauf
La Sortie
1998

La Sortie ironizes one of cinema's original motifs: Under Fruhauf's expert hands, just as in the people's real history, the workers will never manage to leave the factory; instead of escaping into off-screen space, as in the initial three stagings by the Lumière brothers, their movements from foreground to background and simultaneously from left to right and right to left form a plastic cross which refers to the death of manual labor in factories, the figurative erasure of its working class, and the death of cinema. In other words, after the harmonious *mise en scène* of the Lumières who invented an appeased everyday comes a critical elegy.

Two factors add weight to this formal irony. Firstly, a soundscape entirely comprised of groans and wheezes, evoking the painfulness of work, where the Lumière films dealt only with the moment of being freed from it – their mise en scène thus substituting itself for work, since the laborers were asked to repeat their exit thrice for the camera. Secondly, color, perhaps referring to the Lumières' incessant research into this parameter in which they were pioneers, as much in relation to photography as cinema; but, more definitely, as a way of sensually underlining the repetitive and ineluctable nature of seriality itself, in the tradition of Malcolm Le Grice's initiatives, especially in *Berlin Horse* (1970). We must note here the way in which *La Sortie* forms a diptych with the 1984 masterpiece *Motion Picture (La Sortie des Ouvriers de l'usine Lumière à Lyon)* by Peter Tscherkassky, who was Fruhauf's teacher. For that film Tscherkassky projected a single frame from Lumière's very first film onto a rectangle consisting

of fifty strips of unexposed film stock. After developing the film strips, he edited them together. Tscherkassky thus created a film that returns the ensemble of the cinematic dispositif to its photographic determination and transformed the original film into a completely abstract, black-and-white *défilement* in order to measure the crucial role of immobility and intermittence in analogical cinema. Fruhauf, under the same historical banner, proposes three initiatives. He chooses images that differ from the Lumière footage, showing the workers relentlessly marching into a factory corridor and, thus, precisely never quitting work; he adds two "untimely" parameters, sound and color; and he indicates, as much as the workers' suffering, the death of cinema itself, whose *défilement* is interrupted by, on the one hand, freeze-frames and, on the other, that cross created by the movements, asserting itself (via the force of its acceleration) bit by bit, erasing the frame, blocking the *défilement* and signifying (as Tscherkassky himself has noted) "a symbol of death as a *ballet mécanique.*"[3] From such an artistic gesture we can intuit the energy which will allow Fruhauf to negotiate the transition

---

3   This and all further unattributed quotations about Austrian experimental film derive from the online catalogue at http://www. sixpackfilm.com/en/. Some of the catalogue's English translations have been rephrased.

Siegfried A. Fruhauf
Blow-Up
2000

Siegfried A. Fruhauf
Exposed
2001

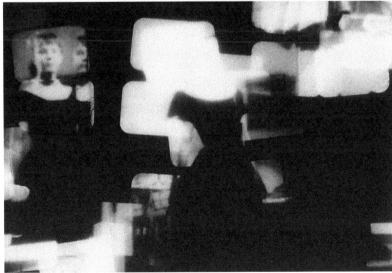

to digital: the refashioning not only of material elements, but also the general presuppositions of representation in movement.

More precisely, as regards the immaterial elements of cinema, Fruhauf further develops an emblematic domain of Austrian experimental cinema: the scopic drive. _Blow-Up_, _Exposed_ and _Mirror Mechanics_ provide precise developments on this score. Each one treats the representation of the body in cinema. _Blow-Up_ indexes the _défilement_ of celluloid within a breathy rhythm that duly organizes the representational ensemble. _Défilement_ is liberated from the dispositif's fatality and the emblematic "24 times a second" of the image, cinema's motor-energy then coming from a deeper, more perennial site: rhythm, even (we must say) the original _ruthmos_, which guides the mouths in _Blow-Up_ to open and shut, the images to expand and retract, phenomena to beat and pulse. Emile Benveniste devoted some crucial pages to distinguishing between rhythm and schema, or _ruthmos_ and _skema_, the latter "defined as a fixed 'form,' realized and viewed in some way as an object. On the other hand _ruthmos_, according to the contexts in which it is given, designates the form in the instant that is assumed by what is moving, mobile and fluid, the form of that which does not have organic consistency; it fits the pattern of a fluid element, of a letter arbitrarily shaped, of a robe which one arranges at one's will, of a particular state of character or mood. It is the form as improvised, momentary, changeable." [4]

While the cinematic dispositif can be associated with the _skema_ – a fixed form ensuring regularity – _Blow-Up_ uncovers and affirms the aspect of it that relates also to _ruthmos_, fluid and ephemeral rhythm, without which the frame would be merely a photograph joined to other photographs in a saccadic progression. And (as Benveniste reminds us) such a dimension presumes a particular conception of the universe, "a representation of the universe in which the particular configurations of movement are defined as 'fluctuations.'" [5]

This takes us to Fruhauf's digital films, which utilize the natural, cyclical motifs par excellence – the sun and the moon – in order to bring out the properties of the digital and the pixel.

But before that, the magnificent works _Exposed_ and _Mirror Mechanics_ also monumentalize and metaphorize celluloid _défilement_. A first inversion is geometrical: _Exposed_ makes the usual vertical _défilement_ horizontal. The second inversion is logical: Instead of starting from a matrix-image and then varying it until all its variables are exhausted (even to the point of disappearance, as in Kirk Tougas' _The Politics of Perception_,1973), _Exposed_ starts from variable elements (black-and-white, relation of part to whole, etc.), and constitutes a shot from them. The third inversion is psychic: By gradual transfers, the editing transforms the image into a puzzle of its own elements; having done this, it alters the nature of the fragmentation, for that has been pegged as fetishistic, an eroticization of detail torn from a whole which does not really exist beyond its libidinal reconstitution. Perforation, the site of iconographic transfer, is in effect designated in such a way that it evokes a Peeping Tom's key-hole. In the film's third movement, a dancing woman and a surfing man are mixed, evoking the profiles of Scottie and Madeleine when the latter first appears in Alfred Hitchcock's _Vertigo_ (1958). The montage of profiles, mismatched in terms of screen-direction, demonstrate the hallucinatory nature of the Madeleine figure: Scottie invents a woman before our very eyes. In _Exposed_, the representation's subject becomes the way in which we hallucinate images, via transfer, re-elaboration and _ruthmos_: While completely respecting the theoretical schema of structural-materialist cinema, the film becomes a poetics of libidinal projection, a dispositif to capture that unfigurable, which is the scopic drive. _Exposed_ constitutes the most beautiful optical caress that cinema has ever given itself. Thanks to this work, Fruhauf found himself freed of the analogical imprint, which is no longer the _source_ of the work but its _horizon_, something that constitutes a way of relativizing the necessity for representation: If every image arises from a psychic elaboration, then the analogical becomes secondary.

---

4   Emile Benveniste, _Problems in General Linguistics_ (Coral Gables: University of Miami Press, 1973), pp. 285–286.
5   Benveniste, p. 286.

Siegfried A. Fruhauf
Mirror Mechanics
2005

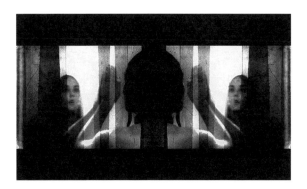

Mirror Mechanics elaborates a kinetic Venus. Firstly, a Venus at the mirror who makes herself up before a *psyché*, in the manner of Rubens or Velázquez; then a Venus emerging from the sea, a Venus Anadyomene in the manner of Sandro Botticelli or especially Titian. On this motif of a young girl, the plastic elements of cinema (horizontal/vertical geometry, single shot/superimposition, positive/negative, full or partial occupation of the frame, etc.) are doubled, one by one, and combined in order to create an ecstatic effect. An equilibrium is created between the motif's classicism – the nude having always been, in the West, the privileged site for plastic experimentation and demonstration – and the structural deployment of the working-through of plastic variation. This time, it is not the analogical image whose status is placed in question within a representational economy, but its referent. The kinetic work on plastic parameters occurs in such a way that *Mirror Mechanics* ends up producing a "Turin Shroud" effect: The force and organizing of reflections affirm the impossible nature of the body that could have left such traces.

To Invent a Plastic Vocabulary for the Digital
Whatever the coherence of Fruhauf's aesthetic initiatives, probably nothing prepared him better for the coming of digital than the sound work accompanying his films – usually composed by

Jürgen Gruber, with whom he has collaborated since *Wk=mMv2/2is* (1997–2006). Partly because the tools of sonic creation have integrated the digital more quickly, but above all because this indicates the aesthetic site from which best to begin in order to create a new plastic vocabulary: not sound per se, but the regime from which both sound recording and image recording equally derive, i.e., mastery of the *wave*. From the time of Thomas Edison, we know that sound recording preceded image recording, and the latter was made to accompany the former. With digital we must go to a higher level and recall that recording techniques in their totality were born with the discovery of electromagnetic wires by Heinrich Hertz, and their transformation into a means of communication by Guglielmo Marconi (among others). In his video and digital films, Fruhauf establishes a visual vocabulary in order to give vision to the signal, the pixel and the image-noise – the characteristic stability of the digital's binary tools opposed to the unstable nature of argentic material.

In 2003 *Structural Filmwaste. Dissolution 1* represents the moment of transition between argentic and digital, a transition which does not at all constitute an abandonment or rupture, but rather a lap dissolve, of which the film gives an image. Its iconography comes from cinema's magnified leftovers, in the firm tradition of Kurt

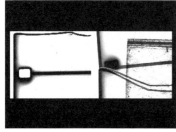

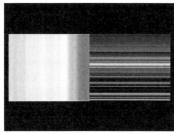

Siegfried A. Fruhauf
Structural Filmwaste. Dissolution 1
2003

Schwitters, of the outtakes, rushes and fragments worked over by the Lettrists, of Ernst Schmidt Jr.'s *Filmreste* (*Film Scraps*, 1966), of Wilhelm and Birgit Hein, Morgan Fisher and Peter Tscherkassky. As textural and geometric work on the celluloid fragments takes place, we are at the heart of structural cinema – but, suddenly, this industrial wasteland is simplified, turns abstract to the point of becoming a pure, abstract kineticism, vertical and horizontal, at the same time as the music becomes simpler and more punctual. The textural specificities of cinema (opacity, transparency, frame lines, scratches) are fused in the incandescence of a whiteness which, instead of re-giving us cinema

as in Tscherkassky's *CinemaScope Trilogy* (1997–2001), takes us over to the side of a whiteness that is computer generated, and a blackness that corresponds to the gathering of a signal, no longer the recording of an imprint. In 2008, *Ground Control* invents the digital equivalent of Schwitters' Merz-bau: a stylistic of the parasite or bug in the program, as if imaged by ants. *Ground Control* and its radar field could be Marconi's nightmare as, stationed in Cornouailles, he listened for whole nights to the electromagnetic waves that he awaited in their broadcast from Canada, and which he could only pick up as a surging static while his antennae swayed back and forth at the mercy of the winds…

Realtime (2002), *Sun* (2003), *Night Sweat* (2008) and *Tranquility* (2010) tackle, each in a different way, a common problem: that of an aesthetic center in this new technological environment. Here, that center is assimilated to the sun, which is revealed as the telescopic lens in *Realtime*, chromatic inconsistency in *Sun* and the sublime height of a swarm of pixels in *Night Sweat*. Peter Kubelka once declared that cinema was more powerful than reality because it can recreate a lightning flash 24 times a second; *Night Sweat* invents a digital tempest that obliges us to reread Immanuel Kant's texts on the sublime, since this time the lightning and its flash come from human fabrication, without ever losing their striking effect.

If the wave allows Fruhauf to structurally seize the digital, this is also due to his culture of seriality. In fact, as he explains it in reference to *Mona Lisa Dissolution* (2004): "The original no longer remains untouchable. In re-using the pictures, there is the possibility of breaking a ruling order, so as to show that every order is only one possible variant of many." Such a culture of the multiplicity of possible orders – which we can summarize by the term *virtual* – has prestigious antecedents: G. W. Leibniz's "compossibles," Blanqui's "bifurcations" in *Eternity According to the Stars*… but also the first principles of seriality as formulated by Arnold Schoenberg. To compose on the basis of the properties of the material itself, such is his first rule: "If we wish to investigate what the relation of tones to each other really is, the first question that

Siegfried A. Fruhauf
Ground Control
2008

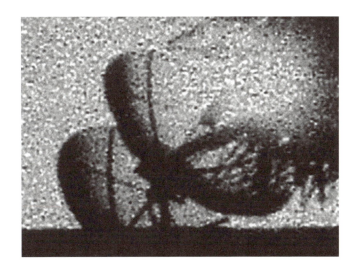

Siegfried A. Fruhauf
Sun
2003

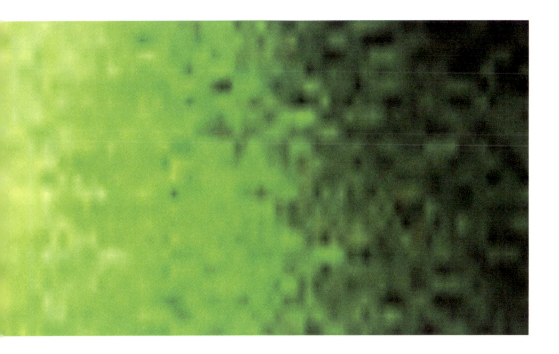

Siegfried A. Fruhauf
Frontale
2002

arises is: what makes it possible that a second tone should follow a first, a beginning tone? How is this logically possible? The question is more important than it seems at first; nevertheless to my knowledge it has not been previously raised. Although all imaginable and far-reaching problems have been considered, no one has yet asked: How after all, can two tones be joined one with another?"[6]

We recognize the consequences of this elucidation: Musical composition becomes the structuring of propositions that make modes of sonic recurrence intelligible. As a proposition, it logically determines a series of possible solutions, from which a composition will organize their selection or exhaustion. For instance: "The further such tones are brought into relation and contrast with each other and with rhythm, the greater is the number of possible solutions to the problem, and the more complex are the demands made on the carrying out of the musical idea."[7]

In Tscherkassky, fulfillment of the structural principles advanced by Schoenberg amounts to knowing how to deploy the power of *narrative*, thus rendering his structuralism so dazzling and immediately accessible – just as in Fruhauf's wonderful *Frontale* (2002), the description of a love story that is at once narrative and reflexive (collusion of two cars/two people in love/two frames). With digital, in *Structural Filmwaste. Dissolution 1* and *2*, Fruhauf returns to the pure

rigor of those first principles: the chain of material – structure – possible solutions – proposition. Since the two basic materials, argentic and digital, are the furthest apart, a diptych was required in order to explore these "possible solutions" in their interlacing, their respective compression/decompression (the subject of *Filmwaste 1*), then to explore the plasticity specific to digital beams (*Filmwaste 2*).

Palmes d'Or (2009) synthesizes argentic textures with the possibilities of digital montage. The film whips up an optical hurricane out of the perfectly calm and orderly iconography of palm trees, based on 800 photos taken during the Cannes Film Festival. The challenge is to create a plastic frenzy, tied to a pure chaos of optical and sonic energy, from representational elements (photography, iconography, programming logistics) that all belong to regimes of stability. *Palmes d'Or* offers a seemingly uncontrollable visual unlinking within a world of computerized programming. This aesthetic of volcanic disorder belongs less with algorithmic

Siegfried A. Fruhauf
Palmes d'Or
2009

---

6   Arnold Schoenberg, "Problems of Harmony,"
http://tonalsoft.com/monzo/schoenberg/problems/problems.htm.
7   Schoenberg.

Siegfried A. Fruhauf
Structural Filmwaste. Dissolution 2
2003

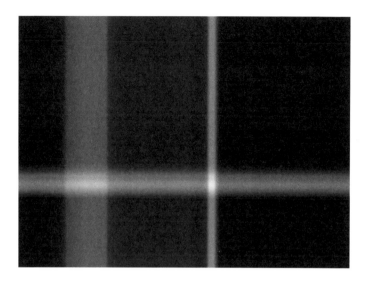

logic than with Blanqui's liberatory Utopias: "And as for this profusion of editions: there's no reason to worry about the infinite, it is rich. As insatiable as one might very well be, it possesses more than enough to satisfy all needs and dreams. Besides, this rainfall of *proofs* isn't a downpour over only one town. It's sprinkled and scattered across fields that are impossible to measure. And it really matters so little whether or not our twins are our neighbours."[8]

Dissolution/Joy

We can now formulate the hypothesis that the extremely Fruhaufian word *dissolution* – which becomes a form in itself across his film titles (beyond *Filmwaste* there are the installation *Mona Lisa Dissolution* [2004] and the filmic miniature *Mozart Dissolution* [2006]) – does not in the least amount to a suppression, not merely to an abstraction and not even truly to a deconstruction: more concretely, it is the expansion of a problem to its multiple possible solutions. It remains to be asked whether such an expansion of variants can, in

Fruhauf's work, create the resonance of something like that true mode of existence, delivered from immediacy, which Blanqui theorized, deep in prison, in order to give himself hope: the perspective of "happy variants." Here is how Adrian Martin describes Fruhauf's most recent work: "*Tranquility* is a typically lyrical, disquieting and mysterious 'mobile collage' of motifs concerning water, bodies and aviation."[9] In the light of Blanqui's hopes – this astounding theorist of the possibilities of the virtual – it is intriguing to see that *Tranquility*, an inverted response to *Palmes d'or*, authorizes a paradox within the logic of his career, and also in Austrian cinema in general, characterized for the most part by iconographic and formal violence: developing the same aesthetic problems, but deploying them from the vantage point of their oneiric and euphoric potential.

Translated from the French by Adrian Martin

8   Blanqui, p. 45.

9   Adrian Martin, "The Austrian Flow," *IF Innovative Film Austria* (Vienna: Federal Ministry for Education, the Arts and Culture, 2010), p. 12.

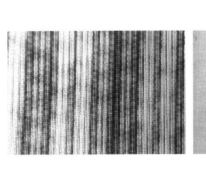  

Michaela Grill. Vibrating Currents.

Steve Bates

Patterns of gray light flicker past in shifting tonal fields. Light and sound move together over time, the one registering and shaping the other. The geometry of images shifts and crackles with continually recalibrating energy fields, the sonic and the visual alternately reinforcing and countering one another, creating a new whole. The work of Michaela Grill holds vibration as its core element. Whether it is the fluid, slightly warped, mathematical grid work of the abstracted videos, the filtered and shimmering pieces derived from archival materials or the carefully composed sound environment of each individual work, perfectly vibrating and oscillating in many registers and timbres at once: Her world of sound and vision resonates with multiple feeds of information. One could describe it as a collection of shimmering signifiers, a term used by Roland Barthes in reference to sound that is interpreted and experienced anew when the materiality of it is pulled from its melodic and rhythmic framework. Material is to be reconsidered once released from its mooring, to shift our experience in new ways, proposing raw potentials, new energy flows, a new time across an electronic and social network created and formed by us.

I first experienced Michaela Grill's work as part of a performing quartet appearing under the name My Kingdom for a Lullaby, composed of Grill, video artist Billy Roisz and musicians Christof Kurzmann and Martin Siewert. I was the director of the sound art festival Send + Receive, and a series of fortunate coincidences made it possible for us to present the work of people I knew of but had yet to experience as an improvisational group. Meeting them for the first time at the airport, beleaguered in the wake of Canadian customs ordeals, it was clear these individuals were very much like their work: refined but street-wise, sophisticated and approachable. Their performance radiated these qualities as well. I introduced them as the Rolling Stones of improvised music, although I should have said, of improvised light and sound instead. Not cold but calculated. It was very elegant, the sound and light bouncing around the granite walled venue of the Winnipeg Art Gallery. The layers of the spectacle felt at home surrounded by stone – tones of gray, white and black providing a geological backdrop. The walls were quarried from the bottom of the ancient glacial Lake Agassiz, which the quartet later visited. During their performance I remember thinking that somehow we had been transported in time, back through flickering image and sound to occupy space as molecules in the glistening lake. The textural elements that first made an impression on me with My Kingdom for a Lullaby come up repeatedly when I consider Grill's other video work.

While one can view Grill's project through the lens of cultural and media art theory, her work is immediately approachable and experiential, on a visceral, phenomenological level. There is a rock'n'roll-ness that makes it immediate and gritty while possessing the elegance of post-minimalism. It exists decidedly as abstract form. While not purposely obtuse, it encourages commitment to analyze and form a response. It is not easy viewing and functions in the space of active dialogue between the work and the viewer. While such an invitation to actively engage is sometimes proffered as an attack on abstraction, a sort of limited/limiting reductionism, Grill would seem to argue that the work is open to anyone willing to look and listen. This may take some time in Grill's visual and sound world.

In *cityscapes* (2007) we see black-and-white images of Viennese streets almost as if through frosted glass. The original footage is culled from archives of the Austrian Film Museum, where Grill was invited to do a residency. People and vehicles drift across the screen while black forms cloud the vision like missing memory codes. This absence forms something new. The past inhabits the current in a ghost-like way, a sort of haunting – perhaps, a "seething presence," as outlined by Avery Gordon, where "experiences (...) are more often than not partial, coded, symptomatic, contradictory, ambiguous. What is it to identify haunting and follow its trajectory?"[1] What is our relationship to the past? This question is not only raised in a broader sense, but also within the more circumscribed context of the cultural production of the moving image. Just as images become clear, they return to shadow again – memory-as-ruin as creative act – a reinterpretation of historical legacy, the crash of modernity – cars and electric guitars. Vibrating lines become more pronounced. Movement, speed increases as the editing quickens. Trains are iron impulses that coordinate time, approaching and departing stations. Precision. Timing. Synchronization. Scan rates. Film frames. Beats per-minute. Time emerges as a global socio-political, technical force. New grids emerge over the city/image highlighting this human fabric/weave within a heavily planned metropolis.

Eventually the fluctuating grid takes over almost completely. Sound and image move back and forth between grit and an urban pastoral. Movement studies of the city continue to fascinate us. The grid bends into roundness, provides structure for a kind of fluidity. There is a break with historical time through the soundtrack here as well. An electronic pulse and stutter by Martin Siewert transports the archival images to a sense of the present. A *meanwhile from the past* moves the image to pixelate and flow into a video grid pattern across the screen. Walter Benjamin's idea that you have to halt the historical flow of images to make them legible and that history dissolves into images as opposed to stories is here translated into audio-visual signals. Grill reprocesses the pure film image yet the street continues to pass by despite the technical shift. The video scan lines make an indelible mark/trace on the image, itself a product of the timing of the scanning apparatus.

There is another way to experience Grill's work – one that perhaps sets the above aside, or assumes it as instinct – whereby one gives oneself up to the sheer thrill of moving image and sound. It's more *minor* than that. But even in this state of phenomenological drift we never completely remove ourselves from the experience of the body and its place in a cultural, social and political whole. When one looks and listens closely, one can discern forms beneath the initial abstraction of Grill's art. Unlike some of her contemporary Austrian video makers who utilize a purely synthetic, computer generated toolset to compose work, Grill's flickering light takes from real world events and images. At the same time she explores ideas of perception – sensual pulses of light on the retina and sound reaching out to move cilia, and also memory and trace. Despite what some call the "flatness" of video – mistakenly compared to the film image – here a desire to reach out and touch the work is still in play. Images slide across the screen with a pulsing tactility that is fleeting and at the same time situated in extended *durées* – like a flickering flame that remains as a trace in your vision – a body memory. In discussing Henri Bergson's ideas of perception, film theorist

---

1   Avery Gordon, *Ghostly Matters: Haunting and the Sociological Imagination* (Minneapolis: University of Minnesota Press, 2008), p. 24.

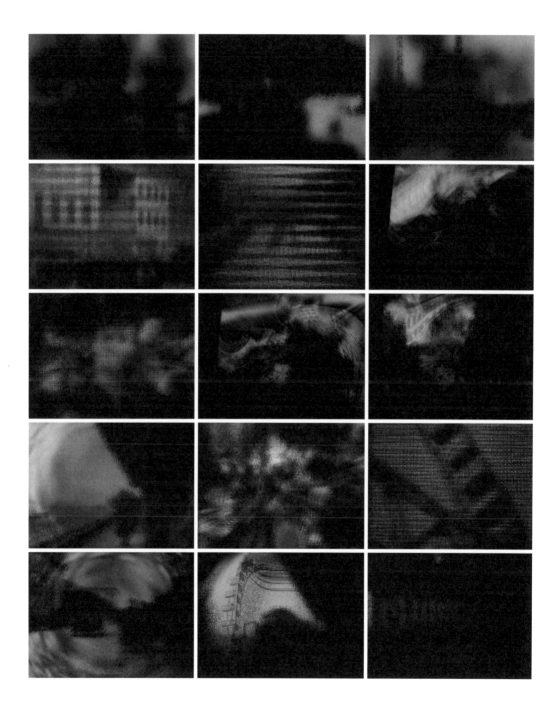

Michaela Grill,
Martin Siewert
cityscapes
2007

Mary Ann Doane outlines a connection between traces of images and memory: "The human experience of perception hence pivots upon a temporal lag, a superimposition of images, an inextricability of past and present. To that extent it is a perverse temporality, a nonlinear temporality that cannot be defined as a succession of instants. According to Gilles Deleuze, 'Bergsonian duration is defined less by succession than by coexistence.' And it is this peculiar temporality that for Bergson is the mark of the human." [2]

Much of Grill's art is not so much abstraction as simultaneous accumulations of past into present, like Henri Bergson's notion of the past being present in every now, currents of past and present always interacting with each other in layers of light and idea. Or it can be seen as speaking to Alva Noë's enactive approach to perception, summarily described in his intro-duction to *Action in Perception*: "The world makes itself available to the perceiver through physical movement and interaction. (...) Perceptual experience acquires content thanks to our possession of bodily skills. *What we perceive* is determined by *what we do* (or what we know how to do); it is determined by what we are *ready* to do." [3]

---

2   Mary Ann Doane, *The Emergence of Cinematic Time: Modernity, Contingency, the Archive* (Cambridge: Harvard University Press, 2002), p. 77.
3   Alva Noë, *Action in Perception* (Cambridge: MIT Press, 2004), p. 1.

From these actions, we create the content that narrates our lives. This approach relies on an active viewer. In Grill's case, the movement of light over retina and sound oscillating cilia, invites us to take a sideways look at the everyday in order to experience forms and structures around us in a new light.

A good example of Grill's visual language is seen in *Kilvo* (2004), an abstracted image of the *real*, sourced from images of Lapland, Finland. Natural elements of the landscape including trees, water, and clouds are reduced to their most minimal outlines and played back in quartered sections of the frame, in white, gray and black. This framing conveys that *nature* is a human construct, and while we are *of it,* we produce it as much as it produces us. Seen from another perspective, the piece presents a transformation of landscape into four quartered sections that move and adjust themselves to the thumping sound of Vienna's remarkable Radian, whose music track gives *Kilvo* its title. The group is in sync with Grill in terms of mixing analog and digital elements and blurring between the two. The piece can be considered as art while also imagined as music video, a paired interpretation that may offend an artist concerned with keeping popular and artistic forms separate. But Grill's rock'n'roll impulse emerges here again.

Grill's sonic collaborators are exceptional *texturists*, with sounds detailing surfaces as her images explore the texture of interlocking, flickering

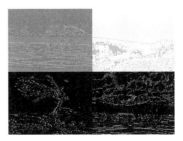

Michaela Grill
Kilvo
2004

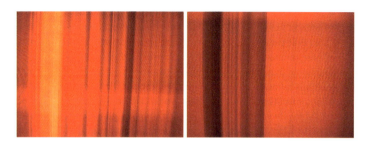

Michaela Grill
Hello Again
2006

pixels of light, pulses of connected energies that detail the grain of the image – grain here in the sense that Barthes considers voice: "The 'grain' is the body in the voice as it sings, the hand as it writes, the limb as it performs."[4] Grill's extensive work performing live with musicians tunes her into the complex relationships between acoustic space and time. Her careful collaboration with musicians on her soundtracks, including the great care given to sonic detail, seamlessly combines with her imagery leading to a sum greater than its parts: "But music is not just an appendage to the visual image. It must be an essential element of the realization of the concept as a whole. Properly used, music has the capacity to change the whole emotional tone of a filmed sequence; it must be so completely one with the visual image that if it were to be removed from a particular episode, the visual image would not just be weaker in its idea and its impact, it would be qualitatively different."[5]

Texture holds a corollary in the visual material. *Hello Again* (2006) takes this quite literally, as the source material is from a road trip Grill shot while on tour in the United States: "The source material is different roads I filmed during a trip around the States, a music trip going from Nashville, Memphis, down the Mississippi Delta to New Orleans and into Cajun country trying to visit as many music-related places as possible. In many commercial music videos the topos of being on the road is featured and as Trapist commissioned me to do a video to this track, I thought that it was like a commercial music video where you have the finished music track and then illustrate it."[6]

When one picks Michaela Grill's work apart, initial abstraction gives way to literalness. We can see Grill's attraction to abstraction as well as real-world experience. There is a consistent tendency to reconcile abstraction with the real – the here and now as imagined through the most *out-there* Neil Young guitar solo. *Hello Again* is a palette of gliding strips of red, orange and yellows

4   Roland Barthes, "The Grain of the Voice," in Roland Barthes, *Image-Music-Text* (London: Fontana Press, 1977), p. 188.
5   Andrei Tarkovsky, *Sculpting in Time* (Austin: University of Texas Press, 1989), p. 158–159.

6   Correspondence with the artist.

acting as a color field for a visceral body encounter with the world along the lines of the classic road film: Time to set off on the open road and take stock of life. Grill's work lives through the solitary understanding of the viewer, but this experience is informed by a social network which provides the means through which it comes into being. There is a belief that our experience of sound, color and movement go into making us who we are both as individuals and a collective. One can filter her work through the lens of Vilém Flusser's *intersubjective field*: "If one holds fast to the image of an inter-subjective field of relations – we is concrete, I and you are abstractions of this – then the new image of the city gains contours. It can be imagined roughly in this way: The relations among human beings are spun of differing densities on different places on the net. The denser they are, the more concrete they are. These dense places develop into wave-troughs in the field that we must imagine as oscillating back and forth."[7]

Grill's *monroc* (2005) is another example of the abstract world crossing or weaving through the concrete. And again quite literally: Monroc is a factory ruin which once produced aggregates, ready-mix and precast concrete in Idaho Falls, Idaho. The soundtrack in the first chapter is nostalgic. A melodic and sad guitar melody is heard. Abstract line, shape, movement and synthetic sound take over. The windows of the Monroc ruin act as a refrain while each chapter takes off on a voyage through another window. Here the window-as-framing-device does not act as a vantage point

for a road movie or classic motion study shot out a train window, but instead serves as a stationary, defiantly immobile, hulking ruin. Monroc acts as the dead weight of an industrial past. Think Detroit, northern England, wedges of the former Soviet Union, sections of industrial Germany. While some of these areas are now transformed into art parks and zones of creative class gentrification, Monroc performs a visitation on the artist in the form of a "lost destination." A website dedicated to *dead spaces*. "Abandoned, unusual, wild and weird" locales.[8] But where *monroc* begins as a piece of nostalgia, complete with melodic guitar lines, it ends with a more subtle outcome, as if to say that, despite the ruin all is not lost. This is perhaps a different kind of nostalgia, kindred to that outlined by Andreas Huyssen, "We are nostalgic for the ruins of modernity because they still seem to hold a promise that has vanished from our own age: the promise of an alternative future."[9]

Grill's work does not evoke nostalgia for the past, whether it is based on the architectural remains of industry, the film archive, or a lost historical Viennese streetscape. Her project is a meditation on the simultaneity of past and present, the co-existence of sound and image, film and video, black, gray and white, life and death: a pulsating, vibrational now.

---

7   Vilém Flusser, "The City as Wave-Trough in the Image-Flood", trans. Phil Gochenour, in *Critical Inquiry*, no. 31, Winter 2005, pp. 325–326. Available at http://independent.academia.edu/ PhilGochenour/Papers/204550/The_City_as_Wave-Trough_in_ the_Image_Flood.

8   Lost Destinations, http://www.lostdestinations.com/ (accessed November 15, 2010).

9   Andreas Huyssen, "Nostalgia for Ruins," *Grey Room*, no. 23, Spring 2006, p. 21. http://www.mitpressjournals.org/toc/grey/-/23

Michaela Grill,
Martin Siewert
monroc
2005

Avant-Garde Now.
Notes on Contemporary Film Art.

Barbara Pichler

At first sight Austrian avant-garde film exhibits two striking phenomena: its long and successful tradition and its astounding vitality and variety. Nevertheless, describing contemporary forms of film art in Austria is no easy task. This is not only due to its dynamic nature, but also because classifying the work presents an even more basic question: Many artists regard the designation "avant-garde" as a form of historicization to which they do not want to adhere, nor does the equally classic concept of "experimental film" seem entirely appropriate. No clear-cut theoretical or social contexts can be determined that would permit the identification of homogeneous (sub)cultures and thereby simple categorization. The interplay between film, art and pop-culture phenomena has intensified, heightening transdisciplinary approaches. Forms and formats overlap, specific references to avant-garde and experimental work methods are evident, though serving less as manifestations of an explicit conceptual progression and more as loose reference points or inspirations for reflection on the medium, its narrative forms and potential.

The following text represents a reaction to this heterogeneity and fragmentation: It does not pretend to be exhaustive or to propose a definition of the parameters of so-called film art or the avant-garde. By means of a discussion concerning several artists, it instead provides an overview of artistic work methods and circumstances of production,

thereby roughly delineating a field of art whose media of choice are film and video.

Scene 1: Film as Material

In the mid-1990s, film still had a strong presence, not just in terms of the cinematic apparatus, but particularly as analog film. Notably, a group of filmmakers who had studied under Peter Kubelka in Germany, at Frankfurt's art academy Städelschule, stimulated Austria's film scene. These artists made an impact through their exploitation of the specific possibilities and ways of working with the Super 8 and 16 mm camera, the relationship of the film apparatus to the object or subject in front of the camera. Their works also examine the materiality and haptic nature of the 16 mm filmstrip, as well as approaches to structural and metric film – all expressed in a personal and often almost lyrical manner.

Albert Sackl investigates the relationship between the camera and the human body. His work is characterized by confrontation: between the human body/actor and the mechanical gaze, between movement examined through the montage of single frames and the playful choreography that results. In *Gut ein Tag mit Verschiedenem* (*A Day Full of Variety*, 1998) the activities of one day are compressed into a few minutes by means of stop-motion photography. The continuous observation of basic elements of everyday life, such as eating and sleeping, is selectively interrupted by the body that breaks out of its daily routine in actions performed directly for the camera. This form of staging creates a distance to the actor and shifts the action from an event to an investigation, a movement study.

Sackl's works are precisely crafted, humorous and "strenuous" in terms of their focus and the attention they require of the spectator. Conceptually, one can see an affinity to the photographs of Eadweard Muybridge, as well as moments in both classic and Austrian avant-garde film tradition. However, this proximity to a specific cinematic history is combined with a healthy dose of critical self-awareness and, most importantly, irony. This is not only evident in individual instances that border on slapstick comedy, but can also be recognized in nach "pièce touchée" (after "pièce touchée," 1998), a "sensuous remake" (Sackl) of pièce touchée (1989), Martin Arnold's classic of found footage manipulation: Sackl reconstructed Arnold's stuttering hopelessness using live bodies.

In his latest work, Im Freien (In the Open, 2011), Sackl expands his field of vision in a literal sense. The film opens with a deserted landscape that delivers overwhelming aesthetic material. Shooting took place in a remote area in Iceland with a computer-controlled 16 mm camera that exposed one frame every three minutes. As a result, some three months (during which Sackl lived in a tent nearby with two assistants) were compressed into 23 minutes. An affinity to structural film of the 1960s and 1970s is evident, particularly to British landscape films. However, in spite of the undeniable interest shown in topographic conditions of light, shade, weather and the color and texture of the landscape, Sackl does not permit us to succumb to the fascination of natural phenomena. This landscape is intruded upon by human bodies and various objects, such as a mirror and a cube, triggering associations with the projection space: The landscape is both a surface of projection and a sphere of activity, but the filmic apparatus and its relationship to this space, the bodies and the objects, remain the focus.

The work of **Thomas Draschan** also shares the central idea of condensing film to such an extent that repeated screenings are required to comprehend it – or even more importantly, the film is not exhausted after several viewings – resulting from intensive craftsmanship and specifically filmic processes. Draschan's 3 filme: baum 3 tage, georg balkon 3 tage, basler platz (tag/nacht) (3 films: tree 3 days, georg balcony 3 days, basel square (day/night), 1998) deals with filmic movement, and might be described as three experimental setups for viewing a film and the possibilities offered by filmic sight. Every other frame of each shot was exposed at a different time of day, transforming relationships between time, space and movement.

Despite the concision of his early works, Draschan was internationally acknowledged only after turning to found footage filmmaking, a practice with an especially long and rich tradition in Austria, under the formative influence of such artists as Peter Tscherkassky, Gustav Deutsch, Lisl Ponger and Martin Arnold. The fact that Draschan does not locate himself solely within this tradition, but aims to broaden the playing field considerably, is evidenced by his statement that the creation of something extraordinary from the banal represents a pivotal achievement of modernism.[1] His palette of images ranges from advertising films and pop-culture references to educational films from former East Germany. At the same time, their materiality seems to be the main focus, their analog nature veritably placed on display. Draschan condenses these images according to formal criteria such as color and movement, and the rhythm of the editing is determined by the accompanying music. In Freude (Delight, 2009) his work with found footage reaches a climax. In a furious staccato, images are liberated from their original message and the spectator is plunged into an associative flood of images, effecting a sensory overload and creating an entirely new perceptive space. The tempo, the surfeit of stimuli, the unbridled delight in the material and connections beyond rational

---

1   Paraphrased from an article by Julie Fried, Die Presse, August 29, 2009.

Albert Sackl
Gut ein Tag mit Verschiedenem
1998

Albert Sackl
nach "pièce touchée"
1998

Albert Sackl
Im Freien
2011

Thomas Draschan
3 filme: baum 3 tage, georg balkon 3 tage, basler platz (tag/nacht)
1998

Georg Wasner
Oceano Nox
2011

arguments as created through the rearrangement of images are for Draschan essential, as "art requires something ecstatic, orgiastic, transgressive, otherwise it's just like everyday life."[2]

After taking an extended break from filmmaking **Georg Wasner**, another former pupil of Kubelka, also turned to found footage with his *Oceano Nox* (2011), employing newsreel footage from 1912 about the sinking of the *Titanic*. However, Wasner ignores the question of its original materiality, subjecting the film to a high-resolution digital scan and focusing instead on documentary gestures from the early days of cinema and their formal and aesthetic conventions. By enlarging details and speeding the film up or slowing it down, his adaptation directs the gaze to the unfamiliar and perplexing, and the seemingly unimportant. This includes figures who attempt to avoid the camera, others who obtrusively force their way into the frame, and shots without a recognizable logic or purpose. Wasner creates a new temporal order and shifts attention, revealing design principles and specific characteristics of early cinema, and probing the "documentary value" of such recordings. At the same time, the film becomes even more closely linked to a reality beyond its originally intended news value, to a lived and filmically experienced reality. Wasner searches for what the material has to say, the "stories" it contains and their significance for the material world, in light of

documentary processes and their lyrical moments.

The film is accompanied by a composition for piano penned by Chandrasekhar Ramakrishnan, as performed and interpreted by Elaine Brennan. While reminiscent of early cinema's live musical accompaniment to silent films, the effect produced by the music is not illustrative, it does not steer or manipulate the emotions. On the contrary, the minimalistic score underlines the focus on specific moments, while at the same time enlarging the atmospheric space the material occupies.

A subsequent generation of filmmakers includes **Johann Lurf**, an artist who repeatedly finds enchanting cinematic forms through which to translate his ideas concerning the construction of filmic perception and grammar. *Vertigo Rush* (2007) is based on a simple idea: a forest, a camera mounted on a dolly and the changing spatial perception rendered by zooming and simultaneously moving the camera backward and forward.[3] This movement is always structured identically, and it employs the simplest possible means to supply contradictory information to the sensory organs, eliciting an unbelievable physical reaction. The rules of spatial perception are no longer in force, space is expanded and simultaneously compressed at an increasing rate until the small section of forest visible on screen has been divested of realistic space, and in an onrush of speed hurtles

---

2   Fried.

---

3   The film's title is, of course, a playful reference to Alfred Hitchcock's famous tower scene in *Vertigo* (1960).

Thomas Draschan
Freude
2009

towards the virtual. As Lurf puts it, *Vertigo Rush* is "a love letter to cinema and the richness of film language," and to the cinematographic apparatus, which can reinvent the object of its gaze according to its own filmic conditions. The associative references of this work do not involve Austrian experimental film so much as structuralist experiments with space and perception, or movement studies, such as those undertaken by Michael Snow in the 1960s and 1970s. The cinematographic exists as an idea of subversion delivering unfamiliar experiences. And the cinematographic also serves as a venue of presentation: This film was created for the screen, and for the cinema, where physical immersion in the film is possible.[4]

This love for cinema can also be found in two other films by Lurf. *Zwölf Boxkämpfer jagen Viktor quer über den großen Sylter Deich 140 9* (*The quick brown fox jumps over the lazy dog*, 2009) is a found footage work consisting of a sequence of single frames Lurf employed to construct his own "feature film." *12 Explosionen* (*12 Explosions*, 2008, video, 12 min.) presents static tableaux shot at night in Vienna and, as betrayed by the title, explosions are to be expected: Lurf engages in humorous play with special effects and cinema's classic dramaturgical element of suspense as liberated from narrative requirements and reduced to the moment of the explosion, a suspense that can never be resolved.

---

4   Both dolly and camera were built by Martin Reinhart (he also constructed the equipment for Sackl's *Im Freien*), whose extraordinary skill in inventing brilliant technical solutions has often benefited domestic avant-garde film production.

Scene 2: Digital Abstraction

But despite such exceptional examples, the expiration date of the film era seems to be approaching. Processes of production and presentation are steadily moving toward the digital. By the mid-1990s, digital processes for creating and editing images gave rise to a movement propelled by a number of young artists working in the borderland between film, art, multimedia production, electronic music and pop-culture. They have been united, not always willingly, under the banner of "Austrian Abstracts": Michaela Grill, Annja Krautgasser, lia, Michaela Schwentner, Tina Frank, Barbara Doser & Hofstetter Kurt, Billy Roisz, Manuel Knapp, Norbert Pfaffenbichler, et al. But regardless of the heterogeneity of their work, it shares some characteristic traits: the intensive examination of relationships between sound and image, the predominance of abstraction and minimalism, an aesthetic marked by formal reduction, the manipulation of found materials or computer-aided construction of visual and acoustic realms, as well as creative exploitation of the technology's possibilities and limitations. That this work cannot be conventionally categorized is not only demonstrated by the methods of its production, but also the venues where it has been presented: Works were either created live in connection with music, or were shown as videos at festivals or visual art in galleries, or presented at cinemas.

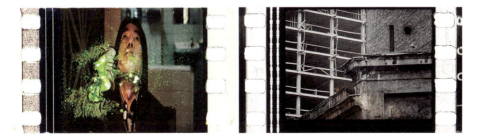

Johann Lurf
Zwölf Boxkämpfer jagen Viktor quer über den großen Sylter Deich 140 9
2009

The question of audiovisual accessibility is central to the works of **Billy Roisz**, so at first it might seem paradoxical that she pursues it through radical abstraction and the visualization of technical means. Her videos are the result of deeply collaborative processes, created through close work with musicians and sometimes other video artists such as Michaela Grill. Acoustic and visual levels carry equal weight and mutually influence each other's creation. Roisz's videos are conceptually clear. Her vocabulary of forms is extremely reduced and limited to graphic shapes, interference effects are used as visual elements, and visual and acoustic feedback. However, terming her work austere would be wrong. The sensuousness and materiality of the video images are of central importance.

smokfraqs (video/sound by Billy Roisz and Dieter Kovacic, 2001) combines eight brief fragments divided by a few seconds of black: These elements refuse to assume a "classic" self-contained form, functioning on their own as well as in a sequence or as a loop. The music provides a pattern of sensory experience that is not only visible, but also tangible in an audiovisual sense. Fine details of the image react to changes in the music. Visual effects created by means of electronic feedback provide the basic material for further digital processing. Technical equipment such as a video mixer is reappropriated to create a new instrument, and the resulting system error becomes productive.

Her pleasure in playing with the sensory experience of sound and image is even more obvious in *brRRMMMWHEee II* (video by Billy Roisz, sound by dieb13, 2010). In a rapid flow of overlapping and interdependent fragments of sound and image, the spectator falls into an ecstasy of perception involving colors, forms and speed that results in rhythmically pulsing afterimages – "fast and furious electronic pop at its best" [5] – in which fun, the development of a synesthetic dramaturgy and examination of the technical means of production seamlessly fit together.

Billy Roisz's work, as well as that created by a number of Austrian Abstracts colleagues, can be regarded as a continuation of modernist ideas using contemporary means. Graphic reduction and a synergetic approach invite associations with the classic avant-garde – such as the work of Hans Richter and László Moholy-Nagy and the early videos of Steina & Woody Vasulka, including their experiments with electronic sound and video. However, these references are more likely evidence of an affinity than a matter of direct quotation. Above all, this work is without any dogmatic sense of "pure" art. Abstraction serves as a means to an end, for presentation of the potential of video as a medium, as well as sensory experiences of seeing and hearing. Abstraction here results from a search for beauty of form which reflects its process.

Manuel Knapp shares an understanding of abstraction resulting from process rather than the production of pure form. His soundtracks, usually generated by Knapp himself using a variety of software, some of it from the field of architecture, play an equally central role in his work to generate virtual spaces that cancel conventional geometric references and categories of perception. He exhausts this software, taking it to its limits: Strictly reduced graphic forms of distortion, interference and dysfunction serve as visual elements in the composition of his images. In this sense Knapp, too, repurposes technical equipment and integrates chance into the process of artistic production as expressions of autonomy, a form of freedom to withdraw from dominant visual aesthetics. The goal of his artistic praxis is not real, but virtual space, which is created when sight no longer delivers reliable information.

In *accelerated lines* (2005) Knapp constructs a fine network of interwoven animated lines in shades of gray and white. Foreground and background overlap, and the resulting acoustic and visual space exposes conventional patterns of perception and their instability, since the space cannot be explained – it can only be experienced by means of the senses. Another work, *stroboscopic noise* (2009), plays with the unfamiliar and

---

5 Christian Höller, review of *brRRMMMWHEee II*, n.d., http://www.filmvideo.at/filmdb_pdf.php?id=1877&len=de.

Johann Lurf
Vertigo Rush
2007

Johann Lurf
12 Explosionen
2008

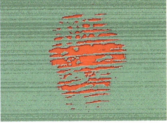

Billy Roisz
smokfraqs
2001

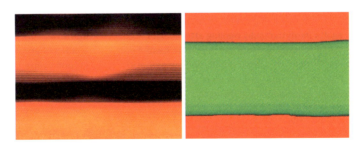

Billy Roisz
brRRMMMWHEee II
2010

perplexing, and the limits of what can be perceived. The visual information comprises no more than two lines oscillating at different rates. Their movement eventually becomes so rapid that the eye is no longer able to perceive it and new spaces are created by the simultaneity of perception and afterimages. At the same time, the relationship between the analog and digital apparatus shifts when the effect of the afterimage, an analog principle, is translated into digital form.

Scene 3: From the Abstract to the Concrete

The distortion or alteration of live images, graphic reduction to the point of total abstraction and computer-aided composition have been of interest to all artists regarded as producing Austrian Abstracts. In the meantime, however, there seems to be a certain amount of weariness with this type of minimalism, and a turn to realistic images.

Lotte Schreiber, in collaboration with Norbert Pfaffenbichler, created a number of wonderful abstract miniatures including *36* (2001), *Piano Phase* (2004) and *a1b2c3* (2003). These works are especially striking in their structural approach, their penchant for mathematical minimalism and preference for clear lines and forms. In solo work likely informed by her background as an architect, Schreiber turned this highly developed analytical and formal attention to a virtually classic theme of experimental film: spaces, topographies and architecture. In 2002 she began a series of works that could be termed filmic cartographies or described as translations of "spatial art" into "film art."

   quadro (2002), a film about a structuralist apartment building in Trieste, is more than a simple portrait of architecture. Schreiber undermines the usual manner of depicting architecture, instead translating the structure and materiality of a constructed space into filmic form. She works in black-and-white, with tightly framed details that are repeatedly interrupted by the movement of a handheld camera, and the montage conforms to a metric principle. To do justice to the building's basic materials, exposed concrete and glass,

Schreiber chose Super 8 and digital video, thus directly comparing the haptic nature and material qualities of these media. An electronic soundtrack by Stefan Németh expands the perceptive space, which results in a film that both represents a translation of one form of expression into another and at the same time wordlessly comments on ideas of social-utopian architecture and its failure.

   The question of the tension between the object of aesthetic reproduction and subjective sensory perception, between traditional pictorial categories and the corporeality that can be conveyed by the subjective gaze of a video camera also represents the focus of *I. E. [site 01-isole eolie]* (2004). The camera is used to survey the island of Stromboli and examine its landscape as both a subjective sensory experience and aesthetic subject matter. The terrain is thereby subordinated to the camera's gaze while a third space is created through montage, a space made possible solely through the camera, a space in which nature and its depiction become one but artificiality and unfamiliarity remain.

In her more recent works **Annja Krautgasser** also deals with the question of perception and the constitution of a world through the medium of video, as well as the influence of the apparatus upon perception – though no longer on the basis of abstraction. In *horizon/1* (2005) the camera scans a city's horizon in abrupt, discontinuous movements. Depiction of the urban space conforms to a recognizable visual paradigm for portrayals of landscape, with the horizon serving as a dividing line. The type of motion, however, remains constant, making the city intangible, "invisible," due to interference and noise. The problem, and also the image's potential, can be found in the tension between the visible and that which withdraws from visibility, thereby undermining the dominant spatial and filmic order.

   These considerations took Krautgasser's work in a direction increasingly concerned not only with apparative prerequisites of the gaze but also the narrative dispositif of cinema. The year 2008 saw the two-part *Beyond* and *Innerer Monolog* (*Stream of Consciousness*). Both works employ the same raw

Manuel Knapp
accelerated lines-
2005

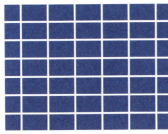

Lotte Schreiber, Norbert Pfaffenbichler
a1b2c3
2004

Lotte Schreiber, Norbert Pfaffenbichler
Piano Phase
2004

Lotte Schreiber
quadro
2002

Lotte Schreiber
I. E. [site 01–isole eolie]
2004

Annja Krautgasser
horizon/1
2005

material, with the exception of the final scene. *Innerer Monolog* could be termed an architectural portrait: The camera glides over a building, registering architectural details in its path and assembling a surface. The visual level of the work is enhanced by an off-screen voice. In the same way that the picture avoids showing the building in a long shot, the soundtrack remains fragmentary, providing hints and creating an indefinable tension. *Beyond*, using the same footage, differs only in its concluding sequence, during which the visual field expands. The title refers to the space of the filmic construction, as the set and the conditions of production are moved into the picture. These two scopic regimes are not differentiated: Both spaces are depicted in the same style, and both realities are exposed as constructions of a filmic universe.

An increasing concern with issues of narrative construction can also be found in the work of **Dariusz Kowalski**, who makes use of an unusual source for his visual material. His point of departure for *Luukkaankangas – updated, revisited* (2005, sound by Stefan Németh) consists of automatically created images devoid of aesthetic interest: downloaded shots of roads taken by a webcam. Kowalski employs this material to create a serial montage of individual images that take on a strangely narrative character and become enchantingly beautiful in a dramaturgy of light and shadow, and under natural influences such as wind, weather and season. Kowalski arranges this automatized gaze according to such aesthetic criteria as graphic elements, colors, moods and motifs. With regard to aesthetic and craftsmanship, he basically follows the praxis of methods used for found footage films, but the source of his images shifts the focus of attention. In contrast to the pool of images taken from home movies and popular culture characteristic of "classic" found footage films, the Web not only provides an archive but also generates visual content that serves practical purposes.

In *Optical Vacuum* (2008) Kowalski focused an aspect of these considerations on the anonymous gaze and surveillance to develop an experimental narrative. His film essays build on images made for

the purpose of monitoring private and public spaces. These documentary and functional images regain an element of the spectacular by being linked in a new way. In combination, the flow of images and the narrator's voice develop into a narrative form that is strongly influenced by moods and associations, as well as the distance between the images and voice. In the rare moments when voice and image match, the constructed nature of the film narrative becomes even more clearly visible.

In the 1990s and the following decade, **Michaela Schwentner** worked primarily on translating musical structures. Her works provide a "legible" plan of musical structure so as to enable the hearing of music on an equivalent visual level. The pleasure of seeing and listening results from a process of free association, of being open and responding to forms, colors and sounds. This way of dealing with the material and processes of perception represents a central theme in both modern art and experimental film. However, after a few years of intensive work with abstraction Schwentner's desire for more concrete material advanced to the fore, despite the fact that the fragile borderline between idea and recognition, between visibility and the image's withdrawal from the visible regime remains decisive. In addition, a fascination with the history and images produced by narrative cinema seems to have influenced the development of her work over the past few years. *Giuliana, 64:03* (2003, sound by Didi Bruckmayr) might be the first film to evidence this shift in interest. The greatly reduced soundtrack and the visual raw material was taken from Michelangelo Antonioni's *Il deserto rosso* (*Red Desert*, 1964). We see the vague outline of a woman's face composed of constantly changing fragments that are continuously rearranged, without ever forming a complete whole, crowded and displaced by graphic elements. The visual contents overlap and the concrete material disappears in abstraction before it is able to manifest itself fully. Schwentner continues her work with narrative cinema's repertoire of gestures and a connection with experimental forms of depiction

Annja Krautgasser
Beyond
2008

Dariusz Kowalski
Luukkaankangas – updated, revisited
2005

Dariusz Kowalski
Optical Vacuum
2008

Michaela Schwentner, Didi Bruckmayr
giuliana, 64:03
2003

in *des souvenirs vagues* (2009). The soundtrack samples a wide range of film roles played by women and is visually juxtaposed with miniaturized scenes, translations of these gestures by the performer in front of the camera.

Scene 4: Performative Staging

Filmic performance art of all different kinds, and especially that done *with* rather than solely *for* the camera, is among the most interesting contemporary work being produced, even if it does not occupy center stage.

For **Sabine Marte** video represents more than just a technology for reproducing images. It is also a "co-performer" with whom to investigate the relationship between the (her) body, in the broadest sense, and the construction of meaning through image and/or language or sound, as well as the role the medium of video plays in this context. In *Ich möchte gerne einmal einen Horrorfilm machen* (*I Would Like to Make a Horror Movie Sometime*, 1999) fragments of narrative unfold in the form of an uncontrollable rant that breaks through the order of both filmic and literary narration, shifting the focus to rhythm, innuendos and insane linguistic perplexities, to recitative and tonal music. We see visually manipulated material, and in place of concrete images that correlate with a possible narrative we see images that foreground the materiality of the video image. As a spectator, one must abandon oneself to this madness or reject it – both reactions revealing structures made visible, perceptible, tangible. One step beyond classic performance art, Marte's work can be seen both in light of feminist discourse and reflections on the construction of the gaze, female bodies and gender, as well as Mara Mattuschka's considerably more dramatic and mannered performances.

Questions regarding the construction of meaning and systems of representation – whether visual, spatial, gestural or linguistic – and language as a system of power are central to all of Marte's works. "Disorder" reigns supreme in the brilliant *b-star, untötbar!* (*b-star, unkillable!*, 2009), visually,

in terms of the video image and the woman depicted; and narratively, as the viewer repeatedly stumbles into information gaps resulting from deceleration, repetition, interruption and fragmentation. In addition, scopic regimes and spatial conventions come under fire through manipulation of real space. Language, the medium of video, the human body and its repertoire of gestures confront each other repeatedly, and are consequently reevaluated, their linguistic and visual expression representing an attack on the dominant order. At the same time various forms of artistic expression are treated equally, their unity maintained by Marte's physical presence, whether as a performer's body, the subject and content of the work or as its voice and narrator.

The body and the question of its audiovisual presence is a common theme in the videos of **Jan Machacek**. Live performances play an important role in his work, and their translation into film involves a question of central importance, namely the difference between live action and video image. *erase remake* (2007, sound by Martin Siewert) is the filmic translation of one such performance. In extreme close-ups the black-and-white video image explores Machacek's body. However, these shots do not result in the complete image of an integral person, they instead remain "surfaces," and as such become the main event. The speed of Martin Siewert's music increases rapidly over the course of this exploratory process, the camera keeps up with the rhythm, and the video turns into a joint and mutually determinative action involving body, sound and camera.

Communication with images of one's own body is also a main focus of *in the mix* (2008), the video version of a dance performance. The camera's continuous circling produces a hypnotic vortex that makes it impossible to concentrate the gaze on the picture's central element, the body. The usual logic of cinematic representation is replaced by a physical experience of seeing. The spectator is not able to avoid a physical reaction; image and body are made one, voluptuously placing the relationship between

Michaela Schwentner
des souvenirs vagues
2009

Sabine Marte
Ich möchte gerne einmal einen Horrorfilm machen
1999

Sabine Marte
b-star, untötbar!
2009

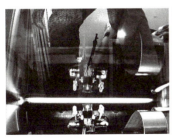

Jan Machacek
erase remake
2007

Jan Machacek
in the mix
2008

the body moving in front of the camera, the camera itself and the audience in question.

Looking Ahead

The essential questions posed by the above-mentioned works have dominated artistic discourse for decades in the field of alternative motion pictures, involving the examination, probing and deconstruction of the medium's conventions. This discussion has been heightened on all fronts by new conditions created with the advent of digital technology and its relationship to film and cinema. The main issues involve the visibility and shifting of meaning; our comprehension, expectation and reception of the image; narrative constructions; and the reality to be found in the image. The ideas, traditions and essential issues of avant-garde and experimental film are alive and kicking in new interpretations made with contemporary means.

In addition to this common ground, one factor unites these filmmakers inhabiting the heterogeneous landscape of contemporary production: No one makes film or video exclusively, and everyone works in a variety of media and presentation contexts, venturing into galleries and venues for visual art, concert halls and the Internet in addition to cinemas. Ironically, a result of this change in or expansion of context and the resulting shift in focus is that some artists are no longer considered in terms of "film," and are instead perceived as part of the art world. This is true in the case of, for example, the performance-oriented works of **Carola Dertnig** and **Maria Petschnig**. One could argue that these are artistic positions, which have always been seen, in aesthetic terms, more in the field of (media) art, though at the same time a kind of migration of artists trained in classic filmmaking can be observed. Some examples, **Kerstin Cmelka**, **Bernhard Schreiner** and **Günter Zehetner**, all of whom studied under Peter Kubelka at the Städelschule, currently have a strong presence at galleries, equal if not greater to the recognition they enjoy in what could be termed the classic film context. On the other hand, there is also movement in the opposite direction, characterized by artists

previously anchored in experimental film turning to more documentary forms. This documentary turn has dominated the art world for years, and now seems to have reached film. Some examples are Annja Krautgasser's _Romanes_ (2010), the recent films of former Ernie Gehr student **Thomas Korschil**, and projects by Dariusz Kowalski and Michaela Schwentner currently in production.

Genre boundaries already of questionable validity keep overlapping. For example, why are Lotte Schreiber's architecture films considered experimental while Sasha Pirker's architectural studies are usually relegated to the documentary category? The connection between art and film is getting closer, while interdisciplinary work methods and approaches on both aesthetic and theoretical levels are undoubtedly becoming more important. Furthermore, changes in contexts of production, presentation and, most importantly, reception as a result of digitalization cannot be ignored. A positive consequence of this change can be found in the greater exposure of a potentially broader spectrum of the public to works frequently marginalized in the realms of underground film and the art world. On the other hand, pressing new questions are arising with regard to the adequate presentation of audiovisual works at art venues and online, the exploitation of works originally conceived for reception in entirely different contexts, and unauthorized distribution – to name a few of the most obvious. All of these issues, whether positive or problematic, are clearly part of the current production landscape and impact individual artistic praxis as well as examination of the work, theoretical and otherwise. The definition of avant-garde or experimental film remains a question, but less as a search for straightforward categorization, demarcation, or canonization. Instead, it is more concerned with the needs and demands of artists in the field of alternative motion picture production and the challenges they face in a steadily growing and rapidly commercializing world of audiovisual production.

Translated by Steve Wilder

Carola Dertnig
Dégueulasse
2009

Maria Petschnig
KIP MASKER
2007

Kerstin Cmelka
Mit Mir
2000

Bernhard Schreiner
Arrêté
2001

Günter Zehetner
Fernsehen, Christine und ich
1993

Annja Krautgasser
Romanes
2010

Thomas Korschil
Artikel 7 – Unser Recht!
2005

Peter Tscherkassky

The Framework of Modernity.
Some concluding remarks
on cinema and modernism.[1]

In 1915, twenty years after the brothers Auguste and Louis Lumière staged the world's first and legendary public film screening in Paris, the most influential pioneer of narrative film completed his magnum opus, *Birth of a Nation*: Like no other director before him, the American D. W. Griffith recognized and developed the potential of cinema as a medium of storytelling. In the official annals of film history, the 190-minute epic *Birth of a Nation* is regarded as the birth of modern cinema.

In the very same year Kasimir Malevich, painter of the famous *Black Square*, wrote his Suprematist manifesto: "Before the advent of Suprematism, all of painting, both past and present, the written word and music were slaves to natural form. They waited for their liberation in order to be able to speak their own language and no longer be dependent upon reason, sense, logic, philosophy, psychology or laws of causality..."[2] It is clearly evident that film and fine art were undergoing two rather distinct developments at that point in time...

How did this come to pass? In order to answer this question we need to briefly define our epoch, the era of modernity. The keyword to understanding modernity is "reason." The modern era can be characterized by a successive marginalization of mythical worldviews, which gradually were replaced by rationalism: Rationality began to permeate all spheres of life.

In the field of philosophy this rationalism corresponds with the ideas of the Age of Enlightenment, the guiding principle of which Immanuel Kant concisely formulated in 1783: "Enlightenment is man's emergence from his self-imposed immaturity."[3] In terms of social history, the French Revolution of 1789 laid the foundation for a new, "rational" social order in Europe. In the place of a government "ordained by God," a democracy was established, resting (ideally) upon the reasonable competition of arguments. Under the auspices of reason, a fundamentally new social order and egalitarian distribution of political power was supposed to be realized. However, rationalism not only became the operative criteria in assessing all activities of society in general, it also increased pressure upon the individual: No longer could a person rely upon unquestioned, established patterns of thought and behavior to make sense of things. Instead, these habits had to be replaced with reasoned decisions and responsible actions. The technical manifestation of modernity's process of rationalization is encountered in the triumphal march of industrialization, transforming the world into raw material. And as demonstrated by the sociologist and political economist Max Weber, the economic system of capitalism, too, is the consequence of a more abstract and rational form of thought than that

---

1   For a comprehensive analysis of the evolution of modern art see the brilliant study by Werner Hofmann *Grundlagen der modernen Kunst* (Stuttgart: Kröner, 1966). English: *Turning Points in Twentieth-Century Art: 1897–1917* (New York: George Braziller, 1967).
2   *Kasimir Malewitsch und der Suprematismus in der Sammlung Ludwig*, eds. Katia Baudin and Elina Knorpp (Cologne: Museum Ludwig/Wienand Verlag, 2011), p. 77.

---

3   In 1783 Kant posed and answered the question "What is Enlightenment?" in his aptly entitled and influential essay. The onset of the modern era is naturally not attached to a specific year; its roots reach back into the late Middle Ages.

which had determined pre-industrial economic systems, in which ethical and moral considerations largely alien to capitalist economies played a decisive role.[4] (One of the paradoxes of modernity is here touched upon: On the one hand, magical worldviews lose their ground; on the other hand, abstract instrumental rationality, which determines our approach to reality gains irrational, that is, self-destructive dimensions.[5])

But what did this process of rationalization mean for art?

For one thing, it meant a radical shift in social status. In Europe the groundwork for this change had been prepared in the revolutionary year of 1789: With the political disempowerment of the Church and progressive secularization of society, art lost its most important patron. Up until the time of the Enlightenment, the institutional representatives of religion had a monopoly on answers. It was the Church that explained the world and its inner workings. The role of art was to depict these metaphysical explanatory models, and to make them available to the senses. The Church proceeded to lose its monopoly to a rational, scientifically based worldview that, instead of proclaiming absolute truth, formulated its theses and models according to the principle of falsifiability, the principle of refutability.[6] With the loss of its function in the service of religion, an entirely new sphere within society began to emerge: a sphere of autonomy for the arts. Liberated from the framework of its traditional role as servant to ecclesiastical tasks art attained a secularized identity as an end in itself: This is the historical moment that autonomous, modern art as we know it today was born.

The disentanglement of art from immediate practical use and its release into a society increasingly conceived and organized along rational lines had dramatic consequences for the development of

its inner structure. The art of the French Revolution known as Classicism was to be the last school of art accepted by all members of society. Parallel to the establishment of a collective imagination of reason as the organizing principle for the shaping of society, a codified and "reasonable" system of artistic guidelines was developed and promulgated. The classicists considered this system of rules to be timelessly valid (the search for such a canon of aesthetic principles beyond the reach of historical change can be found up to the time of the Russian Constructivists).[7] But despite prevalent academicism, progressive artists began to question the inner structure of art itself. The loss of its prior functions and its new autonomous status provoked the self-interrogation of art itself. Artists began to directly reflect their artistic means and the specific capabilities of their media in the works they produced. In the process, everything about the creation of an artwork – *what* is created and *how* – gradually lost an unquestioned and unquestionable "axiomatic" character. Liberated from the catalog of artistic regulations, the function of representation was incrementally abandoned: Art steadily began to develop in a direction of increasing abstraction. In retrospect, this process can be recognized as a crisis of representation directly resulting from the process of rationalization taking place in society as a whole. It represents a development within which art took leave of all inherited – and that means largely representational – norms and prerequisites. This crisis of representation marked and accompanied the development of modern art, and with each step toward abstraction it unlocked new artistic possibilities.

Overall, the year 1910 can be viewed as the culmination of this development during which art withdrew into its own immanent formal history. By this time all aesthetic rules governing representation originating from the Renaissance had been abandoned. With his *Black Square* Malevich demonstrated the new, radically emancipated self-awareness of an art that had become entirely autonomous. (This description of autonomous art that

4   Max Weber, "Die protestantische Ethik und der Geist des Kapitalismus," in *Gesammelte Aufsätze zur Religionssoziologie*, ninth edition (Tübingen: J. C. B. Mohr, 1988; first published in 1904), pp. 17–206; English version: *The Protestant Ethic and the Spirit of Capitalism* (New York: W. W. Norton, 2009).

5   See Theodor W. Adorno and Max Horkheimer, *Dialectic of Enlightenment* (Palo Alto: Stanford University Press, 2002), first published in 1944.

6   See http://en.wikipedia.org/wiki/Falsifiability.

7   One of the incunabular films of the avant-garde, *Symphonie Diagonale* (1925), is the result of such a manic search by its creator, Viking Eggeling, in pursuit of a universal language of forms.

culminated in abstraction is equally valid for neo-realist forms of representation. Here, too, a once axiomatic representational aspiration has been transformed into a *formal principle*: Every "realistic" depiction derives from an individual decision that has no relevance to art in general, beyond this personal choice. That is to say that "realism," in whatever form, is now simply *one* possible method of construction among many in the realm of modern art.)

The cumulative impact of the evolutionary process here roughly outlined, is that *nothing* in art is self-evident. Modernism eradicated any notion of an obligatory formal canon – for any artistic discipline whatsoever. As far as artistic practice is concerned, there are no longer any rules resting upon cultural conventions inherent to any medium. Or to put it more loosely, any notion of "right" and "wrong" ways of making art are no longer tenable. Only acts of censorship can impose restraints upon art and ban it – but the inner structure of art, its fundamental freedom remains intact.

For the sake of terminology: This characterization of modern art also includes art of a so-called postmodern nature. In polemical retrospect we can stipulate that in its day "postmodernism" was often nothing but a trademark used to earn a bunch of money off mediocre art, architecture and eccentrically convoluted philosophy. The effort of postmodernism to push back its time of birth ever further (and to adopt artworks from an increasingly distant past, from Lawrence Sterne's *Tristram Shandy* of the 18th century to Giuseppe Arcimboldo's 16th century mannerist fruit and vegetable faces) is another indication that it was but an additional fold in the multi-layered costume of the modern age. And despite all mischievous postmodern ringing of quotes within quotes, one of the most central categories of the modern – the new, the innovative – continues to challenge all forms of relevant art making.

Back to film: While fine art turned toward its materials and began to include a reflection upon the conditions of its fabricated nature, the trend in cinema took the exact opposite direction. To heighten the realistic illusion of film, its material and processes were effectively rendered "invisible." At the expense of recognizing and reflecting its

materiality and the conditions of its artistic creation, film became a "window onto the world," as French film theoretician André Bazin put it. For a long time, not only prevailing film practice, but also film theory assumed the illusionistic representation of reality as an unquestioned fact – as if the representation of reality naturally was the rightful purpose of cinema. It was only with the linguistic turn in theory at the beginning of the 1960s, and the advent of semiotic methods and models within the field of film studies that the perspective on film began to shift. Suddenly, the seemingly natural connection between film and reality was recognized to be rife with encodings *creating* the illusion of this "natural" bond. However, these new semiotic models in film studies were used to investigate and formalize the syntax of narrative films, and not to describe the use of film as an artistic medium beyond established codes and conventions.

So how can autonomous art be characterized from a semiotic perspective? In semiotic terms, the work of art is distinguished from a referential or "normal" use of language through its self-reflexivity and polysemy.[8] The single work of art sets up its own code, created by the artist: an idiolect. The relationship between the individual work and culture at large is therefore based on a resistance to standardized public expectations in regard to the codes and materials used. The privacy of this unfamiliar code provokes the spectator to look more closely, at *how* the artwork is made in order to recognize *what* it could mean. Instead of effecting unambiguous, referential connections between the sign and the signified, "the aesthetic message," the work of art leaves a number of alternative choices open to the understanding. Also, the material with which a work is made becomes meaningful in its technical and physical substance: It is a signifying component in itself.

But what does all this mean for film as an art form? What does the formulation of self-reflexive and polysemic texts mean for cinema? In the case of the seventh art, the category of materiality plays a perhaps even greater role than in classical art

---

8   Cf. Umberto Eco, *La struttura Assente* [*The Absent Structure: An Introduction to Semiology*] (Milan: Bompiani, 1968); German version: *Einführung in die Semiotik* (Munich: Wilhelm Fink Verlag, 1972), especially pp. 145–167.

forms. Film is based on a technology entailing innumerable apparative codings, which necessarily inscribe themselves upon the work created. The entire cinematographic apparatus, its very inner structure, depends on a precise coordination of individual elements – from image frequency to the optical system (adhering to perspectival rules straight out of the Renaissance) to the loaded film stock and its chemical/physical characteristics – to produce an image, conventionally seen as a "reproduction of reality." When film focuses on its own material in order to interrogate its very nature and realize itself as a modern and autonomous art form, then a host of these seemingly axiomatic characteristics – naturally including technical aspects – become open to questioning. Film as a radical form of art, that is to say, engaged in an investigation of the very heart of its matter, offers a wide array of options for artistic intervention – options that have been extensively exploited especially in expanded cinema works.

From a historical perspective, image content and syntactical structures play an even greater role than the apparative dispositif. Almost exactly 100 years ago, it was on this level that an impressive and ever expanding history of autonomous film art began to unfold. It began with the first hand-painted color experiments of Futurists Bruno Corra and Arnaldo Ginna between 1910 and 1912,[9] with the works of the German Absolute film, the French Cinéma pur, the Dadaist films; followed by Luis Buñuel's ingenious subversion of narrative syntax; the pioneering films of Len Lye, Harry Smith, Jordan Belson, the Whitneys, and Maya Deren; the metric films, the New American Cinema, structural film; the found footage film, which transforms the images and syntax of industrial cinema into material for art; new forms of digitally produced moving images, both abstract and figurative, and so on... In this work we encounter an incredibly multi-layered and multi-faceted class of motion pictures that resists standardized cinematic codes and

instead invents its own. For the purposes of simplification, whenever this process results in the revelation of new and unexpected dimensions that expand the medium and its possibilities of articulation, we use the designation "avant-garde."[10] These works manifest themselves as autonomous aesthetic phenomena that render the notion of cinema as a "window onto the world" transparent as an ideological construct, by revealing that the world behind this "window" is itself a *product* of this window.

In contrast, the feature film adheres to prescribed and standardized rules of narrative syntax in order to function, namely, to be instantly comprehensible and profitably marketable.[11] This means that feature films not only tell a story, but also always *how* to tell a story. It is this implicit and constantly repeated message about how a film *is supposed to look* that cultivates the expectations of the viewer. The near grotesque marginalization of avant-garde film as an art form in terms of public perception is directly connected to these audience expectations in regard to cinematic representation. The association of the individual's perception of reality with their perception of conventional film is so strong that any deviation from conventionalized cinematic technique is experienced as an attack on the individual's *own* perception and its apparent self-evidence. This leads to an aggressive set of

---

9   In the 1916 *Manifesto of Futurist Cinema* by Bruno Corra, et al. (reminiscent of Malevich): "Cinema is an autonomous art. The cinema must therefore never copy the stage. The cinema, being essentially visual, must above all fulfill the evolution of painting and detach itself from reality, from photography." In *Futurist Manifestos*, ed. Umbro Apollonio (New York: Viking Press, 1973), p. 207.

10   For those countries that hosted classical avant-garde art-film movements during the interwar period, the term "avant-garde film" is already taken. In these countries the notion "experimental film" is generally employed. But this designation unavoidably implies a kind of "preliminary investigation with uncertain results" and as such is at least as problematic as the term "avant-garde." Actually, the hegemony of "normal" cinema is here again in evidence, under which no differentiated conceptual index developed for a radical artistic use of the medium (in distinction to all other autonomous art forms with their categories and sub-categories). Whatever term is used, it will ultimately serve only one purpose: to designate the alterity of the work in distinction to the commercial mainstream. For this reason – despite the ongoing debates about the most appropriate designation – the decision as to which term is most apt will remain a matter of personal preference.

11   Naturally, the syntax of the feature film is continually evolving and many productions in this genre are engaging as works of art. When we speak in simple terms of the "feature film," we mean films of a highly conventional nature, commercial industrial productions aimed above all at making a financial profit. Regardless of this distinction, how every feature film is inherently inscribed with the character of a commodity is relevant to its status as a work of art.

expectations – not especially concerned with *what* is depicted, but rather *how* it is represented.

Were one to cite the lowest common denominator of the avant-garde that at the same time clearly distinguishes it from commercial cinema, one would arrive at the specific character of the relationship every film implicitly and unavoidably cultivates between itself and its audience. The pivotal question is: Does the film provoke the viewers to identify with the gaze of the camera *as if it were their own*? Or can an "author" be recognized in the images, as with the writer of a novel or the painter of a picture? In other words: How prominent is the voice of the film's narrator?

In his standard reference work *How to Read a Film: Movies, Media, and Beyond*, James Monaco compares narrative forms of the novel to that of film, and draws the conclusion that in film "the persona of the narrator is so much weaker. There has only been one major film, for example, that tried to duplicate the first-person narration so useful to the novel, Robert Montgomery's *Lady in the Lake* (1946). The result was a cramped, claustrophobic experience: we saw only what the hero saw."[12] Monaco here unintentionally betrays the principle behind the narrative mode of the feature film. The voice of the narrator in film is in no sense weaker than the first-person narrator of the novel. On the contrary! There is a very powerful narrator of the feature film: This narrator is the spectator himself, and thanks precisely to his identification with the gaze of the camera. In feature film, the camera assumes the position of an unseen third party watching events as they unfold. With this representation or "reproduction" the camera establishes a quasi "objective" narrative style behind which the director, screenplay author, etc., virtually disappear. The individual spectator is lured into this artificial and artistically rendered gap, created entirely on purpose, and identifies with the gaze of the camera as if he were a silent eyewitness to events. *He himself* thereby becomes the narrator: Nobody can tell me what I *actually see* – I "tell" it to myself. This identification with the gaze of the camera allows the viewer to become the "ideal,

immaterial 'voyeur' of a filmic pseudo-reality."[13] At the same time this identification establishes the basic prerequisite for a seamlessly functioning narrative. As in *Lady in the Lake*, any attempt to place the actor in the position of the narrator through the use of a so-called subjective camera leads to a collision with the secret "narrators" in the movie house. Monaco's formulation of a "claustrophobic feeling" perfectly describes this involuntary union of the gaze of the actor rendered by the subjective camera with the "narrative" gaze of the viewer.

In order to enable identification with the gaze of the camera and to equip the spectator with the power of the seemingly all-seeing and all-knowing voyeur, certain rules must be followed. On the screen we see a play of light and shadow. This spectacle of fluttering photons initially has *nothing* in common with the qualities of reality we recognize in the images. This is because film does not reproduce reality. Film reproduces *conditions of our perception of reality*. Whether filmic or photographic, the iconic sign in general does not reproduce the object; it reproduces our perceptual model of the object.[14] Even in this formulation the notion "reproduction" is imprecise: Film, and especially narrative film, is constellated by a complex system of various conventionalized codes, which are thus *accepted* as reproducing conditions of the perception of reality. So for instance, the abrupt shift in what is seen that coincides with every single edit conveys an experience that has nothing in common with everyday experience. Nevertheless, even the

---

12   James Monaco, *How to Read a Film* (New York: Oxford University Press, 2004), p. 54.

13   Noël Burch and Jorge Danaf, "Propositions," *Afterimage*, no. 5 (1974), p. 45. In general, we are here referring to the apparatus theory as first formulated by Jean-Louis Baudry in his essay "Le Dispositif," *Communications*, no. 23 (1975); English version: Jean-Louis Baudry, "The Apparatus," *Camera Obscura*, no. 1, Fall 1976: pp. 104–126. See also Jean-Louis Baudry and Alan Williams, "Ideological Effects of the Basic Cinematographic Apparatus," *Film Quarterly* 28, no. 2 (Winter 1974–1975), pp. 39–47, http://www.jstor.org/pss/1211632. Christian Metz authored the standard work on different forms of identification in cinema, *Le Signifiant imaginaire. Psychanalyse et cinéma* (Paris: Union Générale d'Éditions, 1977); English: *Psychoanalysis and Cinema. The Imaginary Signifier* (London: Macmillan Press, 1982); German: *Der imaginäre Signifikant. Psychoanalyse und Film* (Münster: Nodus Publikationen, 2000). Incidentally, it is telling that in a sweeping generalization Monsieur Metz dismisses avant-garde film as overly intellectualized nonsense: His theory of identification fails miserably in regard to avant-garde work.
14   Cf. Eco, p. 213.

most unusual montage strategies have been so widely conventionalized that they are accepted as valid reproductions of space/time continuity. The edit and its associated shift are in effect not perceived as a shift. The history of narrative film is also the history of this codification: on the part of the audience, the willingness to read the filmic image as the reproduction of reality; and on the part of film, the increasing glossing over of appearances and the removal of specific filmic elements that disturb the illusion of reality.[15] In the field of visual arts on the other hand, the author always reveals him- or herself and endeavors to draw the viewer into a discursive process. Often, this "dialogue" revolves around the form of the film, the qualities of *film as film*. It is here that the tradition of the cinematic avant-garde converges with that tradition of modern art whose *sine qua non* is the reflection of its constructed nature, of the process of its own production and thereby its creator. And as we find ourselves in the midst of an age moving beyond chemical film, reaching into digital and virtual realms, this battlefield is expanding into entirely new territories.

In order to become autonomous, visual art had to emancipate itself from its submissive role as a servant of ritual and representational functions. And it had to rebel against all externally predetermined rules and conventions imposed by society. In a similar process, avant-garde film rebels against the hegemony of commercial film production. With the emancipation of cinematic form, the elements of film are disengaged from a prefabricated coherence, and made accessible *in themselves* as artistic material and tools of expression, whether analog or digital – come what may. The same process that demolished the rule of established norms within the visual arts makes way for free artistic access to the elements of cinematography in the construction of avant-garde motion pictures. Its works attain the historical level of articulation reached by modern art and it is alive and well as an autonomous art form.

Translated by Eve Heller

---

15   The so-called "continuity system" serves precisely this purpose, including the 180 degree rule, the eyeline match, the maintenance of smooth shot transitions in temporal sequence including matching on action, the avoidance of jump cuts, rules forbidding actors to look directly into the camera, the horizontal depiction of all horizontals in space, etc., etc.

01

03

02

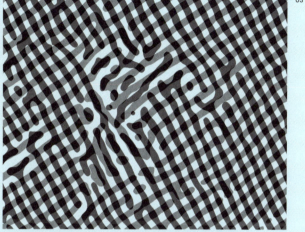

04

05

06

07

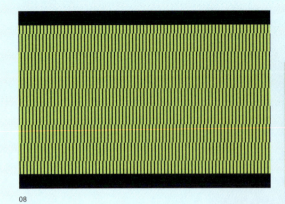

08

09

10

11

12

13

14

15

16

17

18

19

20

21

22

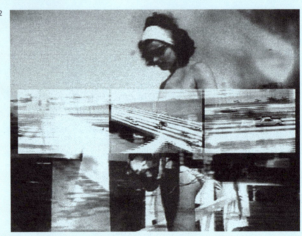

25

23

24

26

27

29

28

30

32

31

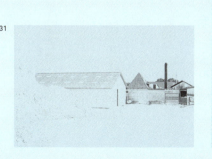

Biographies, Filmographies and Bibliographies

MARC ADRIAN

Born in Vienna in 1930. As a thirteen-year-old pupil drafted into a paratrooper unit. Returned to Vienna on a Russian ammunition transport before it was taken over by the Red Army. From 1950 to 1954 studied at the Academy of Fine Arts in Vienna with sculptor Fritz Wotruba. Began to produce the *Sprungperspektiven* (jumping perspectives) and geometrical *Hinterglasmontagen* (montages behind glass) and became an early exponent of Op-Art. After 1954 involved with kinetics, rhythmic interferences and optical structures. 1957–1960 Audited courses at the IDHEC College of Film in Paris. Since 1960 work with infra- and meta-structures. 1970–1973 Professorship for painting and aesthetic theory at the Academy of Fine Arts, Hamburg. 1980–1981 Worked at the Center for Advanced Visual Studies, Massachusetts Institute of Technology (MIT). *Screenings and Exhibitions* (selection): Marc Adrian, Neue Galerie Graz, 2007; marc adrian: dreaming doll – magic doll, Galerie Hofstätter, Vienna, 2006; Lichtkunst/Kunstlicht, ZKM, Karlsruhe, 2005; Bildlicht, Museum of the 20th Century, Vienna, 1991; Olympiade of Arts, Olympic Rak, Seoul, 1988; Computer Art, National Gallery of Modern Art, New Dehli, 1972; Impulse. Computerkunst, Kunstverein München, 1970; Cybernetic Serendipity, ICA, London, 1968. Member of the Vienna Secession, the Graz Assembly of Authors and the Austria Filmmakers Cooperative. Marc Adrian died in 2008.
Filmography (selection)
2000 Taos 1998 Conundrum 1997 Four Short Pieces 1996 Kenya Newsreel 1994 92 Avignon 1993 Kiln 1990 Stadt-Werk-Statt 1989 Pueblo I 1987 Farewell to Kurt 1983 Der Regen 1977 uarei 1971 Theoria 1969 Blue Movie & Black Movie III 1968 Total 1966 Text III 1964 Text I & Text II 1962–1964 Orange 1963 RANDOM 1959 Black Movie II 1959/1960 Schriftfilm 1958 Wo-Vor-Da-Bei 1958 1. Mai 1958 (with Kurt Kren) 1957 Black Movie I (with Kurt Kren)
Bibliography (selection)
Publications by Marc Adrian: Mozgó Film/ 3 A BBS Mühely Kiadványa [Hungarian] (Budapest), 1998. → "Aber Indianer können

keine Weißen werden… Gedanken zu seinem Film *Pueblo.*" [German] *Blimp. Zeitschrift für Film*, no. 13 (1989). → "film-realität und textrealität. versuch einer synopsis des artistischen prozesses." [German] *Freibord* 52/53, no. 2/3 (1986). → "10. Thesen. Maxime für das andere Kino (zum Filmprogramm der Filmgruppe Rosa-Grün-Blau)." [German] *Chäslager Stans*, no. 3 (1969). → "komputer und die demokratisierung des ästhetischen bewußtseins." [German] In *Kunst und Computer*. Vienna: Zentralsparkasse der Gemeinde Wien, 1969.
Books and Catalogues: Artaker, Anna, and Peter Weibel, eds. *marc adrian*. [German/English] Graz and Klagenfurt: Ritter Verlag, 2007. → Mörth, Otto, ed. *Marc Adrian: Das filmische Werk.* [German] Vienna: Sonderzahl Verlag, 1999.
Articles, Interviews and Essays: Reicher, Isabella. "Bewegung auf Leinwand." [German] *Der Standard* (Vienna), February 7, 2001. → Mudie, Peter. "Thought lines fluid in static frame. The aesthetics of loss in the films of Marc Adrian." [English] *Blimp. Film Magazine*, no. 39 (1998). → Büttner, Elisabeth, and Christian Dewald. *Anschluß an Morgen. Eine Geschichte des österreichischen Films von 1945 bis zur Gegenwart.* [German] Salzburg and Vienna: Residenz-Verlag, 1997. → Weibel, Peter. "Der Wiener Formalfilm." [German] In *Jenseits von Kunst*, edited by Peter Weibel. Vienna: Passagen Verlag, 1997. → Prucha, Martin. "Die Kraft der Negation. Marc Adrians Filme." [German] In *Avantgardefilm Österreich. 1950 bis heute*, edited by Alexander Horwath, Lisl Ponger and Gottfried Schlemmer. Vienna: Verlag Wespennest, 1995. → Grbić, Bogdan. " Ein paar Fragen zur Film- und Weltsicht des Marc Adrian." [German] *Blimp. Film Magazine*, no. 24 (1993). → Hendrich, Hermann. "Der mehrdimensionale Künstler Marc Adrian." [German] *Blimp. Film Magazine*, no. 24 (1993). → Rothschild, Thomas. "Fehldiagnose Wirklichkeitstreue. Ein paar Bemerkungen zur österreichischen Filmkultur (oder was sich dafür hält) und über den Anarcho-Avantgardisten Marc Adrian." [German] *Blimp. Film Magazine*, no. 24 (1993). → Rothschild, Thomas. "Aufstand gegen das Gegebene. Überlegungen des Malers und Filmemachers im Gespräch mit Thomas Rothschild." [German] *Forum*, no. 442/443 (1990). → Luxbacher, Günther. "Filme aus Wörtern. Der Avantgarde-Film und seine Konzepte." [German] *Wiener Zeitung* (Vienna), December 11, 1987. → Schlüpmann, Heide. "Österreichische Filmtage Wels." [German] *epd Film*, no. 12 (1984). → Gassert, Siegmar. "Avantgarde- und Undergroundfilme aus Österreich." [German] *Basler Zeitung* (Basel), June 14, 1980. → Hein, Birgit. "Underground-Film.

Bildende Künstler machen Filme, Avant-Garde-Filmer machen Kunst." [German] *Magazin Kunst*, no. 41 (1971).

MARTIN ANIBAS

Born in Waidhofen an der Thaya, Austria, in 1961. Since 1994 member of the Künstlerhaus Wien. 1987–1992 Master class for painting and experimental creative art under Maria Lassnig at the University of Applied Arts, Vienna, at Studio for Experimental Animation Films. 1992 Diploma with award of honor. 1989 and 1992 Honorable mention award from the federal state of Lower Austria for creative art. 1993 Karl Rössing Award, Rupertinum Salzburg. 2003 Honorable mention award from the federal state of Lower Austria for media art. Numerous exhibitions and film shows in Austria and abroad. www.anibas.at
Filmography (selection)
Animation Films 2000 Pique-Nique 1993 Le trait rouge 1993 Bild 15 & Bild 16 1991 Edge 1991 Spinning-Bild 14 1991 Am Land 1990 Immer-Hin 1990 Fluchtpunkt 1989 La rencontre 1989 60 Seh-Kunden *Documentaries* 2011 Von hier nach dort 2010 Atlantic Hotel 2010 Right here, right now 2009 Schwarze Pferde 2008 Yella Yella 2007 Lisbon Chill out tour 2004 Westport Mayo
Bibliography (selection)
Books and Catalogues: Kurz, Toni, ed. *Martin Anibas: Portriments. Arbeiten auf Papier*. Horn, Austria: Galerie + Edition Thurnhof, 1993.
Articles, Interviews and Essays: Dewald, Christian, Sabine Groschup, Mara Mattuschka and Thomas Renoldner, eds. *Die Kunst des Einzelbilds. Animation in Österreich – 1832 bis heute.* [German] Vienna: verlag filmarchiv austria, 2010.

MARTIN ARNOLD

Born in Vienna in 1959. Studied Psychology and Art History at the University of Vienna. Independent filmmaker since 1988. Taught at art schools and universities including San Francisco Art Institute (1996–1997), Academy of Fine Arts, Städelschule, Frankfurt am Main (1998–1999), Bard College, Annandale, NY (2000–2001), and CalArts, Los Angeles (2008). Gained international recognition through a series of 16 mm films: *pièce touchée* (1989), *passage á l'acte* (1993) and *Alone. Life Wastes Andy Hardy* (1998). Recent years dedicated to digital film installations including *Deanimated* (2002), *Coverversion* (2008) and works on video including *Shadow Cuts* and *Soft Palate* (2010). Represented at several film festivals including Cannes, Rotterdam, New York, and major cinematheques including Centre Pompidou, Cinèmathéque Royale in Brussels, the Tate

Modern and the National Film Theatre in London, the MoMA in New York, and museums including Barbican Art Centre, Witte de With in Rotterdam, Bozar in Brussels, Kunsthaus Zürich and Hamburger Kunstverein.

Filmography and Installations
Installations & 35 mm: 2011 Self Control 2010 Soft Palate, Shadow Cuts Installations: 2007 Coverversion, Cloudy Insulin 2005 Soft Winds 2003 Jeanne 2002 Deanimated, Dissociated, Forsaken Films: 1998 Alone. Life Wastes Andy Hardy 1997 Psycho (Viennale trailer) 1996 Don't – the Austrian Film 1994 Brain again (trailer), Kunstraum Remise (trailer) 1993 Jesus walking on Screen (trailer) passage á l'acte 1989 pièce touchée 1986 O.T. – 2 1985 O.T. – 1

Bibliography (selection)
Books and Catalogues: Matt, Gerald, and Thomas Miessgang, eds. *Martin Arnold: Deanimated.* [German/English] Vienna and New York: Springer Verlag, 2002. *Articles, Interviews and Essays:* Blazicek, Martin. "profil_martin Arnold." [Czech] *Cinepur*, no. 68 (2010). → Désanges, Guilliaume. "Martin Arnold." [French] *DITS. Publication semestrielle du Musée des Arts Contemporains de la Communauté framcaise de Belgique*, no. 5 (Fall–Winter 2010). → Huber, Florian. "Martin Arnold und die Fortschreibung der Avantgarden." [German] In *Bildsatz. Texte zur Bildenden Kunst*, edited by Franz Josef Czernin and Martin Janda. Cologne: DuMont Buchverlag, 2008. → Baross, Zsuzsa. "The Future of the Past: The Cinema." [English] *Angelaki. Journal of Theoretical Humanities* 11, no. 1 (2006). → Herbert, Daniel. "To Mock a Killingbird: Martin Arnold's *passage a l'acte* and the Dissimetries Of Cultural Exchange." [English] *Millenium Film Journal*, no. 45/46 (Fall 2006). → Cahill, James L. "Martin Arnold: From Cineseizure to Silenced Cinema." [English] *Cinematexas*, film festival catalogue, University of Texas, 2005. → Pircher, Wolfgang. "Hollywoods Gespenster – Martin Arnolds filmische Dekonstruktionsarbeit." [German] In *Film Denken*, edited by Brigitte Mayr, Ludwig Nagl and Eva Waniek. Vienna: Synema, 2005. → Mulvey, Laura. "Deanimated. Laura Mulvey in conversation with Martin Arnold." [English] In *Fact Annual 2003*. Liverpool: Fact, 2004. → Carels, Edwin. "Passiespel met pixels." [Dutch] *De Financieel-Economische Tijd* (Brussels), May 3, 2003. → Hickling, Alfred. "Reviews. Deanimated." [English] *The Guardian* (London), July 5, 2003. → Koegel, Alice. "Reviews. Martin Arnold, Kunsthalle Wien." [English] *frieze*, no. 74 (April 2003). → Ploebst, Helmut. "Klonen und morphen in leeren Betten." [German] *Der Standard* (Vienna), September 26, 2003. → Rozendaal, Ernst Jan. "Vleeshal toont experi-

mentele films." [Dutch] *PZC*, April 17, 2003. → Schoonenboom, Merlijn. "Een Hollywood-icoon in een vleeshal." [Dutch] *Volkskrant* (Amsterdam), May 14, 2003. → Traven, Patrick. "Le cinéma au musée: le cinéma médusé!" [French] *Balthazar*, no. 6, (Summer–Fall 2003). → Beckmann, Aki. "Bilder lügen immer." [German] *ray Filmmagazin* (November 2002). → Delorme, Stéphane. "Le cinéma déserté de Martin Arnold." [French] *Cahiers du Cinéma* (December 2002). → Grissemann, Stefan. "Triebsteuerungskino. Der Filmemacher Martin Arnold vollzieht den Übertritt in die bildende Kunst." [German] *profil*, no. 42 (2002). → Huber, Christoph. "Geisterhafte Fahrten durch die Leere: Eine Hinrichtung des Blicks." [German] *Die Presse* (Vienna), October 15, 2002. → Loebenstein, Michael. "Endlich entseelt!" [German] *Falter*, no. 40 (2002). → Philipp, Claus. "Neue Blicke ohne Helden: Auslöschung in Hollywood." [German] *Der Standard* (Vienna), October 10, 2002. → Reiterer, Martin. "Martin Arnold: Deanimated." [German] *springerin*, no. 4 (December 2002). → Vogel, Sabine B. "Critics' Pick. Martin Arnold, Kunsthalle Wien." [English] *Artforum International Magazine* (November 2002). → Delorme Stéphane. "Found footage, mode démploi." [French] *Cahiers du Cinema* (May 2000). → Rosenbaum, Jonathan. "Wrinkles in Time." [English] *Chicago Weekly Reader*, February 18, 2000. → Huston, Johnny Ray. "What makes you tic/Out Loud." [English] *San Francisco Bay Guardian* 33, no. 25 (March 1999). → Kermabon, Jacques. "Martin Arnold, Scratcher Hollywood." [French] *Bref. Le magazine du court métrage*, no. 40, (1999). → Morris, Gary. "Compulsion at 24 frames per second. Films of Martin Arnold at Cinematheque." [English] *The Bay Area Reporter* 29, no. 12 (March 1999). → Noetinger, Jérome. "Martin Arnold." [French] *revue & corrigée*, trimestrial, no. 39 (April 1999). → Grissemann, Stefan. "Maschinelle Erregungen." [German] *Die Presse* (Vienna), March 19, 1998. → MacDonald, Scott. "Martin Arnold." [English] In *A Critical Cinema: Interviews with Independent Filmmakers*. Berkeley, Los Angeles and London: University of California Press, 1998. → Omasta, Michael. "Die Ordnung der Dinge." [German] *Falter*, no. 12 (1998). → Korschil, Thomas. "Iz arhiva / Out of the Archive. The Reinvention of the Past." [Slovenian/German] In *medij v mediju / media in media*, edited by Barbara Borčić, et al. Ljubljana, 1997. → Lippit, Akira M. "Martin Arnold's Memory Machine." [English] *Afterimage. The Journal of Media Arts and Cultural Criticism* 24, no. 6 (1997). → Philipp, Claus. "Ahnung von Apokalypse: Spritzendes Weiß. Ein Gespräch über das Löschen und Auslöschen mit dem Filmemacher Martin Arnold." [German] *Der Standard* (Vienna), Septem-

ber 15, 2007. → Waniek, Eva. "Le cinema et le corps: un art du luxe." [French] In *Florilège Scratch*, edited by Yann Beauvais and Jean-Damien Collin. Paris: Scratch, 1999. → Grissemann, Stefan. "Martin Arnold. *Don't – Der Österreichfilm*. Mysterienmaschine." [German] In *Eine Geschichte der Bilder. Acht Found Footage Filme aus Österreich*, edited by Polyfilm Verleih. Vienna: Polyfilm, 1996. → MacDonald, Scott. "Martin Arnold." [French] In *L'art du mouvement. Collection cinématographique du Musée nationale d'art moderne 1919– 1996*, edited by Centre Pompidou and Jean-Michel Bohours, catalogue. Paris, 1996. → Tscherkassky, Peter. "Brève histoire du cinéma d'avant-garde autrichien." [French] In *L'avant-garde autrichienne au cinéma 1955–1993*, edited by Centre Pompidou. Paris, 1996. → MacDonald, Scott. "Sp.. Sp.. Spaces of Inscription. Scott MacDonald im Gespräch mit Martin Arnold." [German] In *Avantgardefilm Österreich. 1950 bis heute*, edited by Alexander Horwath, Lisl Ponger and Gottfried Schlemmer. Vienna: Verlag Wespennest, 1995. → Philipp, Claus. "Tanz mit Fundstücken. Martin Arnold und seine Filme." [German] In *Gegenschuß*, edited by Peter Illetschko. Vienna: Verlag Wespennest, 1995. → Tscherkassky, Peter. " Die rekonstruierte Kinematografie. Zur Filmavantgarde in Österreich." [German] In *Avantgardefilm Österreich. 1950 bis heute*, edited by Alexander Horwath, Lisl Ponger and Gottfried Schlemmer. Vienna: Verlag Wespennest, 1995. → Turim, Maureen C. "Eine Begegnung mit dem Bild. Martin Arnolds *piéce touchée*. " [German] In *Avantgardefilm Österreich. 1950 bis heute*, edited by Alexander Horwath, Lisl Ponger and Gottfried Schlemmer. Vienna: Verlag Wespennest, 1995. → Geissler, Ulrike. "Wirbel bei Bühne Eröffnung: Kurzfilm schockt Ehrengäste." [German] *Neue Niederösterreichische Nachrichten* (Sankt Pölten, Austria), July 6, 1994. → MacDonald, Scott. "Sp.. Sp.. Spaces of Inscription: An interview with Martin Arnold." [English] In *Film Quaterly* 48, no. 1 (Fall 1994). → Stadler, Hilar. "Das Physische des Kinos: Über 2 Filme von Martin Arnold." [German] *Das Kunst Bulletin*, no. 3 (1994). → Grissemann, Stefan. "Metal Beat. Methoden der Verstümmelung und Neuordnung in Martin Arnolds Film *passage á l'acte*." [German] *Blimp. Film Magazine*, no. 22/23 (1993). → Jutz, Gabriele. "Espace et Cinéma d'Avant-Garde Autrichien." [French] In *Sémiotiques*, no. 4 (June 1993). → Philipp, Claus. "Neuland zwischen den Bildkadern. Zur Weltpremiere von Martin Arnolds Found Footage Film *passage á l'acte.*" [German] *Der Standard* (Vienna), March 3, 1993. → Robnik, Drehli. "Vom Tick zum Stottern." [German] *Falter*, no. 9 (1993). → Weixelbaumer, Robert. "Familie

Hollywood auf der Couch. Avantgarde-Filmemacher Martin Arnold über seine neue Arbeit *passage á l'acte*." [German] *Die Presse* (Vienna), March 4, 1993. → Tscherkassky, Peter. "Die Analogien der Avantgarde." [German/English] In *Found Footage Film*, edited by Cecilia Hausheer and Christoph Settele. Lucerne: Viper/zyklop Verlag, 1992. → Illmaier, Gerhild, and Bogdan Grbić. "*pièce touchée* on the Road. Blimp im Gespräch mit dem Avantgardisten der 3. Generation." [German] *Blimp. Zeitschrift für Film*, no. 14 (1990). → Praschl, Bernhard. "Griff in den Müll. Martin Arnold ist Österreichs erfolgreichster Experimentalfilmer." [German] *Die Presse* (Vienna), June 9/10, 1990. → Horwath, Alexander. "Berührt – Geführt: Heiße Liebe zwischen Technik und Intellekt. Martin Arnold stellt sein neues Werk vor." [German] *Der Standard* (Vienna), October 11, 1989. → Stadler, Tina, Peter Zach and Bogdan Grbić. "Œil Touchée. Blimp im Gespräch mit Peter Tscherkassky & Martin Arnold." [German] *Blimp. Zeitschrift für Film*, no. 13 (1989). *DVD Editions*: *Martin Arnold. The Cineseizure*. Vienna: Index DVD Edition (in cooperation with Re:Voir) 018, 2007.

THOMAS BAUMANN

Born in Salzburg in 1967. *Selected exhibitions and screenings*: 2011 Roboterträume (Kunsthaus Graz); The Constitution of Liberty (Public Project, Detroit). 2010 Roboterträume (Museum Tinguely, Basel); Triennale 1.0 (OK Offenes Kulturhaus, Linz); Play Admont (Museum Stift Admont). 2009 Best of Austria (Lentos, Linz); Rewind / Fast Forward (Neue Galerie, Graz); Romantische Maschinen (Georg Kolbe Museum, Berlin). 2008 Abstract (Museum Moderner Kunst Kärnten, Klagenfurt); Another Tomorrow (Neue Galerie Graz; Slought Foundation, Philadelphia); Balancing the wrong and the true... (Kunsthaus Basel Land); WAK, Unlimited/Public Project (Art Basel). 2007 Hard Rock Walzer (Villa Manin, Italy). 2006 Ordnung und Verführung (Haus Konstruktiv, Zurich); Und es bewegt sich doch.... (Kunstmuseum Bochum); Viennale 06 (Vienna); Diagonale 06 (Graz). 2005 Moving Objects (Museum Jean Tinguely, Basel); Bewegliche Teile (Kunsthaus Graz); Wiener Linien (Wien Museum); Galerie Krobath Wimmer (Vienna). 2002 Persönliche Pläne (Kunsthalle Basel). 2001 Lebt und arbeitet in Wien (Kunsthalle Wien); Ausgeträumt... (Vienna Secession); Raumkörper (Kunsthalle Basel). **Filmography** (selection) 2008-2010 WESTWIENOST 2007 Laufding (with Martin Kaltner) 2005 Odessa (with Kaltner), Zoomahinundher 2004 Motiv/Figur/Grund, Plot:Bach 1998 You Talk / I Listen, Before the heart's too hot

1997 Many PE Many PA (with Kaltner) 1996 La bibliothec francaise und chin. Neujahr (with Kaltner) Hutagang (with Kaltner) 1995 27 (with Kaltner), Toupie (with Kaltner) Ader 1 1994 Pas Trop, Gehfilmen 6 (with Kaltner and Josef Dabernig) 1993 Plato (with Kaltner), Gehfilm (with Kaltner, Norbert Trummer) 1992 Geh! (with Kaltner, Trummer), Aehoui (with Kaltner) 1991 Ashum, Naraf! **Bibliography** (selection) *Articles, Interviews and Essays:* Korschil, Thomas. "Konterbande. Über einige neue kurze und längere Filme aus Österreich." [German] *Meteor*, special issue (1998). → Philipp, Claus. "Gehfilme." [German] *StadtkinoProgramm*, no. 298 (1996).

MOUCLE BLACKOUT

Born in Prague, Czech Republic, in 1935. 1948–1954 Studied sculpture under Fritz Wotruba at Vienna's Academy of Fine Arts. 1948 First sculptures, from 1949 onwards various exhibitions, 1952–1954 Studied in Milan and Paris (Académie de la grande Chaumière, Prof. Ossip Zadkine). 1957–1958 Unaccredited student at the IDHEC College of Film in Paris. As of 1953 studies in film; as of 1954 involved with kinetics, rhythmic interferences and problems of optical structures; as of 1960 work with infra-structures and meta-structures; 1965 Studied perceptive psychology at the University of Vienna. 1970–1973 Professor of Painting and Aesthetic Theory at the College of Fine Arts in Hamburg; numerous lectures at American universities. 1980–1981 Worked at the Center for Advanced Visual Studies at Massachusetts Institute of Technology, Cambridge, USA. 1988–1989 Visiting Professor for visual communication at the University of Hessen and at the Polytechnic University in Kassel. Member of the Vienna Secession, the Graz Assembly of Authors and the Austria Filmmakers Cooperative. **Filmography** (selection) 1984–2004 Break 1998 Loss 1996 Neue Wege bricht neue Welt aus 1992 Der galaktische Nordpol liegt im Haar der Berenice 1987 O.K. 1979 Stoned Vienna 1972 Die Geburt der Venus 1969 walk in **Bibliography** (selection) *Articles, Interviews and Essays:* Mudie, Peter, ed. *Below the Centre*. [English] Perth: Austria Filmmakers Cooperative and School of Architecture and Fine Arts, University of Western Australia, 1994. → Perthold, Sabine, ed. *Rote Küsse. Film-Schau-Buch*. [German] Tübingen: Konkursbuch-Verlag, 1990. → Preschl, Claudia, ed. *FRAUEN und FILM und VIDEO Österreich*. [German] Vienna: filmladen, 1986. → Gassert, Siegmar. "Avantgarde- und Undergroundfilme aus Österreich." [German] *Basler Zeitung* (Basel), June, 14, 1980. → Schmidt Jr., Ernst. *Österreichi-*

scher Avantgarde- und Undergroundfilm 1950–1980. [German] Vienna: Österreichisches Filmarchiv, 1980.

DIETMAR BREHM

Born in Linz in 1947. 1967–1972 Studied painting at the University of Fine Arts, Linz. Professor at the University of Fine Arts, Linz. Experimental films, drawing + painting and photography. Numerous film screenings, awards and exhibitions at home and abroad. *Solo Exhibitions* (selection): 2009 Museum Nordico, Linz; 1988/1993/2008 Landesgalerie am Oberösterreichisches Landesmuseum, Linz; 2005 Museum Moderener Kunst Stiftung Wörlen, Passau; 2002–2003 Künstlerhaus Wien/Austrian Film Museum, Vienna; 1986 Neue Galerie der Stadt Linz. *Collections* (selection): Austrian Film Museum, Vienna; Filmarchive Austria, Vienna; Lentos Kunstmuseum, Linz; Oberösterreichisches Landesmuseum, Linz; The Royal Filmarchive, Brussels; Kali-Film, Cologne; Film-Makers' Cooperative, New York. Since 1984 numerous film presentations and TV portraits in ORF, 3sat, Kunstkanaal Amsterdam, ARTE, Channel 4, London, VOX, SBS TV, Australia, TIV-TV-Station Wien, RTV-Slovenia, OKTO, Vienna, Dorf TV, Linz. *TV* (selection): → *Georg Ritter im Gespräch mit dem Filmemacher, Maler und Zeichner Dietmar Brehm*. Dorf TV, Linz, 2011. *Dietmar Brehm. Blick + Zwang*. ORF *Kunst-Stücke*, 2000. → *Dietmar Brehm. Blickzwang*. ORF *Kunst-Stücke*, 1996; 3sat, 1997. → *Vom Blickpunkt der Beschattung. Eine Beobachtung zu den Zeichnungen, Malereien und Filmen von Dietmar Brehm*. ORF *Kunst-Stücke*, 1990. **Filmography** (selection) *Videos* (selection): 2011 XXX!, Praxis-9, Praxis-10 2010 Praxis-7, Praxis-8 2009 OZEAN, Verdrehte Augen – Videoversion 2, Praxis-4, Praxis-5, Praxis-6. 2008 Praxis-2, Praxis-3, Verdrehte Augen – Videoversion 1, Fliege 2007 Praxis-1 2006 Videokalkito-1 *16 mm Films* (selection): 2007 Halcion 2005 Selektion, Peng-Peng, Blah Blah Blah 2004 Black Death Filter + Shining, Basis pH, Fit 2002 Verdrehte Augen, Prima 2001 Camera Girls, Satina 2000 Blitze, Mix-3, MIX-4 1992–1999 Schwarzer Garten: The Murder Mystery/Blicklust/Party/Macumba/Korridor/Organics 1997 Kamera, Mix-2 1994 Mix-1 1993 Ostafrika, Job 1991 DIRT + VENUS 1990 Roter Morgen *Super 8/16 mm Blow-Ups* (selection): 1976/2003 Huh Huh 1988/1996 Who loves the sun 1986/1993 Color de Luxe 1982/1996 Perfekt 1–3 1976/1996 Insch-1, Interview ohne Ton 1981/1994 Sekundenfalle 1977/1994 Film Path-1, Film Path-2 1974/1994 Filmweg *Super 8 Films* (selection): 1989 Job 1987/1988 The Murder Mystery. 1st Version 1978–1980 Die Sensible 1978 Normal-2 1977 Normal-1

1976 <u>Heavy Heat</u> 1975 <u>Rolle-1</u> 1974 <u>Total</u>
Bibliography (selection)
Books and Catalogues: Nordico-Museum
der Stadt Linz, ed. *Dietmar Brehm. Film +
Video 1974–2009, Malerei 2004–2009.*
[German] 2009. → Brehm, Dietmar, ed.
Dietmar Brehm. Sekundenfalle. [German]
Linz: Artbook Verlag, 2008. → Wipplinger,
Hans-Peter, Museum Moderner Kunst –
Stiftung Wörlen, ed. *Dietmar Brehm.
Blickzwang.* [German] Passau, 2005.
→ Horwath, Alexander, ed. *Dietmar Brehm.
Party. Filme 1974–2003.* [German] Vienna:
Triton Verlag, 2003. → Künstlerhaus Wien,
ed. *Dietmar Brehm: Job. Malerei, Arbeiten
auf Papier, Fotografie, Film.* [German]
2002. → Schlemmer, Gottfried, ed. *Dietmar
Brehm: Perfekt.* [German] Vienna: Sonder-
zahl Verlag, 2000. → Pappernigg, Michaela.
*Dietmar Brehm. Blickfalle. EXP-Filme,
Zeichnungen, Malerei, Fotografie.* [Ger-
man] Master's thesis, Vienna, 1997. →
Oberösterreichisches Landesmuseum
and Peter Assmann, eds. *Dietmar Brehm.
Blicklust. Zeichnungen 1988–1993,
Malerei 1989–1993, Fotografie 1976–1993,
Film 1974–1992.* [German] Linz, 1993.
→ Tscherkassky, Peter. "Brakhage, Warhol,
Brehm." [German] In *Dietmar Brehm.
Blicklust.* → Oberösterreichisches Landes-
museum and Wilfried Seipel, eds. *Dietmar
Brehm. Malerei, Zeichnung, EXP-Filme.*
[German] Linz, 1988.
Articles, Interviews and Essays: Rebhandl,
Bert. "Gewaltexzess trifft Bildwelten-
sturz." [German] *Der Standard* (Vienna),
March 21, 2011. → Grissemann, Stefan.
"Dietmar Brehm – Programm #44."
[German] In *Was ist Film. Peter Kubelkas
Zyklisches Programm im Österreichischen
Filmmuseum*, edited by Stefan Grisse-
mann, Alexander Horwath and Regina
Schlagnitweit. Vienna: Filmmuseum-
SynemaPublikationen, 2010. → Büttner,
Elisabeth. "Letzter Ausgang: Verwesung.
Im Würfelwurf: Hand Hirn, Auge. Zu
Dietmar Brehms *Organics*." [German]
In *Filmhimmel Österreich*, edited by
Christian Dewald. Vienna: verlag filmar-
chiv austria, 2008. Program notes no. 084.
→ Grissemann, Stefan. "Dietmar Brehm."
[Czech] *Film a doba* (2008). → Schlemmer,
Gottfried. "Nicht versöhnt. Strukturelle
Bezüge im Tacoma-Film von Dietmar
Brehm." In *Filmhimmel Österreich*, edited
by Christian Dewald. Vienna: verlag filmar-
chiv austria, 2007. Program notes no. 069.
→ Büttner, Elisabeth. "Filmhimmel, A
2004." [German] In *Filmhimmel Österreich*,
edited by Christian Dewald. Vienna: verlag
filmarchiv austria, 2005. Program notes
no. 001. → Büttner, Elisabeth, and Christi-

an Dewald. "Eindringen in den Abfall der
Geschichte, Dietmar Brehm im Gespräch
mit Elisabeth Büttner und Christian
Dewald." [German] *kolik.film*, no. 5 (2005).
→ Clark, George. "Arnold, Brehm, Deutsch
and Tscherkassky. Four Contemporary
Austrian Avant-garde Filmmakers."
[English] *senses of cinema*, no. 28 (2003).
→ Höller, Christian. "Dietmar Brehm. Loch
im Kino." [German] *springerin* 1/03, no. 9
(2003). → Omasta, Michael, and Michael
Loebenstein. "Man muss es aushalten.
Dietmar Brehm." [German] *Falter*, Decem-
ber 13, 2002. → Horwath, Alexander.
"Magic and Loss." [German] *Schnitt.
Das Filmmagazin*, no. 22 (2001). → Müller,
Matthias. "Rauschzustände – Die Hirn-
filme des Dietmar Brehm." [German]
epd Film 1/01 (2001). → Schifferle, Hans.
"Menschen aus zweiter Hand. Mysteriös
und unberechenbar: Dietmar Brehms
Underground-Kino." [German] *Süddeut-
sche Zeitung* (Munich), March 1, 2001.
→ Grissemann, Stefan. "Hinter all den
bleichen Körpern und Gesichtern – die
Verschwisterung von Tod und Eros im
Irritationskino des Dietmar Brehm."
[German] *Die Presse* (Vienna), March 18,
2000. → Rebhandl, Bert. "Maskenball. Zu
den Filmen von Dietmar Brehm." [German]
In *Diagonale*, film festival catalogue. Graz,
2000. → Grissemann, Stefan. "Magische
Räume, sinistre Welten – Brehms wunder-
liche Filme." [German] *Die Presse* (Vienna),
March 30, 1998. → Steiner, Ulrike. "In
den Unerklärlichkeitsbereich weisen –
Eine andere Schule des Sehens ist Blickzwang mit Dietmar Brehm." [German]
OÖ Nachrichten (Linz), October 15, 1996.
→ Schlemmer, Gottfried. "Letztlich ist
man ein Leichenpumpe." [German] In
Avantgardefilm Österreich. 1950 bis heute,
edited by Alexander Horwath, Lisl Ponger
and Gottfried Schlemmer. Vienna: Verlag
Wespennest, 1995. → Schlemmer, Gott-
fried. "*The Murder Mystery* – Ein Doku-
ment der Angst und des Grauens." [Ger-
man] In *Avantgardefilm Österreich. 1950
bis heute*, edited by Alexander Horwath,
Lisl Ponger and Gottfried Schlemmer.
Vienna: Verlag Wespennest, 1995. →
Gyöngyösi, Stefan. "Gespräch mit Dietmar
Brehm – Zur Blicklust." [German] In *Art of
Vision*, edited by Stefan Gyöngyösi for
Kulturverein Zeitfluß. Salzburg, 1993. →
Steppan, Dorothea. "Gespräch mit Diet-
mar Brehm." [German] *Filmkunst – Zeit-
schrift für Filmkultur und Filmwissen-
schaft*, no. 137 (1993). → Palm, Michael.
"Chirurgische Eingriffe in das versehrte
Kino." [German] *Der Standard* (Vienna),
October 1, 1990. → Schlemmer, Gottfried.
"Blickstücke der Angst und des Grauens.
Dietmar Brehm." [German] *Der Standard*
(Vienna), October 18, 1989. Part of the
series "Die Kinomacher – 16 österrei-
chische Regisseure für die 90er Jahre."

→ Preschl, Claudia, and Dietmar Brehm.
"Blicklust. Zu den Filmen von Dietmar
Brehm." [German] *Blimp. Zeitschrift für
Film*, no. 15 (1986).
DVD Editions: Praxis 1–4, 2006–2008.
Linz: Dietmar Brehm DVD private edition,
vol. 1, 2011. → *Praxis 5–8, 2008–2009.*
Linz: Dietmar Brehm DVD private edition,
vol. 2, 2011. → *Dietmar Brehm. Perfekt.
Der Österreichische Film*, no. 110, Vienna:
Edition Der Standard/Filmarchiv Austria/
Hoanzl, 2008. Nine experimental films,
1976–2008. → *Dietmar Brehm. Black
Garden.* 1987–1999. Vienna: Index DVD
Edition 016, 2006.

DIDI BRUCKMAYR

Born in Linz in 1966. PhD in Commercial
Science, founder of the musical group
Fuckhead. Singer, musician, Action artist
and media artist at international clubs.
His media art focuses on realtime 3D
rendering and A/V performances. Grand
prize at 2004 Diagonale in the category
Innovative Cinema. Work on avatars for
use on stage, and realization of the project Imago with Jörg Diessl and Michael
Strohmann for the 2005 Ars Electronica.
Presentation of an expanded version at
SIGGRAPH2007 in San Diego. Finalization
of the project with the experimental
film *Fragmented*. 2011 Realization of a
realtime 3D 360° projection at Vienna's
mediaOpera. Currently working on various
albums, audiovisual performances
and experimental films. www.fuckhead.
at/bruckmayr

Filmography
2010 <u>Fragmented</u> 2009 <u>Drauf</u>, <u>Trend-
follower</u> 2008 <u>Flexible Cities</u> 2007 <u>My
Personality Hates Me!</u> 2005 <u>Collider2</u> 2004
<u>ich bin traurig</u> (with Michael Strohmann),
<u>Sinus_passage</u> 2003 <u>Giuliana 64:03</u>
Bibliography (selection)
*DVD Editions: Sonic Fiction. Synaesthetic
Videos from Austria.* Vienna: Index DVD
Edition 014, 2004.

GÜNTER BRUS

Born in Ardning, Styria, in 1938. 1958–
1960 University of Applied Arts, Vienna,
left without degree. 1958–1964 Informal
graphics and paintings, friendship with
Alfons Schilling, Otto Muehl, Adolf Frohner, Hermann Nitsch, Rudolf Schwarzkogler, Kurt Kren. In 1961 Brus met his future
wife, Anna. 1964 First Action, *Ana*, Vienna.
1965 Several Actions, including *Selbstverstümmelung (Self-Mutilation)*, Vienna;
and *Wiener Spaziergang (Vienna Walk)*.
1966 Participant in the Destruction in Art
Symposium, London; radicalization of
Action art; first productions of Action
scores. 1968 Action *Der helle Wahnsinn
(Sheer Madness)*, Aachen; Action *Kunst
und Revolution (Art and Revolution)*;
sentenced to six months prison. 1969

Escaped to Berlin. 1970 Last Action: *Zerreißprobe (Breaking Test)*, Munich. 1970–1975 Returned to drawing; edited several magazines, interaction of text and drawing. 1976 Prison sentence converted to a fine after an audience of Anna Brus with the federal president. Since 1976 completed several text-drawing cycles, called "picture poems," as a separate genre; writes novels, poetry and prose. 1979 Returned to Graz. 2008 Launch ceremony of the BRUSEUM, a museum of Brus works at the Landesmuseum Joanneum in Graz. Numerous exhibitions in Austria and abroad (including documenta 5, 6 and 7 in Kassel; Centre Pompidou, Paris; MAK, Vienna). Since 2008 draws cartoons for the Austrian magazine *DATUM*.

Filmography (selection)
1970 <u>Zerreißprobe</u> 1969 <u>Impudenz im Grunewald</u> (with Otmar Bauer), <u>Die Verbesserung von Oswald Wiener</u> (with Otmar Bauer), <u>Intelligenztest</u>, <u>Körperanalyse I</u> 1967 <u>Mit Schwung ins neue Jahr</u> (with Otto Muehl and Rudolf Schwarzkogler), <u>Einatmen und Ausatmen</u>, <u>Pullover</u>, <u>Osmose</u> 1966 <u>Totalaktion</u> 1965 <u>Transfusion</u>, <u>Starrkrampf</u> <u>Selbstverstümmelung</u>, <u>Selbstbemalung – Selbstverstümmelung</u>, <u>Wiener Spaziergang</u>

Bibliography (selection)
Publications by Günter Brus: *Das gute alte Wien*. [German] Salzburg and Vienna: Jung und Jung, 2007. → *Die gute alte Zeit*. [German] Salzburg and Vienna: Jung und Jung, 2002. → *Writings of the Vienna Actionists*. [English] Edited and translated by Malcolm Green. London: Atlas Press, 1999. → *Amor und Amok*. [German] Salzburg and Vienna: Residenz Verlag, 1987. → *Die Geheimnisträger*. [German] Salzburg and Vienna: Residenz Verlag, 1984. → *Irrwisch*. [German] Frankfurt am Main: Kohlkunst-Verlag, 1971. → *Patent Merde*. [German] Vienna: private edition, 1969. → *Patent Urinoir*. [German] Vienna: private edition, 1968.
Books and Catalogues: Brucher, Rosemarie. *Durch seine Wunden sind wir geheilt. Selbstverletzung als stellvertretende Handlung in der Aktionskunst von Günter Brus*. [German] Vienna: Löcker Verlag, 2008. → Haubernhofer, Dietmar, ed. *Günter Brus. Kratzspuren. scratchmarks. (Radierungen und Lithographien, etchings and lithographs, 1971–2007)*. [German/English] Vienna and New York: Springer Verlag, 2008. → Noever, Peter, ed. *Günter Brus. aurore de minuit, midnight dawn, Mitternachtsröte*. [French/English/German] Vienna: MAK Wien, 2008. → Schwanberg, Johanna. *Günter Brus: Bild-Dichtungen*. [German] Vienna and New York: Springer Verlag, 2003. → *Sammlung Essl Privatstiftung*, ed. *Günter Brus. Werke aus der Sammlung Essl*. [German] Klosterneuburg,

Austria, 1998. → Amanshauser, Hildegund, and Dieter Ronte, eds. *Günter Brus. Der Überblick*. [German] Salzburg: Residenz Verlag, 1986.
Articles, Interviews and Essays: Schröder, Gerald. *Schmerzensmänner: Trauma und Therapie in der westdeutschen und österreichischen Kunst der 1960er Jahre; Baselitz, Beuys, Brus, Schwarzkogler, Rainer*. [German] Paderborn, Germany: Fink, 2011. → Scheugl, Hans. *Erweitertes Kino. Die Wiener Filme der 60er Jahre*. [German] Vienna: Triton Verlag, 2002. → Rönnau, Jens. "Günter Brus: Die Realität hat heute eine Form angenommen, die einem wie ein Traum vorkommen muß." [German] *Kunstforum International* no. 152 (2000). → Noever, Peter, ed. *Out of actions – Aktionismus, Body Art & Performance 1949–1979*. [German] Ostfildern, Germany: MAK Wien, Cantz Verlag, 1998. → Wailand, Markus. "Ich war kein Chorknabe." [German] *Falter*, no. 39 (1998). → Schwanberg, Johanna. "Dicht-bildungen. Günter Brus. Vom Aktionisten zum Bild-Dichter – Vom meistgehaßten Österreicher zum Staatspreisträger." [German] *Parnass*, no. 2 (1997). → Schwanberg, Johanna. "Ich war Spezialist im Erröten." [German] *Die Presse* (Vienna), April 26, 1997. → Ferentschik, Klaus. "Biographarium. Günter Brus." [German] In *austria im rosennetz. Eine Ausstellung von Harald Szeemann*, edited by Peter Noever. Vienna and New York: Springer Verlag, 1996. → Grenier, Catherine. "Interview with Günter Brus." [French/English] In *Limite du visible*. Paris: Éditions du Centre Pompidou, 1993. → Klocker, Hubert, ed. *Wiener Aktionismus. Wien 1960–1971*. [German] Klagenfurt: Ritter Verlag, 1989. → Schmidt Jr., Ernst. *Österreichischer Avantgarde- und Undergroundfilm 1950-1980*. [German] Vienna: Österreichisches Filmarchiv, 1980. → Scheugl, Hans, and Ernst Schmidt Jr. *Eine Subgeschichte des Films. Lexikon des Avantgarde-, Experimental- und Undergroundfilms*. [German] Frankfurt am Main: edition suhrkamp, 1974. → Weibel, Peter, and Valie Export, ed. *bildkompendium wiener aktionismus und film*. [German] Frankfurt am Main: Kohlkunstverlag, 1970.
DVD Editions: Brus, Günter. *Bodyanalysis / Actions 1964–1970*. [German/English] Berlin: Edition Kröthenhayn, 2010. Book and DVD.

LINDA CHRISTANELL
Born in Vienna in 1939. Studied Painting at Vienna's Academy of Fine Arts. 1965–1974 Taught Art Education. Works in a number of genres: textile objects, installations, slideshows with sound, performances, object art in the form of books. Texts: visualized wordplay accompanied by object artworks, diary entries, texts dealing with film. Photographs and films

since 1975, at present focused on possibilities offered by new media, such as redefinition of content and condensation of visual material. Since 1966 numerous exhibitions, film screenings and awards in Austria and abroad. 1987 Jury member at the International Short Film Festival, Oberhausen. 1993 Taught a seminar in Film Studies at the University of Zurich; 2002–2003 Guest lecturer at the universities of Vienna, Liverpool and Dresden. Joined the Austria Filmmakers Cooperative in 1982, the Künstlerhaus Wien in 1980, and the Graz Assembly of Authors (GAV) in 1984. 1977 Founding member of IntAkt. Films distributed by sixpackfilm, Vienna; Medienwerkstatt, Vienna; Light Cone, Paris; Kinothek Asta Nielsen, Frankfurt am Main; Freunde der deutschen Kinemathek, Berlin.

Filmography (selection)
2012 <u>reflections inside-out</u> 2002 <u>Picture again</u>, <u>A rose is a rose</u> 2000 <u>Carrousel Deux</u> 1998 <u>Carrousel</u> 1996/2000 <u>NS-Trilogie: Ende-Film</u> 1997 <u>Gefühl</u> <u>Kazet</u> 1998 <u>Wunschkonzert</u> 1995 <u>Moving Picture</u> 1993 <u>Rouge et noir</u>, <u>My Moviestar</u> 1992 <u>All can become a rose</u> 1990/1991 <u>Aline Carola</u> 1988 <u>Meomsa</u> 1985 <u>Film Nr. 5</u>, <u>Zum Geburtstag</u> 1984/1985 <u>Der Schlüsselbund</u> 1984 <u>Federgesteck</u>, <u>Home</u>, <u>For You</u> 1982–1984 <u>Fingerfächer</u> 1980/1981 <u>Anna</u> 1979 <u>Es war ein merkwürdiger Tag</u> 1978 eight short films 1976 <u>Objektassoziationen</u> 1975 <u>Szenen zur Bezüglichkeit der Berührung</u>, <u>Fingerhäute</u>, <u>Bewegung – Weiß ist so gut wie Erde</u>.

Bibliography (selection)
Publications by Linda Christanell:
"Über meine Filme und ein Blick auf den Film *Carrousel deux*." [German] In *25 Jahre Medienwerkstatt Wien*. Vienna, 2003, http://www.medien-werkstatt-wien.at. → "... Von der Präsenz der Erinnerung ..." [German] *Frauen und Film*, no. 62 (2000). → "Gedanken zu meiner Arbeit." [German] In *Die andere Eva*, edited by Horst Schwebel and Heinz-Ulrich Schmidt. Menden, Germany: Trapezverlag, 1985. → "Gedanken zur Berührung." [German] In *Berührungen*, edited by Renate Bertlmann, Linda Christanell, Rita Furrer, et al. Feldkirch, Austria: Palais Liechtenstein, 1983. → "Mir genügt die Bezeichnung 'Kunst von Frauen.'" [German] *Das Pult*, no. 67 (1983). → "Text 1," "Text 2" and "Text 3." [German] In *Liebesgeschichten*, edited by Christel Göbelsmann and Jochen Schimmang. Frankfurt am Main: Suhrkamp, 1982. → "Persönliches." [German] In *Unbeschreiblich weiblich*, edited by Anna Rheinsberg and Barbara Seifert. Hamburg: rororo, 1981.
Books and Catalogues: Synema, Tanja Widmann and Linda Christanell, eds. *Linda Christanell. Wenn ich die Kamera öffne, ist sie rot*. [German] Vienna:

Synema, 2011. → Galleria Tommaseo, ed. *Linda Christanell*. [Italian] Trieste, 1977. *Articles, Interviews and Essays:* Mayr, Brigitte. "Linda Christanell – Wenn ich die Kamera öffne, ist sie rot." [German] In *Diagonale*, film festival catalogue. Graz, 2011. → Noll Brinckmann, Christine. "Der Wolfshund des Offiziers: Gedanken zu Linda Christanells NS-Trilogie." [German] In *Filmhimmel Österreich*, edited by Christian Dewald. Vienna: verlag filmarchiv austria, 2008. Program notes no. 080. → Dertnig, Carola, and Stefanie Seibold, eds. *Let's twist again. Performance in Wien 1960 bis heute*. [German/English] Vienna: D.E.A. Verlag, 2006. → Büttner, Elisabeth. "Am Gewebe des Sichtbaren spinnen – *Picture Again*." [German] In *Filmhimmel Österreich*, edited by Christian Dewald. Vienna: verlag filmarchiv austria, 2005. Program notes no. 012. → Wiederspahn, Katja. "Nomadinnen der Lüste. Feministische Film- und Kinoarbeit im 21. Jahrhundert – Avantgarde ohne Publikum?" [German] In *Screenwise. Film, Fernsehen, Feminismus*, edited by Monika Bernold, Andrea B. Braidt and Claudia Preschl. Marburg, Germany: Schüren Verlag, 2004. → Aigner, Silvie. "*Fingerfächer*." [German] *Beredte Hände*, edited by Gabriele Groschner. Salzburg: Residenzgalerie, 2003. → Haider, Hans. "*Picture again* als Zerstörungsakt." [German] *Die Presse* (Vienna), October 25, 2003. → Horwath, Alexander. "Zu Linda Christanells Film *Carrousel deux*." [German] In *Gibt es eine Lust jenseits des Bildes?* Dresden: Hochschule für Bildende Künste Dresden, 2003. → Rathner, Elfriede. *Zwischenbilder – Gegenbilder. Ein Rezeptionsversuch der Filme von Linda Christanell*. [German] Master's thesis, University of Salzburg, 1996. → Sladek, Ulrike. "*Moving Picture. Ein Film von Linda Christanell*." [German] *Auf*, no. 91 (1996). → Leitich, H. C. "*Rouge et Noir*." [German] *Der Standard* (Vienna), May 25, 1995. → Perthold, Sabine. "Schönheit ist der Glanz der Wahrheit. L.C. und ihre Filme." [German] In *Avantgardefilm Österreich. 1950 bis heute*, edited by Alexander Horwath, Lisl Ponger and Gottfried Schlemmer. Vienna: Verlag Wespennest, 1995. → Perthold, Sabine. "Die Suche nach der anderen Frau – *Aline Carola* von Linda Christanell." [German] In *Blaue Wunder: Neue Filme und Videos von Frauen 1984 – 94*, edited by Eva Hohenberger and Karin Jurschik. Hamburg: Argument Verlag, 1994. → Cargnelli, Christian. "Das Häkeln und der Fingerfächer." [German] *Falter*, no. 1/2 (1990). → Cargnelli, Christian. "Fernsehen: Filme von L.C." [German] *Falter*, no. 1/2 (1990). → Gehrke, Claudia. "Linda Christanell." [German] In *Rote Küsse. Ein erotisches Frauen Film Schaubuch*. Tübingen, Germany: Konkursbuch Verlag, 1990. → Rybarski, Ruth.

"Linda Christanell." [German] *profil*, no. 8 (1990). → Sykora, Katharina. "Filme von L.C." [German] *Falter*, no. 8 (1990). → Rick, Karin. "*Meomsa*. Die dunkle Seite der Sehnsucht." [German] *Blimp. Zeitschrift für Film*, no. 13 (1989). → "Interview." [German] In *Einfach den Gefahren ins Auge sehen. Künstlerinnen im Gespräch*, edited by Heidemarie Seblatnig. Vienna, Cologne and Graz: Böhlau Verlag, 1989. → Maderna, Maria. "Artista estremiste." [Italian] *X. Incontro Internazionale di cinema e donne*. Florence: 1988. → Lippert, Renate. "Blickwechsel." [German] *Frauen und Film*, no. 40 (1986). → Pellikan, Christine. "Linda Christanell." [German] *filmlogbuch*, no. 2 (1985). → Sykora, Katharina. "Filme von Linda Christanell, Cathy Joritz und Christine N. Brinckmann." [German] *Journal Film*, edited by Kommunales Kino Freiburg, no. 9 (1985). → Preschl, Claudia. "Apropos Frauenfilm. Gespräch mit Linda Christanell, Valie Export, Lisl Ponger, Gisela Scheubmayr." [German] In *Der weibliche Blick*, edited by Edith Almhofer. Vienna, 1984. → Christanell, Linda, Karin Mack and Margot Pilz. "Wir über uns." [German] In *Haut*, edited by Frauenmuseum Bonn, 1983. → Waechter-Böhm, Liesbeth. "Da sitzen die Frauen. Sie häkeln ihr Leichentuch. Über Linda Christanells Film *Anna*." [German] *Frauen und Film*, no. 35 (1983). → Gorsen, Peter. "Schritte zur weiblichen Emanzipation der Künstlerin." [German] In *Frauen in der Kunst*. Vol. 2, edited by Peter Gorsen. Frankfurt am Main: Suhrkamp Verlag, 1980. → Waechter-Böhm, Liesbeth. "Renate Bertlmann/Linda Christanell: Performances." [German] *heute Kunst*, no. 25 (1979). → Wisniewski, Jana. "Gespräch mit Linda Christanell." [German] *Falter*, no. 41 (1979). → Alinovi, Francesca. "La ricerca dell' identità." [Italian] In *La Performance*, edited by Galleria Communale d'Arte Moderna, Bologna, 1977. → Schwarzbauer, Georg Friedrich. "Performance Linda Christanell." [German] *Kunstforum International*, no. 24 (6/1977). → Lüthi, Kurt. "Linda Christanell. Schwarze Kunst – Deutung ihrer Objekte." [German] In *Alte und moderne Kunst*, edited by Kurt Rossacher. Salzburg and Vienna: AMK Verlag, 1972. *DVD Editions: Linda Christanell. The Nature of Expression*. Vienna: Index DVD 025, 2006.

KERSTIN CMELKA

Born in Mödling, Austria, in 1974. 1999–2005 Studied at the Academy of Fine Arts, Städelschule, Frankfurt am Main, under Monika Schwitte, Thomas Bayrle and Simon Starling. 2005 Postgraduate studies in Fine Arts under Prof. Simon Starling. Lives in Berlin. *Awards and Scholarships:* 2011 Residency in New York (Federal Ministry of Education, Arts and Culture, Vienna); 2008 Residency in Rome (Federal Ministry of Education, Arts and Culture, Vienna); 2007 Travel grant (Hessische Kulturstiftung); 2005 dynamo. eintracht studio scholarship in Dresden; 2004 Bethmann Bank award in the frameworks of Rundgang/Städelschule; 2003 Award for Media and Experimental Filmmaking (Lower Austria); 2002 Travel grant (Freunde der Städelschule); 2002 Peter Wilde Award for most technically innovative film, Austin, Texas; 2001 Diagonale, Festival for Austrian Film: Award selected by the young jury/production grant (ORF *Kunststücke*).

Filmography

Microdramas (performances and performance videos since 2008) 2011 Disconnecting entirely (loop) 2010 Who's afraid?/Final Fight 2009 Micromusical #1, Change 2008 Nora, Ich liebe Dich (I love you), Liebelei (Flirtations), 2008 Tap Dance 2005–2007 2006 A Mechanical Theatre 2005 He is back, Rape 2004 Untitled (16 mm film installation) 2003 Hallowe'en, Laufband (Loop) 2002 camera 2001 Ohne Titel 2000 Et In Arcadia Ego, In einem Raum, Mit mir 1998 Neurodermitis, Kerstin/Johannes

Bibliography (selection)

Books and Catalogues: Cotten, Ann, and Kerstin Cmelka. *I, Coleoptile*. [English] Berlin: Broken Dimanche Press, 2010. *Articles, Interviews and Essays*: "Kerstin Cmelka Male!" [English] *Fantom*, no. 07 (Spring–Summer 2011). → Bool, Shannon. "Re-Actionism." [English] *cmagazine 97. International contemporary art* (Spring 2008). All-interview issue. → Behm, Meike. "Kontextverschiebungen und ihre Folgen." [German] In *Kerstin Cmelka. Non-Identical Twins*, edited by Kunst Raum Niederösterreich. Vienna, 2006. → Bool, Shannon. "Re-action as Expression." [English] In *Kerstin Cmelka. Multistability*, edited by Dresdner Bank AG. Frankfurt am Main: Revolver, Archiv für aktuelle Kunst, 2006. → Slanar, Claudia. "Land in Sicht. Beobachtungen zur Ikonografie der Landschaft in neueren, experimentellen Videos und Filmen aus Österreich." [German] In *moving landscapes. Landschaft und Film*, edited by Barbara Pichler and Andrea Pollach. Vienna: Synema, 2006. → Glienke, Olivia. "Close-up: Kerstin Cmelka." [English] *filmwaves. the magazine for independent filmmakers*, no. 18 (Spring 2002).

JOSEF DABERNIG

Born in Kötschach-Mauthen, Austria, in 1956. Visual artist, graduated in Sculpture in 1981. Short films since 1994. Lives in Vienna. *Solo exhibitions* (selection): 2010 MAK – Austrian Museum of Applied Arts/Contemporary Art, Vienna. 2006 Galerie im Taxispalais, Innsbruck; National Museum

Matthias. "Camera Obscura auf Aegina, Griechenland." [German] *architektur. aktuell*, no. 284, 2003. → Feldmann, Sebastian. "Ordnung gestiftet in der Welt als Scherbenhaufen." [German] *Rheinische Post* (Düsseldorf), April 9, 2002. → Grissemann, Stefan. "Das Schweigen erklärt nichts." [German/English] In *Film ist. 7–12.* Vienna, 2002. → Grissemann, Stefan. "Kommen, sehen und sichten: Die Welt im Brennglas des Kinos." [German] *Die Presse* (Vienna), March 18, 2002. → Gunning, Tom. "*Film ist.* Eine Fibel für eine sichtbare Welt." [German] *Stadtkino Zeitung*, no. 379 (2002). → Huber, Christoph. "Die Straße taumelt, und das Zimmer gleich mit: Eine unendliche Archäologie von Kinowundern." [German] *Die Presse* (Vienna), April 13, 2002. → Loebenstein, Michael. "*Film ist.* Die Freuden des Schneidetischs." [German] *Falter*, no. 15 (2002). → Omasta, Michael, and Michael Loebenstein. "Der Mann ohne Kamera." [German] *Falter*, no. 15 (2002) → Philipp, Claus. "Auf der Suche nach dem unverdorbenen Blick." [German] *Der Standard* (Vienna), April 13/14, 2002. → Pichler, Dieter. "*Film ist. 7–12.*" [German] *ray Filmmagazin* (April 2002). → Grissemann, Stefan. "*Film ist.* DVD Installation im Künstlerhaus." [German] *profil*, November 18, 2002. → Seibel, Alexandra "Unter der Haube." [German] *Kurier* (Vienna), November 13, 2002. → Sallmann, Bernhard. "Diagonale." [German] *Filmforum*, no. 17 (1999). → Horwath, Alexander. "Die Weitergabe des Feuers." [German] *profil* (Vienna), October 10, 1999. → Grissemann, Stefan. "Das wunderbare Chaos: Was das Kino-Auge sieht." [German] *Die Presse* (Vienna), November 11, 1998. → Philipp, Claus. "Spielformen eines Sammlers." [German] *Der Standard* (Vienna), October 22, 1998. → Bianchi, Paolo. "Wüste-Welt-Oase, Gustav Deutsch & Hanna Schimek." [German] *Kunstforum*, no. 137 (1997). → Amarante, Leonor. "Cinema de Bolso: sessões de anarquia e humor." [Portuguese] *Jornal da Tarde São Paolo*, May 21, 1996. → Healy, Isabel. "Discrete charm of the pocket cinema." [English] *The Examiner* (Dublin), November 18, 1996. → Jobin, Thierry. "Passez le film à votre voisin." [French] *Le Nouveau Quotidien* (Lausanne), October 10, 1996. → Remke de Lange. "Gustav Deutsch: *Taschenkino* is uiteindelijk mijn persoonlijke viering van hoderd jaar film geworden." [Dutch] *Daily Tiger* (Rotterdam), no. 1 (1996). → Zwaan, Dineke de. "*Taschenkino*: Met een gif groen viewertje in de Bioscoop." [Dutch] International Film Festival Rotterdam 1996, http://iffrotterdam.nl/FFR/96 (site now discontinued). → Zuilhof, Gertjan. "Zakbioskoopjes." [Dutch] *De Groene Amsterdamer* (Amsterdam), February 14, 1996. → Philipp, Claus. "Man hat Töne." [German] In *Eine Geschichte der Bilder*, edited by

Alexander Ivanceanu. Vienna: polyfilm Verleih, 1996. → Büttner, Elisabeth. "Diese Augen kenn' ich doch." [German] *Falter*, no. 40 (1995). → Grissemann, Stefan. "Das taktlose Kino. Notizen zu den jüngsten Vertretern der österreichischen Avantgarde. Ein Spaziergang, nahe der Sonne." [German] In *Avantgardefilm Österreich. 1950 bis heute*, edited by Alexander Horwath, Lisl Ponger and Gottfried Schlemmer. Vienna: Verlag Wespennest, 1995. → Voester, Conny E. "Duisburger Filmwoche: Ein Forum für den Nachwuchs." [German] *epd Film*, no. 1 (1995). → Philipp, Claus. "Erweiterung des Horizonts – mit Augenklappen." [German] *Der Standard* (Vienna), November 20, 1995. → Retzek, Ilse. "Einfach lustiges Kino." [German] *OÖ Nachrichten* (Linz), December 6, 1995. → Wailand, Markus. "Nur keine Witze." [German] *Falter*, no. 46 (1995). → Rudolf, Irene. "Dunkel des Bildes." [German] *Multimedia*, no. 22 (1994). → Büttner, Elisabeth, and Christian Dewald. "Gustav Deutsch über die Fort/Bewegung und ihre vielfältige Praxis." [German] In *Filmbrunch*. Mödling, Austria: Filmbühne Mödling, 1993. → Geißler, Karlheinz A. "Internationaler Sendeschluß." [German] *Universitas*, no. 12 (1994). → Rebhandl, Bert. "Hypnotische Schleifen." [German] *Der Standard* (Vienna), December 17, 1994. → Walden, Fritz. "Rituale." [German] *Arbeiter Zeitung* (Vienna), October 2, 1982.

DVD Editions: Gustav Deutsch. Film ist. (1–12) DVD Version. Vienna: Index DVD Edition 012, 2004.

BARBARA DOSER
Born in Innsbruck in 1961. Artist, living and working in Vienna. 1989 PhD. in Art History, University of Innsbruck. Artistic focus: experimental video art, video/space installations, paintings and print works – all based on video-feedback materials. Since 1998 in the field of experimental art video collaboration with Hofstetter Kurt (Parallel Media): optoacoustic synesthetic video works using video-feedback materials and Möbius sounds. Participation in festivals for film, video, new media in more than 40 countries. *Solo Shows* (selection): 2010 Palais Kabelwerk Art Space Vienna, 2008 Landesmuseum Ferdinandeum Innsbruck; Andechsgalerie Innsbruck; Diagonale – Festival of Austrian Film: Barbara Doser + Parallel Media, 2000 Gallery T19 Vienna, 1996 Museum of Applied Art – MAK/Vienna. *Group Shows and Events* (selection): 2011 Kro Art Gallery Vienna; 2009 Venice Biennale/collateral project; 2008 Musée d'art contemporain Bordeaux; 2007 Music Biennale Venice; Moscow Museum of Modern Art; 2006 Kunsthalle Basel; 2005 Future Design Institute Tokyo, Super-Deluxe Tokyo; 2005 Ovalhalle MQ Vienna.

Filmography (selection)
2009 frameframer 2008 evolverevolve 01, evolverevolve Y02 2004 even odd even 2002 image[s] ... loss, don't piss down my back and tell me it's raining 2001 see you see me, The Sunpendulum Time-Eyes by H.K. 1996/1997/1998 moments (12 sec, about 50 moments) 1997 balkans Trilogy, Integration II, samples 1996 Integration I, samples, mind the mind 1994 created circular course
With Hofstetter Kurt (aka Parallel Media): 2011 nowwhere, 2011 Ada 2010 zart_B 2008 time no time 2007 dream'sdreams 2006 order-re-order 2005 You breathe life into my bosom Oleander 2002 facing time. parallel in an orbit 2001 runtime one 1995 crossover

Bibliography (selection)
Books and Catalogues: Video-Feedback – Lyricism in Patterns of Light. [German/English] Edited by Barbara Doser. Vienna: Zwei Kongruent Null, 2010.
Articles, Interviews and Essays: Kurt, Hofstetter, ed. *time no time.* [German/English] Vienna: Kiesler Foundation Vienna, Two Congruent Zero, 2008. DVD & Book. → Thiel, Wolf Guenter. "Bewegung – Zeit – Gleichzeitigkeit." [German] *Diagonale Materialien*, no. 041, Graz: Diagonale, 2008, http://2008.diagonale.at/fetchfile/MAT41_barbaradoser_web.pdf.
DVD Editions (selection)*: VISIONary. Contemporary Short Documentaries and Experimental Films from Austria*, DVD, Index DVD Edition 034, 2009. → *Video Edition Austria. Release 02*, Medienwerkstatt Wien, 2009. → *The Gift of Sound and Vision*, DVD Edition Der Standard/Hoanzl, *Der österreichische Film*, Vienna, 2007. → *Video Edition Austria. Release 01*, Medienwerkstatt Wien, 2002.

THOMAS DRASCHAN
Born in Linz in 1967. 1992–1998 Studies film under Peter Kubelka at the Academy of Fine Arts, Städelschule, Frankfurt am Main. 1995 Cooper Union N.Y.C. 1996 Civil Service 2005 Foundation of exhibition series Apartment Draschan, Vienna (two annual exhibitions for Viennafair). 2011 Organized group exhibition, Drei Zähne. 2008 Art purchase by Federal Ministry of Art and Culture. 2010 Collection DZ Bank. *Exhibitions* (selection): 2012 Weltkunst (Kunstforum Rheinhessen). 2011 "Frieze!" (Carter Presents, London). 2010 Ideal State (L.A. Galerie, Frankfurt Main); Lebt und arbeitet in Wien, Kunsthalle Wien. 2009 Videorama (Austrian Cultural Forum New York, Kunsthalle Wien); Negative Capability (Kunstverein Heppenheim). 2008 All New (Galerie Wildwechsel, Frankfurt Main). 2007 Hybride Praxen, Sampling, Mixing, Blending (NBK, Berlin). 2006 Exploding Television (Witte de With Contemporary Art Center, Rotterdam).

"Hinausgehen aus dem sicheren Hafen." [German] *Der Standard* (Vienna). May 15/16, 2010. → Feldman, Avi. "VALIE EXPORT's Films." [Hebrew/English] In *VALIE EXPORT: Jerusalem Premiere,* catalogue. Jerusalem: The Israel Museum, 2009. → Hallensleben, Markus. "Importing VALIE EXPORT. Corporeal Topographies in Contemporary Austrian Body Art." [English] *Performance* 42, no.3 (2009). → Viola, Eugenio. "VALIE EXPORT." [English] *ARTFORUM,* September 13, 2009, http://www.artforum.com/picks/section=world#picks23442. → Thunedal, Jenny. "Laddad leck med kvinnorollerna." [Swedish] *Aftonbladet* (Stockholm), November 29, 2008. → Burger-Utzer, Brigitta, and Sylvia Szely. "In der Erweiterung liegt die Möglichkeit zur Veränderung." [German] Interview. *ray Filmmagazin,* no. 3 (2007). → Halter, Ed. "MOMA's Best Week Ever." [English] *Village Voice* (New York), February 28–March 6, 2007. → Reicher, Isabella. "Die Erweiterungskünstlerin." [German] *Der Standard* (Vienna), May 18, 2007. → Meyer, Petra Maria. "Medialisierung und Mediatisierung des Körpers. Leiblichkeit und mediale Praxis bei VALIE EXPORT und Nan Hoover." [German] In *Performance im medialen Wandel,* edited by Petra Maria Meyer. Munich: Wilhelm Fink Verlag, 2006. → de la Villa, Rocío. "VALIE EXPORT. Después de la provocación." [Spanish] *Exit Expres, Periódico Mensual de Informción y Debate Sobre Arte,* no. 2 (April 2004). → Molina, Ángela. "Valie Export: la mirada resistente." [Spanish] *El País* (Madrid), January 17, 2004. → Breerette, Geneviève. "Les installations et actions subversives de la pèrchesse VALIE EXPORT." [French] *Le Monde* (Paris), October 9, 2003. → Hess, Barbara. "Immer und überall." [German] In *Women artists. Künstlerinnen im 20. und 21. Jahrhundert,* edited by Uta Grosenick. Cologne, London, Madrid, New York, Paris and Tokyo: Taschen-Verlag, 2001. → Labelle, Charles. "VALIE EXPORT." [English] *frieze,* no. 60 (June–August 2001). → Frieling, Rudolf, and Dieter Daniels. "VALIE EXPORT. Differenzen der Widersprüche – Interview mit femme total." [German/English] In *Medien Kunst Interaktion. Die 80er und 90er in Deutschland / Media Art Interaction. The 1980s and 1990s in Germany.* Vienna and New York: Springer Verlag, 2000. → Sicinski, Michael. "VALIE EXPORT and Paranoid Counter-Surveillance." [English] *Discourse. Journal for the Theoretical Studies in Media and Culture,* no. 2 (Spring 2000). → Huck, Brigitte. "VALIE EXPORT. Expanded Cinema – Expanded Arts." [German] *Parnass,* no. 15 (1999). Special edition. → Noever, Peter, ed. *Out of actions – Aktionismus, Body Art & Performance 1949– 1979.* [German] Ostfildern, Germany: MAK

Wien, Cantz Verlag, 1998. → Christoph, Horst. "Splitterkunst. Das 20er Haus zeigt das Werk der Aktionistin, Medienkünstlerin und Feministin Valie Export." [German] *profil,* April 21, 1997. → Lübbke, Maren. "Künstlerische Passagen zum Strukturwandel der Öffentlichkeit. Ein Interview mit VALIE EXPORT." [German] *Noema Art Journal,* no. 44 (1997). → Schor, Gabriele. "Riss im Raum – VALIE EXPORT im Wiener Museum Moderner Kunst." [German] *Neue Zürcher Zeitung* (Zurich), May 15, 1997. → Weibel, Peter. "Der Wiener Formalfilm." [German] In *Jenseits von Kunst,* edited by Peter Weibel. Vienna: Passagen Verlag, 1997. → Jurschick, Karin. "Die Spur der Begriffe am Körper. Eine Retrospektive der multimedialen Künstlerin VALIE EXPORT." [German] In *Feminale. Internationales Frauenfilmfestival,* film festival catalogue. Cologne, 1996. → Folie, Sabine. "VALIE EXPORT. Ikonen des Schmerzes und Wundmaschinen." [German] *Texte zur Kunst,* no. 18 (1995). → Prammer, Anita. "Avantgarde – Die Lust des Geistes." [German] In *Avantgardefilm Österreich. 1950 bis heute,* edited by Alexander Horwath, Lisl Ponger and Gottfried Schlemmer. Vienna: Verlag Wespennest, 1995. → Buchmann, Sabeth, Isabelle Graw, Judith Hopf, Jutta Koether and VALIE EXPORT. "Anläufe, Eine Gesprächsrunde über Künstlerinnen, Institutionen und Formen von Sexismus im Kunstbereich." [German] *Texte zur Kunst,* no. 15 (1994). → Prammer, Anita. "VALIE EXPORT. Künstlerin zwischen Tradition und Trends." [German] In *Rote Küsse. Frauen-Film-Schaubuch,* edited by Claudia Gerhrke. Tübingen, Germany: konkursbuch Verlag, 1990. → Hershman, Lynn. "Lust and Anger: The Commodification of Marginality (excerpts from Seven Deadly Sins)." [English] *Cinematograph. A Journal of Film and Media Art* 3 (1987/1988). → Rötzer, Florian, and Sara Rogenhofer. "Mediale Anagramme. Ein Gespräch mit VALIE EXPORT." [German] *Kunstforum International* 97 (1988). → Kienan, Joanna. "Films by VALIE EXPORT." [English] *Millennium,* 1986. 20th anniversary special edition. → Lippert, Renate. "Ein Millimeter schmerzfreie Zone. VALIE EXPORTS ....Remote....Remote...." [German] *Frauen und Film,* no. 39 (1985). → Hoberman, Jim. "Sex! Violence! Fun!" [English] *Village Voice* (New York), 1982. → Christoph, Horst. "Biennale von Venedig: Frauenkörper, Frauenblut." [German] *profil,* no. 23 (1980). → Schmidt Jr., Ernst. *Österreichischer Avantgarde- und Undergroundfilm 1950–1980.* [German] Vienna: Österreichisches Filmarchiv, 1980. → Riedl, Jochen. "Gegner in Sicht. VALIE EXPORT Erfolgsfilm *Unsichtbare Gegner* veranlasste die Kulturkämpfer, aus dem Versteck zu kriechen." [German] *profil,* no. 48 (1977). → Koch, Gertrud.

"Unsichtbar macht sich die Unterdrükkung der Frauen, indem sie ungeheure Ausmaße annimmt." [German] *Frauen und Film* (1976). → Scheugl, Hans, and Ernst Schmidt Jr. *Eine Subgeschichte des Films. Lexikon des Avantgarde-, Experimental- und Undergroundfilms.* [German] Frankfurt am Main: edition suhrkamp, 1974. → Schmölzer, Hilde. "VALIE EXPORT." [German] *Das böse Wien. 16 Gespräche mit österreichischen Künstlern.* Munich: Nymphenburger Verlagshandlung, 1973. → Hein, Birgit. *Film im Underground. Von seinen Anfängen bis zum unabhängigen Kino.* [German] Frankfurt am Main, Berlin and Vienna: Ullstein, 1971.

DVD Editions (selection): *VALIE EXPORT. 3 Experimental Short Films. 1970–1984.* Vienna: Index DVD Edition 004, 2004. → *VALIE EXPORT. Invisible Adversaries. 1977.* Vienna: Index DVD Edition 021, 2006.

TINA FRANK

Born in Tulln in 1970. Mother of a daughter. Studied graphic design at Vienna's graphic art college, the Graphische Lehr- und Versuchsanstalt. Self-employed designer since the middle of 1990, working in the fields of corporate design and web design. Founding member of U.R.L. Agentur für Informationsdesign Vienna & Berlin, Design by Frank Scheikl as well as Tina Frank Design. Member of multimedia formation Skot until 2000. Art director of electronic music label Mego until 2005. Professor for Graphic Design as well as chair of the Department of Graphic Design and Photography at the University of Artistic and Industrial Design Linz since 2008. Visual artist working in the fields of music visualization/video performance. *Festivals* (selection): Hong Kong International Film Festival, Lovebytes Digital Art Festival, ars electronica Linz, ICC/NTT Japan. Artistic collaboration with Florian Hecker, Peter Rehberg, Mia Zabelka and many more. 2006 Prize for Innovative Cinema at Diagonale Graz. 2010 Organized the international symposium REAL FAKE on design and mapping reality. Lives and works in Vienna and Linz.

Filmography (selection)
2010 <u>vergence</u> (with Florian Hecker) 2007 <u>don't stop</u> 2006 <u>grounded</u> (with Florian Hecker) 2005 <u>chronomops</u> 2004 <u>Goosing – live in york</u> 2003 <u>starlight 1</u> 2003 <u>intro</u> 2003 <u>kidds fuzz series: Puppet Soup</u> 2003 <u>kidds fuzz series: Stripes no Stars</u> 2003 <u>kidds fuzz series: High Heels</u> 2003 <u>kidds fuzz series: Letter Solo</u> 2003 <u>kidds fuzz series: Wisdom of S.A.R.S.</u> 2003 <u>kidds fuzz series: Türkisches Bad</u> 2002 <u>vigil</u> 2001 <u>glambox</u> 2001 <u>pitbudp</u> 2001 <u>reconnaissance : processing</u> 2000 <u>end of skot</u> (with Mathias Gmachl, Skot) 1999 <u>Skot vs. Hecker</u> (with Mathias Gmachl, Klaus Voltmer, Skot) 1998 <u>High-</u>

[German] *Spike*, no. 01 (October 2004). → Pichler, Barbara. "Die Kunst der Abstraktion." [German] *kolik.film*, no. 1 (October 2004). → Reicher, Isabella. "Metamorphosen und Energiefelder. Digitale Filmkunst im Kino: 'Goldt trifft Grill.'" [German] *Der Standard* (Vienna), September 28, 2004. → Schöny, Roland. "Michaela Grill/Christof Kurzmann: Place Becomes Time, Space Becomes Mine." [German/English] Edited by OK Centrum für Gegenwartskunst and Roland Schöny. Linz, 2004. → Benzer, Christa. "Rock'n'Roll Will Never Die. Zu den Musikvideos, Live-Visuals und Installationen der Videokünstlerin Michaela Grill." [German] *springerin* (Summer 2003). → Webber, Mark. "Counting the Waves: A Summery of Activity." [English] *senses of cinema*, no. 28 (2003), http://www.sensesofcinema.com/2003/28/counting_the_waves. → Erdmann, Petra. "Weiß auf Weiß im Videomix. Aktuelle Electronica-Videos bei der Diagonale." [German] *springerin* III, no 2 (2000). → Pichler, Barbara. "Von New Electronica zum Transgender-Cyborg." [German] *Telepolis. Zeitschrift für Netzkultur*, March 29, 1999. *DVD Editions*: *VISIONary. Contemporary Short Documentaries and Experimental Films from Austria*. Vienna: Index DVD Edition 034, 2009. → *The Gift of Sound and Vision*, DVD Edition Der Standard/Hoanzl, *Der österreichische Film*, Vienna, 2007. → *Sonic Fiction. Synaesthetic Videos from Austria*. Vienna: Index DVD Edition 014, 2004.

FRIEDL VOM GRÖLLER (KUBELKA)
Born in London in 1946. Childhood in Vienna and Berlin. 1965–1969 Studied photography at the School of Graphic Arts, Vienna. 1971 Masters certificate and commercial atelier for photography. 2005 National award for photography. 1990 Founder and director of School for Artistic Photography, Vienna (until 2010). 2006 Founder and director of School for Independent Film, Vienna. First films in 1968.
Screenings (selection): Generali Foundation, Vienna, Anthology Film Archives, New York, documenta 12, Austrian Film Museum, Toronto International Film Festival, 2009, 2010; Hong Kong International Film Festival, 2010, 2011; Berlin Biennale, 2010; Diagonale 2009, 2010, 2011; Retrospective in Media City, Canada, 2010.
Filmography (selection)
2011 Gutes Ende, Menschen am Sonntag, Ulrich Gregor und Heidi Kim at W Hong Kong Hotel, La Cigarette 2010 Paris June 2009, Heidi Kim at W Hong Kong Hotel, Polterabend, Passage Briare, Boston Steamer, Hochzeit, Delphine de Oliveira, Der Phototermin 2006 Vue Tactile 2005 Psychoanalyse ohne Ethik 1995–2005 Secret Identities of a Psychoanalyst

2001–2005 Eingreifen 2004 Allegorie, Le Baromètre 2003 Mirjam Ploteny und Ariane, Sebastian Mekas 2001 Dreyer's Zitat 2000 Spucken, L'Ecluse – Die Schleuse 1997–1999 Eltern (Mutter; Vater) 1993 Peter Kubelka und Jonas Mekas 1981 Ohne Titel 1974 Heidi 1969 Graf Zokan (Franz West) 1968–1969 Erwin, Toni, Ilse
Bibliography (selection)
Books and Catalogues: *Friedl vom Gröller/ Friedl Kubelka. Dem Zufall eine Chance geben. Fotografie/Film*. [German/English] Edited by Dietmar Schwärzler. (Vienna, 2012). → Reutner, Brigitte, Lentos Kunstmuseum, eds. *FRIEDL VOM GRÖLLER, Paris +33 621 24 11 37*. [German/English] Linz and Weitra, Austria: Verlag Bibliothek der Provinz, 2011. → Saloranta, Elina, Finnish Academy of Fine Arts, eds. *Secret Identities of a Psychoanalyst. Viewpoints on the works of Friedl Kubelka (Friedl vom Gröller)*. [English] Helsinki, 2010.
Articles, Interviews and Essays: Schwärzler, Dietmar, and Sylvia Szely. "Ein Film ist beendet, wenn die Spule aus ist. Interview mit Friedl Kubelka." [German/English] In *Rohstoff. Eine filmhistorische Recherche nach der kleinen Form*. Vienna: Sonderzahl Verlag, 2006. → "Friedl Kubelka." [German/English] In *Occupying Space. Sammlung / Collection Generali Foundation*, edited by Sabine Breitwieser. Cologne and Vienna: Verlag der Buchhandlung Walther König, 2003.

SABINE GROSCHUP
Born in Innsbruck in 1959. Artist, filmmaker, writer. Lives and works in Vienna and Berlin. 1978–1980 Studied Archaeology, Prehistory, Early History and Architecture at the University of Innsbruck. 1980–1982 Studied Architecture at the University of Applied Arts Vienna (under Wilhelm Holzbauer). 1982–1989 Studied Painting and Experimental Animation at the University of Applied Arts Vienna (under Maria Lassnig). 1984 Audited classes at the Düsseldorf Art Academy (video art with Nam June Paik). 1989–1992 Studied Ethnology at the University of Vienna. Since 1980 short films on Super 8, 16 mm, 35 mm and video. Has realized more than 35 films and videos to date. 1983 Founding member of ASIFA Austria. Since 1984 exhibitions with film loops, cell animation paintings, video and mixed-media installations. 1993 Juror at the 34th Festival Internacional de Cine de Bilbao. Since 1997 narrative literature. 2003 Juror at Tricky Women, Vienna. 2005 First novel, *Alicia und die Geister*. 2007 Tricky Women film and video award for the animation film *Gugug*. 2008 *Teufels Küche* (novel). 2009 *Tim und die Blumen* (novel). 2010 Co-editor of *Die Kunst des Einzelbilds. Animation in Österreich – 1832 bis heute*. http://sabinegroschup.mur.at;

http://sabinegroschup.at (blog)
Filmography (selection)
In production A View of Ears (with Georg Weckwerth) 2006 Gugug 2005 Schöner Wohnen (with Welzig/Steixner) 2000 Ghosts – Nachrichten von Wem 1999 Wideawake – Hellwach 1996 sonambiente – festival für hören und sehen (documentary) 1994 Attwengerfilm (short film contribution), Call Ester All (with Christa Angelmaier) 1993 Abitiamo Insieme, Denkwürdigkeiten eines Nervenkranken (part 3; compilation film by Ernst Schmidt Jr., posthumously produced by Peter Tscherkassky; short film contribution) 1992 10-13-Nur Lügen vielleicht, Das unsagbare Sagen (Film by Valie Export, Oswald Wiener, Ingrid Wiener, animation contribution) 1990 Vahnzinn – aus den Augen außerhalb ist der Sinn, Das Attentat (live film by Florian Flicker, short film contribution) 1989 Guten Morgen Madam Mona, All das All 1988 Liebe, Haus, Denkwürdigkeiten eines Nervenkranken (part 2; compilation film by Ernst Schmidt Jr., posthumously finished by Susi Praglowski; short film contribution) 1987 Geld, Messer, Nudeln, I love my dentist (with Bady Minck and Pascale Velleine) 1985 Kloppun Kunfes 1984 OgameO 1983 Komeru Kanfas, 1220 1982 Kopfsteinpflaster, Wiener Walzer
Bibliography (selection)
Publications by Sabine Groschup: "Das Kind ohne Zunge." [German] *Die Presse* (Vienna), May 17, 2008. → *Teufels Küche*. [German] Vienna: Czernin Verlag, 2008.
Books and Catalogues: Groschup, Sabine, and Galerie Michaela Stock, eds. *The Hidden, Etc*. [German/English] Exhibition catalogue. Vienna, 2011.
Articles, Interviews and Essays: Schlocker, Edith. "Gerichte aus Teufels Küche." [German] *Tiroler Tageszeitung* (Innsbruck), June 23, 2008. → Renoldner, Thomas. "Pocta Sabine Groschup." [Czech/English] *Rakousky Program AniFest*, catalogue. Třeboň, Czech Republic: 2004. → Preschl, Claudia, ed. *Frauen und Film und Video Österreich*. [German] Vienna: filmladen, 1986.

JOHANNES HAMMEL
Born in Basel in 1963. Studied cinematography at the Vienna Film Academy. Since 1986 lives and works in Vienna as a freelance filmmaker, cameraman and producer. 1992 Founder of Navigator Film, 1998 Founder of hammelfilm. As cameraman work includes *Way of Passion* by Joerg Burger, *The Future will not be capitalist* by Sasha Pirker, *Into the World* by Constantin Wulff and *Volver la Vista – The Gaze Back* by Fridolin Schönwiese. Several short films were followed by his feature film debut as director, *Folge mir*, screened at the Berlinale 2011 (Forum section).

Filmography
2011 Jour Sombre (The Gloomy Day) 2010
Folge mir (Follow Me), Shooting Stars
(Trailer) 2005 Abendmahl (Last Supper)
2004 Die Liebenden (The Lovers) 2003 Die
Badenden (The Bathers), Mazy – System
of Transition 1997 Abschnitt (Trailer)
1992 Die schwarze Sonne (Black Sun)
Bibliography (selection)
Articles, Interviews and Essays: Bra-
datsch, Reinhard. *"Folge Mir."* [German]
ray Filmmagazin, no. 05 (2011). → Felperin,
Leslie. "Berlinale Review Follow Me."
[English] *Variety* (New York), December 4,
2011. → Gromes, Dominique. "No Direction
Home – *Folge mir*, ein radikales Debüt
aus Österreich." [German] *thegap*, no. 116
(May 2011). → Kamalzadeh, Dominik, and
Isabella Reicher. "Streifzüge ins Univer-
sum und in die Nachbarschaft." [German]
Der Standard (Vienna), May 4, 2011. →
Kohler, Birgit, and Karin Schiefer. "Religion
is a rather sad affair – Interview with
Johannes Hammel." [German] In *Berlinale
Forum*, film festival catalogue. Berlin,
2011. → Schätz, Joachim, and Michael
Pekler. "The Dark Side of the Familienaus-
flug in Super 8." [German] *Falter*, May 13,
2011. → Schiefer, Karin. "Religion ist eine
ziemlich traurige Angelegenheit – Interview mit Johannes Hammel." [German]
Stadtkino Zeitung, no. 489 (April 2011).
→ Flos, Birgit. "Solange man träumt, gibt
es immer einen Ausweg. Zu den Filmen
von Johannes Hammel." [German] *kolik.
film*, no. 14 (October 2010). → Reicher,
Isabella. "Familienglück gibt's nur auf
Super-8 – Johannes Hammels entdrama-
tisiertes Familiendrama *Folge mir*." [Ger-
man] *Der Standard* (Vienna), October 18,
2010. → Matt, Gerald, Angela Stief and
Gerhard Johann Lischka, eds. *Videorama.
Kunstclips aus Österreich/Artclips from
Austria* [German/ English] DVD exhibition
catalogue. Bern: Benteli Verlag, 2009.
→ Gardner, Belinda Grace, Michael Buhrs,
Dirk Luckov and Gerald Matt, eds. *True
Romance – Allegorien der Liebe von der
Renaissance bis heute.* Cologne: DuMont
Buchverlag, 2008. → Olcèse, Rodolphine.
"La cène de Johannes Hammel." [French]
Bref. le magazine du court métrage, no. 71
(2006). → Reicher, Isabella. "Spinnenwe-
sen vor der Kamera." [German] *Der Stan-
dard* (Vienna), July 27, 2003. → Berndt,
Sven. "Love like Blood – *Die Schwarze
Sonne*." [German] *Splatting Image*, no. 14
(June 1993). → Natschläger, Bernhard.
"Dark Space." [German] *Multi Media*, no.
13 (1993).
Online Articles: Bach, Lida. "Grauer Hafen
Heimat." [German] *Titel-Magazin*, Februa-
ry 6, 2011, http://www.titel-magazin.de/
artikel/17/8662/berlinale-forum---folge-
mir.html. → "Digitale Filme auf der Berlinale, Interview mit Johannes Hammel."
[German] *Slashcam netLOUNGE DV.11*,

February 2011, http://www.netloungedv.
de/index.php?id=288. → Frieler, Felix.
"*Folge mir* – Ein Leben zwischen Religion,
Angst und kleinen Sonnenstrahlen."
[German] *critic.de*, January 28, 2011,
http://www.critic.de/film/folge-mir-2505/.
→ "Johannes Hammel und Heinz Ditsch
im Gespräch mit David Krems." [German]
*Mica-Interviewreihe: Film Musik Gesprä-
che*, July, 20, 2011, http://www.musicau-
stria.at/musicaustria/weltmusik/film-
musik-gespraeche-johannes-hammel-
heinz-ditsch. → Behn, Beatrice. "Folge
mir." [German] *kino-zeit.de*, February 13,
2010, http://www.kino-zeit.de/blog/
berlinale/folge-mir.

EVE HELLER
Born in Northampton, MA, USA, in 1961.
1978–1982 Filmmaking, photography and
cinema studies at S.U.N.Y. Buffalo Department of Media Studies and New York
University. 1987 BA summa cum laude in
German Literature and Interdisciplinary
Studies, Hunter College N.Y.C. 1993 MFA in
Filmmaking from Bard College. Teachers
included film avant-gardists Paul Sharits,
Tony Conrad, Keith Sanborn, Abigail Child,
Peggy Ahwesh and Peter Hutton, as well
as photographer Roy DeCarava. 1987–
1993 Co-manager at state-subsidized film
and video production facility Film/Video
Arts in New York. Member of N.Y.C. under-
ground filmmaker group Opium Den there.
1993–1996 Equipment manager and
workshop instructor at Bard College,
Annandale, NY. Two residencies at Phil
Hoffman's Independent Imaging Retreat,
Mount Forest, Ontario. 2005 Expatriated
to Vienna, where she lives and works
as a filmmaker, touring, teaching work-
shops, giving lectures and gardening.
2008 Founded Tather Gang.
Screenings and retrospectives (selection):
Whitney Museum of American Art,
Museum of Modern Art, New York Film
Festival 2001/2004/2005/2010, London
Film Festvial, Pacific Film Archives,
Cinematheque Ontario, Rotterdam Inter-
national Film Festival 2002/2005/2006,
Louvre (Paris), Austrian Film Museum,
ACMI Melbourne, Cinematheque Mexico
City. Films distributed by sixpackfilm,
Light Cone (Paris) and Canyon Cinema
(San Francisco). www.eveheller.com
Filmography
Tender Science (work in progress)
Word By Word (work in progress)
1982/2010 Juice 1981/2010 Self-Exami-
nation Remote Control 1978/2010 One
2005 Ruby Skin 2004 Behind This
Soft Eclipse 2001 Her Glacial Speed
1997 Astor Place 1996 Last Lost
Bibliography (selection)
Articles, Interviews and Essays: Boltin,
Kylie. "Dark Room and Dreamscapes:
Eve Heller interview." [English] *SBS*, July

2011, http://www.sbs.com.au/films/
movie-news/single/895351/Dark-Room-
and-Dreamscapes-Eve-Heller. → Chow,
Lesley. "The Biggest and Smallest." [Eng-
lish] *Bright Lights Film Journal*, no. 74
(November 2011), http://www.bright-
lightsfilm.com/74/74ffmelbourne_chow.
php. → Martin, Adrian, and Conall Cash.
"Interview with Eve Heller and Peter
Tscherkassky." [English] Conducted July
25, 2011, http://www.screenmachine.
tv/2011/07/28/interview-with-eve-heller-
and-peter-tscherkassky. → Woels, Michael-
Franz. "This Is Not Film. This Is Not Cinema." [German] *FAQ*, no. 15 (December
2011). → Harrer, Gudrun. "Mit der Leber im
Koffer." [German] *Der Standard*, *Rondo*
supplement (Vienna), September 24, 2010.
→ McElhatten, Mark. "A Decade in the
Dark: Avant-Garde Film & Video 2000–
2009. Top 50 Filmmakers." [English] *Film
Comment* 46, no. 3 (May/June 2010),
http://www.filmlinc.com/film-comment/
article/best-of-the-decade-avant-garde.
→ Laskin, A. Lee. "Breach Birth: The Hygie-
ne of Screen Skins: An Introduction to
the DVD Insert." [English] *Octopus*, no. 4
(2008). → Sandlos, Karyn, ed. *Waiting ...
and Wanting: Curating, Pedagogy and the
Media Arts: Works on Film and Video.*
[English] Toronto: Canada Council, 2004.

HERMANN HENDRICH
Born in Vienna in 1934. Studied mechanical engineering at the University for
Technology in Vienna; MA in 1961. Worked
as an engineer and machine-tool distributor until 2000. Started writing professio-
nally in 1959, some of his short theatrical
pieces were performed in 1961. 1962
Purchase of a 16 mm camera. Developed
a number of multi media programs beginning in 1968; in 1972 he used one of the
first SONY ½" video cameras in Austria.
Founder of the group alternative medien,
who participated in the first large video
project in Austria, IFI, in 1976. In 1980 he
founded with Valie Export the Valie Export
Filmproduktion Company, and was its
manager until 1985, producing two of
Export's feature films and some promotional films. Co-founder of the Austria Filmmakers Cooperative in 1982. Served on
the board in various positions until the
mid-1990s. Since 1999 produces digital
video for many documentary and some
avant-garde productions.
Filmography (selection)
2005 Ein Platz in Europa (A space in
Europe) 2004 identität? (identity?)
2002 Lake Powell, Zwei Plätze in Guadala-
jara (Two spaces in G.) 1996 handschuhen
(gloves) 1986 mnemosyne 1981 project s
(multimedia) 1974 14 long shots
1973 gray day, Frame for a movie
1971 49 steine (49 stones) 1970 Chicago 70
1962 cleinview experiment

Bibliography (selection)
Articles, Interviews and Essays: *Re-Play. Anfänge internationaler Medienkunst in Österreich*. [German/English] Edited by Sabine Breitwieser. Vienna: Generali Foundation, 2000. → *Avantgardefilm Österreich. 1950 bis heute.* [German] Edited by Alexander Horwath, Lisl Ponger and Gottfried Schlemmer. Vienna: Verlag Wespennest, 1995.

SABINE HIEBLER & GERHARD ERTL
Sabine Hiebler and Gerhard Ertl have worked together since studying at the Academy of Artistic and Industrial Design in Linz. They have written screenplays and produced experimental films to international acclaim. Their collaborations have also been presented at a number of exhibitions, such as the Ars Electronica, the Theseustempel/Kunsthistorisches Museum in Vienna and the Biennale de l'image in Paris. 2002 Hiebler and Ertl made their first fiction film, *Nogo*, with actors Jürgen Vogel, Jasmin Tabatabai, Meret Becker, Oliver Korittke, Mavie Hörbiger, Michael Ostrovsky, et al. The film was invited to festivals around the world, including Berlin, New York, Los Angeles, San Francisco, Sidney, Rotterdam and London, and received numerous honors and awards, including the Variety Critics' Choice and the Diagonale award for Innovative Production. Hiebler and Ertl have received the state of Upper Austria's culture award for film, the state of Lower Austria's young artist's award for media art and the Thomas Pluch Screenplay Award. In December 2011 their new fiction film, *Anfang 80*, starring Karl Merkatz and Christine Ostermayer, premiered.
Filmography (selection)
2011 Anfang 80 2002 Nogo 1998 Transcoder(understanding Lydia) 1996 Komakino 1995 Prost 1994 Spot-Check 1993 General Motors 1992 Definitely Sanctus 1991 Livingroom 1990 Schönberg, Crossover, Crossover 2
Bibliography (selection)
Publications by Hiebler & Ertl: Gegenwartsarchäologie/Archeology of the Present. [German/English] Edited by Kunsthistorisches Museum. Vienna, 1993. *Articles, Interviews and Essays*: Philipp, Claus. "Ein Plädoyer für persönliche Freiheit. Sabine Hiebler und Gerhard Ertl im Gespräch." [German] Geyrhalterfilm, interview, Vienna, 2011, http://www.geyrhalterfilm.com. → Philipp, Claus. "Action, automatisiert." [German] In *Eine Geschichte der Bilder. Acht Found footage Filme aus Österreich*, edited by Alexander Dumreicher-Ivanceanu. Vienna: Polyfilm Verleih, 1996. → Grissemann, Stefan. "Das taktlose Kino." [German] In *Avantgardefilm Österreich. 1950 bis heute.* [German] Edited by Alexander Horwath, Lisl

Ponger and Gottfried Schlemmer. Vienna: Verlag Wespennest, 1995. → Kerbel, Karl, and Peter Weibel, eds. *Genetische Kunst – künstliches Leben. Genetic art – artificial life.* [German/English] Linz: ars electronica, PVS Verleger, 1993.

PAUL HORN
Born in Amstetten, Lower Austria, in 1966. 1987–1992 University of Applied Arts, Experimental Design (Maria Lassnig) in Vienna. 1992–1998 Worked as set designer for different film and theater productions (Mara Mattuschka, Kurt Palm, Niki List; several productions at the Stadttheater Basel, etc.). 1998–2009 Assistant teacher and lecturer at the University for Art and Industrial Design Linz (Department of Art and Cultural Studies). *Exhibitions* (selection): 2011 moving stories. Hund&Horn, Offenes Kulturhaus, Linz; 2010 Hund+Horn, Kasseler Architekturzentrum im Kulturbahnhof, Kassel, Germany; b-sides and rarities, Kunsthal Antwerp; 2007 The Happiness of Objects, SculptureCenter, New York.
Filmography (selection)
Films in cooperation with Harald Hund:
2011 Apnoe 2010 Mouse Palace 2007/2008 Dropping Furniture 2005 All people is plastic 2002 Habibi Kebab 2001 Tomatenköpfe (Tomatoheads)
Film in cooperation with Barbara Kraus/fishy: 2005 Ungeklärte Verhältnisse
Bibliography (selection)
See Harald Hund's bibliography.

HARALD HUND
Born in 1967. Studied new media at the University of Applied Arts and the Academy of Fine Arts, both in Vienna. Works with video and film, photography and animation. His works deal mostly with utopian aspects of modern life. Hund is part of the artist duo Hund & Horn, which has collaborated on a number of film, video and exhibition projects. Their films *Tomatoheads, Dropping Furniture, Apnoe* and *Mouse Palace* form part of Hund & Horn's Living Space Series, which portrays human existence under absurd conditions. Hund & Horn's works have been shown internationally at a wide range of exhibitions and film festivals. *Festivals* (selection): Mostra Internazionale d'Arte Cinematografica Venice, International Film Festival Rotterdam, Ann Arbor Film Festival, USA, Victoria Film Festival, Canada, Hong Kong International Film Festival. *Awards* (selection): Best Experimental Short at the Dallas Film Fest and the Festival du court-métrage, Lille, France; Local Artist Award at Crossing Europe Film Festival, Linz.
Filmography
Films in cooperation with Paul Horn:
2011 Apnoe 2010 Mouse Palace 2008

Dropping Furniture, All People Is Plastic, Habibi Kebab – From The Life Of An Artist 2002 Tomatenköpfe (Tomatoheads) *Solo works:* 2007 My Favourite Actors 2 2006 My Favourite Actors 1 2004 Red Planet (music clip for Villalog) 2000 Dackel Du 2000 Holidays (Urlaub) 1999 Gorilla wants to eat 1998 Warm Humans (music clip for Le Car) 1996 Green Girl (music clip for Planet E) 1996 Emma Pad (music clip for Planet E)
Bibliography (selection)
Articles, Interviews and Essays: Schwarz, Gertraud. "Schwerkraft-Experimente." [German] *Film & TV Kameramann*, no. 5 (2011). → Thek, Birgit. "Familienalltag, der im wahrsten Sinn ins Wasser gefallen ist." [German] *Neues Volksblatt* (Linz), April 14, 2011. → *Die Kunst des Einzelbilds. Animation in Österreich – 1832 bis heute.* [German] Edited by Christian Dewald, Sabine Groschup, Mara Mattuschka and Thomas Renoldner. Vienna: verlag filmarchiv austria, 2010. → Grissemann, Stefan. "Flimmern im Negativland." [German] *profil*, no. 36 (2010). → Robnik, Drehli. "Sozialismus oder Barbarei. Von Mäusen und Menschen." [German] *Falter*, no. 41 (2010). → Seibel, Alexandra. "Österreichs Avantgarde in Venedig." [German] *Kurier* (Vienna), August 31, 2010. → Graf, Lorenz. "Zerstörte Wohnzimmer, gesellschaftlicher Wandel und Antifeminismus." [German] *peng! Magazin*, no. 03 (2008). → McNamara, T. C. "Benefits of the business." [English] *nzherald.co.nz*, May 2, 2007, http://www.nzherald.co.nz/arts-literature/news/article.cfm?c_id=18&objectid=10437218. → Benzer, Christa. "Six Degress of Separation." [German] *springerin*, no. 03 (2001).

MARTIN KALTNER
Born in Bruck an der Mur, Austria, in 1961. 1980–1985 Academy of Fine Arts, Vienna. 1990 Scholarship at the Cité des Arts, Paris. Studied Animation Film at the Academy of Applied Arts, Vienna. *Exhibitions and Screenings (selection):* 2010 Polite, Palazzo delle Sperimentazioni, Naples; Le Comfort Modern, Portiers. 2009 Rewind / Fast Forward, Neue Galerie Graz; end of the court, Asifakeil, Vienna. 2008 Another Tomorrow – Young Video Art from the Collection of the Neue Galerie am Landesmuseum Joanneum, Slought Foundation, Philadelphia. 2007 Laufding (with Thomas Baumann), Stift Admont, Austria; Kunsthistorisches Museum, Vienna – Raum für künstlerische Intervention. 2006 Strip – images in line, Kunsthaus Baselland, Switzerland; halflight, JesuitenFoyer, Vienna. 2005 Napoli Presente–Walking Project, Palazzo delle Arti, Naples; M City – European Cityscapes, Kunsthaus Graz; The one two master, Gallery of the City Schwaz, Austria; Wiener Linien, Wien–

Filmen aus Österreich." [German] In *moving landscapes. Landschaft und Film*, edited by Barbara Pichler and Andrea Pollach. Vienna: Synema, 2006.

KARL KOWANZ

Born in Vienna in 1951. 1971–1975 Academy for Applied Art, Vienna. As of 1975 made films, videos and music. One of the first filmmakers of the third generation of Austrian avant-garde cinema. A prolific filmmaker who was among the first to make the transition to video. 1993 Würdigungspreis for the Art of Video of the Ministry for Art.

Filmography (selection)
1984 Vier Tänze 1983 Liebe, Last und Leidenschaft 1982 Skizzen nach Motiven der Hecke 1980/1982 Ein Film ist eine Woche 1979 Ein Film hat viele Standpunkte, Ein Film hat viele Darsteller, Ein Film hat viele Male 1978 Abendjournal für meine Katze 1977 Film-Ende 1976 Miles Smiles, Zitronenbäumchen 1975 Kontur

Bibliography (selection)
Books and Catalogues: Kowanz, Karl, Helmut Mark and Helmut Rainer. *Dissipative Inszenationen* [German] Vienna: Museum Moderner Kunst Wien, 1991.
→ Kowanz, Karl. *Karl Kowanz*. Vienna: Galerie Grita Insam, 1990.
Articles, Interviews and Essays: Schmidt Jr., Ernst. *Österreichischer Avantgarde- und Undergroundfilm 1950–1980*. [German] Vienna: Österreichisches Filmarchiv, 1980. → Weibel, Peter. "Transformationen des Films." [German] In *Die Schatten im Silber. Österreichische Avantgarde-Filme 1976–1987*, edited by Lisl Ponger. Vienna: Museum of the 20th Century, 1987.

ANNJA KRAUTGASSER

Born in Tyrol in 1971. Lives and works in Vienna. Video artist. 1996–2002 Studied Visual Media at the University of Applied Arts, Vienna. *Video and Media Installations* (selection): Galerie im Taxispalais, Innsbruck; OK Centrum für Gegenwartskunst, Linz; Künstlerhaus, Vienna; Lothringerhalle 13, Munich and MediaLab, Madrid. Various artist in residence programs in London; Los Angeles (MAK Schindler); Paliano, Italy; and Amsterdam. 2003–2004 Assistant at the Institut für Künstlerische Gestaltung, Technical University of Graz. Since 2006 Assistant Professor at the Department of Art and Digital Media, Academy of Fine Arts, Vienna. State Scholarship for Fine Art 2009. RLB Art Award 2010. www.annjakrautgasser.net

Filmography (selection)
2009–2010 Romanes 2009 Zandvoort, Le Madison Lessions 1–3, What Remains, void.seqz 1 2008–10 Fragments 2008 La Sagra, Beyond, Innerer Monolog 2007 Prelude, Prologue, around and around, void.seqz 5 2006 Cruising around, Vegas Dashed.Film II 2005 void.seqz 3, horizon/1 2004 Dashed.Film I 2002 frame 2001 track 09 2000 rewind 1999 perceiving faculty 2

Bibliography (selection)
Books and Catalogues: Krautgasser, Annja, ed. *Verzeichnis*. [German/English] Vienna: Schlebrügge Editor, 2010.
Articles, Interviews and Essays: Krejs, Christiane, ed. *Übersetzung ist eine Form.* | *Translation is a mode.* [German/English] Vienna: Kunstraum Niederösterreich, 2010. → Beck, Martin, Adrian Bremenkamp, Joerg Franzbecker and Arsenal – Institut für Film und Videokunst, eds. *fake or feint*. [German/English] Berlin: argobooks, 2009. → Frank, Rike, Olaf Möller, Norbert Pfaffenbichler and Lotte Schreiber. *Cineplex. Experimentalfilme aus Österreich*. [German/English] Vienna: Vienna Secession, 2009. → Pamperl, Brigitte, and Barbara Höller, eds. *zeitraumzeit*. [German] Vienna: Gesellschaft bildender Künstler Österreichs, Künstlerhaus, and Folio Verlag, 2008. → Sunkovsky, Beatrix, ed. *Stelle, Siedelung, Lager*. [German/English] Vienna: Edition Selene, 2008. → Bidner, Stefan, and Kunstraum Innsbruck eds. *Ca. 1000m2 Tiroler Kunst*. [German] Innsbruck: Skarabaeus Verlag, 2007. → Droschl, Sandro, and Kunstverein Medienturm, eds. *CrossMedia*. [German/English] Bolzano, Italy, and Vienna: Folio Verlag, 2007. → Droschl, Sandro, Vitus H. Weh and Kunstverein Medienturm, eds. *Abstracts of Syn*. [German/English] Bolzano, Italy, and Vienna: Folio Verlag, 2007. → Droschl, Sandro, Christian Höller, Harald A. Wiltsche and Kunstverein Medienturm, eds. *Techno-Visionen. Neue Sounds, Neue Bildräume*. [German] Bolzano, Italy, and Vienna: Folio Verlag, 2005. → Fiedler, Elisabeth, Christa Steinle and Peter Weibel, eds. *Postmediale Kondition*. [German] Graz: Neue Galerie am Landesmuseum Joanneum, 2005. → Rosen, Margit. "The Chronofile-Society." [English] In *Making Things Public*, edited by Bruno Latour and Peter Weibel. Cambridge, MA: MIT Press, 2005. → Volkart, Yvonne. "Rechnen und rechnen lassen." [German] *springerin*, no. 4 (2004). → Pfaffenbichler, Norbert, Sandro Droschl and Künstlerhaus Wien, eds. *Abstraction Now*. [German/English] Graz: Verlag Edition Camera Austria, 2004. → Rosen, Margit, and Christian Schoen, eds. *The Chrono Files. From Time Based Art to Database*. [German] Berlin: Revolver Verlag, 2003. → Höller, Christian. "Clip Archive." [German] *springerin*, no. 1 (2003). → Eiblmayr, Silvia, and Galerie im Taxispalais, eds. *Variable Stücke*. [German] Vienna: Triton Verlag, 2002. → Klanten, Robert, Hendrik Hellige and Birga Meyer, eds. *anime. 72-dpi*. [English] Berlin: Die Gestalten Verlag, 2002. → Erdmann, Petra. "Digitaler Spielplatz." [German] *springerin*, no. 1 (2000).

→ Höller, Christian. "Flimmern im Kollektiv." [German] *springerin*, no. 4 (2000).

KURT KREN

Born in Vienna in 1929 to a German mother and an Austrian father of Jewish decent. In 1939 the ten-year-old was sent via *Kindertransport* (organized by the British Refugee Children Movement) to Rotterdam. In 1947 Kren returned to Vienna and was given a job at the National Bank by way of reparation. Shortly afterwards associated with members of the Art Club, a circle of progressive artists. In 1955 Kren bought his first Regular 8 camera and became a member of an amateur filmmakers' club, Klub der Kinoamateure. Some of his first artistic experiments with film were made in collaboration with the poet Konrad Bayer. As of 1957 Kren created his first 16mm film and in 1960 made his first serial montage film of many to follow. It is due to these early serial works that Kren is considered one of the most influential pioneers of structural filmmaking. From 1964 through 1966 Kren made films based on Material Actions staged by Otto Muehl and Günter Brus performed exclusively for Kren and several photographers. In 1966 he participated in the Destruction in Art Symposium in London, during which the Viennese Actionists made their first international appearance. In 1968 Kren took his first trip to America to present his films in New York and St. Louis. In the same year, he was wrongly accused of filming the scandalous Action Art and Revolution staged at the University of Vienna, directly leading to the termination of his bank job. In 1971–1976 Kren lived in Cologne. In 1972–1973 he produced a series of 5 boxes, each containing a Super 8 print of one of his films, a copy of its handwritten score and several stills. In 1976 he moved to Munich, participated in Kassel's documenta 6 in 1977, and emigrated to the US in 1978. In 1979 Kren married Marnie Rogers and they lived for a few months in Europe on a DAAD scholarship. After returning to America they divorced in 1980 and Kren moved to California, without a steady address and sometimes living out of his car. In 1981 he worked with a group of housewreckers in New England, making money from wood they salvaged. Kren subsequently moved to Austin and then relocated to Houston, Texas. From 1983 to 1989 Kren worked as a security guard at the Museum of Fine Arts in Houston. His films were presented in many different cities and prints sold to numerous international collections. In 1989 Kren returned to his homeland and was provided an apartment and a small pension by the Austrian government. In 1997 he worked as an actor and cinematographer for

Christoph Schlingensief's *Die 120 Tage von Bottrop*. Co-founder of the Vienna Institute of Direct Art (1966) and of the Austria Filmmakers Cooperative (1968). Member of the Vienna Secession, the London Filmmakers' Coop (1967), the New York Film-Makers' Cooperative (1968), P.A.P. Munich (1969) and Graz Assembly of Authors (GAV). Films distributed by sixpackfilm (Vienna), Light Cone (Paris), LUX London, Canyon Cinema (San Francisco) and New York Film-Makers' Cooperative. Kurt Kren died in 1998.

Filmography (selection)
1996 50/96 Snapspots (for Bruce) 1994 49/94 Fragment W. E. 1995 48/95 tausendjahrekino 1991 47/91 Ein Fest 1990 46/90 Falter 2 (commercial for the weekly newspaper *Falter*) 1988 45/88 Trailer (for ORF *Kunststücke*) 1985 44/85 Foot'-age shoot'-out 1984 43/84 1984 1983 42/83 no film 1981 40/81 Breakfast im Grauen, 39/81 Which Way to CA? 1982 41/82 Getting warm 1979 38/79 Sentimental Punk 1978 36/78 Rischart 37/78 Tree Again 1977 33/77 Keine Donau, 34/77 Tschibo 1976 32/76 An W+B 1975 31/75 Asyl 1973 30/73 Coop Cinema Amsterdam, 29/73 Ready-made, 28/73 Zeitaufnahme(n) 1971 27/71 Auf der Pfaueninsel, 26/71 Zeichenfilm – Balzac und das Auge Gottes, 25/71 Klemmer und Klemmer verlassen die Welt 1970 24/70 Western 1969 23/69 Underground Explosion, 22/69 Happy-end 1968 20/68 Schatzi, 18/68 Venecia kaputt, 17/68 Grün-rot 1967 16/67 20. September, 15/67 TV, 13/67 Sinus Beta 1966 12/66 Cosinus Alpha 1965 11/65 Bild Helga Philipp, 10c/65 Brus wünscht euch seine Weihnachten, 10b/65 Silber – Aktion Brus, 10/65 Selbstverstümmelung 1964 9/64 O Tannenbaum, 8/64 Ana – Aktion Brus, 7/64 Leda mit dem Schwan, 6/64 Mama und Papa 1962 5/62 Fenstergucker, Abfall, etc. 1961 4/61 Mauern pos.-neg. und Weg 1960 2/60 48 Köpfe aus dem Szondi-Test, 3/60 Bäume im Herbst 1957 1/57 Versuch mit synthetischem Ton (Test), Mobiles, Klavier Salon 1. Stock 1956 Das Walk

Bibliography (selection)
Books and Catalogues: Trummer, Thomas, ed. *Kurt Kren. Das Unbehagen am Film.* [German] Vienna: Atelier Augarten. Zentrum für zeitgenössische Kunst der Österreichischen Galerie Belvedere, 2006. → Hummel, Julius, ed. *Kurt Kren. Film Foto Wiener Aktionismus / Film Photography Viennese Actionism.* [German/English] Vienna: Galerie Julius Hummel, 1998. → Rhomberg, Kathrin, ed. *Kurt Kren. tausendjahrekino.* [German/English] Vienna: Vienna Secession, 1996. → Scheugl, Hans, ed. *Ex Underground Kurt Kren, seine Filme.* [German] Vienna: PVS Verleger, 1996. *Articles, Essays and Interviews:* Burger-Utzer, Brigitta. "Kurt Kren – Lord of the

Frames (1929–1998)." [Slovenian] *kinotecnik*, program notes. Slovenska Kinoteka, March–April, 2011. → Büttner, Elisabeth. "Form als Protest. Stichproben Wiens im Avantgardefilm." [German] In *Wien im Film. Stadtbilder aus 100 Jahren*, edited by Christian Dewald, Michael Loebenstein and Werner Michael Schwarz. Vienna: Wien Museum, Czernin Verlag, 2010. → Grill, Michaela. "Kurt Kren. Sentimental Punk." [French/English] *Montreal – Festival du Nouveau Cinéma*, film festival catalogue, Montreal, 2009. → Burger-Utzer, Brigitta. "Kurt Kren – Lord of the Frames (1929–1998)." [German/English] In *European Media Art Festival*, catalogue. Osnabrück, Germany, 2008. → Lavin, Mathias. "Copyright Kren." [French] In *Austriaca. Cahiers universitaire d'information sur l'Autriche*, edited by Christa Blümlinger. Mont-Saint-Aignan Cedex, France: Université de Rouen, 2007. → Tscherkassky, Peter. "Ikkunasta kurkkijoita, roskia yms. Kurt Krenin hasstattelu." [Finnish] *Avanto Festival*, film festival catalogue. Helsinki, 2004. → Scheugl, Hans. *Erweitertes Kino. Die Wiener Filme der 60er Jahre*. [German] Vienna: Triton Verlag, 2002. → LeGrice, Malcolm. *Experimental Cinema in the Digital Age.* [English] London: BFI Publishing, 2001. → Tscherkassky, Peter. "Die kleine Ewigkeit des Augenblicks. Sieben Anmerkungen zu Person und Werk von Kurt Kren." [German] *Diagonale*, film festival catalogue. Graz, 1999. → Tscherkassky, Peter. "Lord of the Frames: Kurt Kren." [English] *filmwaves*, no. 8 (1999). → "Eine Frage zum Abschied: 'Kennen Sie diesen Mann?'" [German/English] *Der Standard* (Vienna), July 3, 1998. Compiled by sixpackfilm with texts by Martin Arnold, Valie Export, Stephen Dwoskin, Robert Fleck, Birgit Hein, Richard Linklater, Hans Scheugl, Gottfried Schlemmer, Phil Solomon, Maureen Turim and Amos Vogel. → Grissemann, Stefan. "Von Körpern, Köpfen und dem Kamera-Auge." [German] *Die Presse* (Vienna), July 29, 1998. → Kochenrath, Hans-Peter, and Franz Novotny. "Servus Kurti! Meine Zeit mit Kurt Kren." [German] *Falter*, no. 27 (1998). → Löser, Claus. "Kurt Kren." [German] *film-dienst*, no. 15 (1998). → Tscherkassky, Peter. "Lord of the Frames: Kurt Kren." [French] *Trafic*, no. 28 (1998). → Tscherkassky, Peter. "Pán filmových okének: Kurt Kren." [Czech] *Film a doba*, no. 4 (1998). → Büttner, Elisabeth, and Christian Dewald. *Anschluß an Morgen. Eine Geschichte des österreichischen Films von 1945 bis zur Gegenwart.* [German] Salzburg and Vienna: Residenz-Verlag, 1997. → Weibel, Peter. "Der Wiener Formalfilm." [German] In *Jenseits von Kunst*, edited by Peter Weibel. Vienna: Passagen Verlag, 1997. → Tscherkassky, Peter. "Kurt Kren." [French] In *L'art du*

mouvement – collection cinématographique du Musée national d'art moderne, 1919–1996, edited by Jean-Michel Bouhours. Paris: Centre Pompidou, 1996. → Ferentschik, Klaus. "Biographarium. Kurt Kren." [German] In *austria im rosennetz. Eine Ausstellung von Harald Szeemann*, edited by Peter Noever. Vienna and New York: Springer Verlag, 1996. → Gorsen, Peter. "Touristen im Tausendjahrekino." [German] *Frankfurter Allgemeine Zeitung* (Frankfurt am Main), February 29, 1996. → Grissemann, Stefan. "Steine um die Ohren." [German] *Die Presse* (Vienna), April 6, 1996. → Omasta, Michael, and Markus Weiland. "Die Kamera erschießen." [German] *Falter*, no. 4 (1996). → Tscherkassky, Peter. "Lord of the Frames: Kurt Kren." [German/English] In *Kurt Kren. tausendjahrekino*, edited by Kathrin Rhomberg. Vienna: Vienna Secession, 1996. → Büttner, Elisabeth. "Diese Augen kenn' ich doch." [German] *Falter*, no. 40 (1995). → Hurch, Hans. "Framework. Anmerkungen zu einigen Filmen von Kurt Kren." [German] In *Avantgardefilm Österreich. 1950 bis heute*, edited by Alexander Horwath, Lisl Ponger and Gottfried Schlemmer. Vienna: Verlag Wespennest, 1995. → Tscherkassky, Peter. "Die rekonstruierte Kinematografie. Zur Filmavantgarde in Österreich." [German] In *Avantgardefilm Österreich. 1950 bis heute*, edited by Alexander Horwath, Lisl Ponger and Gottfried Schlemmer. Vienna: Verlag Wespennest, 1995. → Tscherkassky, Peter. "Kren. Peter Tscherkassky im Gespräch mit Kurt Kren." [German] In *Avantgardefilm Österreich. 1950 bis heute*, edited by Alexander Horwath, Lisl Ponger and Gottfried Schlemmer. Vienna: Verlag Wespennest, 1995. → Jutz, Gabriele. "Die Poetik der Zeit. Kurt Kren und der strukturelle Film." [German] In *The Art of Vision*, edited by Stefan Gyöngyösi. Salzburg: Kulturverein Zeitfluß, 1993. → Resch, Thomas. "Ich habe keine Donau." [German] *Die Presse* (Vienna), April 25, 1992. → Gidal, Peter. *Materialist Film.* [English] London and Boston: Routledge, 1989. → Horwath, Alexander. "44 Versuche in moderner Filmlyrik. Kurt Kren, der vielleicht einflußreichste heimische Filmemacher ist nach Österreich zurückgekehrt." [German] *Der Standard* (Vienna), September 29, 1989. → Scheugl, Hans. "Interview mit Kurt Kren." [German] *Stadtkino Programm*, no. 132 (1988). → Gerstein, David, and David Levi Strauss. "Kurt Kren, Interview." [English] *Cinematograph. A Journal of the San Francisco Cinematheque* 1 (1985). → Hoffmann, Hilmar, and Walter Schobert, eds. *W+B Hein: Dokumente 1967–1985. Fotos, Briefe, Texte.* [German] Frankfurt am Main: Kinematograph no. 3, Deutsches Filmmuseum, 1985. → Levi Strauss, David. "Kren: Cutting

Through Structural Materialism; or, 'Sorry. It had to be done.'" [English] *Cinematograph. A Journal of the San Francisco Cinematheque* 1 (1985). → Hein, Birgit, and Wulff Herzogenrath, eds. *Film als Film. 1910 bis heute. Vom Animationsfilm der zwanziger zum Filmenvironment der siebziger Jahre.* [German] Cologne: Kölnischer Kunstverein, 1977. → LeGrice, Malcolm. *Abstract Film and Beyond.* [English] Cambridge, MA: MIT Press, 1982. First published in 1977. → LeGrice, Malcolm. "Kurt Kren." [English] In *Structural Film Anthology*, edited by Peter Gidal. London: BFI Publishing, 1976. → Dwoskin, Stephen. [English] *Film Is.* London: Overlook TP, 1975. → Scheugl, Hans, and Ernst Schmidt Jr. *Eine Subgeschichte des Films. Lexikon des Avantgarde-, Experimental- und Undergroundfilms.* [German] Frankfurt am Main: edition suhrkamp, 1974. → Curtis, David. *Experimental Cinema. A fifty year evolution.* [English] London: Studio Vista, 1971. → Hein, Birgit. *Film im Underground. Von seinen Anfängen bis zum unabhängigen Kino.* [German] Frankfurt am Main, Berlin and Vienna: Ullstein, 1971. → Hein, W & B, Christian Michelis and Rolf Wiest, eds. *XSCREEN. Materialien über den Underground.* [German] Cologne: Phaidon Verlag, 1971.
DVD Editions: Kurt Kren. Which Way to CA? Bonus track: Hans Scheugls' documentary *Keine Donau – Kurt Kren and his films.* Vienna: Index DVD Edition 020, 2007. → *Kurt Kren. Action Films.* Vienna: Index DVD Edition 001, 2004. → *Kurt Kren. Structural Films.* Vienna: Index DVD Edition 002, 2004.

PETER KUBELKA

Born in Vienna in 1934. Upbringing in the Upper Austrian village Taufkirchen. 1941 The experience of a mobile cinema screening in the farming village left a lasting impression. 1944–1947 Member of the Vienna Boys' Choir. As of 1949 hitchhiked through most European countries. Acquired several languages. Interested in music, literature, philosophy, ethnology. Began the long process of liberation from religious indoctrination. 1949–1967 Competitive sports: track and field, judo. 1951 While still in high school decided to pursue filmmaking as a profession. Studied film in Vienna and Rome. 1955 Rejection of his first film, *Mosaik im Vertrauen*, by the film establishment, pushed him into the avant-garde. 1956 Participated in the Biennale di Venezia for Vietnam. 1957–1960 Created his Metric Films *Adebar, Schwechater, Arnulf Rainer*. 1958 First real film exhibition, Forum Alpbach: *Adebar* pinned onto wooden haystacks as a three-dimensional object. 1962 In desperation destroyed the scores of his Metric Films. 1964 Co-founder of

the Austrian Film Museum. 1966 First visit to the USA. Finished *Unsere Afrikareise.* As of 1966 began despecialization and commenced with autodidactic reeducation. Taught film at numerous American universities. Formulated his theory on food preparation as the most ancient medium of communication, the Edible Metaphor. 1968 Cooking Concert in New York, also Eating the Universe, a TV lecture on Channel 13. 1970 Co-founder of Anthology Film Archives. Designed the Invisible Cinema. 1973 Restored Vertov's *Enthusiasm.* 1976 Established the collection of avant-garde cinema for the Centre Pompidou in Paris. 1978–1999 Professor for Cinema at the Academy of Fine Arts, Städelschule, Frankfurt am Main. 1980 Changed the name of his master class to Film and Cooking as an Art Form. 1980 Founder of the musical ensemble Spatium Musicum. Concerts in Europe and USA. 1996 Established the cycle "What Is Film" for the Austrian Film Museum. 2010–2012 *Film ist Analog* (in progress). Peter Kubelka's Metric Films preceded the international movement of Structural Cinema. His Metaphoric Films define a purely cinematographic language, articulated between the elements of sound and image. Kubelka is also known as a non-writing theorist, using non-verbal elements, such as mimic, music, food, objects, tools in his lectures. 2012 Premiere of *Fragments of Kubelka*, a four-hour documentary, by Martina Kudlácek at International Film Festival Rotterdam.

Filmography
2012 <u>Antiphon</u> 1996/2003 <u>Dichtung und Wahrheit</u> (Poetry and Truth) 1977 <u>Pause!</u> 1966 <u>Unsere Afrikareise</u> (Our Trip to Africa) 1960 <u>Arnulf Rainer</u> 1958 <u>Schwechater</u> 1957 <u>Adebar</u> 1955 <u>Mosaik im Vertrauen</u> (Mosaic in Confidence)

Bibliography (selection)
Books and Catalogues: Was ist Film. Peter Kubelkas Zyklisches Programm im Österreichen Filmmuseum. [German] Edited by Stefan Grissemann, Alexander Horwath and Regina Schlagnitweit (Vienna: FilmmuseumSynemaPublikationen, 2010). → *Peter Kubelka.* [Czech/English] Edited by Martin Mazanec. Olomouc, Czech Republic: Edice PAF, 2008. → F. G. Zenker. *Nicht mehr als sechs Schüsseln! Ein Kochbuch für die mittleren Stände.* [German]. Edited by Peter Kubelka. Vienna: Czernin Verlag, 2006. → Adriano, Carlos and Bernardo Vorobow. *Peter Kubelka – A Essência do Cinema.* [Portuguese] São Paulo: edições Babushka, 2002. → *Peter Kubelka.* [German] Edited by Gabriele Jutz and Peter Tscherkassky. Vienna: PVS Verleger, 1995. → *Peter Kubelka.* [French] Edited by Christian Lebrat. Paris: Paris Experimental Editions, 1990.
Articles, Interviews and Essays: Rebhandl,

Bert. "Der Zeigefinger ist eines der ersten Kunstmedien. Gespräch mit Peter Kubelka." [German] *Cargo*, no. 10 (2011). → *Bild für Bild. Film + zeitgenössische Kunst. Image by Image. Film + contemporary art.* [German/English] Edited by Kurt Wettengl. Dortmund, Germany, and Paris: Museum Ostwall + Centre Pompidou, 2010. → Kubelka, Peter. "Jede gute Kunst ist eine angewandte Kunst." [German] *20er. Die Tiroler Straßenzeitung* (Innsbruck), no. 118 (September 2010). → Chodorov, Pip. "Peter Kubelka. Una Lezione di cinema. Intervista a cura di Pip Chodorov." [Italian] In *Visionari. Lo sguardo del cinema e del video tra arte, realtà e utopia*, edited by Andrea La Porta. Recco, Italy: Le Mani, 2009. → Hatzinikolaou, Konstantinos. "Peter Kubelka. Hitting the Screen." [Greek/English] *6th Athens Avant-Garde Film Festival*, catalogue. Athens, 2009. → Lebrat, Christian. "En finir avec le cinéma experimental?" [French] *L'Art meme* (Brussels), no. 42 (March/May 2009). → "Transcript, 'Round Table #1.'" [English] In *Food for Thought: Thought for food. All el Bulli dishes 1987–2007*, edited by Richard Hamilton and Vicente Todoli. Barcelona and New York: Actar, 2009. → Camper, Fred. "Peter Kubelka." [Croatian] In *Austrijska filmska avangarda*, edited by Mirna Belina and Marina Kozul. Zagreb: 25fps Association, 2008. → Kubelka, Peter. "Über das Wiener Schnitzel." [German] *Genuss bei Tisch. Für literarische Feinschmecker*, edited by Evelyine Polt-Heinzl. Vienna: Hauptverband des Österreichischen Buchhandels, 2008. → Sperlinger, Mike, and Ian White. *Kinomuseum. Towards an Artist's Cinema.* [English] Cologne: Verlag der Buchhandlung Walther König, 2008. → Kubelka, Peter. "Architektur und Speisenbau." [German] In *Der Architekt, der Koch und der gute Geschmack*, edited by Petra Hagen Hodgson and Rolf Toyka. Basel, Boston and Berlin: Birkhäuser, 2007. → Kubelka, Peter. "Die eßbare Metapher." [German] *Geschmackssache*. Vol. 6 of Schriftenreihe Forum series, edited by Kunst- und Ausstellungshalle der Bundesrepublik Deutschland. Göttingen, Germany: Steidl Verlag, 2006. → Mekas, Jonas. "Entrées de mon Journal: Peter Kubelka." [French] In *Jonas Mekas – Anecdotes*, edited by Jérôme Sans. Paris: Scali, 2007. → Boerger, Britta. "Interview Peter Kubelka." [German] In *Revolver. Kino muss gefährlich sein*, edited by Marcus Seibert. Frankfurt am Main: Verlag der Autoren, 2006. → Brougher, Kerry. "Hall of Mirrors." [English] In *Art and Film since 1945*, edited by Museum of Contemporary Art. Los Angeles, 2006. → Païni, Dominique. "Ballet d'ombres. Autour d'Adebar de Peter Kubelka." [French] *cinéma. Revue semestrielle d'esthétique et d'histoire du cinéma*, no. 12 (Fall 2006). → Philipp, Claus. "Das Kino digital (v)erschließen? Der Schein trügt. Peter Kubelka im Gespräch mit Claus Philipp." [German] *kolik.film*, no. 5 (March 2006). → Pinent, Antoni. "Arnulf Rainer" [Spanish/English] In *Xcèntric. 45 pellícules contra direcció / 45 películas contra dirección*, edited by Centre de Cultura Contemporània de Barcelona i Institut d'Edicions de la Diputació de Barcelona, 2006. → Börger, Britta. "Interview Peter Kubelka." [German/English] *European Media Art Festival*, catalogue. Osnabrück, Germany, 2004. → Horwath, Alexander. "Peter Kubelka. This Side of Paradise." [English] *Film Comment* 40, no. 5 (September/October 2004). → Kubelka, Peter. "Die essbare Metapher. Kochen als Ursprung der Künste und des Denkens." [German] *Schlaraffenland? Europa neu denken*, edited by Hubert Christian Ehalt. Weitra, Austria: edition seidengasse/Bibliothek der Provinz, 2004. → Kubelka, Peter. "Ursprünge von Kunst: Suchen, finden, begreifen. Ein Gesprächstext aufgezeichnet von Christian Reder." [German] In *Sahara. Test- und Bildessays*, edited by Christian Reder and Elfriede Semotan. Vienna and New York: Springer 2004. → MacDonald, Scott. "His African Journey – An Interview with Peter Kubelka." [English] *Film Quarterly* 57, no. 3 (Spring 2004). → Sitney, P. Adams. "Peter Kubelka und die neue Welt." [German/English] *European Media Art Festival*, catalogue. Osnabrück, Germany, 2004. → Bullot, Érik. "Virtualité du montage." [French] *Cinéma. Revue semestrielle d'esthétique et d'histoire du cinéma*, no. 6 (Fall 2003). → La Porta, Andrea. *Metafore della visione. Sperimentalismo cinematografico e formazione artistica.* [Italian] Bologna: Edizioni Pendragon, 2003. → Jocks, Heinz-Norbert. "Peter Kubelka. Kochen, die älteste bildende Kunst." [German] *Kunstforum International*, no. 159 (April–May 2002). → Bardon, Xavier Garcia. "1963 – Un traitement de choc." [French] *EXPRMNTL – Festival hors normes, Knokke 1963, 1967, 1974*, Revue Belge du Cinéma (RBC), no. 43 (December 2002). → Sitney, P. Adams. *Le Cinéma visionnaire – L'avant-garde américaine 1943–2000*. [French] Paris: Paris Experimental, 2002. → Sitney, P. Adams. "The Graphic Cinema: European Perspectives." [English] In P. Adams Sitney. *Visionary Film. The American Avant-Garde 1943–2000*. New York: Oxford University Press, 2002. → Kubelka, Peter. "Beschreibung einer Speise." [German] In *Mensch und Tier. Geschichte einer heiklen Beziehung*, edited by Ursula Wolf. Frankfurt am Main: Suhrkamp, 2001. → Gaigg, Christine. "The Edible Metaphor. An interview with Peter Kubelka." [English] *On Cooking: Performance Research*, issue editor: Richard Gough. 4, no. 1 (Spring 1999). → Kubelka, Peter. Introduction to Breuss,

Renate. *Das Maß im Kochen. Mengen- und Maßangaben in Kochrezepten von der Antike bis zur Einführung der metrischen Maße im 19. Jahrhundert und deren Parallelität zu künstlerischen Gestaltungsprinzipien.* [German] Innsbruck: Haymon, 1999. → Lebensztejn, Jean-Claude. "Entretien avec Peter Kubelka." [French] *Les Cahiers du Musée national d'art modern*, no. 65 (Fall 1998). → Heindl, Bernhard. *Einwärts – Auswärts. Vom Hegen der Erde.* [German] Innsbruck: Edition Löwenzahn, 1997. → Weibel, Peter. "Der Wiener Formalfilm." [German] In *Jenseits von Kunst*, edited by Peter Weibel. Vienna: Passagen Verlag, 1997. → Kubelka, Peter. "Making Landscapes Into a Brilliant Ironic Actor." [Japanese/English] *Image Forum Festival*, catalogue. Tokyo, 1997. → Vogel, Amos. *Film als subversive Kunst. Kino wider die Tabus – von Eisenstein bis Kubrick.* [German] St. Andrä-Wördern, Austria: Hannibal, 1997. → Kubelka, Peter. "Was bedeutet Essen und Kochen für die Menschen?" [German] In *Erd- und Herdgeschichten*, edited by Arge Bio-Landbau and die umweltberatung. Vienna, 1996. → Sitney, P. Adams. "Peter Kubelka." [French] In *l'art du mouvement. Collection cinématographique du Musée national d'art moderne*, edited by Jean-Michel Bouhours and Centre Pompidou. Paris, 1996. → Kubelka, Peter. "Die essbare Metapher. Kochen als Ursprung der Künste und des Denkens." [German] In *Instanzen, Perspektiven, Imaginationen, Interventionen*, edited by Jörg Huber and Alois Müller. Basel and Frankfurt am Main: Stroemfeld/Roter Stern and Museum für Gestaltung Zürich, 1995. → Tscherkassky, Peter. "Die gefügte Zeit. Peter Kubelkas metrische Filme." [German] In *Avantgardefilm Österreich. 1950 bis heute*, edited by Alexander Horwath, Lisl Ponger and Gottfried Schlemmer. Vienna: Verlag Wespennest, 1995. → Tscherkassky, Peter. "Die rekonstruierte Kinematografie. Zur Filmavantgarde in Österreich." [German] In *Avantgardefilm Österreich. 1950 bis heute*, edited by Alexander Horwath, Lisl Ponger and Gottfried Schlemmer. Vienna: Verlag Wespennest, 1995. → Tscherkassky, Peter. "hand made." [German] *Media Biz*, no. 12 (March 1995). → Tscherkassky, Peter. "Peter Kubelka oder Vom Sinn der Sinne." [German] In *Kunst in Österreich*, edited by Robert Fleck and Noemi Smolik. Cologne: Kiepenheuer & Witsch, 1995. → Tyler, Parker. *Underground Film. A Critical History.* [English] Cambridge, MA: Da Capo Press, 1995. First published 1969. → Tscherkassky, Peter. "The Light of Periphery. A brief history of Austrian avant-garde cinema." [English] *Austrian Avant-Garde Cinema 1955–1993*, edited by Martin Arnold and Peter Tscherkassky. Vienna: Sixpack Film, 1994. → Kubelka, Peter. "Gasthaus in der

Kunsthalle." [German] In *Zur Zeit*, edited by Kunst.Halle.Krems. Krems, Austria: Kunst.Halle.Krems, 1993. → Tscherkassky, Peter. "The Analogies of the Avant-Garde/ Die Analogien der Avantgarde." [German/English] In *Found Footage Film*, edited by Cecilia Hausheer and Christoph Settele. Lucerne: Viper/zyklop Verlag, 1992. → Kubelka, Peter. "Schlag klar die Schnee nach deinem Gedanken." [German] In *Das Riegersburger Kochbuch*, edited by Peter Noever. Vienna: Orac Verlag, 1988. → Turim, Maureen Cheryn. *Abstractions in Avant-Garde Films.* Ann Arbor, MI: UMI Research Press, 1985. → Moore, Barry Walter. *Aesthetic Aspects of Recent Experimental Film.* [English] New York: Arno Press, 1980. → Noguez, Dominique. *Éloge du cinéma expérimental.* [French] Paris: Centre Pompidou – Musée national d'art modern, 1979. → Masi, Stefano. "Tutto Kubelka, film e lezioni." [Italian] *L'Unità* (Rome), May 10, 1978. → Weibel, Peter. "Der Wiener Formalfilm. Entstehungsgeschichte und Leistungen." [German] In *Film als Film. 1910 bis heute. Vom Animationsfilm der zwanziger zum Filmenvironment der siebziger Jahre*, edited by Birgit Hein and Wulff Herzogenrath. Cologne: Kölnischer Kunstverein, 1977. → Mekas, Jonas. "Peter Kubelka." [English] In *Structural Film Anthology*, edited by Peter Gidal. London: BFI Publishing, 1976. → Simon, Elena Pinto. "The Films of Peter Kubelka." [English] *Artforum*, no. 8 (April 1972). → Tyler, Parker. *Underground Film. Eine kritische Darstellung.* [German] Frankfurt am Main: März Verlag, 1970. → "Peter Kubelka." [German] In *Neuer Österreichischer Film*, edited by Kuratorium Neuer Österreichischer Film. Vienna: Viennale, 1970. → Patalas, Enno. "Der Untergrund drängt nach oben." [German] *Filmkritik*, no. 1 (1969). → Sitney, P. Adams. "Structural Film." [English] *Film Culture*, no. 47 (1969). → Bodien, Earl. "The Films of Peter Kubelka." [English] *Film Quarterly*, no. 2 (1966/1967). → Mekas, Jonas. "On the Supreme Mastery of Peter Kubelka." [English] *Village Voice* (New York), October 13, 1966. → Lachenay, R. "Comment peut-on être jeune turc?" [French] *Cahiers du Cinema*, no. 57 (1956).

WOLFGANG KUDRNOFSKY

Born in Vienna in 1927. Studied Psychology and Anthropology. Obtained the master craftsman's certificate as a photographer in 1950. Journalist for *Stern-Wiener Illustrierte* and was editor-in-chief of the German periodical *Die Bunte Illustrierte* (*Bunte* as of 1972). Producer, screenwriter and cameraman for Kurt Steinwender's Edgar Allan Poe adaptation, *Der Rabe* (1951), and appeared in Franz Novotny's adaptation of Elfriede Jelinek's *Die Ausgesperrten* (1982). As a photographer he was a member of Hundsgruppe (Dogs Group), an artists' association formed around Ernst Fuchs, Arnulf Rainer, et al. in 1950. During this time produced two series of photographs. 1951 Created in collaboration with Arnulf Rainer a collection of photographs entitled "Perspektiven der Vernichtung." In addition to the famous porn parody *Fifi Mutzenbacher* he wrote numerous other books, including *Bubis Hochzeit oder die Unreifen* (1967), *Zur Lage des österreichischen Schriftstellers* (1973), *Vom Dritten Reich zum Dritten Mann* (1975), *Schandl, Schubirsch & Co: Kriminalfälle der Zweiten Republik* (1994) and *Natur, oh Natur* (2000). Also wrote radio plays, etc., for the ORF. Wolfgang Kudrnofsky died on December 20, 2010.

Filmography
1951 Der Rabe (cinematography; dir.: Kurt Steinwendner)

Bibliography (selection)
Publications by Wolfgang Kudrnofsky: *Vom dritten Reich zum dritten Mann*. [German] Vienna, 1983.
Articles, Interviews and Essays: Büttner, Elisabeth, and Christian Dewald. *Anschluß an Morgen. Eine Geschichte des österreichischen Films von 1945 bis zur Gegenwart*. [German] Salzburg and Vienna: Residenz-Verlag, 1997. → Fritz, Walter. *Kino in Österreich. 1945–1983. Film zwischen Kommerz und Avantgarde*. [German] Vienna: Österreichischer Bundesverlag, 1984.

MARIA LASSNIG
Born in Carinthia, Austria, in 1919. 1941–1944 Studies at the Academy of Fine Arts in Vienna (classes with Wilhelm Dachauer, Ferdinand Andri and Herbert Boeckl). 1951 Scholarship in Paris: acquaintance with Gisèle and Paul Celan, André Breton and Benjamin Péret. 1952 Second sojourn in Paris. Member of the Art Club, Vienna. 1954 Returned to Vienna to the Academy of Fine Arts (class of A. P. Gütersloh); acquaintance with writers of the Vienna Group (Friedrich Achleitner, H. C. Artmann, Konrad Bayer, Gerhard Rühm, Oswald Wiener). 1956 Contact with Monsignore Otto Mauer and the artists of his newly founded Galerie nächst St. Stephan in Vienna. 1961–1968 Studio in Paris. 1968–1980 Studios in New York. 1970–1972 Attended an animation film class at the School of Visual Arts, New York. Used her "body-awareness paintings" as models for her first animated films. 1980 Represented Austria at the Venice Biennial together with Valie Export. 1980–1997 Chair at the Academy for Applied Arts, Vienna. 1981 Introduced animation into the curriculum and founded the first teaching studio for animation film as part of her master class for painting. 1982 & 1997 Participated at documenta, Kassel. *Awards* (selection): 1988 Grand Austrian State Prize for Art,

Vienna; 1998 Oskar Kokoschka Award, Vienna; 2002 Roswitha Haftmann Award, Zurich. Ring of Honor, University of Applied Arts, Vienna; 2004 Max Beckmann Award of the City of Frankfurt am Main, Germany; 2005 Austrian Cross of Honour for Science and the Arts, Vienna. Numerous solo and group exhibitions in Austria and abroad. Lives and works in Vienna and Carinthia.

Filmography (selection)
1992 Maria Lassnig Kantate (with Hubert Sielecki) 1976 Art Education 1970–1974 Baroque Statues 1973 Palmistry 1972 Couples, Shapes 1971 Selfportrait, Chairs, Iris

Bibliography (selection)
Publications by Maria Lassnig: *Maria Lassnig. Die Feder ist die Schwester des Pinsels. Tagebücher 1943–1997.* [German] Edited by Hans Ulrich Obrist. Cologne: DuMont, 2000.
Books and Catalogues: Maria Lassnig. [English] Edited by Helmut Friedel. Berlin: Die Gestalten Verlag, 2010. → *Das neunte Jahrzehnt.* [German] Edited by Wolfgang Drechsler. Vienna: Museum Moderner Kunst, 2009. → *Maria Lassnig.* [English] Edited by Melissa Larner. London: Koenig Books, Serpentine Gallery, 2008. → *Maria Lassnig. Körperbilder. Body awareness painting.* [German/English] Edited by Andrea Madesta. Cologne: Snoeck Verlagsgesellschaft, 2006. → *Zwei oder Drei oder Etwas. Maria Lassnig, Liz Larner.* [German/English] Edited by Peter Pakesch. Cologne and Graz: Verlag der Buchhandlung Walther König, Kunsthaus Graz, 2006. → *Maria Lassnig. body. fiction. nature.* [German/English] Vienna: Sammlung Essl, 2005. → *Maria Lassnig. Kunstfiguren.* [German] Edited by Kasper König and Johannes Schlebrügge. Cologne: Verlag der Buchhandlung Walther König, 1995. → *Murken, Christa. Maria Lassnig. Ihr Leben und ihr malerisches Werk: Ihre kunstgeschichtliche Stellung in der Malerei des 20. Jahrhunderts.* [German] Herzogenrath, Germany: Murken-Altrogge Verlag, 1990. → *Maria Lassnig.* [German] Edited by Museum Moderner Kunst Wien. Klagenfurt: Ritter Verlag, 1985.
Articles, Interviews and Essays: Schurian, Andrea. "Ich weiß um die Flüchtigkeit von Prominenz." [German] *Der Standard* (Vienna), September 8, 2009. → Wege, Astrid. "Body and Soul. Über Maria Lassnig im Museum Ludwig, Köln." [German] *Texte zur Kunst*, no. 74 (June 2009). → *Wack! Art and the Feminist Revolution.* [English] Edited by Lisa Gabrielle Mark and Elizabeth Hamilton. London and Los Angeles: MIT Press, MoCA, 2007. → McKechneay, Maya. "Werkschau Maria Lassnig." [German] *Diagonale*, film festival catalogue. Graz, 2006. → Grissemann, Stefan. "Der Schrecken kommt an einen

heran, ganz langsam." [German] *profil*, no. 18 (2005). → Schmitz, Rudolf. "Maria Lassnig – Kompromisslos jung." [German] *Frankfurter Allgemeine Zeitung* (Frankfurt am Main), February 18, 2004. → Jones, Ronad. "Maria Lassnig." [English] *frieze*, no. 73 (2003). → Gorsen, Peter. "Die Kunst der guten und schlechten Gefühle. Maria Lassnig. Kunstfiguren." [German] *Kunstforum International*, no. 89 (1995). → Christoph, Horst. "Den Stil verwerfen." [German] *profil*, no. 6 (1985).
DVD Editions (selection): *Maria Lassnig. Animation Films*. Vienna: Index DVD Edition 033, 2009.

LIA
Digital artist since 1995, upon graduating from the Academy for Students of Music in Graz, Austria and moving to Vienna. Since then divides her time between visual design, web art, video and realtime visual performances, apparently different activities she manages to bind together through her unique approach to creativity and production. In recent years lia also teaches at universities in Austria, Portugal, Norway and Switzerland. *Exhibitions* (selection): 2010/2009 Decode: Digital Design Sensations, CAFA Art Museum; Beijing/Victoria and Albert Museum, London; 2010 Mind and Matter, Künstlerhaus, Vienna; 2009/10 See this Sound – Promises in Sound and Vision, Lentos Kunstmuseum, Linz; 2009 A Secret Understanding, Kunsthaus Graz; Rewind, Fast Forward, Neue Galerie Graz; 2008 Art Machines Machine Art, Museum Tinguely, Basel; 2007/2008 Art Machines Machine Art, Schirn Kunsthalle Frankfurt am Main; 2007 NetSpace, MAXXI, Museo nazionale delle arti del XXI secolo, Rome; 30x1, Casa Da Musica, Porto, Portugal; 2006 Further Processing, Kunstverein Medienturm, Graz; 2005 Generative X, ICA, London; 2003 Design Interactif, Centre Pompidou, Paris.

Filmography (selection)
2010 Machination 84 2008 Construction 76, o68 2006 Study #40, flow 2005 int.16/45//son01/30x1, VS_process, radio_int.14/37 2004 int.5_27/G.S.I.L.XXX, v3/G.S.I.L.XXIX. visualisation of an interview with p.m. 2003 E.V.A./G.N.S.I.L, hardVideo/G.S.I.L.XIX 2002 untitled 2002 G.S.I.L.XII 2001 walking on ice (with Miguel Carvalhais), STALLT, G.S.I.L.VI / almada 2000 tixotorp 1999 liaZzone

Bibliography (selection)
Publications by lia: Frank, Tina, and lia. "Audiovisual Parameter Mapping in Music Visualizations." [German/English] In *See This Sound – Audiovisuology Compendium*, edited by Dieter Daniels and Sandra Naumann. Cologne: Walther König, 2010. → "Some Ingredients Of Some Generative Works." [Portuguese/English] In *Mono 1*,

Monodisperso. Porto, Portugal: School of Arts, University, 2007.
Articles, Interviews and Essays: Holler-Schuster, Günter. and Christa Steinle, eds. *Rewind / Fast Forward, Die Videosammlung*. [German] Graz: Neue Galerie Graz am Landesmuseum Joanneum, 2009. → Dohm, Katharina, Heinz Stahlhut, Max Hollein and Guido Magnaguagno, eds. *Kunstmaschinen Maschinenkunst / Art Machines Machine Art*. [German/English] Heidelberg: Kehrer Verlag, 2007. → Tenenbaum, Ilana, and Christiane Paul. *NETworking – Net Art from the Computer Fine Arts Collection*. [Hebrew/English] Exhibition catalogue. Haifa: Haifa Museum of Art, 2007.
DVD Editions: *Sonic Fiction. Synaesthetic Videos from Austria*. Vienna: Index DVD Edition 014, 2004.

JOHANN LURF

Born in Vienna in 1982. 2002 Acadamy of Fine Arts, Vienna (Obholzer/Bohatsch/Margreiter/Farocki). 2008 Slade School of Fine Art, London. 2009 Diploma with Harun Farocki. www.johannlurf.net
Filmography
2009–2012 * 2011 Kreis Wr. Neustadt 2010 Endeavour 2009 Zwölf Boxkämpfer jagen Viktor quer über den großen Sylter Deich 140 9 2008 12 Explosionen 2007 Vertigo Rush 2005 pan 2003 (ohne Titel)
Bibliography (selection)
Articles, Interviews and Essays: Grissemann, Stefan. "Mindfuck – Der Bilderstürmer und Filmemacher Johann Lurf." [German] *kolik.film*, no. 15 (2011). → Payne, Simon. "Vienna Report." [English] *sequence*, no. 1 (2010). → Grissemann, Stefan. "Mosaik im Misstrauen." [German] *kolik.film*, no. 11 (2009). → Pfaffenbichler, Norbert. *Cineplex, Experimentalfilme aus Österreich*. [German/English] Catalogue. Vienna: Vienna Secession, 2009.

JAN MACHACEK

Born in Vienna in 1975. Studied Sculpture and Stage Design in Vienna and Karlsruhe, Germany. Works at the interface between media and performance art integrating video. In his atmospherically dense works familiar technology takes on a life of its own and turns away from seamless reference. Has performed at festivals in Austria, Germany, France, Italy and England. His videos have been screened at the Viennale, Vienna; Sonic Acts Festival, Amsterdam; Avanto, Helsinki; etc. Has collaborated with Oliver Stotz, Billy Roisz, Sabine Marte, Peter Kozek, dieb13 and Martin Siewert. Also has developed installations and video works for public spaces.
Awards: 2009 Video > 10 min, Flex Festival, Gainesville, FL. 2007; Preis für Innovatives Kino, Diagonale, Graz; 2006 International Prize for Performance, Trento, Italy.

Filmography (selection)
2009 words 2008 in the mix 2007 erase remake (with Martin Siewert)
Bibliography (selection)
Articles, Interviews and Essays: Benzer, Christa. "Ganze Körperarbeit. Zu einer kleinen Auswahl jüngster Performance-Videos." [German] *kolik.film*, no. 11 (2009).
DVD Editions: *VISIONary. Contemporary Short Documentaries and Experimental Films from Austria*. Vienna: Index DVD Edition 034, 2009.

MARA MATTUSCHKA

Born in Sofia, Bulgaria, in 1959. 1974 Awarded Golden Compass for Higher Mathematics. 1977 General Certificate of Education, University of London. 1977–1983 Studied Ethnology and Linguistics, Vienna. 1990 Awarded Magister Artis degree at Vienna's University of Applied Arts after studying under Maria Lassnig in Painting and Animation Film. Adolf Schärf Award for her work in film. Austrian Film Promotion Award 1990. Birth of son Max Viktor. 1994–2001 Professor of Fine Art at Braunschweig University of Art. 2001 Birth of son Leo August. 2005 Austrian Award of Recognition for Film Art. 2010 City of Vienna's Fine Art Award. Also known as Mimi Minus, Madame Ping Pong and Mahatma Gobi.
Filmography (selection)
2010 Burning down the palace – The making of Burning Palace 2009 Burning Palace (with Chris Haring) 2008 Running Sushi (with Chris Haring) 2007 Part Time Heroes (with Chris Haring) 2005 Comeback, Mozart Minute – Königin der Nacht 2004 Plasma, Legal Errorist (with Chris Haring) 2003 ID 2001 Cabinet 9 – 60 000 sind begeistert (with G. Szekatsch, SiSi Klocker) 1996 Unternehmen Arschmaschine (with G. Szekatsch) 1994 Suvlaki ist Babylon: komm, iß mit mir 1993 Beauty and the Beast, S.O.S. Extraterrestria 1989 Der Einzug des Rokoko ins Inselreich der Huzzis (with A. Karner und H. W. Poschauko) Loading Ludwig (with M. Petrov) 1986 Pascal – Gödel, Die Schule der Ausschweifung (with H. W. Poschauko), Parasympathika, Furchtbar-schrecklich (with B. Neubauer), contributions to Denkwürdigkeiten eines Nervenkranken (parts 1, 2 and 3 by Ernst Schmidt Jr.), Les Miserables, Danke, es hat mich sehr gefreut, Kaiser Schnitt 1985 Cerolax, Untergang der Titania, Kugelkopf, Begegnungen der vierten Art 1984 Nabel-Fabel 1983 Ten short animation films
Bibliography (selection)
Articles, Interviews and Essays: Ballhausen, Thomas. "Die Frau ohne Frisur, die unter die Haut schneidet." [German] *Falter*, no. 3 (2009). → Braidt, Andrea, and Barbara Liebhardt. "Auf der Suche nach der bewussten Unschuld." [German/

English] In *Diagonale*, film festival catalogue. Graz: 2009. → Kamalzadeh, Dominik. "In Wirklichkeit ist es geistiger Hedonismus." [German] *Der Standard* (Vienna). March 16, 2009. → Schwärzler, Dietmar. "Aneinander entlang gleiten, Mara Mattuschka und Chris Haring im Gespräch." [German] *kolik.film*, no. 11 (2009). → Von Reden, Sven. "Unraffiniert bis zum Exzess." [German] *taz* (Berlin). March 29, 2009. → Bast, Gerald, ed. *Mit eigenen Augen. With Their Own Eyes. KünstlerInnen aus der ehemaligen Meisterklasse Maria Lassnig. Former Students of Maria Lassnig*. [German/English] Vienna and New York: Springer Verlag, 2008. → Dertnig, Carola, and Stefanie Seibold, eds. *Let's twist again. Performance in Wien 1960 bis heute*. [German/English] Vienna: D.E.A. Verlag, 2006. → Kremski, Peter. "Man sucht nach einem eigenen Zeichensystem, mit dem man Geschichten neu formulieren kann. Ein Gespräch mit Mara Mattuschka." [German] In *Überraschende Begegnungen der kurzen Art. Gespräche über den Kurzfilm*. Cologne: Schnitt Verlag, 2005. → Vogel, Juliane. "Cutting. Schnittmuster weiblicher Avantgarde." [German] In *Schluss mit dem Abendland!* edited by Thomas Eder and Klaus Kastberger. Vienna: Zsolnay, 2001. → Blümlinger, Christa. "Die Gesichter der Mara Mattuschka." [German] In *Avantgardefilm Österreich. 1950 bis heute*, edited by Alexander Horwath, Lisl Ponger and Gottfried Schlemmer, Vienna: Verlag Wespennest, 1995. → Knecht, Doris. "Je grösser die Frau, desto kleiner die Welt. Die Sprache der Körper in den Filmen Mara Mattuschkas." [German] *Neue Zürcher Zeitung* (Zurich), 1995. → Tscherkassky, Peter. "Mimi Minus oder Die angewandte Chaosforschung." [German] In *Gegenschuss. 16 Regisseure aus Österreich*, edited by Peter Illetschko, Vienna: Verlag Wespennest, 1995. → Klippel, Heike. "Starring: Mimi Minus. Die Kurzfilme von Mara Mattuschka." [German] In *Blaue Wunder. Neue Filme von Frauen 1984–94*, edited by Eva Hohenberger and Karin Jurschik. Argument Verlag, 1994. → Mudie, Peter, ed. *Below the center*. [English] Perth and Vienna, 1994. → Renoldner, Thomas. "Im Dschungel der Kategorien." [German] *Austrian Film News*, no. 8/9 (1994). → Erenz, Benedikt. "Stroh zu sein bedarf es wenig..." [German] *Die Zeit* (Hamburg), 1990. → Schödel, Helmut. "Seid frisch zueinander!" [German] *Die Zeit* (Hamburg), 1990. → Thurnher, Armin. "Mara Mattuschka – Diva der 90-er Jahre." [German] *Falter* (1990). → Ankowitsch, Christian. "Im Reich der Huzzis." [German] *Der Standard* (Vienna), 1989. → Horwath, Alexander. "Sonnenstürmer und Sternsinger." [German] *Der Standard* (Vienna), September 23/24, 1989. → Omasta, Michael. "So eine Art Recycling Film."

[German] In *Blimp. Zeitschrift für Film*, no. 13 (1989). → Preschl, Claudia. "Das Kichern der Mimi Minus." [German] *Frauen und Film*, no. 46 (1989). → Schöllhammer, Georg. "Die Schwerkraft der Worte zeigen." [German] *Der Standard* (Vienna), October 19, 1989. → Settele, Stephan. "Mit dem Herzen drucken." [German] *Falter* (1989). → Hein, Birgit. "Mara Mattuschka." [German] *epd Film*, no. 3 (1988). → Hein, Birgit. "Mara Mattuschka." [German] In *Die Schatten im Silber. Österreichische Avantgarde-Filme 1976–1987*, edited by Lisl Ponger. Vienna: Museum of the 20th Century, 1987. → Weinberger, Richard. "Phönix aus der Asche." [German] *Film-logbuch*, no. 2 (1985).

DVD Editions (selection): *Mara Mattuschka & Chris Haring. Burning Down the Palace*. Vienna: Index DVD Edition 038, 2011. → *As She Likes It. Female Performance Art from Austria*. Vienna: Index DVD Edition 023, 2007. → *Mara Mattuschka. Iris Scan*. Vienna: Index DVD Edition 006, 2004.

SABINE MARTE

Born in Feldkirch, Austria, in 1967. Video artist, performer, musician. Lives and works in Vienna. Film screenings, performances, installations, concerts in Austria and abroad. Member of the performance band SV Damenkraft (2003–2008). Member of the mixed-media band Pendler (since 2005).
1991–1993 Attended Beverly Piersol's master class, University of Applied Arts, Vienna. 1993 Completed graduation project for Beverly Piersol master class with Gertrude Moser-Wagner, at the Galerie ON, Poland, and University of Applied Arts, Vienna. 1987–1991 Vienna Graphic Art College. 1990 Salzburg Summer Academy scholarship. 1993 Progetto Civitella D'Agliano, Italy, Grant of the Federal Ministry for the Arts. 1999 Chicago studio scholarship, Austrian Federal Chancellery/art section. 2006 Česky Krumlov studio scholarship, Austrian Federal Chancellery/art section. 2009 State scholarship for video and media art. 2010 Diagonale Award for Innovative Cinema. sabine.klingt.org, www.sixpackfilm.com, pendler.klingt.org, www.myspace.com/svdamenkraft
Filmography (selection)
2011 Do we need to have an accident? (trailer for the Austrian Film Festival Diagonale 2011) 2009 B- Star, unkillable! reloaded, B- Star, unkillable! 2007 Finale 2006 Helen A/B + the Sea 2004 Grass A/B 2003 Stewardessenclip 2000 Art is a bear and she bites who she wants to, Sprung (with Billy Roisz, Oliver Stotz and Klaus Filip), me-ju (with Markus Marte) 1999 I Would Like to Make a Horror Movie Sometime 1998 Me Thing – You Dog 1996 I am Working 1993 Free Fall,

A Woman Alone at Home, Ragazzi con Juke-Box (with Bernadette Dewald)
Bibliography (selection)
Books and Catalogues: Hollerer/Marte. Brauchen wir einen Unfall? / Do we need to have an accident? [German/English] Edited by Katrin Bucher Trantow and Peter Pakesch. Graz: Kunsthaus Graz, Universalmuseum Joanneum, 2011. *Articles, Interviews and Essays*: Dietrich, Christa. "Filmischer Horror höchster Güte." [German] *Vorarlberger Nachrichten* (Bregenz), February 3, 2011. → Benzer, Christa. "Ganze Körperarbeit. Zu einer kleinen Auswahl jüngster Performance-Videos." [German] *kolik.film*, no. 11 (2009). → *Matrix. Geschlechter, Verhältnisse, Revisionen / Gender, Relations, Revisions.* [German/English] Edited by Sabine Mostegl and Gudrun Ratzinger. Vienna and New York: Springer Verlag, 2008. → Eismann, Sonja. "Pomp, Fuck?&?Circumstance." [German] *Jungle World,* no. 03 (January 17, 2008). → Wasner, Georg. "Paarkonstellationen unter Druck." [German] *Diagonale Materialien*, no. 021 (2006). → *Work the Room. Ein Handbuch zu Performance-strategien. Handbook of Performance Strategies.* [German/English] Edited by Ulrike Müller. Berlin: b_books, 2006.

BADY MINCK

Born in Inari, Lapland, in 1959. 1962 Relocation to Luxembourg. Works as an artist, filmmaker and producer in Vienna and Luxembourg. Studied Sculpture at Vienna's Academy of Fine Arts (Prof. Bruno Gironcoli) and Experimental Film at the University of Applied Arts. In 1989 as a student at the Academy, she realized her first film, *The Man with Modern Nerves*. The film was invited to the Cannes Film Festival and the Berlinale; it was purchased by Centre Pompidou Paris for their collection of avant-garde films. Her surreal short film *Mécanomagie* won awards in 1996 and was invited to 70 international film festivals. For her film *In the Beginning was the Eye*, she collaborated with scientific researchers in an exchange of knowledge between art and science. The film was premiered at the Director's Fortnight at the Cannes Film Festival 2003, recieved invitations to over 100 film festivals, and won several awards. Her films have been presented in more than 30 international retrospectives. *In the Beginning was the Eye* was selected as one of the top ten best films of East and Central Europe as well as for the top ten best films 2003 in Melbourne, Australia. Working as a visual artist, her work *Free Radicals* premiered in 2007 at Biennale di Venezia and other works have been presented at the Moscow Biennale, the Chelsea Art Museum in New York, Centre Pompidou, Paris; the Expo '98 in Lisbon;

the Museum of Fine Arts in Houston; the Moscow Museum of Modern Art; Manchester Art Gallery; and Lincoln Center in New York. 2009 Member of the Orizzonti Jury at the Venice Film Festival. A book about her films was published in 2008 by Sonderzahl Verlag. www.badyminck.com
Filmography (selection)
2008 Schein Sein (Seems to Be) 2007 Das Sein und das Nichts (Being and Nothingness) 2007 Free Radicals 2006 Roll Over Mozart 2005 La Belle est la Bête (The Beauty is the Beast) 2003 Im Anfang war der Blick (In the Beginning was the Eye) 2000 Elektroansprache 1998 Seeen sehen (look the lakes!) 1996 Mécanomagie 1996 Attwengers Luft (The Air of Attwenger) 1989 Der Mensch mit den modernen Nerven (The Man with Modern Nerves; with Stefan Stratil)
Bibliography (selection)
Books and Catalogues: Dumreicher, Heidi, and Olaf Möller, eds. *Im Anfang war der Blick. Ereignishorizont eines Films.* [German] Vienna: Sonderzahl Verlag, 2008. *Articles, Interviews and Essays:* Noe, Paola. "Bady Minck, Giuria di Orizzonti / Jury at Venice Film Festival." [Italian/English] *L'Uomo Vogue*, July 23, 2009. → Kozinn, Allan. "Dishes From a Recipe for Eye and Ear." [English] *The New York Times*, April 2009. → Martin, Serge. "Le spectaculaire ou l'intime: Free Radicals." [French] *Le Soir* (Brussels), April 7, 2008. → Buchanan, Jason. "Being and Nothingness." [English] *The New York Times*, June 30, 2007. → Schifferle, Hans. "Menschen mit modernen Nerven – Filme von Bady Minck." [German] *Süddeutsche Zeitung* (Munich), December 7, 2006. → Hofmann, Katja. "Women drive alternative cinema – Radical femme Focus." [English] *Variety*, May 16, 2005. *Daily Cannes Film Festival issue.* → Godfrid, Federico. "A traversando la mirada – Entrevista a Bady Minck." [Spanish] *Kane-Magazine*, Buenos Aires, August 1, 2004. → Meils, Cathy. "Austria: Empresses of the Alps." [English] *Variety*, May 17, 2004. *Daily Cannes Film Festival issue.* → Roy, Jean. "La bataille de Graz a bien eu lieu." [French] *L'Humanité* (Paris), March 10, 2004. → van Bueren, P. "Que Pasa?" [Spanish] *Sin Aliento* (Buenos Aires), April 20, 2004. → Cielova, Hana, and Stefan Uhrik. "New Austrian Cinema." [Czech] *Czech TV*, November 2003. Television broadcast. → Danks, Adrian. "Polls Best Films." [English] *Senses of Cinema*, March 27, 2003. → Linssen, Dana. "In the Beginning was the Eye." [Dutch] *NRC Handelsblad* (Amsterdam), November 2003. → Losilla, Carlos. *En busca de Ulrich Seidl*. [Spanish] Gijon, Spain: El Camino, 2003. → Sander, Robin. "Court Circuit / KurzSchluss: Portrait Bady Minck." [German/French] *Arte*, Strasbourg and Cologne, May 5, 2003. Television broadcast.

→ Blouin, Pierre & Hélène Frappat. "
Découverte: Amour Fou Filmproduktion."
[French] *Cahiers du cinéma*, Dossier
Cannes 2003, June 4 (2003). → Meils,
Cathy. "Amour Fou in Cannes." [English]
Variety (Los Angeles), May 2003.
→ Schmerkin, Nicolas. "Cannes 2003:
La Quinzaine – Coté Courts." [French]
Répérages, May 12, 2003. → Turan, Ken-
neth. "Countdown in Cannes." [English]
Los Angeles Times, May 14, 2003.
→ Kothenschulte, Daniel. "Die Tage, an
denen wir nicht existieren – warum wir
Österreich um seine Filmkultur beneiden
müssen." [German] *Frankfurter Rund-
schau* (Frankfurt am Main), October 30,
2002. → Daum, Pierre. "Soutien à l'autre
Autriche." [French] *Libération* (Paris),
January 23, 2001. → Granica, Martin.
"On ne bady pas avec la *minck...*" [French]
Répérages, June 7 (2001). → Horwath,
Alexander. "elektrofrühstück." [German]
Kursiv Art Magazine (September 2001).
→ Kellermann, Kerstin. "Kampflust: Kein
Don Quijote sein." [German] *an.schläge*,
January 26, 2001. → le Rider, Jacques.
L'Autriche de M. Haider. [French] Paris:
Presses Universitaires, 2001. → Schmer-
kin, Nicolas. "Graz mâtinée de résistance."
[French] *Répérages*, May 8 (2001). → Jungk,
Peter Stephan. *Österreich – Berichte aus
Quarantanien*. [German] Frankfurt am
Main, edition suhrkamp, 2000. → Ebner,
Martin. "Zeichen der Zeit an den Wänden."
[German] *Süddeutsche Zeitung* (Munich),
June 10, 2000. → Goldberg, Marcy. "Kalime-
ra." [German] *Neue Zürcher Zeitung*
(Zurich), August 29, 2000. → Miessgang,
Thomas. "Im Land der Lächler." [German]
Die Zeit (Hamburg), June 29, 2000. → Rothe,
Marcus. "La résistance autrichienne
cherche un second souffle." [French]
L'Humanité (Paris), October 27, 2000.
→ Schmidtmaier, Irmgard. "Kunst unter
Hochspannung – Politisch frühstücken."
[German] *taz* (Berlin), December 7, 2000.
→ Poos, Francoise. "TV-Portrait Bady
Minck." [Luxembourgish] *RTL-TV Luxem-
bourg*, October 14, 1999. Television broad-
cast. → Scheffen, Jean-Louis. "Wer hat
Angst vor Bady Minck?" [German] *Télécran*
(Luxembourg), October 20, 1999. → Schmid-
maier, Irmgard. "Der mehrdimensionale
Blick." [German] *Mediabiz*, July 6 (1999).
→ Eiblmayr, Markus, Martin W. Draxler and
Franziska Maderthaner. "Film in Wien in
den frühen achtziger Jahren. Interview mit
den österreichischen Regisseuren Franz
Novotny, Niki List, Harald Sicheritz and
Bady Minck." [German] In *Idealzone Wien.
Die schnellen Jahre (1978–1985)*, edited
by Markus Eiblmayr, Martin Drexler and
Franziska Maderthaner. Vienna: Falter
Verlag, 1998. → Bouhours, Jean-Michel,
ed. *L'art du mouvement – collection ciné-
matographique du Musée national d'art
moderne, 1919–1996*. [French] Paris:

Centre Pompidou, 1996. → Rist, Pipilotti.
"Carte Blanche à Pipilotti Rist: Bady
Minck." [German] *DU*, May (1997).
→ Bouhours, Jean-Michel. "La caméra
expérimente la ville." [French] In *Visions
urbaines*, edited by Centre Pompidou.
Paris, 1994. → Savasci, Özlem. "Der
Mensch mit den modernen Nerven. Inter-
view with Bady Minck." [Turkish] *Hürriyet
Gösteriy* (Istanbul), April, 2, 1991.
→ Illetschko, Peter. "In Österreich sind
wir vater- und mutterlos – sie sind die
Zukunft des österreichischen Films.
Portrait Bady Minck & Stefan Stratil."
[German] *Der Standard* (Vienna), April 20,
1989. → Ruzowitzky, Stefan. "Besuch
bei der Filmkünstlerin Bady Minck."
[German] *ORF, Okay*, September 1987.
Television broadcast.

OTTO MUEHL

Born in a small village in Burgenland,
Austria, in 1925. Before finishing school
he was drafted into the German army. In
1952 he completed his studies in German
and History at the University of Vienna,
and began to study art education at the
Academy of Fine Arts, Vienna. From 1954
to 1963 Muehl worked as a drawing teacher and therapist. 1960 First solo exhibition and met Günter Brus and Alfons
Schilling. In 1962 he published the *Blut-
orgelmanifest* (Blood Organ Manifesto)
together with Adolf Frohner and Hermann
Nitsch: This manifesto pointed out ideas
on developing a performative and materi-
al-oriented art that includes the body.
From 1963 to 1973 Muehl executed a large
number of private and public Actions;
many Actions were documented by the
photographer Ludwig Hoffenreich. 1964
Met Kurt Kren, who filmed a number of his
Material Actions. In 1966 he founded
together with Günter Brus the Institut für
Direkte Kunst (Institute for Direct Art).
In 1968 he was arrested as a consequence
of the Action Kunst und Revolution (Art
and Revolution). In 1970 he took part in
the exhibition Happening and Fluxus,
curated by Harald Szeemann, and in 1972
in documenta V. Together with friends he
founded a commune for collective life at
the Friedrichshof. From 1975 to 1991 he
produced a large number of paintings and
drawings in the retreat of the commune.
In 1991 Muehl was convicted for "criminal
acts against morality" and drug abuse and
sentenced to seven years of prison. After
being released in 1997 he left Austria and
since then has lived and worked in the
commune Art and Life Family in Portugal.
Filmography (selection)
1986/1987 Back to Fucking Cambridge
(with Terese Schulmeister) 1985 Pablo
1974 Die Kirschen in Nachbars Garten
1971 SS und Judenstern 1970 Manotest,
Investmentfonds, Der geile Wotan, Oh

Sensibility, Manopsychisches Ballett 1,
Manopsychisches Ballett 2 1969 Apollo
10, Campagnerreiterclub, Scheißkerl,
Stille Nacht 1968 Mit Schwung ins neue
Jahr, Amore, Satisfaction, Libi, Fountain,
1967 Grimuid, ZOCK Exercises, Wehrer-
tüchtigung 1966 Nahrungsmitteltest,
St. Anna, 2. Totalaktion, Funebre 1965
Turnstunde in Nahrungsmitteln, Penis-
aktion, Gehirnoperation, Astronaut, Kopf
1964 Klarsichtpackung, Gesäßpanierung
Bibliography (selection)
Publications by Otto Muehl: Roussel,
Danièle, ed. *Otto Muehl. Aus dem Gefäng-
nis*. [German] Klagenfurt: Ritter Verlag,
1997. → Muehl, Otto. *Lettres de prison.
Otto Muehl*. [French] Dijon, France: Les
presses du réel, 1994.
Books and Catalogues: Falckenberg,
Harald, ed. *Otto Muehl. Retrospektive.
Jenseits von Zucht und Ordnung*. [German/
English] Berlin: revolver, 2007. → Badura-
Riska, Eva, and Hubert Klocker, eds.
Otto Muehl. Aspekte einer Totalrevolution.
[German/English] Vienna and Cologne:
Museum Moderner Kunst Wien, Walther
König, 2004. → Busse, Bettina M., and
Peter Noever, eds. *Otto Muehl. Leben /
Kunst / Werk. Aktion Utopie Malerei
1960–2004*. [German] Vienna and Cologne:
MAK Wien, Walther König, 2004.
Articles, Interviews and Essays: Roussel,
Danièle, ed. *L'Actionnisme viennois et les
autrichiens*. [French] Dijon, France: Les
presses du réel, 2008. → Vogel, Amos.
Film as a Subversive Art. [English] London:
C. T. Editions, 2005. First published 1974.
→ Scheugl, Hans. *Erweitertes Kino.
Die Wiener Filme der 60er Jahre*. [German]
Vienna: Triton Verlag, 2002. → Roussel,
Danièle, ed. *Der Wiener Aktionismus und
die Österreicher. Gespräche*. [German]
Klagenfurt: Ritter Verlag, 1995. → Green,
Malcolm, ed. *Brus, Muehl, Nitsch,
Schwarzkogler: Writings of the Vienna
Actionists*. [English] London: Atlas Press,
1999. → Noever, Peter, ed. *Out of actions
– Aktionismus, Body Art & Performance
1949–1979*. [German] Ostfildern, Germany:
MAK Wien, Cantz Verlag, 1998. → Klocker,
Hubert, ed. *Wiener Aktionismus. Wien
1960–1971/Viennese Actionism. Vienna
1960–1971*. 2 vols. [German/English]
Klagenfurt: Ritter Verlag, 1988. → Scheugl,
Hans, and Ernst Schmidt Jr. *Eine Subgeschichte des Films. Lexikon des Avant-
garde-, Experimental- und Undergroundfilms*. [German] Frankfurt am Main: edition
suhrkamp, 1974. → Hein, Birgit. *Film im
Underground. Von seinen Anfängen bis
zum unabhängigen Kino*. [German] Frankfurt am Main, Berlin and Vienna: Ullstein,
1971. → Weibel, Peter, and Valie Export,
eds. *bildkompendium wiener aktionismus
und film*. [German] Frankfurt am Main:
Kohlkunstverlag, 1970.

MANFRED NEUWIRTH

Born in 1954. Studied journalism, informatics and history. Director, producer, cinematographer, media artist in the areas of film, video, sound, installation. Founding member of Medienwerkstatt Wien, business manager of loop media. Visiting Professor at University for Art and Industrial Design, Linz.

Filmography & Installations (selection)
Territorium (work in progress), 2011 scapes and elements 2010 Michael Pilz – Filmartist 2006 Aquarium 2005 Tibet Revisited 2003 Pictures of a fleeting world, Pictures that make the heartbeat faster, Private News 2002 HH 2000 Balkan syndrome 1999 magic hour 1998 manga train 1988–1995 Tibetan Recollections 1995 In memory 1994 barkhor round 1993/1994 Picture Maker 1993 The End Of The Gang Of Four 1992/1993 About Living Loving Dying – Experiences with Aids (with Walter Hiller) 1991 Minutes of Vienna 1990 Collected Views (with Gerda Lampalzer) 1988 Reminiscences of a lost land 1987 Pilot 1986 Experts 1985 Healing strokes 1982 Asuma (with Gerda Lampalzer and Gustav Deutsch) 1983–1984 Wossea Mtotom – The meadow is green in the garden of Wiltz (with Gerda Lampalzer and Gustav Deutsch)

Bibliography (selection)
Publications by Manfred Neuwirth:
"Mission Statement. Anmerkungen zur Zukunft des Audiovisuellen." [German] *Diagonale*, film festival catalogue. Graz, 2008. → Lampalzer, Gerda, and Manfred Neuwirth. "Medienlabor. Zum Verhältnis von Technologie und alternativer Medienarbeit." [German] *Montage*, no. 1 (1992). → Lampalzer, Gerda, and Manfred Neuwirth. "Digitallandschaft mit Einzelhändlern. Persönliche Montagen zur Entwicklung der dokumentarischen Film/Videoästhetik." [German] In *Sprung im Spiegel, Filmisches Wahrnehmen zwischen Fiktion und Wirklichkeit*, edited by Christa Blümlinger. Vienna: Sonderzahl, 1990. → "Gegenkultur durch Video. Zur Entwicklung des unabhängigen Videos in Österreich." [German] In *Medienkultur in Österreich*, edited by Hans H. Fabris und Kurt Luger. Vienna: Böhlau Verlag, 1988. → "Video-Dokument-Experiment. Ein Aufsatz zu den genreübergreifenden Möglichkeiten des Mediums Video." [German] In *Dokumentarfilmschaffen in Österreich*, edited by Stefan Aichholzer, Christa Blümlinger and Michael Stejskal. Vienna: filmladen, 1986.
Articles, Interviews and Essays: Hofer, Sebastian. „Tibet Revisited." [German] *ray Filmmagazin* (December 2005). → Omasta, Michael. „Gebet und Gymnastik." [German] *Falter*, no. 48 (2005). → Omasta, Michael. „Zweimal Weltkino." [German] *Falter*, no. 10 (2005). → Goldberg, Marcy, and Yann-Olivier Wicht. „[ma] trilogie." [German/

man/English/French] In *Visions du Réel*, film festival catalogue. Nyon, Switzerland, 2000. → Omasta, Michael. „Von Tokyo bis Kritzendorf." [German] *Falter*, no. 40 (2000). → Cargnelli, Christian. „Lichtspuren in Zeitlupe." [German] *Falter*, no. 40 (1999). → Reicher, Isabella. „Magische Bewegung. Manfred Neuwirths *magic hour* komplettiert eine Trilogie der Zwischenräume." [German] *Der Standard* (Vienna), October 1999. Special Edition for the Viennale film festival. → Wulff, Constantin. „Tibetische Souvenirs." [German] *Kunstforum*, no. 137 (1997). → Flos, Birgit. „Der zweite Blick." [German] Catalogue for recipients of State of Lower Austria's Culture Award, 1997. → Flos, Birgit. „Vertrauen in die Kraft des Optischen. Der Bildermacher." [German] In *Gegenschuss. 16 Regisseure aus Österreich*, edited by Peter Illetschko. Vienna: Verlag Wespennest, 1995. → "Medienwerkstatt. Gespräch zur Geschichte der unabhängigen Videoarbeit." [German] *Eikon*, no. 6 (1993). → "Das Sinnliche im Filmemachen. Ein Gespräch mit dem Regisseur, Kameramann und Produzenten Manfred Neuwirth." [German] *Montage*, no. 3 (1992). → "Die Region und das Zentrum. Ein Gespräch mit Gottfried Schlemmer zum Begriff Heimat im Film." [German] In *Medium Film. Lauf. Bild. Buch. Niederösterreich*, Vienna: Amt der Niederösterreichischen Landesregierung, 1990. → "Die Welt, heil wie noch nie." [German] *Falter*, no. 13 (1989). → Grissemann, Stefan. "Die elektromagnetische Erinnerung. Zehn Jahre Medienwerkstatt Wien. Eine vorläufige Bilanz." [German] *Blimp. Film Magazine*, no. 39 (1988). → "Videoauge. Elisabeth Loibl und Christine Gaigg vom Falter im Gespräch mit Gustav Deutsch, Gerda Lampalzer und Manfred Neuwirth von der Medienwerkstatt." [German] *Falter*, no. 7 (1982).
DVD Editions: *Manfred Neuwirth. [ma]Trilogy*. Vienna: Index DVD Edition 011, 2004.

DIETMAR OFFENHUBER

Born in 1973. Artist and urban researcher with a background in urban studies and digital media and architecture. Interested in spatial aspects of cognition, representation and behavior. Holds a degree from TU Vienna and from the MIT Media Lab. 1996 Founding member of the Ars Electronica Futurelab. 2004 Japan Foundation Fellow at the IAMAS institute in Gifu, Japan, followed by a professorship at the University of Applied Sciences in Hagenberg, Austria. 2007–2009 Professor at the University for Art and Industrial Design, Linz, and Researcher at the Ludwig Boltzmann Institute for Media Art Research. Currently Research Fellow at the Senseable City Lab in the Department of

Urban Studies at Massachusetts Institute of Technology. In his artistic practice, Dietmar frequently collaborates with sound artist Markus Decker as well as composers Sam Auinger and Hannes Strobl, as the group stadtmusik. Exhibitions at MoMA, New York, ZKM Karlsruhe, Ars Electronica, Sundance Film Festival, Vienna Secession, the Seoul International Media Art Biennale and Arte Contemporaneo, Madrid etc.

Filmography (selection)
2009 boston buzz (with stadtmusik) 2007 Zurückbleiben bitte!/please stand back! (with stadtmusik) 2006 paths of g, kapitel 3 (with stadtmusik) 2005 Heinz Weiss (naredmanet) (with Nina Wenhart & Sam Auinger), felsen m18 (with stadtmusik), mauerpark (with stadtmusik) 2001 besenbahn (with stadtmusik) 1999 bike (with Markus Decker)

Visual Music
2005 *Philip Glass & Steve Reich: Images 4* – Music DVD ars electronica; Randonnée – Orquestra Simfònica de Barcelona i Nacional de Catalunya, *Sónar* (with Nina Wenhart). 2004 *Steve Reich, Music for 18 Musicians*, Brucknerorchester Linz, Ars Electronica. 2000 *image manipulation soundtrack* – Ars Electronica (with Markus Decker & Joachim Schnaitter). 1999 *L-void weekenders*, Blasthaus San Francisco (with Markus Decker).

DVD Editions: *VISIONary. Contemporary Short Documentaries and Experimental Films from Austria*. Vienna: Index DVD Edition 034, 2009.

ASTRID OFNER

Born in Linz in 1966. 1985–1987 Studies in Paris (Sorbonne Nouvelle III). 1987–1989 Studies at the Film Academy in Vienna. 1989–1994 Studies at the German Film and Television Academy in Berlin. 1990–1991 Collaboration with Jean-Marie Straub and Danièle Huillet for the staging of *Antigone* and as Antigone in their film *Antigone*. Worked as an actor at the Schaubühne Berlin. Since 1997 film curator and program advisor for the annual Viennale film festival. Since 1998 editor of books for retrospectives at the Viennale (including Jean-Luc Godard, Jaques Rivette, Danièle Huillet and Jean-Marie Straub, Andy Warhol – Filmmaker, Jacques Demy and Agnès Varda, Chantal Akerman, et al.).

Filmography
2012 Abschied von den Eltern (Leavetaking) 2007 Sag es mir Dienstag (Tell Me on Tuesday) 1994 Jetzt und alle Zeit (Now and for all times) 1993 Ins Leere (Into Emptiness) 1990 Savannah Bay

Bibliography (selection)
Articles, Interviews and Essays: Dominik Kamalzadeh. "Schuldenberg und Sehnsuchtsfahrten. Zwei lyrische Kurzfilme aus Österreich." [German] *Der Standard*

(Vienna), March 11, 2008. → Grissemann, Stefan. "Über Menschenkraft." [German] *Stadtkino Zeitung*, no. 450 (2008). → Huber, Christoph. "Die Geduld der Welt." [German] *Die Presse* (Vienna), March 5, 2008. → Schätz, Joachim. "Schule des Sehens." [German] *Falter*, no. 10 (2008). → Omasta, Michael. "Häuser mit und ohne Menschen." [German] *Falter*, no. 43 (2007). → Blümlinger, Christa. "Wohin mit der Wirklichkeit? Der neue österreichische Dokumentarfilm." [German] *Blimp. Film Magazine*, no. 30 (1994). Borgfeld, Wolfgang. "40. Internationale Kurzfilmtage Oberhausen. Wehmütiger Blick zurück." [German] *Kameramann*, no. 5, May 20 (1994). → Rebhandl, Bert. "Filmische Seelenlehre mit Brevier und Peitsche." [German] *Der Standard* (Vienna), September 20, 1994. → Sowada, Richard. "Now and for all times." [English] *Melbourne International Film Festival*, catalogue. Melbourne, 1994. → Grissemann, Stefan. "Die Form der Seele." [German] *Die Presse* (Vienna), September 1993. → Klabacher, Heidemarie. "Faszination des Geschlossenen und der strengen Regeln." [German] *Salzburger Nachrichten* (Salzburg), December 6, 1993. → Philipp, Claus. "Mit einigen Denkwürdigkeiten ins Leere." [German] *Der Standard* (Vienna), December 9, 1993. → Weixlbaumer, Robert. "Drei Schritte vor, einer zurück." [German] *Die Presse* (Vienna), December 9, 1993.

MICHAEL PALM
Born in Linz in 1965. Filmmaker, film editor, sound designer, writer and lecturer on film theory and film history. Studied at Vienna's Film Academy (Film and Video Editing) and at the University of Vienna, focusing on Film and Media Theory. Since 1988 freelance editor, composer and sound designer. Since 2001 has concentrated on directing. His films have received several awards at international film festivals and are screened in theatres and on TV. Author of numerous lectures and articles on theory and aesthetics of film and cinema. From 1990 to 1994 worked as film critic (*Der Standard*, *Falter*). Since 1998 lecturer at the University for Music and Arts, Vienna. Lectures and conducts filmmaking workshops, film theory seminars and film education programs at the Austrian Film Museum, the Viennese Medienzentrum, at the School for Independent Film and the Vienna Film College. Founding member of PVS Verleger and Navigator Film and member of Synema – Society for Film and Media, Austrian Editors Association (AEA), and of dok.at, the association of documentary filmmakers. He lives and works in Vienna.
Filmography
2011 Low Definition Control – Malfunctions #0 2009 Laws of Physics, body trail

(choreography by Willi Dorner), body trail CCTV (choreography by Willi Dorner) 2005 Mozart Sells 2004 Edgar G. Ulmer – The Man Off-screen 2003 Sim Movie (trailer for the 2003 Diagonale film festival) 2001 Sea Concrete Human – Malfunctions #1
Bibliography (selection)
Publications by Michael Palm: "Flux Aeterna. Stanley Kubrick in der musikalischen Leihanstalt." [German] In *Film und Musik*, edited by Regina Schlagnitweit and Gottfried Schlemmer. Vienna: Synema, 2001. → "Southern Comfort. Über einige Annehmlichkeiten in Terrence Malicks *Days of Heaven*." [German] *Meteor*, no. 14 (1999). → "Is the Audience Listening? Einige Samples zum Einhören, unter Vernachlässigung streng musikalischen Schalls." [German] *Meteor*, no. 15 (1999). → Palm, Michael, and Drehli Robnik. "Schutt und Asche: 100 Jahre Katastrophenfilm." [German] *Meteor*, no. 9 (1997). → Palm, Michael, and Drehli Robnik. "Das Verblödungsbild. Parodistische Strategien im neueren Hollywoodkino." [German] *Meteor*, no. 3 (1996). → "Liebesfilme. Zu einigen Arbeiten von Peter Tscherkassky." [German] In *Avantgardefilm Österreich. 1950 bis heute.* Edited by Alexander Horwath, Lisl Ponger and Gottfried Schlemmer. Vienna: Verlag Wespennest, 1995. → "Which Way? Drei Pfade durch das Bild-Gebüsch von Kurt Kren." [German] In *Ex Underground Kurt Kren, seine Filme*, edited by Hans Scheugl. Vienna: PVS Verleger, 1996. → *Und immer wieder geht die Sonne auf. Texte zum Melodramatischen im Film.* [German] Edited by Christian Cargnelli and Michael Palm. Vienna: PVS Verleger, 1994. → Palm, Michael, and Drehli Robnik, eds. *Und das Wort ist Fleisch geworden. Texte über Filme von David Cronenberg.* [German] Vienna: PVS Verleger, 1992. → "Quartett zu Fünft." [German] In *Der siebente Kontinent. Michael Haneke und seine Filme*, edited by Alexander Horwath. Vienna: Europaverlag, 1991.
Articles, Interviews and Essays: Alderete, Marcelo. "Rarezas y sorpresas de un anfitrión." [Spanish] *Otros cines*, November 6 (2011). → Huber, Christoph. "Zukunftskino mit Gegenwartsbildern." [German] *Die Presse* (Vienna), October 19, 2011. → Jensen, Erik. "Big Brother ser helt ind i din sjæl." [Danish] *Politiken* (Copenhagen), November 12, 2011. → Jurtschitsch, Aurelia. "Triumph der Tierschützer." [German] *artmagazine*, November 14 (2011). → Pauleit, Winfried. "Filmische Theorie jenseits von Kontrolle. *Low Definition Control* von Michael Palm." [German] *kolik.film*, no. 16 (2011). → Kamalzadeh, Dominik. "Die abgespeckte Selbstverständlichkeit." [German] *Der Standard* (Vienna), March 23, 2009. → Reicher, Isabella. "Achtung, gleich

kracht und blitzt es." [German] *Der Standard* (Vienna), March, 2009. Diagonale film festival supplement. → Siefen, Claudia. "Dropping Films and Burning Palaces." [English] *Senses of Cinema*, no. 60 (2009). → Rosenbaum, Jonathan. "Global discoveries on DVD." [English] *cinema scope*, no. 29 (February 2007). → Wittmann, Matthias. "Fragmente aus der Zukunft. Michael Palms Fake-Doku *Sea Concrete Human – Malfunctions #1*." [German] *Fotogeschichte. Beiträge zur Geschichte und Ästhetik der Fotografie*, no. 106 (2007). → Pichler, Barbara, and Andrea Pollach. "Zur Produktion von Landschaft. Ein Gespräch mit den Filmschaffenden Gustav Deutsch, Michael Palm, Hanna Schimek und Lotte Schreiber." [German] In *moving landscapes. Landschaft und Film*, edited by Barbara Pichler and Andrea Pollach. Vienna: Synema, 2006. → Dargis, Manohla. "A B-Movie Auteur Toiling in Hollywood's Shadows." [English] *The New York Times*, July 29, 2005. → Stinn, Renate. "Angeber oder Genie?" [German] *epd Film*, no. 70 (September 2004). → Lueken, Verena. "Was kann man schon mit Geld anfangen?" [German] *Frankfurter Allgemeine Zeitung* (Frankfurt am Main), September 4, 2004. → Göttler, Fritz. "Billig in Hollywood." [German] *Süddeutsche Zeitung* (Munich), September 4, 2004. → Halter, Ed. "Tracking Shots." [English] *Village Voice*, July 26 (2004). → Grissemann, Stefan. "Sand im Getriebe, Schäden in den Bildern." [German] *Die Presse* (Vienna), March 25, 2002. → Loebenstein, Michael. "Sea Concrete Human." [German] *Falter*, no. 13 (2002). → Reicher, Isabella. "Transformationen, Erinnerungsbilder." [German] *Der Standard* (Vienna), October 2001. Viennale film festival supplement.

MARIA PETSCHNIG
Born in Klagenfurt, Austria, in 1977. Moved to New York in 2003. Studied painting at the Academy of Fine Arts in Vienna and at the Royal College of Art and the Wimbledon School of Art in London. Petschnig's videos, performances and video installations confront dominant ideals and norms surrounding gender and sex, simultaneously revealing and thwarting the desire for an idealized feminine identity. Her work has been shown at numerous solo and group shows and film festivals internationally. Most recently, her videos were included in Commercial Break, Garage Projects at the 54th Venice Biennale; Erolastika, On Stellar Rays, New York; Greater New York 2010, MoMA PS1, New York; Western Exhibitions, Chicago; Maria Petschnig Video Performances, Stadtturmgalerie Innsbruck; Beauty Contest, Austrian Cultural Forum, New York; Queering Sex, Human Resources, Los Angeles; and the Triennale Linz 1.0, at Lentos,

Museum of Modern Art, Linz.
She lives and works in New York.
http://maria.petschnig.cc
Filmography
2010 De Niña A Mujer, Episoden Windows
2009 Born To Perform 2008 Pareidolia
Holodeck 2007 Minnie, Kip Masker
2006 Scopophilic 2003 peep 2002 saucy
slips & kinky curves
Bibliography (selection)
Books and Catalogues: *Maria Petschnig.*
Master Bedroom. [English/German]
Edited by Stadtturmgalerie Innsbruck.
Comet Books, 2011.
Articles, Interviews and Essays:
Kley, Elisabeth. "Naughty and Nice."
[English] *Artnet.com* (February 2011).
→ Amir, Yaelle. "NADA Art Fair." [English]
Artslant.com (December 5, 2010).
→ Douglas, Sarah. "The New Professio-
nals." [English] *Art + Auction* (September
2010). → Halle, Howard. "Greater New
York." [English] *Time Out New York*, June 3,
2010. → *Triennale Linz 1.0* [German/
English] Edited by Stella Rollig, Martin
Hochleitner and Martin Sturm. Nurem-
berg: Verlag Moderner Kunst, 2010.
→ *Greater New York 2010*. [English] Edited
by Klaus Biesenbach, Connie Butler and
Neville Wakefield. New York: MoMA PS1,
2010. → Benzer, Christa. "Ganze Körper-
arbeit. Zu einer kleinen Auswahl jüngster
Performance-Videos." [German] *kolik.film*,
no. 11 (2009). → Cole, Lori. "The Happiness
of Objects." [English] *Artforum.com* (June
2007). → Schwendener, Martha. "Proof
That Things Are People Too." [English]
The New York Times, May 18, 2007.
DVD Editions: *Just Say No to Family Values.*
Vienna: Index DVD Edition 036, 2011.

NORBERT PFAFFENBICHLER
Born in Steyr, Austria, in 1967. Artist,
filmmaker and curator. Studied at the
University of Applied Arts in Vienna,
master class for Media. *Exhibitions and
Festivals* (selection): 2011 Mostra d'Arte
Cinematografica Venezia (Orizzonti); 2010
Silent Alien Ghost Machine Museum,
Medienturm Graz; Triennale 01, OK Linz;
2009 Cineplex, Vienna Secession; See This
Sound, Lentos, Linz 09; 2008 Wavelengths,
Toronto International Film Festival;
International Film Festival Rotterdam;
Melbourne International Film Festival;
2007 Rencontres Berlin/Paris/Madrid,
Paris; Austrian Film Museum; 2006 Digital
Transit, Arco, Medialab Madrid; 2005
Kunstverein Medienturm, Graz; 2004 ars
electronica, Linz; 2003 Sound Spectral,
OK Centrum für Gegenwartskunst, Linz;
ars electronica, Linz; 2002 International
Film Festival, Rotterdam; Intercultural
Videoart Exhibition, Tokyo; 59th Mostra
d'Arte Cinematografica Venezia; Museum
der Wahrnehmung, Graz; 2001 Under-
ground Film Festival, New York; 2000

Sonar Festival, Barcelona; Medienturm,
Graz; 1999 Viper Film and Video Festival,
Basel; 1997 Chichester Film Festival,
Chichester; Circles of Confusion, Berlin;
1996 Chromapark, Berlin.
Filmography
2011 Intermezzo. notes on film 04,
Conference. notes on film 05 2007 Mosaik
Mécanique 2006 Notes on Film 02, a1b2c3
(with Lotte Schreiber) 2004 Piano Phase
(with Lotte Schreiber) 2003 notes on Mazy
2002 notes on film 01 else 2001 36 (with
Lotte Schreiber) 1998 traxdata (with Jürgen
Moritz), santora (with Jürgen Moritz)
1997 Wirehead (with Timo Novotny)
Bibliography (selection)
Publications by Norbert Pfaffenbichler:
*Cineplex, Experimentalfilme aus Öster-
reich*. [German/English] Catalogue.
Vienna: Vienna Secession, 2009. → Künst-
lerhaus Wien, Norbert Pfaffenbichler
and Sandro Droschl, eds. *Abstraction Now.*
[German/English] Vienna and Graz:
Edition Camera Austria, 2004.
Books and Catalogues: Droschl, Sandro,
ed. *Silent Alien Ghost Machine Museum*.
[German/English] Monograph. Graz: Kunst-
verein Medienturm, Folio Verlag, 2010.
Articles, Interviews and Essays: Daniels,
Dieter, and Sandra Naumann, eds. *See this
Sound. Audiovisuology. Essays, Histories
and Theories of Audiovisual Media and Art:
2*. [English] Cologne: Walther König, 2010.
→ Rainer, Cosima, Stella Rollig and Dieter
Daniels, eds. *See This Sound. Verspre-
chungen von Bild und Ton / Promises in
Sound and Vision*. [German/English] Linz
and Cologne: Lentos Museum, Walther
König, 2010. → Morandi, Iman, Ant Scott,
Joe Gilmore and Christopher Murphy, eds.
Glitch: Designing Imperfection. [English]
London, 2009. → Loebenstein, Michael.
"Notationen. Zu den Kinofilmen des
Videokünstlers Norbert Pfaffenbichler."
[German] *kolik.film*, no. 9 (2008).
→ Droschl, Sandro, and Vitus H. Weh,
eds. *Abstracts of Syn*. [German/English]
Bolzano, Italy, and Vienna: Folio Verlag,
Kunstverein Medienturm, 2007.
→ Höller, Christian. "Clip Archiv." [German]
springerin, no. 1 (2003). → Klanten, Robert,
Hendrik Helige and Birga Meyer, eds.
72-dpi Anime. [English] Berlin: Die Gestal-
ten Verlag, 2001. Book & DVD. → Höller,
Christian. "Flimmern im Kollektiv."
[German] *springerin*, no. 4 (2000).
→ Erdmann, Petra. "Digitale Patina"
[German] *springerin*, no. 4 (1998).
DVD Editions: *The Gift of Sound and Vision*,
DVD Edition Der Standard/Hoanzl,
Der österreichische Film, Vienna, 2007.

MICHAEL PILZ
Born in Gmünd, Austria, in 1943, near the
former Iron Curtain between Austria and
Czechoslovakia. 1954 Began taking photographs. 1956 Moved to Vienna, began

working with 8 mm film. 1964 Began
working with 16 mm film. Early years
marked by encounters with Catholicism,
Soviet newsreel propaganda films,
Gregorian chants, Thelonious Monk, Miles
Davis, Albert Camus, Samuel Beckett,
Henry Miller, Sigmund Freud, Robert
Frank, Jackson Pollock, Karl Prantl,
Jean-Luc Godard, Michelangelo Antonioni,
Robert Bresson, the New American Cinema. Growing interest in the technical and
material as well as in the spiritual aspects
of cinematography and in the various
ways of expressing the unconscious in
film. Most cinematographic experiments
of the 1960s, mainly Regular 8 films,
lost since 1985. Since 1983 occasional
lectures and workshops on aesthetics and
experimental filmmaking in Austria and
abroad. Artistic consultant for films of
Claudia von Alemann (*War einst ein
wilder Wassermann*, 1998–2000), Othmar
Schmiderer (*Josef Hauser. Klang und
Raum*, 1988; *Am Stein*, 1997: *An Echo
from Europe*, 1998; *Im toten Winkel*, 2002),
Gabriele Hochleitner (*Die Stadt und die
Erinerung*, 2000; *Autisti*, 2003; *Luigi oder
der geheime Garten*, 2001–2003), Regina
Höllbacher (*Ganz Normal*, 2002–2005),
Kenan Kilic (*Nachtreise*, 2002), Angela
Summereder (*Baustelle*, 2004; *Ort–Ried*,
2004; *Vermischte Nachrichten*, 2005), etc.
Filmography (selection)
1988–2012 Curtains (work in progress)
2011 Roman Diary 2006–2010 Rose and
Jasmine 2009 Invocation of Bliss 2006–
2008 Yemen Travelogue – Days at Shibam
and Seiyun 2006–2008 Jewel of the Valley
– Dourat Al-Wadi 1966–2008 Unter
Freunden 2 1997–2007 Für Keith Goddard
2005 Windows, Dogs and Horses 1988–
2004 That's All There Is 1995–2004 28
April 1995 Aus Liebe (For Love) 1997–
2004 Across the River 1994–2003 Siberian
Diary – Days at Apanas (short version)
1997–2002 Gwenyambira Simon Mashoko
2001 La Habana 2000–2001 Indian Diary
– Days at Sree Sankara 1995–2000 Da
Capo al Fine – Was ich erinnere nicht was
ich sehe (Da Capo al Fine – What I recall
and not what I see) 1988–1999 Pieces of
Dreams 1996–1998 Bridge to Monticello
1996 Was übersetzt ist noch nicht ange-
kommen (Facts for Fiction) 1995 Irgendwo
hätt' ich sonst hingewollt (I would've
otherwise liked to be in some other place)
1994–1995 Prisyadim na Dorozhku
(Let's sit down before we leave) 1993–
1995 Sibirisches Tagebuch (Siberian diary)
1987–1994 All the Vermeers in Prague
1992 Eigentlich spreche ich ja eine andere
Sprache, und trotzdem haben wir immer
gut miteinander gesprochen (Although
I speak another language, we have always
managed to understand each other)
(with Walter Stach) 1991–1993 State of
Grace 1990 Für Sebastian Prantl 1987–

1990 Feldberg 1986–1989 80 cm 5 t
1986–1988 Der Lauf des Wassers (Water-
course Way), Parco delle Rimembranze
(Parc of Remembrance) 1985 Noah Delta II
1984 Wels 1979–1982 Himmel und Erde
(Heaven and Earth) 1977 Franz Grimus,
How the Ladies Pay (Lou Reed), Die
Generalin 1974–1976 Langsamer Sommer
(with John Cook) 1971 Wienerinnen,
Easy Feeling 1969 Maskerade
1968–1969 Voom 1968 Für Peter Noever
und Achille Castiglione 1967 Haus-
Rucker-Co. Ballon für zwei 1965 Unter
Freunden 1964 Plakatkleber
Bibliography (selection)
Books and Catalogues: Möller, Olaf, and
Michael Omasta, eds. *Michael Pilz. Auge
Kamera Herz*. [German] Vienna: Film-
museumSynemaPublikationen, 2008.
Articles, Interviews and Essays: Rebhandl,
Bert. "Eine Kamera, die sich die Welt nicht
anders wünscht, als sie ist." [German]
Frankfurter Allgemeine Zeitung (Frankfurt
am Main), February 22, 2011. → Nield,
Anthony. "Himmel und Erde (1982). DVD
Video Review." [English] *thedigitalfix*,
http://homecinema.thedigitalfix.co.uk/
content/id/73365/himmel-und-erde.html.
→ Glaser, Christina. "Von der einen bis zur
anderen Ewigkeit. Michael Pilz' unverges-
slicher Film *Himmel und Erde* über die
Menschen in einem Bergbauerndorf und
sich selbst." [German] *ray Filmmagazin*,
no. 10 (2010). → Stöhr, Mark. "Video – Ich
sehe." [German] *ray Filmmagazin*, no. 11
(2009). → Young, Neil. "Berlin Wrapup :
Six From The Archive. Includes Slow
Summer/1976, Clinch/1978, The Dancing
Hawk/1977, Araya/1959, Stars of the
Day/1968 and Little Valentino/1979."
[English] *Neil Young's Film Lounge*, June 2
(2009), http://www.jigsawlounge.co.uk/
film/content/view/1019/1/. → Martin,
Corinne. "Windows, Dogs and Horses."
[German/English/French] *Visions du Réel*,
Festival International du Cinéma, film
festival catalogue. Nyon, Switzerland,
2006. → Kamalzadeh, Dominik. "Bis sich
ein Ausdruck verdichtet. Michael Pilz'
meditativer Bilderbogen *Windows, Dogs
and Horses*." [German] *Der Standard*
(Vienna), March 21, 2006. → Guyot, Sophie.
"Siberian Diary – Days at Apanas." [Ger-
man/English/French] *Visions du Réel*,
Festival International du Cinéma, film
festival catalogue. Nyon, Switzerland,
2003. → Stöhr, Mark. "Nothing left to tell."
[German] *Schnitt. Das Filmmagazin*
(March 2001). → Rothschild, Thomas.
"Wie die Pause zur Musik." [German]
Filmbulletin, no. 229 (2000). → Zuilhof,
Gertjan. "Een varkentje villen." [Dutch] *De
Groene Amsterdammer* (Amsterdam), April
12, 1997. → Visarius, Karsten. "Eine Arche
in der Bilderflut." [German] *Frankfurter
Allgemeine Zeitung* (Frankfurt am Main),
January 23, 1986. → Egger, Christoph.

"Himmel und Erde." [German] *Neue Zür-
cher Zeitung* (Zurich), September 14, 1983.
DVD Editions: Michael Pilz. *Himmel und
Erde (Heaven and Earth)*. Vienna: Edition
Filmmuseum, no. 62, 2010. → *Michael Pilz.
Facts for Fiction. Parco delle Remembranze.*
Vienna: Index DVD Edition 027, 2006.

LISL PONGER
Born in Nuremberg, Germany, in 1947.
Lisl Ponger's work concerns stereotypes,
racism and the construction of the gaze.
It is located at the interface between art,
art history and ethnology in the mediums
of photography, film and installation. She
lives and works in Vienna, Austria. *Solo
Shows* (selection): 2011 ...it belongs in a
museum (Indiana Jones III), Charim Galerie, Vienna; 2010 Werkschau XV, Fact or
Truth, Fotogalerie Wien; 2008 Lasst tau-
send Blumen blühen, Kunsthaus Dresden;
Happy History, History, CUC, Berlin;
2007 Imago Mundi, Landesgalerie Linz;
2004 Place Myths, Galerie Charim, Vienna;
2004 Si j'avais eu l'autorisation..., Dak'art
Off, Dakar, Senegal; 2004 Phantom Fremdes Wien, Wien Museum; 1999 Musée
d'Ethnographie, Genève; 1996 Museum
of Ethnology, Vienna; 1993 Kunsthalle
Exnergasse, Vienna. *Group Exhibitions*
(selection): 2011 Sowing and Weeding,
Folk Culture and Contemporary Art, Cobra
Museum, Amstelveen, NL; Haut, Kunsthaus Hamburg; Bleiben und Gehen/Rester
et Partir/Toso any ka taka, Musée de
Bamako, Mali; 2008 Beyond Paradise,
Stedelijk Museum Bureau Amsterdam;
2007 documenta XII (film program), Kassel,
Germany; 2005 Projekt Migration, Kölnischer Kunstverein, Germany; 2005 Die
Regierung, Vienna Secession; 2004 Black
Atlantic, House of Cultures, Berlin; Tour-
ism, Tapies Foundation, Barcelona; 2002
documenta XI, Kassel, Germany. www.
lislponger.com, www.charimgalerie.at
Filmography
2007 Imago Mundi – Challenging what is
accepted 2005 If the Lumiére Brothers....
Mozart-Minute 2004 Phantom Foreign
Vienna 1999 déjà-vu 1998 Panorama
(trailer for Diagonale, Festival of Austrian
Films) 1996 Passages 1990 Semiotic
Ghosts 1988 Train of Recollection
1988 Lichtblitze 1987 Substantial
Shadows 1986 Sound of Space 1985
Container-Contained 1984 Tendencies
to Exist 1983 Film – An Exercise in Illusion
II 1981 Souvenirs 1981 The Four Corners
of the World 1980 Film – An Exercise
in Illusion I 1979 Space Equals Time –
Far Freaking Out
Bibliography (selection)
Publications by Lisl Ponger: *Phantom
Fremdes Wien / Phantom Foreign Vienna.*
[German/English] Klagenfurt/Celovec:
Wieser Verlag, 2004. → Handke, Peter, and
Lisl Ponger, eds. *Ein Wortland.* [German]

Klagenfurt/Celovec: Wieser Verlag, 1998.
→ Horwath, Alexander, Lisl Ponger and
Gottfried Schlemmer, eds. *Avantgardefilm
Österreich. 1950 bis heute.* [German]
Vienna: Verlag Wespennest, 1995.
→ *Xenographische Ansichten.* [German]
Klagenfurt/Celovec: Wieser Verlag, 1995.
→ *Fremdes Wien.* [German] Klagenfurt/
Celovec: Wieser Verlag, 1993. → *Dopp-
leranarchie. Wien 1967–1972.* [German]
Vienna: Falter Verlag, 1990.
Books and Catalogues: Hochleitner,
Martin, Lisl Ponger, Landesgalerie Linz
and Kunsthaus Dresden, eds. *Lisl Ponger
Foto- und Filmarbeiten. Photos and Films.*
[German/English] Klagenfurt/Celovec:
Wieser Verlag, 2007.
Articles, Interviews and Essays: Gürses,
Hakan. "Die Verfremdung der Fremdheit."
[German] *IDM Kulturführer Mitteleuropa*
(2010). → Schedlmayer, Nina. "Schnitzel-
jagd." [German] *profil*, no. 49, 2007.
→ Huck, Brigitte. "Die große Schere."
[German] Opening speech, Museum in
Progress. 2005, http://www.mip.at/attach-
ments/40. → *Der Black Atlantic.* [German]
Berlin: Haus der Kulturen der Welt, 2004.
→ "Laudatio an Lisl Ponger anlässlich der
Verleihung des Goldenen Ehrenzeichens
der Stadt Wien." [German] Speech at
award ceremony, 2004, http://www.basis-
wien.at/avdt/pdf/211/00062419.pdf.
→ Sharp, Tim. "Traveling Shots." [English]
Austria Kultur 11, no. 1 (2001). → A.C. "Lisl
Ponger: Voyage dans la réalité de l'illusion
cinématographique." [French] *Hors-Champ*,
no. 3 (1999). → Blümlinger, Christa. "Fest-
stellungen über das Reisen." [German]
springerin V, no. 3 (1999). → Blümlinger,
Christa. "Sagbares und Sichtbares."
[German] *Neue Zürcher Zeitung* (Zurich),
1999. → Heim, Christoph. "Der Blick der
weißen Mittelklasse auf die Welt." [Ger-
man] *Basler Zeitung* (Basel), 1999.
→ Perret, Jean. "Lisl Ponger." [French/
German/English] In *Visions du Réel*, film
festival catalogue. Nyon, Switzerland,
1999. → Stecher, Thorsten. "Eine Reise
hinter die Bilder." [German] *WOZ Die
Wochenzeitung* (Zurich), 1999. → Horwath,
Alexander, "Memories are made of this."
[German] In *Avantgardefilm Österreich.
1950 bis heute*, edited by Alexander Hor-
wath, Lisl Ponger and Gottfried Schlem-
mer. Vienna: Verlag Wespennest, 1995.
→ Jutz, Gabriele. "Der polymorphe Raum,
Lisl Pongers *Semiotic Ghosts*." [German] In
Avantgardefilm Österreich. 1950 bis heute,
edited by Alexander Horwath, Lisl Ponger
and Gottfried Schlemmer. Vienna: Verlag
Wespennest, 1995. → Blümlinger, Christa.
"Schattenschrift zu Lisl Pongers *Semiotic
Ghosts*." [German] In *Blaue Wunder. Neue
Filme von Frauen 1984–94*, edited by
Eva Hohenberger and Karin Jurschik.
Argument Verlag, 1994. → Blümlinger,
Christa. "Die illusionären Räume der

Welt." [German] *Der Standard* (Vienna), 1989. → Horwath, Alexander. "Memories Are Made Of This." [German] *Blimp. Zeitschrift für Film*, no. 11 (1989). → Horwath, Alexander. "Die dritte Generation." [German] *Falter* (1987). → Preschl, Claudia. "Tendencies to Exist." [German] *Frauen und Film*, no. 40 (1986).
CD-ROM/DVDs (with Tim Sharp): 2007 *Logbook, A Bulgarian Journey*, EVN Collection. 2006 *Hidden Histories – remapping Mozart*, Wiener Mozartjahr. 2004 *ImagiNative*, Haus der Kulturen der Welt, Berlin.
DVD Editions: Lisl Ponger. Travelling Light. Vienna: Index DVD Edition 010, 2004.

URSULA PÜRRER

Born in Vienna in 1962. 1965–1982 Raised in Southern Germany. 1982–1984 Studied Medicine at the University of Vienna, Austria. 1984–1989 Studied Visual Media under Peter Weibel at the Academy of Applied Arts in Vienna. 1986–1989 Electroacoustics and Composition at the Academy of Music and Performing Arts, Vienna, Prof. Dieter Kaufmann. 1989 MA. 1991–1994 New York, USA. Since 1995 video editor for *Spiegel-TV* (Germany's leading political magazine) Berlin and Hamburg. 2011/12 Lecturer at the Institute of Theater, Film and Media Studies, University of Vienna: "Recreation of Actuality and Factuality by Means of Editing. Iconic Turn, Speed and Image in the Realm of Editing."
Filmography (selection)
Bella am Kyritzer See (work in progress) 2001 Blueprint 1992 Flaming Ears (with A. Hans Scheirl and Dietmar Schipek) 1989 The Drift of Juicy 1986 Originally coloured (with Angela Scheirl) 1982–1985 Super-8-Girl Games (with A. Hans Scheirl) Approx. 25 short films shot in Super 8.
Bibliography (selection)
Articles, Interviews and Essays: Finkelstein, David. "Super 8 Girl Games. DVD." [English] *filmthreat*, November 11, 2009, http://www.filmthreat.com/reviews/11976/
DVD Editions: *Flaming Ears. Ursula Pürrer, A. Hans Scheirl, Dietmar Schipek*. Vienna: Index DVD Edition 031, 2008. → *Pürrer / Scheirl. Super–8–Girl Games*. Vienna: Index DVD Edition 026, 2006.

FERRY RADAX

Born in Vienna in 1932. Member of the Vienna Boys' Choir. Attended music high school in Frankfurt am Main. Textile college in Vienna. Jazz pianist. Worked in architecture and as a press photographer. Exhibition of photographs and paintings at Vienna's Art Club. As of 1951 engaged with filmmaking, first as assistant for productions of documentaries. Attended film academies in Vienna and Rome (Centro Sperimentale di Cinematografia). 1953 Collaboration with colleagues at the

Film Academy. Since then screenwriter, cameraman, editor, director and producer of documentary, experimental, advertising, fiction and music films and series. Spent many years working in Switzerland, Germany and Italy – rarely in Austria – and regularly working on film in Japan, Peru, St. Helena, the US, New Zealand, etc. Numerous festivals and awards. Retrospectives at the Austrian Film Museum, Vienna; the National Film Theatre, London; Centre Pompidou, Paris; Die Lupe, Berlin; Irish Film Center, Dublin; Gasteig, Munich; Zurich, Rome and Tokyo. 2003 Austrian Cross of Honour for Science and Art. 2007 Otto Breicha Award for Photography, Museum der Moderne Salzburg. Lives, works and paints in Vienna and Krems. www.ferryradax.at
Filmography (selection)
1995–1998 Hundertwasser in Neuseeland 1990 Jenseits von Österreich 1984 Auf der Spur des Erich von Däniken (3 sequences) 1980 Attentat in Gastein 1977 Unter Freunden 1975 Ludwig Wittgenstein (2 sequences) 1972 Der Italiener 1970 Wiener Phantastische Realisten (2 sequences) 1970 Der Kopf des Vitus Bering 1968/1969 Konrad Bayer oder die welt bin ich, und das ist meine sache 1967 H. C. Artmann 1967 Testament 1966 Große Liebe 1965/1966 Hundertwasser 1964–1980 Wer sind Sie, Mr. Joyce? 1961–1963 Am Rand 1960 Schindler in der Schweiz 1959–1962 Sonne, halt! 1955 Mosaik im Vertrauen (cinematography; dir.: Peter Kubelka) 1954 Das Floß (The Raft; unfinished)
Bibliography (selection)
Articles, Interviews and Essays: Nau, Peter. "Ferry Radax. *Sonne Halt!*" [German] *kolik.film*, no. 8 (2007). → Vogel, Juliane. " 'Ich bin so groß und Du bist so klein'. Allmachtsphantasien in Ferry Radax' *Sonne Halt!*" [German] In *Psyche im Kino. Sigmund Freud und der Film*, edited by Thomas Ballhausen, Günter Krenn and Lydia Marinelli. Vienna: verlag filmarchiv austria, 2006. → Büttner, Elisabeth, and Christian Dewald. *Anschluß an Morgen. Eine Geschichte des österreichischen Films von 1945 bis zur Gegenwart*. [German] Salzburg and Vienna: Residenz-Verlag, 1997. → Weibel, Peter. "Der Wiener Formalfilm." [German] In *Jenseits von Kunst*, edited by Peter Weibel. Vienna: Passagen Verlag, 1997. → Omasta, Michael. "Stichwortlexikon zu Bayer, Radax, *Sonne Halt!*" [German] In *Avantgardefilm Österreich. 1950 bis heute*, edited by Alexander Horwath, Lisl Ponger and Gottfried Schlemmer. Vienna: Verlag Wespennest, 1995. → Omasta, Michael. "Ferry Radax. Die Erste." [German] *Falter*, no. 18 (1990). → Omasta, Michael. "Ferry Radax. Die Zweite." [German] *Falter*, no. 19 (1990). → Rudle, Ditta. "Gerupfter Doppel-

adler." [German] *Wochenpresse*, no. 48 (1990). → Schweikhardt, Josef. "Dr. Wittgensteins Vilm – Tractatus Radax Philosophicus." [German] *Falter*, no. 43 (1989). → Blomberg, Catharina. "Ferry Radax at Ottenstein Castle." [English] *Sight and Sound*, no. 1 (Winter 1984/1985). → Radax-Ziegler, Senta. "Mein Mann, der Surrealist. Beobachtungen aus der Nähe." [German] *morgen*, no. 35 (1984). → Schweikhardt, Josef. "Der Cineast als Einzelgänger. Ferry Radax, ein Klassiker der Avantgarde." [German] *morgen*, no. 35 (1984). → Schmidt Jr., Ernst. *Österreichischer Avantgarde- und Undergroundfilm 1950–1980*. [German] Vienna: Österreichisches Filmarchiv, 1980. → Prager, Michael. "*Testament*." [German] *Action*, no. 1 (1969).
DVD Editions: *Ferry Radax. Thomas Bernhard – Three Days*. Vienna: Index DVD Edition 035, 2010.

MARTIN REINHART

Born in Vienna in 1967. Studied at Vienna's University for Applied Arts under Bernhard Leitner. Extensive work with practical, theoretical and historical aspects of film and filmmaking in a wide range of contexts: as a specialist writer, lecturer and instructor, curator for film and photography at the Vienna Technical Museum, expert on historically significant cameras at WestLicht-Auction, technical work on films in Hollywood and Munich, co-founder and CEO of Indiecam GmbH, inventor, and experimental and documentary filmmaker. In addition to his own works, collaboration, conception, technical work and artistic consultation for various experimental films, such as Johann Lurf's *Vertigo Rush* (2007), and for numerous other Austrian filmmakers, such as Martin Arnold, Alfons Schilling, Linda Christanell, Georgia Kraemer, Günther Selichar, Elke Groen, Bady Minck, Christian Brunner, et al.
Filmography
2012 Revolution im Ton (working title, in progress. With Thomas Tode) 2002 tx-dance 2000 Pinocchio – Er hat Euch nicht belogen, tx-transformator (installation) 1998 tx-transform (with Virgil Widrich)
Bibliography (selection)
Articles, Interviews and Essays: Vanvolsem, Maarten. *The Art of Strip Photography. Making Still Images with a Movie Camera*. [English] Leuven: Leuven University Press, 2011. → *Future Cinema. The Cinematic Imaginary After Film*. [English] Edited by Jeffrey Shaw and Peter Weibel. Cambridge, MA: MIT Press, 2003.

THOMAS RENOLDNER

Born in Linz in 1960. 1979–1983 Studied Psychology and Educational Theory at universities in Innsbruck and Salzburg. 1989–1994 Studied Painting and Animation Film at the Academy of Applied Art, Vienna. Since the age of sixteen has worked in the areas of music, painting, film, installation and performance. Numerous experimental and animated films and some commercials. Since 2000 producer of animated films for artists including Sabine Groschup and Heimo Wallner, and graphic designers including Nicolas Mahler, Christoph Abbrederis and Heinz Wolf. Since 1992 animation workshops and seminars with children, youngsters and adults. After a one-year lectureship for animation at the Arts University in Linz (2002) has held regular animation seminars as head of animation studios at the Vienna Art School (since 2003) and the Academy of Fine Arts in Vienna (since 2004). Several research projects about the history of animation in Austria since 1998. Last publication: *Die Kunst des Einzelbilds – Animation in Österreich 1832 bis heute,* together with Sabine Groschup, Mara Mattuschka and Christian Dewald. Animation and avant-garde programs at Vienna Independent Short Film Festival since 2009. Selection and jury member at numerous international animation film festivals.

Filmography (selection)
2012 Sunny Afternoon 2007 Rosenmäd-chen Seelenclown (portrait of Gerlinde Zickler) 2004 Plato & Tao (artist portrait of Helene Avramidis and Chen Xi) 1998 Sophia's Year, SC01 – Belo Horizon-te.April.97 1997 Zeit Raum (Time Space) Hiroshima.August.92 1996 Picnic in the green 1994 Rhythmus 94 (Rhythm 94) 1992 Lonely Cowboy in 1992 1991 Bunt (Colorful) 1990 Würfel (Cubes) 1989 Struktur/Auflösung (Structure/Dissolution), Ein Schlag zuviel (Too many strokes), Shark in the City, Haus/Frau (House/Woman) 1988 Der Dialog (The Dialogue – between film & reality) 1987 Das Fenster (The Window), Filmplastik (Film Sculpture) 1985 Warten Sie auf etwas Besonderes? (Are you waiting for something special?) 1986 Sehnsucht: Wildnis (Desire: Wilderness) 1984 Il carnevale 1983 Die Begrenzungslinien der Projektionsfläche (The borders of the projection screen) 1982 Sie haben 15 Sekunden Zeit, etwas besonders Wichtiges zu sagen (You have 15 seconds time to say something extremely important) 1981 Kobbla Manfred 1980 Atemnot (Shortness of Breath)

Bibliography (selection)
Publications by Thomas Renoldner:
Dewald, Christian, Sabine Groschup, Mara Mattuschka and Thomas Renoldner, eds. *Die Kunst des Einzelbilds. Animation in Österreich – 1832 bis heute.* [German] Vienna: verlag filmarchiv austria, 2010. → Renoldner, Thomas. "Between conceptualism and humour. A selection of mostly animated films by Thomas Renoldner

1983–2002." [Serbian/English] *Balkanima. International Animated Film Festival,* catalogue. Belgrade: Balkanima, 2005. → Renoldner, Thomas. "Juror's Section. Thomas Renoldner." [Czech/English] *AniFest. International Festival of Animated Films,* catalogue. Třeboň, Czech Republic: AniFest, 2004.
Articles, Interviews and Essays: Korschil, Thomas. "Konterbande. Über einige neue kurze und längere Filme aus Österreich." [German] *Meteor,* special issue (1998). → Büttner, Elisabeth, and Christian Dewald. "Filme von Thomas Renoldner." [German] In *filmbrunch 1–19,* edited by Judith Wieser-Huber and Ralph Wieser. Mödling and Vienna: filmbühne Mödling, 1992. → Quehenberger, Peter. "Magie der Dinge hinter der Fassade des Alltags – Experimentalfilm im Treibhaus." [German] *Tiroler Tageszeitung* (Innsbruck), June 20, 1987. → Stadler, Michael. "Achterbahn mit der Kamera. Thomas Renoldner zeigte seinen Film *Sehnsucht: Wildnis*." [German] *Salzburger Nachrichten* (Salzburg), May, 24, 1986.

BILLY ROISZ
Born in Vienna in 1967. Lives and works in Vienna. Specialized in feedback video and video/sound interaction, using monitors, cameras, video mixing desks, a self-built video synthesizer, computer, bass guitar and turntables for generating video and sound. Her video works are distributed by sixpackfilm. Co-organizer/programmer of the annual Reheat Festival. Member of NotTheSameColor (with dieb13), Avva (with Toshimaru Nakamura), Cilantro (with Angélica Castelló), kutin|roisz (with Peter Kutin), Skylla (with Silvia Fässler), etc. Has also performed with Sachiko M., Michaela Grill, Mario de Vega, Martin Brandlmayr, Burkhard Stangl, Otomo Yoshihide, eRikm, Martin Siewert and Metamkine, etc.
Film and Music Festivals (selection):
IFF Rotterdam 2002/2003/2005/2007/2009/2010, EXiS Seoul 05/07/09, Imageforum Tokyo 2003/2008, Feedback: Order from Noise UK tour 2004, Unyazi 2005, FBI 05, Sonic Acts XI 2006, Donaufestival 2006/2009/2010, THE LONG Weekend/Tate Modern 2007, Relay Seoul 2007/2010, Cimatics Brussels 2008, Tokyo<->Wien Modern 2010, Signal & Noise 2010, Suoni per il popolo 2010, etc. http://billyroisz.klingt.org
Filmography (selection)
2011 Chiles en Nogada 2010 brRRMMM-WHEee II 2009 Close Your Eyes 2008 Tilt, Not Still 2007 elesyn 15.625 2006 Avva:ragtag, Bye Bye Bice (audio & video: NotTheSameColor [with dieb13]) 2004 sources 2003 my kingdom for a lullaby #2 (with Michaela Grill) -2.20, i/o: flies. circles. glyphs 2002 blinq 2001 smokfraqs (audio & video: Billy Roisz & Dieter Kovacic)

Bibliography (selection)
Articles, Interviews and Essays: Trantow, Katrin Bucher, ed. *Catch Me! Geschwindigkeit fassen.* [German/English] Graz: Kunsthaus Graz, 2010. → Höller, Christian. "Smelling Sounds, Hearing Images." [German] *springerin,* no. 2 (2010). → Kasman, Daniel. "Rotterdam 2010. Digital Mescaline & Urns of Film." [English] *Mubi.* February 5, 2010, http://mubi.com/notebook/posts/rotterdam-2010-digital-mescaline-urns-of-film. → Moradi, Iman, Ant Scott, Joe Gilmore and Christopher Murphy. *Glitch: Designing Imperfection.* [German/English] New York: mbp, 2009. → Komary, David. *Sound Alliances II – Iconophonic.* [German] Krems, Austria: Galerie Stadtpark, 2009. → Komary, David. *noise reduction: off.* [German] Vienna: galerie dreizehnzwei, 2007. → Thiel, Wolf Guenter. "*wieder modern.*" zu den Arbeiten von Billy Roisz und Manuel Knapp. [German] Vienna: galerie dreizehnzwei, 2007. → "Interview w/ Billy Roisz." [Korean/English] *N'Avant. Experimental Film & Video Magazine,* no. 03 (2007). → Montgomery, Will. "AVVA:gdansk queen." [English] *Wire Magazine,* no. 274 (2006). → Collins, Nicolas. "Visual Music." [English] In *Handmade Electronic Music – The Art of Hardware Hacking.* New York: Routledge, 2006. → Wellins, Matt. "Sound Eye, Sound Body: Interviews with Artists Bridging the Gap between Sound and Image." [English] *Dusted Magazine,* 2005, http://www.dustedmagazine.com/features/369
DVD Editions: *VISIONary. Contemporary Short Documentaries and Experimental Films from Austria.* Vienna: Index DVD Edition 034, 2009. → *Sonic Fiction. Synaesthetic Videos from Austria.* Vienna: Index DVD Edition 014, 2004.

CONSTANZE RUHM
Born in Vienna in 1965. Artist, filmmaker and author based in Vienna and Berlin. 1987–1993 Studied at the Academy of Applied Arts Vienna. Postgraduate studies at the Institute of New Media, Städelschule, Frankfurt am Main. 1996–1997 Visiting Professor for Visual Communication at the Offenbach University of Art and Design, Offenbach am Main. 1998 Schindler grant/residency, MAK Center for Art and Architecture in Los Angeles. 1999–2006 Board Member of the Vienna Secession, Vice-President from 1999 to 2001. Curator of the exhibition Fate of Alien Modes at the Vienna Secession in 2003; curatorial projects in the framework of the haus.0 program at Künstlerhaus Stuttgart (with Fareed Armaly); at the ZKM Karlsruhe and Neue Galerie Graz. 2004–2006 Professor for Film and Video at Merz Academy Stuttgart. Since 2006 Professor for Art and Media at the Academy of Fine Arts Vienna. 2008–2011 Adjunct Professor at

Gleichzeitig nackt* 1984 anna alpha nacht, Men & Masks II Ostern '84*, Piß in Rosa* Bauchtanz*, Wald- und Wiesenfilm* Anna wackelt*, Metall & Blumen* Sex & Crime*, Kampf & Kuß* Hochhaus & Reißverschluß*, Nacht-Plakat-U-Bahn* Maria Meistert Metall & Anna Arbeitet Anständig*, LGP* 1983 DNA, Jocasta taucht auf, Orlando , Frau Zemo 1982 Bei dieser Geschwindigkeit fetzen die Haare 1981 Straße II (loop, sound on cassette tape), The Ascension, Tigerin 1980 Men & Masks, Noch Kokoseis, Saxophone & Spione, Charles tanzt, Paris, Meyva Suyu, Gerüstfilm (part of an installation in the beleben exhibition, Forum Stadtpark, Graz), For Men 1979 Straßenbilder, Hände Hoch!, Artistin in der Zirkuskuppel und Herzattacke
* with Ursula Pürrer, ** with Dietmar Schipek, *** with Ursula Pürrer & Dietmar Schipek
Bibliography (selection)
Publications by Hans Scheirl: Scheirl, Hans, and Andrea B. Braidt. "Kunstschnee – Manifesto zu *Dandy Dust.*" [German] *Urtux – Kunst als Utopie*, no. '01/'02, Institut der Modernen Kunst Nürnberg. → "cyber-comix-splatter cinema." [German/English] *Coil*, no. 8 (1999). *Books and Catalogues*: Braidt, Andrea B., ed. *[cyborg.net/z] – Katalog zu Dandy Dust.* [German/English] Vienna, 1999. *Articles, Interviews and Essays*: de Philo, Johnny. "To Tremble the Ejaculate." [English] *Bigmag. III Polytopia*, no. 08 (2008). → Doderer, Yvonne, ed. *Doing Beyond Gender. Interviews zu Positionen und Praxen in Kunst, Kultur und Medien.* [German] Münster: Monsenstein & Vannerdat, 2008. → Volkart, Yvonne. *Fluide Subjekte. Anpassung und Widerspenstigkeit in der Medienkunst.* [German] Bielefeld, Germany: Transkript Verlag, 2006. → Dertnig, Carola, and Stefanie Seibold, eds. *Let's twist again. Performance in Wien 1960 bis heute.* [German/English] Vienna: D.E.A. Verlag, 2006. → Schaffer, Johanna, and Dietmar Schwärzler. "Rot Weiß Rot: oder die Eingrenzung der potentiell ausufernden roten Farbe. Ein Gespräch mit Hans Scheirl." [German/English] *Rohstoff* (December 2005). → Wiese, Doro. "Das Zerschlagen todbringender Eindeutigkeit im Film *Dandy Dust* oder: Wie man aus dem Körper ein Vermögen macht." [German] In *Gewalt und Geschlecht: Konstruktionen, Positionen, Praxen*, edited by Frauke Koher and Katharina Pühl. Opladen, Germany: Leske + Budrich, 2003. → Kuzniar, Alice. *The Queer German Cinema.* [English] Stanford, CA: Stanford University Press, 2000. → Kamalzadeh, Dominik. "Sonne, Mond und Sperma – *Dandy Dust,* Hans Scheirl's Splatter/ Trans-Gender/Science Fiction/Road-Movie." [German] *Der Standard* (Vienna),

June 18, 1999. → Armstrong, Dr. Rachel. "Cyborg Film Making." [English] *Cybersociology*, no. 5 (1999), http://www.cybersociology.com/files/5_cyborgfilmmaking. html. → Pichler, Barbara. "Der Film *Dandy Dust*, ein 'Transgender-Cyberlesben-Horror-Comix.'" [German] *Telepolis*. June 16, 1999, http://www.heise.de/tp/artikel/3/3387/1.html. → Braidt, Andrea B. "The New (Media-)Technology of Gender – Remarks on the film *Dandy Dust* by the Austrian Director Hans Scheirl." [German] *springerin*, no. 3 (1998). → Braidt, Andrea B. "The stuff that gender is made of...Dandy Dust." [German/English] *Blimp. Film Magazine*, no. 39 (1998). → Valerio, Max Wolf. "Dandy Dust." [English] *TNT – Transsexual News Telegraph*, no. 12 (1998). → Armstrong, Dr. Rachel. "Cyborg Artists." [Polish] *Magazyn Sztuki*, no. 2 (1998). → Michelotti, Gabriela. "Repulsa e atração." [Portuguese] *Revista da Folha* (São Paolo), November 8, 1998. → "Dandy Dust als Fernsehrauschen. Interview with Vina Yun." [German] *Volksstimme* (Vienna), June 24/25, 1998. → Scheirl, Hans. "Cyborg Manifesto." [English] In *The Eight Technologies of Otherness*, edited by Dr. Sue Golding. New York: Routledge, 1997. → *Talking Pictures – Interviews with Contemporary British Filmmakers.* [English] Edited by Graham Jones and Lucy Johnson. London: BFI, 1997. → Grissemann, Stefan. "Die aquarellierten Androiden – Bemerkungen zu *Rote Ohren Fetzen Durch Asche* von A.H. Scheirl, D. Schipek und U. Pürrer." [German] In *Der Neue Österreichische Film*, edited by Gottfried Schlemmer. Vienna: Verlag Wespennest, 1994. → Lombardi, Fred. "*Rote Ohren Fetzen Durch Asche.*" [English] *Variety* (Los Angeles), June 15, 1992. → Halberstam, Judith. "Some Like It Hot – The New Sapphic Cinema." [English] *The Independent – Film & Video* (November 1992). → Guthmann, Edward. "Austrian Sci-fi Fantasy Featured in Gay Festival." [English] *San Francisco Chronicle*, June 25, 1992. → Dougherty, Cecilia. "An Earful." [English] *San Francisco Bay Guardian*, June 24, 1992. → Philipp, Claus. "Blutrote Nonnen, tödliche Poetinnen." [German] *Der Standard* (Vienna), March 20, 1992. → Perthold, Sabine. "*Rote Ohren Fetzen Durch Asche.*" [German] *Falter*, no. 10, 1992.
DVD Editions: Flaming Ears. Ursula Pürrer, A. Hans Scheirl, Dietmar Schipek. Vienna: Index DVD Edition 031, 2008. → *Pürrer / Scheirl. Super–8–Girl Games.* Vienna: Index DVD Edition 026, 2006.

HANS SCHEUGL

Born in Vienna in 1940. 1961–1963 Film Academy Vienna. 1964 Apprenticeship at the Cinémathèque in Paris. Filmmaker since 1966. Published articles on film together with Ernst Schmidt Jr. and Peter Weibel in periodicals such as *Caligari* and *Film* between 1964 and 1969. 1967 First public screening of his films. 1967/1968 Participated in the Fourth Experimental Film Festival in Knokke, Belgium. 1968 Founded the Austria Filmmakers Cooperative (with Schmidt Jr., Weibel, Valie Export, Kurt Kren and Gottfried Schlemmer). Screenings in London, Amsterdam, Zurich and Berlin; Expanded Cinema in Hamburg, Munich and Vienna. Stopped making films in the 1970s and published various books. 1984 Attended film festivals in Rotterdam, Berlin, London, New York, Calcutta, etc. Participated in Arts Dialogue, Kennedy Center, Washington, D.C. 1985 Returned to filmmaking. *Exhibitions* (selection): 2006 Big Bang. La Pelicule du Chaos, Centre Pompidou; 2005 Open Systems: Rethinking Art around 1970, Tate Modern, London; 2004 Wiener Linien – Kunst und Stadtbeobachtung seit 1960, Wien Museum; 2003/2004 X-Screen. Film Installationen und Aktionen der Sechziger- und Siebzigerjahre, Museum moderner Kunst Stiftung Ludwig, Vienna. Lives in Vienna.

Filmography
1993 Prince of Peace 1993 (Calcutta) GO 1993 Rutt Deen 1990 Black/White 1988 Keine Donau – Kurt Kren und seine Filme 1986 Was die Nacht spricht 1985 Der Ort der Zeit 1968 Sugar Daddies, Der Voyeur, Eroticon sublim, zzz: hamburg special, Safety Film 1967 Hernals, Wien 17, Schumanngasse 1966 Miliz in der Früh

Bibliography (selection)
Publications by Hans Scheugl: Sex und Macht. Eine Metaerzählung des amerikanischen Films des 20. Jahrhunderts. [German] Stuttgart: Schmetterling-Verlag, 2007. → "Der Film der frühen Jahre. Herbert Vesely und der neue deutsche Film." [German] In *Viennale*, film festival catalogue. Vienna, 2006. → *Erweitertes Kino. Die Wiener Filme der 60er Jahre.* [German] Vienna: Triton Verlag, 2002. → *Das Absolute. Eine Ideengeschichte der Moderne.* [German] Vienna and New York: Springer Verlag, 1999. → *Ex Underground. Kurt Kren, seine Filme.* [German] Edited by Hans Scheugl. Vienna: PVS Verleger, 1996. → Scheugl, Hans, and Ernst Schmidt Jr. *Eine Subgeschichte des Films. Lexikon des Avantgarde-, Experimental- und Undergroundfilms.* [German] Frankfurt am Main: edition suhrkamp, 1974. → *Show Freaks & Monster.* [German] Cologne: DuMont Buchverlag, 1974. *Articles, Interviews and Essays*: Büttner, Elisabeth. "Form als Protest. Stichproben Wiens im Avantgardefilm." [German] In *Wien im Film. Stadtbilder aus 100 Jahren*, edited by Christian Dewald, Michael Loebenstein and Werner Michael Schwarz. Vienna: Wien Museum, Czernin Verlag,

2010. → Michalka, Matthias, ed. *X-Screen. Filmische Installationen und Aktionen der Sechziger und Siebzigerjahre.* [German/English] Vienna: Museum Moderner Kunst Stiftung Ludwig, 2003. → Büttner, Elisabeth, and Christian Dewald. *Anschluß an Morgen. Eine Geschichte des österreichischen Films von 1945 bis zur Gegenwart.* [German] Salzburg and Vienna: Residenz-Verlag, 1997. → Hrachovec, Herbert. "Hans Scheugl: *Der Ort der Zeit*." [German] In *Avantgardefilm Österreich. 1950 bis heute,* edited by Alexander Horwath, Lisl Ponger and Gottfried Schlemmer. Vienna: Verlag Wespennest, 1995. → Hein, Birgit, and Wulff Herzogenrath, eds. *Film als Film. 1910 bis heute. Vom Animationsfilm der zwanziger zum Filmenvironment der siebziger Jahre.* [German] Cologne: Kölnischer Kunstverein, 1977. → Hein, Birgit. *Film im Underground. Von seinen Anfängen bis zum unabhängigen Kino.* [German] Frankfurt am Main, Berlin and Vienna: Ullstein, 1971. → Weibel, Peter, and Valie Export, eds. *bildkompendium wiener aktionismus und film.* [German] Frankfurt am Main: Kohlkunstverlag, 1970.
DVD Editions: Hans Scheugl. The Seconds Strike Reality. Vienna: Index DVD Edition 029, 2008. → *Kurt Kren. Which Way to CA?* Bonus track: Hans Scheugl's documentary *Keine Donau – Kurt Kren and his films.* Vienna: Index DVD Edition 020, 2007.

GOTTFRIED SCHLEMMER
Born in Vienna in 1934. Professor h.c. Co-founder of the theatre group werkstatt. Received a degree for performance and stage direction in 1963. He staged plays for experimental and avant-garde theater and multimedia experimental theater, such as *versuche 1*, in 1965 (with Peter Schweiger), in 1966 *drive in für konrad bayer* (with Peter Weibel), in 1967 *experimentaltheater deutschland 1914– 1927*, in 1968 *Time Art* (with Rudolf Kohoutek), in 1969 *Mystery*. Took part in national and international exhibitions of visual poetry: 1968 in Alpbach, Tyrol, in Vienna (Galerie nächst St. Stephan) and Innsbruck (Galerie im Taxispalais); 1969 in La Plata, Argentina, and Resistencia, Argentina. Co-founder of the Austria Filmmakers Cooperative in 1968. National and international film presentations. Awarded the Förderungspreis des Wiener Kunstfonds and the Sonderpreis der 2. Maraisiade in 1968. From 1967 to 1984 he was on the scientific staff of the Austrian Film Museum. From 1971 to 2006 taught at various universities in Austria and held lectures on film theory and history and the history of perception. 1981 Founded the Gesellschaft für Filmtheorie, later renamed Synema – Gesellschaft für Film und Medien.

Filmography
1968 8h01 – 8h11, Film (slide as film), Rot 1969 The Time for ACTION has come (expanded cinema)
Bibliography (selection)
Publications by Gottfried Schlemmer: "Verdrehte Augen." [German] *Maske und Kothurn. Falsche Fährten in Film und Fernsehen.* Vienna, Cologne and Weimar: Böhlau Verlag, no. 2–3 (2007). → Schlemmer, Gottfried, ed. *Dietmar Brehm: Perfekt.* [German] Vienna: Sonderzahl Verlag, 2000. → "Gespräch mit Dietmar Brehm. Die Kunst des Abstrahierens." [German] In *Dietmar Brehm: Perfekt.* → "Von Paris nach Dallas im flackernden Pumping Screen. Die Perfekt-Trilogie." [German] In *Dietmar Brehm: Perfekt.* → "The Time for ACTION has come." [English] In *X-Screen. Filmische Installationen und Aktionen der Sechziger und Siebzigerjahre,* edited by Matthias Michalka. Vienna: Museum Moderner Kunst Stiftung Ludwig, 2003. → "Gegen die Perfektion der Kinomaschine. Destruktion als Prinzip." [German] In *Avantgardefilm Österreich. 1950 bis heute*, edited by Alexander Horwath, Lisl Ponger and Gottfried Schlemmer. Vienna: Verlag Wespennest, 1995. → "Gespräch mit Dietmar Brehm. Letzlich ist man eine Leichenpumpe." [German] In *Avantgardefilm Österreich.* → "The Murder Mystery. Ein Dokument der Angst und des Grauens." [German] In *Avantgardefilm Österreich.* → "Dokument." [German] In *Das Licht der Peripherie. Österreichische Avantgarde Filme 1957–1988*, edited by Peter Tscherkassky. Vienna: Museum of the 20th Century, 1988. → "Anmerkungen zum Undergroundfilm." [German] In *Begriffslexikon zur bildnerischen Erziehung*, edited by Walter Stach and Herwig Zens. Vienna and Munich: Jugend und Volk, 1981. → *Avantgardistischer Film 1951– 1971: Theorie.* [German] Edited by Gottfried Schlemmer. Munich: Hanser Verlag, 1973.

ERNST SCHMIDT JR.
Born in Hadersdorf am Kamp, Austria, in 1938. Attended Vienna's Film Academy for 2 1/2 years, leaving in 1963 when a film project proposal was denied (which later became his second film, *P.R.A.T.E.R.*). After 1963 numerous 16 mm films. Countless screenings, including Experimental Film Festival Knokke, Berlin Film Festival, Centre Pompidou, Paris, Kunstmesse Basel and the Viennale. 1964 Edited the hectographic film journal *Caligari* (two issues). As of 1966 contributed to film journals in Austria, Switzerland and West Germany (including *Film* and *Blimp*), writing articles about Sergej Eisenstein, Kurt Kren, Erich von Stroheim, G. W. Pabst, et al. Co-founder of the Austria Filmmakers Cooperative in 1968

(with Hans Scheugl, Valie Export, Peter Weibel, Kren and Gottfried Schlemmer). 1968 Wrote the first encyclopedia of new European avant-garde and underground film, *Das andere Kino* (in the *Film 1968* yearbook). 1974 Co-authored the most comprehensive book about avant-garde film to date, *Eine Subgeschichte des Films* (two vols., Frankfurt am Main: Suhrkamp) with Hans Scheugl. 1976 Completed his first full-length film, *Wienfilm 1896–1976*, in collaboration with Joe Berger, Ernst Jandl, Gerhard Rühm, Peter Weibel, Friedrich Achleitner, Padhi Frieberger, et al. 1980 Edited the catalogue *Österreichischer Avantgarde- und Undergroundfilm 1950–1980* for the Austrian Film Archive on the occasion of a retrospective at the Z-Club Alternativ. 1981 35 mm feature film *Die totale Familie* based on a novel by Heimito von Doderer. 1986–1988 Worked on a filmic adaptation of the book *Denkwürdigkeiten eines Nervenkranken* by Daniel Paul Schreber, which took the form of a three-part compilation film. Died during the completion of part two, on February 9, 1988. Part two was finished by his assistent, Susi Praglowski, part three realized by Peter Tscherkassky in 1993.
Filmography (selection)
1987–1988 Denkwürdigkeiten eines Nervenkranken (Part 2) (unfinished) 1987 Denkwürdigkeiten eines Nervenkranken (Part 1) 1984 Berühmte Wienerinnen, nackt (Part 3) 1983 Berühmte Wienerinnen, nackt (Part 2), Berühmte Wienerinnen, nackt, (Part 1), Graf//Kowanz 1981 Die totale Familie, Die Tauben, Kriminalfilm 1979 Gertrude Stein, Gesammelt von Wendy 1978 12 Uhr Mittags – High Noon, The Merry Widow, Mein Begräbnis ein Erlebnis, N 1976 Wienfilm 1896–1976 1975 Ichfilm, Herr über 230 Autos, Wien in Namen 1974 Eine Subgeschichte des Films, Burgtheater – Stempelfilm, 50 x Basel 1973 Anfänge, Blumen, Landschaft, Reduziertes Stilleben, 3 Nächte 1971 Filmisches Alphabet, Blauer Ton, Roter Ton 1970 Burgtheater, Farbfilm 2, Farbfilm 3 1969 Doppelprojektion, Das Frühstück im Grünen 1968–1973 Abstraktionen (parts 1+2) 1968 Tonfilm, Denkakt, Ja/Nein, Schnippschnapp, Prost, Schöpfung, David& Zorro, 1967 Filmtext, Farbfilm, Rotweißrot, Weiß, Filmkritik oder Prädikat werttlos, Nothing, Kunst und Revolution, Loin du Vietnam, Loin du Jackie, Fernsehen, Dracula, Filmtagebuch 1966/1967 Filmreste 1 966 15. Mai 1966 1965–1968 Einszweidrei 1965/1966 Bodybuilding 1964/1965 Steine 1963–1966 P.R.A.T.E.R.
Bibliography (selection)
Publications by Ernst Schmidt Jr.: "Avant-garde- und Undergroundfilm sowie Expanded Cinema in Österreich: Theorie und Praxis einer extremen Kunst." [German] In

Kinoschriften. Jahrbuch der Gesellschaft für Filmtheorie, edited by Georg Haberl. Vienna: Synema, 1988. → "Kommerz und Avantgarde. Zur Situation des österreichischen Films." [German] In *Österreich zum Beispiel*, edited by Otto Breicha and Reinhard Urban. Salzburg: Residenz-Verlag, 1982. → *Österreichischer Avantgarde- und Undergroundfilm 1950–1980*. [German] Vienna: Österreichisches Filmarchiv, 1980. → "Aufstieg und Fall des Jean-Luc-Godard." *Falter*, nos. 59 & 60 (1975). → Scheugl, Hans, and Ernst Schmidt Jr. *Eine Subgeschichte des Films. Lexikon des Avantgarde-, Experimental- und Undergroundfilms*. [German] Frankfurt am Main: edition suhrkamp, 1974. → "Kino und Film." [German] *Kinema*, no. 7 (1968). → Schmidt Jr., Ernst, Hans Scheugl and Peter Weibel. "Wiener Filmhappenings. Bildende Kunst und Film. Experimente der Wiener Gruppe." [German] *Film*, no. 12 (1966).

Books and Catalogues: Bilda, Linda, and Vienna Secession, eds. *Drehen Sie Filme, aber keine Filme: Filme und Filmtheorie 1964 bis 1987*. [German/English] Monograph. Vienna: Triton Verlag, 2001. *Articles, Interviews and Essays*: Büttner, Elisabeth. "Form als Protest. Stichproben Wiens im Avantgardefilm." [German] In *Wien im Film. Stadtbilder aus 100 Jahren*, edited by Christian Dewald, Michael Loebenstein and Werner Michael Schwarz. Vienna: Wien Museum, Czernin Verlag, 2010. → Taanila, Mika. "Taide ja vallankumous." [Finnish] *Avanto Festival, film festival catalogue*. Helsinki: avanto, 2004. → Scheugl, Hans. *Erweitertes Kino. Die Wiener Filme der 60er Jahre*. [German] Vienna: Triton Verlag, 2002. → Weibel, Peter. "Expanded Cinema: Materialfilme, Filmaktionen (ohne Film), Projekt- und Konzept-Filme." [German] In *Jenseits von Kunst*, edited by Peter Weibel. Vienna: Passagen Verlag, 1997. → Schlemmer, Gottfried. "Gegen die Perfektion der Kinomaschine. Destruktion als Prinzip." [German] In *Avantgardefilm Österreich. 1950 bis heute*, edited by Alexander Horwath, Lisl Ponger and Gottfried Schlemmer. Vienna: Verlag Wespennest, 1995. → Tscherkassky, Peter. "Aufruf statt Nachruf: Tradiert Ernst Schmidt jr.!" [German] *Stadtkino Programm*, no. 203 (1991). → Trencak, Heinz, and Bogdan Grbić. "Lieber Ernstl!" [German] *Blimp. Zeitschrift für Film*, no. 9 (1988). → Weibel, Peter. "Der Fremde in der Heimat. Zum Tode von Ernst Schmidt jr." [German] *Falter*, no. 7 (1988). → Scheugl, Hans. "Schmidtfilm. 1963–1984. Retrospektive in der Albertina." [German] *Falter*, no. 4 (1984). → Geyrhofer, Friedrich. "Doderers reiner Tisch auf der Leinwand." [German] *Stadtkino Programm*, no. 16 (1982). → Gassert, Siegmar. "Wienfilm 1896–

1976." [German] *Basler Zeitung* (Basel), June, 17, 1980. → Hein, Birgit, and Wulff Herzogenrath, eds. *Film als Film. 1910 bis heute. Vom Animationsfilm der zwanziger zum Filmenvironment der siebziger Jahre*. [German] Cologne: Kölnischer Kunstverein, 1977. → Manola, Franz. "Avantgarde im Umbruch." [German] *Die Presse* (Vienna), January 31, 1977. → Hein, Birgit. *Film Underground. Von seinen Anfängen bis zum unabhängigen Kino*. [German] Frankfurt am Main, Berlin and Vienna: Ullstein, 1971. → Weibel, Peter, and Valie Export, eds. *bildkompendium wiener aktionismus und film*. [German] Frankfurt am Main: Kohlkunstverlag, 1970. → Patalas, Enno. "Der Untergrund drängt nach oben." [German] *Filmkritik*, no. 1 (1969).

LOTTE SCHREIBER

Born in Mürzzuschlag, Austria, in 1971. Lives and works in Vienna as a visual artist and filmmaker. 2011 Received Outstanding Artist Award for Experimental Film from the Austrian Federal Ministry for Education, Arts and Culture. *Exhibitions* (selection): 2011 Gallery Maerz, Linz; 2010 Fundacja Art Transparent, Warsaw; 2009 Cineplex, Vienna Secession → See this Sound, Lentos Museum, Linz. 2008 We declare: Spaces of Housing, gallerygachet, Vancouver, Canada 2007 art_clips.ch.at.de, ZKM, Karlsruhe, Germany. 2006 Digital Transit, ARCO, Medialab Madrid. 2005 Now's the time, Kunsthaus, Graz. 2004 MAK Night at Contemporary Art Tower, Vienna. 2003 24!, O.K Centre for Contemporary Art, Linz 2002 Video Art Center Tokyo. *Festival Screenings* (selection): 2011 Viennale; 2010 Vienna Independent Shorts; 2009 Vision du Reel, Nyon, Switzerland; Hong Kong International Film Festival; 2008 IDFA, Amsterdam; Jihlava Documentary Film Festival, Czech Republic; 2007 Moving Patterns, ACF, New York; 2006 Cinéma du réel, Paris; 2004 Viennale; 2003 EMAF – European Media Art Festival, Osnabrück, Germany; 2002 Toronto International Film Festival; 2001 International Film Festival, Leeds.

Filmography 2011 <u>Tlatelolco</u>, <u>Git Cut Noise</u> (with Radian) 2008 <u>Borgate</u> 2006 <u>a1b2c3</u> (with Norbert Pfaffenbichler) 2005 <u>Domino</u> 2004 <u>Piano Phase</u> (with Norbert Pfaffenbichler) 2003 <u>I.E. [site 01 – isole eolie]</u> 2002 <u>quadro</u> 2001 <u>36</u> (with Norbert Pfaffenbichler)

Bibliography (selection)
Publications by Lotte Schreiber: "City – Migration – Identity." [German/English] *Crossing Europe Filmfestival Linz*, catalogue. Linz: Crossing Europe Filmfestival, 2011. → "Reclaiming Space." [German/English] *Crossing Europe Filmfestival Linz*, catalogue. Linz: Crossing Europe Filmfestival, 2010.

Articles, Interviews and Essays: Rainer, Cosima, Stella Rollig and Dieter Daniels, eds. *See This Sound. Versprechungen von Bild und Ton / Promises in Sound and Vision*. [German/English] Linz and Cologne: Lentos Museum, Walther König, 2010. → Pfaffenbichler, Norbert. *Cineplex, Experimentalfilme aus Österreich*. [German/English] Catalogue. Vienna: Vienna Secession, 2009. → Öhner, Vrääth. "Architektur in Ansichten. Zu Sascha Pirkers *Angelica Fuentes, The Schindler House* und Lotte Schreibers *Borgate*" [German] *kolik.film*, no. 11 (2009). → Droschl, Sandro, and Vitus H. Weh, eds. *Abstracts of Syn*. [German/English] Bolzano, Italy, and Vienna: Folio Verlag, Kunstverein Medienturm, 2007. → Pichler, Barbara, and Andrea Pollach. "Zur Produktion von Landschaft. Ein Gespräch mit den Filmschaffenden Gustav Deutsch, Michael Palm, Hanna Schimek und Lotte Schreiber." [German] In *moving landscapes. Landschaft und Film*, edited by Barbara Pichler and Andrea Pollach. Vienna: Synema, 2006. → Bianchi, Paolo & Eckermann, Walter. "Grosses Welttheater, Stadt und Zufall on display." [German] *Kunstforum International*, no. 179 (2006). → Künstlerhaus Wien, Norbert Pfaffenbichler and Sandro Droschl, eds. *Abstraction Now*. [German/English] Vienna and Graz: Edition Camera Austria, 2004. → Beckmann, Aki. "Kurze Begegnungen mit fremden Orten – Über fünf aktuelle österreichische Kurzfilme." [German] *kolik.film*, no. 1 (2004). → *Konstruiertes Leben / Constructed life* [German/English] Internationaler Medienkunstpreis, catalogue & DVD, edited by Barbara Könches and Peter Weibel. Karlsruhe: ZKM, SWR, 2003. → Klanten, Robert, Hendrik Helige and Birga Meyer, eds. *72-dpi Anime*. [English] Berlin: Die Gestalten Verlag, 2001. Book & DVD.

DVD Editions: *VISIONary. Contemporary Short Documentaries and Experimental Films from Austria*. Vienna: Index DVD Edition 034, 2009. → *The Gift of Sound and Vision*, DVD Edition Der Standard/Hoanzl, *Der österreichische Film*, Vienna, 2007.

BERNHARD SCHREINER

Born near Vienna in 1971. Currently lives in Frankfurt am Main. 1991–1998 Studied at the Academy of Fine Arts, Städelschule, Frankfurt am Main, under Peter Kubelka, and where he later became an assistant lecturer for film/video. Until 1999 he primarily produced documentary-based, experimental Super 8 and 16 mm film works and curated film programs in Germany, Austria and Italy. In 2001 he received a yearlong travel grant from the Hessische Kulturstiftung. Stopovers in Italy, Portugal, Gibraltar, etc. 2004 Founded the label feld-records (http://feld-records.com/). Co-curator of *Dictionary of War* (Frankfurt,

Munich, Graz and Berlin, 2006/2007). Co-curator at steirischer herbst, 2006–2011. To date he works mainly on installations, photography, compositions, sounds, and film/video, often incorporating found materials.

Filmography
2006 Don't forget that you are dealing with air!, dying toy piano 2005 Dissection, Bonham Ghost Loop (installation) 2003–2004 News (installation) 2003–2004 CageCar 2002–2004 Black Robe Rmx. (installation) 2001 Dian, Paito, Arrêté 2000 Hwa-Shan District, Taipei 1998 Reise durch Italien 1997 Schönbrunn, Neapel 96 (Aktion Nitsch) 1996 Fenster #4, Hochberg 1995 Karl Kels 1995 1992–1994 Holland 92 1992 Polizist, Perchtoldsdorfer Turm, Kirche in Bornheim

Bibliography (selection)
Articles, Interviews and Essays: Schütte, Christoph: "Warteschleife, tanzbar: Bernhard Schreiners Installation Holding Patterns in der Galerie Middendorff." [German] *Frankfurter Allgemeine Zeitung* (Frankfurt am Main), October 15, 2010. → *The Art of Programming. Film, Programm und Kontext*. [German] Edited by Heike Klippel. Berlin, Münster, Vienna and Zurich, London: LIT Verlag, 2008.

MICHAELA SCHWENTNER
Born in Linz in 1970. Lives and works in Vienna and Linz. Media artist (focusing on experimental film and video works, audio-visual projects/performances). Studies in Philosophy, History, Art History, Drama in Vienna. Teaches at Kunstuniversität Linz. Director of mosz records. Schwentner experiments with different forms of perception, forms of projections, and focuses on phenomena of illusion and imagination. Under the moniker Jade she works on compositions for audiovisual performances with Peter Rehberg and Electric Indigo. *Festival and Exhibitions* (selection): Sundance Film Festival, London Film Festival, Kurzfilmtage Oberhausen, Viennale, Transmediale Berlin, Videonale Bonn, EMAF European Media Art Film Festival Osnabrück, VideoEx Zürich, Cork Filmfest, Evolution Film Festival Leeds, New York Underground Film Festival, Edinburgh Film Festival, Film Festival Rotterdam, WRO Biennale Wroclaw, Crossing Europe Film Festival Linz, Triennale Linz 1.0, Edith Russ Haus für Medienkunst, Shedhalle Zürich, ACF New York. Awards: Local Artists Award, Crossing Europe Film Festival Linz, 2004. Austrian Promotional Award for the art of film, 2007. www.jade-enterprises.at

Filmography (selection)
2011 Prospects 2010 mouvements/caduques III, Canranc 2009 des souvenirs vagues 2008 alpine [an]notation, alpine passage, bellevue 2006 swinging,

la petite illusion, composition set // image transformed // mozart moved 2005 der tränenwärmer 2004 der kopf des vitus bering 2003 how do you want m.? / MAZY, giuliana 64:03, forest of the moon 2002 Jet, the future of human containment, take the bus 2001 grainbits, sZ 2000 r4, transistor 1997 Orchester 33 1/3

Bibliography (selection)
Articles, Interviews and Essays: "Michaela Schwentner." [French] *37. Festival du Film de La Rochelle*, catalogue. La Rochelle, France, 2009. → *Cover Art By: New Music Graphics*. [English] Edited by Adrian Shaughnessy. London: Laurence King Publishing, 2008. → Nemec, Christina. "Mosz – wenn es auch noch rockt, fein!" [German] *springerin*, no. 03 (2006). → "Michaela Schwentner im Gespräch mit Barbara Pichler und Claudia Slanar." [German] *Diagonale Materialien*, no. 13 (2005). → Benzer, Christa. "Abstraction Now." [German] *springerin*, no. 04 (2003). → Weber, Gerald. "Kurzes in die Länge ziehen." [German] *pool magazin*, no. 02 (2003). → Erdmann, Petra. "Weiß auf Weiß im Videomix." [German] *springerin*, no. 02 (2000). → Fluch, Karl. "Nur keine Wellen schlagen: Sitz-Disco und Dancefloor." [German] *Der Standard* (Vienna), November 22, 2000. *DVD Editions*: VISIONary. Contemporary Short Documentaries and Experimental Films from Austria. Vienna: Index DVD Edition 034, 2009. → The Gift of Sound and Vision, DVD Edition Der Standard/Hoanzl, *Der österreichische Film*, Vienna, 2007. → Sonic Fiction. Synaesthetic Videos from Austria. Vienna: Index DVD Edition 014, 2004.

HUBERT SIELECKI
Born in Carinthia in 1946. 1968–1973 Studied at the University of Applied Arts, Vienna. 1975–1976 Scholarship at the Film University (Animation Film) and at the Art University (Painting) in Łódź, Poland. Since 1973 freelance work with experimental color photography, electronically, mechanically and acoustically reacting objects, environments, performance, posters without commercial purposes, old photographic techniques and music. Various exhibitions. Since 1982 lecturership for Experimental Animation Film at the University of Applied Arts in Vienna: Responsible for the installation of its animation studio (the only one of its kind at an Austrian art university), and also serving as its mangaging director and instructor. 1984 Co-Founded ASIFA Austria. 1986–1991 Member of the Austrian Film Support Committees. 1988 Founded the film production company Animotion Films. 1990–1991 Lectureship at the University of Fine Arts in Braunschweig and Ludwigsburg, Germany.

Filmography (selection)
2011 Der Prediger, Der Kurator, Der Minister 2010 Radetzkyplatz 2009 Foul 2007 Sehen (Seeing) 2006 Drei Stücke (Three Pieces) 2001 Österreich! 1997 Love TV 1996 Book Factory 1995 Air Fright 1995 Dachbodenstiege 1994 Nitweitaget (Nowayout) 1992 Maria Lassnig Kantate (with Maria Lassnig) 1989 Drunk 1985 Festival 1983 Nachrichten (News), Die Suppe (The Soup)

Bibliography (selection)
Articles, Interviews and Essays: Bruckner, Franziska. *Malerei in Bewegung. Studio für experimentellen Animationsfilm an der Universität für angewandte Kunst Wien*. [German] Vienna: Springer Verlag, 2011. → Bruckner, Franziska. "Neugierig sein, experimentieren, Musik und Filme machen." [German] In *Die Kunst des Einzelbilds. Animation in Österreich – 1832 bis heute*, edited by Christian Dewald, Sabine Groschup, Mara Mattuschka and Thomas Renoldner. Vienna: verlag film-archiv austria, 2010.

THOMAS STEINER
Born in 1956. Studied at the University of Artistic and Industrial Design in Linz and the University of Fine Arts, Vienna, under Maria Lassnig, Studio for Experimental Animation Film. Member of Oberösterreichischer Kunstverein, ASIFA Austria and Künstlerhaus Wien. Since 1990 exibitions of fine art. Since 1984 participation with international film festivals. *Selected Festivals and Screenings:* Diagonale, Salzburg and Graz; VIS Vienna Independent Shorts; Riga International Film Festival; O.K., Linz; L'Alternativa, Barcelona; Istanbul International Short Film Festival; Melbourne International Film Festival; Viennale, Vienna; International Film Festival Rotterdam; Humboldt International Filmfestival; Onion City Film Festival, Chicago; Telluride Film Festival; Cinematexas; Corona Cork Film Festival; CINANIMA, Espinho, Portugal; São Paulo International Film Festival; Muu Media Festival, Helsinki; Tate Gallery of Modern Art, London; International Animation Festival Hiroshima; Austrian Film Museum, Vienna; Ann Arbor Film Festival; Central Florida Film and Video Festival, Orlando; Denver Film Festival; Cinematheque, San Francisco; LA Freewaves, Los Angeles; Berlinale, Berlin; 2nd Bangkok Experimental Film Festival, Museum of Fine Art, Chiang Mai, Thailand; Asian Art, Hong Kong; Imperialkino, Vienna; Crossing Europe Filmfestival, Linz; La Enena Marron, Madrid, Viper Film and Video Festival, Basel; Animafest Zagreb animation film festival; Pittsburgh Filmmakers; Moderna Muset, Stockholm; Austrian Cultural Forum New York, etc.

Filmography
2011 36 Views 2009 Camping Cezanne
2008 Vanishing Room, Cervinara
2007 notes on the economy of art
2006 romance, TAU II 2005 Weltraum-
brüder, Flow 2004 Chew, Paradiesvögel,
Alferjewo 2003 War, Studio, O.T. 10, SOL,
2000 Walk II, 1999 Walk 1998 Schwenk
1997 Zócalo, Halle II 1993 Ikonostasis II
1990–1992 Ikonostasis 1990–1994 O.T.
(9 films) 1989 Ballett 1, Ballett 2
Bibliography (selection)
Books and Catalogues: Steiner, Thomas,
ed. *Video/Bilder. 2001–2006*. [German]
Weitra, Austria: Bibliothek der Provinz,
2007. Book and DVD. → Steiner, Thomas,
ed. *Film / Bilder / Bilder / Film*. [German]
Linz, 2000. Book and DVD.
Articles, Interviews and Essays:
Dewald, Christian, Sabine Groschup,
Mara Mattuschka and Thomas Renoldner,
eds. *Die Kunst des Einzelbilds. Animation
in Österreich – 1832 bis heute*. [German]
Vienna: verlag filmarchiv austria, 2010.
→ Korschil, Thomas. "Konterbande.
Über einige neue kurze und längere
Filme aus Österreich." [German] *Meteor*,
special issue (1998).

KURT STEINWENDNER
Born in Vienna in 1920. 1942–1943 Studied
Painting at Vienna's Academy of Fine Arts.
1943–1945 Military service. 1945–1949
Master classes in Painting under Albert
Paris von Gütersloh, and in Sculpture
under Fritz Wotruba. 1946 Founding
member of the Art Club. Researched the
reproducibility of movement in art. 1948
Theater Studies. Attended lectures in Film
Studies. 1949–1950 Press photographer,
apprentice film editor, set painter and
set designer. With the expressionistic
short film *Der Rabe* (1951), based on the
poem "The Raven" by Edgar Allan Poe,
Steinwendner created the first independent art film in Austria, breaking formal
ground and paving the way for the avant-
garde tradition soon to follow. 1951
Der Rabe won awards at film festivals in
Venice and Edinburgh. 1952 Theatrical
release of his debut feature film, *Wienerinnen* [Viennese Women]. 1955 His ballet
film, *Gigant und Mädchen* [Giant and Girl]
was invited to screen at the Venice film
festival. 1957 Married Burgtheater actress
Antonia Mittrowsky, who became his
most important collaborator and actress.
Founded Kurt-Steinwendner-Filmproduk-
tion, which produced more than 60 educational and industrial films. 1962 Received
Berlinale's Silver Bear for his experimental
city portrait *Venedig* [Venice] (1962).
Started making object art. 1966 Participated at the XXXIII Biennale, Venice.
1969 Changed name to Curt Stenvert.
1971 Began working with bio-cybernetic
painting. 1977 Moved to Germany. 1983

Established a studio hall as a production
and exhibition space in Cologne.
Attained international renown as an artist.
Kurt Steinwendner died in 1992.
Filmography (selection)
1977 Vorstoss ins Niemandsland – Auf
der Suche nach der neuen Humanitas
1961 Venedig 1959 Auf allen Strassen
1955 Gigant und Mädchen 1953 Flucht ins
Schilf, Die fünf Karnickel 1952 Wienerin-
nen 1951 Der Rabe
Commissioned Works: 1964 Situation 1964
– Ein Film über Franz Schubert, VÖEST –
Das Werk an der Donau 1962 Glückliches
Österreich 1959 Die Kugel und der Mensch
1958 Impressionisten, Fast zwei Poeten,
Das Geld liegt auf der Straße 1957 Land
im Schatten, Was wäre ohne..?!, Der
Amerikaner 1956 Die Straßenbahndebatte
1955 Alfred Kubin – Abenteuer einer
Zeichenfeder 1953 Freiheit für den
Menschen
Bibliography (selection)
Books and Catalogues: Maurer, Lukas, ed.
Taschenkino #6: Kurt Steinwendner.
Vienna: verlag filmarchiv austria, 2011.
Book and DVD.

STEFAN STRATIL
Born in Vienna in 1963. At a time of vast
sociocultural change, Stefan Stratil was
determined to engage in a rather versatile
artistic career right from the beginning.
He takes his inspiration and themes from
the most diverse areas of life – including
the martial arts discipline of judo, in
which he became Austrian champion
following periods of training in Japan.
Frequent stays in Brazil have likewise
made a strong contribution to his personal development. His cultural coming of
age took place during the early 1980s, in
an environment characterized by punk,
new wave and the new "ligne claire"
drawing style of the up-and-coming
French comic book scene. It was during
his art studies with Maria Lassnig that
he made the leap from the two-dimensio-
nality of painting into the world of moving
pictures, experimenting with various
animated film techniques. The evenhan-
ded employment of music and a film's
actual soundtrack has often played a
determining thematic role in his films,
as is the case in the animated, Frank
Sinatra-inspired biopic *I'm a Star!* Stratil
is a successful draughtsman, illustrator
and comic book author. His print and film
works for the advertising industry have
won prizes, including the Global Award
in New York and several Golden Venuses
from the Art Directors Club of Austria.
A number of music videos and short
films round out his filmic oeuvre to date.
Stratil's short films, such as *The Man
with Modern Nerves* and *I'm a Star!*, were
screened at film festivals such as Cannes,

Rotterdam, Berlin and Clermont-Ferrand.
Stratil is working on an animated
feature-length film, heads the animated
film association ASIFA Austria, and works
as a curator at quartier21 in Vienna's
MuseumsQuartier.
Filmography (selection)
2002 I'm a Star! 2001 Spacy (commercial)
1992 Sad Mood (commercial) Vivus Fune-
ratus 1989 Der Magen und der Darm (commercial), The Man with Modern Nerves
(with Bady Minck) 1986–1994 The secret
of the grey cells 1986 Tichy (commercial)
Bibliography (selection)
Articles, Interviews and Essays: Höller,
Christian. "Song, Improvisation, Sampling.
Formen musikbezogener Bild-animation."
[German] In *Die Kunst des Einzelbilds.
Animation in Österreich – 1832 bis heute*,
edited by Christian Dewald, Sabine
Groschup, Mara Mattuschka and Thomas
Renoldner. Vienna: verlag filmarchiv
austria, 2010. → Steinlechner, Gisela. "Der
Puls der Bilder. Poetiken und Erzählstra-
tegien im österreichischen Animations-
film." [German] In *Die Kunst des Einzelbilds*. Vienna: verlag filmarchiv austria,
2010. → Ulver, Stanislav. "Testy a resty
rakouského avantgardního filmu." [Czech]
Film a doba (April 2005). → Jessen, Taylor.
"Fresh from the Festivals: December
2003's Film Reviews." [English] *Animation
World Magazine,* December 15, 2003,
http://mag.awn.com/index.php?ltype=
pageone&article_no=1949&page=2.
→ Ivanceanu, Alexander. "L'Homme aux
nerfs modernes." [French] In *L'art du
mouvement – collection cinématographique du Musée national d'art moderne,
1919–1996*, edited by Jean-Michel Bou-
hours. Paris: Centre Pompidou, 1996.
→ Bouhours, Jean-Michel. "La caméra
expérimente la ville." [French] In *Visions
urbaines*, edited by Centre Pompidou.
Paris, 1994. → Ivanceanu, Alexander.
"Moderne Menschen mit modernen
Nerven." [German] *Die Presse* (Vienna),
May 30/31, 1992. → Savasci, Özlem.
"Der Mensch mit den modernen Nerven.
Interview with Bady Minck." [Turkish]
Hürriyet Gösteriy (Istanbul), April, 2, 1991.
→ Illetschko, Peter. "In Österreich sind wir
vater- und mutterlos – sie sind die Zu-
kunft des österreichischen Films. Portrait
Bady Minck & Stefan Stratil." [German]
Der Standard (Vienna), April 20, 1989.

DANIEL ŠULJIĆ
Born in Zagreb, Croatia, in 1971. Animation
film artist and musician. Since 1992 lives
in Vienna. Began studying at Academy of
Fine Arts in Zagreb, and from 1992 to 1998
studied Painting and Animation at the
University of Applied Arts in Vienna under
Christian Ludwig Attersee. Makes animation, music, illustrations and sound design, works as a DJ. 2005–2008 Lecturer

for Classical Animation at the Institut for Mediendesign, Timebased Media Department at the University of Artistic and Industrial Design, Linz. Since March 2009 lecturer for Animation at the Academy of Fine Arts, Zagreb. Since 2010 artistic consultant for animated film at Croatian Audiovisual Centre. 2011 Artistic director of Zagreb's world festival of animated films, AnimaFest. His films have been shown at numerous (animation) film festivals, earning 20 awards to date. www.danielsuljic.com
Filmography (selection)
2011 In Chains 2007 Short Life (with Johanna Freise) 2003 I Can Imagine It Very Well 2000 A Film With a Girl 1997 The Cake 1997 Sun, Salt and Sea 1996 Highway 59 1995   Leckdonalds 1994 Walzer 1993 Evening Star
Bibliography (selection)
Articles, Interviews and Essays:
Dewald, Christian, Sabine Groschup, Mara Mattuschka and Thomas Renoldner, eds. *Die Kunst des Einzelbilds. Animation in Österreich – 1832 bis heute.* [German] Vienna: verlag filmarchiv austria, 2010.

NANA SWICZINSKY
Born in Vienna in 1969. 1985–1989 Trained as graphic designer at Vienna Graphic Art College. Numerous screenings and awards worldwide. 1989–1991 Courtroom sketch artist for daily newspaper *Arbeiterzeitung.* 1989–1996 Studied Animation Film and Painting at the Academy of Applied Arts in Vienna. Since 1991 illustrator. 1993–1994 Studied at the Institut St-Luc in Brussels, Comics Department. 1996 Degree. Since 1996 filmmaker and animation artist. 1996–1999 Postgraduate study at the Kunsthochschule für Medien Köln, Television and Film Department. Since 1996 teaches at various Austrian universities and universities of applied sciences. Since 1998 storyboard artist. 2009 Founded illuskills – die illustrationsausbildung.
Filmography
2008 Lezzieflick 2005 Vanishing Points 1999 Screen Opener Fudge (Diagonale 99 trailer) 1998 Points of View 1997 Wieder Holung 1994 Aids Affects Us All (with Gert Tschuden) 1993 Käpt'n Knödl im Dreck (with Georg Dienz and Pepi Öttl) 1992 Trailer (for Mörderinnen Filmfestival) 1991 Bio-Grafics 1990 That To You, Das ungehobelte Pack
Bibliography (selection)
Articles, Interviews and Essays:
Dewald, Christian, Sabine Groschup, Mara Mattuschka and Thomas Renoldner, eds. *Die Kunst des Einzelbilds. Animation in Österreich – 1832 bis heute.* [German] → Öhner, Vrääth, "Entscheidende Differenzen. Nana Swiczinskys *Wieder Holung.*" [German] *Meteor* (1998).

PETER TSCHERKASSKY
Born in Vienna in 1958. 1977–1979 Studied journalism and political science at University of Vienna. 1979 Moved to Berlin, studied philosophy at Freie Universität Berlin and started making Super 8 films. 1984 Return to Vienna. Continued studying philosophy at University of Vienna. 1986 PhD: "Film and Art – Towards a Critical Aesthetic of Cinematography." Since 1984 has authored numerous essays on avant-garde film. Started teaching in 1988. 1990 Co-founder of sixpackfilm. Organized several film festivals and curated countless film programs. 1995 Co-editor (with Gabriele Jutz) of the monograph *Peter Kubelka* (Vienna: PVS Verleger). As of 1997 established dark room studio called Manufraktur and produced his CinemaScope trilogy (1997–2001). 2005 *Instructions for A Light And Sound Machine* premiered at the Cannes Film Festival and the bilingual (English/German) monograph *Peter Tscherkassky* was published, edited by Alexander Horwath and Michael Loebenstein. As of 2006 has produced light-box installations that have been exhibited throughout the world, including a one-person show at the renowned Gallery nächst St. Stephan/Rosemarie Schwarzwaelder. 2007 documenta XII (film program), Kassel, Germany. 2008 Lecture and world premiere of the original 35 mm version of *Parallel Space: Inter-View* (1992) at the Louvre in Paris. 2010 World premiere of *Coming Attractions* at the 67th Venice Film Festival. To date more than 50 awards, including Golden Gate Award (San Francisco), Main Prize at Oberhausen, Germany, and Best Short Film at the Venice Film Festival. www.tscherkassky.at
Filmography (selection)
2010 Coming Attractions 2006 Nachtstück (Nocturne) 2005 Instructions for a Light and Sound Machine 2001 Dream Work 1999 Get Ready (Viennale '99 trailer), Outer Space 1997/1998 L'Arrivée 1996 Happy-End 1992 Parallel Space: Inter-View 1987/1989 tabula rasa 1987 Shot-Countershot 1986 kelimba 1985 Manufraktur 1984 Motion Picture (La Sortie des Ouvriers de l'Usine Lumière à Lyon), Ballett 16 1983 Miniaturen – viele Berliner Künstler in Hoisdorf, Freeze Frame, Urlaubsfilm 1982 Liebesfilm, Erotique 1981 Aderlass, Rauchopfer 1980 Portrait 1979/1980 Kreuzritter
Bibliography (selection)
Books and Catalogues: From a Dark Room. The Manufactured Cinema of Peter Tscherkassky. [English/Spanish] Edited by Maximiliano Cruz and Sandra Gómez. Mexico City: Interior 13, 2012. → Dorner, Patrick. *Die Charakteristika des Avantgarde- und Experimentalfilms in Österreich: Die Arbeit des Filmemachers und Filmwis-*

senschafters Peter Tscherkassky. [German] Munich: Grien Verlag, 2011. → *Peter Tscherkassky.* [English/German] Edited by Alexander Horwath and Michael Loebenstein. Vienna: FilmmuseumSynemaPublikationen, 2005. → *Peter Tscherkassky – CinemaScope Trilogy & Miniaturen.* [English/French] VHS-booklet, edited by Nicole Brenez. Paris: re:voir, 2004. → Faucon, Térésa. "*Outer Space* de Peter Tscherkassky." [French] In *Lycéens au cinéma en région Centre,* edited by Serge Caillet. Orléans, France: Livret pédagogique enseignants – Edition APCVL, 2003. DVD booklet. → *Peter Tscherkassky.* [Chinese] Edited by Chin Thom. Guangzhou: Knife Fucktory Matters, 2002.
Articles, Interviews and Essays: Gunning, Tom. "Peter Tscherkassky Manufactures Two Minutes of (Im)Pure Cinema." [English/Spanish] In *From a Dark Room. The Manufactured Cinema of Peter Tscherkassky,* edited by Maximiliano Cruz and Sandra Gómez. Mexico City: Interior 13, 2012. → Woels, Michael-Franz. "This is not film, this is not cinema!" [German] *FAQ,* no. 15, December 2011. → Kamalzadeh, Dominik. "Das Zucken der Blitze zur Abenddämmerung. Peter Tscherkasskys Filme." [German] *Der Standard* (Vienna), March 2011. Diagonale special edition. → Bachmann, Alejandro. "Man erkennt einen Tscherkassky innerhalb weniger Kader." [German] *Diagonale,* film festival periodical (Graz), 2011. → Nüchtern, Klaus, and Michael Omasta. "Ich möchte etwas machen, was so schön ist wie ein Ton von Miles Davis!" [German] *Falter,* no. 11 (March 2011), http://www.falter.at/web/print/detail.php?id=1355. Interview. → Von Reden, Sven. "Berauschend sinnliche Qualität." [German] *taz* (Berlin), March 29, 2011. → Reicher, Isabella. "Kopf des Tages: Peter Tscherkassky, Filmavantgardist mit ausgeprägtem Geschmackssinn." [German] *Der Standard* (Vienna), September 13, 2010. → Loebenstein, Michael. "Die Leidenschaft des Historiographen. Über Peter Tscherkasskys *Coming Attractions.*" [German] *kolik.film,* no. 14 (October 2010). Also in *From a Dark Room. The Manufactured Cinema of Peter Tscherkassky.* [English/Spanish] Edited by Maximiliano Cruz & Sandra Gómez. Mexico City: Interior 13, 2012. → Grissemann, Stefan. "Flimmern im Negativland. Peter Tscherkassky in Venedig." [German] *profil,* no. 36 (September 2010). → Jutz, Gabriele. "Gegen die Verleugnungsversuche des Tatsächlichen. Man Rays *Le Retour à la raison* (1923), Marcel Duchamps *Anémic Cinéma* (1926), Peter Tscherkasskys *Dream Work* (2001)." [German] In *Cinéma brut. Eine alternative Genealogie der Filmavantgarde,* edited by Gabriele Jutz. Vienna and New York: Springer Verlag, 2010. → Blümlinger, Christa. "Lumières Nachleben (Al Razutis

HERBERT VESELY

Born in Vienna in 1931. Studied Theatre and Art History at the University of Vienna. 1951 Studied Film at the Academy of Performing Arts, Vienna, under Walter Kolm-Veltée. Took acting classes and got involved in theater productions. 1952 During an extensive screening tour of German film clubs with his second short *An diesen Abenden* he met the producer Hans Abich who raised the money for his first feature *nicht mehr fliehen* (1955). 1957 Together with Harald Braun and Haro Senft founded the company filmform in Munich and produced several low-budget films by young filmmakers. He was one of the signatories of the Oberhausen Manifest in 1962 together with 25 other young German film directors. Shortly after this significant act, his film *Das Brot der frühen Jahre* (based on the novel by Heinrich Böll) premiered at the Cannes Film Festival in 1962 and initiated the Young German Cinema movement. Thereafter mainly worked for German TV stations and made numerous fiction films, documentaries, TV series, ballet and music films, feuilletons, etc. In 1980 he directed a film about Egon Schiele, his first film made in Austria since 1952. Herbert Vesely died in Munich in 2002.

Filmography (selection)

1966 Im Wartesaal zum grossen Glück, Der grüne Salon 1963 Sie fanden ihren Weg 1961/1962 Das Brot der frühen Jahre 1960 Düsseldorf – Modisch, heiter, im Wind verspielt 1959/1960 Die Stadt 1958 Ein Wochenende 1957 Autobahn 1956/1957 Prélude – Portrait einer Pause 1955 nicht mehr fliehen 1952 An diesen Abenden 1951 Und die Kinder spielen so gerne Soldaten
Bibliography (selection)
Articles, Interviews and Essays: Scheugl, Hans. "Der Film der frühen Jahre. Herbert Vesely und der neue deutsche Film." [German] In *Viennale*, film festival catalogue. Vienna, 2006. → Büttner, Elisabeth, and Christian Dewald. *Anschluß an Morgen. Eine Geschichte des österreichischen Films von 1945 bis zur Gegenwart.* [German] Salzburg and Vienna: Residenz-Verlag, 1997. → Jung, Fernand. "Von der Verfilmung zum wirklichen Film." [German] In *Avantgardefilm Österreich. 1950 bis heute*, edited by Alexander Horwath, Lisl Ponger and Gottfried Schlemmer. Vienna: Verlag Wespennest, 1995. → Fuhrmann, Susanne, and Heinrich Lewinski. "Poesie ist das, was bleibt. Der Filmregisseur Herbert Vesely." [German] *filmwärts*, no. 27 (1993). → Jung, Fernand. "Das Kino der frühen Jahre. Herbert Vesely und die Filmavantgarde der Bundesrepublik." [German] In *Zwischen Gestern und Morgen. Westdeutscher Nachkriegsfilm 1946 – 1962*, edited by Hilmar Hoffmann und Walter Schobert. Frankfurt am Main: deutsches filmmuseum, 1989. → Schmidt Jr., Ernst. *Österreichischer Avantgarde- und Undergroundfilm 1950–1980.* [German] Vienna: Österreichisches Filmarchiv, 1980. → Scheugl, Hans, and Ernst Schmidt Jr. *Eine Subgeschichte des Films. Lexikon des Avantgarde-, Experimental- und Undergroundfilms.* [German] Frankfurt am Main: edition suhrkamp, 1974. → Rohrbach, Günter. "*Das Brot der frühen Jahre*." [German] *Filmkritik*, no. 6 (1962). → Ungureit, Heinz. "Veselys Versuch mit Böll." [German] *Frankfurter Rundschau* (Frankfurt am Main), May 21, 1962. → "Existentialismus. In der Zone Null." [German] *Der Spiegel* (Hamburg), July 13, 1955. → Hanres, Jacobi. "*An diesen Abenden*. Ein Trakl-Film eines Wiener Avantgardisten." [German] *Neue Zürcher Zeitung* (Zurich), January 11, 1953. → Patalas, Enno. "Filmischer Totentanz. *An diesen Abenden*, Experiment – oder mehr?" [German] *Filmforum* (1953).

PETER WEIBEL

Born in Odessa in 1944. Studied Literature, Medicine, Logic, Philosophy and Film in Paris and Vienna. He became a central figure in European media art due to his various activities as artist, media theorist and curator. Since 1984 Professor at the University of Applied Arts, Vienna, from 1984 to 1989 head of the digital arts laboratory at the Media Department of New York University in Buffalo. 1989 Founded the Institute of New Media at the Academy of Fine Arts, Städelschule, Frankfurt am Main, which he directed until 1995. Between 1986 and 1995 in charge of the Ars Electronica in Linz, and commissioned the Austrian pavilions at the Venice Biennale from 1993 to 1999. From 1993 to 1998 chief curator at the Neue Galerie Graz, Austria, and since 1999 Chairman and CEO of the ZKM | Center for Art and Media, Karlsruhe. 2002 Großes Ehrenzeichen für Verdienste um die Republik Österreich, 2007 Honorary Doctorate by the University of Art and Design Helsinki, 2008 French order Officier dans l'Ordre des Arts et des Lettres (Order of Arts and Literature). 2008 Artistic Director of the Biennial of Sevilla (Biacs3). 2009 Friedlieb Ferdinand Runge-Preis für unkonventionelle Kunstvermittlung of Stiftung Preußische Seehandlung, the Verdienstmedaille des Landes Baden-Wuerttemberg and the Europäische Kultur-Projektpreis of the Europan Foundation for Culture. 2009 Full member of the Bavarian Academy of Fine Arts Munich. From 2009 to 2012 Visiting Professor at the University of New South Wales, Sydney, Australia. 2010 Österreichisches Ehrenkreuz für Wissenschaft und Kunst 1. Klasse. 2011 Artistic Director of the Fourth Moscow Biennial of Contemporary Art.

Filmography and TV Works (selection)
1988 Stimmen aus dem Innenraum (with Susanne Widl) 1987 Clip, Klapp, Bum. Von der virtuellen Musik zum Musikvideo 1986 Kurt Gödel – ein mathematischer Mythos (ORF) 1984 Die Landschaft des 21. Jahrhunderts 1983 Casablanca I und II 1975 Videotexte (Video Texts)1973–1975 Zum Theorem der Identität (On the Theorem of Identity) 1971–1975 Körperwerke (Bodyworks) 1968–1975 Wor(l)d Cinema. Ein Sprachfest (with Valie Export) 1974 Komxxikxxxxx (ORF) 1967–1974 radio plays and video texts 1973 Lichtseil (expanded cinema) 1969–1972 VT and TV works 1971 Kino, Prä- und Parakino (text-film action with plotting projector) 1967–1972 text Actions – Action texts 1970 Manirieren (with Otto Muehl) 1969 Prozeß als Produkt (Process as Product) 1966–1968 Gut und Gerne (expanded cinema) 1966/1967 Nivea (expanded cinema) 1965/1966 Welcome
Bibliography (selection)
Publications by Peter Weibel: Vasulka, Woody, and Peter Weibel, eds. *Buffalo Heads. Media Study, Media Practice, Media Pioneers, 1973–1990.* [English] Cambridge, MA: MIT Press, 2008. → "Marc Adrian. Vater der österreichischen Medienkunst." [German/English] In *marc adrian*, edited by Anna Artaker and Peter Weibel. Graz and Klagenfurt: Ritter Verlag, 2007. → "Seeing Sound. Synästhetiken, Synchronien und Synchromien." [German] In *Zapping Zone*, edited by Gerhard Johann Lischka. Bern and Zurich: Benteli, 2007. → Weibel, Peter, ed. *Jenseits von Kunst.* [German] Vienna: Passagen Verlag, 1997. → Weibel, Peter, ed. *Inklusion, Exklusion: Versuch einer neuen Kartografie der Kunst im Zeitalter von Postkolonialismus und globaler Migration.* [German] Graz and Cologne: steirischer herbst, DuMont, 1997. → "Warum der Wiener Film so gut ist – zum geflissentlichen geleit. (1970)." [German] In *Avantgardefilm Österreich. 1950 bis heute*, edited by Alexander Horwath, Lisl Ponger and Gottfried Schlemmer. Vienna: Verlag Wespennest, 1995. → Weibel, Peter, and Veruschka Bódy, eds. *Clip, Klapp, Bum. Von der visuellen Musik zum Musikvideo.* [German] Cologne: DuMont, 1991. → Rötzer, Florian, and Peter Weibel, eds. *Strategien des Scheins. Kunst, Computer, Medien.* [German] Munich: Boer Verlag, 1991. → "Der Wiener Formalfilm." [German/French] In *Weltpunkt Wien. Un regard sur Vienne: 1985*, edited by Robert Fleck. Vienna and Munich: Löcker Verlag, 1985. → Weibel, Peter, and Valie Export, eds. *bildkompendium wiener aktionismus und film.* [German] Frankfurt am Main: Kohlkunstverlag, 1970.
Books and Catalogues: Buol-Wischenau, Karin, and Christa Steinle, eds. *Peter Weibel. das offene werk 1964–1979.* [German/English] Ostfildern, Germany: Hatje Cantz Verlag, 2006. → Kolleritsch, Alfred, and Christa Steinle, eds. *Peter Weibel. X-Dream.* [German] Graz: Literaturverlag Droschl, 2004. → Meusburger, Wilhelm, ed. *B–Picture. Ein Film über Peter Weibel von Markus Huemer, nach einem Treatment von Peter Weibel.* [English] Frankfurt am Main: Revolver, 2004. → Schuler, Romana, ed. *Peter Weibel. Bildwelten 1982–1996.* [German] Vienna: Triton Verlag, 1996.
Articles, Interviews and Essays: López, Raúl Molín. "BIACS3: Interview with Peter Weibel." [English] *artfacts.net*, December 23 (2008), http://www.artfacts.net/index.php/pageType/newsInfo/newsID/4558/lang/1. → Schuler, Romana. "Peter Weibel – Die Wiederkehr des Verdrängten." [German] *Peter Weibel*, June, 11, 2011, http://www.peter-weibel.at/index.php?option=com_content&view=article&id=118&catid=9&Itemid=7. → Böckem, Jörg. "Der Künstler und Kurator Peter Weibel, 65. Über Streber, Sport und eine Uni-Ferkelei." [German] *KulturSpiegel*, no. 5 (2009). → Kapfer, Herbert, and Margit Rosen, eds. *der künstler als junger hund. peter weibel tribute album.* Munich: Bayerischer Rundfunk, intermedium records,

2009. Three CDs and booklet. → Böckem, Jörg. *Mit 17 hat man noch Träume.* [German] Munich: dtv Verlag, 2006. *DVD Editions: Peter Weibel – Mediapoet.* Sulgen, Switzerland: Benteli, 2011. → *Peter Weibel. Depiction is a Crime. Video Works 1969–1975.* Vienna: Index DVD Edition 024, 2008.

VIRGIL WIDRICH
Born in Salzburg in 1967. Has worked on numerous films and multimedia productions. His first feature film *Heller als der Mond* (*Brighter than the Moon*, 2000) received several awards. His short film *Copy Shop* won 35 prizes and was nominated for an Academy Award. His animated short *Fast Film* won 36 awards and was shown at 285 festivals. In 2006 it was included in the list of the 100 most important short animation films of the past 100 years by 30 leading film critics at the Annecy Animation Festival. From 2001 to 2007 partner in Amour Fou film production company in Vienna and from 2004 to 2007 chairman of the Austrian Film Directors' Association. Co-founder and CEO of checkpointmedia AG in Vienna. Has taught and given guest lectures at Vienna Graphic Art College, the Danube University in Krems, the institutes of higher education in Salzburg, Hagenberg and Graz, the SAE institutes in Vienna and Munich, the Medialab at the Technical University in Munich, the ISPA Philosophicum in Vienna and many more. 2007–2009 Professor of digital art at the University of Applied Arts in Vienna and since 2009 Professor for the department Art & Science at the same institution. www.widrichfilm.com
Filmography
2003 Fast Film 2001 Copy Shop, linksrechts 2000 Heller als der Mond (Brighter than the Moon) 1998 tx-transform (with Martin Reinhart) 1983–1985 Vom Geist der Zeit (feature) 1982 Monster in Salzburg 1981 Auch Farbe kann träumen (animated short) 1980 My Homelife, Gebratenes Fleisch, Drei Mal Ulf
Bibliography (selection)
Articles, Interviews and Essays: Museum Tinguely, ed. *Fetisch Auto. Ich fahre, also bin ich.* [German] Basel, Heidelberg and Berlin: Kehrer Verlag, 2011. → Schafer, Mirko Tobias. *Bastard Culture! How User Participation Transforms Cultural Production.* [English] Amsterdam: Amsterdam University Press, 2011. → Museum Tinguely, ed. *Roboterträume.* [German] Basel, Heidelberg and Berlin: Kehrer Verlag, 2010. → Dewald, Christian, Sabine Groschup, Mara Mattuschka and Thomas Renoldner, eds. *Die Kunst des Einzelbilds. Animation in Österreich – 1832 bis heute.* [German] Vienna: verlag filmarchiv austria, 2010. → Unterberger-Probst, Carola.

Der Filmische Hypertext: Links im Film– Film als Link. [German] Munich: Grin Verlag, 2009. → Halle, Randall, and Reinhild Steingröver, eds. *After the Avant- Garde: Contemporary German and Austri- an Experimental Film.* [English] Rochester, NY: Camden House, 2008. → Furniss, Maureen. *The Animation Bible: A Guide to Everything – from Flipbooks to Flash.* [English] London: Laurence King, 2008. → Nelmes, Jill. *An Introduction to Film Studies.* [English] New York: Routledge, 2007. → Rasche, Hermann, and Christiane Schönfeld. *Processes of Transposition. German Literature and Film.* [English] Amsterdam: Editions Rodopi, 2007. → Wells, Paul. *Basics Animation: Script- writing.* [English] Lausanne: Ava Publis- hing, 2007. → Dorschel, Andreas, and Institut für Wertungsforschung, Akademie für Musik und Darstellende Kunst in Graz, eds. *Tonspuren: Musik im Film: Fallstudien 1994–2001.* [German] Vienna: Universal Edition, 2005. → Pauker, Manfred, and Dominik Orieschnig. *Rollenspiele. Öster- reichische Filmkünstler im Portrait.* [German] Raaba bei Graz, Austria: Cm Medienverlag, 2005. → Bär, Gerald. *Das Motiv des Doppelgängers als Spaltungs- phantasie in der Literatur und im deutschen Stummfilm.* [German] Amsterdam: Editi- ons Rodopi, 2005. → Buchan, Suzanne, and Andres Janser. *Trickraum – Space- tricks.* [German/English] Hamburg: Merian, 2005. → Rihl, Gerhard. *Science / Culture: Multimedia.* [German] Vienna: facultas. wuv Universitätsverlag, 2007. → Shaw, Jeffrey, and Peter Weibel, eds. *Future Cinema. The Cinematic Imaginary After Film.* [English] Cambridge, MA: MIT Press, 2003. → Brouwer, Joke, and Arjen Mulder, eds. *Machine Times.* [English] Rotterdam: NAi Publishers, 2001.

GÜNTER ZEHETNER
Born in Wels, Austria, in 1965. Filmmaker and curator. Based in Frankfurt am Main since completing his studies under Peter Kubelka at the Academy of Fine Arts Städelschule in 1992. Since 1993 Zehetner has organized and presented numerous film screenings, lectures and exhibitions, mainly in Europe and the US. In 1998 a large part of his Super 8 work was sold to the permanent collection of the Austrian Film Museum, Vienna. In 1996 he began the project Gefundene Filme (Found Films), thoughtfully constelling pro- grams based on amateur films, giving them voice without editorial interference. Since 2011 has composed ten different film programs along these lines. In 2001 completed his first 16 mm film *Meine Verehrung* (My Adoration) which to this day remains singular in Zehetner's work – all his other films are edited entirely in camera. 2003 Began shooting with DV

formats, culminating in 2009 with the shortest works of his oeuvre, with running lengths of approximately 5 to 8 seconds. In 2009 the Austrian Film Museum in Vienna included a program of Super 8 films by Zehetner as part of its ongoing screening series, the cyclical program What Is Film. In 2010 Günter Zehetner started to work on an adaptation of Alfred Döblin's *Berlin Alexanderplatz* under the title *Franz Biberkopf*.
Filmography (selection)
2009 Es bleibt genauso wie das jetzt ist (It Stays Like It Is Now), Machen sie was immer sie wollen (Do Whatever You Want), Okay, Gifted Daylight, Wo ist meine Tasche? (Where Is My Bag?), Is schön; ne? (It Is Beautiful; Isn't It?), Yes, oooooo oohoo oooooo, Hi, Wwwhhhhhh 2006 I send you a love letter straight from my heart fucker You wan' know what a love letter is? It's a bullet from my fucking gun you fucker! 2005 Sometimes 2001 Meine Verehrung (My Adoration) 2000 Existenz I – immer nur lächeln und immer vergnügt (Existence I – always smiling and always amused) 1998 Maria 1997 Hin zum Besonderen (On The Way To The Extraordinariness), Die Zeit heilt alle Wunder (Time Heals All Wonder) 1996 Für Roy Black (Dedicated to Roy Black) 1995 Wir hätten gern eins (We Would Like To Have One), ...a blede Sau (...A Stupid Pig)
Bibliography (selection)
Articles, Interviews and Essays:
Grissemann, Stefan. "8 mm Films of Günter Zehetner." [German] In *Was ist Film. Peter Kubelkas Zyklisches Progamm im Österreichischen Filmmuseum*, edited by Stefan Grissemann, Alexander Horwath and Regina Schlagnitweit. Vienna: FilmmuseumSynemaPublikationen, 2010.

General Bibliography

Books and Catalogues (selection):
→ *Die Kunst des Einzelbilds. Animation in Österreich – 1832 bis heute.* [German] Edited by Christian Dewald, Sabine Groschup, Mara Mattuschka and Thomas Renoldner. Vienna: verlag film-archiv austria, 2010.
→ *Was ist Film. Peter Kubelkas Zyklisches Progamm im Österreichischen Filmmuseum,* edited by Stefan Grissemann, Alexander Horwath and Regina Schlagnitweit. Vienna: FilmmuseumSynemaPublikationen, 2010.
→ Jutz, Gabriele. *Cinéma brut. Eine alternative Genealogie der Filmavantgarde.* [German] Vienna: Springer Verlag, 2010.
→ Blümlinger, Christa. *Kino aus zweiter Hand. Zur Ästhetik materieller Aneignung im Film und in der Medienkunst.* [German] Berlin: vorwerk 8, 2009.
→ *Austrijska filmska avangarda.* [Croatian] Edited by Mirna Belina and Marina Kozul. Zagreb: 25fps Association, 2008.
→ *Abstracts of Syn.* [German/English] Edited by Sandro Droschl and Vitus H. Weh. Bolzano, Italy, and Vienna: Folio Verlag, Kunstverein Medienturm, 2007.
→ *Le cinéma autrichien.* [French] In *Austriaca. Cahiers universitaire d'information sur l'Autriche.* Edited by Christa Blümlinger. Mont-Saint-Aignan Cedex, France: Université de Rouen, 2007.
→ *Abstraction Now.* [German/English] Edited by Künstlerhaus Wien, Norbert Pfaffenbichler and Sandro Droschl. Vienna and Graz: Edition Camera Austria, 2004.
→ Tscherkassky, Peter. "The Greatest Story Never Told – 50 Jahre Filmavantgarde in Österreich." [German] In *Österreich 2005. Das Lesebuch zum Jubiläumsjahr,* edited by Bundeskanzleramt/Bundespressedienst Österreich. Salzburg: Residenz-Verlag, 2004.
→ *X-Screen. Filmische Installationen und Aktionen der Sechziger und Siebzigerjahre.* [English] Edited by Matthias Michalka. Vienna: Museum Moderner Kunst Stiftung Ludwig, 2003.
→ Scheugl, Hans. *Erweitertes Kino. Die Wiener Filme der 60er Jahre.* [German] Vienna: Triton Verlag, 2002.
→ Horwath, Alexander, and Peter Tscherkassky. *crossing the front lines. austrian independent film + video.* [German/English] Vienna: sixpackfilm, 2001.
→ *Re-Play. Anfänge internationaler Medienkunst in Österreich.* [German/English] Edited by Sabine Breitwieser. Vienna: Generali Foundation, 2000.

→ Tscherkassky, Peter. "Ausztria." [Hungarian] In *álommásolatok – középeurópai filmavantgárd,* edited by Balázs Béla Studio. Budapest: Balázs Béla Studio, 1999.
→ *avant-garde films and videos from central europe.* [English] Edited by Peter Tscherkassky. Vienna: sixpackfilm, 1998.
→ *vanguarda cinema 1995–1997.* [Portuguese] Edited by Martin Arnold and Peter Tscherkassky. Rio de Janeiro: Centro Cultural Banco do Brasil, 1998.
→ Büttner, Elisabeth, and Christian Dewald. *Anschluß an Morgen. Eine Geschichte des österreichischen Films von 1945 bis zur Gegenwart.* [German] Salzburg and Vienna: Residenz-Verlag, 1997.
→ *avantgardecinema: Austria/Slowenia.* [Italian/English] Trieste: Alpe Adria Cinema, 1996.
→ *Cinéma expérimental autrichien.* [French] Edited by Martin Arnold and Peter Tscherkassky. Paris: Centre Pompidou, 1996.
→ *Avantgardefilm Österreich. 1950 bis heute.* [German] Edited by Alexander Horwath, Lisl Ponger and Gottfried Schlemmer. Vienna: Verlag Wespennest, 1995.
→ *Gegenschuss. 16 Regisseure aus Österreich.* [German] Edited by Peter Illetschko. Vienna: Verlag Wespennest, 1995.
→ *Austrian Avant-Garde Cinema 1955–1993.* [English] Edited by Martin Arnold and Peter Tscherkassky. Vienna: sixpackfilm, 1994.
→ *En el frente de las imagenes – Cine de Vanguardia en Austria.* [Spanish] Edited by Peter Tscherkassky. Vienna: sixpackfilm, 1993.
→ Tscherkassky, Peter. "morgenlicht." [German] In *morgenlicht. Österreichischer Avantgardefilm von Kubelka bis heute,* edited by Sixpack Film. Vienna: Sixpack Film, 1993.
→ Drechsler, Wolfgang, and Peter Weibel. *Bildlicht. Malerei zwischen Material und Immaterialität.* [German] Vienna: Museum of the 20th Century, 1991.
→ *The Middle of Europe. The festival of avant-garde films and video art from Austria, Czecho-Slovakia, Hungary and Poland.* [English] Edited by Ryszard W. Kluszczynski. Warsaw: Centre of Contemporary Art, Ujadowski Castle, 1991.
→ *Das Licht der Peripherie. Österreichische Avantgarde-Filme 1957–1988.* [German] Edited by Peter Tscherkassky. Vienna: Museum of the 20th Century, 1988.
→ *Wiener Aktionismus. Wien 1960–1971/ Viennese Actionism. Vienna 1960–1971.* 2 Volumes. [German/English] Edited by Hubert Klocker. Klagenfurt: Ritter Verlag, 1988.
→ *Die Schatten im Silber. Österreichische Avantgarde-Filme 1976-1987.* [German]

Edited by Lisl Ponger. Vienna: Museum of the 20th Century, 1987.
→ *Aria di Vienna.* [Italian] Edited by Annamaria Percavassi and Leonardo Quaresima. Florence: 1986.
→ *Frauen und Film und Video Österreich.* [German] Edited by Claudia Preschl. Vienna: filmladen, 1986.
→ Bilek, Robert. "Der Wiener Undergroundfilm der 60er Jahre. Realitätsbezüge und kritische Funktion." [German] Master's thesis, Vienna, 1983.
→ Fleck, Robert. *Avantgarde in Wien. Die Geschichte der Galerie nächst St. Stephan Wien 1954–1982. Kunst und Kunstbetrieb in Österreich.* [German] Vienna: Löcker, 1982.
→ LeGrice, Malcolm. *Abstract Film and Beyond.* [English] Cambridge: MIT Press, 1977. Reprint 1982.
→ *Österreich zum Beispiel.* [German] Edited by Otto Breicha and Reinhard Urban. Salzburg: Residenz Verlag, 1982.
→ *Der Art Club in Österreich. Zeugnisse eines Aufbruchs.* [German] Edited by Otto Breicha. Vienna, 1981.
→ Schmidt Jr., Ernst. *Österreichischer Avantgarde- und Undergroundfilm 1950–1980.* [German] Vienna: Österreichisches Filmarchiv, 1980.
→ *Film als Film. 1910 bis heute. Vom Animationsfilm der zwanziger zum Filmenvironment der siebziger Jahre.* [German] Edited by Birgit Hein and Wulff Herzogenrath. Cologne: Kölnischer Kunstverein, 1977.
→ Dwoskin, Stephen. *Film Is... The International Free Cinema.* [English] Woodstock, NY: The Overlook Press, 1975.
→ Scheugl, Hans, and Ernst Schmidt Jr. *Eine Subgeschichte des Films. Lexikon des Avantgarde-, Experimental- und Undergroundfilms.* [German] Frankfurt am Main: edition suhrkamp, 1974.
→ Hein, Birgit. *Film im Underground. Von seinen Anfängen bis zum unabhängigen Kino.* [German] Frankfurt am Main, Berlin and Vienna: Ullstein, 1971.
→ *bildkompendium wiener aktionismus und film.* [German] Edited by Peter Weibel and Valie Export. Frankfurt am Main: Kohlkunstverlag, 1970.
→ Schmidt Jr., Ernst. „Das andere Kino. Ein Lexikon des neuen europäischen Films." [German] *Film 1968. Chronik und Bilanz des internationalen Films,* yearbook of the periodical *FILM.* Velber bei Hannover: Friedrich Verlag, 1968.

Articles and Essays (selection):
→ Reicher, Isabella. "Avantgardefilm startet Welttournee." [German] *Der Standard* (Vienna), February 21, 2012.
→ Grissemann, Stefan. "Planvoll verwischt. Zur Allgegenwart der Filmavantgarde

im österreichischen Kino." [German] *film-dienst*, no. 22 (2010).

→ Payne, Simon. "Vienna Report." [English] *sequence*, no. 1 (2010).

→ Barber, Stephen. "The Films Of The Vienna Action Group." [English] *Vertigo*, Autumn/Winter (2004).

→ Greuling, Matthias. "Filmkunst abseits des Spielfilms." [German] *Die Furche* (Vienna), March 4, 2004.

→ Rebhandl, Bert. "The Avant-Garde and Beyond. Omaggio alla Sixpack Film." [Italian/English] *40. Mostra Internazionale del Nuovo Cinema*, film festival catalogue. Pesaro, Italy, 2004.

→ Webber, Mark. "Counting the Waves: A Summary of Activity." [English] *senses of cinema*, http://www.sensesofcinema.com/2003/28/counting_the_waves.

→ Jutz, Gabriele. "Film als Kunst – Zur österreichischen Filmavantgarde." [German] *Geschichte der Bildenden Kunst in Österreich. Das 20. Jahrhundert*, edited by Wieland Schmid. Munich, London and New York: Prestl Verlag, 2002.

→ Pichler, Barbara. "Digitaler Augenschmaus. Austrian Abstracts III – computergenerierte Bild- und Tonwerke auf der Diagonale, Graz." [German] *telepolis*, March 31, 2001, http://www.telepolis.de/deutsch/inhalt/sa/7258/1.html.

→ Steinkellner, Eva. "Herumwüten auf der Leinwand." [German] *celluloid*, no. 1 (2001).

→ Korschil, Thomas. "Konterbande. Über einige neue kurze und längere Filme aus Österreich." [German] *Meteor* (1998). Diagonale special edition.

→ Sallmann, Bernhard. "Anmerkungen zum neuen österreichischen Filmschaffen." [German] *Filmforum*, no. 14 (1998).

→ Roth, Wilhelm. "Avantgarde aus Österreich." [German] *epd Film*, no. 7 (1997).

→ Tscherkassky, Peter. "Das Kreisen der Kader. Avantgardefilm in Österreich." [German] *neue bildende kunst – Zeitschrift für Kunst und Kritik* (Berlin), no. 5 (1997).

→ Tscherkassky, Peter. "Die österreichische Schule des Experimentalfilms." [German]. In *Kunst in Österreich*, edited by Robert Fleck and Noemi Smolik. Cologne: Kiepenheuer & Witsch, 1995.

→ Buchschwenter, Robert. "40 Jahre Filmgeschichte abseits des Silberwaldes." [German] *Die Presse* (Vienna), June 19, 1995.

→ Buchschwenter, Robert. "Die Brust in der Schachtel." [German] *Die Presse* (Vienna), July 22, 1995.

→ Reicher, Isabella. "Österreich ist frei. Ein Überblick. Heimspiel nach US-Tournee: Große Avantgarde-Kinoschau in Wien." [German] *Der Standard* (Vienna), June 19, 1995.

→ Tscherkassky, Peter. "hand made. Avantgardefilm in Österreich." [German] *media biz,* March 1995.

→ Wolff, Kurt. "Viennese Waltzes." [English] *The San Francisco Bay Guardian*, January 11–17, 1995.

→ Anker, Steve. "Getting Under the Skin." [English] *Austria Kultur* 4, no. 5. IX/X (1994). Introduction to *Austrian Avant-Garde Cinema, 1955–1993*.

→ Tscherkassky, Peter. "Geburtstag feiern in Amerika. Austrian Avant-Garde Cinema: 1954–1993." [German] *Filmfolder, no. 1* (1994).

→ Philipp, Claus. "Strahlende Peripherien des Kinos." [German] *Der Standard* (Vienna), March 12/13, 1994.

→ Scharres, Barbara. "Austrian Avant-Garde Cinema, 1955–1993." [English] *The Film Center Gazette* 22, no. 3 (1994).

→ Weixelbaumer, Robert. "Mama und Papa in Amerika." [German] *Die Presse* (Vienna), March 11, 1994.

→ Freitag, Barbara. "Das Experiment Film." [German] *Salto*, no. 49, 1992.

→ Tscherkassky, Peter. "Berührt, weitergeführt... – ein Blitzlicht auf Geschichte und Gegenwart des österreichischen Avantgardefilms." [German] In *Audiovisionen Österreich 1992*, edited by Christoph Nebel. Basel: Kunsthalle Basel, 1992.

→ Tscherkassky, Peter. "Filmavantgarde in Österreich." [Italian/German] In *Austria (In)Felix*, edited by Francesco Bono, Rome: Associazione Italiana Amici Cinema d'Essai, 1992.

→ Tscherkassky, Peter. "16mm und International: Das Format des österreichischen Experimentalfilms." [German] *Film+Video* (special edition "FILM, Vision – Realität"), no. III (1991).

→ Tscherkassky, Peter. "Nekoliko Imena, Nekoliko Podataka: Austrijski Avangardni Film." [Serbian] In *alternative Film-Video 90* (festival catalogue). Belgrade: AFV, 1990.

→ Tscherkassky, Peter. "avant-garde film." [English/Dutch] In *AVE – 5. International AudioVisual Experimentalfestival 1989* (festival catalogue). Arnhem: AVE, 1989.

→ Lehner, Wolfgang, and Bernhard Praschl. "Stellen Sie sich einen österreichischen Film vor! Zur Entwicklung der filmischen Avantgarde nach 1945." [German] *Medienkultur in Österreich. Film, Fotografie, Fernsehen und Video in der Zweiten Republik*, edited by Hans H. Fabris and Kurt Luger. Vienna, Cologne and Graz: Böhlau, 1988.

→ Schmidt Jr., Ernst. "Avantgarde- und Undergroundfilm sowie Expanded Cinema in Österreich: Theorie und Praxis einer extremen Kunst." [German] *Kinoschriften. Jahrbuch der Gesellschaft für Filmtheorie*, edited by Georg Haberl. Vienna: Synema, 1988.

→ Tscherkassky, Peter. "Alguns nomes, alguns factos." [Portuguese] In *Audiovisual Lisboa* (festival catalogue), edited by António Cunha. Lisbon: Audiovisual Lisboa, 1988.

→ Tscherkassky, Peter. "überBlick – Eine Retrospektive auf die Zukunft der Avantgarde." [German] *Filmlogbuch* 10 (Vienna), special edition "Österreichische Filmtage 1987," (1987).

→ Tscherkassky, Peter. "Die Lust am Film sieht anders aus – Notizen zum Stand der Filmavantgarde" [German] *Falter* (Vienna), no. 15, 1985.

→ Tscherkassky, Peter. "Film in Österreich." [German] *Kometen.Folge.Lawinen. Orte*, edited by Galerie Ropac. Salzburg: Galerie Ropac, 1984.

→ Weibel, Peter. "Der Wiener Formalfilm – Entstehungsgeschichte und Leistungen." [German] In *Film als Film. 1910 bis heute*, edited by Birgit Hein and Wulff Herzogenrath. Cologne: Kölnischer Kunstverein, 1977.

→ Hein, Birgit. "Return to Reason. On Experimental Film in West Germany and Austria." [English] *Studio International*, no. 11/12 (1975).

Contributors

STEVE ANKER

Steve Anker studied with Ken Jacobs, Larry Gottheim, Nicholas Ray and Ernie Gehr at SUNY Binghamton from 1967 to 1972 and received his MFA in Filmmaking from Columbia University in 1975. He began or directed avant-garde screening series at the Boston Film/Video Foundation (1977–1980), San Francisco Cinematheque (1982–2002) and Los Angeles' REDCAT Theater (2002–present). He has curated for festivals and museums in New York City, Vienna, Toronto, London, Brussels, San Francisco and Los Angeles, including the touring series *Austrian Avant-Garde Film: 1955–1993*, MoMA's 76-program survey of American 8 mm filmmaking, *Big As Life* (1998–2000) and *Radical Light: Alternative Film and Video in the San Francisco Bay Area, 1945–2000* (2010). Anker has written for *Film Comment* and *Film Quarterly*, among other journals, and for catalogues on Gunvor Nelson, Valie Export and American avant-garde cinema (*Independent America*, AMMI, 1988; Black Maria 25th Anniversary Catalogue, 2006). He recently co-edited the anthology *Radical Light: Alternative Film and Video in the San Francisco Bay Area, 1945–2000* with Kathy Geritz and Steve Seid (Berkeley: University of California Press, 2010). Steve Anker is currently Dean of the School of Film/Video at the California Institute of the Arts, Valencia.

STEVE BATES

Steve Bates is an artist and musician. An early infatuation with punk rock eventually led to more experimental practices working with sound. He founded and directed *Send + Receive: A Festival of Sound* international sound-art festival (Winnipeg) from 1998 to 2004. From 2005 to 2011 he was the Sound Coordinator at the Hexagram Institute for Research/Creation in Media Arts and Technologies at Concordia University. Recent projects include *concertina*, exhibited as part of the Québec Triennial, Musée d'art contemporain de Montréal; and in collaboration with Douglas Moffat *Okta*, a public art commission in conjunction with the City of Toronto for its first permanent outdoor sound installation. He has released music on Oral Records and his work has been exhibited in Canada, the US and Europe. He lives and works in Montréal.

LIVIO BELLOÏ

Livio Belloï is a Research Associate at the FNRS (Fonds National de la Recherche Scientifique, Brussels) and teaches Film Studies at the University of Liège. His books include *Poétique du hors-champ* (Brussels: APEC, 1992); *La Scène proustienne. Proust, Goffman et le théâtre du monde* (Paris: Nathan, 1993); *Le Regard retourné. Aspects du cinéma des premiers temps* (Québec and Paris: Nota Bene/Méridiens-Klincksieck, 2001); *L'Œuvre en morceaux. Esthétiques de la mosaïque* with Michel Delville (Paris and Brussels: Les Impressions Nouvelles, 2006). He is also the author of several essays on early cinema, film history and experimental film (see http://orbi.ulg.ac.be/simple-search?query=belloi). His forthcoming publications include a book-length essay on contemporary experimental filmmaker Gustav Deutsch (Lausanne: L'Age d'Homme, 2012), as well as a collection of essays entitled *La Mécanique du détail. Approches interdisciplinaires* with Maud Hagelstein (Lyon: ENS Éditions, 2012).

CHRISTA BLÜMLINGER

Christa Blümlinger is Professor of Film Studies at the University of Paris 8 / Vincennes-Saint-Denis. Her past teaching positions include an assistant professorship at the University of Paris 3 and a guest professorship at the Free University Berlin. She has worked extensively as a curator and critic in Vienna, Berlin and Paris. Her publications include editions of the writings of Harun Farocki in French: *Reconnaître et poursuivre* (Quetigny: THTY, 2002) and Serge Daney in German: *Von der Welt ins Bild. Augenzeugenberichte eines Cinephilen* (Berlin: Vorwerk 8, 2000), and books about the essay film, media art, avant-garde cinema and film aesthetics. Her most recent publication is about appropriation, entitled *Kino aus Zweiter Hand. Zur Ästhetik materieller Aneignung im Film und in der Medienkunst*, in German (Berlin: Vorwerk 8, 2009), and in French *Théâtres de la mémoire. Mouvement des images*, co-edited with Sylvie Lindeperg, Michèle Lagny, et al. (Paris: Presses Sorbonne Nouvelle, "Théorème 14," 2011).

NICOLE BRENEZ

Nicole Brenez is Professor at the University of Paris 3/Sorbonne Nouvelle. Graduate of the Ecole Normale Supérieure, *agrégée* of Modern Literature. She is a Senior Member of the Institut Universitaire de France. Her publications include *De la Figure en général et du Corps en particulier. L'invention figurative au*

cinéma (Paris and Liège, Belgium: De Boeck Université, 1998), *Jeune, dure et pure. Une histoire du cinéma d'avant-garde et expérimental en France* (Paris and Milan: Cinémathèque française/Mazzotta, 2001), *La Vie nouvelle/nouvelle Vision* (Paris: Leo Scheer, 2004), *Cinéma/Politique Série 1* (Liège, Belgium: Labor, 2005), *Jean-Luc Godard: Documents* (co-editor, Paris: Centre Pompidou, 2006), *Abel Ferrara* (Champaign: University of Illinois Press, 2007), *Traitement du Lumpenproletariat par le cinéma d'avant-garde* (Paris: Séguier, 2007), *Cinémas d'avant-garde* (Paris: Cahiers du Cinéma, 2007), *Abel Ferrara. Le Mal mais sans fleurs* (Paris: Cahiers du Cinéma, 2008). *Jean Epstein. Bonjour Cinéma und andere Schriften zum Kino* (co-editor, Vienna: FilmmuseumSynemaPublikationen, 2008), *Le cinéma critique. De l'argentique au numérique, voies et formes de l'objection visuelle* (co-editor, Paris: Publications de la Sorbonne, 2009). Curator of the Cinémathèque française's avant-garde film sessions since 1996. In 2000 recipient of the Film Preservation of the Anthology Film Archives Award in New York, has organized many film events and retrospectives, notably *Jeune, dure et pure, A History of Avant-Garde Cinema in France* for the French Cinémathèque in 2000, and curated series in Buenos Aires, Rio de Janeiro, New York, Tokyo, Vienna, London, Madrid, etc.

STEFAN GRISSEMANN

Stefan Grissemann, born in 1964, works as a film critic and journalist in Vienna, Austria. From 1989 to 2001 he was critic for the daily newspaper *Die Presse*. Since 2002 he works as department head of the arts section of *profil* magazine. He regularly writes reviews and articles for books and catalogues, and works as a book editor. Grissemann pieced together the life and work of mythical B-movie director Edgar G. Ulmer in his biography *Man in the Shadows* (Vienna: Zsolnay, 2003) and in 2007 published a book on the provocative works of Austrian filmmaker Ulrich Seidl (*Sündenfall*, Vienna: Sonderzahl Verlag), which will be updated in a second edition in 2012. He also edited the first comprehensive assessment of the cinematic work of artist/photographer Robert Frank in 2003 together with Brigitta Burger-Utzer (*frank films*, Zurich, Berlin and New York: Scalo. Re-issued in a revised and updated edition in 2009), and together with Regina Schlagnitweit and Alexander Horwath published an extensive catalogue on Peter Kubelka's weekly avant-garde film series "Was ist Film" in the Austrian Film Museum,

Was ist Film. Peter Kubelkas Zyklisches Programm im Österreichischen Filmmuseum (Vienna: Filmmuseum-SynemaPublikationen, 2010). As an editor Grissemann was also responsible for the 2001 book *Haneke | Jelinek: The Piano Teacher* (Vienna: Sonderzahl). Grissemann teaches journalism and lectures regularly at the Vienna Film Academy and the School for Independent Film.

CHRISTOPH HUBER

Christoph Huber, born in Vöcklabruck, Austria, in 1973. Academically qualified engineer. Grew up in Attnang-Puchheim, studied Physics at the Technical University of Vienna and graduated with a thesis about the magnetoinductive characteristics of steel sheets. He lives in Vienna, where he works as the main film critic for the daily paper *Die Presse*. Also writes program notes for the Austrian Film Museum and is the European editor of the Canadian film magazine *Cinema Scope*. Regular contributor to various international magazines and websites that involve film, author of articles for numerous books on film (forthcoming: essays on Hugo Fregonese and Abel Ferrara), curator of diverse film series, most recently Classic Finnish Films for the Ljubljana International Film Festival together with the other members of the Ferroni Brigade, Olaf Möller and Barbara Wurm. Co-author (with Olaf Möller) of the book *Taschenkino #4: Peter Kern* (Vienna: filmarchiv austria, 2011). Ferronian.

ADRIAN MARTIN

Associate Professor Adrian Martin teaches Film and Television Studies and is Co-Director of the Research Unit in Film Culture and Theory, Monash University (Melbourne, Australia). He is the author of five books: *Phantasms: The Dreams and Desires at the Heart of Our Popular Culture* (Carlton, Australia: McPhee Gribble, 1994), *The Mad Max Movies* (Strawberry Hills, Australia: Currency Press Pty Ltd, 2003), *Once Upon a Time in America* (London: BFI, 2008), *What is Modern Cinema?* (Santiago, Chile: Uqbar 2008), and *Raúl Ruiz: Magnificent Obsessions* (Altamira 2004), hundreds of essays (translated into over twenty languages), and thousands of reviews relating to cinema and the other arts. He is co-editor of the book *Movie Mutations: The Changing Face of World Cinephilia* (London: BFI, 2003) and the website LOLA (www.lolajournal.com). His forthcoming book is the literary-poetic project *A Secret Cinema* (Victoria, Australia: re.press, 2012). He is also

working on books about Terrence Malick and Brian De Palma, as well as a guidebook to creative film criticism. His archive website will be launched in 2012: http://www.filmcritic.com.au/

MAYA MCKECHNEAY

Maya McKechneay was born in Munich in 1974 and attended school in Hummelstown, PA. Studied German Literature, History, and Theater and Film Studies in Munich and Vienna. Works for the Viennale and Kino unter Sternen, editor of the catalogue for Linz's Crossing Europe Film Festival. Freelance film journalist, since 2000 regularly writes for Vienna's weekly newspaper *Falter*, Austrian correspondent for the trade magazine *Blickpunkt:Film*, co-founder of the film magazine *ray*. Chosen for the IFFR Rotterdam's Young Film Critics Trainee Project in 2001. Member of the international association of critics Fipresci, member of the juries at the Thessaloniki Documentary Film Festival, the Viennale, the IFFR Rotterdam, etc. Member of the advisory board of the Federal Chancellor's office, film division. Works for sixpackfilm. Has given lectures on film theory at the University of Vienna, the University of London, the Volksbühne Berlin, etc. on Spaces of Fear. Works as a photographer and is a mother of two children.

NORBERT PFAFFENBICHLER

Norbert Pfaffenbichler, born in 1967, is a freelance filmmaker, artist and curator living in Vienna. His curatorial work includes Austrian Abstracts (Diagonale, 1999 through 2002), Abstraction Now (Künstlerhaus Wien, 2003), Maths In Motion (10 film programs, Künstlerhaus-kino, 2003), Re-Modern (Künstlerhaus Wien, 2005), Blank (Medienturm Graz, 2005), MedienWERKSTATTGESPRÄCHE (Medienwerkstatt Wien, 2007–2010), Wunschmaschine Orient (Regionale, 2008), Concept Film (ARTI Amsterdam, 2009), VISIONary (touring film program, 2009) and Cineplex (Vienna Secession, 2009). Pfaffenbichler's texts have been published by *springerin*, *kolik.film*, sixpackfilm, Diagonale, Vienna Secession, Künstlerhaus Wien, departure, Kunstverein Medienturm and the Museum Moderner Kunst Kärnten.

ANDRÉA PICARD

Andréa Picard is a curator and writer based in Toronto. A member of the programming team at TIFF Cinematheque (née Cinematheque Ontario) from 1999 to 2011, she has curated numerous directors'

retrospectives and thematic shows, and oversees The Free Screen, a series exploring the intersections between film, video art and other artistic disciplines. Since 2006, she is the curator of Wave-lengths, the celebrated avant-garde sidebar of the Toronto International Film Festival, as well as a regular contributor to TIFF's installation program, Future Projections, and its features selection. In addition to her curatorial work Picard has published internationally on art, architecture and film, and writes a quarterly "Film/Art" column for *Cinema Scope* magazine.

BARBARA PICHLER

Barbara Pichler, born in 1968, received her MA in Film Studies from British Film Institute/London University and has been involved with film since the mid-1990s as a curator, author, (copy-)editor and in the field of film education. Conception of film programs (i.e., moving landscapes, VideoVisions, embodiment of the gaze, framed 1–8) and educational programs on film, work for various film festivals, lecturer at the University of Vienna 2006–2008, and co-editor of *moving landscapes*. *Landschaft im Film* (Vienna: Synema Publikationen, 2006) and *James Benning*, a monograph on the American filmmaker's work (Vienna: FilmmuseumSynema-Publikationen, 2007). Since 2008 she has been serving as director of the Diagonale – Festival of Austrian Film. Lives in Vienna, Austria.

BERT REBHANDL

Bert Rebhandl, born in Upper Austria in 1964, studied Literature, Catholic Theology and Philosophy. Freelance journalist, writer and translator. Film critic for the *Frankfurter Allgemeine Zeitung* and contributes to the newspaper *Der Standard* and numerous other publications. He is the author of *Orson Welles. Genie im Labyrinth* (Vienna: Paul Zsolnay Verlag, 2005) and the editor of *Western. Genre und Geschichte* (Vienna: Paul Zsolnay Verlag, 2008). He is currently working on a book about Jean-Luc Godard. Co-founder and co-editor of the quarterly *CARGO Film/Medien/Kultur* (www.cargo-film.de). Lives in Berlin. cargooner@web.de

JONATHAN ROSENBAUM

Jonathan Rosenbaum was film critic for the *Chicago Reader* from 1987 to 2008. His books include *Goodbye Cinema, Hello Cinephilia: Film Culture in Transition* (Chicago: University Of Chicago Press, 2010), *The Unquiet American: Transgressive Comedies From The U.S.*

(Marburg, Germany: Schüren Verlag, 2009), *Discovering Orson Welles* (Berkeley: University of California Press, 2007), *Essential Cinema: On the Necessity of Film Canons* (Baltimore: The Johns Hopkins University Press, 2004), *Abbas Kiarostami* with Mehrnaz Saeed-Vafa (Champaign: University of Illinois Press, 2003), *Movies as Politics* (Berkeley: University of California Press, 1997), *Dead Man* and *Greed* (both London: BFI, 2008), *Midnight Movies* with J. Hoberman (Cambridge: Da Capo Press, 1982), *Film: The Front Line 1983* (Denver: Arden Press, 1983), *Placing Movies: The Practice of Film Criticism* and *Moving Places: A Life at the Movies* (both Berkeley: University of California Press, 1995). He has also edited *Discovering Orson Welles* (Berkeley: University of California Press, 2007) and co-edited *Movie Mutations: The Changing Face of World Cinephilia* with Adrian Martin (London: BFI, 2008). Since 2008 he has maintained a website at jonathanrosenbaum.com and taught film courses in Chicago and Richmond, Virginia.

HANS SCHEUGL

Hans Scheugl, born in Vienna in 1940, was a prominent member of the second generation of Austrian avant-garde filmmakers and, in addition to Ernst Schmidt Jr., penned the most significant works on this subject, writing numerous books on themes specific to film (see his bibliography in the appendix). The two-volume encyclopedia of more than 1,300 pages, *Subgeschichte des Films – Lexikon des Avantgarde-, Experimental- und Undergroundfilms* (Frankfurt am Main: Suhrkamp, 1974), which he co-wrote with Schmidt Jr., remains the most comprehensive description of the history and aesthetic of the subject to this day. In 1999 Scheugl published a cultural history, *Das Absolute. Eine Ideen-geschichte der Moderne* (Vienna and New York: Springer Verlag), in which the development of subjectivity in the Modern age, from the birth of the Renaissance to the present, is outlined in terms of philosophy, art and art theory.

PETER TSCHERKASSKY

Peter Tscherkassky, born in Vienna in 1958, earned his Ph.D. in Philosophy in 1986 with a dissertation entitled "Film und Kunst. Zu einer kritischen Äthetik der Kinematografie" [Film and Art. A Critical Aesthetic of Cinematography]. Subsequently and parallel to his own filmmaking, Tscherkassky emerged as a voice of the third generation of the Austrian avant-garde film scene, publishing over 100 articles and essays, primarily in the 1980s and 1990s, that contributed to the widespread dissemination of an understanding of the new film aesthetic of this young generation. His writings have been translated into twelve languages. In addition to comprehensive texts covering the third generation, he has focused especially on the films of Peter Kubelka, Kurt Kren and Dietmar Brehm. In 1995 Tscherkassky co-edited the first monograph on the work of Peter Kubelka (together with Gabriele Jutz), *Peter Kubelka*, (Vienna: PVS-Verleger). For more information visit www.tscherkassky.at

MAUREEN TURIM

Maureen Turim is Professor of Film and Media Studies in the Department of English at the University of Florida. She has published over 90 essays in journals, anthologies and museum catalogues which focus on theoretical, historical and aesthetic issues in cinema and video, art, cultural studies, feminist and psychoanalytic theory, and comparative literature. Books: *The Films of Oshima Nagisa. Images of a Japanese Iconoclast* (Berkeley: University of California Press, 1998); *Flashbacks in Film: Memory and History* (New York: Routledge, 1989); *Abstraction in Avant-Garde Films* (Ann Arbor, MI: UMI Research Press, 1985). Currently completing *Desire and its Renewals in Cinema*.

Index of Persons

Index of Films

A book by sixpack**film**

Film Unframed

Published in the series
FilmmuseumSynemaPublikationen

© Vienna 2012
SYNEMA – Gesellschaft für Film und Medien
Neubaugasse 36/1/1/1
A-1070 Wien

Design, Layout: Karl Ulbl
Assistant: Flora Watzal
Project Management: Brigitta Burger-Utzer
Sub-Editor: Eve Heller
Translators: Eve Heller, Steve Wilder,
Adrian Martin, Fabrice Leroy
Proofreaders: Eve Heller, Kellie Rife,
Steve Wilder, Ute Katschthaler
Appendix: Brigitta Burger-Utzer and the filmmakers

Printed by: REMAprint
Printed and published in Vienna, Austria
Printed on paper certified in accordance with the rules
of the Forest Stewardship Council
ISBN 978-3-901644-42-9

This book was supported by
the Austrian Federal Ministry for Education,
the Arts and Culture (Department for Innovative Film),
the City of Vienna (Department for Cultural Affairs:
Sciences and Research) and the Regional Government
of Upper Austria (Directorate for Cultural Affairs)

Österreichisches Filmmuseum (Austrian Film Museum)
and SYNEMA – Society for Film & Media
are supported by BM:UKK – Abteilung VI/3 Film
and by Kulturabteilung der Stadt Wien.

Acknowledgments

Peter Tscherkassky and sixpackfilm wish to thank:
Helmut Benedikt, Giulio Bursi, Pia Bolognesi, Stefan Grissemann,
Tom Gunning, Peter Hell, Vivian Heller, Ute Katschthaler, Joseph Sepp Kloucek,
Ralph McKay, Hans Scheugl, Phil Solomon, Aldo Tambellini Archive, as well
as the Federal Ministry for Education, Culture and the Arts (Andrea Ecker,
Barbara Fränzen, Carlo Hufnagl), Filmarchiv Austria (Ernst Kieninger,
Lukas Maurer, Peter Spiegel), Synema – Gesellschaft für Film und Medien
(Brigitte Mayr, Michael Omasta) and the Austrian Film Museum (Andrea
Glawogger; Roland Fischer-Briand, Stills Collection; Elisabeth Streit, Library;
Barbara Vockenhuber, Ephemeral Paper Collection; Georg Wasner; frame
enlargements).

Illustrations

All reproductions of stills courtesy of the filmmakers
or the rightholders.
Unless noted below, all photographs and illustrations
are from the collection of sixpackfilm.

Austrian Film Museum, Stills Collection: pp. 14, 18 (left),
25 (photos: Gertraude Wolfschwänger), 85 (left).
Filmarchiv Austria: pp. 44, 49, 50, 53.
Hans Scheugl Collection: pp. 5, 17, 23 (photo: Hans Scheugl),
51, 104, 128, 133 (below), 137, 139 (below).
Ernst Schmidt Jr. Collection (Estate Executor Helmut Benedikt): p. 24.
Collection Centre national d'art moderne, Centre Pompidou: p. 56.

Marc Adrian stills (Estate Executor Dorothee Frank)
Kurt Kren stills (Estate Executors Martin Arnold and Hans Hurch)
Ernst Schmidt Jr. stills (Estate Executor Helmut Benedikt)

We are committed to respecting the intellectual property rights of others.
While all reasonable efforts have been made to credit copyright
holders for material used in this book, any oversight will be corrected
in future editions, provided the publishers are duly informed.

Front cover (from right): Peter Kubelka, *Mosaik im Vertrauen*;
Ernst Schmidt Jr., *15. Mai 1966*; Michael Petrov, Mara Mattuschka,
Loading Ludwig; Siegfried A. Fruhauf, *Ground Control*
Back cover (from left): Kurt Kren, *6/64 Mama und Papa*;
VALIE EXPORT, *Unsichtbare Gegner*; Michaela Schwentner, *Grain Bits*;
Gustav Deutsch, *Film Ist. [1-6]*.